HOUGHTON MIFFLIN SOCIAL STUDIES

America Will Be

U.S. Custom House. 1805.

O yes,

I say it plain,

America never was America to me,

And yet I swear this oath—

America will be!

An ever-living seed,

Its dream

Lies deep in the heart of me.

Langston Hughes

Beverly J. Armento
Gary B. Nash
Christopher L. Salter
Karen K. Wixson

America
Will Be

Houghton Mifflin Company • Boston

Atlanta • Dallas • Geneva, Illinois • Princeton, New Jersey • Palo Alto • Toronto

Consultants

Program Consultants

Edith M. Guyton
Associate Professor of Early
  Childhood Education
Georgia State University
Atlanta, Georgia

Gail Hobbs
Associate Professor of Geography
Pierce College
Woodland Hills, California

Charles Peters
Reading Consultant
Oakland Schools
Pontiac, Michigan

Cathy Riggs-Salter
Social Studies Consultant
Hartsburg, Missouri

Alfredo Schifini
Limited English Proficiency Consultant
Los Angeles, California

George Paul Schneider
Associate Director
  of General Programs
Department of Museum Education
Art Institute of Chicago
Chicago, Illinois

Twyla Stewart
Center for Academic Interinstitutional
  Programs
University of California—Los Angeles
Los Angeles, California

Scott Waugh
Associate Professor of History
University of California—Los Angeles
Los Angeles, California

Teacher Reviewers

David E. Beer (Grade 5)
Weisser Park Elementary
Fort Wayne, Indiana

Jan Coleman (Grades 6–7)
Thornton Junior High
Fremont, California

Shawn Edwards
  (Grades 1–3)
Jackson Park Elementary
University City, Missouri

Barbara J. Fech (Grade 6)
Martha Ruggles School
Chicago, Illinois

Deborah M. Finkel
  (Grade 4)
Los Angeles Unified
  School District,
  Region G
South Pasadena,
  California

Jim Fletcher (Grades 5, 8)
La Loma Junior High
Modesto, California

Susan M. Gilliam
  (Grade 1)
Roscoe Elementary
Los Angeles, California

Vicki Stroud Gonterman
  (Grade 2)
Gibbs International
  Studies Magnet School
Little Rock, Arkansas

Lorraine Hood (Grade 2)
Fresno Unified School
  District
Fresno, California

Jean Jamgochian
  (Grade 5)
Haycock Gifted and
  Talented Center
Fairfax County, Virginia

Susan Kirk-Davalt
  (Grade 5)
Crowfoot Elementary
Lebanon, Oregon

Mary Molyneaux-Leahy
  (Grade 3)
Bridgeport Elementary
Bridgeport, Pennsylvania

Sharon Oviatt
  (Grades 1–3)
Keysor Elementary
Kirkwood, Missouri

Jayne B. Perala (Grade 1)
Cave Spring Elementary
Roanoke, Virginia

Carol Siefkin (K)
Garfield Elementary
Sacramento, California

Norman N. Tanaka
  (Grade 3)
Martin Luther King Jr.
  Elementary
Sacramento, California

John Tyler (Grades 5, 8)
Groton School
Groton, Massachusetts

Portia W. Vaughn
  (Grades 1–3)
School District 11
Colorado Springs,
  Colorado

Acknowledgments

Grateful acknowledgment is made
for the use of the material listed below.
    The material in the Minipedia is
reprinted from *The World Book*
Encyclopedia with the expressed permission of the publisher. © 1990 by World
Book, Inc.

–Continued on page 604.

From Your Authors

*T*he hunters shiver as an icy wind blows across the empty land. It is flat and treeless here, covered only with moss and small shrubs. Far away, the hunters can see a tall range of mountains covered with ice and snow.

So begins an imaginary account of the first humans who ever crossed over the ice from Asia to North America. For periods of time during the Ice Age long ago, a land bridge connected the two continents. Historians think musk ox crossed over first, and hunters looking for game followed them. In Chapter 4 of this book, you will have the chance to read more about the ancestors of present-day Native Americans.

Most of the people you will meet in this book lived long ago in places that may seem very far away from home. But they all had feelings just like yours and faced many of the same challenges you will face in your life. And whether they were great leaders or ordinary people, their decisions and actions helped shape your nation and your world.

As you read about these people, places, and events, we hope you will ask many questions. Some questions may be about history: "What caused these people to make the decisions they did?" or "How do we know about these events?" Other questions may be about geography: "What are the land and weather like in that place?" or "Why did people choose to settle there?" Still other questions may be about economics: "How did people meet their needs for food and shelter?" or "How did people work out ways for using limited resources?"

Most of all, we hope you catch the excitement of thinking, questioning, and discovering answers about your world—now and in the 21st century.

Beverly J. Armento
Professor of Social Studies
Director, Center for Business and
Economic Education
Georgia State University

Christopher L. Salter
Professor and Chair
Department of Geography
University of Missouri

Gary B. Nash
Professor of History
University of California—Los Angeles

Karen K. Wixson
Associate Professor of Education
University of Michigan

Contents

Understanding Skills

Each "Understanding Skills" feature gives you the opportunity to learn and practice a skill related to the topic you are studying.

Understanding Concepts

Each "Understanding Concepts" feature gives you more information about a concept that is important to the lesson you are reading.

Making Decisions

Much of history is made of people's decisions. These pages take you step-by-step through fascinating problems from history and today. What will you decide?

Literature

Throughout history people have expressed their deepest feelings and beliefs through literature. Reading these stories, legends, and shorter passages that appear in the lessons will help you experience what life was like for people of other times and places.

Primary Sources

Reading the exact words of the people who made and lived history is the best way to get a sense of how they saw themselves and the times in which they lived. You will find more than 50 primary sources throughout this book including the following:

Exploring

The story of the past is hidden all around you in the world of the present. "Exploring" pages tell you the secrets of how to find it.

A Closer Look

Take a closer look at the objects and pictures spread out on these special pages. With the clues you see, you'll become a historical detective.

A Moment in Time

A person from the past is frozen at an exciting moment. You'll get to know these people by reading about where they are, what they're wearing, and the objects around them.

Charts, Diagrams, and Timelines

These visual presentations of information help give you a clearer picture of the people, places, and events you are studying.

Maps

The events of history have been shaped by the places in which they occurred. Each map in this book tells its own story about these events and places.

Starting Out

What makes this textbook so much more interesting than others you've used? In this book, the people of the past speak directly to you, through their actual words and the objects they used. You'll walk inside their houses and look inside their cooking pots. You'll follow them as they go to school, build cities, fight wars, work out settlements for peace.

When and where? The timeline at the beginning of each lesson and the lesson title tell you the time and place.

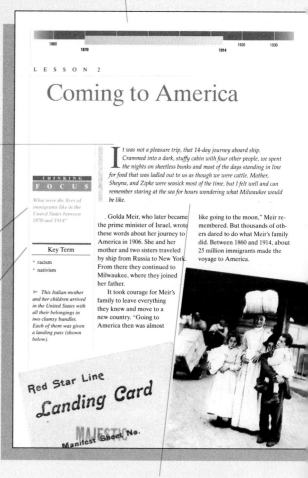

LESSON 2

Coming to America

THINKING
FOCUS

What were the lives of immigrants like in the United States between 1870 and 1914?

Key Term

• racism
• nativism

➤ *This Italian mother and her children arrived in the United States with all their belongings in two clumsy bundles. Each of them was given a landing pass (shown below).*

I t was not a pleasure trip, that 14-day journey aboard ship. Crammed into a dark, stuffy cabin with four other people, we spent the nights on sheetless bunks and most of the days standing in line for food that was ladled out to us as though we were cattle. Mother, Sheyna, and Zipke were seasick most of the time, but I felt well and can remember staring at the sea for hours wondering what Milwaukee would be like.

Golda Meir, who later became the prime minister of Israel, wrote these words about her journey to America in 1906. She and her mother and two sisters traveled by ship from Russia to New York. From there they continued to Milwaukee, where they joined her father.

It took courage for Meir's family to leave everything they knew and move to a new country. "Going to America then was almost like going to the moon," Meir remembered. But thousands of others dared to do what Meir's family did. Between 1860 and 1914, about 25 million immigrants made the voyage to America.

From unit to chapter to lesson— each step lets you see history in closer detail. The maps and photos show you where events happened. The art introduces you to the people.

Right from the beginning the lesson opener pulls you into the sights, the sounds, the smells of what life was like at that time, in that place. Here it is 1906 aboard a ship traveling from Russia to America.

Like a road sign, the question that always appears here tells you what to think about while you read the lesson.

Look for these key terms. They are listed here so that you can watch for them. The first time they appear in the lesson they are shown in heavy black print and defined. Key terms are also defined in the Glossary.

Letters, diaries, books—short passages from these primary sources let people from the past speak to you. When you see a tan background, a red initial letter, and a gray bar, you know that the quotation is a primary source.

Giving you the inside story is the purpose of two special paragraphs. Across Time & Space connects what you're reading to things that happened centuries ago or continents away. Its companion, How Do We Know?, tells you where information about the past comes from. (See page 496 for an example.)

of these people could not speak English. Most were unskilled workers who wanted jobs in American factories. Look at the article on page 557 of the Minipedia to learn more about these new immigrants.

Some European immigrants had relatives and friends who had already settled in America. They sometimes sent money home for the boat trip. They offered to help friends from their villages find housing and jobs in America.

To unskilled European workers struggling to support their families, America promised plenty of jobs. In Eastern Europe, Jews were often persecuted for their religion. To them, America offered the promise of a place where all religions would be allowed.

With these hopes and plans, millions left their homes, fam-

▲ *Immigrants often brought items from their homeland with them to America. These painted Easter eggs, for example, came from Russia.*

Across Time & Space

A hundred years ago, most immigrants to the United States came from Europe. Today, about one-third of all immigrants come from Mex-

America with their small savings and their most precious possessions—things like family portraits, an ancestor's wedding ring, and a grandmother's silver candlesticks.

A New Home for Immigrants

Immigrants faced many hardships when they arrived in America. Many were too poor to leave the crowded tenements of port cities like New York or Boston. Others traveled to cities where family members or friends lived. They settled in neighborhoods with other people from their home countries. Soon, many American cities had Jewish, Italian, Polish, and other ethnic neighborhoods.

Life in these neighborhoods gave immigrants some of the comforts of their home lands. Anna Federovi...

*T*he Russian Church was in the Hill District then. So every Sunday morning my brother would take me and we would walk over the bridge to church. . . . And there were all kinds of Russian stores. So, we bought herring and black bread and we got together. That's how we met people.

Nicolette DiLucente told how her neighborhood celebrated an Italian saint's day. "All the people were from the same town," she said. "We decorated the whole street, made special foods, and we celebrated."

Immigrant neighborhoods were often run down and overcrowded. But they were also filled with familiar languages, customs,

◀ *This shop in San Francisco's Chinatown sold such ethnic foods as Chinese cabbage, mushrooms, tea, and ginger.*

and foods of the old country. These ethnic neighborhoods helped make the immigrants' new land seem a little less strange. To learn more about the lives of immigrants look at A Closer Look at Immigrant Children on page 490. ■

■ *Why did immigrants often settle in ethnic neighborhoods?*

Immigrants and Politics

As immigrant neighborhoods became more crowded, they needed more city services. People needed protection from fire and crime. They needed garbage collection, street repairs and schools.

Bosses Help Immigrants

Many immigrants turned to local politicians, called bosses, to get these services. These politicians often made important improvements in the immigrant neighborhoods. In return, immigrants would vote for the boss that helped them in the next election.

Many immigrants had never before had the right to vote in Europe. Voting meant little to them

at first. But as time went on, they were happy to give their votes to whomever would help them.

Bosses Help Themselves

Bosses became very powerful as a result of these immigrant votes. Some bosses took advantage of the immigrants and made themselves very rich.

The most famous of these bosses was William Tweed of New York. Tweed promised to make city improvements, just as all bosses did. But Tweed kept the money he raised. After he swindled New York out of millions of dollars, Tweed was arrested and sent to jail.

Immigration to the United States, 1870-1910

Mercator Projection
0   1500   3000 mi.
0 1500 3000 km

	1870	1890	1910
Northern Europe			
Southern Europe			
Eastern Europe			
Asia			

Number of Immigrants (in thousands)
0 50 100 150 200 250 300   0 50 100 150 200 250 300   0 50 100 150 200 250 300 350 400 450

Immigrants in the United States

The immigrants who came to the United States after the Civil War were different from those who came earlier. Early immigrants had come from Great Britain, Germany, and other countries of northern Europe. Many had moved from overcrowded European cities in search of a better living. Many of these immigrants already spoke English or learned it quickly. They settled on farms or in cities and lived much as their American neighbors did.

A New Wave of Immigrants

After the Civil War, however, most immigrants came from eastern and southern Europe. These people escaped from economic hardships and political problems in their home countries. The map and graphs on this page show where these immigrants came from. Many

▲ *This map shows where most immigrants to the United States came from. The graphs show how many immigrants arrived from different parts of the world between 1870 and 1910.*

The titles outline the lesson. The red titles tell you the main topics discussed in the lesson on "Coming to America." The blue titles tell you the subtopics.

Every map tells a story. The maps in the book tell the story of where people came from and what the land was like. Here three bar graphs add to the map's story of immigration to the United States from 1870 to 1910.

Continuing On

Frozen at a moment in time, the school reformer captures your attention. You learn all about her, through her clothes, her badge, and the things she holds in her hands.

As you get to know the people of the past, you'll want ways of understanding and remembering them better. This book gives you some tools to use in learning about people and places and remembering what you've learned.

The things people make and use tell a great deal about them. In this book you'll find lots of photographs of the paintings and statues people made and the coins, tools, and weapons they used.

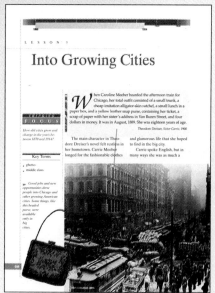

Every age has its great storytellers. Each chapter includes short examples of fine writing from or about the period. The literature is always printed on a tan background with a blue initial letter and a multicolored bar.

Take a closer look, in this case at immigrant children. Look at the games they played, the food they ate, and the schoolbooks they read.

Some tools you'll always use. The Understanding pages walk you through skills that you will use again and again, as a student and later on in life.

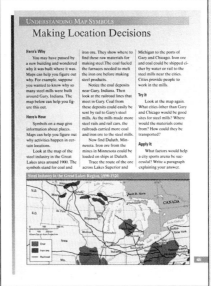

You're in charge of your reading. See the red square at the end of the text? Now find the red square over in the margin. If you can answer the question there, then you probably understood what you just read. If you can't, perhaps you'd better go back and read that part of the lesson again.

A special kind of Understanding page looks at concepts—the big ideas that help put all the pieces together. This section helps you understand ideas like Land Use, the Frontier, and in this case, Mechanization, or using machines to do work.

A picture is worth a thousand words. But just a few words in a caption can help you understand a picture, a photograph, a map, or in this case, a cartoon.

After you read the lesson, stop and review what you've read. The first question is the same one you started out with. The second question connects the lesson to what you've studied earlier. Other questions and an activity help you think about the lesson you've read. Chapter Review questions help you tie the lessons together. (See pages 508 and 509 for an example.)

Also Featuring

Some special pages show up only once in every unit, not in every lesson in the book. These features continue the story by letting you explore an idea or activity, or read a story about another time and place. The Time/Space Databank in the back of the book brings together resources you will use again and again.

School isn't the only place where you can learn social studies. This feature gives you a chance to explore history and geography outside the classroom—at home or in your own neighborhood.

EXPLORING

Early Photography

people in the picture know they were being photographed? Why do you think the picture was taken? Can you tell what time of day it was?

Compare your answers about the 1800s photographs to your answers about the current ones. Make a list of the differences you observed.

▼ *The photographer poses his client for a portrait in the 1800s.*

► *Only two of these early cameras exist in the United States. This one dates from 1839.*

Chapter 18

472

MAKING DECISIONS

Immigration: Open or Restricted?

L*et them come, then, as the waves come . . . It is easy for every man of them to have a farm which they can soon call their own.*

Boston Evening Transcript

W*e need to keep our voting power and our reserves of public land out of the reach . . . of the hordes of half-educated and wholly unreliable foreigners now bribed to migrate here.*

John Murray Forbes, railroad builder

Background

Anna Maria Gavin came to America in 1866. As a child, she had heard that in America you could become rich, practice the religion you chose, and eat meat and bread every day! In Ireland Anna Maria often ate only dry bread with watercress, a plant like lettuce.

The 40 million immigrants who poured in from 1820 to 1920 had high hopes. Most, like Anna Gavin, became citizens.

But for citizens born in America, the waves of immigration were disturbing, even frightening. The newcomers would compete for jobs, housing, and land. They might dress and speak differently. No one knew what political beliefs they might have. Would they really be loyal to this country rather than to the place where they were born? Would they understand how democracy worked?

Many immigrants had been extremely poor. Would they work for less money and bring down wages of native-born American workers? Would they take over whole towns and neighborhoods with their different ways of life?

Conflict Over Immigration

The argument over immigration was heating up by the time Anna Gavin arrived. From one point of view, it seemed that the nation's doors must remain open. The country's founders were, after all, immigrants or the children of immigrants. They had come to escape poverty and unjust laws.

More than that, they had come to find freedom and opportunity. How could they or their children turn away other people who shared the same goals? Railroads were opening the West. Industry was growing rapidly. Surely, there were jobs and space enough for anyone willing to work. Why not let the immigrants come in?

On the other hand, numbers are important in a democratic country. What if the newcomers took control of the country with their votes? They might want to change the laws and customs. They might settle in the crowded cities and take the jobs the native-born Americans wanted. Pressure was building for new laws, laws that would limit immigration. Americans were pleased with the new nation they were building, and they wanted to keep it as it was.

Immigration: Open or Restricted?

• Promise of America
• Variety of cultures
• Refuge for the oppressed

• Job competition
• Cultural differences
• Expanded population

Open

Restricted

In 1882, Congress passed the first law to limit immigration. Was the land of the free now less free? Or was freedom being protected?

Decision Point

1. What made immigration disturbing to "born" Americans?
2. What goals and values of the American-born citizens helped them accept the newcomers?
3. Find a newspaper or magazine article about immigration today.
4. What goals and values make present-day immigrants want to come to America?
5. What information could help you decide about open immigration? Where might you find this information?

Life in a Changing America

493

What would you do? The Making Decisions pages show you an important decision from the past. Then you practice the steps that will help you to make a good choice.

Stories have always been important parts of people's lives. Each unit in the book has at least one story about the time and place you're studying. In this case, it's a story of an immigrant boy who goes to live in Nebraska.

LITERATURE

An Orphan for Nebraska

Charlene Joy Talbot

You have learned that the cities grew in the late 1800s because of immigration and movement of people from farms. The problem of homeless children grew as well, and a Children's Aid Society was formed to take orphans from the cities and settle them in the towns and farms of the western United States. The Society found homes or work for them. In this story, Kevin, an Irish orphan who worked as a newspaper boy and lived on the streets of New York City, finds a new life in Nebraska in the 1860s.

Millions of immigrants came to America with their dreams of a better life. Here is a story about an 11-year-old immigrant boy.

T*he next thing Kevin knew, Elizabeth was screeching, "Be we there, Mister? Is this Nebraska?"* He threw back the buffalo robe to see sun streaming through the depot window. Elizabeth, George and Maggie were crowding out the door. He heard them running on the platform. Kevin tied his shoes. Fumbl—

buffalo robe a blanket made of buffalo skins

The Time/Space Databank is like a reference section of a library at your fingertips. It's the place to go for more information about the places, people, and key terms you meet in this book. Some of your country's most prized documents are reproduced here too.

What's a minipedia? It's a small version of an encyclopedia, one that you don't have to go to your library to use. It's bound right into the back of your book so you can quickly look up its articles, charts, and graphs.

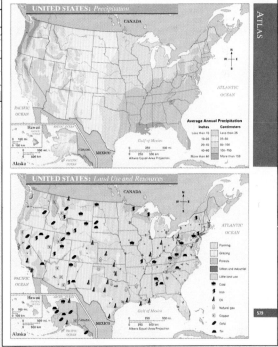

The Atlas maps out the world. Large-scale maps show the political divisions and the geographic areas of the world and of the United States. Special maps tell you about the climate, vegetation, population, and resources of the United States.

"Berries!" she screeched. The red-orange rose hips did indeed look like fruit. She bit one. Her face scrunched, and she spat.

"Breakfast!" Mr. Carter called from the platform. "Whoever wants breakfast, come along!" Hannah, Mr. Carter and Peter set out along the road to town. The others straggled after, running from side to side, making tracks in the unmarked snow.

The hotel, which was the largest building in town, was beginning to stir when the group trailed across the porch. A man opened the door, exclaiming, "Land alive, these must be the orphans! Molly!" he called over his shoulder. "Breakfast customers!" He directed them to a hallway where they hung their coats. A bench held two big washpans and a bucket of water. A girl came from the kitchen with a steaming kettle and poured hot water into the basins. Beside the bench hung a long strip of toweling. A mirror was nailed beside it. Hands and faces were washed; Hannah combed the girls' hair and Peter's, and the comb was passed among the rest of the boys. From the neck up, they looked respectable, Kevin thought. The boys had barber's haircuts before leaving New York. Their clothes, however, were a different story—wrinkled, dirty and even torn, having been lived in so many days and nights.

They sat on either side of a long, bare table. Pitchers of milk and coffee came from the kitchen, followed by platters of wheat cakes and sausage, with syrup

rose hips part of a rose bush

Unit 1

The United States: Past and Present

The story of America is a story of people and the land. From 2000 B.C.—when American Indians had settled throughout North America—to today, people from all over the world have come to America. They crossed rivers, climbed mountains, and built homes from one coast to another. The people who settled this land created our nation. The people and land continue to shape the United States today.

2000 B.C.

Thomas Moran, Green River Wyoming, 1907.
Collection of The Gerald Peters Gallery, Santa Fe, New Mexico.

Today

Chapter 1

A Nation of Many Peoples

About 200 years ago, a French settler named Michel Jean de Crèvecoeur asked, "What then is the American?" Crèvecoeur believed that the United States was a land where people from different places could live together. From the earliest time, America has been a land of many peoples. This rich mix of cultures has shaped every part of life in the United States today.

The first people to arrive in America 30,000 years ago were American Indians. These peoples remain an important part of the mix of cultures in America today.

Benjamin Banneker (right) was an important American astronomer, inventor, and writer in the 1700s. His ancestors came from Africa.

BANNAKER

2000 B.C.

Before 1900, most people moving to the United States came from Europe. The photograph above shows two Swedish-Americans in the early 1900s.

Today, many people in the
United States practice the
customs of their homelands.
Here, a group of Mexican-
Americans celebrate a
festival in Phoenix, Arizona.

Many different religions
thrive in the United States
today. This toy, called a
dreidel, is used during
the Jewish festival of
Chanukah.

More than 200,000 Chinese came
to the United States during the
1800s. The brush shown above
is used to paint the characters
of the Chinese language.

Today

L E S S O N   1

A Tale of One City

What makes New Orleans an example of pluralism?

Key Terms

- culture
- pluralism

▼ *Jazz bands and church choirs entertain at a New Orleans music festival.*

In the tent over here, a crowd is tapping its feet to the beat of a Dixieland band. Dixieland is a kind of jazz that was born in New Orleans nearly 100 years ago. On the stage over there, a string band is playing spirited Cajun *(KAY juhn)* tunes. This kind of music can be traced to the French-Canadian settlers who came to New Orleans in the 1700s.

In another tent, a band made up of a guitar, an accordion, and a washboard is playing zydeco *(ZY dih koh)* music. This kind of music mixes French and Caribbean tunes with the blues.

As you walk around, you see brass bands like the ones that march through New Orleans during jazz funerals. You also see parades of people dressed up like the Chickasaw, Choctaw, and Natchez Indians who settled in Louisiana many thousands of years ago.

It is spring and you are among many people in the city of New Orleans, Louisiana. Together you are celebrating the history of this city at the New Orleans Jazz and Heritage Festival. For more facts about some of the musical instruments at the festival, see A Closer Look on page 7.

Now step up to one of the food stands. Try New Orleans dishes such as gumbo, jambalaya, alligator po-boy sandwiches, and stewed rabbit. All in all, this festival shows you the many people, sights, sounds, and tastes that make up this wonderful city. It also gives you an idea of the rich mixture of people—the ethnic diversity—that can be found all around these United States.

Where Is New Orleans?

Why does the city of New Orleans have such a rich and diverse mixture of people? Take a look at its location.

As you can see on the map below, New Orleans lies at the mouth of the Mississippi River. The Mississippi begins in Minnesota and flows south to the Gulf of Mexico. People of different backgrounds—American Indians and European explorers—came down the Mississippi from the north. From the south, people from many different countries entered the Mississippi through the Gulf of Mexico. These people all met in New Orleans.

◄ *The wide bend of the Mississippi River stretches out behind New Orleans.*

▼ *Find New Orleans on this map. Why do you think its location attracted so many different people?*

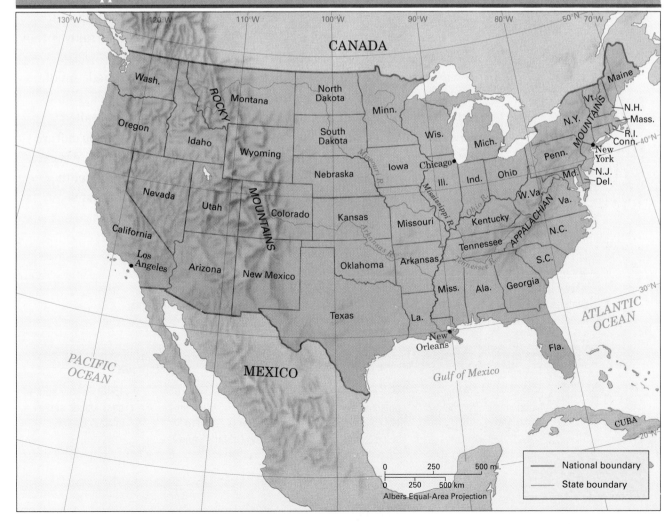

The Mississippi River and New Orleans

■ *How did the Missis-*
sippi River help to make
New Orleans an impor-
tant city?

At different times, France and Spain governed New Orleans. During these times, French, German, and Spanish soldiers, frontiersmen, and black slaves arrived in New Orleans. More people came during the War of 1812 and during the Civil War. In both wars New Orleans was a key battleground. During times of peace, trade on the river made New Orleans an important seaport. ■

Who Lives in New Orleans?

Across Time & Space

Cajuns are an important ethnic group in New Orleans. The word Cajun *originally came from the word* Acadian. *Acadia was a region of Canada settled by people from France. However, the British forced the Acadians to leave Canada in the 1750s. Many of them moved to Louisiana. Today, the Cajun culture still has traces of its French-Canadian roots.*

■ *What is pluralism?*

▼ *According to this timeline, how many different ethnic groups played a part in the history of New Orleans?*

A book written in 1817 had this to say about the people of New Orleans:

> Here in half an hour you can see and speak to Frenchmen, Spaniards, Danes, Swedes, Germans, Englishmen, Portuguese, Hollanders, Mexicans, Kentuckians, Tennesseans, Ohioans, Pennsylvanians, New Yorkers, New Englanders, and a motley group of Indians, quadroons, Africans. . . .

These people gave and still give New Orleans a special **culture** or way of life. Look at the timeline on this page. Notice the many people who have left their mark on New Orleans.

One group of people—the Creoles—have a special place in New Orleans's history. Having both French and black backgrounds, they form an important culture.

In many ways, Creoles show the great diversity of New Orleans. Creoles mix both French and African ways of life, and their food comes from a number of cultures. They cook with spices from Spain and the West Indies. Their meals often include long, crusty loaves of French bread. They also serve the kind of wild game— turkeys, rabbits, squirrels—that American Indians hunted. Their cooks are famous for the wonderful way they prepare many foods.

New Orleans is made up of people from many backgrounds. This kind of culture is called **pluralism,** or a pluralistic culture. In a pluralistic culture, life is exciting. People work, join together, struggle, learn, and grow. ■

Key Events in the History of New Orleans

Before 1682, Chickasaw, Choctow, and Natchez live in the area.

1764, Acadians begin arriving soon after France gives city to Spain.

1851, Over 50,000 immigrants, mostly German and Irish, arrive.

1867, The first Chinese immigrants arrive.

1700	1750	1800	1850	1900	1950	2000

1718, New Orleans founded in French territory.
1720, Numbers of Africans arrive.

1800, France regains Louisiana from Spain then sells it to the United States in 1803.

1887–1914, Several thousand Italian immigrants come to New Orleans yearly.

1980s, Many Southeast Asians settle in New Orleans.

Musical Instruments

When you turn on your boom box, you're listening to history. The music you hear is made by instruments created long ago in other parts of the world.

Crash, splash, pang, swish, sizzle, and ride are names for different cymbals that drummers use today. Musicians played the first cymbals 3,000 years ago in southwest Asia.

Out of the Congo region of Africa came conga drums. Latin American workers went to work in the Congo in the early 1900s. They created exciting dance beats to play on the congas, and brought the music and the drums back across the ocean.

Musicians kept tinkering with the Chinese mouth organ after it was brought to Europe in 1777. Eventually they turned it into something new: the accordion. German immigrants took their accordions to Louisiana. Today the accordion plays a key part in Louisiana's spicy regional music.

Arabs brought instruments called *gitterns* when they invaded Spain in A.D. 711. From gitterns, the Spaniards developed the guitar, and they took guitars with them when they colonized America. Later, American jazz musicians plugged guitars into electric amplifiers and turned them up *loud!*

How Is America Like New Orleans?

New Orleans is only one example of pluralism in the United States. In fact, you can find people from different backgrounds living together all over the nation.

Find Los Angeles on the map on page 5. People with Irish, German, English, Chinese, Japanese, African, Mexican, and other backgrounds have settled there.

A woman named Harriette Lane Levy wrote a book about growing up as a Jew in San Francisco in the late 1800s. Here Levy describes the people of many different backgrounds who lived in her neighborhood:

The baker was German; the fish man, Italian; the grocer, a Jew; the butcher, Irish; the steam laundryman, a New Englander. The vegetable vendor and the regular laundryman who came to the house were Chinese.

Harriette Lane Levy, 902 O'Farrell Street, 1937

The United States is a pluralistic culture. This was true in the past, and it is true today. You will see this as you study the stories of the many people who make up the United States. ■

■ *Why do historians say that the United States is a pluralistic culture?*

▼ *According to the graph, which ethnic group is largest in New York?*

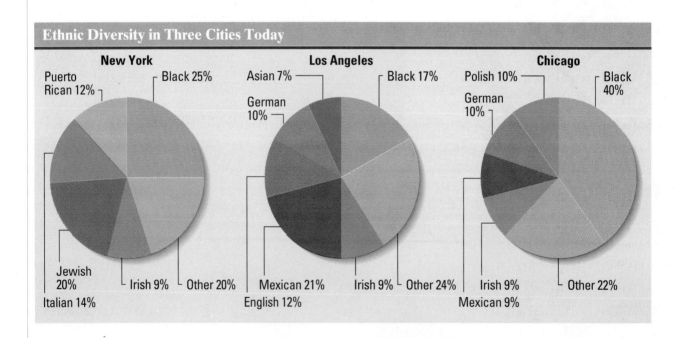

Ethnic Diversity in Three Cities Today

New York
- Puerto Rican 12%
- Black 25%
- Jewish 20%
- Irish 9%
- Other 20%
- Italian 14%

Los Angeles
- Asian 7%
- Black 17%
- German 10%
- Mexican 21%
- Irish 9%
- Other 24%
- English 12%

Chicago
- Polish 10%
- Black 40%
- German 10%
- Irish 9%
- Other 22%
- Mexican 9%

REVIEW

1. **FOCUS** What makes New Orleans an example of pluralism?

2. **GEOGRAPHY** How did the location of New Orleans lead to its becoming a pluralistic culture?

3. **CRITICAL THINKING** Do you consider your town or city to be a pluralistic community? Explain.

4. **ACTIVITY** Find three examples of how your community has borrowed from other cultures. Examples may include the name of a town or building, holidays the community celebrates, local heros, or popular foods. What ethnic groups contributed to your community's history?

Using Encyclopedias

Here's Why

You often need to use reference materials to get information. Encyclopedias are reference books with information about many subjects. This chapter tells about the New Orleans Jazz and Heritage Festival. Suppose you want to know more about that city. An encyclopedia can give you an overview of New Orleans.

Here's How

Articles in an encyclopedia are arranged alphabetically. A one-volume encyclopedia has an index in the back that lists all its topics or articles with their page numbers. If an encyclopedia has many volumes, its entire last volume may be an index.

The part of an index below shows N:278—volume N, page 278—as the location of the main article about New Orleans. Part of the article on page 278 is shown below. It is divided into sections to make it easier to understand. Each section has its own title or subhead.

At the end of the article, this encyclopedia tells you about articles related to your topic. It also lists additional resources.

Try It

In the back of this book is a Minipedia, reference material arranged like an encyclopedia. Find the article Immigration on page 557.

This article includes graphs and charts. Look at the graph on current immigration to find how many immigrants come to the U.S. from Mexico each year. Look at the chart of major waves of immigration to find out which group came because of religious persecution.

Apply It

Use an encyclopedia to find information about your state. When did it become part of the United States? Does a natural feature or historical event make it special? What is its major crop or industry?

Heading   Pronunciations   More information in the encyclopedia

New Orleans

New Orleans, *AWR lee uhnz, awr LEENZ,* or *AWR luhnz,* is the largest city in Louisiana and one of the world's busiest ports. It is also a leading business, cultural, and industrial center of the Southern United States. New Orleans lies along the Mississippi River about 100 miles (160 kilometers) north of where the river flows into the Gulf of Mexico.

Subhead ———— **The city**

New Orleans covers 364 square miles (943 square kilometers), including 165 square miles (427 square kilometers) of inland water. The city occupies all of Orleans parish and has the same boundaries as the parish. In Louisiana, counties are called *parishes.*

Related articles in *World Book* include:
Armstrong, Louis
Civil War (Capture of New Orleans)
Blenville, Sieur de
Louisiana Purchase

Additional resources ——— Other places to find information
Fodor's New Orleans. McKay, 1983.
Huber, Leonard V. *New Orleans:
    A Pictorial History.* Crown, 1982.

Index ——— Guide to the encyclopedia
New Orleans [Louisiana] **N:278**
    with pictures and maps
Civil War (Capture of New Orleans)
    Ci:629
Louisiana (Territorial Days) **l:502;**
    picture on L:503

Adapted from the World Book *Encyclopedia. © 1990 World Book, Inc. by permission.*

The Immigrant Experience

I nterviewing an immigrant to the United States will help you understand the dreams and hopes that built America. People came here from all over the world for many different reasons. Each one has a story to tell.

Get Ready

The person you interview can be a relative, friend, neighbor, fellow student, or teacher. If you don't know anyone who is an immigrant, ask your family or your teacher to help you. Be sure to have your notebook, a list of questions, a pencil or pen, and possibly a tape recorder. Ask permission to record the interview.

Find Out

The person you're interviewing may be eager to tell you an interesting story. If so, listen to the story before you go on with your questions. Remember to ask about the journey

1. Where were you born?
2. When did you come to America?
3. Who was your first American friend?

to America and the reasons for immigrating. How did the person feel? Scared? Excited? Where did he or she live? Go to school? Get his or her first job? Learn to speak English?

Move Ahead

Tape a large world map to the classroom wall. Use pins or colored pens to show where the people you interviewed came from. Mark the places in this country where they first settled. How many people came directly to your community?

Read your interview to the class. If someone else interviewed the same person, combine your information and take turns reading aloud. If you heard a very exciting story, turn it into a short play. Ask some classmates to help you act it out.

Explore Some More

After sharing your interviews, you may have more questions about the immigrant experience. Choose a particular ethnic group and find out as much as you can about it.

Learn what foods, customs, music, arts, or crafts this group brought to America. Are immigrants from this country still coming to America in large numbers?

You can arrange another interview with someone who knows a lot about the ethnic group you've chosen. Museums, cultural centers, churches, and libraries can also be sources of information as can some special programs featuring ethnic groups.

Foreign language newspapers help people keep in touch with their countries of origin.

L E S S O N   2

A Land of Immigrants

THINKING
FOCUS

How has immigration made the United States a pluralistic country?

Key Terms

- immigrant
- descendant

➤ *Ernesto Galarza became a university professor and an expert on the experiences of immigrants.*

> T hat night we shared a small room. . . . with two ladies and their children. There was little space for anything besides the army cots lined up in two rows. There were no windows in the adobe room and the only light came from the kitchen. . . . Our wet clothes and shoes were arranged near the stove to dry.
>
> In the sunny morning of the next day we walked back to the station. Our train was still there, the flats and the boxcars and coaches deserted, Mexican and American soldiers walking back and forth. "Look, the American flag," my mother said. It was flying over a building near us. Down the street, beyond the depot, there was a Mexican flag on a staff. "We are in the United States. Mexico is over there."

The story you just read is by Ernesto Galarza from his book *Barrio Boy.* As a young boy in the early 1900s, Galarza traveled with his family from Mexico to their new home in the United States. They arrived late one night in the city of Nogales, Arizona.

Ernesto Galarza begins his story by describing his early years in a small mountain village in Mexico. *Barrio Boy* goes on to tell how Galarza and his family were forced to leave their village and move to a nearby city. Galarza's book also explains why his family finally decided to leave Mexico and come to the United States to live. After a difficult journey by train, the Galarza family settled in Sacramento, California.

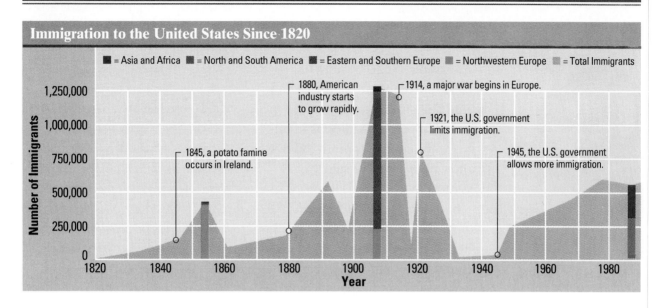

Immigration to the United States Since 1820

■ = Asia and Africa ■ = North and South America ■ = Eastern and Southern Europe ■ = Northwestern Europe ■ = Total Immigrants

Number of Immigrants (y-axis): 0, 250,000, 500,000, 750,000, 1,000,000, 1,250,000

Year (x-axis): 1820, 1840, 1860, 1880, 1900, 1920, 1940, 1960, 1980

1845, a potato famine occurs in Ireland.

1880, American industry starts to grow rapidly.

1914, a major war begins in Europe.

1921, the U.S. government limits immigration.

1945, the U.S. government allows more immigration.

America's Many People

One reason America is so diverse is that it was settled by immigrants. An **immigrant** is a person who moves permanently from one country to live in another.

A Land of Immigrants

Everyone who lives in the United States is either an immigrant or the descendant of immigrants. **Descendants** are the children and grandchildren of earlier generations.

Even American Indians, the first people to live in America, came from Asia many thousands of years ago. Since then people from many lands have moved to this country.

All of us, somewhere in our past, have relatives who immigrated to this land. Some of us are descendants of people who came willingly to the United States in search of a new life. Others are descendants of people who were forced to come to America—perhaps on slave ships. Together,

immigrants and their descendants make up the people of the United States today.

People from Many Nations

English people were among the first Europeans to come to North America. They first arrived during the 1600s and built towns in areas that are now Massachusetts and Virginia. Many Irish and German people came to America in the 1840s. They settled in cities like New York and Philadelphia.

In the early 1900s, millions of immigrants arrived from southern and eastern Europe and Asia. Italians, Russian Jews, Greeks, Poles, Chinese, and Japanese all came to the United States at that time.

Study the timeline on this page. Where did most of the immigrants come from between 1820 and 1914? Where have most come from since 1950? These people came to the United States from many different places and for many different reasons. ■

▲ What events—in the United States or elsewhere—affected immigration? How did those events affect immigration?

How Do We Know?

HISTORY *We know a lot about the immigrants who came to the United States from records kept at Ellis Island in New York. Ellis Island was an arrival center for immigrants from 1892 through 1954. Today it is being restored and will serve as a museum for the immigrant experience in America.*

■ *Why do you think historians call the United States a "nation of immigrants?"*

13

Why People Came

Most people who came to America loved their countries and would have liked to remain in them. However, conditions in immigrants' countries often did not allow people to live safely or comfortably.

In the 1600s, some English people were persecuted for their religious beliefs. In 1840, the Irish suffered crop failures that caused much starvation. In the 1880s, Russian Jews were made to leave their country by a government that didn't like their religion.

No one story can describe every immigrant's experiences. However, in telling his story, Ernesto Galarza describes feelings that were shared by other immigrants. For example, troubles at home forced Galarza's family to leave Mexico. Galarza remembered his family's poverty.

▲ *This Jewish immigrant came to New York from Russia around 1900.*

■ *Why did the Galarza family decide to leave Mexico and go to the United States?*

*A*nother kind of news that Jose brought us was about the scarcity of work in the town. More peasants were coming down from the mountain villages to find a safe place for their families and to work. Gustavo came back one weekend from his job at the sugar mill to tell us he had been laid off.

Galarza's family was also caught in a revolution, a war between people and their government. "There was gunfire in some part of the town every night. . . . Schools closed and there was no sewing for my mother to do."

Like the English immigrants of the 1600s and the Irish of the 1840s, Galarza's family decided to leave their homeland. They wanted to start a new life in the United States. ■

The Trip to America

Traveling from one's homeland to a new country has often been hard. From the 1600s to the 1900s, millions of European immigrants crossed the Atlantic Ocean to America by ship. Usually the conditions on board were very uncomfortable. People were packed into dark, wet areas of the ship. Food was poor and there was often very little water.

In *Journey to Pennsylvania,* published in 1750, Gottlieb Mittelberger described a voyage made by German immigrants at that time.

▼ *An Irish man reads a poster advertising opportunities in America.*

*A*t length, when, after a long and tedious voyage, the ships come in sight of land. . . . all creep from below on deck to see the land from afar, and they weep for joy, and pray and sing, thanking and praising God. The sight of land makes the people on board the ship, especially the sick and the half-dead, alive again. . . .

Ernesto Galarza's family traveled from Mexico to the United States by train. This journey also was difficult. Their trip was

◄ Nearly nine million immigrants arrived in the United States between 1900 and 1910. Most came from Europe on ships like this one.

Across Time & Space

The United States continues to accept immigrants who have left home because of political troubles and wars. These people are called refugees. In recent years the United States has accepted refugees from Cuba, Central America, the Soviet Union, and Southeast Asia.

interrupted for several weeks when Galarza became sick with measles. He stayed in a tent near the tracks with other sick children until he was well enough to travel.

When Galarza's journey began again, the train moved slowly and only during the day. At one point the tracks had been destroyed by revolutionary soldiers and had to be repaired before the train could move on.

Galarza's first memory of the United States was the sight of the American flag flying over the town of Nogales, Arizona. After 1886, the first sight of America for most European immigrants was the Statue of Liberty in New York Harbor. Whether they came by ship or by train, though, all immigrants wondered the same thing: What would their lives be like in this strange new country? ■

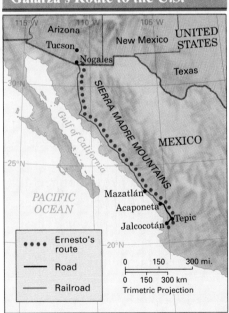

Galarza's Route to the U.S.

- •••• Ernesto's route
- —— Road
- —— Railroad

0   150   300 mi.
0 150 300 km
Trimetric Projection

◄ In Ernesto Galarza's boyhood, there were only a few ways to go from Mexico to the United States: on a train, in a cart or wagon, or on foot.

■ In what ways did Galarza's trip differ from the one described by Mittelberger? In what ways was it the same?

Life in a New Country

From Nogales, the Galarza family moved to Sacramento, California. They found life there very different from life in Mexico. The family moved to a *barrio,* a neighborhood where other Mexican people lived. But people from other countries lived there as well.

15

A Nation of Many Peoples

Most immigrants began their new lives in American cities. Sacramento, California, shown here in the 1920s, was just one of many cities where immigrants settled.

■ *How did Galarza's life in the United States differ from his life in Mexico?*

The women walked on the street in kimonos, wooden sandals, and white stockings, carrying neat black bundles on their backs and wearing their hair in puffs with long ivory needles stuck through them. When they met, they bowed.

The lower quarter [of the city] was not exclusively a Mexican barrio but a mix of nationalities. Between L and N Streets two blocks from us, the Japanese had taken over. Their homes were in the alleys behind shops.

Galarza was fascinated by the way the Japanese women in his neighborhood dressed and acted.

Galarza found not only Japanese in his neighborhood, but also Filipinos, Portuguese, Italians, Poles, Yugoslavs, Koreans, and blacks. He described his neighborhood as a joyful mixture. "It was a kaleidoscope [changing pattern] of colors and languages and customs that surprised and absorbed me at every turn."

Most immigrants who arrived in America in the 1800s and 1900s shared Galarza's interest in the new country. Like Galarza, most of these people had left countries where people looked and acted in similar ways and where everyone shared a similar culture. But here in America, they found a new kind of life.

In America people looked different, spoke different languages, and had different customs. These people had become part of America's pluralistic culture. ■

R E V I E W

1. **FOCUS** How has immigration made the United States a pluralistic culture?
2. **CONNECT** Why would both New Orleans and Sacramento be considered examples of pluralism?
3. **HISTORY** What kinds of conditions might cause a person to leave his or her country and come to America?
4. **CRITICAL THINKING** When a person lives in a neighborhood with many different nationalities, what should he or she do to understand and get along well with others?
5. **ACTIVITY** After the class has had time to answer question number four, collect your classmates' ideas and make a list of helpful hints called "Living Together in a Neighborhood of Many Cultures."

L E S S O N   3

A Country of Many Cultures

Nine o'clock sharp the next morning, Shirley sat in the principal's office at P. S. 8. Her mother and the schoolmistress were talking. Shirley didn't understand a word. It was embarrassing. Why hadn't she, too, studied the English course on the records that Father had sent? But it was too late now. She stopped trying to understand. Suddenly, mother hissed, in Chinese. "Stop that or else!"

Shirley snapped her head down. She had been staring at the stranger. But she could not keep her eyes from rolling up again. There was something more foreign about the principal than about any other foreigner she had seen so far.

Bette Bao Lord, *In the Year of the Boar and Jackie Robinson*

The character in this story is an immigrant from China. She speaks little English and has a hard time making friends at school. However, she does learn to play baseball. When she learns about Jackie Robinson, the first black player to break into the major leagues, she feels ". . . as if she had grown as tall as the Statue of Liberty."

THINKING FOCUS

How does a pluralistic culture benefit America? How does it challenge America?

Key Terms

- ethnic custom
- prejudice

◄ *When this picture was taken, Bette Bao Lord was about the age of Shirley, the character in her story.*

Benefits of Many Cultures

In a society made up of many cultures, people borrow music, foods, clothes, and other things from each other. But one of the most important things they borrow is language.

17

▲ Greek and Syrian immigrants brought pita bread to America.

➤ Dark rye bread came from northern Europe.

➤ French bread came with French immigrants to New Amsterdam (New York) and North Carolina in the 1600s.

▼ American Indians baked corn bread long before Europeans arrived in America.

You may not know that words you use every day have come from other cultures. The word *kindergarten* is German, meaning "children's garden." *Cookie* comes from Holland. *Mosquito* is Spanish. *Corral*, a place where horses are kept, comes from the African word *kraal*. Early settlers in the Western United States learned the word

UNDERSTANDING CULTURE

*I*mmigrants to the United States often begin living just like other Americans. They buy the clothing, furniture, and foods used by their native-born neighbors. In this way immigrants come to feel that they share in the culture of America.

Similar Cultures

Culture is the way of life shared by a group of people. For example, many Japanese people share similar ideas about how a person should behave. These beliefs have been handed down from generation to generation. They are cultural beliefs.

A group of people who share a culture often live in the same area. However, people who live in the same area do not always have the same culture. If the people in an area do not share the same beliefs, outlooks, and values, they do not have the same culture.

Pluralistic Cultures

Pluralistic cultures are made up of many subcultures, or cultures within a culture. For example, Japanese immigrants may practice Japanese customs while still being part of American culture.

People who are part of a culture have a sense of belonging. Even in America, with its pluralism, people share many beliefs and want many of the same things in life.

from black pioneers. The next time you order a hamburger, remember that it is named after Hamburg, a city in Germany.

Like language, culture itself changes slowly over time. People who immigrated to America did not simply drop their ways of life. They kept many of their customs. A custom that is special to a group of immigrants is called an **ethnic custom.** Ethnic customs have enriched our country and given us diversity in our daily lives.

Claudia DeMonte, an artist who was raised in Astoria, an Italian neighborhood in New York, speaks fondly of her ethnic customs.

Although my life style today is far removed from Astoria, I am still attached to my roots, to the foods and customs. I think it is great to have lasagna for Thanksgiving and to have fish on Christmas Eve. That is a wonderful part of my life, and I hate to think that it might be lost. What makes America great is that each ethnic group still loves and eats the dishes their parents and grandparents ate. If we all dropped that and ate hamburgers . . . I think it would be tragic.

Claudia DeMonte,
Growing Up Italian

Across Time & Space

During the 1950s, teachers in the United States often forbade students to speak a foreign language in school. Today students are encouraged to express themselves in foreign languages and in English.

Ethnic customs, such as special holiday celebrations or foods like the breads you see here, help people to remember their ancestors' way of life. Bette Bao Lord, the

▽ Jewish settlers brought matzo to New Amsterdam (New York) in 1654.

◀ Italian bread like this may first have been made by Roman bakers 2,000 years ago.

▽ Indians in Mexico and Central America first made tortillas.

◀ Croissants have a French name, but they were first baked in Vienna, Austria, in 1686.

author of the story about the Chinese immigrant Shirley, explained how she felt about keeping her Chinese customs. She said,

"I think we hyphenated [immigrant] Americans are doubly blessed. We can choose the best of both [cultures]." ■

Challenges of Many Cultures

As you have learned, pluralism has many benefits. However, pluralism also has created some challenges for America. Much of the history of the United States is the story of how America has met the challenges of pluralism.

One challenge of pluralism is the many languages spoken by people in America. You have read that Americans borrow words from other cultures. This makes our culture more rich and interesting. Sometimes, however, it is hard for Americans to understand the languages spoken by all the people they meet. You may hear different languages in your own classroom. In many places, students in a class speak several different languages.

Immigrants who come to America often feel as if they have to change. They think they must leave behind the ways of their own ethnic groups.

For example, Elizabeth Wong's family came to California from China. Her parents sent Elizabeth to Chinese school after regular school, so she could learn Chinese writing and customs. Elizabeth hated Chinese school. She wanted to be an "all-American girl." Later, however, she felt sad because she had lost her Chinese customs. Here is what she says about her experience.

Public places, like zoos, often put up signs that can be easily understood by everyone.

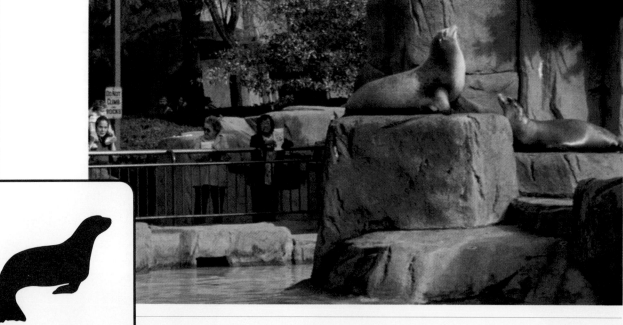

I thought of myself as multicultural. I preferred tacos to egg rolls; I enjoyed Cinco de Mayo [a Mexican celebration] more than Chinese New Year.

At last I was one of you; I wasn't one of them.

Sadly, I still am.

Elizabeth Wong, "The Struggle to Be an All-American Girl"

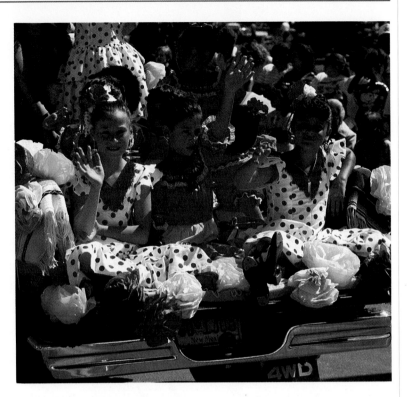

▲ *Today life in America is enriched by immigrant cultures. Here a group of Mexican-Americans ride in a parade in Sante Fe, New Mexico.*

When cultures mix, people sometimes have a hard time understanding one another. Ernesto Galarza tells of an American habit he found hard to understand:

We had to get used to the Americans. They did not listen if you did not speak loudly, as they always did. In the Mexican style people would know you were enjoying their jokes tremendously if you merely smiled and shook a little, as if you were trying to swallow your mirth. In the American style there was little difference between a laugh and a roar, and until you got used to them you could hardly tell whether the boisterous Americans were roaring mad or roaring happy.

Maybe the hardest problem in a pluralistic culture is **prejudice,** disliking a person without knowing anything about them. You will learn how immigrants, Native Americans, and blacks have met with prejudice.

Pluralism is good for a nation. However, it also presents challenges. This textbook tells the story of a nation that faced those challenges as it grew. The special story of the American nation is how the people built a united country in spite of their great diversity. ■

■ *What challenges do immigrants face in the United States?*

REVIEW

1. **FOCUS** How does pluralism benefit America? How does it challenge America?
2. **CONNECT** Do you think a language problem was a challenge in New Orleans? Explain.
3. **CITIZENSHIP** Why is prejudice a problem in a country of many cultures?
4. **CRITICAL THINKING** Elizabeth Wong did not want to practice the customs of her parents. Why do you think young students sometimes prefer to be like their classmates rather than be seen as part of a special group?
5. **WRITING ACTIVITY** Together with a partner write a short story using at least seven words that come from languages other than English.

21

A Nation of Many Peoples

Gooseberries to Oranges

Barbara Cohen

A new beginning in America—this was the dream of many who came and of many who still come. America provides freedom, hope, and opportunities for education and work. Our country is woven together with the threads of many stories like this one of eight-year-old Fanny as she leaves her familiar village to join her father in New York.

As you have learned, immigrants from many nations came to America. Like Ernesto in Lesson 2, Fanny in this story gives up one life for a strange new one.

gooseberries small sour berries

mezuzah (muh ZUZ uh) a small box holding papers with words from the Bible written on them

scroll a roll of paper with writing on it

polluted not clean

epidemic rapid spread of a disease

cholera a serious disease of the stomach and intestines

cubbyhole a small, enclosed space

Listen, darlings, and I'll tell you a story about what happened to me when I was a little girl. I lived far away, in Europe, in a village named Rohatyn. My mother was dead. My father had gone to America. I lived with Aunt Rebecca. She couldn't have loved me more if I had been her own child.

My cousin Leah loved me too. She had blue eyes and white skin, like an angel. She washed my hair. She took me for walks. In the spring we picked wild strawberries from the fields. In the summer we ate gooseberries right off the bushes. In the fall we sucked brown pears that grew on trees in front of Aunt Rebecca's little house.

But winter came, and war. We put feather pillows around the walls of the rooms so if bullets hit our house they wouldn't hurt us. Soldiers in steel helmets searched every corner, looking for boys to take away to the army. They tore the mezuzah off the door jamb because they thought gold was hidden inside. There was no gold inside the mezuzah, only a little scroll inscribed with words from the Bible.

We had nothing to eat. The well became polluted. An epidemic of cholera roared through Rohatyn. Aunt Rebecca died. Cousin Leah died. Half the village died. I was eight.

A letter arrived from Papa. "America is the golden land," he said. "Here is a ticket so that you can come to America too."

Did I want to leave my village? Did I want to leave the gooseberries and the little brown pears? But when my Aunt Elke came to get me, I went. So did Aunt Elke's children, Cousin Sylvia, Cousin Sam, Cousin Rose, and Cousin Betty.

The ship carried more people than lived in our whole village. The six of us stayed in a tiny little cubbyhole down deep inside the ship. It had no windows. There were no beds to sleep on, only hammocks, and nothing to eat except moldy bread and Swiss cheese.

Every day on the deck I saw a man studying from a book or rocking back and forth in prayer. He never spoke to me, but I liked to look at him. Papa had written that in America everyone could get an education. Everyone could be learned.

One day I saw another man holding a round, bright thing. "What kind of little ball is that?" I asked him.

"It's not a ball," the man said. "It's an orange. It's to eat." Very slowly, very carefully, he peeled away the skin. Underneath the bumpy skin were plump, juicy sections of fruit. He threw the skin over the railing and into the ocean. He pulled one section away from the others and popped it into his mouth. He chewed it slowly, and then he swallowed it. He did that with another section and another section and another section until the whole orange was gone.

A few days later I saw the orange man again. "Have you seen the man with the book?" I asked him.

"Didn't you hear?" the orange man said. "He threw himself overboard. He drowned."

"Why?" I cried. "Why did he do that?"

The orange man shrugged. "He was very sick. He was coughing blood. He knew that when he got to America they would send him back. He decided he'd rather be dead."

Every night I prayed that I wouldn't get sick, and that Aunt Elke and Sylvia, Sam, Rose, and Betty wouldn't get sick.

The ship pulled into New York harbor. We passed the Statue of Liberty. All the passengers stood on the deck and cheered.

We came to Ellis Island. Inspectors opened our bundles and examined every candlestick, every feather bed, inside and out. They screamed questions at us. We couldn't understand what they said. They grabbed us by the arms and shoulders and pushed and shoved us where they wanted us to go.

I stood in a dark corner of a huge room. A woman in a uniform took scissors and cut off my two long braids, snip, snap, snip, snap. I shoved the braids into my coat pocket. She pulled my hair this way and that way, peering at my scalp.

Then she rolled up the sleeves of my dress. She stared at my arms. They were covered with spots. I hadn't taken my dress off the whole time I was on the ship. I hadn't even known I had a rash.

Did the rash mean I was sick? I couldn't understand what anyone was saying. They pushed and shoved me to a tall brick building with a thousand windows. Inside, the rooms were very white, so white they blinded my eyes, and very clean. They were the cleanest white rooms in the universe.

For days I lay on a white bed, wearing a white gown. I cried

Ellis Island   the place in New York Harbor where immigrants entered the United States

23

peddlers person who travels around selling goods

P.S. public school

Yiddish Germanic language spoken mainly by Jews

tsatskeleh (TSAH tskeh leh) my favorite

the whole time. I was sure they were going to send me back to the old country. What would I do there all alone?

After a week the rash had disappeared from my arms and they gave me back my clothes, all wrinkled, but clean.

A man came into the long white room. He looked familiar to me, but I didn't know who he was.

He walked over to my bed. "Fanny," he said, "don't you know me? Don't you know who I am?"

"Papa?" I whispered.

"Yes, Papa," he said. He put his arms around me and hugged me. I put my arms around him and hugged him back.

Then Papa took me home. He lived on Attorney Street, in a two-room apartment with his new wife. He worked in a garment factory where he earned three dollars a week.

The street was crowded with people and shops and peddlers and cats. Voices screamed from the windows. Laundry hung from the fire escapes.

Papa had said America was a golden land. I had thought that meant the streets were paved with gold. They weren't. They were paved with garbage—huge barrels so stuffed with old newspapers and rotting apples and potato peels that they overflowed—and wherever I walked, I stepped on something hard or rustly or squishy.

I went to school. I learned to speak English. I learned to read it and write it too. I went to the library. They gave you books for nothing. You had to bring them back, but when you did, they let you take others.

I made a friend. Her name was Selma and she went to P.S. 174, just like me. In the summer, if it was very hot, Selma and I slept outside on the fire escape.

Next door, Mrs. Ludwig sewed sleeves into coats. One day she said to me, "Fanny, if you take this bundle of coats to the factory for me, I'll give you two nickels."

"I'll take it for you, Mrs. Ludwig," I said. "I'll take it for you anywhere."

The bundle was so big I couldn't see over it. It was heavy too. But when I got back from the factory, Mrs. Ludwig gave me two nickels, just as she had promised. I looked at the nickels for a long time. Then I went back to our flat.

My father was sitting at the kitchen table. I held out my hand to him. The two nickels were lying in my palm. He looked up from the Yiddish paper he was reading. He saw the nickels in my hand. "Where did you get two nickels, Fanny?" he asked me.

"Mrs. Ludwig gave them to me because I took a bundle of coats over to the factory for her," I said. "They're for you."

Carefully he closed my fingers over the nickels. "No, tsatskeleh," he said, "they're for you."

I took one nickel and put it under my pillow. I would use it to go with Selma to see a Charlie Chaplin movie. The other nickel I held tight in my fist.

I ran out of our flat and down five flights of steps. I ran out on the street. A fruit peddler usually stood near the curb.

Yes, she was there. I rushed over to her. "Two oranges, please," I said. I held out my nickel.

She took the nickel. "Pick out your own oranges," she said. "Pick whichever oranges you want."

I stared at the oranges for a long time. Finally I chose the two that seemed to me to be the brightest, the largest, and the roundest.

Then I ran back into our building and up the five flights of steps to our flat. I put one orange on the table in front of my father. Then I sat down next to him. I peeled the other orange very, very slowly. I pulled it apart, section by section. I sucked each section until it was dry, and then I chewed and swallowed what was left. It tasted like heaven.

If at that very moment a gate had opened, and on the other side of the gate were the wild gooseberries and little brown pears of Rohatyn, I would not have walked through that gate.

I was already home.

Further Reading

Child of the Owl. Lawrence Yep. Casey is sent to live with her grandmother in San Francisco's Chinatown. She knows nothing of her Chinese heritage and faces many puzzling situations.

Hello, My Name Is Scrambled Eggs. Jamie Gilson. Harvey's family is the sponsor of a newly arrived Vietnamese family. Harvey is determined to help the son, a boy his own age, become an instant American, but his plans get "scrambled."

Chapter Review

Reviewing Key Terms

culture (p. 6)
descendant (p. 13)
ethnic custom (p. 19)
immigrant (p. 13)
pluralism (p. 6)
prejudice (p. 21)

A. Read the sentences below. Rewrite each sentence using a key term in place of the underlined words.

1. <u>Groups of people from many different backgrounds</u> can make a city colorful and interesting.
2. Ernesto Galarza's family were <u>people who moved from one country to another</u>.
3. The people of New Orleans give the city an exciting <u>way of life</u>.
4. <u>Disliking a person without knowing anything about them</u> is a very unfair way to judge someone.

B. Each statement below describes a descendant, an ethnic custom, or a prejudice. Using information from the chapter, explain your choice.

1. A child's grandparents came to America from Russia.
2. Special foods are part of holiday celebrations for many people.
3. Brass bands sometimes march in funerals for people in New Orleans.
4. During the 1840s, many Boston businesses refused to hire Irish immigrants.
5. The way people dress and greet each other can be different from place to place.
6. The first Indians who came to America were originally from Asia.

Exploring Concepts

A. Copy the following chart on your paper. Fill in the empty columns with facts from the chapter.

Immigrant group	Why they left their homeland	Where they settled in America
French	To explore America	Louisiana
Mexican		
English		
Russian		
Irish		
Black		

B. Write one or two sentences to answer each of the questions below.

1. What did New Orleans, New York City, and Sacramento have in common during the 1800s and early 1900s?
2. Why did Russian Jews come to the United States during the 1880s?
3. According to Mittelberger, how did Germans feel when they reached America?
4. What did Ernesto Galarza and Elizabeth Wong do to help themselves fit into the American culture?
5. Why do the descendants of immigrants follow their ethnic customs?
6. How has pluralism in New Orleans influenced music in that city?
7. List three challenges Americans face in a pluralistic culture.

Reviewing Skills

1. Look in the Minipedia article on Mexico. Find out what the three colors in the Mexican flag stand for, and write them down.
2. Continue studying the Minipedia article on Mexico. Then answer the following questions: What is the estimated 1990 population of Mexico? What percent of the people live in cities? What are two important national holidays? When did Mexican women win the right to vote?
3. Interview a relative or a neighbor and ask them questions about their ancestors. What county or countries did they come from? Does their family follow any special traditions or customs from that country? Ask them if they feel it is important to keep traditions.
4. Suppose you want to learn more about immigration. You are curious about the millions of immigrants who came to Ellis Island in New York City. How would you learn about it? In what kind of book would you find this information?

Using Critical Thinking

1. Martin Luther King, Jr., once said: "I have a dream that my four little children will one day live in a nation where they will not be judged by the color of their skin, but by the content of their character." What challenge to American culture was King talking about? Do you think King was referring only to his children or to all children? Explain.
2. The Sioux Indians have the following saying: "A people without history is like the wind on the buffalo grass." This means people without customs or tradition are like people without a past. Think about the saying. Do you think Elizabeth Wong and Claudia DeMonte would agree with the Sioux? Give reasons for your answer using information from the chapter.
3. You probably have heard people say, "Wouldn't life be boring if everyone were the same?" And likely it would be boring. Think about all the ethnic influences in your life today. Food, popular music, and clothing styles are three areas where you can see the mark of different ethnic groups. List three countries or regions of the world that you think have put their mark on our culture. Then decide how each country has given us food, music, or clothing choices that make our lives more interesting.

Preparing for Citizenship

1. **WRITING ACTIVITY** Use restaurants to measure the diversity of your town or city's culture. Find the restaurant listings in your local Yellow Pages. First, write down four types of ethnic restaurants, such as Chinese, French, or Italian. Then, list two or three restaurants under each group. Hold a discussion with four to five other students. Write down the names of some dishes served by the different restaurants.
2. **COLLABORATIVE LEARNING** Form two-person teams to look at immigrant groups in the United States today. Have each team cover a specific immigrant group, such as Mexican, Vietnamese, or Pakistani. Cut out newspaper articles and watch television programs to collect information. Research the country's flag, national holidays, or other symbols of their homeland. Write your report and display your articles.

Chapter 2
This Land of Ours

"From sea to shining sea . . ." The song "America the Beautiful" gives us many different pictures of our land: amber waves of grain, purple mountains, and fruited plains. Americans have explored this land, made maps of it, moved across it, and built homes on it. Each place has shaped the people who lived there and the events that happened there. In many ways the story of America is the story of its land.

Europeans first learned about the land of America by exploring it. This map, made in 1527, shows what Europeans knew about North America after 35 years of exploration.

Sarah Warren's needlework from the 1700s shows a garden in Boston, Massachusetts. Warren saw the America that attracted many people to move here: a land of plenty.

2000 B.C.

Today, satellite pictures give us new views of earth and the United States. Compare this image of America with the map from 1527.

Pioneers—like the woman shown above—settled the western United States during the 1800s. Life in this land, right down to the cowboy's spurs, was shaped by the western frontier.

Today

L E S S O N   1

Understanding Geography

What types of questions do geographers seek to answer about a place?

Key Term

• geography

➤ *The Colorado River winds its way through the Grand Canyon. Notice the many layers of rock that make up the canyon walls.*

> W e are three-quarters of a mile in the depths of the earth, and the great river shrinks into insignificance, as it dashes its angry waves against the walls and cliffs, that rise to the world above; they are but puny ripples, and we but pigmies [small people], running up and down the sands, or lost among the boulders.
>
> We have an unknown distance yet to run; an unknown river yet to explore. What falls there are, we know not; what rocks beset the channel, we know not; what walls rise over the river, we know not. . . . With some eagerness, and some anxiety, and some misgiving, we enter the cañon below, and are carried along by the swift water. . . .

So wrote the famous American wilderness explorer John Wesley Powell in his diary on August 17, 1869. He led a group of eight men into the Grand Canyon in Arizona. Powell and his men became the first white men to travel down the Colorado River the entire length of the canyon.

After successful trips through the Grand Canyon, Powell became the director of the U. S. Geological Survey. In 1888, he helped found the National Geographic Society.

Studying Places and Location

John Wesley Powell was keenly interested in the geography of his native land. **Geography** is the study of the earth and the distribution of life, including people, on the earth. Geographers study the interactions of people with their environment.

Nature and People

The Grand Canyon is a place created by natural forces. It was formed over millions of years by the cutting action of the Colorado River. Many other places on the earth also have been created by nature. The Hawaiian Islands were created by volcanoes in the Pacific Ocean. Lake Michigan and the other Great Lakes were formed by melting glaciers.

Many places on the earth have been created by people. For example, the city of San Diego didn't exist until pioneers settled the area in the middle 1700s and built the Mission of San Diego.

Physical and Cultural Features

Every place on earth has its own special features. The physical features of a place include its climate, landforms, lakes, and rivers. The cultural features of its people include their languages, homes, food, and clothing.

Consider the Grand Canyon, which stretches for 277 miles. In some places, this deep gorge in the surface of the earth is over one mile deep and 18 miles wide. The

▲ *These storehouses for grain were cut into the walls of the Grand Canyon by Anasazi Indians between A.D. 1000 and 1300. The Anasazi were the ancestors of modern-day Pueblo Indians.*

These are pieces of Indian pottery. Each Indian village had its own special pottery design; today, we can tell which village made a piece of pottery by looking at the design.

■ *What features make up the physical characteristics of a place?*

canyon is made up of many folded layers of granite, sandstone, limestone, and shale.

The canyon has its own climate, too. The floor of the canyon can be 25° F warmer than the rim.

The Indians of the Grand Canyon also make this place special. Powell described the ruins of one Indian village he saw:

Here, on a terrace of trap [dark rocks], we discover another group of ruins. There was evidently quite a village on this rock. Again we find mealing stones, and much broken pottery, and up in a little natural shelf in the rock, back of the ruins, we find a globular basket, that would hold perhaps a third of a bushel. It is badly broken, and, as I attempt to take it up, it falls to pieces. There are many beautiful flint chips, as if this had been the home of an old arrow maker.

Location

Geographers are also interested in the location of any place they are studying. Location is talked about in two ways. The absolute location of a place is its exact location. For example, you might say that a house is located at 945 North Hastings. The relative location of a place is where that place is in relation to other places. You might say that a house is located across the street from the fire station.

As Powell traveled through the Grand Canyon, he always checked his location. He did this with a sextant, an instrument that people use to figure out exactly where they are on the earth. Whenever Powell came upon an interesting place in the canyon, he marked its location in his journal. This way, later explorers would know exactly where to find such places in the Grand Canyon as Bright Angel Falls and Havasu Canyon. ■

Studying Movement and Interaction

In addition to the physical and cultural features of a place, geographers study the movement that takes place in and around an area. They also study interaction, the ways that people and the environment affect each other.

The Movement of People

Geographers study all kinds of movement, including the movement of consumer goods, wildlife, ideas, fads, and people. Through these studies they gain a clearer understanding of how different

places are joined together and how people in these places communicate with one another.

As a geographer, John Wesley Powell was curious about the movement of Indian tribes into the Grand Canyon. He knew that some Indians had lived in the canyon for thousands of years. Others, however, had come to make their homes there just a few hundred years before Powell's trip. Why, Powell wondered, did these Indians choose to move into such a harsh environment?

It is ever a source of wonder to us why these ancient people sought such inaccessible places for their homes. . . . We know that, for a century or two after the settlement of Mexico, many expeditions were sent into the country now comprised in Arizona and New Mexico, for the purpose of bringing the town building people under the dominion of the Spanish government. Many of their villages were destroyed, and the inhabitants fled to regions at that time unknown; and there are traditions . . . that the cañons were these unknown lands.

▲ *John Wesley Powell talks with an Indian in the Grand Canyon in this 1873 photograph. Powell had lost his right arm during the Civil War. However, he never let this injury keep him from exploring America.*

Changing the Environment

When people move to a place, they often make lasting changes there. Geographers observe these changes and study the effects they have on the geography of the land.

How do people interact with their environment? They may clear land for farms and roadways, or dam rivers to establish power plants. They might dig canals or tunnel through mountains to build railroads.

Powell observed the effects the Indians had on the Grand Canyon.

In northern Arizona, the inhabitants [people] have actually built little terraces along the face of the cliff, where a spring gushes out, and thus made their sites for gardens. It is possible that the ancient inhabitants of this place made their agricultural lands in the same way.

In this way the Indians changed the environment of the canyon when they began to farm there. ■

■ *What are some ways in which people interact with the environment?*

R E V I E W

1. **THINKING FOCUS** What types of questions do geographers seek to answer about a place?
2. **CONNECT** Why would geographers be interested in immigration and migration?
3. **GEOGRAPHY** When geographers study a place, what features do they observe?
4. **CRITICAL THINKING** Suppose one town was located on a river that led to the sea. Another town was located in the desert, near a beautiful canyon. Which town might become an important center for trade? Which town might become a place that tourists would visit? Why?
5. **ACTIVITY** Make a two-column chart titled "Places in My State." In one column, name five places created by nature. In the second column, name five places created by people. Give each column a title.

33

This Land of Ours

L E S S O N   2

Regions of America

How do geographers define regions within the United States?

Key Terms

* cartographer
* region

➤ *Tom Sawyer and his friends floated across the United States in a hot-air balloon like the one in this engraving.*

One bright, clear, sunny day, Tom Sawyer and his two buddies, Huck Finn and Jim, set off on a grand adventure. They took to the sky in a hot-air balloon. As the trio drifted across the midsection of the United States, Huck began to worry that they weren't making much progress.

We ought to be past Illinois, oughtn't we?"

"Certainly."

"Well, we ain't."

"What's the reason we ain't?"

"I know by the color. We're right over Illinois yet. And you can see for yourself that Indiana ain't in sight."

"I wonder what's the matter with you, Huck. You know by the *color?*"

"Yes, of course I do."

"What's the color got to do with it?"

"It's got everything to do with it. Illinois is green, Indiana is pink. You show me any pink down here, if you can. No sir; it's green."

"Indiana *pink?* Why, what a lie!"

"It ain't no lie; I've seen it on the map, and it's pink."

You never see a person so aggravated and disgusted. He says:

"Well. If I was such a numskull as you, Huck Finn, I would jump over. Seen it on the map! Huck Finn, did you reckon the States was the same color out of doors as they are on the map?"

Mark Twain,
Tom Sawyer Abroad

Defining Regions

Poor Huck Finn! He kept waiting for the ground to turn pink so he would know he was over Indiana. Huck expected the land below his hot-air balloon to look just as it did on the maps he had studied in his school. He didn't realize that **cartographers**—mapmakers—often fill their maps with lines and colors to show different regions, or areas, of the world. A **region** is any area of land or water with certain characteristics that make it different from other areas.

Look at the map on the bottom of this page. This map shows land regions of the United States where different ethnic groups have settled. Notice how different regions are marked by different colors.

Regions Show Differences

To better understand the idea of regions, think of a large stadium where basketball games are held. A stadium contains many different regions, where different activities take place. For example, there is the area where the audience sits, the area where the athletes perform, and areas where merchants sell souvenirs and snacks.

These large regions are divided into smaller regions. Within the area where the audience sits, some of the seats are on the main floor, close to the action. That's one region. Other main floor seats are farther away from the court. That's a second region. Depending on which region you choose to sit in, your ticket may cost you as little as $10 or as much as $35. Each of these differences—the activities in an area, its location, and the price of a ticket—makes one region different from another.

Regions Reveal Patterns

Geographers identify regions in order to make the world easier to study. Identifying regions helps

▼ *As the colors on this map show, different ethnic groups settled in different regions of the United States.*

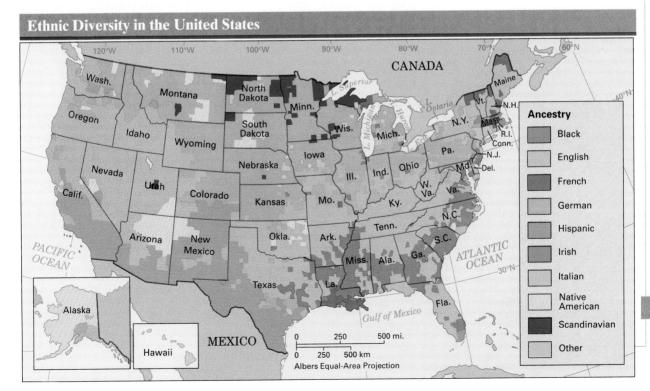

Ethnic Diversity in the United States

Ancestry
- Black
- English
- French
- German
- Hispanic
- Irish
- Italian
- Native American
- Scandinavian
- Other

geographers to see patterns in nature as well as patterns in human actions.

For example, geographers can divide the world into regions based on physical features such as annual rainfall or temperature. Some areas of the world always receive more moisture than other areas. Some areas are always much colder or hotter than other areas. A map that shows these regions can help you to understand more clearly the earth's climate. This, in turn, can help you to see why some areas have more people than other areas, or are better suited for growing crops.

Geographers also study regions to learn more about the people who live in those regions. For example, geographers might divide a country into regions based on the languages people speak, the kinds of work they do, or the annual incomes they earn. ■

■ *What are regions, and what do they show?*

Regions of the United States

Geographers can divide the United States into many different kinds of regions depending on what they are interested in studying. Geographers may define regions of the United States according to its types of land, its many climates, or the characteristics of its people.

Land

Look at the map at the bottom of this page. It shows the many land-form regions of the United States. Notice that the eastern and southeastern areas of the United States are made up of coastal plains, plateaus (elevated areas of flat land), and the hilly Appalachians.

▼ *The United States can be divided into regions based on its different types of land.*

Geographic Regions of the United States

These two photographs—Vermont on the left and Hawaii on the right— were taken at the same time of year. Notice the difference in climate.

In contrast, the center of the country is mostly wide stretches of flat land called plains. This area includes the Central Plains and the Great Plains.

The West is home to several great mountain ranges, including the Rockies, the Cascades, and the Sierra Nevada. Two huge plateaus, the Columbia and the Colorado, surround a vast low-lying area called the Great Basin.

All of these landforms have different physical features. That is why they are considered different regions of the United States. To see how cartographers put together a map showing landform regions of the United States, see A Closer Look on page 38.

Climate

The United States not only includes a variety of landforms but also enjoys many different climates. For much of the year, northern Alaska is locked in ice and snow. In the southern states, the heat and humidity can be almost tropical. Hurricanes sometimes cause destruction on the East Coast. In the west, desert temperatures soar as high as 120° F. Actually, the United States includes every major type of climate that exists on the earth.

Look at the climate map of the United States in the Atlas on page 577. Think about the different ways that climate can affect people's lives. What can you learn about the United States by studying the country's different climate regions?

People

In order to better understand the population of the United States, geographers often divide the country into regions based on the different characteristics of its people. For example, the map on page 35 shows regions of the United States based on where different ethnic groups settled after they came to this country. Compare this map to the map on page 39, which shows how many people 18 years of age and younger live in different parts of the country.

The Layers of a Map

How is a modern map made? Just like a cake—one layer at a time. The picture below shows how the map on page 36 was assembled. Each layer of information was drawn onto see-through pieces of plastic. Then the pieces were put together to form the finished map.

To make sure each line goes exactly where it should, mapmakers use a magnifying lens.

What if a layer was missing? The information on this map would be incomplete. Mapmakers think about each layer, putting in the information that the readers will need.

Label layer—words naming places on the map

Subject layer—colors showing special information

Political layer—boundaries of states and countries

What's my line? Longitude and latitude lines, coastlines, and state and country borders—these are just a few of the lines added to a map, layer by layer.

How is it done? With this scribing tool, mapmakers trace pencil lines, scratching them into one of the map's plastic layers.

Grid layer—longitude and latitude lines

Outline layer—map boxes and scales

Who might find this information on regions based on age useful? Why?

Language is another characteristic of Americans that geographers identify and study. Nearly all Americans speak at least some English. However, not everyone speaks English the same way. Americans in different parts of the country speak English in different ways. To study these variations, geographers divide the United States into regions based on language. These regions are sometimes called dialect regions.

For instance, if you walked into a restaurant in New York and asked for a "hero," you would get a sandwich on a long roll containing meats, cheeses, and relishes. If you walked into a restaurant in Florida and asked for a "hero," you might get only blank stares. In Florida, such a sandwich is called a Cuban sandwich. In New Jersey, it's called a "hoagie"; in Iowa, a "Dagwood"; in Illinois, a "sub"; and in Rhode Island, a "grinder." In New Orleans, where the sandwich is likely to contain some seafood, it's called a "poor boy," or "po' boy." ◼

◄ *Hoagie, grinder, sub, or po' boy? The sandwich remains pretty much the same, but the name changes in different parts of the country.*

◼ *Name three types of regions into which the United States can be divided.*

Population Under the Age of 18

Population Under 18 by County

- 35% or more
- 30–35%
- 25–30%
- 20–25%
- 20% or less

Alaska

Hawaii

CANADA

MEXICO

PACIFIC OCEAN

ATLANTIC OCEAN

GULF OF MEXICO

| 0 | 250 | 500 mi. |
| 0 | 250 | 500 km |

Albers Equal-Area Projection

Based on Historical Atlas of the United States. National Geographic Society, 1988.

UNDERSTANDING INTERDEPENDENCE

*E*ach region of the United States makes its own special contribution to our nation. For example, farming regions produce food and other crops, while industrial regions provide manufactured goods. The people of each region both produce goods themselves and depend on other regions to provide other goods. In this way, the regions of our nation are interdependent.

Global Interdependence

Just as the regions of the United States are interdependent, the nations of the world also depend on one another to supply their needs. No nation can hope to produce all of the goods its people need to survive. Some nations lack important raw materials. Others have poor climates for growing food. And some countries have no industry for manufacturing the consumer goods they need. By trading with one another, the nations of the world have become linked in a network of global interdependence.

Other Connections

In addition to trade, our ability to communicate and move about rapidly also binds together the nations of the world. Communication satellites can beam telephone and television signals instantly to any part of the globe. Similarly, jet travel allows people to reach distant places quickly and easily. Thanks to modern transportation and communication, events and ideas today can quickly affect many parts of the world.

REVIEW

1. **THINKING FOCUS** How do geographers define regions within the United States?
2. **CONNECT** Explain how the movement of people into an unsettled region can affect the area.
3. **GEOGRAPHY** Into how many regions can the United States be divided based on its landforms?
4. **CRITICAL THINKING** Why do geographers identify and study different regions within a country?
5. **ACTIVITY** Does your town have different regions? Make a two-column chart that shows how your town might be divided up into regions. One column should be a list of areas. The second column should tell what type of region each area belongs to.

L E S S O N 3

Studying Globes and Maps

On December 21, 1968, three American astronauts rocketed into space bound for the moon. After ten orbits of the lunar surface, the crew fired the service engine of the Apollo spacecraft and headed home. As they approached the earth, astronaut Jim Lovell radioed Mission Control to describe what he saw.

I n the center is South America—all the way down to Cape Horn. I can see Baja California and the Southwestern part of the U.S. It appears now that the East Coast is cloudy. I can see clouds over parts of Mexico, and parts of Central America are clear.

For colors, waters are all sort of a royal blue. Clouds, of course, are bright white. The land areas are generally a brownish, sort of dark brownish to light brown in texture.

THINKING FOCUS

How do globes and maps represent the real world?

Key Terms

- hemisphere
- parallel
- meridian
- latitude
- longitude
- projection

◄ *As astronauts returned from the moon, they snapped this picture of planet Earth, one of nine planets in our solar system.*

41

This Land of Ours

Finding Location in the World

Equator

Prime Meridian

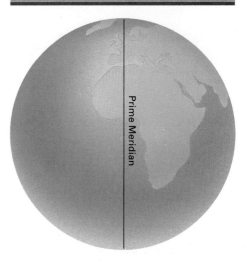

> *The equator, shown on the globe at near right, circles the globe. The Prime Meridian, on the globe at the far right, runs from the North Pole to the South Pole.*

Unlike Apollo astronaut Jim Lovell, you can't rocket into space to look at the earth from far away. You can, however, get much the same view that astronauts see by looking at a globe. A globe is a model of the earth that shows all of the earth's landforms and water features. Like the earth, a globe is a sphere that spins on its axis.

Water and Land

When you look at a globe, you can see that two-thirds of the earth's surface is covered with water. Oceans and seas surround large areas of land called continents. Other bodies of water, lakes and rivers, run through the continents.

Most geographers agree that there are seven continents: Africa, Antarctica, Asia, Australia, Europe, North America, and South America. Some geographers, however, prefer to think of Europe and Asia as two parts of one large continent. They call this

supercontinent Eurasia. These geographers point out that Europe and Asia are not separated by any body of water. In addition, Europe and Asia are not connected by just a narrow strip of land as are North and South America.

The Poles and the Hemispheres

The earth has two geographic poles. These are the North Pole and the South Pole. Exactly halfway between these two geographic poles lies the equator. The equator is an imaginary line that circles the earth and divides it into two **hemispheres.** The word *hemisphere* comes from two Greek words, *hemi* and *sphaira. Hemi* means "half," and *sphaira* means "ball." Thus, a hemisphere is half of the earth.

The half of the earth that is north of the equator is called the Northern Hemisphere; the half that is south of the equator is called the Southern Hemisphere. Look at the maps of the Northern and

Northern Hemisphere

Southern Hemisphere

Eastern Hemisphere

Western Hemisphere

Southern hemispheres at the top of this page. Which two continents are located completely within the Southern Hemisphere?

Just as the equator divides the earth into northern and southern hemispheres, two other imaginary lines divide the earth into the Eastern Hemisphere and the Western Hemisphere. One of these lines, the Prime Meridian, runs from the North Pole to the South Pole, passing through the city of Greenwich, England. On the other side of the globe, a second imaginary line also runs from the North Pole to the South Pole. This line passes through the Pacific Ocean near New Zealand. This line is called the 180° meridian.

Parallels and Meridians

The lines that divide the earth into hemispheres are part of a series of lines called parallels and meridians. On a globe, these lines cross to form a grid.

The idea of a grid on the globe began with Chang Heng, a Chinese scientist and inventor who was a royal astronomer during the Han Dynasty in the A.D. 200s. Heng thought of his grid as "throwing a net over the earth."

Parallels circle the globe in an east-west direction. They are used to measure distance north and south of the equator, which is also a parallel of latitude. Like all parallel lines, parallels of latitude never meet.

▲ *The equator, the Prime Meridian, and the 180° meridian divide the globe into four hemispheres.*

◄ *The globe at the far left shows parallels of latitude. In what ways are they different from the meridians of longitude shown on the globe at the near left?*

Latitude

Longitude

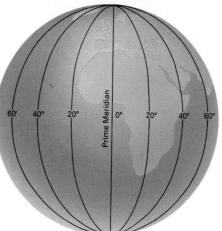

43

This Land of Ours

Meridians run north and south on a globe from the North Pole to the South Pole. Unlike parallels, which completely circle the globe, meridians go only halfway around it. Parallels never meet. Meridians, however, do meet—at the North and South poles.

Latitude and Longitude

Latitude is the measure of distance north or south of the equator. **Longitude** is the measure of distance east or west of the Prime Meridian. Geographers measure distances of latitude and longitude by degrees, which are shown by the degree symbol (°).

Latitude is measured starting at the equator, which is latitude 0°. From the equator, degrees of latitude go as far north as the North Pole, which is latitude 90° north, and as far south as the South Pole, which is latitude 90° south. Each

degree of latitude equals about 70 miles.

Distances of longitude are also measured in degrees. The Prime Meridian is longitude 0°. Any place in the world that is east of the Prime Meridian up to the 180° meridian has east longitude. Any place west of the Prime Meridian up to the 180° meridian has west longitude. East and West meet at the 180° meridian.

Because the meridians are not parallel, each degree of longitude is equal to 70 miles only at the equator. As the meridians get closer to the North and South poles, the distance between them gets smaller and smaller, until the meridians finally meet at the poles.

Latitude and longitude are important place locators. When you know the latitude and longitude of a place, you know exactly where that place is located on a globe. ■

■ *Explain the grid system that divides the earth into hemispheres and allows places to be located exactly on a globe.*

▼ *Parallels and meridians form a grid that makes it possible to locate places on a globe precisely.*

Robinson Projection

Globes to Maps

Because the earth and a globe are both spheres, a globe can show the shapes and sizes of the continents and oceans just as they are on the earth. Many times, however, a flat map is easier to use than a globe. When cartographers try to draw the curved surfaces of the earth on a flat surface, they make a **projection.**

Unfortunately, no projection can show the curved surface of the earth without changing it in some way. Arthur Robinson is a cartographer at the University of Wisconsin. He explains the problem of creating a projection by asking what would happen if a person drew a human face on an orange and then tried to remove the peel in one piece and flatten it against a table. "You'll see," Robinson says, "that in making a two-dimensional [flat] object out of a round one, something has to give." Either the face will become crooked or the

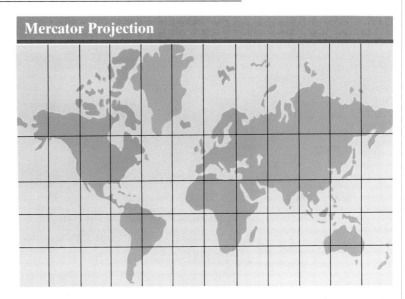

Mercator Projection

peel will break up, dividing the face into several parts.

The Mercator projection above is a good example of this problem. This projection was drawn in 1569 by Gerardus Mercator, a Flemish mathematician. Mercator's projection shows the oceans quite accurately. However, it changes the sizes of large areas of land, especially those areas near the North and South poles.

▲ *Compare the size of Greenland on this Mercator projection to the size of Greenland on the Robinson projection on page 44.*

Alaska appears to be in the center of the Pacific Ocean.

Europe and northwest Africa have been split. Asia appears much wider than it really is.

Antarctica has broken up into six pieces, one at the bottom of each section. It is difficult to see its real shape.

◄ *When a round object like this orange (or a globe) is made into a flat, object like a map, breaks and distortions occur. Compare the way the continents appear here with the way they look on the Robinson projection on page 44.*

45

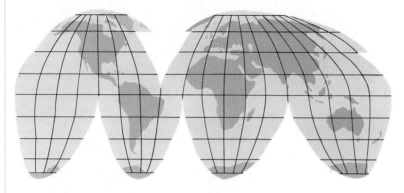

On this Goode's projection, the sizes of the continents are correct, but portions of the oceans are not shown.

▪ Why do many projections show a false view of the earth?

Across Time & Space

In 1988, the National Geographic Society, which publishes National Geographic magazine, adopted a new world map as its standard. The society had not changed its standard world map since 1943. A panel of experts looked at more than 20 different projections before choosing the Robinson projection.

Look back at the Mercator projection. Notice that Greenland appears to be larger than the whole continent of South America. In fact, Greenland has an area of 840,000 square miles, just a little bit larger than Mexico's 760,000 square miles. Looking at the

Mercator projection, you'd never know that Greenland and Mexico are about the same size.

A projection like the Goode's projection on this page divides the world into sections. This is what Robinson was talking about when he described the orange peel breaking up. This kind of projection can show the sizes and shapes of land fairly accurately. However, some people dislike using a map with parts of the oceans cut away.

To solve these problems, Arthur Robinson made his own projection in 1964. Cartographers think the Robinson projection is a major improvement in mapmaking. It is much more accurate than other projections. ▪

The Language of Maps

Every map, whether it shows the world or a plan of a shopping mall, presents a great deal of information. Some maps help you to find your way around an area. Other maps present information about the climate of an area, its population, or its points of interest. Some maps present information about important past events. In order to make full use of this information, you must first understand how to read a map.

Titles and Legends

Look at the map on page 53. What is the title of this map? The title of a map tells you its subject. Some map titles name the geographic area shown on the map. Other titles explain the purpose of the map.

Another important part of a map is the legend. The legend explains the meaning of any special lines, drawings, symbols, or colors on the map. Study the map showing ethnic settlement patterns on page 35. How many items are shown in the legend of this map? Which color does the map use to show areas where people of French origin live? Where Italian people live?

Scale

Suppose you want to know the distance between the cities of San Francisco and Bakersfield, California. You can calculate distance on a map by using a map scale. A map scale helps you to figure out distances on a map as miles or kilometers.

A map scale usually looks a little bit like a ruler. Look at the map scale on the Fault Line Cities map on page 51. The top line of the scale shows how many miles each section of the scale stands for. The bottom line of the scale shows metric measurement.

A simple way to measure distance with a scale requires using a sheet of plain, white paper. First, lay the piece of paper on the map so that the top edge runs through San Francisco and Bakersfield. Then make a pencil mark on your paper at the point where San Francisco is located. Make another pencil mark on the paper at the point where Bakersfield is located.

Now, put the first pencil mark at 0 on the scale, and line up the edge of the paper along the scale. Where on the scale does the second pencil mark fall? That is the distance between the two places.

If the distance you want to measure is longer than the scale itself, you will have to multiply. Move the paper along the scale as many times as you must in order to reach your pencil mark. Then multiply the largest number of miles on the scale by the number of times you moved the paper. The answer is the distance you are looking for.

Direction

When you look at a map of the world, it's fairly easy to see which direction is north, south, east, or west. You just look for the North and South geographic poles. However, on a map that shows a smaller area—just the states of Indiana and Ohio, for example,—the geographic poles aren't shown. How can you find direction on a map where the poles cannot be seen?

It's easy, once you find the compass rose, a small drawing that uses one or more arrows to show the four cardinal directions: north, south, east, and west. In addition to the cardinal directions, a compass rose can also help you find intermediate, or in-between, directions: northwest, northeast, southwest, and southeast. ■

This elaborate compass rose appeared on a map from 1600. The design at the top always points north.

■ *What are the various devices maps use to present information?*

R E V I E W

1. **THINKING FOCUS** How do globes and maps represent the real world?

2. **CONNECT** One way geographers talk about a place is to describe its location. If you wanted to describe the exact location of a place on a globe, what information would you give?

3. **GEOGRAPHY** What are parallels and meridians? How are they different?

4. **CRITICAL THINKING** If a friend told you that his town was exactly 2° due north of your town, how could you figure out the distance from your town to your friend's town?

5. **ACTIVITY** On a globe or world map, locate the Prime Meridian. Then make a two-column chart. Label one column "European Countries" and the other "African Countries." In the proper columns, list the European and African countries that the Prime Meridian passes through.

47

This Land of Ours

Locating Cities

Here's Why

If you were an air-traffic controller, you would often use latitude, longitude, and altitude. With these measurements, you could describe the locations of aircraft to avoid midair collisions.

You can also use latitude and longitude to describe locations on the ground. Suppose you want to locate a city based on its latitude and longitude. How do you use that information to find the city on a map?

Here's How

Suppose you want to discover what city is located at 38°N, 98°W. Notice that the latitude markers on this map begin with 45°N. Count down the latitude lines to find 38°N latitude (between the 35° and 40° lines). Place a finger at the right of the map at 38°N latitude.

Now find the longitude 98°W. Begin at the 125° longitude line on the left, and count across by fives until you get to 100°. Longitude 98° falls between 100° and 95°. Place another finger at 98°W longitude at the top of the map. Then slide your fingers down the longitude line and across the curved latitude line to find Hutchinson, Kansas, at the intersection of 38°N and 98°W.

Try It

Look at the map of the United States and name the cities at these locations:
33°N, 85°W
47°N, 123°W
43°N, 79°W
37°N, 122°W
30°N, 90°W

Apply It

Choose five U.S. cities from the Gazetteer starting on page 582. Write the latitude and longitude of each city on your paper.

Then work with two or three other students. Take turns naming the latitude and longitude of a city. Locate and name each person's city.

United States: Latitude and Longitude

L E S S O N   4

Stories Maps Tell

On a sunny June afternoon in 1849, a lone eagle wheels silently in the sky above the North Platte River. Along the river's edge, 16 covered wagons roll slowly along a dry, rutted road. Trailing a small herd of dairy cattle and swaybacked pack horses, the wagon train makes its way toward Fort Kearny. It is one of the last military outposts before the Rocky Mountains. This wagon train is following the California Trail to gold country.

Seated in the back of the lead wagon, a young man studies a well-worn map. With a finger he traces the journey of the wagon train from its start in Independence, Missouri, across the Kansas River, and on toward the Continental Divide. As he looks at his map, the young man thinks about the challenges, the dangers, and the hardships ahead.

The train is in Indian country now. Scouting parties have been formed to ride ahead of the wagons and make sure the trail is clear and the people safe from attack. Ahead on the map loom the Rocky Mountains. Crossing them is probably the most difficult and dangerous part of the trip.

Despite the dangers and hardships, the young man cannot help thinking about the wagon train's

THINKING FOCUS

What types of stories do maps tell?

Key Terms

- physical map
- fault
- historical map

◀ *Gold seekers used maps like this one to find their way to northern California.*

This Land of Ours

49

final destination—the Sacramento River Valley in northern California. As the wagons lumber on, the young man studies his map and dreams of gold nuggets and incredible riches. For the moment, the danger and hardship of his journey seem far away.

Stories About Places

Like the young gold miner's map of the California Trail, all maps have stories to tell. Maps tell stories about places, people, and history.

The Fall-Line Cities

The map at the top left of page 51 tells a story about the location and growth of some important cities near the East Coast of the United States. These cities include Trenton, New Jersey; Richmond, Virginia; and Augusta, Georgia.

This map is a **physical map**—one that shows land features such as mountains, rivers, and lakes. Notice that cities are located on rivers, at points where the rivers have rapids or falls. Why did cities grow up at these points?

The land along the East Coast of the United States is called the Atlantic Coastal Plain. This area is shown on the map on page 36. Where the Atlantic Coastal Plain meets the hard rock of the Piedmont Plateau, rivers and streams flowing toward the Atlantic Ocean form rapids and waterfalls. Geographers call this area the fall line. It stretches from Pennsylvania in the north all the way to Georgia in the south.

Indians paddling their canoes up the rivers along the fall line could not pass the rapids and falls. So they built villages at these points. When Europeans came to settle North America, they too found their ships blocked by the rapids and falls. Like the

▼ *These two maps tell different stories about New York City. The large map shows how the island of Manhattan and the other neighborhoods of New York are related to each other geographically. What is the title of the smaller map? What story does it tell?*

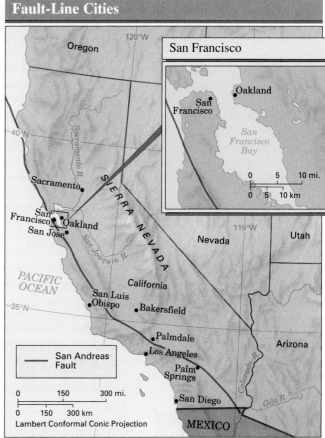

Indians before them, the Europeans also built towns at these sites.

The cities along the fall line could be reached easily from the sea, so many became important trading centers. Also, the cities were located near waterfalls, which were used at that time to make the power to run machinery. In this way, many of the cities built by European settlers became important manufacturing centers.

The Fault-Line Cities

The location of a city can have an important effect on its history, as the map at the top right of this page shows.

Just after 5:00 A.M., on April 18, 1906, a terrible earthquake rocked the city of San Francisco.

The quake caused stoves and gas lamps to overturn and gas lines to explode, spreading fires throughout the city that burned for days.

The quake and the fires destroyed more than 28,000 buildings. About 700 persons lost their lives. The 1906 San Francisco earthquake remains one of the worst natural disasters in the history of the United States.

Eighty-three years later, on October 17, 1989, at 5:04 P.M., another major earthquake shook the city of San Francisco. This time, the damage caused by the quake was not as bad as in 1906. Still, many buildings in the city were damaged beyond repair and had to be destroyed. A mile-long section of a double-decker freeway collapsed, as did a section of the Bay

▲ *These maps show the fall-line and fault-line cities. What rivers run through the city of Philadelphia? Why are the cities along the fault line in danger?*

51

This Land of Ours

Bridge connecting San Francisco with Oakland. Again, as in 1906, broken gas lines fed fires that destroyed homes and businesses.

Back in 1906, no one knew that San Francisco had been built directly over a fault. A **fault** is a break, or crack, in the earth's surface. Notice the line on the map that runs along the west coast of California. This line shows the San Andreas Fault.

Faults happen at places where different parts of the earth's crust, called plates, rub together. The map on page 51 shows the San Andreas Fault, where the Pacific plate meets the North American plate. When the pressure caused by the rubbing of these plates becomes too great, the plates slip past each other slightly, causing the violent movement of the ground called an earthquake. That's what happened in San Francisco.

Earth scientists are keeping a close watch on the San Andreas Fault, making maps to aid their study. They predict that another major earthquake—an even bigger one than the quake of 1989—will take place along this fault sometime in the near future. Scientists are now mapping the fault and measuring the pressure building up along its edges. They hope they might be able to predict when the next major earthquake is likely to take place. This could save many lives and much property. ■

These Anasazi Indian ruins are over 800 years old. Important Indian cultures like the Anasazi flourished here long before Europeans came.

■ *How can the location of a place affect what happens there?*

Stories About the Past

Maps can also tell us something about the past. Each of the four maps shown on page 53 is an **historical map**—a map that gives information about an earlier time in history. These four maps tell a story about Indian lands lost between 1775 and today.

When the earliest European explorers reached North America, they found a land with an estimated three to ten million native people who spoke some 200 languages. As more Europeans began settling the continent, they took over lands that had belonged to the Indian tribes for centuries.

Sometimes the settlers bought this land, as in 1626 when Peter Minuit purchased the island of Manhattan from the Canarsec Indians. At other times, the Indians gave their land to settlers by signing treaties that promised the Indians other lands in return. Often, however, the Indians lost their land in bloody battles with settlers who thought the land was theirs for the taking.

The first map on page 53 shows the United States in 1775. Indians held nearly all of the land in North America. The only exceptions were the areas along the East Coast where the original 13 colonies had been established and some land along the Gulf of Mexico. By 1819, however, much of the Midwest and the South was held by the government or the settlers and their descendants.

The second map shows more Indian land disappearing, especially along the West Coast. This took

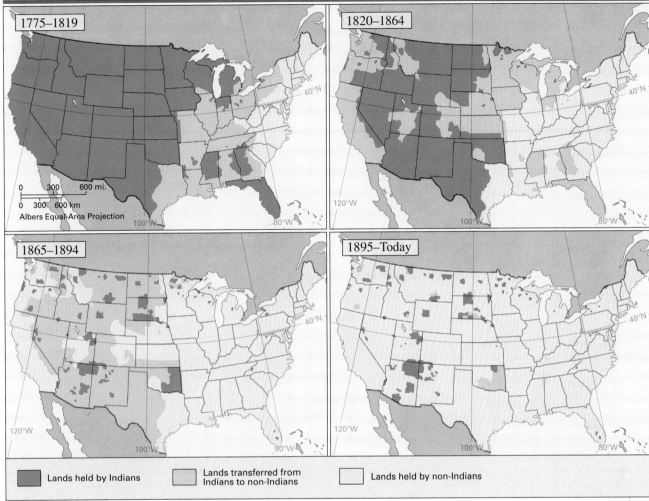

1775–1819

0   300   600 mi.
0   300   600 km
Albers Equal-Area Projection

1820–1864

1865–1894

1895–Today

| Lands held by Indians | Lands transferred from Indians to non-Indians | Lands held by non-Indians |

Based on Historical Atlas of the United States, *National Geographic Society, 1988.*

place because of the California gold rush of the 1850s and the opening of the Oregon Territory. During this time, the U.S. government signed many treaties with the Indian tribes on the West Coast. The government promised the Indians new territory in exchange for their land on the coast, which was thought to hold valuable gold deposits. The promises were not kept, and the Indians were left with only small areas of land.

The third map shows that the Indians had lost most of their land by the beginning of the 1900s. And today, as the fourth map shows, nearly all of the land that makes up the United States is non-Indian land. In just over 200 years, North America's native peoples have become almost completely landless. ■

▲ *American Indians once claimed nearly the entire continent as their home. Today, Indians in the U.S. own very little land.*

■ *During which historical period was the least amount of Indian land lost?*

R E V I E W

1. **THINKING FOCUS** What types of stories can maps tell?
2. **CONNECT** What historical regions of the United States are shown on the four maps on this page?
3. **GEOGRAPHY** What is the difference between a physical map and an historical map?
4. **CRITICAL THINKING** Explain how the location of a city can influence its growth and its historical importance.
5. **WRITING ACTIVITY** Imagine you are a television news reporter. Your assignment is to deliver a three-minute broadcast about the cities in California that have a high risk of experiencing an earthquake. Write your broadcast, using the map on page 51 as a visual aid.

53

This Land of Ours

Chapter Review

Reviewing Key Terms

cartographer (p. 35) longitude (p. 44)
fault (p. 52) meridian (p. 44)
geography (p. 31) parallel (p. 43)
hemisphere (p. 42) physical map (p. 50)
historical map (p. 52) projection (p. 45)
latitude (p. 44) region (p. 35)

A. Be sure you understand the meanings of the key terms. Then use the words in each pair in a sentence that gives accurate information.
1. longitude, meridian
2. parallel, latitude
3. region, geography
4. hemisphere, geography
5. cartographer, projection

B. Be sure you understand the meanings of the key terms. Then answer each question by writing one or more sentences.
1. In what two ways are parallels and meridians different?
2. What kind of information does a physical map provide?
3. What does it mean to say that a historical map can tell a story?
4. Why is it important for people to know if their city is on a fault line?
5. What are climate regions?
6. How is a map projection like "throwing a net over the earth"?

Exploring Concepts

A. On your own paper, copy this map and compass rose. You may sketch or trace the outline of a map of the United States from the chapter or from the Atlas map on pages 572 and 573. Then use information from the chapter to complete the map by following the instructions in the next column.

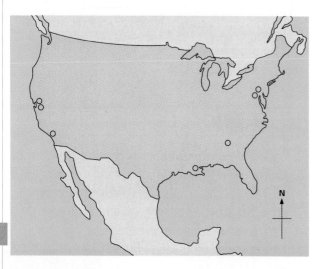

1. Color a region where little rain falls.
2. Draw and label the lines of longitude and latitude that pass through New Orleans.
3. Label the compass rose.
4. Draw and label two mountain ranges.
5. Label three fall-line cities and three fault-line cities.

B. Support each statement with facts and details from the chapter.
1. Geographical features result from natural forces.
2. Geographers study movement.
3. Regions reveal patterns.
4. The North American continent includes a wide variety of landforms.
5. Maps have many helpful features.
6. Globes and maps represent many characteristics of the real world.
7. The Mercator projection distorts the sizes of certain land masses.

Reviewing Skills

1. What does 40°N, 110°W mean? What city on the map of Utah is located there?
2. Use the map of Utah to identify the city at each of the following locations:
   38°N, 112°W
   39°N, 110°W
   41°N, 112°W
   40°N, 112°W
3. In which cardinal direction would you go to get from 45°N, 100°W to 45°N, 110°W?
4. Use an encyclopedia to find information on the Grand Canyon National Park. What special things could you do there?
5. If you wanted to describe the exact location of Santa Fe, New Mexico, on a map, what would be the best information to give?

Using Critical Thinking

1. Look at the two maps on page 560 in the Minipedia. The regions on one map show different culture areas. The regions on the other show how people got food. Looking at these maps, describe how the boundaries of the regions in the two maps are similar. Then summarize the relationships you find. For example, "Most Eastern Woodlands people got food through a combination of hunting, gathering, and farming."

2. Geographers study the movements of many things, including people. Recently in the United States there has been a gradual movement of population from the Northeast to the Southwest. One result is that Los Angeles, California, has overtaken Chicago, Illinois, as the nation's second-largest city. List five questions a geographer might ask to find out causes of this type of movement.

Preparing for Citizenship

1. **ARTS ACTIVITY** Learn about the history of map-making, or cartography. Use an encyclopedia or ask a librarian for help. Look at the maps on pages 102–103 and 126–127 to find out what maps from long ago look like. Notice the rich detail in their lettering and decoration. Based on your research, make a map in the style of ancient maps. You may make a map of a zoo or park, your town, or any geographical area you choose.

2. **COLLABORATIVE LEARNING** Some wild animals—including mammals, birds, fish, reptiles, and amphibians—live only in certain regions of the United States. In groups, list some of these animals. Discuss with your group how you could divide a map into wildlife regions. Name and sketch one wildlife region. Make a large class map showing all the wildlife regions the groups have found. On the map, make colorful pictures of an animal for each region.

Chapter 3
Clues to Our Past

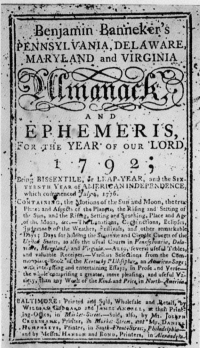

American history is found not only in textbooks. It can be found in museums or in diaries. It may also be found in a box of photographs in your attic, or in the stories your grandparents tell. Even games and toys can help you understand how people felt and lived long ago. Almost everywhere you look you can find clues to America's past. Understanding America's past can help you understand America today.

Books, letters, and diaries tell us how people in the past lived. Thousands of Americans bought this popular almanac in 1792 for its entertaining writing and scientific information.

This toy carving from the late 1700s shows how important George Washington was to Americans at that time.

2000 B.C.

Photographs give us clues about the past. This picture, taken in Oregon in 1912, tells what students wore, what their schoolrooms were like, and even what they studied.

Some objects can help us understand people from different cultures. This cornhusk mask is an important part of the culture of the Seneca Indians who live in New York.

The coins that colonists used in the 1600s show their close ties to England.

Today

LESSON 1

What Is History?

Snow covers King Street in Boston on the morning of March 6, 1770. As you walk down the street, you notice hundreds of footprints in the dirty snow. You see a spot of red in the middle of the road. You see bullet holes in the wall of a shop across the street. You hear the excited voices of people rushing up and down the frozen street. From their words you discover that 100 people from the town fought with a group of British soldiers in King Street late last night. Several of the townspeople are dead.

Everything you have seen and heard tells you that something happened on King Street. What really happened?

Key Terms

- evidence
- history
- historian
- interpret
- chronology

➤ *John Adams's search for evidence of the Boston Massacre might have led him to these musket balls.*

Knowing What Happened

John Adams, a young Boston lawyer, asked that same question. Adams defended the British soldiers in the trials that followed the shootings of March 5, 1770. This event is known as "the Boston Massacre."

John Adams first looked for **evidence,** or proof of what happened that night. Next, he talked to people who saw the shooting. Surely their stories would tell Adams what happened.

During the trial, however, Adams discovered that no two witnesses to the shooting told the same story. A man named Calef said that he heard the British officer tell the soldiers to fire. "I looked the officer in the face when he gave the word and saw his mouth," Calef said.

A man named Hickling said that the officer could not have given the order to fire. "I was within a yard of him and must have heard him had he spoken it."

Even with these conflicting stories Adams was able to prove that the soldiers had not murdered the people in King Street. Adams also explained why no one had agreed on what happened. Passion and imagination, he said, "may account for variations in the testimony of honest men." He meant that many people could see the same thing, yet each could remember it differently.

The trial taught John Adams an important lesson: no one would ever know all of what happened in King Street that night. That lesson is true of all events in the past. We learn about the past through evidence and stories. Sometimes we find little evidence; sometimes we find a mountain of it. But no matter what evidence or stories exist, we can never know everything that happened. ■

■ *Why isn't it possible to know everything about a past event?*

Studying the Past

We cannot hope to know everything about the past. But it is important to study what we do know about the past. The study of things done and said in the past is called **history.** A person who studies the past is called a **historian.** The first thing a historian must do is look closely at the evidence of the past.

Interpretation

Historians **interpret** evidence. This means that they decide if it is important and how it should be understood. Historians ask: Will this evidence help me understand the past? Where did the evidence come from?

Knowing where evidence came from helps historians understand it. For example, look at the stories told during the trial after the Boston Massacre. If historians learn that the man named Calef hated the British soldiers in Boston, that changes their understanding of his story. Calef probably wanted to make the British soldiers look as guilty as possible.

If historians learn that the man named Hickling was the brother of a British soldier in Boston, that changes their understanding of his

▼ *Several victims of the Boston Massacre are buried in the Granary Burial Ground, shown here. A death certificate for one of them (left) is important evidence for historians.*

59

Clues to Our Past

➤ *Paul Revere's engraving of the massacre tells the story many Bostonians wanted to hear. People who hated the soldiers eagerly purchased this picture of the British as villains.*

story. Hickling would want to make the soldiers on King Street that night look innocent.

Knowing why somebody said or did something is important. This can be shown by looking at the color print to the right and the drawing on page 61. Both show the shooting on King Street. Both were made by Paul Revere. Yet each shows a very different version of what happened that night. As the captions explain, Paul Revere made the two pictures for different reasons. Therefore, they mean different things.

UNDERSTANDING HISTORICAL PERSPECTIVE

*I*n 1770, the Boston Massacre was an important event. Ten years later in 1780, few Americans remembered it so clearly. Then, it was seen as just one in a series of events leading up to the American Revolution.

The Boston Massacre was seen one way by people living in 1770. It was seen in another way in 1780. These changes in the way that people see the events of the past are called changes in historical perspective.

Meanings Change

Changes in historical perspective do not change facts. The fact that five people died in the Boston Massacre does not change over time. But the meaning and importance of those facts *does* change.

You probably see the world differently than your grandparents do. In the same way, today's historians understand the past differently than the historians of 50 years ago. Today, they see new things in the past and ask new questions.

Times Change

Fifty years ago, historians studying the American West wrote about cowboys, Indians, even buffalo, but not about women. As the role of women in our society has grown, the story of women in the West has been told. This knowledge has changed our understanding of how the West was settled. Our perspective on history has changed.

So, the meaning of events may change as time passes and as we ask new questions about the past. It is important to remember that when studying the Boston Massacre—or any event of the past.

Chronology

Another way historians learn about the past is to find the order in which events happen. This is called **chronology.** Timelines show chronology and how one event leads to another. The timeline below shows fights between colonists and British soldiers and their supporters, called Tories. Here, chronology helps us to understand what happened.

Understanding History

Figuring out the order of events and interpreting evidence are basic skills used by all historians to understand the past. Those tools are also helpful to students who study history. Historians think carefully about where evidence comes from. Students should think carefully about how history is written. A student of history should know how historians do their job. ■

■ *Why is interpretation important to historians?*

◄ *Paul Revere drew this diagram of the shooting in King Street for the trial of the British soldiers. Here Revere tried to show where the victims of the shooting fell. He also shows the soldiers gathering on a corner on the right side of the street.*

▼ *This timeline shows the events leading up to the Boston Massacre. Here we can see the tensions between Bostonians and the British increasing from month to month.*

Unrest in Boston, 1765–1770

October 1768, British troops arrive in Boston.

October 1769, About 20 colonists attack two Tories. Both are wounded.

March 1770, Seven soldiers clash with 100 angry colonists in King Street. The soldiers fire, killing five people and wounding six others.

| 1769 | 1770 | 1771 |

September 1769, Several colonists and soldiers start a fight in the British Coffee House.

February 1770, Over 100 colonists attack Tory businesses. In the riot, a Tory shoots and kills an 11-year-old boy.

REVIEW

1. **FOCUS** How do people learn about the events of the past?

2. **CONNECT** Paul Revere's sketch of the Boston Massacre is really a kind of map of King Street. What does this "map" tell you about the shooting that Revere's engraving does not? What does the engraving tell you that the "map" does not?

3. **HISTORY** What is the past? What is history? How is history different from the past?

4. **CRITICAL THINKING** Look at the timeline above. How does this timeline help historians understand the Boston Massacre?

5. **WRITING ACTIVITY** Tonight, write an account of two things that happened in your classroom today. Tomorrow, compare your account with three of your classmates'. How and why do your stories differ?

Clues to Our Past

Comparing Art and Photos

Here's Why

It is impossible to know every detail about events from the past. Each type of historical evidence has its limitations. Each has its own advantages. Every piece of evidence is limited by the viewpoint of the person who made it. Books, newspapers, letters, and journals can reveal only what the writers of these documents know. Drawings and photographs can also reveal only the viewpoints of their creators.

You can more easily "read" the information in a drawing or in a photograph if you know how the two differ. When can you rely on a drawing or a painting? When can you rely on a photo?

Here's How

Look at the two pictures at the right. At the top is a photograph of a Pony Express rider. At the bottom is a painting of one of the first Pony Express riders around 1860. Only the painting shows the horse in motion. This is because in 1861, when the photograph was taken, cameras could not operate as fast as they can today.

Compare the two pictures. How are the two riders different? How do the horses differ? What details are different? What does each picture tell you about a Pony Express rider's life?

Try It

Look at the painting of slaves working in the field on page 442. Compare it with the photo of slaves on page 408. Use questions like those from Here's How. Write a paragraph describing what you discover.

Apply It

Study a photo. List its purpose, details that may be missing, and what was going on at the time. How would you draw the same scene? What could you express in your drawing that might be missing from the photo?

L E S S O N   2

What Does a Historian Do?

amuel Argell, governor of the English colony of Virginia, issued an order in 1618. He required "every man to set [plant] two acres of corn." Governor Argell then said that anyone in the colony who did not obey the order would be made a slave.

At first glance, this order does not seem very important. It is just one of hundreds of orders issued by the governor of Virginia in the 1600s. It has not been a law for more than 300 years. Most of us would not see anything meaningful or interesting in the governor's order.

But a historian studying life in colonial Virginia cannot ignore that order. To the historian, that law is a mystery waiting to be solved. The governor's order forces the historian to ask one question

THINKING FOCUS

How do historians study the past?

Key Terms

- primary source
- archives
- oral history
- artifact

◄ *These coins and engravings of corn and tobacco are examples of primary sources. Objects like these help historians solve the mysteries of the past.*

after another: Why did the governor have to order people to grow corn? Were the colonists unwilling or unable to grow corn? What was going on in the colony of Virginia in 1618?

A Trail of Questions

Historians make sense of the past by asking questions like these. The answers are often found in the records of the people who took part in past events. These records are called **primary sources.**

Many primary sources from colonial Virginia have been lost over the last 350 years. But some sources have survived. They can be found in books or in collections of records called **archives.**

A Little Corn

A historian named Edmund Morgan found enough sources to begin to make sense of Governor Argell's order. Some sources make the order even more mysterious. Morgan read one pamphlet that said:

> *O*ne man in 48 hours may prepare as much ground and set [plant] such a quantity of corn that he may be secure for want of bread all the year following.

After reading this the historian asks: "If corn was so easy to grow, why did the governor have to threaten the colonists with slavery to make them grow it?"

The answer turns up in the records of the Virginia Company of London. This company organized and paid for the settling of Virginia. Their records show that in May 1611, nothing had been planted in Virginia except for a "few seeds put into a private garden or two."

John Smith, one of the leaders of the colony, said that Governor Argell bought 600 bushels of corn from the Indians. This "did greatly relieve the whole colony."

It is clear that corn was easy to grow and that it was needed to feed the colony. Yet, for some reason the colonists did not grow corn. That helps

Captain John Smith wrote about his experiences in A Generall Historie of Virginia. *It is one of the most important sources about life in the colony.*

explain the governor's order. But if the colonists didn't plant corn, what did they do?

A Lot of Tobacco

A clue to this mystery is found in Governor Argell's description of Jamestown, Virginia, in 1617. Argell said that he found "the market-place, and streets, and all other spare places planted with tobacco." Why did the colonists grow tobacco when they wouldn't raise enough corn to feed themselves?

Most people came to Virginia hoping to get rich. After they made their fortunes, they would return to England. The records of the Virginia Company show that a tobacco farmer could become rich with one year's harvest.

Between 1619 and 1622, nearly 4,000 people moved from England to Virginia. Most of the settlers hoped to find wealth in the new colony. The records of the Virginia Company show that by 1622, the colony had "lost 3,000 persons in three years." Virginia had a death rate of nearly 80 per cent.

Death was a risk for colonists everywhere in the New World. In

Tobacco, sold in Europe with labels like this one, was one of the only ways to make money in the Virginia colony.

the Plymouth colony of New England, almost half of the people died in the first difficult years. But 15 years after the beginning of the Virginia colony, eight out of every ten people died.

The historian looks at these facts and sources and sees a new picture of life in colonial Virginia. Virginians chose to grow tobacco rather than corn. This made the colony a deadly place for most of the people who came there. A few Virginians got rich. Most of them died. No governor's order could change that. ∎

How Do We Know?

HISTORY *In the 1930s, writers interviewed black Americans who had been slaves just before the Civil War. The stories they told had never been written down before. Today, those oral histories are some of the most important sources about slavery in the United States.*

∎ *Why are primary sources important to historians?*

Other Sources, Other Questions

Official documents—laws, business records, a governor's order—tell us about the public side of history. But in order to get the whole story of the past, historians must look at these and many other sources. Study A Closer Look at Primary Sources on pages 66–67 to learn more about these sources.

Oral history is a source of history that official documents often miss or ignore. Oral history is not based on what a person has written. Instead it is based on what a person says during an interview. Oral histories preserve the experiences of people who can't write them down—slaves and servants.

Clues to Our Past

Primary Sources

Documents, journals, photos, and objects are all primary sources of historical information. They give historians a firsthand look at the past. You may want to throw away old letters, magazines, or buttons. But, in 100 years, they could become a historian's valued primary sources.

Two tickets to information is how historians would view these. Some of the towns listed here grew and faded with the railroads. How many names on the tickets do you recognize?

What do you see in this picture? Historians may look at this 1903 photo from the Tuskegee Institute in Alabama and see an equal number of men and women students. Historians might also look at the people's clothing and hair styles, or even the kind of laboratory equipment they used.

Curiosity is what this cat gives historians. Sometimes artifacts create new questions. This wooden statue of a panther was found in Florida in 1884. Archaeologists believe the carving was made by American Indians, but they're not yet sure when or why.

In the days before television, campaign buttons helped to tell people about a political candidate's positions. In 1896, Republicans were called "goldbugs" because they believed that the value of the U.S. dollar should be based on the value of gold.

Though his face has been worn by the play of time, this drummer was once someone's favorite toy. A historian specializing in toys could tell the soldier was made before 1850 by noting how the crank moves the soldier's arms.

What did little girls do in 1896? According to this girl's journal, they got their clothes dirty and spied on their big sisters. Journals are useful because they tell how people thought and felt about everyday matters.

➤ *Even the maps people drew can tell us about the past. This map was made by a man named Hondius in the 1600s. What does this map tell you about Virginia at that time?*

▲ *This doll was made from corn husks. This would tell a historian that the doll was made in a place where corn was plentiful and that it was probably a handmade gift for a child.*

■ *How do literature and artifacts help historians understand the past?*

Poems, stories, myths, and novels can also tell us things about the past.

V irginia,
    Earth's only paradise,
Where nature hath in store
Fowl, venison, and fish,
And fruitfullest soil.

This poem was written by a man named Michael Drayton in 1607. He wrote it before he sailed from England for Virginia. We know that Virginia was no paradise. But Drayton's poem tells us what he expected to find there and why he might have wanted to go.

Historians also look at the things people made. These are called **artifacts.** Paintings, tools, clothing, and furniture tell us about the people who made and used them. For example, historians have found very few chairs from Virginia in the 1600s. In the harsh conditions of the colony, people considered chairs a luxury. They sat on the floor or on boxes or benches.

Artifacts, oral histories, poems, and documents all contain clues about the past. Like detectives, historians look for clues. Then they interpret the evidence to "solve" or make sense of the past. ■

R E V I E W

1. **FOCUS** How do historians study the past?
2. **CONNECT** Define primary source. Give two examples of primary sources used in the first lesson of this chapter.
3. **HISTORY** Why is oral history an important source of information for a historian studying slavery during the 1800s?

4. **CRITICAL THINKING** Interpret the map at the top of this page as an artifact. What do the decorations and drawings on this map tell you?
5. **WRITING ACTIVITY** Each chapter of this book has literature and primary source excerpts. Choose one and read it. Write out two questions that come to your mind after reading the source.

Chapter 3

Interpreting Information

Here's Why

Studying artifacts can help us experience history by understanding the lives of people in the past. When you visit a museum or an old building that has been re-stored, you often see artifacts—clothes, tools, and other objects that were used in the past. Looking at tools used during the colonial period, for example, could help you to understand more about what life was like for the people who lived in the colonies.

Here's How

Look at the objects on this page. They are used in similar ways but come from different times in history.

When you examine arti-facts, ask yourself these questions:
1. What is the object used for?
2. What is the object made from?
3. How was it made?
4. What parts does it have?
5. What does it tell you about the people who used it?

The top picture shows a butter churn from the early 1900s. Churns were used to make butter from cream. This churn was made of wood, metal, and glass. The style of the churn and the cast iron parts tell you it was probably made by machine.

How did the churn work? The cream was poured into the glass container. As the wooden paddle was turned, the butter slowly thickened and had to be removed.

The way this churn works suggests an important thing about the people who used it. Making butter was a hard job that took one person a long time. Butter must have been valuable enough to people for them to spend the time needed to make it. They had to give up many hours to make a product you can quickly buy today at the grocery.

Try It

Study the picture of the food processor. Ask yourself the questions listed in Here's How.

Apply It

Borrow an object from the past such as a piece of clothing or jewelry, a tool or a piece of sports equip-ment. Inter-view the person who pro-vides your object and find out its use and historical background. Bring the object to school and show it to your class. Have your classmates take turns trying to explain what the object is and how it was used. Then share the in-formation you learned about the object from its owner.

Butter Churn

Food Processor

Clues to Our Past

L E S S O N   3

Why Study History?

THINKING
F O C U S

How does studying history help you understand the people and events of today's world?

Key Terms

- journal
- empathy

➤ *In this painting by Karl Bodmer, Prince Maximillian meets Minnetaree chiefs at Fort Clark.*

In April 1833, Prince Alexander Philipp Maximilian set out to study the Plains Indians in the western United States. The German prince left St. Louis and sailed up the Missouri River. On the boat with Maximilian were his two trained pet bears, a music box, and a thermometer to record every day's temperature in his **journal,** or daily record of his travels.

The prince also brought two helpers along with him. One of those helpers was a Swiss artist named Karl Bodmer. Bodmer's job was to draw and paint all of the sights and people that the prince wrote about. During the trip Bodmer painted wonderful landscapes, huge herds of buffalo, and Indians.

Bodmer painted many pictures of Indians. The Indians had no word for "draw." But a translator told Maximilian that the Indians thought that Bodmer could "write very correctly."

Understanding Other People

Bodmer's paintings and Maximilian's journal record the lives and habits of the Plains Indians. The explorers hoped to understand the actions, customs, and feelings of the Indians. This understanding is called **empathy.**

Different Yet Similar

It is sometimes hard to feel empathy with the people we read about in Maximilian's journal. The Plains Indians lived in a different time and place. How can we begin to understand them?

The skills of the historian can be helpful when trying to understand people from other times and other places. Looking closely at stories or pictures helps us feel empathy with others.

Look at Karl Bodmer's painting of a young Blackfoot girl on this page. At first this girl may seem somewhat different from you or your classmates. But look more closely. The expression on her face is one you might see on any of your friends' faces. Her clothes and jewelry look like clothing and jewelry worn today. Perhaps she already seems more familiar.

Other parts of the lives of the Plains Indians also seem very familiar. Maximilian wrote that one hot, summer afternoon "the Indians bathed in the river in great numbers, including women, girls, and children." They swam to a boat and jumped from it into the river, said Maximilian. "The noise from all this was very great."

Past and Present

People living in other times and places had fun the same way you do. History was made by people who felt the same things you feel.

◄ *Karl Bodmer painted this Blackfoot girl in 1833. Bodmer's detailed drawings provide historians with important information about the Plains Indians.*

▼ *This leather ball and shirt were made by the Plains Indians of the 1800s. How are they like items found in your home? How are they different?*

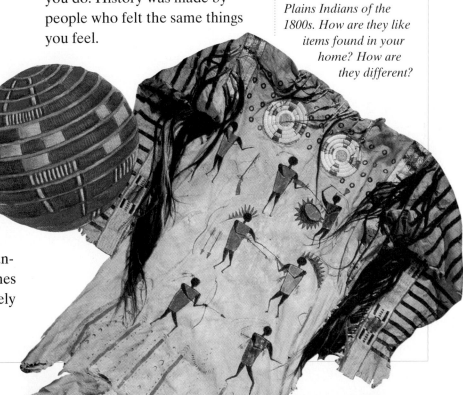

How does history help you to feel empathy for other people?

Every person you read about in this book was once the same age that you are. Many of them went to school. They all laughed, cried, slept, and ate. If you read their stories, you can begin to see why they acted as they did. In this way, understanding the past is a way of understanding yourself and the people around you. That is the first step towards understanding your world. ■

Understanding Your World

In 1781, Thomas Jefferson wrote that studying history made people good "judges of the actions and designs [plans] of men." Two hundred years later, events still need to be examined and understood. Studying the Plains Indians may help us understand the people around us. In the same way, studying yesterday's world may help us understand the world today. The skills of the historian can help us to do that.

The Skills of History

Let's look at an event that occurred not long ago. In the summer of 1988, a series of fires burned large parts of Yellowstone National Park. Thousands of primary sources on these fires exist. In September 1988, for example, *Newsweek* magazine reported:

> Since the beginning of the summer, the worst fires in several centuries have ravaged more than 400,000 acres of Yellowstone National Park land.

The *Wall Street Journal* described "flaming destruction" and "a fire-blackened ruin." The *Chicago Tribune* said that "damage to a treasured national park has been devastating." According to the *Los Angeles Times*, people complained that the park had "let the situation

The Yellowstone fires of 1988 were so large that crews of firefighters (center) could not put them out. A year later, plant life returned to burned areas of the park (right).

get out of hand."
These people said that
the park was wrong to follow its "policy to let natural
fires burn their course."

In the autumn of 1988, the National Park Service issued a statement. Yellowstone would be "a
more interesting and educational
national park" after the fires,
according to the statement.

A newsletter called the *Greater
Yellowstone Report* said that the
fires were smaller "than reported."
Dr. Linda Wallace, a scientist,
agreed that the fires were not "a
national tragedy as some would
believe." She wrote that the fires
were part of a "natural process of
renewal."

The Uses of History

These are just a few of the
sources a future historian will use
to study the fires in Yellowstone

National Park during the
summer of 1988. That historian
will ask many questions: What
happened? Why did it happen?
What does this evidence say about
the event? Did the fires ruin Yellowstone? Or did the fires make
the park better?

Professional historians will be
asking those questions 50 or 100
years from now. You can start asking questions right now.

Just as historians will never
learn everything about the past,
you will never learn everything
about the Yellowstone fires—or
any event in the past or present.
You can, however, learn enough to
understand some of the events and
people of your world. Studying history will give you some of the skills
you need to do this. ■

*Newspapers, maga-
zines, and even T-shirts
expressed opinions about
the Yellowstone fires.*

■ *How are the skills of
the historian useful in
making sense of current
events?*

R E V I E W

1. **FOCUS** How does studying history help you to understand the people and events of today's world?
2. **CONNECT** How do the skills of the historian help you
   to feel empathy with the Plains Indians?
3. **HISTORY** Why are Bodmer's paintings and Maximilian's journals helpful to a historian studying the
   Plains Indians?

4. **CRITICAL THINKING** Several sources about the Yellowstone National Park fires are printed in this lesson.
   Which sources present the facts of the event most
   clearly? Which convey an opinion?
5. **ACTIVITY** Prepare a one-minute speech answering the
   question: "Why Study History?" Use examples from
   this lesson and the rest of the chapter.

Clues to Our Past

Chapter Review

Reviewing Key Terms

archives (p. 64)
artifact (p. 68)
chronology (p. 61)
empathy (p. 71)
evidence (p. 58)
history (p. 59)
historian (p. 59)
interpret (p. 59)
journal (p. 70)
oral history (p. 65)
primary source (p. 64)

A. Decide which key term is described in each case below.

1. In a hole her dog had dug, Ann found an object that looked like a very old arrowhead.
2. Was it a real arrowhead or just a stone? If it was real, what did that mean?
3. Ann decided to look into what had been on the site of her house long ago. Who had lived there?
4. In the library she discovered a room filled with old town records and papers.
5. There were maps, diaries, contracts, and other papers from colonial times.
6. On one map she found proof that an Indian settlement had once stood on the site of her house. It seemed likely that her arrowhead was real!

B. Use each word below in a sentence that shows what the word means. Write your sentence as if it began a story.

1. journal
2. empathy
3. chronology
4. history
5. oral history
6. primary source

Exploring Concepts

A. Write one or two sentences to answer each of the following questions. Use the information in the chapter.

1. What information can artifacts like clothes or furniture give to historians?
2. What sources other than artifacts do historians use?
3. What use is it to study items like these and other parts of history?
4. What primary sources do you come into contact with from day to day?
5. Consider the clothes you wore to school today. What would they tell a visitor from the future about your life?
6. If you write letters to a friend, imagine that a historian finds them 100 years from now. How would historians find them useful?

B. Write whether you agree or disagree with each of the following statements. If you disagree, give your reasons.

1. If we have enough evidence, we can know exactly what happened in a past event.
2. Historians need to know where a piece of evidence came from.
3. It is important to determine the order in which past events occurred.
4. It is the historian's job to study the past, not to ask questions about it.
5. As historical evidence, a personal diary is as valuable as a business contract.
6. Historians usually ignore what everyday people have to say about the past.
7. Studying history helps us to understand other people.

Reviewing Skills

1. Compare the painting of a Blackfoot girl on page 71 with the photo here. The photo has a painted background. How does the girl on the right in the photo appear different from the Blackfoot girl?
2. Look at the photograph on page 383 of George Northrup, a Minnesota teacher. Use details from the photo to state what you think are Northrup's plans.
3. Look at the ball on page 71. What does it tell you about what materials were available to Plains Indians in 1870? What ball do you think has replaced it today?
4. Where would you look to find the latitude and longitude of the site where the Boston Massacre took place?
5. Imagine you discovered some tools that had been used 300 years ago but had not been touched since 1690. How would you learn about the people who had used them?

Using Critical Thinking

1. Think about your gym shoes, a T-shirt, or any other piece of clothing that says something about you. Pretend you are a historian in the future. Ask questions about this piece of clothing. What would it tell you about people in the 1990s?
2. Historical evidence can be misleading. Choose a drama, a comedy, or a game show on TV. Suppose historians living in the year A.D. 2200 saw a tape of the program. What might they misunderstand about our lives based on that program?

Preparing for Citizenship

1. **COLLECTING INFORMATION** In an encyclopedia, you can read about the money we use in the United States and how it came to look as it does. Choose a slogan or picture from an American coin or bill. Do some research and find out why that slogan or picture was used. Study money from another country. Are there any similarities between its design and that of the American money you researched? Write a paragraph summarizing what you found out.

2. **COLLABORATIVE LEARNING** In groups of four, choose a past event in your school or town—perhaps an accident, an unexpected sports victory, or a visit from a famous person. Investigate it as historians would. Assign one member of the group to research primary sources, one to interpret what happened, one to put the incidents in order, and the fourth to write the story of the event. Then the writers should meet to decide which stories will be recorded in a class History Scrapbook.

Exploring and Settling America

"Men of strange appearance have come across the great water." These words describe a dream an American Indian had sometime in the 1500s. Yet for many American Indians those words tell of a real event: the arrival of Europeans in America. At first the Europeans wanted the land's riches. Later they took the land itself. Once the Europeans came, life for the American Indians was never again the same.

2000 B.C.

Unknown American Indian artist, wall painting of Spanish explorers. Canyon del Muerto, Arizona. Photo by Jerry Jacka.

A.D. 1682

The First People of the Americas

In A.D. 1200, North America was home to millions of people. These people settled in every region and climate. Some lived in small hunting villages. Some lived in huge cities of stone. Each group worshiped its own gods and spoke its own language. In A.D. 1200, these many active peoples shared the land of North America—a place that had been their home for almost 30,000 years.

2000 B.C. Some groups of American Indians get most of their food and clothing by hunting caribou (above), buffalo, deer, and other animals.

Throughout this period, American Indians invented new tools. This knife was sharper than earlier stone tools, and this bone flute shows the Indians' interest in music.

2000	1500	1000	500

2000 B.C.

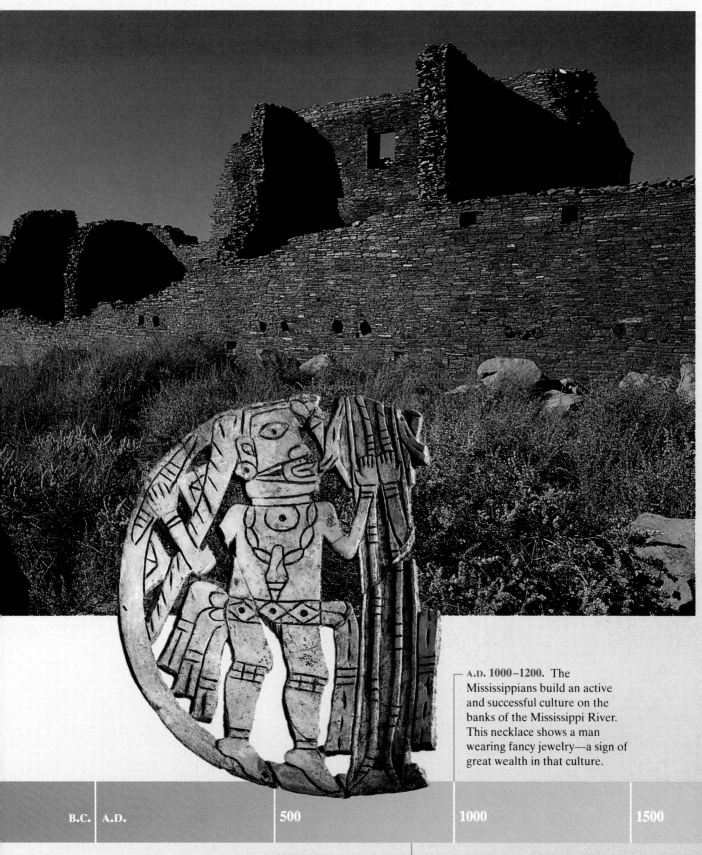

A.D. 1000–1200. The Mississippians build an active and successful culture on the banks of the Mississippi River. This necklace shows a man wearing fancy jewelry—a sign of great wealth in that culture.

B.C.	A.D.		500		1000		1500

A.D. 920 The Anasazi people begin building a community called Pueblo Bonito (top) deep in the desert of present-day Arizona.

A.D. 1500

L E S S O N   1

People Come to the Americas

THINKING
F O C U S

How did the changing environment affect the first Americans?

___

Key Terms

- glacier
- epoch
- agriculture

The hunters shiver as an icy wind blows across the empty land. It is flat and treeless here, covered only with moss and small shrubs. Far away, the hunters can see a tall range of mountains covered with ice and snow.

The hunters are closing in on a herd of musk oxen. The bravest men circle several oxen, each one larger than a bull. The frightened animals run, and the hunters throw their spears. The fight is long and bloody, but when it is over, three huge oxen lie dead.

Now the hunters can begin the feast. They eat the meat and divide the skins, which are cut into rough coats and blankets. They chip new tools out of the bones. They rest and prepare for the next hunt.

For as long as the hunters can remember, they have searched for food across this bare land. This day, however, they have done something that has never been done before. Although they do not realize it, these hunters are the first humans ever to set foot on North America.

From Asia to the Americas

Today, people can no longer walk from Asia to North America. The land bridge those hunters once walked across now lies beneath the icy waters of the Bering Strait. The Bering Strait is a narrow strip of ocean that separates the continents of Asia and North America.

No one is sure exactly when, but perhaps about 28,000 B.C., a bridge of land connected the two continents. At that time, almost one-third of the earth's surface was covered with huge sheets of ice called **glaciers.** Glaciers were sometimes up to a mile thick. They held much of the world's water in their frozen grip. As a result of these glaciers, the surface of the oceans was about 300 feet lower than today.

The highest parts of the Bering Strait were above water at that time. This dry land stretched from Asia to North America. Several different groups of humans walked across this bridge of land at different times.

The land bridge existed until about 10,000 B.C. At that time temperatures rose and caused the glaciers to melt. Over time, water from the melting glaciers covered the land bridge. People may have kept crossing the Bering Strait in boats. But the time when hunters in search of food could walk from Asia to North America was over. ■

■ *How was it possible for humans to walk from Asia to the Americas?*

▼ *The photograph and the locator map show (1) Asia, (2) the Bering Strait, and (3) North America as they appear today.*

▼ *The drawing is an artist's idea of what the Bering land bridge may have looked like in 28,000 B.C. Find the land bridge that existed where the waters of the Bering Strait lie today (2). Red lines show the coastline today.*

From Hunting to Farming

How Do We Know?

HISTORY *The first Americans left no written records of their lives. Scientists have pieced together their story from spear points, bones, and other objects they left behind. By looking closely at these objects, scientists can tell how they were made, what they were used for, and how old they are.*

▼ *The progress of the first Americans from traveling hunters to settled farmers was long and slow, as this map and timeline show.*

The hunters who walked across the land bridge into North America were the ancestors of the people we now call American Indians. Their story can be divided into four **epochs,** or very important periods of history.

Hunting and Gathering

The Beringian *(bur IHN jee uhn)* epoch (28,000–12,000 B.C.) began when the main group of hunters came to North America. These people found a land different from the land today. **Glaciers,** large masses of ice and snow, covered most of what is now Canada. Forests stretched across the United States. Grasslands swept south into Mexico.

North America had many of the animals that the hunters had followed from Asia—wooly mammoths and musk oxen. Hunters followed these animals away from the glaciers to warmer lands in the south. The paths these American Indians may have followed are shown in the map below.

Warming weather changed these lands during the Paleo-Indian epoch (12,000–6000 B.C.). Glaciers melted and raised the levels of oceans. The western grasslands of North America became hot deserts. As the land changed, large grass-eating animals died out for want of food.

American Indians who had hunted these animals now had to search for new sources of food. Hunters made smaller and better weapons, like the spear thrower on page 83. With weapons like these, Americans Indians could hunt animals that were smaller and faster.

First Human Settlement in the Americas

28,000 B.C.
Beringian epoch

- Main group of humans arrive in North America
- Hunting-and-gathering tribes travel through the Americas

12,000 B.C.
Paleo-Indian epoch

- Hunters use improved tools
- Humans inhabit southernmost part of South America

6,000 B.C.
Archaic epoch

- Humans live in permanent settlements
- Corn is grown in North America

500 B.C.
Postarchaic epoch

- Agriculture spreads through the Americas
- Distinct cultures develop in the Americas
- Postarchaic epoch ends A.D. 1500

These included bison, caribou, and deer.

American Indians learned new ways to live off the land during the Archaic *(ahr KAY ihk)* epoch (6000–500 B.C.). People who lived near water, for example, built boats for fishing. Those who lived in forests gathered wild nuts and berries.

Farming and Settling

During the Archaic epoch, American Indians also learned to plant and harvest corn, beans, and other crops. After the birth of **agriculture,** as this discovery is known, they could settle in one spot and grow crops in nearby fields. These new food crops allowed American Indian groups to grow in number.

These groups developed into many different cultures during the Postarchaic epoch (500 B.C.–A.D. 1500). By A.D. 1500, American Indians wore clothing made of everything from animal skins to cloth made from plants. Some lived in simple huts made of tree bark and mud or in wooden houses on stilts. Others lived in cities made of stone.

Some American Indians lived like the hunters who crossed the Bering land bridge. One group, called the Chipewyans *(chihp uh WY uhns)* hunted caribou across the cold, bare regions of what is now northern Canada. Other groups, like the Aztecs of Mexico, grew into powerful societies. The center of Aztec culture was the city of Tenochtitlan *(tay nawch tee TLAHN)*. In this city perhaps as many as 100,000 people lived among canals, temples, and islands. These and thousands of other American Indian cultures lived in every region of North America around A.D. 1500. ∎

▼ *Weapons like this spear thrower made hunting easier. A hunter (shown above) would (1) load the spear into the spear thrower, (2) propel the spear, and (3) release the spear. In this way, hunters could throw farther and harder than before.*

∎ *How did the discovery of agriculture change American Indian groups?*

R E V I E W

1. **FOCUS** How did the changing environment affect the first Americans?

2. **CONNECT** How was North America different during the Beringian epoch than it is now?

3. **GEOGRAPHY** List three ways that the first Americans changed with their environment.

4. **CRITICAL THINKING** The search for food led ancient hunters throughout North and South America. How did agriculture and the development of a steady supply of food affect later American Indians?

5. **WRITING ACTIVITY** Today, scientists look for clues to how people lived long ago. Pick three objects that belong to you. In a short paragraph, describe each object. Explain why you chose it and what it would tell a scientist 3,000 years from now about how you lived.

The First People of the Americas

How the Turtle Beat the Rabbit

A Cherokee Folktale

You have learned something about American Indian society and way of life. American Indians used stories to teach what they considered proper behavior. In this familiar story of the turtle and the rabbit from "Myths of the Cherokee" by James Mooney, you see what the Cherokee thought of boastfulness. If you were a young Cherokee hearing it, how would you change your behavior?

Folktales like this one show the liveliness of Indian culture.

warrior a person who fights
boastful speaking with too much pride
dispute to discuss, argue

lodges small houses

humility lack of pride

The rabbit was a great runner, and everybody knew it. No one thought the turtle anything but a slow traveler, but he was a great warrior and very boastful, and the two were always disputing about their speed. At last they agreed to decide the matter by a race. They fixed the day and the starting place and arranged to run across four mountain ridges. The one who reached the last ridge first would be the winner.

Rabbit felt so sure of victory that he said to Turtle, "You know you can't run. You can never win the race, so I'll give you a headstart to the first ridge and then you'll have only three to cross while I will have to go over four."

The turtle said that would be all right. They then both returned to their lodges for the night. Turtle, however, sent for his turtle friends and family, telling them that he needed their help.

"I know that I cannot outrun the rabbit, but I am tired of his always boasting about his great speed. It is time someone taught him a little humility. Come listen to my plan."

All his friends agreed to help out. When the day came, all the animals were there to see the race. The rabbit was at the starting point, but the turtle had already gone ahead toward the first ridge, as had been agreed to earlier. The rabbit started off with a roar from all the crowd as he sprang into action. He started off with long jumps and soon was climbing the first ridge, expecting to win the race before the turtle could get down the other side. But before he got up the mountain, he saw Turtle go over the next ridge ahead of him.

Rabbit ran on. When he reached the top he looked all around, but he could not see the turtle because of the long grass below. He kept going down the mountain and climbed the second ridge, but when he looked up again there was Turtle just going over the top. Now he was both surprised and angry. He began making his longest leaps to catch up, but when he got to the top of the ridge, there was the turtle away in front going over the third ridge.

The rabbit was getting tired now and nearly out of breath, but he kept on down the mountain and up the other ridge until he got to the top. And he was just in time to see Turtle cross the fourth ridge and win the race!

The rabbit could not make another jump, but fell over on the ground, as the rabbit does ever since when he is too tired to run anymore. A ribbon was given to the turtle for winning the race and all the animals wondered how he could win against the rabbit. The turtle wasn't about to tell either. It was easy because all the turtle's family and friends looked just alike, and he had simply had one of them climb to each ridge before the race began. They then waited until the rabbit came in sight before hiding themselves in the long grass. That is how the turtle taught Rabbit not to be too boastful.

Further Reading

And It's Still That Way: Legends Told to Arizona Indian Children. Byrd Baylor. These are stories from several Native American tribes.

And Me, Coyote! Betty Baker. This tale, based on the creation myths of the Native Americans in California, reveals how the coyote tries to take the credit for what his brother, a World Maker, has done.

Conquista. Clyde Bulla. The story of how the Indians may have gotten their first horse is told through the experiences of Little Wolf, a young boy.

The Sound of Flutes and Other Indian Legends. Richard Erdoes. The author collected these stories from Native American storytellers.

L E S S O N   2

Four American Indian Cultures

Key Terms

- mesa
- potlatch
- mound

R ichard Wetherill squinted in the bright December light. The winter of 1888 had just begun, and Wetherill was looking after one of his family's herds of cattle. The herd wandered across the **mesa,** one of the many steep, flat-topped mountains in that part of Colorado. Every so often, a cow strayed from the herd and got lost in the deep, twisting canyons that separated the mesas.

Wetherill searched for one of these lost cattle in some pine trees near the edge of the mesa. As he reached the rim of the canyon, he saw something on the other side that made him forget about lost cattle. A city made of stone, with towers and walls, was built into the canyon wall.

When Richard Wetherill saw that city, he saw something that had been forgotten for hundreds of years. He had found Mesa Verde, the main city of an American

➤ *More than 1,000 people lived in the cliff city at Mesa Verde during the 1100s.*

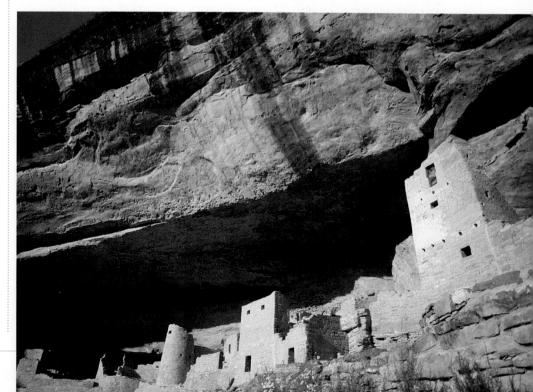

Indian culture called the Anasazi *(ah nuh SAH zee)*.

The discovery of Mesa Verde helped many people at that time understand that a people of an age-old culture once lived in the canyons of the southwestern United States. The Anasazi were just one of the thousands of groups in North America by A.D. 1500. The story of these peoples is where the story of America begins.

In the pages that follow, you will read about four of these cultures. The map on page 88 shows where the Anasazi, the Makah *(MAHK uh)*, the Mississippians, and the Creek settled. As you read about these groups, think about where they lived. Also think about how their surroundings affected what they ate, what they lived in, and how they made sense of the world.

Anasazi: People of the Desert

The Anasazi first arrived in the deserts of the Southwest in about A.D. 100. They raised corn, beans, and later cotton near their homes on the mesas.

After about 1,000 years, the Anasazi left their settlements on the mesa tops and moved to cliff dwellings. Historians believe that the Anasazi may have feared an enemy culture. They then moved to homes that were easier to defend from enemies. From these cities— like Mesa Verde—the Anasazi climbed up the canyon walls to tend their crops on top of the mesas.

Corn was the Anasazi's most important food. But their corn would not survive without rain. Over time the Anasazi learned to tame the dry, desert land. They learned to "catch" rain in ditches, which carried the water to their crops.

This poem from the Tewa *(TAY wuh)* culture, another desert people, shows how important rain was in that region.

L ong ago in the north
Lies the road of emergence!
Yonder our ancestors live,
Yonder we take our being.

Yet now we come southward
For cloud flowers blossom here
Here the lightning flashes,
Rain water here is falling!

▲ *The zig-zag design on this Anasazi pitcher may represent lightning and rain. Without rain, the Anasazi would not have been able to grow corn (shown below) in their desert environment.*

Rain also played an important part in Anasazi religion. The Anasazi believed that ceremonies, like exciting rain dances, would bring rain. If the rain came, their crops would grow and they would live.

Sometime in the 1200s, the rain stopped falling on the mesas. This caused the Anasazi to leave their homes in the cliffs. After leaving these cities, the Anasazi moved into smaller villages closer to water.

Today, the descendants of the Anasazi still live in the southwestern United States. But they no longer live in cliff dwellings. Those structures were useful only when the Anasazi had enough water to grow their crops. ■

■ *How was the importance of rain shown in Anasazi culture?*

Makah: People of the Coast

The Makah lived on what is now called the Olympic Peninsula in the state of Washington. In this land of tall cedar forests, the Makah were surrounded by water—the Pacific Ocean, lakes, rivers, and streams. The fish and animals in these waters provided the Makah with food all year.

The Makah hunted and fished for these animals throughout the year. In spring and fall, the Makah lived along streams and fished for salmon. In summer, the Makah moved nearer the ocean. The Makah rowed into the sea in big canoes. Armed with harpoons, they hunted whales, sea lions, and sea otters in the warm waters of the Pacific Ocean.

The Makah moved to an inland village for the winter. There they were able to enjoy all of the food they had gathered over the year. The Makah lived on dried salmon and seal oil in their warm cedar

▲ *These drawings of whales show the importance of the sea to Makah culture.*

➤ *The American Indians discussed in this lesson lived in different environments and different parts of North America.*

North American Cultures, 500 B.C–A.D. 1500

Hudson Bay

Makah

PACIFIC OCEAN

Great Lakes

Mississippi R.

Anasazi

•Cahokia
Mississippian

Creek

ATLANTIC OCEAN

Gulf of Mexico

Tropic of Cancer

0   400   800 mi.
0   400   800 km
Lambert Conformal Conic Projection

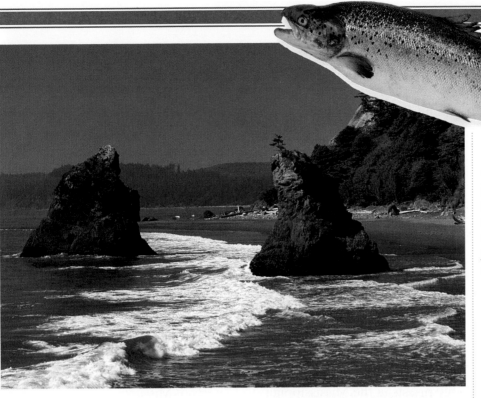

In the mild, rainy land of the Makah, fish was an important source of food. Salmon (shown above) was the most important fish of all to the Makah.

houses. During the winter, they made baskets, boxes, masks, and other objects of wood. This wood was cut from the cedar trees of the forests surrounding the Makah villages.

The Makah often had extra food and art objects. They celebrated this wealth in a **potlatch** ceremony. In this ceremony a village chief proved his wealth and generosity by giving gifts to his guests.

The Makah were able to celebrate their wealth in potlatches most of the time. But, sometimes they did not have enough food. The years when they ran out of food reminded the Makah that they needed the salmon to survive. They believed that the salmon gave up its life to feed them. Each year the Makah held a ceremony to honor the salmon and its return to the rivers of their land. ■

■ What do potlatch ceremonies tell us about the Makah?

Mississippians: People of the River

Rivers connected the Mississippians to people of other lands. The most important of these rivers was the one we call the Mississippi. Along its branches the Mississippians built a network of trade. They traded with people from the Great Lakes to the Gulf of Mexico, from the Atlantic Ocean to what is now Oklahoma.

The Mississippians traded a kind of stone used for weapons and tools to these faraway peoples. This stone is called chert. In return, the Mississippians got shells, copper, and jewelry. They brought these things back to their homes along the Mississippi River.

On the banks of the river, the Mississippians raised corn, beans, and other crops. They also built villages and towns. The largest of these towns was Cahokia. As many as 40,000 people lived there by

The First People of the Americas

The Mississippians traded goods with many distant peoples. This mica sculpture of a bird's claw came from the east coast of North America.

■ *Why was the river an important part of Mississippian life?*

This drawing shows what Cahokia may have looked like in A.D. 1200. The mound that stood in the center of town can still be seen today in East St. Louis, Illinois (right).

A.D. 1200. Like other Mississippian towns, Cahokia was built around a huge, steep platform called a **mound.** This mound was more than 1,000 feet long and 700 feet wide. It was larger than the Great Pyramids of Egypt.

The mounds of Mississippian towns tell us a lot about their culture. Historians think that it may have taken Cahokians up to 200 years to build their mound. Only a powerful class of rulers, historians say, could lead the many workers needed to make such mounds.

Artifacts from these mounds tell us that these rulers were probably priests in the Mississippian religion. Headdresses, pipes, and masks have also been found in the mounds in recent centuries. These things, say historians, tell us that religion was an important part of Mississippian life.

These artifacts also tell us that some parts of the Mississippian culture may have come from other places. Pictures of feathered snakes, winged warriors, and spiders are often found in Mississippian art. These forms also exist in the art of other American Indian societies. Some Central American societies, like the Aztec culture of Mexico, built cities around huge buildings that look like Mississippian mounds.

This evidence tells us that some important parts of Mississippian life may have been brought to North America by traders. These traders may have visited the Aztecs and other groups. It is possible that parts of Mississippian culture came up the river in boats along with seashells, copper, and jewelry. ■

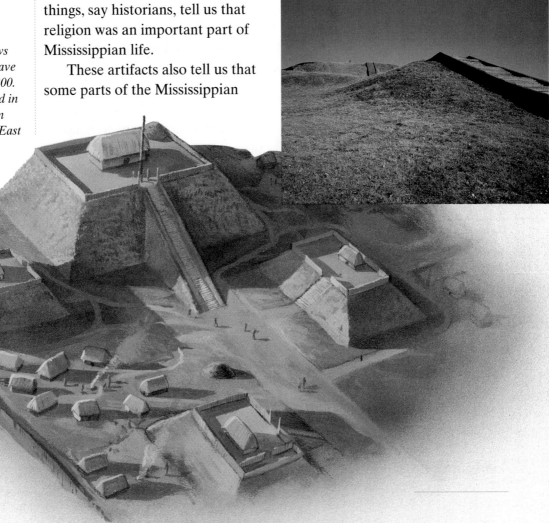

Chapter 4

Creek: People of the Forest

The Creek had much in common with the Mississippians. Both cultures, for example, built mounds. Both groups lived along rivers and streams. But because they lived in a different region, the Creek were different from the Mississippians in many ways.

The Creek lived in the forests of what are now Alabama and Georgia. There, the Creek hunted, fished, and gathered fruits and nuts. They planted corn and beans in forest clearings. Nearby, they built villages surrounded by tall wooden fences. These fences protected them from enemies.

Inside the village stood dozens of small houses, each belonging to one family. The houses were built on pieces of ground, much like the houses of today. Two houses stood on some lots. One was a light, airy house for summer. The other was a warm, solid house for winter. The houses were arranged around a plaza.

The town council met in this plaza. The council was made up of men who had shown their bravery or wisdom. One of these men was chosen town chief. The chief and the council ruled the village together.

Creek religious ceremonies also took place in the plaza. The Green Corn Dance, for example, was a feast held after the corn harvest in late summer. In this ceremony, people put aside any anger with one another and vowed to live in peace for the coming year. The Creek, filled with new hope, danced and then feasted on the corn. It was a festival of people living in harmony with nature. ■

■ *How did the Creek use the central plaza of their towns?*

◄ *In the forests of what is today the southeastern United States, the Creek hunted deer and gathered foods like persimmons, blackberries, raspberries, and pecans (above).*

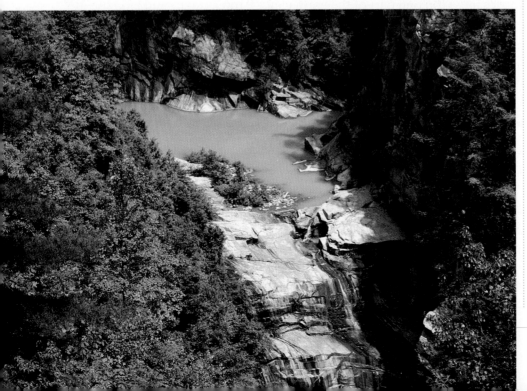

UNDERSTANDING LAND USE

American Indian cultures respected the land. The land and its products were a part of the religions of many cultures. As you have read, the Makah honored the salmon in their ceremonies.

These feelings affected how American Indians used the land. They believed, for example, that the land was made for all people and that it should be shared by all people.

A Local Decision

Land use refers to how a group—like the Anasazi, the Creek, or the English—feels about the land and what they do with it. Do they build cities or live in caves? Do they grow corn in fields or do they gather berries in the forest? Do they believe that the land can be bought, sold, and owned?

American Indians did not believe that land could be owned, but other groups did. In Europe, for example, land was owned by a few powerful people. The first Europeans in North America wanted to own the land.

In this century, groups have argued about the amount of land that is to be set aside for U.S. national parks. Some people feel this land is best used to preserve forests and wildlife. Others think the land should be used for farming, mining, and building.

A Global Issue

Today, the debate over how land is used involves the entire world. We have learned that what happens on one part of the earth can affect other parts. Factories in the United States can cause pollution in Canada.

A nuclear accident can affect the entire planet. How land is used anywhere on the earth is an important matter for everyone.

How people feel land should be used is an important part of their culture. American Indians, for example, often held ceremonies connected with land use. Both the Creek and the Anasazi held corn festivals after the harvest. These cultures celebrated land use as a part of their religions. This shows they respected the land and how it was used.

REVIEW

1. **FOCUS** How were American Indian cultures affected by their environments?

2. **CONNECT** What do the artifacts found in mounds tell us about the Mississippians?

3. **HISTORY** How is the environment of the Anasazi people shown in their arts and religion? How is the environment of the Makah people shown in their arts and beliefs?

4. **CRITICAL THINKING** Compare and contrast Creek and Mississippian towns.

5. **ACTIVITY** Look at the article on American Indians in the Minipedia on pages 558–560. Choose an American Indian group that is not discussed in this lesson. Find the following: clothing, housing, and crafts. Look at the map on page 560 to see where this group was located.

Observing the Seasons

Here's Why

Activities change with the seasons. Thousands of years ago, American Indians based their lives on the seasons. They planted in the spring and gathered crops in the fall. They knew when the seasons changed, but they did not know why. Do you?

Here's How

Many people think seasons change because the distance between the earth and the sun changes. This is not so. What really makes the seasons change is that the angle at which the sun's rays strike the earth changes.

The diagram on this page shows the angle of the sun's rays during the year. Look at the earth on June 20 or 21 in the diagram. The Northern Hemisphere tilts toward the sun; it is summer there. The Southern Hemisphere tilts away and receives the sun's rays at an angle. It is winter there. On the diagram, a line through the center of the earth represents the earth's axis. The tilt of the axis never changes.

By September 22 or 23, the earth completes one-fourth of its orbit around the sun. Northern and Southern hemispheres are both half-way between summer and winter. The sun's direct rays hit the equator. September 22 or 23 is the first day of autumn in the Northern Hemisphere and of spring in the Southern Hemisphere.

Try It

Find the part of the diagram that shows the earth when it is summer in South America. How can you tell it is summer there? What season is it in North America?

Apply It

Suppose it is summer in the United States. What kind of clothing would you need for a trip to Australia?

March 20
or March 21

North Pole

June 20
or June 21

Equator

Sun

December 21
or December 22

Equator

September 22
or September 23

The First People of the Americas

L E S S O N   3

Life in an Iroquois Village

What were the major features of Iroquois daily life?

Key Terms

- confederation
- long house

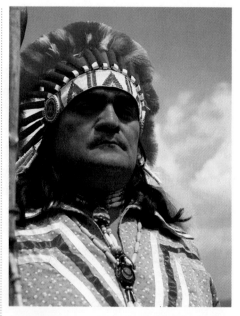

▲ *Many Iroquois still live in the United States and Canada today. This man wears his traditional Iroquois clothing only for special occasions.*

T he scene is Heathrow International Airport in London, England. Passengers arriving from all over the world are passing through the customs gate.

A tall man hands his passport to a guard. It bears the stamps of more than 20 countries. In it she reads the words: *Nawyayh nenh genh awhyawk nee hoe nonh nwenh jaw gayh.*

"What country are you from?" asks the guard.

"I am from the Iroquois *(IHR uh kwoy)* Nation," he answers.

The guard looks closely at the passport. "Where is that?"

"Between the United States and Canada."

"What brings you to England?" the guard asks.

The man says that he has come to see the Iroquois team play the English team in lacrosse, an American Indian game something like hockey and soccer. The guard looks behind the man. Sure enough, several lacrosse players are wearing uniforms that say "Iroquois Nationals."

The man smiles and tells the guard, "If we can beat Team England, Team Canada, and Team USA, our country will be the lacrosse champion of the world."

"Good luck," says the guard as she returns the passport, "and welcome to our country."

"Thank you very much," answers the man. "Perhaps one day I can welcome you to the Iroquois Nation. It is one of the oldest countries in the world."

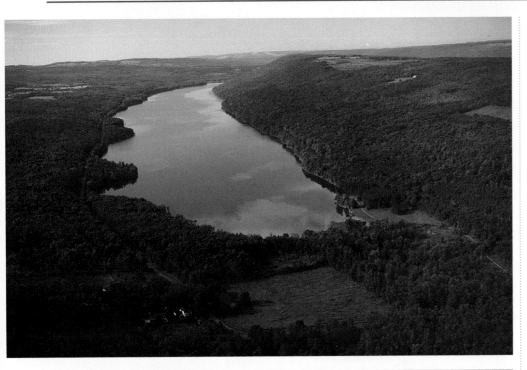

The Iroquois settled in what is today called the Finger Lakes region of New York state.

People of the Long House

The Iroquois Nation began in the 1400s. At that time, five tribes formed a **confederation,** a group of societies that united for a common goal. Those tribes are shown on the map on page 97. They hoped to make peace among their tribes. They called themselves "People of the Long House."

The **long house** was the building where the Iroquois lived. Several family groups lived in a long house. Women were often the most important people in these groups. When an Iroquois man and woman married, for example, they lived in the long house of the woman's family. Look at the Moment in Time on page 96 to learn more about an Iroquois woman.

Work

The Iroquois who lived together in the long houses also worked together in the fields and forests outside the village. They divided their work equally between men and women.

Iroquois men cleared land around the village for farming and fished in nearby streams. They also hunted deer and other animals.

The long house was the center of life in Iroquois villages.

95

An Iroquois Clan Leader

*5:45 P.M., September 17, 1597
In a long house on Onondaga Lake*

Feather
She placed her feather at the back of her headband when she married during her 15th summer, 13 years ago.

Headband
The beadwork advertises her position as clan matron. She'll use her authority tonight to settle an argument between her husband and her brother over winter hunting plans.

Green Corn Leaves
The homemade dressing under her sleeve covers a gash. She cut herself while harvesting squash this morning.

Buckskin Dress
All her clothes give off a smoky scent from the indoor fire that burns 24 hours a day.

Buckskin Cord
She wears this string to secure her wraparound dress and to bring good luck. Her husband gave her the cord after he last went hunting.

Corn Cake
Available to snackers and guests all day, the food will taste good to her younger brother. He has just arrived from his wife's long house for the clan council meeting.

Moose-Hide Moccasin
She decorated her shoes with fine moose hair and porcupine quill embroidery especially for tonight's meeting. She wants to look like the strong leader she must be to decide her husband's and her brother's claims.

The food and hides brought back by the men were shared by everyone who lived in the village. The men also fought other tribes when the Iroquois were at war.

While the men hunted, the women raised corn, beans, and squash in fields near the village. They also took charge of daily life. They made sure that everyone in the village had food, clothing, and a place to live.

Values

The Iroquois felt very close to nature as they hunted and farmed in the land around their village. They believed that every part of nature—every tree and plant, every animal—had its own spirit. They prayed to these spirits and asked for their help in hunting and farming. The Iroquois honored the land and the animals. They believed that a person should take only what was needed from nature and nothing more.

The Iroquois honored the needs of other people just as they honored the land and animals. Sometimes the harvest was small and food was scarce. Everyone in the village, however, would share their food before any one person went hungry. The Iroquois helped all the people of the village, even in the hardest times.

In every part of their lives, the Iroquois people worked together. Cooperation was an important part of the Iroquois Nation from the beginning. ∎

▲ *The Iroquois raised squash as well as corn in the fields around their villages.*

■ *Find evidence to support this statement: The Iroquois valued cooperation.*

The Iroquois Nation

Without cooperation the Iroquois knew that their people could not survive. The five tribes of the Iroquois were often at war with one another before they became a single nation.

If a member of the Cayuga *(kay YOO guh)* tribe killed a Seneca *(SEHN ih kuh)*, the Seneca tribe got even by killing a Cayuga. After that each tribe would keep trying to get even.

◄ *The five tribes of the Iroquois Nation were all located in the same region near Lake Ontario.*

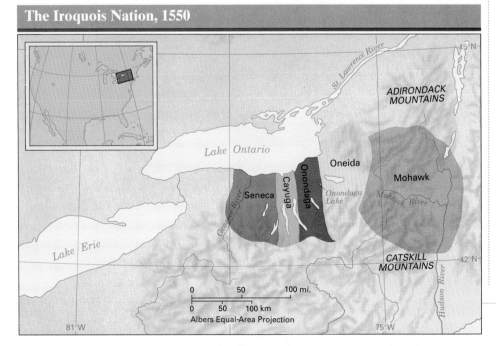

The Iroquois Nation, 1550

ADIRONDACK MOUNTAINS
St. Lawrence River
Lake Ontario
Oneida
Mohawk
Seneca
Cayuga
Onondaga
Onondaga Lake
Mohawk River
Genesee River
Lake Erie
CATSKILL MOUNTAINS
Hudson River
45°N
42°N
81°W
75°W

0   50   100 mi.
0   50   100 km
Albers Equal-Area Projection

The Iroquois used wampum belts as ornaments and as a way to remember important events. The symbols on this belt show the five tribes joining together into one Iroquois Nation.

Across Time & Space

About 50,000 Iroquois live as citizens in the United States or Canada today. However, they hold Iroquois passports and call the town of Onondaga, near Syracuse, New York, their capital.

■ *Why did the five tribes unite to form the Iroquois Nation?*

The Legend of Hiawatha

An Iroquois tale tells of an Onondaga *(ahn uhn DAW guh)* chief named Hiawatha. Tired of the endless fighting, Hiawatha lived alone in the forest. There he met the god Dekanawida *(dee kahn uh WEE duh)*. This god said that the way to bring peace to the tribes was to form a single Iroquois nation. Hiawatha went from tribe to tribe and explained Dekanawida's plan. He told them:

> We bind ourselves together by taking hold of each other's hands so firmly and forming a circle so strong that if a tree should fall upon it, it could not shake nor break it, so that our people and grandchildren shall remain in the circle in security, peace, and happiness.
>
> from an Iroquois legend

After hearing Hiawatha's words, the tribes formed a single Iroquois Nation. The new nation was like an imaginary long house, with all five tribes living together under the same roof.

Hiawatha's Legacy

No one has been able to prove that a chief named Hiawatha ever lived. Sometime in the 1400s, however, the Mohawk, Oneida *(oh NY duh)*, Onondaga, Cayuga, and the Seneca united. They formed a Great Council of 49 chiefs. Each tribe had an equal voice in the Council.

The Council brought an end to the wars and other fights. They resolved differences with words instead of blood. The Iroquois people brought many other problems before the Council. The chiefs talked about each problem until all agreed on an answer, following rules laid down in the story of Hiawatha.

The story of Hiawatha was important to the Iroquois. It helped them in times of trouble. It showed how one person could make a difference in the world. Remembering the words of Hiawatha, the Iroquois worked together and built a great nation. ■

R E V I E W

1. **FOCUS** What were the major features of Iroquois daily life?
2. **CONNECT** Which American Indian culture discussed in Lesson 2 is most like the Iroquois? Why?
3. **HISTORY** How did the Iroquois resolve differences between tribes, villages, and individuals?
4. **CRITICAL THINKING** The Iroquois view of nature was based on sharing and cooperation. Where else is this attitude seen in Iroquois life and history?
5. **WRITING ACTIVITY** In this lesson you have learned about the Iroquois. Imagine that you live in an Iroquois village. Write an account of your day: what you eat, what you wear, what you are taught.

Using Timelines

Here's Why

Timelines can give you a sense of sequence and may suggest cause-and-effect relationships. Using a timeline also can help you to relate events that occur in different places at the same time. For example, the timeline on this page shows important events among American Indian tribes between 700 B.C. and A.D. 1500.

Here's How

We use the abbreviations B.C. and A.D. when we refer to years in history. Christians in Europe started this way of referring to dates. Dates B.C. are those that occur before the birth of Christ. The letters A.D. stand for the Latin phrase *Anno Domini*, which means "in the year of our Lord." Dates A.D. are those

that occur after the birth of Christ.

Most dates for events that happened B.C. are not specific. The calendar as we know it had not yet been developed, so the people who lived then did not leave dated records. When we do not know the precise year something happened, we give an approximate year and say, for example, *about* 500 B.C.

The timeline below shows 700 years in the B.C. period and 1,500 years in the A.D. period. Each major division on the timeline represents a period of 500 years. Dates are written at the beginning of each time period. Each event is written on the timeline at the date when it took place. For an event that spans a period of time, you would place marks on the

timeline at the beginning and end of that period and shade the line between the marks.

Try It

Copy the timeline below onto your own paper. Then add the following events:
- A.D. 1200, Mississippian city of Cahokia reaches population of about 40,000.
- About 250 B.C., Eastern Plains Indians live in permanent villages.
- A.D. 1070–1130, Anasazi build apartment buildings with impressive architecture.
- A.D. 1050, Anasazi grow cotton.

Apply It

Make a timeline that shows five to ten events in your own life. Use *about* for any dates you are unsure of.

700 B.C.– A.D. 700, Anasazi build pithouses

About A.D. 600, Anasazi make pottery and use bows and arrows

About 1168, Aztec culture begins

About 1300, Anasazi migrate from San Juan River area.

| 500 | B.C. | A.D. | 500 | 1000 | 1500 |

About 500 B.C., Postarchaic Epoch begins

About 700, Creek culture begins

800–1500, Mississippians develop most powerful culture in North America

About 1400, Hiawatha leads founding of Iroquois Great Council

99

Chapter Review

Reviewing Key Terms

agriculture (p. 83)   long house (p. 95)
confederation (p. 95)   mesa (p. 86)
epoch (p. 82)   mound (p. 90)
glacier (p. 81)   potlatch (p. 89)

A. The following clues refer to key terms. Use a dictionary to help you figure out the answers. Then use each term in a sentence that shows you understand the meaning.

1. Which term comes from the Latin word *mensa*, meaning "table"?
2. Which term comes from two words— *ager* and *cultur*?
3. Which term is related to *glacé*, "having a glazed, glossy surface"?
4. Which term comes from the word *patshatl*?
5. Which term means "highly significant or important"?
6. Which term begins with three letters that mean "together" and has an ending that means "an action or process"?
7. Which term refers to something larger than the pyramids of Egypt?

B. Imagine you are visiting an Iroquois family. Write a paragraph in your diary to describe your activities. Include these terms:

1. long house
2. agriculture

Exploring Concepts

A. Write one paragraph to summarize each lesson in this chapter.

Lesson 1: Tell about changes in environment for each of the following epochs:

    Beringian   Paleo-Indian
    Archaic   Postarchaic

Lesson 2: Give examples of how the people of these American Indian cultures used their environment:

    Anasazi   Makah
    Mississippians   Creek

Lesson 3: Tell about the accomplishments of the Iroquois people using these concepts:

    family   work   values

B. Answer each question with information from the chapter.

1. How is the Bering Strait different today than it was about 30,000 years ago? What changes explain the difference?
2. How did the early American Indians get food to eat before they learned the skills of agriculture?
3. What was Richard Wetherill's discovery and why was it important to people?
4. What did the Anasazi do to save the precious water they needed? What happened when the water supply stopped?
5. How were the Makah and the Mississippians more fortunate than the people of the desert?
6. What did Makah ceremonies celebrate and why?
7. What three questions did each American Indian culture answer in its own way?
8. How did the Iroquois people work toward keeping peace among their tribes?
9. Who were the leaders of Iroquois clans? What were some of their responsibilities?

Reviewing Skills

1. Use the diagram to answer the following questions: What season is it in the Northern Hemisphere? How can you tell this from the diagram? What season is it in the Southern Hemisphere? How is this shown in the diagram?
2. Use the diagram to explain why the seasons north and south of the equator are opposite.
3. Use the map on page 82 to make a timeline showing the following events:
   - Humans arrive in North America
   - Humans reach the tip of South America
   - Paleo-Indian epoch begins
   - Migration of hunting and gathering tribes throughout the Americas
   - Agriculture spreads throughout the Americas

4. What headings would you check in an encyclopedia to find articles about the changing seasons?
5. Suppose you are asked to tell about the technology that existed among the five American Indian cultures covered in this chapter. What type of visual evidence from the past would help you?

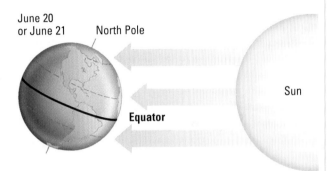

June 20 or June 21 North Pole

Sun

Equator

Using Critical Thinking

1. Imagine that you lived during the time of the American Indian cultures that you studied in this chapter. Which culture would you choose to belong to? Give reasons for your choice.
2. The Creeks and the Europeans had different ideas about how the land should be used. Compare the Creeks' ideas with those of the Europeans. Which ideas do you think are better? Explain your opinion.
3. The Iroquois nation provides passports for their people, even though they are citizens of the United States or Canada. Why do you think some Iroquois people feel strongly about this? Do you agree or disagree with their system?

Preparing for Citizenship

1. **WRITING ACTIVITY** Imagine that you are a planter who is desperate for rain. Without rain, your crops will die and you will not have food for your family. Write a poem, song, or story that tells how important the rain is to your life.
2. **ARTS ACTIVITY** Make a diorama to represent a dwelling or activity of one American Indian group. You may choose a group from the chapter or a group from pages 558 and 559 of the Minipedia.
3. **COLLABORATIVE LEARNING** Help to create a radio program called "Voices of the Past." Form small groups based on the Indian cultures you studied in this chapter. Each group will prepare a script, appoint an announcer, and choose speakers to represent members of the culture. The announcer will ask each speaker questions about the culture they were part of, when they lived, where their lands were, and something about their daily life.

Chapter 5

The Age of Exploration

For centuries Europeans had dreamed of a faster route to the riches of Asia. In the 1400s new ships, inventions, and discoveries made that dream a reality. Soon, almost every kingdom in Europe sent explorers across the western ocean. Those earliest explorers did not find a new route to Asia. Instead, they discovered a whole new world.

Throughout this period, improved instruments help explorers sail ships more accurately. The cross-staff (above) and this compass of the 1620s (below) made longer ocean voyages possible.

| 1300 | 1350 | 1400 | 1450 |

1356

1469 Ferdinand of Aragon and Isabella of Castile marry and become king and queen of Spain. The rulers, shown above holding court, grant large sums of money for exploration.

1543 An Italian mapmaker named Battista Agnese makes the map above. It shows the routes Spanish ships took on the first voyage around the earth 20 years earlier.

1500	1550	1600	1650

1492 Christopher Columbus is granted money by Ferdinand and Isabella. After a voyage of two months Columbus reaches the New World.

1650

Europe in the Age of Exploration

Key Terms

- technology
- navigate

➤ *This illustration from an ancient map of the world shows a sea monster swallowing a ship.*

I magine an island where monsters 28 to 30 feet tall live. In 1356, Sir John Mandeville told of such a place in his *Travels,* a book that told stories of things supposedly seen by travelers to Asia and Africa.

> A nd they have no clothes to wear except the skins of beasts, which they cover their bodies with. They eat no bread; but they eat raw flesh. . . . They will more readily eat human flesh than any other. Thanks to them no pilgrim dare enter this isle; for if they see a ship in the sea with men aboard, they will wade into the sea to take the men.

Strange tales also told of a snake that

lived in the Atlantic Ocean. Flames sprang from around its neck. Eyes 16 feet across glared at its enemies. Another rhinoceros-like creature was said to gobble up crabs 12 feet wide.

Most Europeans in the 1400s knew little about the world beyond their own villages. Many believed that monsters roamed over distant lands and seas. But in the 1400s, Europeans began to explore these unknown areas. Within 50 years, exploration changed the way Europeans saw the world.

How Europeans Saw the World

The map on page 105 shows the European idea of the world in the 1400s. Like most maps of the time, this one mixed real geographical knowledge with stories and guesses. People knew of only

▼ *A beautiful compass rose like this often decorated early maps.*

three continents—Europe, Africa, and Asia.

Educated people knew that the earth was round and that Asia lay across the Atlantic. Not everyone believed that monsters hid underwater or that the sea near the equator was boiling hot. But even those who did not believe the stories did not think it would be possible to sail across the ocean.

Sailors didn't have the skills needed for long voyages. Once they were out of sight of land, they could not tell how far they had gone or in what direction.

However, political events and trade awakened new interest in the outside world. Also, developments in **technology,** knowledge used for making things, let nations begin to explore the world's oceans. ■

■ *How much did Europeans in the 1400s know about the world around them?*

Reasons for Exploration

The changes in European society began with a series of religious wars called the Crusades. From 1095 to about 1300, European Christians fought Muslims, people who believed in the religion of Islam. Christians fought to gain control of Jerusalem and other areas they believed were holy.

The Crusades took Europeans to the Mediterranean area, northeast Africa, and southwest Asia. There they discovered Italian and Arab merchants in control of busy trade centers. These merchants traded spices, fine silks, and gems from India, China, and Japan.

Desire for Trade

Word of these riches excited Europeans, and they dreamed of trading with Asia themselves.

These fine goods would make life in Europe better. For example, before refrigeration, people could use spices like pepper and nutmeg from Asia to slow the rotting process and hide the taste of rotting meat.

Europeans also learned of the riches of Asia by reading. They read, for example, this description of an Indian king:

> The king is no more clothed than the rest, except that he has a piece of richer cloth, and is honorably distinguished by various kinds of ornaments, such as a collar set with jewels, sapphires, emeralds, and rubies, of immense value. He also wears . . . a fine silken string containing 104 large handsome pearls and rubies. . . . On each arm he wears three gold bracelets, adorned with pearls and jewels; on three different parts of the leg, golden bands ornamented in the same manner; and on the toes of his feet, as well as on his fingers, rings of great value.
>
> Marco Polo, *Description of the World*, 1298

■ *What did Europeans hope to gain from their explorations?*

▼ *As the timeline shows, events over 400 years combined to produce the age of exploration.*

The invention of the printing press in the 1400s made books such as Marco Polo's journals available to the public for the first time. Polo, an adventurer from Venice, Italy, traveled through India, China, and Japan in the late 1200s. His book described the people and things he found there. Europeans dreamed of having such things for themselves.

Duty to Spread Christianity

Besides dreams of riches, Europeans had other reasons for wanting to open routes to Asia and Africa. They saw exploration as a way to spread Christianity.

The Crusades had not won Jerusalem from the Muslims. However, Europeans had not lost their crusading spirit. They were certain that Christianity was the only true religion. Therefore, they believed it was their duty to convert all non-Christians to Christianity. ■

Developments Leading to the Age of Exploration

About 1000, Use of Arabic triangular sails enables European ships to sail into the wind.

1090, Magnetic compass comes into use in Europe.

| 1000 | 1100 | 1200 |

1095–1291, Crusades expose Europeans to new technology and luxury goods.

About 1200, Development of rudder enables one person to steer ship.

Technological Developments

Contact between Europe and Asia did more than create the desire for trade and for spreading Christianity. It also led to important developments in shipbuilding and in the ability to **navigate,** or chart the course of a journey.

In the 1400s, even the most experienced sailors feared sailing in strange waters. An unexpected rock formation or ocean current could cause a shipwreck or take a ship off course. Also, sailors never knew when they might be in enemy territory. Before they could undertake long voyages, explorers needed the equipment to get them safely home.

Ships and Sails

For about 1,000 years, European ships moved by means of square-rigged sails. These ships could hold their own against tossing waves during short trips along the coast. However, they could sail only in the same direction as the wind. Thus they could not make long voyages without being blown off course.

About A.D. 1000, Arab sailors introduced the lateen *(luh TEEN)* sail to the Mediterranean area. A lateen sail looked like a triangle and was rigged along the length of a ship. It could catch winds from the sides and from the rear. The development of the rudder allowed sailors to steer lateen ships, which were called caravels *(KAR uh vehls),* without a large crew of oarsmen.

Portuguese shipbuilders joined European and Arab techniques to create a new ship called a carrack *(KAR uhk).* The ship shown on page 113 is a carrack. These ships

About 1300, Cannons first used aboard ships.

About 1400, New astrolabe measures distance more accurately.

1469, Marriage of Ferdinand and Isabella unites Spain.

1300   1400   1500

1271, Marco Polo travels to the Orient.

1454, Gutenberg's printing press improves the spread of information.

The Age of Exploration

A sailor could find latitude by measuring the angle of the horizon in relation to the North Star. To do this he used a cross-staff. The sailor aimed the crosspiece so that it lined up with the star at its top and the horizon at its bottom. The lower the North Star in the sky, the farther south the ship.

■ *What major technological developments made exploration possible in the 1400s?*

had two or three adjustable square-rigged masts, one lateen-rigged mast, and a rear rudder. Carracks had the speed and flexibility of lateen ships and the strength to stand pounding waves and high winds. They also had room for cargo and living space.

Navigation

Exploration needed more than ships, however. Sailors had to know where they were going and how far they had come, especially when out of sight of land.

European sailors had used the compass to find direction since about 1100. They measured latitude by turning the pointer on a metal disk called an astrolabe

(AS truh layb) toward the sun. However, astrolabes were designed for use on land. Sailors could not get accurate readings on the bouncing deck of a ship. The drawing on this page shows how sailors used the more reliable cross-staff to figure latitude.

Although sailors could figure out their latitude, they had no way to measure longitude. Along the shore, landmarks allowed sailors to correct a course. But on the open sea, they could only guess longitude by figuring how long and how far they had traveled.

Weapons

As explorers set out on unknown seas, they depended on another kind of technology: weapons. Sailors did not know what enemies they might meet. They needed a way to defend themselves against attack. Sailors on the first overseas ships carried weapons familiar to them—swords, spears, bows, and armor. As technology improved, more powerful weapons such as guns and cannons came into use. These weapons made Europeans feel nearly all-powerful over the peoples they met. ■

R E V I E W

1. **FOCUS** Why did Europeans look for new sea routes to Asia in the 1400s?
2. **CONNECT** How did sailors use the cross-staff to figure their latitude?
3. **HISTORY** What influence did the writings of Marco Polo have upon Europeans?
4. **CULTURE** Why was the triangular lateen sail an improvement over the old square-rigged sail?
5. **CRITICAL THINKING** New technology was necessary for

early exploration. What exploration today depends on new technology?

6. **ACTIVITY** Make up a story such as a traveler at the time of the Crusades might have told to frighten and impress his listeners. Include some frightening monster or force of nature such as a sea serpent or boiling water at the equator. Share your story with the class.

L E S S O N   2

Portuguese and Spanish Exploration

W hy did Prince Henry of Portugal choose to live in the town of Sagres *(SAH greesh),* in southwest Portugal? He had once shown promise as a military leader. At 21, Henry had boldly fought the North African Muslims and captured the city of Ceuta *(SAY oot uh)* for the Portuguese.

But in 1420, at age 26, Henry almost never left Sagres. He liked to stay with the mathematicians, map-makers, shipbuilders, and captains at the school of navigation he had started there.

Members of the court of King John, Henry's father, wondered why Henry chose such a quiet,

lonely life. They did not see that the scholars at Sagres would start the greatest period of exploration in history.

THINKING FOCUS

What were the most important results of Portuguese and Spanish explorations?

Key Terms

- expedition
- colony

▲ *Prince Henry the Navigator never went on a voyage of discovery himself. However, he devoted his life to studying the coast of Africa.*

Portuguese Exploration

Henry had not forgotten the sights he saw while fighting in North Africa. The Muslims there controlled a great trading center. They sold gold and ivory from African lands south of the Sahara, and spices and silks from India,

China, and Japan. If only Portugal could share in these riches, Henry thought.

Muslims controlled the land routes to Asia. The Portuguese also wanted to have spices and silks, but they didn't have enough money to buy them from the Arabs. They couldn't send their own traders to Asia because they couldn't get past the armed Muslims. However, Prince Henry thought they might be able to reach Asia and Africa by sea.

Henry ordered the experts at Sagres to find a sea route to Africa and Asia. Then he searched for sailors brave enough to lead these voyages. Henry paid for a series of **expeditions,** or organized journeys, down the west coast of Africa. His captains returned bearing gold and ivory. But Henry wanted them to go farther south. He would not be happy until one of his ships sailed all the way to the Indian Ocean.

Henry the Navigator, as he was called, died in 1460. In 1488, Bartholomeu Días reached the southern tip of Africa. Then, in 1497, Vasco da Gama began a voyage that would match Henry's dreams. He sailed all the way around Africa to India. The map on page 111 shows the routes Días and Da Gama took.

The journey to India and back to Portugal covered over 27,000 miles and lasted over two years. Along the way, Da Gama and his crew battled disease, storms, and even attacks by rival traders. But in the end, Da Gama succeeded in opening the door to Portuguese trade with Asia. ■

Early Spanish Exploration

Christopher Columbus, a captain from Genoa, Italy, had learned to sail aboard Portuguese trade ships. He knew that the Portuguese were trying to reach Asia by sailing around Africa. However, Columbus had studied maps of Ptolemy *(TAHL uh mee),* a Greek geographer who lived around A.D. 150. Columbus became convinced that the shortest route to Asia, or the Indies, was straight west across the Atlantic.

Voyages of Columbus

Columbus knew that such a voyage would cost a great deal of money. For eight years he tried to persuade European rulers to pay for his voyage. Everyone said his idea was too dangerous and would cost too much. Finally, in 1492, Columbus heard that King Ferdinand and Queen Isabella of Spain would give him the money he needed to sail.

The king and queen wanted to spread Spanish power. After years of war, they had driven the North African Muslims out of southern Spain. Now they wanted to bring Christianity to other lands—and to win a share of the rich trade with Asia.

Columbus left Palos, Spain, on August 3, 1492, with his crew and three ships. After a stop at the Canary Islands off Africa, he set a course straight across the Atlantic.

Because he was afraid that the crew would refuse to go on, Columbus kept his own secret records

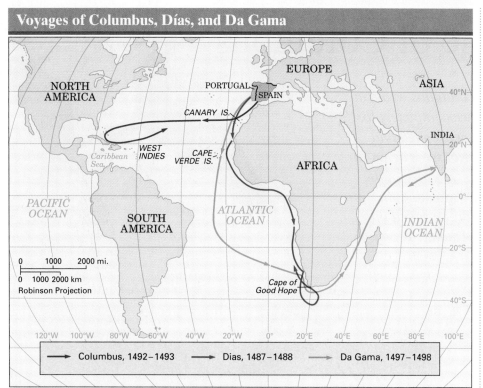

Voyages of Columbus, Días, and Da Gama

NORTH AMERICA
EUROPE
ASIA
PORTUGAL
SPAIN
CANARY IS.
INDIA
WEST INDIES
Caribbean Sea
CAPE VERDE IS.
AFRICA
PACIFIC OCEAN
SOUTH AMERICA
ATLANTIC OCEAN
INDIAN OCEAN
Cape of Good Hope

0   1000   2000 mi.
0   1000 2000 km
Robinson Projection

→ Columbus, 1492–1493   → Dias, 1487–1488   → Da Gama, 1497–1498

◄ This map shows Columbus's first voyage and the voyages of Días and Da Gama. Which routes led to Asia?

▲ This painting of Columbus, done about 20 years after his death, was probably copied from an earlier portrait.

of how far he believed they had sailed each day. He insisted that they sail on.

They sailed and sailed as
    winds might blow,
Until at last the blanched mate
    said,
"Why, now not even God
    would know
Should I and all my men fall
    dead.
These very winds forget their
    way,
For God from these dread seas
    is gone.
Now speak, brave Admiral,
    speak and say—"
He said: "Sail on! sail on! and
    on!"

Joaquin Miller, from "Columbus"

On October 12, Columbus landed on a tiny Caribbean island that is today one of the Bahama Islands. He named it "San Salvador"—Holy Savior. Columbus believed he had reached the Indies. He called the people he met at San Salvador "los Indios" (Indians). The people ran away at first, frightened of the ships landing on their shore. But when they saw men get off the ships, they welcomed them with gifts of gold.

When Columbus returned to Spain in March 1493, he brought plants and gold from the islands to Ferdinand and Isabella. They were so impressed that they gave him 17 ships and 1,200 men to form a **colony,** a settlement governed by a distant country, in the Indies. For more information about Columbus's voyage, see A Closer Look on the next two pages.

Columbus made three more voyages. He explored Caribbean islands and the coast of what he thought was China.

Across Time & Space

Columbus was not really the first European to explore the Americas. In the late 900s, a group of Norse, or Scandinavian, explorers sailed to Iceland and Greenland. A few settled briefly in what is now Newfoundland, Canada. But few Europeans ever knew of that settlement, and it was only remembered as a legend in Scandinavia by 1400.

The Voyage of Columbus

On September 9, 1492, Columbus wrote in his ship's log: "This day we completely lost sight of land, and many men sighed and wept for fear they would not see it again for a long time." The log tells the story of the trip aboard the Niña, *the* Pinta, *and the* Santa Maria, *as the expedition sailed into unknown regions of the Atlantic Ocean.*

Coastal birds like the ones the sailors saw

September 21, 1492
The sailors grew afraid their ships would get stuck in thick seaweed, called sargassum.

Sargassum

Niña

September 22, 1492
". . . The crew is agitated, thinking that no winds blow in these parts that will return them to Spain."
The Log of Christopher Columbus

Santa Maria

Deck—where the men worked and slept

Pinta

September 24, 1492
"I am having serious trouble with the crew. . . . I am told by a few trusted men (and these are few in number) that if I persist in going onward, the best course of action will be to throw me into the sea some night."
The Log of Christopher Columbus

Crow's nest—for the lookout to stand in

October 11, 1492
The explorers had not seen land for 33 days. On this night, Columbus finally heard a boom from the *Pinta*'s gun—the signal that land had been sighted!

Captain's cabin—where Columbus slept, dined with his officers, and wrote in his log

October 9, 1492
All night the men could hear birds flying overhead and see them against the moon. The birds gave the men hope that they were nearing land.

Hold—where food, water, and other supplies were stored

Lead weight and marked rope for measuring depth of water so the ships wouldn't run aground

However, he failed to find the riches of Asia. He never knew that he had found a continent new to Europeans.

Explorers After Columbus

News that Columbus had reached land by sailing west led other voyagers to try to claim new lands for Spain. But geographers soon understood that Columbus had not landed in Asia. In 1507, a German map-maker named the new continent "America," after an Italian explorer, Amerigo Vespucci *(vays POOT chee)*. Vespucci made two voyages for Spain and wrote a book in which he called the lands he saw a "New World."

In 1513, Vasco de Balboa proved that Columbus had not reached Asia. Balboa crossed Panama on foot and arrived at the Pacific. Another ocean stood between Spain and the Indies! Not until 1519 did a Portuguese explorer named Ferdinand Magellan reach Asia by sailing west. ■

■ *Why did Columbus believe he had reached Asia?*

How Do We Know?

Cortés's victory over the Aztecs is one of the best-documented military campaigns in history. A Spanish soldier, Bernal Díaz, kept a journal that describes Cortés's mistakes and cruelties. Aztec written histories of the conquest also survive.

The Search for Gold

Even though America was not Asia, the Spanish kept searching for riches. In 1519, Hernando Cortés went to Mexico, which was said to have huge gold mines.

With 17 horses and about 600 soldiers, Cortés marched inland from the east coast of Mexico to the huge Aztec capital city of Tenochtitlan *(tay nawch tee TLAHN)*.

UNDERSTANDING EXPANSION

The rulers of Spain sent explorers all over the world. They wanted to expand the influence of their country. Historians use the word *expansion* to describe the actions of a country that occupies or controls another country. As a country expands, people often move from that country into the new land.

Kinds of Expansion

Expansion often involves war. One country may start a war to expand into land owned by another country.

A country may buy land for expansion. In 1803, President Thomas Jefferson was able to expand the United States by buying a large part of America from France.

Today, a country might expand its influence by trading with other countries. For example, Japan now sells its products around the world. Your family may own a car or a stereo produced by a Japanese company. In this way, Japanese culture expands its influence as Japanese business expands.

Expansion and Change

Expansion often has dramatic effects. When one country occupies another, it usually changes the land it occupies.

The expansion of Spain into the Americas greatly reduced the number of Indians on these lands. The culture of Spain—Spanish language, food, and architecture—became dominant in the lands Spain occupied.

Thousands who had been defeated by the Aztecs joined this passing army. A messenger to Moctezuma *(mahk tuh ZOO muh)*, the Aztec king, announced that light-skinned men had come on "small mountains floating on the waves of the sea."

Aztec Defeat

Moctezuma waited to fight off the invaders, believing they might be the gods of Aztec legend. By the time Moctezuma understood

what was happening, Cortés's army had entered the city and blocked off its exits. With no way to get food, the Aztecs were trapped.

Cortés's army took gold and jewels from every building. Then they destroyed the buildings. The city lay flat when the last Aztecs gave up in 1521. After four months of battle, Cortés had beaten an empire of four million. On the ruins he built Mexico City, which became the capital of a Spanish empire.

Treasure Hunters

After Cortés's victory, other Spaniards came to the Americas to find treasure. In South America, they defeated both the Inca and the Chibcha *(CHIHB chuh)* in present-day Peru and Colombia, and took over gold and silver mines there.

In North America, Francisco Coronado and Hernando de Soto searched for but did not find cities of gold and silver. These expeditions brought no wealth. But they allowed Spain to claim the lands across southern North America. By the mid-1500s, Spain had passed Portugal as the most powerful nation in Europe. ■

▲
Objects like this gold lizard from Peru fed the dreams of explorers who searched for cities of gold.

◄ *The painting on the left shows Indians leaving their village as the Spanish approach on horseback.*

■ *What were the consequences of the Spaniards' search for gold in the Americas?*

R E V I E W

1. **FOCUS** What were the most important results of Portuguese and Spanish explorations?
2. **CONNECT** How did Prince Henry the Navigator's experiences in North Africa influence him to look for a route to Asia?
3. **GEOGRAPHY** Find Mexico City on the map of North America on page 576 of the Atlas. Use the distance scale on the map to estimate how far Mexico City is from the east coast of Mexico, which was where Cortés landed.
4. **CRITICAL THINKING** Why do you think Columbus was considered a failure at the time of his death?
5. **ACTIVITY** Tell about a place—Antarctica, the bottom of the ocean, the moon—that you would like to explore. What dangers might there be in getting there? What would you expect to find there?

Money for Exploration

▼ *Ferdinand and Isabella provided money for Columbus's voyage. They are shown in the painting and coins below. Columbus gave coins like these to natives on his arrival in America.*

> The end of Spain and the beginning of India are not far distant but close, and it is evident that this sea is navigable in a few days with a fair wind.
>
> *Imago Mundi [A World Geography], c. 1410*

> His (Columbus's) promises and offers were impossible and vain and worthy of rejection . . . (I)t was not . . . proper . . . for their royal authority to favor an affair that . . . appeared uncertain and impossible to any educated person . . . "
>
> Bartolomé de las Casas, on the report of the royal committee

Background

Christopher Columbus was sure he could sail west, circle the earth, and reach the Indies—the European name for eastern Asia. But Columbus had a hard time persuading any European rulers to fund his voyage.

In trying to persuade Ferdinand and Isabella of Spain, Columbus explained how Spain could benefit. He pointed out that a better trade route to Asia could bring Spain great wealth and power. Spanish merchants would have wonderful new metals, cloth, and spices to sell. Spanish products would find new buyers. The Spanish flag would lead the way across the "western ocean." The power of Spain would circle the globe. And along the way, the Spanish could bring Christianity to foreign places.

Ferdinand and Isabella's committee of advisors foresaw other results. They warned that the earth was far larger than Columbus thought. The "western ocean" was huge and dangerous and could not be crossed. Supporting Columbus's plan would waste Spanish lives and money. The country and its government would be laughed at for believing such nonsense.

Conflict over Exploration

Would Ferdinand and Isabella listen to their advisors or would they grant Columbus's request? The decision was a difficult one. We cannot know what line of thinking finally led them to support Columbus. However, they must have carefully considered the possible consequences of each alternative.

The safe choice would have been to reject Columbus's request. The advantages of saying no would include putting money to other uses such as strengthening the army and navy, improving roads and public buildings, and funding the arts. The main disadvantage would be giving up the possibility of gaining wealth and trading advantages.

Saying yes was the high-risk choice. If Columbus succeeded, Spain would get all of the benefits that Columbus had promised. If he failed, Spain might suffer just as the royal advisors had warned.

Ferdinand and Isabella finally decided to risk giving Columbus ships and money. Their decision had one major consequence that no one could have predicted—the discovery of a world entirely unknown to Europeans.

Flag from The World Book Encyclopedia. © 1980 World Book, Inc. By Permission

Should we pay for Columbus' voyage?

- Expand Spain's power
- Christianize the Indies
- Trade with the east
- Discover new lands

↓

Pay

- Fear of failure
- Dangers of journey
- Waste of money

↓

Don't pay

Decision Point

1. What advantages and disadvantages might Ferdinand and Isabella have considered before making their decision?
2. Why do you think Ferdinand and Isabella decided to support Columbus? Do you think you would have made the same decision? Why or why not?
3. Based on this example, do you think it is possible to predict all the consequences of a decision? Explain.
4. For more than 30 years, the United States has launched missions to explore outer space (see Mini-pedia p. 553). What are some advantages to continuing this exploration? What are some disadvantages?
5. Do you think that space exploration might lead to an unpredictable discovery? If so, how might that affect your decision about whether to spend billions of dollars on space exploration?

▲ *The Spanish flag (above) carried a castle and a lion, symbols of Ferdinand and Isabella. Modern explorers like astronauts have used flags to mark their discoveries.*

L E S S O N   3

French, Dutch, and English Voyages

THINKING FOCUS

Why did the French, Dutch, and English decide to begin exploring in the Western Hemisphere?

Key Terms

- Northwest Passage
- contagious disease

➤ *The supplies listed here were expected to feed 190 sailors for three months. How would you like eating these foods for three months?*

What's for dinner? For sailors on long sea voyages in the 1500s, the food seldom changed. Night after night, month after month, voyagers lived on a diet of salted meat, dried beans or peas, and hard biscuits. If the crew stopped on land during the journey, they might enjoy fresh fruit or meat. Only dried or heavily salted foods would keep for more than a few days. And the sailors had no way to keep rats or insects out of their food. Sailors on Columbus's ships ate after dark so as not to see the worms.

Bad food was not the only hardship sailors faced. Lack of vitamin C in the diet caused scurvy, a painful and often fatal disease. Over half the crew on Vasco da Gama's voyage to India in 1497 died of scurvy.

Barrels holding the precious supply of fresh water often sprang leaks. Frequent storms made life miserable. Yet despite such conditions, exploration grew rapidly during the 1500s.

Food for a Voyage
8000 pounds salt beef
2800 pounds salt pork
600 pounds salt cod
20,000 biscuits
30 bushels oatmeal
40 bushels dried peas
1 barrel salt
100 pounds fat
1 barrel flour
11 wooden casks butter
10,500 gallons beer
3,500 gallons water
2 casks cider

Exploration of North America

When asked why he risked crossing an unknown ocean, Spanish explorer Bernal Díaz replied, "To serve God and His Majesty . . . and to grow rich, as all men desire to do." By the mid-1500s, overseas

◄ *Compare this map made in 1527 to the one shown on page 105. How are the Indian and Atlantic oceans on the later map different? How much of the coast of North America does this map show?*

travel was still dangerous but not quite so mysterious. Although Spanish and Portuguese explorers tried to keep their knowledge secret, information leaked out. Maps like the one above showed that explorers had new knowledge of the American coastline.

In addition to learning of new lands and routes, French, Dutch, and English rulers knew that exploration had made Spain and Portugal rich. Portugal controlled the eastern routes to Asia and Africa, and Spain had claimed Central and South America. Other explorers, therefore, decided to sail to the northern part of America to seek fame and fortune.

French Voyages

The French sent out the first of several voyages in 1524. King Francis I hired an Italian, Giovanni da Verrazano *(vehr uh ZAH noh),* to search for the **Northwest Passage,** a legendary water route to China through North America. Verrazano landed near what is now North Carolina and mapped the coast as far north as Maine.

Jacques Cartier *(kahr TYAY)* continued the search for the Northwest Passage in 1535. Cartier sailed up the St. Lawrence River, in the hope that it might lead him to China. His route is shown on the map on page 120. The river's rapids and ice stopped his ship.

Cartier and his crew spent a winter in an Iroquois village at the place that is now Montreal. He discovered that this land, which the Indians called Canada, was rich

◄ *This drawing from the late 1500s shows a French explorer with his Indian hosts.*

The Age of Exploration

➤ *This 1663 Dutch painting shows a parrot brought from the Indies. The lady wears a jacket trimmed with fur that probably came from North America.*

▼ *How many years did it take Drake to sail around the world?*

with fish, game, and furs. Indians taught the visitors how to make cornbread and how to cure scurvy by drinking tea made from herbs. However, the harsh winters and the lack of gold and silks discouraged the French from settling in North America.

Dutch Voyages

The Dutch began exploring more than 100 years after Columbus's voyages. In 1595, the Dutch sent ships to take over Portuguese trade centers in Asia. To manage their growing trade, the Dutch started the East India Company in 1602. The company paid for expeditions to Australia and to islands in the South Pacific.

Managers of the East India Company thought that finding the Northwest Passage to Asia would give them even greater control over trade. In 1609, the company hired an English sailor named Henry Hudson to lead the first

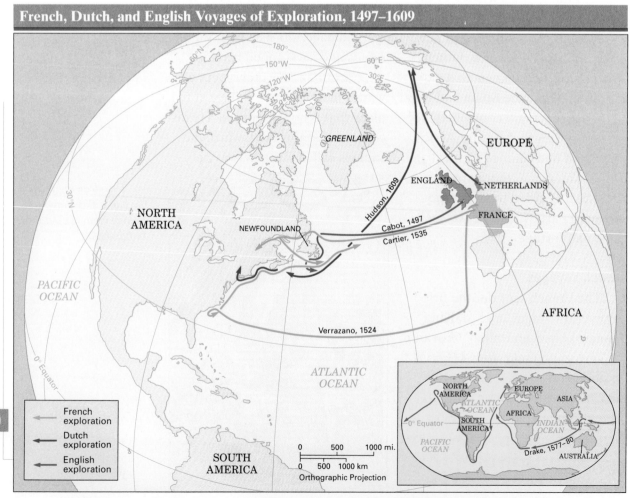

French, Dutch, and English Voyages of Exploration, 1497–1609

GREENLAND

EUROPE

ENGLAND NETHERLANDS

NORTH AMERICA

FRANCE

NEWFOUNDLAND

Hudson, 1609

Cabot, 1497

Cartier, 1535

PACIFIC OCEAN

AFRICA

Verrazano, 1524

ATLANTIC OCEAN

SOUTH AMERICA

French exploration
Dutch exploration
English exploration

0   500   1000 mi.
0   500 1000 km
Orthographic Projection

NORTH AMERICA   EUROPE
ATLANTIC OCEAN   ASIA
AFRICA
SOUTH AMERICA   INDIAN OCEAN
PACIFIC OCEAN
Drake, 1577–80   AUSTRALIA

Dutch expedition to North America. Look at the map on page 120 to see Hudson's route. Hudson explored the river, later named for him, near what is now New York City. The Indians he met were interested in fur trading.

In 1610, the Dutch set up trading posts at places that are now Albany and New York City. However, this trade did not bring the Dutch as much money as trading centers in southeast Asia, western Africa, and the South Pacific.

English Voyages

As with the Dutch, the English were slow to get started on overseas exploration. King Henry VIII had paid for one voyage in 1497. He hired John Cabot, an Italian sea captain, to sail west to Asia, discover unknown lands, and establish trade there.

On one voyage, Cabot landed on an island he called "New Found Land," or Newfoundland. There he found cod and salmon but no gold or spices.

After Cabot's voyages, most English exploration stopped. Throughout the 1500s, the English were busy with problems at home and battles with other nations. England and Spain had become enemies.

In 1577, England's Queen Elizabeth sent Francis Drake, a sailor with the English navy, on a secret voyage. Drake sailed around the tip of South America and up its western coast. Along the way, he stole from Spanish ships and trading centers and loaded his own ship with treasures.

Drake sailed north along the coast of present-day California and claimed this land for England. He returned home by crossing the Pacific. Thus, he became the first Englishman to sail around the world. Like other explorers, Drake cared more about wealth and glory than about settling a new land. ■

▲ *This drawing of corn shows one of the first foods brought to Europe from the Americas.*

■ *What areas did the French, Dutch, and English explore, and why?*

Impact on American Indians

The first contact between Europeans and Indians had great impact on both peoples. Some Europeans became rich from the gold, silver, furs, and fish they got from the Indians. The foods Europeans ate changed. Corn, potatoes, cocoa, and other foods such as those listed at the right were shipped to Europe.

However, contact with Europeans did a great deal of harm to Indian groups throughout the Americas. The explorers exposed Indians to contagious diseases. A

Items Exchanged Between Indians and Europeans	
From Europeans to Indians	**From Indians to Europeans**
Bananas	Catfish
Cattle	Chocolate
Chickens	Corn
Horses	Pineapples
Pigs	Potatoes
Sheep	Pumpkins
Sugar cane	Squash
Wheat	Sweet potatoes
	Tobacco
	Tomatoes

◄ *This chart shows items that were exchanged between the Americas and Europe.*

This Mexican drawing from the 1500s shows the deadly effects of smallpox. When Cortés invaded Mexico, about 25 million people lived in the Aztec empire. Fifty years later, only about one-tenth this number lived in Mexico.

■ How did the lives of Europeans and Indians change after explorers established contact between the two groups?

contagious disease is a sickness that spreads from one person to another. These diseases swept through Indian communities, killing many thousands.

Smallpox was the most contagious and most deadly of these diseases. By 1650, smallpox had killed three-fourths of the Indians who once lived in North and South America.

Europeans' force and violence also killed thousands of Indians. European colonists in South and Central America pushed Indians off their lands and forced them to work long hours on farms and in mines. Many died of exhaustion.

For those Indians who survived disease and forced labor, life changed greatly. Many explorers believed everyone should be Christian. They even used force to make Indians become Christians.

Some Indian groups tried to fight the Europeans, but few succeeded. Spears and arrows were weak against European guns. Also, Indians had never seen horses before. At first, horses terrified Indians and allowed Europeans to escape attack.

As more Europeans sailed to America, contact between Europeans and Indians steadily increased. Indians were especially interested in trading for weapons, tools, and cooking utensils. They also began to breed horses, sheep, cows, pigs, and chickens, and to grow wheat and rice. Many of these items improved the lives of Indians, and relations between Indians and Europeans were often friendly.

However, in the 1600s, more and more Europeans settled in America. Fights and trouble grew as the Europeans claimed lands that had belonged to the Indians for thousands of years. ■

REVIEW

1. **FOCUS** Why did the French, Dutch, and English decide to begin exploring the Western Hemisphere?

2. **CONNECT** What did the first French, Dutch, and English explorers learn from the Spanish and Portuguese explorers?

3. **HISTORY** How did the introduction of contagious diseases carried by European explorers and settlers affect American Indians?

4. **CRITICAL THINKING** Compare the results of French,

Dutch, and English exploration with those of the Spanish and Portuguese.

5. **WRITING ACTIVITY** Imagine you are an Iroquois living in Canada in the 1500s. Three ships carrying European explorers arrive on the shore of your community. Write a description of the people, their ships, and the things they brought with them. Also describe your reaction to these new sights.

Tracing Routes

Here's Why

If you understand how a map shows directions, you can use a map to see and describe a route from one place to another. For example, you can describe the route of Ferdinand Magellan's crew as they sailed all the way around the earth. The map on this page shows the route they followed.

Here's How

Look for the direction arrow at the bottom center of the map. The arrow shows which direction is north, which is south, which is east, and which is west. North, south, east, and west are cardinal, or main, directions. Between cardinal directions are intermediate directions. For example, the direction between north and east is northeast. You can use intermediate directions to describe Magellan's route.

From Spain, Magellan sailed southwest across the Atlantic Ocean and along the coast of South America to its tip. Then he sailed into the Strait of Magellan.

Try It

Use cardinal and intermediate directions to finish describing Magellan's voyage. Leaving the Strait of Magellan, he sailed ___?___ across the Pacific. From the Philippines, he sailed ___?___ to Timor. His crew continued ___?___ to the Cape of Good Hope and from there ___?___ to Spain.

Apply It

Refer to the world map on pages 566 and 567, and trace an outline of continents. Then locate Miami, Florida, on the U.S. map on pages 572 and 573. Mark Miami on your outline. Draw a line to show a route from Miami to New Zealand. Then use cardinal and intermediate directions to describe the route.

Magellan's Route Around the Earth

The Age of Exploration

Chapter Review

Reviewing Key Terms

colony (p. 111)
contagious disease (p. 122)
expedition (p. 110)
navigate (p. 107)
Northwest Passage (p. 119)
technology (p. 105)

A. Imagine you are keeping a log, or journal, on a sea voyage. Five log entries that refer to key terms are started below. Add one sentence to each entry, using the key term. Be sure your sentences show you understand the meaning of the terms.

1. We heard about a possible water route to China through North America.
2. Tools that were recently invented are helping us reach these new lands.
3. Every day more sailors are becoming sick, suffering from the same terrible illness.
4. In planning our course, we knew we might face dangerous waters.
5. Our journey was organized and paid for by a wealthy prince.
6. Soon we'll form a settlement that will be governed by our native country.

B. Write a sentence for each pair of key terms. Write each sentence as if it were the beginning of a newspaper article.

1. Northwest Passage, navigate
2. technology, expedition
3. contagious disease, colony

Exploring Concepts

A. You can show important achievements of European explorers on a chart. Copy and complete the following chart on your own paper. The first row has been done for you. Use information in the chapter to help you fill in the rest of the chart.

    If you wish to expand the chart, look at page 553 of the Minipedia. You will find information about famous explorers of North America as well as modern-day space explorers.

Country	Explorer's Name	Area Explored
Italy (Venice)	Marco Polo	India, China, Japan
Portugal		
Spain		
France		
Holland (Dutch)		
England		

B. Support the following statements with facts and details from the chapter.

1. Lack of knowledge and fear affected the way Europeans thought about the world.
2. One reason that Europeans went out to explore the world was similar to the reason for the Crusades.
3. Important improvements for ships were developed by Arab sailors and Portuguese shipbuilders.
4. Unless Prince Henry found a water route to Asia, Portuguese traders could not get to the riches of India, China, and Japan.
5. Columbus called the people he met Indians because he had a wrong idea.
6. The arrival of the Europeans was a tragedy for American Indians.
7. Francis Drake was one of the people who proved the European belief that the earth was a sphere.

Reviewing Skills

1. Look at the map of Verrazano's voyage. Use cardinal and intermediate directions to answer the following questions:
   a. In what direction did Verrazano sail from France to the Madeira Islands?
   b. What direction was he going as he sailed from the Madeira Islands to North America?
   c. What direction did he go along the coast of North America to Newfoundland?
2. Find the latitude and longitude of the Madeira Islands on the map.
3. Suppose you want to tell about European exploration. What visual device would best help you to show European voyages of exploration in chronological order?

Verrazano's Voyage of Exploration, 1524

Using Critical Thinking

1. Today, many Native Americans object to reading or hearing that Christopher Columbus "discovered" America. Native Americans do not agree with the European explorers who called America a "new world." Why do you think Native Americans feel this way? Do you agree or disagree with their objection? Explain your answer.

2. Describe European ideas of the world before the explorers began their voyages. Compare those ideas with the ideas of later Europeans after the voyages of exploration. Then predict how people's ideas about the earth, the solar system, and the universe may change as the exploration of space continues. Think about finding new planets and perhaps other forms of life.

Preparing for Citizenship

1. ARTS ACTIVITY Create a mural about Aztec life. The first scenes can show what life was like before the Spanish conquered the Aztec empire. The next group of scenes can show the battle between the Aztecs and Cortés's army. The last part can show what their capital city looked like after the battle. Invite other classes to see the mural.

2. GROUP ACTIVITY Work with a few classmates to create food items from American Indian cultures or from one of these countries: Spain, Italy, France, Holland, or England.

Check the library for recipes in cookbooks or magazines.

3. COLLABORATIVE LEARNING Prepare a television documentary called "You Were There." Imagine that a few reporters meet one of Columbus's ships after its return voyage. The crew members answer the reporters' questions about the "new world." Join a group to work on researching the script; writing the dialogue; and acting out the roles of Columbus, the reporters, and crew members.

Chapter 6
Settling a New World

By 1585, the race to settle the New World had begun. In the South the Spanish had grown wealthy from gold and silver. In the North the French had become rich trading with Indians for furs. In between, the English tried to start their own colonies. Though the English were slow to settle the New World, their colonies became the most powerful in America.

1585 Sir Walter Raleigh (above) sends a group of English colonists to settle Roanoke Island in what is now North Carolina. The colony fails within five years.

1575

1600

1625

1585

1619 The Spanish build the mission of San Gerónimo in present-day New Mexico (above). The Spanish have come to America to find gold and silver and to convert Indians to Christianity.

Throughout this time, forts
protected European colonists
from American Indians and other
settlers. The fort shown above
was built by the English on St.
John's Island, Virginia, in 1585.

1650

1675

1700

1664 The Dutch surrender
their colony of New
Netherlands to the British,
who rename it New York.

1682 French explorer Sieur de
la Salle reaches the mouth of
the Mississippi River. He
claims the surrounding land for
France and calls it Louisiana.

1682

L E S S O N   1

Spanish and French Colonization

THINKING
F O C U S

Why did the Spanish and the French establish colonies in North America?

Key Terms

- colonization
- encomienda
- mission
- tax
- fort

Ten-year-old Cristobal de Oñate *(aw NYAH teh)* drooped under the weight of his leather armor. He glanced up at his father—Juan de Oñate, governor of a new colony and captain-general in the army of Philip II, King of Spain. How proudly his father sat in his velvet saddle!

Immediately, Cristobal straightened. Hadn't his father appointed him lieutenant governor? A high Spanish official must be strong to inspire the colonists.

Cristobal turned to look at the hundreds of men, women, and children journeying north along the Rio Grande. He saw the determination in their faces. For months they had pushed forward across the Mexican highlands and through the desert. It had been a difficult trip! Eighty-three creaking wagons carried the colonists' household goods. Some 7,000 farm animals—cattle, horses, hogs, oxen, mules, goats, and sheep— had plodded along beside them.

When the caravan reached the shady, green banks of the Rio Grande, the colonists' spirits had soared. Already they were imagining the silver from mines that Cristobal's father said they would find in the new colony. Cristobal knew the 11 priests traveling among them were counting the Indian souls they would save.

> ➤ *Spanish soldiers wore vests made of seven layers of leather. The vest protected the soldiers from Indian arrows.*

128

Chapter 6

On April 30, 1598, Juan de Oñate commanded the expedition to halt near the site of the future town of El Paso. A priest raised his cross high above the river, and Oñate formally claimed the land for Spain. Henceforth, the land north of the Rio Grande would be called New Mexico. Spain would rule this land and all its native Indians with the "power of life and death, over high and low, from the leaves of the trees to the stones and sands of the river. . . ."

Spanish Settlers in New Mexico

When he claimed New Mexico for Spain, Oñate was helping Spain colonize part of North America. In **colonization,** a country sends settlers to a distant land and rules the settlements from afar.

To govern its new territory, Spain placed wealthy Spanish settlers in charge of **encomiendas** *(ehn koh mee EHN dahs),* huge estates that often included several Indian villages. The landowners forced Indians to work on their estates while they searched for mines.

Oñate never found mines in New Mexico. He did find dozens of Indian villages that the Spanish called pueblos. The people who lived in the pueblos belonged to Indian tribes, such as the Zuni and the Hopi. They lived in flat-roofed houses made of stone and plastered with dried mud.

Before Oñate arrived in 1598, the Indians lived in peace. They worked hard tending crops of corn, beans, and squash in the dry desert climate. They also grew cotton and wove it into cloth for shirts and dresses. Much of the Indians' social life centered around religion. They worshiped spirits in nature that they believed sent rain and good harvests.

But along with the settlers, Oñate also brought priests to

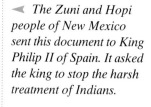

◄ *The Zuni and Hopi people of New Mexico sent this document to King Philip II of Spain. It asked the king to stop the harsh treatment of Indians.*

129

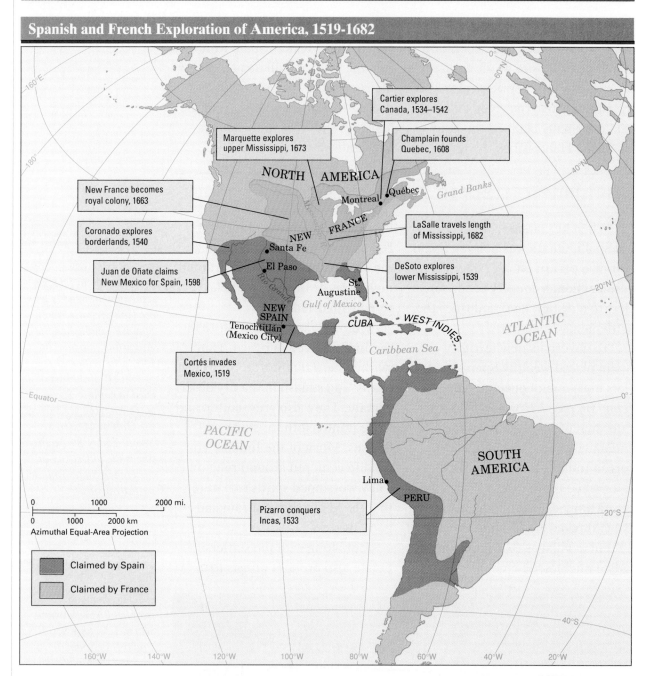

Cartier explores
Canada, 1534–1542

Marquette explores
upper Mississippi, 1673

Champlain founds
Quebec, 1608

NORTH   AMERICA

New France becomes
royal colony, 1663

Québec

Montreal

Grand Banks

FRANCE

NEW

LaSalle travels length
of Mississippi, 1682

Coronado explores
borderlands, 1540

Santa Fe

El Paso

DeSoto explores
lower Mississippi, 1539

Juan de Oñate claims
New Mexico for Spain, 1598

Rio Grande

St.
Augustine

Gulf of Mexico

WEST INDIES

ATLANTIC
OCEAN

NEW
SPAIN

Tenochtitlán
(Mexico City)

CUBA

Caribbean Sea

Cortés invades
Mexico, 1519

Equator

PACIFIC
OCEAN

SOUTH
AMERICA

0   1000   2000 mi.

0   1000   2000 km

Azimuthal Equal-Area Projection

Lima

PERU

Pizarro conquers
Incas, 1533

Claimed by Spain

Claimed by France

▲ *Trace Oñate's route north along the Rio Grande to El Paso. Notice that Oñate's claim spread Spanish control into what is now the southwestern United States.*

■ *How did the Spanish in New Mexico meet their needs for food and housing?*

130

New Mexico. The priests set up **missions,** churches and schools to teach the Indians about the Roman Catholic faith. However, many Indians secretly continued to worship their own gods.

The Indians put up buildings and tended orchards for the priests. They also grew crops and herded cattle for Spanish landowners. Spanish soldiers made sure the Indians did their work.

The Indians even paid taxes to the government in Sante Fe, New Mexico's capital. A **tax** is money or property that a person must pay to the government. The money was used to pay the salaries of soldiers and government officials. The Indians paid their taxes in the form of cotton shirts and wool blankets. Many Spanish officials grew rich by selling these goods in Mexico. ■

French Traders in Canada

While the Spanish were colonizing the southern part of North America, the French were exploring the northern part. Like the Spanish, the French hoped to find precious metals. Instead they found other riches—fish and fur.

Fishing and Fur Trading

During John Cabot's 1497 voyage to North America, he explored the shallow waters off what is now Newfoundland. He reported that "the sea there is swarming with fish." By the early 1500s, fishing fleets from all over Europe were harvesting these rich fishing grounds, which mapmakers named the Grand Banks.

Many French fleets fished in the Grand Banks and along Canada's east coast. Often the fishermen came ashore. Indians offered to trade beaver furs for the Frenchmen's axes, knives, and other metal goods. In France, the fishermen sold the furs for as much as 200 times the cost of the axes and knives. By 1600, fur trading was France's chief interest in North America. The Indians benefited from these exchanges as well, because they got useful metal goods.

Champlain and Quebec

Other Europeans besides the French wanted a share of the fur trade. Traders gave guns and alcohol to the Indians. They hoped these gifts would win the Indians' friendship—and trade. The French decided they needed a **fort,** or military post, in North America to protect their interests. Explorer and geographer Samuel de Champlain founded Quebec in 1608 at a narrow point on the St. Lawrence River. At Quebec, the French could easily stop rival traders from bringing their furs down the river.

Champlain thought of Quebec as more than a fort and a trading post. He asked the French government to send farmers and families. About 100 French soldiers, workers, wives, and children arrived in Quebec in 1633 to start to build a settlement. By the 1660s, about 2,500 people lived in Quebec. ■

▲ *This hat of wool and beaver fur was made in Europe in the early 1600s. Hats like this were so valuable they were often kept in one family for generations.*

▲ *Traders used tokens in their trading practices with Indians.*

■ *How did trade with the Indians lead to French settlements in North America?*

R E V I E W

1. **FOCUS** Why did the Spanish and the French establish colonies in North America?
2. **CONNECT** How did Oñate's conquest of the Hopi and Zuni people in New Mexico differ from Cortés's conquest of the Aztec of Mexico?
3. **GEOGRAPHY** How did geography affect Samuel de Champlain's choice of a settlement?
4. **CRITICAL THINKING** Why were the Indians in Canada willing to trade beaver furs for axes and knives?
5. **ACTIVITY** Spanish settlers in the Southwest and in Florida gave Spanish names to many towns and other geographical features, such as bodies of water. They also influenced the food, language, and building styles of these regions. Study a map of these areas and list the Spanish place names you find. Also list other examples of Spanish influence.

L E S S O N   2

English Settlement in the South

What were early contacts like between Indians and English colonists?

Key Terms

- investor
- profit

➤ *In the lower right corner of White's painting is an Algonquin prayer ceremony. Dancers move in a circle around wooden stakes carved at the top with men's faces. Their bodies are decorated with designs painted in bright colors.*

John White landed on sandy Roanoke Island off the coast of present-day North Carolina in 1585. He and 107 other colonists built cottages, planted corn, and traded with the Indians. When White went back to England for supplies in 1587, he took with him dozens of drawings and paintings he had made while exploring the region. They showed daily life in the small villages of the Algonquin *(al GAHNG kwihn)* people.

White's paintings, like the one on this page, show that the Algonquin lived in long houses. The curving roofs of the houses were held up by a frame of bendable young trees. This frame was covered with bark or mats of cattail stalks. The mats could be rolled up for light and air. The floors of the houses were hard-packed dirt, with raised platforms for resting and sleeping.

In the upper right corner of White's painting is a field of ripe corn. It is guarded by a watchman in a small hut. The watchman was a human scarecrow. His cries kept birds and other animals from eating the corn.

Origins of English Settlement

The Algonquin people had lived in peace for many years along the Atlantic coast. English explorers like John White who came to America in the 1580s hoped to use the Indians to make money. English merchants wanted to trade wool cloth and other things made in English factories for Indian products. They knew they could sell corn, furs, tobacco, and beaded necklaces for a high price in England. The English also knew that Indian slaves in Mexico had mined gold and silver for Spain. As a result, Spain had become very wealthy. The English hoped their colonies would make them rich as well.

Plans for Colonies

An English geographer named Richard Hakluyt was excited about the idea of English colonies in America. He was convinced that England could not allow Catholic Spain and France to control North America. In the 1580s, he wrote several small books that described America's riches and beauty. The books asked Protestant English settlers to move there. In America, Hakluyt wrote, "the earth bringeth fourth all things in abundance, as in the first creation, without toil or labour."

The English colonists did not want to claim land for farming, as Spanish colonists had done. Instead, the English planned at first to make their money through trade. They hoped to set up trading posts at the heads of rivers.

Indians would bring furs, corn, and tobacco to these posts to trade for European products. Only friendly Indians would be good trading partners. Therefore, Hakluyt wrote that the Indians were peaceful people who were willing to trade fairly.

Failures at Roanoke

In 1585, Hakluyt's friend Walter Raleigh arranged to send a group of English settlers to

English settlers came to North America for different reasons. The settlers who founded Jamestown wanted to make money through trade. The settlers who started Plymouth came to find religious freedom. The English took over Dutch New Amsterdam to get its fine harbor.

English Colonies, 1607–1690

New England colonies

Middle colonies

Southern colonies

America. Raleigh was a rich member of the court of England's Queen Elizabeth I. He paid for the settlers' ship and supplies. However, the colony they started on Roanoke Island was not a success. The island was off the shore of what is now the state of North Carolina. The colonists who came to Roanoke in 1585, like John White, returned to England.

A second group of 100 colonists came to Roanoke in 1587. They expected to live on English supplies. But a war between England and Spain prevented supply ships from reaching the settlers for three years. When John White arrived in 1590, he found only traces of the settlers. They had all mysteriously disappeared. Perhaps the colonists went to live with the Chesapeake Indians. If so, they were probably killed when Powhatan, a powerful chief, attacked the Chesapeake Indians in 1607. ■

▲ *This gold coin dates from the reign of Queen Elizabeth I (1558-1603) and carries her portrait.*

➤ *John White drew this map of Virginia in 1585. It shows the location of Roanoke Island and several Indian villages.*

■ *Why did the English want to start colonies on the coast of North America?*

▼ *This English soldier's helmet was dug up near the site of the Jamestown settlement.*

The English Arrive in Virginia

The Roanoke settlers were not able to start an English colony. But the rich land of North America soon made other colonists willing to try. In April 1607, about 104 English colonists landed near Chesapeake Bay, Virginia. They named their new settlement Jamestown, after King James I of England.

The Jamestown colony was paid for by 100 rich **investors**—people who put up money for a business. These investors formed the Virginia Company. Its purpose was to start an English settlement that would earn a **profit,** money made by a business after all expenses have been met.

At first the colonists were hopeful and excited. But by January 1608, only 38 of the 104 settlers who started Jamestown were still alive. You will read more about what happened to the colonists in Chapter 7. However, one important reason the colony failed was that the English hoped to repeat the success of the Spanish. The settlers did not want to work planting crops. Instead, they searched for gold and silver. But they found neither. The Algonquin had no gold and silver treasures for the English to take. Since the English had only a few soldiers, they could not even force the Indians to work for them as the Spanish had done. The Jamestown colonists had planned to trade with the Indians. But in the early years they could only beg, borrow, or steal food from the Indians to try to stay alive. ■

◄ *This deerskin cloak decorated with shells was brought to England from Jamestown in the 1600s. It is believed to have belonged to the powerful chief Powhatan.*

■ *In what ways was Jamestown different from Spanish colonies in the Americas?*

Maryland and the Caribbean

Another new English colony was more successful than Jamestown. In 1632, George Calvert, later called Lord Baltimore, was given land by King Charles I of England. Calvert planned to start a colony north of Chesapeake Bay. The first group of colonists arrived on the Potomac River in 1634. Many of the settlers were Catholics, as was Calvert. They wanted to leave England because Protestants there often treated Catholics cruelly. Unlike the Jamestown colonists, the first thing the Maryland settlers did was to plant gardens to grow food.

Other English colonists tried to take over islands in the Caribbean Sea. Their first efforts, on the islands of St. Lucia and Grenada, failed. Indians who lived on these islands forced the English to leave. However, in 1627, the English started a colony on Barbados, where no Indians were living. They set up plantations for growing tobacco and sugar cane. ■

■ *How were the early years at the Maryland colony different from the early years at Jamestown?*

1. **FOCUS** What were early contacts like between Indians and English colonists?
2. **CONNECT** How did English plans for making money in America differ from the methods used by the Spanish? Which colonists made the most money? Give reasons for your answer.
3. **HISTORY** In what ways were the reasons the Jamestown colonists came to America different from the reasons the settlers in Maryland came?
4. **CRITICAL THINKING** By 1600, people in England had heard stories about the cruelty of the Spanish colonists toward the Indians in Mexico. What effect do you think these stories had on English colonists thinking of settling in America?
5. **ACTIVITY** Make up the kind of advertisement that Hakluyt might have written to make people want to colonize Virginia. Add pictures that might have caught the eye and held the interest of settlers.

Settling a New World

Combining Information

Here's Why

When you do research about a topic, you often find that two books or articles include different information about the same subject. When this happens, you need to know how to summarize and combine the information from those sources.

Look at the painting on the next page. It gives you a picture of the life of Hopi Indians before the Europeans arrived. You get a clearer idea from this painting than you would from looking at a portrait of one Hopi. Just as the painter combined images into one painting, you can combine the main ideas from several written sources into one document. This gives you a more complete idea about what the life of Indians was like than you would get from reading only one source.

Suppose you wanted to learn about the lifestyle of the Hopi before they had contact with the Spanish. This chapter gives you some information. But you may wish to learn more about the Hopi from other sources. Then you will need to combine the information from your sources.

Here's How

The paragraphs on the left and right sides of this page summarize information from two different sources.

Read the paragraph on the left. It summarizes a section from a book about North American Indians. It tells about the peaceful ways of life and the farming methods of the Hopi.

Now read the paragraph on the right. It summarizes a section from a different book about North American Indians. This summary contains information about the Hopi agriculture, art, and mining.

Finally, read the paragraph in the tinted box. It summarizes and combines the information from the two sources.

To summarize information, write sentences in your own words that briefly state

Hopi means "peaceful ones." The Hopi could, and did, fight fiercely to defend their homes and freedom, but they did not begin war against others. Instead, they focused their energy on farming. They developed methods of irrigation to water their crops. They were able to grow corn, squash, beans, and cotton in the desert.

The Hopi achieved a high level of cultural development before contact with Europeans. They were especially skillful in the areas of agriculture, mining, and art. Their methods of farming allowed them to grow corn, beans, and squash in the desert. They mined and used coal for cooking their food, for preparing pigments for their art, and for firing their pottery. Their name meant "peaceful ones," and although they would fight to protect their homes, they did not start wars.

In the 300 years before Europeans came to North America, the Hopi developed skills: agriculture, mural and pottery painting, and coal mining. They grew plants with deep roots in the dry soil. They mined and used coal for cooking, heating, and firing pottery. They used earth and plant colors to paint pottery and colorful murals.

the main ideas. After writing summaries of all your sources, combine the information into one statement. Use the following steps:

1. List the main ideas from the paragraph on the left:
   a. The Hopi were willing and able to defend themselves.
   b. The Hopi did not start wars.
   c. The Hopi irrigated the desert and grew crops of corn, squash, beans, and cotton there.
2. List the main ideas from the paragraph on the right:
   a. Before the Europeans came to North America, the Hopi had developed their own advanced culture.
   b. They grew plants in the desert.
   c. They mined and used coal.
   d. They made pottery and painted with pigments.
3. Combine the main ideas of both sources. The new paragraph, in the tinted box, tells more about Hopi life than either of the summary paragraphs.

Try It

Zuni and Hopi houses were different from those of the Algonquin. For your

source on the Algonquin, reread the paragraph on page 132 that tells about the Algonquin long houses. Write the main ideas of the paragraph.

For your source on Hopi and Zuni dwellings, read the description in the paragraph at the top of the second column on page 129. Write the main ideas from this source.

Combine the information from your two summaries. Create a new paragraph that compares the Algonquin dwellings with the Hopi and Zuni dwellings.

Apply It

Look at the pages on North American Indians in the Minipedia on pages 558-560. Write a summary of the information you find there about the Plains Indians.

Then look up information about the Plains Indians in an encyclopedia or book of your choice and briefly summarize the additional information you find. Finally, write a paragraph or two combining information from your two summaries.

137

LESSON 3

English Settlement in New England

*O*ur harvest being gotten in, our Governor sent four men on fowling [hunting for ducks, geese, and turkeys] that we might after a more special manner rejoice together, after we had gathered the fruit of our labours. They four in one day killed as much fowl as, with a little help beside, served the Company almost a week. At which time, amongst other recreations, we exercised our arms [shot off guns], many of the Indians coming amongst us, and amongst the rest their greatest king, Massasoit with some 90 men, whom for three days we entertained and feasted.

THINKING FOCUS

Why did Puritan settlers start colonies in New England?

Key Terms

- Puritan
- Separatist
- Pilgrim

These words are from a letter written by Edward Winslow in the fall of 1621. Winslow and 50 other

English colonists were celebrating a bountiful harvest—their first at the new Plymouth Colony.

Why the Pilgrims Came

Today we remember the harvest feast celebrated by the Plymouth colonists as the first

Thanksgiving. In fact, one reason the settlers came to Plymouth was to start a colony where they could

Events Leading to the Settlement of the Northern Colonies

1547–1553, Protestantism becomes official religion of England under King Edward VI.

1558, Elizabeth I becomes Queen of England. Protestants return to England and become known as Puritans.

1500   1525   1550   1575

1517, Protestant Reformation begins.

1534, King Henry VIII establishes the Anglican Church.

1553–1558, Queen Mary I restores Catholicism and exiles Protestants to Switzerland.

both keep English customs like the harvest feast and practice their kind of Christianity.

To understand why the colonists came to Plymouth, you need to know something about English church history. In 1534, King Henry VIII broke away from the Roman Catholic Church and started the Church of England. However, religious services in the new church didn't change a great deal. They were still very much like Catholic services.

Some English people wanted to purify the Church of England. They wanted to get rid of all reminders of Catholic services, such as the rich clothing worn by priests. They said that Bible study and sermons were more important than beautiful ceremonies. Because they wanted to purify the church, these people were known as **Puritans.**

Some Puritans formed separate churches, and so were known as **Separatists.** English law said that everyone in the country must belong to the Church of England. Because they were afraid of being put in prison, three Separatist groups left England for the Netherlands.

One Separatist group moved to Leyden in 1609. William Bradford,

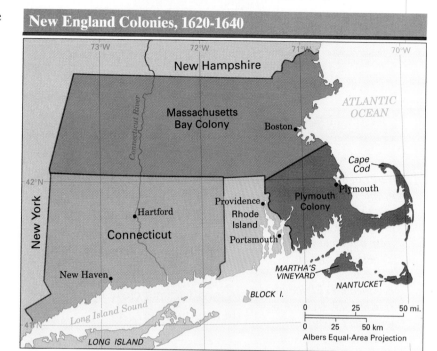

New England Colonies, 1620-1640

a leader of the group, wrote that his followers "knew they were pilgrims"—people on a holy journey. Thus, this group of Separatists became known as **Pilgrims.** Because they could not speak Dutch, the Pilgrims never felt at home in the Netherlands.

In 1619, the Virginia Company gave the Pilgrims permission to settle in Virginia. A group of London merchants, hoping to earn money from the new colony, agreed to pay expenses. When the *Mayflower* left England in September 1620, it carried 35 Pilgrims and 67 hired workers. ■

▲ *Study this map of the New England Colonies. What present-day state includes both Plymouth Colony and Massachusetts Bay Colony?*

■ *Why did the Pilgrims leave England and, later, the Netherlands?*

▼ *Events in English church history led the Pilgrims to settle in Massachusetts.*

1617, Puritans, sometimes called Pilgrims, decide to sail to North America.

1629, Charles I dissolves Parliament. Puritans form Massachusetts Bay Company.

1630–1642, Over 16,000 Puritans move to New England.

| 1600 | 1625 | 1650 |

1608–1609, Puritans move to Holland.

1620, Pilgrims sign Mayflower Compact and settle at Plymouth.

The Pilgrim Experience

The Pilgrims never reached Virginia. Strong ocean storms drove the *Mayflower* off course. On November 11, after 11 weeks at sea, the ship dropped anchor off the tip of Cape Cod. This curved peninsula is on the Atlantic coast of what is now Massachusetts. Though the Pilgrims knew they were hundreds of miles north of Virginia, they were too tired and sick to travel farther. They decided to look for land close by to start their settlement.

Mayflower Compact

Not every passenger on the *Mayflower* was happy with the Pilgrims' decision. Some of the hired workers said that they had only agreed to settle in Virginia. To end this argument, the Pilgrims wrote an agreement called the Mayflower Compact. It said that for the general good of the colony, everyone would go along with its leaders' decisions.

Plymouth Plantation

Next, the Pilgrims sent a group of men to look for a place to settle. The men explored a small bay on the western edge of Cape Cod. Captain John Smith of Jamestown had discovered this bay in 1614. Smith had named the bay "Plymouth" and the whole region "New England." The men found a swift-running stream with clear, fresh drinking water. The area seemed ideal for a settlement. On December 26, the Pilgrims anchored the *Mayflower* in the bay and began building Plymouth Plantation.

The Pilgrims had to make everything they needed for their colony. Read A Closer Look to discover how they made furniture.

➤ *The Pilgrims lived aboard the* Mayflower *until they built houses. These reconstructed buildings in Plymouth, Massachusetts, show the settlement as it looked in 1627.*

Pilgrim Woodworking

The Pilgrims weren't able to bring much furniture with them on their tiny ship. Would they have to sit on the floors of their new homes? No, they wouldn't—they did bring their furniture-making tools.

How precious tools like this hammer must have been to the Pilgrims! They also brought axes, chisels, and hatchets to the timber-rich land.

The Pilgrims stored Bibles in hand-carved boxes like these. The carving on the lid of this box used to show the lion and unicorn symbol of England. Later, when America was at war with England, someone scraped off the lion.

With only a saw to help you turn trees into furniture, you'd want the blade to last. A good cover like the one here kept the saw blade from rusting.

Poles made of sturdy Massachusetts ash

Woven rush seat, added later

A small man, colonist Myles Standish sawed the legs off this chair. He probably cut the chair down so his feet could reach the floor.

Wood pieces joined without nails

By Charles Hoftbauer "Samoset Bids Pilgrims Welcome" collection: New England Mutual Life Insurance Co.

➤ Samoset Bids Pilgrims Welcome, *a painting by Charles Hoftbauer, shows the first Indian to visit the Pilgrims. Samoset had learned to speak English from fishermen who visited the New England coast from time to time.*

■ *What were the advantages and disadvantages of the Pilgrims' choice of Plymouth as a place to settle?*

The Pilgrims had a difficult time surviving the first winter. The weather was freezing, and food supplies were low. Half the colonists died of sickness.

When spring came, many Indians visited the Pilgrims. The most important was Massasoit, chief of the Wampanoag (*wahm puh NOH ag*). Massasoit allowed an Indian named Squanto to live at Plymouth. Squanto taught the Pilgrims the best places to hunt and fish. He also taught them how to plant corn by putting a fish in each hill of seeds as fertilizer. ■

The Founding of Massachusetts Bay

▲ *An Indian is pictured on the official seal of the Massachusetts colony.*

■ *Why did many Puritans move to Massachusetts in 1630?*

While the Pilgrims were building their settlement at Plymouth, events in England made many other Puritans think about moving to North America.

Charles I became king in 1625. He kept up the pressure and threatened to put all Puritans in prison. Moreover, England was going through economic hard times. A large number of Puritan farmers and shopkeepers were losing money. Many Puritans liked the idea of starting a colony in North America. There they could build their own churches and, at the same time, run businesses that would earn a profit.

In 1628, the Massachusetts Bay Company got from King Charles I the right to settle north of Plymouth. The company elected John Winthrop, a Puritan landowner, governor of the Massachusetts Bay Colony. In 1630, Winthrop's ship the *Arbella* led a fleet of 17 ships to New England. The ships carried nearly 1,000 men, women, and children. The Puritans built settlements at Boston and Cambridge. ■

R E V I E W

1. **FOCUS** Why did Puritan settlers start colonies in New England?
2. **CONNECT** How did the Puritans' reasons for colonization differ from those of the Virginia colonists?
3. **HISTORY** In what ways did the Pilgrims and the Wampanoag help each other? How did each group benefit from their contact?
4. **CRITICAL THINKING** The Pilgrims at Plymouth Colony

and at Massachusetts Bay Colony came to America with strong religious beliefs. How do you think these beliefs affected the settlers' ability to survive the hardships of life in a new colony?

5. **ACTIVITY** Imagine that you are a young Wampanoag coming to the Pilgrims' harvest feast. You have never seen European people before. What questions would you would want to ask the Pilgrims?

English Settlement in the Middle Colonies

*I*n 1653, war broke out between England and Holland. At once, [Dutch Governor Peter] Stuyvesant began construction of a wall at the north end of town, from the East River to the Hudson River, to keep out the enemy. It was a wall made of wood, twelve feet high, with a sloping platform inside. Soldiers could climb on the platform and look over the wall for approaching enemies. The soldiers on guard made a path along the wall and this became known as "Wall Street."

Robert Quakenbush, *Old Silver Leg Takes Over*

THINKING FOCUS

How did English settlers come to live in New York, New Jersey, and Pennsylvania?

Key Terms

- Quaker
- pacifism

Wall Street is one reminder that the old Dutch town of New Amsterdam once occupied the southwestern tip of Manhattan Island. Today, Manhattan Island is the busiest part of New York City.

Bustling Wall Street is now a canyon of skyscrapers. The New York Stock Exchange and many other financial businesses line the street. Only its name recalls Wall Street's Dutch past.

◄ *Colonists from the Netherlands, Germany, France, Denmark, Portugal, and Spain lived in New Amsterdam. A French priest visiting the town in 1643 said he heard 18 different languages spoken as he walked down the street.*

143

The Colony of New Netherland

New Amsterdam was the capital of the Dutch colony of New Netherland. The colony was started by Dutch merchants. Since the late 1500s, the Dutch had been among the most successful sailors and traders in the world.

Dutch merchants were always looking for more business. They knew that English and French sailors shipped valuable cargoes of fish and furs to Europe. To get part of this trade, the Dutch needed an American colony.

The Dutch Found New Amsterdam

In 1624, a group of Dutch merchants formed the Dutch West India Company. The company sent about 30 families to settle near the Hudson River in what is now New York State. Because the Netherlands was a small country, the company advertised for settlers all over Europe.

By 1650, New Amsterdam was an important business center.

Merchants had a profitable trade with the Iroquois, exchanging knives and guns for furs. The city hummed with successful businesses like shipbuilding. Farmers settled on rich lands that are now part of New Jersey, Delaware, and Connecticut. There they raised cattle and corn for trade.

The English Take Over

King Charles II of England noticed the success of New Amsterdam. Charles was eager to take the fine harbor at New Amsterdam away from the Dutch. He wanted English merchants to control its rich trade in beef, pork, wheat, tobacco, fish, and furs. Moreover, the geography of New Netherland interested the king. If England could make the Dutch leave, it could unite its American colonies. New England in the north would be connected to Virginia and Maryland in the south.

In 1664, King Charles directed his brother, the duke of York, to send English warships to New Amsterdam. When the people of the city saw the ships' cannons aimed at their homes, they begged Peter Stuyvesant, the governor, to surrender. The Dutch had only 350 soldiers in one fort to defend New Amsterdam. Stuyvesant had no choice but to give up without a fight.

The new English governor, Richard Nicolls, quickly changed the name of New Amsterdam. He called the settlement New York in honor of the duke of York. ■

■ *Why did England take control of the Dutch colony of New Netherland?*

▼ *The Dutch colony of New Netherland was sandwiched between New England to the east and Pennsylvania and New Jersey to the south and west.*

Middle Colonies, 1650–1690

L. Huron

L. Ontario

L. Erie

Hudson R.

Connecticut R.

New Netherland (New York)

New Amsterdam (New York)

Pennsylvania

New Jersey

Philadelphia

Susquehanna R.

Ohio R.

Potomac R.

Delaware

ATLANTIC OCEAN

0   100   200 mi.

0   100   200 km

Lambert Conformal Conic Projection

The Founding of Pennsylvania

After the English took control of New Netherland, a few English farmers moved to the hills and valleys of what is now Pennsylvania. But this region was still mostly empty of white settlers when an Englishman named William Penn founded a colony there. Penn started this colony to make a home for another religious group that was persecuted in England.

The Quakers

The **Quakers,** or the Religious Society of Friends, were founded in 1647 by an Englishman named George Fox. Fox taught that all people were equal in God's sight and therefore should be treated with equal love and respect. Fox also believed that each person has a little bit of God inside. For this reason, he said, people do not need priests or services to get in touch with God. Quakers also thought that war was wrong. Because of this belief, called **pacifism,** Quakers would not join the army or pay taxes to support it.

Like the Puritans, the Quakers were often fined, jailed, and even killed by the English government. Between 1661 and 1680, about 15,000 of the 60,000 Quakers in England had been sent to jail for their beliefs. Once, George Fox himself was on trial. He told the judge "to tremble at the word of the Lord." Since Fox had mentioned trembling, the judge called him a "Quaker." Soon all of Fox's followers were being called Quakers. The Quakers' simple beliefs attracted many English people. One of the best-known Quakers was a rich young man named William Penn.

Quaker women often wore bonnets like the one above. They also wore hats like those the women in the painting are wearing.

◄ A Quaker Meeting *was painted in 1640 by Egbert van Heemskerk. At religious services like this, anyone who wanted to could speak to the congregation.*

Settling a New World

William Penn

William Penn was born in London in 1644. His father was an admiral in the English navy. Like many young Englishmen from important families, Penn went to Oxford University. But Penn had to leave Oxford because he would not go to Church of England services. Instead, he held private prayer meetings with some of his friends. When Penn was in his early twenties, he started going to Quaker meetings. He also spoke in public about Quaker beliefs. He was put in jail many times for these actions.

Penn saw that there was "no hope in England" for people who did not belong to the Church of England to lead a peaceful life. King Charles II owed a large sum of money to Penn's father. Penn asked the king to repay the debt by

➤ *This portrait shows William Penn when he was 65 years old. Francis Place, the artist, did the portrait entirely in chalk.*

UNDERSTANDING COLONIALISM

England wanted colonies in North America. It wanted to compete with the French, Spanish, and Dutch for trade in Indian products such as tobacco, corn, and beaver furs.

A policy of setting up colonies in another country is called colonialism. The colonizing country supports its colonies by sending new settlers and supplies and sometimes soldiers for military protection. It also passes laws for its citizens in the colony.

The ruling country is often far away from its colonies. Its laws may or may not suit the people in the colony.

The Reasons for Colonies

Some countries want colonies in order to gain large areas of land to use for farming or to mine precious metals. Other countries want to establish military bases in a distant part of the world.

Many countries have had colonies. In 142 B.C., Rome established a colony in Palestine, today's Israel. The Romans enslaved the Jews there and forced them to build cities. Some countries still have colonies today. Guam, an island in the Pacific, is an American colony. The United States has Navy and Air Force bases there.

The Importance of Colonies

Colonies help a country expand its territory. With more land, a country can make larger profits from farming and manufacturing. A country with more land and resources often has more military power as well.

Because of these benefits, the English, French, Spanish, and Dutch sent settlers to North America. These settlers helped build the United States.

146

giving him a large piece of land in North America to start a colony for English Quakers. In 1681, the king agreed. He granted Penn an area just south of New York. It became known as Pennsylvania. ■

■ *What were William Penn's reasons for founding the colony*

Relations with the Indians

G od has written his law in our hearts, by which we are taught and commanded to love, and to help, and to do good to one another, and not to do harm and mischief one unto another. Now this great God has been pleased to make me concerned in your parts of the world; and the King of the country where I live has given me a great province therein; but I desire to enjoy it with your love and consent, that we may always live together as neighbors and friends.

These words are from a letter written by William Penn to the Delaware Indians of Pennsylvania. Because of his belief that all people are equal in God's sight, Penn wanted to keep peace between white settlers and Indians. In 1681, Penn asked a friend in Pennsylvania to read this letter to the Delaware in their own language. He hoped his letter would show the Delaware that he intended to treat them fairly.

When Penn arrived in Pennsylvania in 1682, he worked out a treaty with the Delaware. Penn promised to pay the Indians for their land and to respect their rights. However, after Penn's death in 1718, thousands of colonists poured into Pennsylvania. Many of these new settlers did not have the Quakers' beliefs. These settlers did not always follow Penn's practice of treating the Indians fairly. ■

How Do We Know?

HISTORY *Mrs. Preston, an early Pennsylvania colonist, described William Penn in her letters. She told how on his first meeting with the Delaware, Penn sat on the ground and ate corn with them. She also said that the Indians held a jumping contest and that Penn won.*

■ *How did William Penn establish peaceful relations with the Indians in Pennsylvania?*

◄ *Tamanend, the chief of the Delaware people, gave Penn a beaded friendship belt. On the belt was a picture of a Quaker and an Indian clasping hands.*

R E V I E W

1. **FOCUS** How did English settlers come to live in New York, New Jersey, and Pennsylvania?
2. **CONNECT** In what ways were William Penn's reasons for founding Pennsylvania similar to John Winthrop's reasons for founding the Massachusetts Bay Colony?
3. **HISTORY** What were the main beliefs of the Quakers? How did these beliefs affect relations between the Quakers and the Delaware?

4. **CRITICAL THINKING** List some general reasons why countries establish colonies. Then tell which of these reasons best apply to the colonies of New Netherland, New York, and Pennsylvania.
5. **WRITING ACTIVITY** Write a news story for a Philadelphia newspaper in 1682. The article should describe William Penn's meeting with the Delaware to work out a treaty of friendship.

147

Settling a New World

Choosing the Right Scale

Here's Why

Statistics, which are facts using numbers, can be shown in several different ways. In this textbook and in newspapers and magazines, you have seen information presented in charts, tables, bar graphs, line graphs, and pie graphs.

Graphs differ from charts and tables because they show visually the relationship between two sets of numbers. Line graphs are used to show changes that occur in the numbers over time. If, for example, you wanted to show how the beaver fur trade in Canada changed between 1675 and 1685, would you

know how? By learning how to make your own line graphs, you will be able to show these changes.

Here's How

First, collect your data. The table below gives the information on the beaver trade that was used to make the two line graphs on this page.

Next, create the grid for your graph. A grid is a pattern of evenly spaced horizontal and vertical lines. A well-drawn grid has squares that are exactly the same size. You can also use specially marked graph paper for this purpose.

A line graph has two base lines, or axes. The horizontal axis is the base line that goes across the bottom of the graph, from left to right. Look at the two graphs below. In both these graphs, the horizontal graph is marked in one-year sections, from 1675 to 1685.

The vertical axis is the base line that goes up the left side of the graph, from bottom to the top. On the graph at the left, the amount of beaver fur sold each year is shown in increases of 100,000 pounds, from 0 to 500,000. On the graph on the right, the fur sold is shown in increases of 25,000 pounds,

Beaver Trade (in thousands of pounds)										
Year	1675	1676	1677	1678	1679	1680	1681	1682	1683	1684	1685
Pounds	61	70	92	80	68	69	83	90	95	49	138

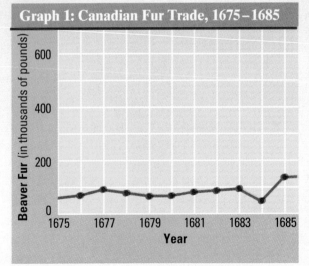

Graph 1: Canadian Fur Trade, 1675–1685

Graph 2: Canadian Fur Trade, 1675–1685

Fur Trade at Fort Albany, 1710–1780

Year	Beaver Furs Traded	Year	Beaver Furs Traded	Year	Beaver Furs Traded
1710	4	1735	32	1760	30
1715	14	1740	37	1765	28
1720	28	1745	30	1770	26
1725	27	1750	27	1775	10
1730	41	1755	25	1780	4

from 0 to 125,000. As you can see, the scale used for the vertical axis of the graph shown on the left is four times greater than the scale used for the vertical axis of the graph on the right.

These two graphs show the importance of choosing the right scale for your graph. The information presented on these two graphs is the same. To check this, use the graph on the left to find out how many pounds of fur were exported in the year 1683. To do this, move your finger up from the 1683 mark on the horizontal axis till you reach the data line. Now move your finger left across the graph to the numbers on the vertical axis. You can see that the data line is at about 95,000 pounds at the year 1683. Now try the same thing on the right-hand side of the graph. Did you get the same data? You should.

Although both graphs give you the same information, the one on the right is much easier to read. Because

the vertical scale on the left graph is so large, you can only guess at the actual amount of fur sold each year. Also, the graphs do not look the same. The graph on the left shows little change over the 10-year period. The graph on the right more clearly shows the rapid increase. The fur trade was five times bigger in 1685 than it was in 1675.

In deciding what scale to use for a graph that you are making, think about the highest and lowest values you have to graph. Each axis should be numbered so that the complete set of points and connecting lines cover most of the graph. Use standard increases, such as 1, 5, or 10 years and 5, 10, 25, or 50,000 pounds.

Try It

Use the information from the table on this page to make a graph of fur trade at Fort Albany during the years 1710 to 1780. Notice that in this table the numbers of furs

traded at just one trading station are given. Find a horizontal axis that gives you 15 sets of information. Find a vertical axis that allows you to show the number of beaver furs traded from 0 to 40 in 8 increases.

Apply It

Follow the steps used in Here's How to make a graph showing some data that change over time. For example, show the change in your height over a period of years. Or show the change over years of the number of students in your class, or the batting average of your favorite baseball player.

Chapter Review

Reviewing Key Terms

colonization (p. 129)   Pilgrim (p. 139)
encomienda (p. 129)   profit (p. 134)
fort (p. 131)   Puritan (p. 139)
investor (p. 134)   Quaker (p. 145)
mission (p. 130)   Separatist (p. 139)
pacifism (p. 145)   tax (p. 130)

A. The following quotations express beliefs. Write the key term that identifies each speaker or belief.

1. "All people should be treated equally."
2. "Bible study is more important than beautiful church ceremonies."
3. "The resources in the colonies will make me rich."
4. "I would rather risk jail than belong to the Church of England."
5. "All war is wrong."
6. "We went on a holy journey to America."

B. Write an explanation of why the following items could be important to you if you were either a European settler or an Indian.

1. colonization
2. tax
3. mission
4. profit
5. fort
6. encomiendo

Exploring Concepts

A. Copy and complete the chart by writing any missing information. The first line has been completed for you.

Date	Who?	From Where?	What?
1598	Juan de Oñãte	Spain	Settled New Mexico
1600s			Founded Quebec
1620		England	
1624	Thirty families		
1630	Puritans		
1664		England	

B. Study the following pairs of words. Write two or three sentences that describe how the two items are connected.

1. pueblos
   long houses
2. John White
   Richard Hakluyt
3. Thanksgiving
   Squanto
4. Puritans
   Separatists
5. Charles I
   Henry VIII
6. beaver furs
   knives and axes
7. *Mayflower*
   Arbella
8. William Penn
   Peter Stuyvesant

Reviewing Skills

1. Read on pages 129 and 130 about how the Spanish treated Indians in New Mexico. Then read the two paragraphs at the top of page 142 about how the Wampanoag and the Pilgrims got along. Summarize and combine details from the two sections. Write your own paragraph, explaining how Indians treated, and were treated by, colonists.
2. Graph the population of Quebec based on the table. Put the dates one-half inch apart per 10 years on the horizontal axis. Place your population figures one-half inch apart per 1,000 people on the vertical axis.
3. To stress how quickly the population grew, which scale of your graph would you change? How would you change it?
4. What artifacts might you find in a museum of French Canadian history?
5. Where would you look to find the latitude and longitude of the Spanish colony at St. Augustine, Florida?

French Population of Quebec, 1610–1700			
Year	Population (estimated)	Year	Population (estimated)
1610	18	1663	2,500
1620	60	1673	6,705
1630	100	1680	9,719
1640	359	1686	11,130
1650	675	1700	15,000

Using Critical Thinking

1. As you know, Manhattan was once the Dutch colony of New Amsterdam. Today, it is home to the United Nations, an organization of countries from all over the world. Could you say that, in a way, the New Amsterdam of the 1600s was also home to a kind of united nations? Why was this possibly true? Give historical facts from the chapter as reasons.
2. William Penn had unusual ideas for his time about how the Indians who lived near English settlements should be treated. He believed that settlers should pay the Indians for their land, respect their rights, and be good neighbors to them. Would Penn's beliefs be more popular today? Name some ways that people's treatment of other ethnic groups has improved in 300 years.

Preparing for Citizenship

1. WRITING ACTIVITY Imagine that you are an explorer preparing to lead a voyage of exploration to a planet many light-years from Earth. The time is the distant future. Earlier trips have revealed life on the planet. Think about the mistakes European explorers made in their approach to the American Indians. Then create a list of guidelines for the explorers who will go with you to use in approaching the people they find on the planet. What is the most important thing they can do to be sure of a peaceful meeting?
2. COLLABORATIVE LEARNING Plan "An Update on European Settlements in North America." Each group of three students should choose a colony. Assign one person to research what that area is like today, one to study its history, and one to decide in what form you'll present your report. For example, if you chose New York you might write a brochure encouraging tourists to visit. In that case, you would want to emphasize cultural and recreational activities that are likely to appeal to your readers.

Unit 3

Life in the
English Colonies

English settlers who came to America in the 1600s often faced disease, hunger, and battles with Indians. But as the English colonies grew, life for many settlers improved. New York merchant William Denning and his family, shown here, had found what many colonists found during the 1700s: wealth, comfort, and success.

1607

*William Williams, The Dennings, 1772.
Private Collection.*

1759

Chapter 7

The Southern Colonies

The Englishmen who landed in Virginia in 1607 expected to get rich. But instead of gold or silver, the colonists found a plant called tobacco. After a slow and difficult start, some Virginians were able to make money growing tobacco. Some planters even bought African slaves and put them to work in their fields. Using this system, a few Virginians soon became the wealthiest people in the colonies.

During this time, English colonists settled along the east coast of Virginia and the Carolinas, shown in the map above.

A TOBACCO PLANTATION

1600	1625	1650

1607

1614 John Rolfe sends the first shipment of Virginia tobacco to England. Though growing and harvesting the plant (above) is difficult, tobacco sells for six times the price of wheat.

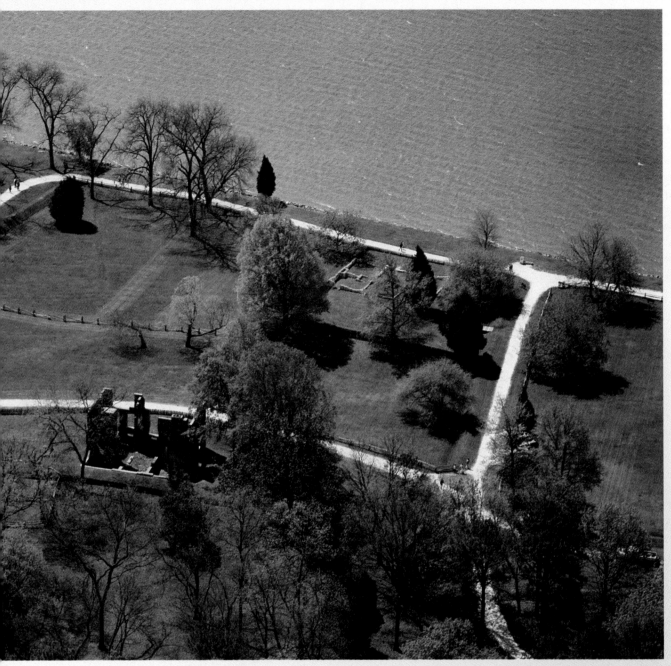

Throughout this period, Jamestown was the capital of Virginia. This photograph shows all that remains of the settlement today.

1675 About 4,000 slaves now live in Virginia and Maryland.

| 1675 | 1700 | 1725 |

1676 Colonist Nathaniel Bacon leads a revolt against the English governor of Virginia. Bacon demands more protection from Indian attacks on the colony.

1682

	1575		1600		1625		1650		1675		1700

1607   **1622**

LESSON 1

A New Settlement in Virginia

➤ *The Virginia Company's advertisements praised the fertile land of Virginia.*

Think of a place where the winters are "dry and fair" and the summers have "many great and sudden showers of rain." In this place, the woods and fields are filled with "rare and delectable [tasty] birds," and the rivers "abound with fish both great and small."

This is how preacher Alexander Whitaker described Jamestown in 1613 in his essay "Good News from Virginia." The Virginia Company of London printed reports by Whitaker and other settlers. They wanted to make people wish to move to Virginia.

NOVA BRITANNIA.
OFFERING MOST
Excellent fruites by Planting in VIRGINIA.
Exciting all such as be well affected to further the same.

LONDON
Printed for SAMVEL MACHAM, and are to be sold at his Shop in Pauls Church-yard, at the Signe of the Bul-head.
1 6 0 9.

Richard Frethorne is one person who did sail from England to Virginia. He was a servant who wanted to start a new life. In a letter written in 1623, Frethorne said of Virginia:

I have nothing to comfort me, nor is there is nothing to be gotten here but sickness and death . . . I have nothing at all —no, not a shirt to my back but two rags.

In fact, Virginia was just as beautiful as Whitaker had described. However, the land was also dangerous and unhealthy. Men like Frethorne found little "good news" there.

Dangers Hide in the Land

The Virginia Company sent men who wanted to make money to Virginia. At first, these men delighted in the land. As they sailed along the coast they enjoyed the "fair meadows." At night they camped on shore. Once they found oysters "thicke as stones." One passenger, George Percy, described the landscape and wildlife.

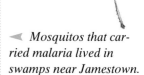

◄ *Mosquitos that carried malaria lived in swamps near Jamestown.*

There are also great store [numbers] of Vines in bignesse of a mans thigh, running up to the tops of the Trees in great abundance. We also did see many Squirels, Conies [rabbits], Black Birds with crimson wings . . .

George Percy, *Observations*, 1607

These men stood in wonder at the beauty of Virginia. They had no reason to think that danger was hiding in the land.

Choosing a Place to Settle

The men decided to build their settlement on the James River. The place they chose had many advantages. First, the settlement was far enough up the river to protect the settlers from ocean attack. Second, the river would provide an easy escape route from the Indians if one was needed. Third, the river could be used to carry goods to and from the settlement. In other ways, however, the place, which the settlers called Jamestown, was a poor choice.

Illness and Hard Times

During high tide, salt water from the ocean poured into the James River. When the men drank from the river, the salty water made them sick. Also the swampland they settled on was full of mosquitos

▼ *John Smith, one of the principal founders of Jamestown, made this surprisingly accurate map of Virginia in 1606.*

carrying germs that caused malaria, typhoid fever, dysentery, and other deadly diseases. The **life expectancy**—the number of years a man could expect to live—was low because of disease. Just as bad, the men had no idea how to grow crops on the swampy land.

■ *What were the advantages and disadvantages of Jamestown as a location for settlement?*

The men thought they would find gold quickly and then return to England. However, they found no gold. When winter came, they shivered in their drafty, poorly made homes. Many wondered if they could survive the hidden dangers of this strange land. ■

John Smith Leads the Settlers

By December 1607, just six months after landing at Jamestown, 66 of the original 104 settlers had

➤ *John Smith saved Jamestown from complete starvation the winter of 1607.*

died. This first group of settlers were soldiers, gentlemen adventurers, and convicts who wanted to get rich and return to England. The gentlemen adventurers were not used to doing hard work such as farming and chopping wood. They did not bring their wives or children with them. So, the men did not settle down in families. They bickered and fought with one another.

Among the early settlers was an able soldier named John Smith. Because he had traveled widely and fought in many wars, John

Smith was used to making decisions. He was a short man who always stood up very straight. His beard and curled moustache gave him a stern and serious look. During the first winter in 1607, when the settlers argued and refused to work, John Smith took control. He realized that the settlers needed direction in order to survive. He was very strict with the settlers, making everyone work. He declared, "You must obey this for a law, that he that will not worke, shall not eate." If Smith heard a man swear, he poured water down his sleeve.

Smith not only directed the settlers, but also tried to bargain with

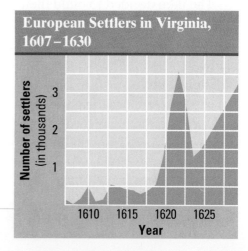

➤ *The population of Virginia went up and down, as new settlers arrived and others died of disease.*

European Settlers in Virginia, 1607–1630

Number of settlers (in thousands)

3

2

1

1610   1615   1620   1625

Year

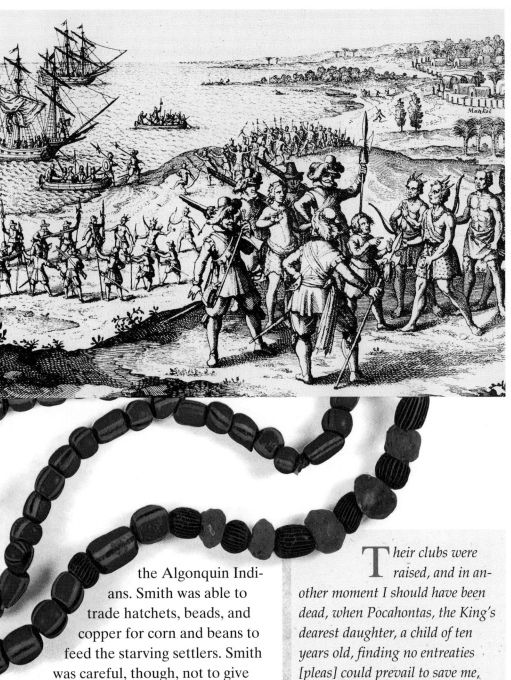

the Algonquin Indians. Smith was able to trade hatchets, beads, and copper for corn and beans to feed the starving settlers. Smith was careful, though, not to give guns to Chief Powhatan. The tall chief towered above Smith. Powhatan wanted to take guns from the settlers. At one point Powhatan's men tied Smith up and almost killed him. Here is how Smith wrote about his adventure:

> Their clubs were raised, and in another moment I should have been dead, when Pocahontas, the King's dearest daughter, a child of ten years old, finding no entreaties [pleas] could prevail to save me, darted forward, and taking my head in her arms, laid her own upon it, and thus prevented my death.
>
> John Smith, *A Generall Historie of Virginia,* 1624

■ *Who were the people who first settled in Virginia? What were their backgrounds? Why did they come to Virginia?*

The Colony Changes

John Smith sailed back to England late in 1609 to heal the severe wounds he suffered in a gunpowder accident. He also returned because some officials of the Virginia Company did not like his stern ways and wanted him to leave. Jamestown then suffered the worst winter yet. It was called the "starving time." People ate dogs, rats, and mice. The terrible winter is described in a novel by Scott O'Dell:

> *W*e ventured outside the fort only to bury our dead, but only at night in shallow graves, for the earth was frozen and we feared death from savage arrows. Inside the fort stalked famine and pestilence [hunger and disease]. Huts of the dead and pickets from the stockade were burned for firewood.
>
> Scott O'Dell, *The Serpent Never Sleeps*

New Ideas to Save the Colony

Hunger, disease, no gold! By 1609, Jamestown was a complete failure as far as the Virginia Company was concerned. The company knew it had to do something. Maybe if the colony had more hard-working settlers, it would do well.

In 1609, the company had begun sending **indentured servants** to Virginia. These servants signed an indenture, or agreement, promising the company five to seven years of unpaid labor. In return, the servants received free passage across the ocean. At the end of their service, the servants got 100 acres of land and their "freedom dues"—clothing, tools, and often a gun.

The need to find good workers continued. By 1616, the Virginia Company did even more to get settlers who were eager to work. The company made a promise to people: 100 acres of land, plus 50 acres

➤ *This drawing shows how a typical Virginian settlement of the 1600s might have looked. How did settlers defend themselves from attacks?*

Watchtower

Fort

Company barn

Cannon platform

Company compound

Cottage

Corral

Because tobacco is an annual crop, new seeds had to be planted each spring.

Tobacco plants were carefully tended. After about 24 weeks, the plants were ready to be cut down.

Tobacco stalks were hung in the sun for a brief period to wilt the leaves.

After wilting, tobacco was hung inside barns to dry, or cure.

Cured tobacco leaves were stripped from their stalks.

Tobacco leaves were layered into barrels. A heavy weight packed the leaves down tightly. The barrels of tobacco were then shipped to warehouses to await inspection.

◄ *Planters needed many workers to grow, dry, and cure the tobacco plant. When full, tobacco barrels like the one shown here weighed about 1,000 pounds.*

for every indentured servant they brought. Men came across the Atlantic Ocean with many indentured servants. They received hundreds of acres of land. The large farms they owned were called **plantations.** In time, Virginia became a colony in which a few rich planters owned most of the land by the rivers.

The Virginia Company also decided to give the people a voice in the government. In this way, settlers would have to care about the success of the colony. In 1619, the company formed a law-making body. It was called the **House of Burgesses.** A burgess was a type of **representative**—a person who spoke for the settlers and voted on laws for the colony. All free white men could vote for a representative. The House of Burgesses was the first time the English in America had a representative government.

A Profitable Crop

The settlers never found gold in Virginia. But with tobacco, Virginians did finally find a crop that would make some of them very rich. Smoking had become popular in Europe, so many people wanted to buy tobacco. In 1613, a settler named John Rolfe found a high-grade tobacco from the West Indies. This tobacco grew well in Virginia.

Across Time & Space

King James I of England thought smoking was unpleasant and dangerous. But he still welcomed the money the tobacco trade brought to his treasury. Today, we know that tobacco is a leading cause of lung cancer, responsible for about 300,000 deaths a year.

161

Maloaks als Rebecka daughter to the mighty Prince Powhatan Emperour of Attanoughkomouck als Virginia converted and baptized in the Christian faith, and Wife to the wor.¹¹ M.ʳ Tho: Rolff.

▲ *After Pocahontas married John Rolfe, she toured England. The English treated her as a princess.*

■ *How did the discovery of tobacco as a crop affect Virginia?*

John Rolfe not only found the ideal crop for Virginia, but he also found a way to improve conditions with Chief Powhatan. In 1614, he married Powhatan's daughter, Pocahontas. The settlers hoped that this marriage would bring a lasting peace in the colony. Pocahontas's marriage to John Rolfe did bring some peace to Jamestown, but not a lasting peace. Pocahontas died from smallpox only three years after her marriage. Strange as it may seem, it was John Rolfe's crop of tobacco that made things worse with the Powhatans.

The problem was land. The settlers demanded more and more Indian land for growing tobacco. The Indians feared that they would soon have no place to live. They had to protect their homeland.

Tensions between settlers and Indians increased. In 1622, the settlers killed a Powhatan war chief and religious leader named Nemattanew. In response, the Indians launched a surprise attack on farms up and down the James River. They killed 347 settlers, almost one-fourth of all the settlers in Virginia at that time.

The Indians wanted to drive the settlers into the Atlantic, and they almost succeeded. The settlers fought back fiercely, however. By the end of the year, the Indians were in retreat.

After this attack, the Virginia Company failed. King James blamed the company for not building enough forts. He decided to rule the colony himself. As for the settlers—they wanted to drive the Indians from Virginia. ■

R E V I E W

1. **FOCUS** In what ways were early settlers unprepared for what they found in Jamestown?
2. **CONNECT** Compare the attitude of the first settlers of Jamestown to Spanish adventurers in the New World.
3. **HISTORY** In what ways did Pocahontas help Jamestown settlers?
4. **CRITICAL THINKING** John Smith hoped that Jamestown would one day become a great city. However, the town never had more than 175 permanent residents. Why do you think this was the case?
5. **WRITING ACTIVITY** Imagine that you are hired to write a motto for Jamestown. Finish this sentence several times with your ideas. "Jamestown: the city. . . ."

LESSON 2

Rebellion in Virginia

Elizabeth Bacon sat down and wrote her sister-in-law a letter to calm her nerves. She wrote about her husband:

> The country does so really love him, that they would not leave him alone anywhere; there was not anybody against him but the Governor and a few of his great men. . . . Surely if your brother's crime had been so great all the country would not have been for him.
>
> Elizabeth Bacon, letter dated 1676

What was Nathaniel Bacon's crime? Why was the governor against him? And why did "all the country" love him?

Nathaniel Bacon had stood up to the governor of Virginia, William Berkeley. Bacon was a talented leader who wanted to be allowed to organize attacks against the Susquehannock *(suhs kwuh HAN nahk)* and other Indians on the Virginia frontier. He was not happy with the way Governor Berkeley handled Indian attacks on settlers who lived far from Jamestown. Bacon was not satisfied with the government of Virginia.

THINKING FOCUS

What caused Bacon's Rebellion?

Key Terms

- council
- rebel

The Government of Virginia

William Berkeley, the king's chosen governor, kept a firm grip on the government of Virginia. He hand-picked his advisers, or the members of his **council.** He personally chose people to run the courts, lead the militia, build forts, and trade with the Indians.

No Elections

The governor also had the power to call meetings of the House of Burgesses. Berkeley did

not like the idea of common people having a voice in the government. So he did not call a new election of the House from 1660 until 1676. For 16 years, the people in Virginia did not have a chance to vote for new members.

High Taxes

For a long time, Berkeley was able to get the House to do as he liked. He raised taxes. The small planters hated the taxes. They

▲ *Nathaniel Bacon stood up for frontier settlers but brutally attacked American Indians.*

163

The Southern Colonies

> William Berkeley traded with the Indians for beaver furs. Traders dried and stretched beaver pelts like this one. The hoop is made from a tree branch.

■ Find examples from the text to support Nathaniel Bacon's statement, "All the power and sway is got into the hands of the rich."

felt that the government took their money but did not give them protection in return.

Berkeley even talked the House into changing the voting laws, so that men without land could not vote. Remember that before 1670, all the free men in the colony could vote for the House of Burgesses. Berkeley did not trust poor people who did not own land. He thought they might stand up to him and cause trouble. So the House took their vote away. ■

The Fight for Land

Men needed land in order to vote. However, large landholders already owned most of the good land near the rivers. Any remaining land was very expensive or hard to get. So ordinary settlers found it harder and harder to become landowners. Even indentured servants who finished their terms of work were forced deep into the frontier to claim their 100 acres of land. These parcels of land were far from water and thick with forest. Algonquin Indians still lived in these areas, too.

By 1675, land-hungry settlers outnumbered the Indians. Many thought that destroying the Indians would solve their land problems.

In the summer of 1675, frontier settlers slaughtered several Doeg Indians. The Doeg fought back by killing several settlers. A group of planters and soldiers attacked the Doeg again. Each attack led to another attack by the other side.

> White settlers cut trees, cleared fields, and built houses on Indian land in Virginia.

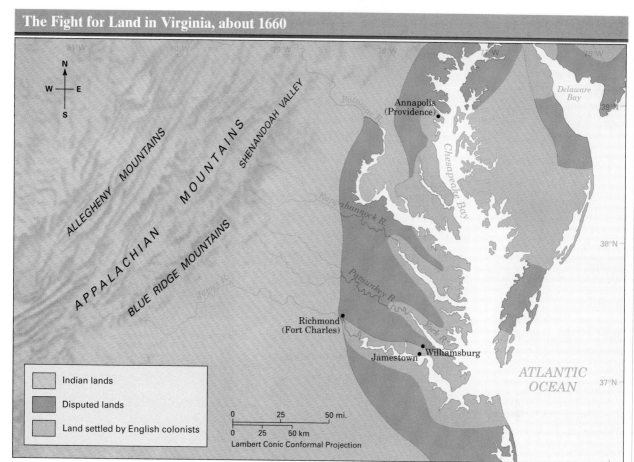

Indian lands

Disputed lands

Land settled by English colonists

0   25   50 mi.
0 25 50 km
Lambert Conic Conformal Projection

Tempers were hot. The settlers asked Governor Berkeley to make the Indians leave the frontier. Instead, the governor ordered a string of forts built to separate the two groups.

The settlers were not happy with the governor's idea. They knew that the governor and plantation owners in eastern Virginia did not have to fear the Indians. Almost all the tribes now lived on the frontier. Frontier settlers accused the governor of building the forts so he could give jobs to his friends. Worse yet, they thought that he secretly wanted to protect the Indians. For years, people whispered that Berkeley was growing even richer as he traded for beaver skins with the Algonquin tribes. The Indian attacks continued. That's when Nathaniel Bacon took charge of the fight. ■

As the number of settlers increased in the late 1600s, the Indians were pushed farther and farther west.

■ *Why was land ownership so important to the Virginia settlers?*

Bacon's Rebellion

Nathaniel Bacon was not a poor man. As a matter of fact, he owned a big plantation, and he sat on the Governor's council. However, as a new settler to the colony, Bacon had new ideas.

The settlers wanted Bacon to lead them against the Indians, even though they did not have the governor's orders to march. After attacking several Indian villages, Bacon and his followers returned to Jamestown. There, Governor Berkeley declared him a **rebel,** one who uses violence to fight the government. Berkeley cried, "Now I behold the greatest rebel that ever was in Virginia!"

> *Bacon and his men burned Jamestown to the ground. "It should harbor no more rogues [evil men]!" Bacon exclaimed.*

■ *Why was Bacon's Rebellion important to the struggle of common men?*

Jamestown Burns

Bacon and Berkeley could never really come to an understanding. Bacon wanted more power to protect frontier settlements. Berkeley continued to hold back. At one point, Bacon and 500 men stormed into a council meeting in Jamestown. Berkeley boldly faced Bacon, tore open his own coat and cried out, "Here, shoot me—'fore God, fair mark!"

Bacon refused to kill him, saying:

> *Sir, I come not, nor intend, to hurt a hair of your honor's head . . . I come for a commission [order] against the heathen who daily inhumanly murder us and spill our brethren's blood.*
>
> Nathaniel Bacon,
> reported speech, 1676

At one point, in their terrible fight, Bacon and his men burned Jamestown to the ground. They did not want the governor to control it. The flames danced in the sky and lit the river waters.

King Charles I then sent troops to control Bacon. By the time they arrived, though, Bacon had died of swamp fever. His men had gone back to their plantations.

After the Rebellion

Bacon's Rebellion showed that common men would not stand by and let the government control them. The rebellion also showed that frontier settlers could be cruel to native people.

Life in Virginia slowly settled down. More women came to the colony. The number of families grew. The colonists wanted to stay and find success in Virginia. ■

R E V I E W

1. **FOCUS** What caused Bacon's Rebellion?
2. **CONNECT** From the time of John Smith, the relation of Algonquin tribes and Virginia's settlers was filled with tension. Why did it get worse by 1675?
3. **GEOGRAPHY** Why was life on the frontier more difficult than life near a town?
4. **CRITICAL THINKING** Do you think if Nathaniel Bacon had never come to Virginia, Governor Berkeley would never have faced a rebellion?
5. **ACTIVITY** Choose two of your classmates to role play with you the roles of Bacon, Berkeley, and a Susquehannock chief. Discuss your problems and hopes for the future.

LESSON 3

Slavery in the Southern Colonies

T he slave ship "filled me with astonishment, which was soon converted into terror." A man named Olaudah Equiano wrote these words. As a young man Equiano was taken from his home in Africa and sold to an English slave trader. The trader brought him across the ocean to America. There he became a slave.

Years later, Equiano described his ocean journey in a book. Once aboard the ship, he wrote, "The heat of the climate, added to the number in the ship, being so crowded that each had scarcely room to turn himself, almost suffocated us."

Some Africans chose death over slavery. Equiano watched as two men "who were chained together, preferring death to such a life of misery, somehow made through the netting, and jumped into the sea."

THINKING
FOCUS

How did the slave trade begin and develop in the southern colonies?

Key Terms

- slavery
- export
- cash crop

▼ *Planters often put slaves in shackles like these.*

The Beginnings of Black Slavery

Olaudah Equiano was one of about 10 million Africans who were sold into slavery between the 1500s and the 1800s. **Slavery** is a system in which people are made to work without pay for their masters. Slaves have no rights.

Slavery did not begin in North America or even in the New World. Slavery existed in the ancient world, too. In the ancient world, prisoners taken in wars were sometimes enslaved. These slaves came from many different places. Some of them earned their freedom after working for a number of years.

The Southern Colonies

Slaves were brought to the New World to raise sugar. Refined sugar, molasses, and rum came from the sugar cane.

In the New World, however, slavery was different—and in some ways more cruel. Only non-Europeans—Africans and Native Americans—were slaves. Once a person became a slave that person was a slave for life. And any child of a slave mother was also a slave for life.

The Spanish were the first people to use African slaves in the New World. In the late 1400s, Spain founded colonies in the West Indies. The Spanish discovered a new form of wealth there in sugar. Sugar was an **export**—a crop sent overseas to Europe for sale. It brought so much money that it quickly became known as white gold.

The Spanish needed strong workers to do the hard work of stooping to plant and cut sugar cane. They tried to make slaves of the Indian people of the West Indies. Most of these people died of disease. The Spanish then turned to using African slaves in their fields.

The Dutch, French, and English also founded colonies in the West Indies and followed the same path. At first, the English used

UNDERSTANDING SLAVERY

*E*uropean colonists were not the first people to use slaves. Slavery, a system of forced labor in which people work without pay for their masters, had existed nearly as long as human civilization.

The first known slaves lived about 3500 B.C. in western Asia. In the Greek empire, in the 400s B.C., up to one-third of the population were slaves. Societies in China, India, and Africa also practiced slavery.

Before the 1500s, most slaves were criminals or prisoners captured in wars. Those who served their masters loyally could win freedom. In Africa, slaves had some of the same legal rights as free citizens. Africans viewed slavery as a temporary condition that was not limited to any one racial group.

However, this view differed greatly from the one in the English colonies. As colonists bought more and more African slaves, slavery became a system of white ownership of black laborers.

By the early 1700s, colonies had passed laws that made all blacks slaves and that forbade masters from giving their slaves freedom.

Slavery remained legal in the southern United States until 1865, after the Civil War. Today, all but a few societies throughout the world have outlawed slavery.

indentured servants to grow sugar. But few of these people would put up with the hard work in the hot and wet West Indies. They preferred to work in North America instead. Eventually, the English followed the example of other European colonials and began trading for African slaves. ■

▲ Planters bought African slaves to do backbreaking work on sugar plantations.

■ How did the colonization of the West Indies lead to the European slave trade?

The Slave Trade

The English traders bought slaves on the west coast of Africa. There, the traders usually found leaders of African kingdoms who had captured prisoners after battles with their enemies.

The village was surrounded by enemies, who attacked us with clubs, long spears, and bows and arrows. After fighting for more than an hour, those who were not fortunate enough to run away were made prisoners.

Charles Ball, *A Narrative of the Life and Adventures of Charles Ball*, 1854

The English slave traders exchanged guns, cotton cloth, and other items for the African prisoners.

First Passage

The traders marched their African prisoners to slave factories along the ocean. This part of a slave's journey was called the first passage.

Prisoners from many different African cultures often came together at the slave factories. A Closer Look at West African Culture on the next two pages tells of some of these cultures.

169

The Southern Colonies

West African Culture

Before the slave trade hit its peak, West Africa boasted cities as large as those in Europe. Powerful African kings ruled over many different peoples. Some peoples governed themselves. During this period, agriculture, art, music, architecture, and trade all flourished.

The Ashanti people founded their fortunes on gold. When Europeans came looking for gold in Africa, they traded with the Ashanti for gold dust and beautiful objects like these.

Ibo women wore these beautiful brass anklets to show off family wealth. The Ibo ruled them selves democratically in small groups.

Tucolor
Woloff
• Dakar
Bondu
Nioro
Massina
• Gao
Dogon
Songhay
Segu •
Wagadugu
• Dinguiraye
Bambara
Sokoto •
• Katsina
• Kano
Mandinka
Mossi
Hausa
• Zaria
Dialonke
Sierra Leone
Tallensi
Temne
Kong •
Old Oyo
OYO
Jukun
Kru
Domaa
Ashanti
Abomey
Dan
Ilorin •
Ife
Lokoja
• Kumasi
Yoruba
Edo
Denkyira
Fon
Egba
Benin
Baule
Fante
Dahomey
Ibo
Nzima •
Accra
Ouidah
Lagos
Ibibio
• Calabar
Cape Coast
Porto Novo
Jekri
Bonny

BENIN

Cape Lopez •

Bakuba
Loango
Matamba
Yaka
Congo
Ndongo

Each Ashanti king had his own gold-decorated stool. The stool was very important because it stood for the soul of the Ashanti people. When the king died, the stool was carefully kept in a special place to protect it.

The ancient city of Benin astonished early European visitors with its wide streets and roomy houses. Benin's artists crafted many bronze images of their kings. This one shows the ideal Benin king, calm and watchful.

Carved in the Congo region, this tortoise played a part in the ceremony marking a boy's entrance into manhood. A traditional African art, wood carvings often celebrated important moments like birth, marriage, or death.

BENIN Empire

Lagos Major City

Ashanti People

171

The Southern Colonies

▲ Slaves were chained together and tightly stacked in the ships. Overcrowding allowed diseases to spread throughout the slave cargo.

■ Describe the treatment of slaves as they were taken from Africa to North America.

Middle Passage

Once the Africans had boarded the slave ship they began the middle passage. This was the journey across the Atlantic Ocean to America.

The slave ship was terribly crowded. Equiano described the smell and the sickness and the horrible fear—the shouts and groans of the dying. Olaudah Equiano had never seen white people before. He did not understand English. He thought he had "got into a world of bad spirits."

Third Passage

Africans who survived the long voyage faced another terror in the American port. The third passage was the slave auction. Equiano wrote about the sale of slaves:

> On a signal given, such as the beat of a drum, the buyers rush at once into the yard where the slaves are confined, and make choice of that parcel they like best.
>
> Olaudah Equiano, *narrative*, published in 1814

Slavery in the Southern Colonies

Not all the blacks who came to North America in the 1600s were slaves. The first blacks arrived in Virginia in 1619. However, records tell us that many of the first Africans came as indentured servants. In the first years some who were brought over as slaves could later buy their freedom.

A Free Black

Anthony Johnson arrived in Virginia in 1621 and worked as a slave on the Richard Bennett plantation for 20 years. In the 1640s, Johnson and his wife Mary gained their freedom. They probably earned money for their freedom by selling vegetables they grew. Once free, Johnson became a successful planter. He bought 250 acres and a herd of cattle. He even had two servants.

By the late 1650s, though, Johnson saw that life for black people in Virginia was changing. Between 1660 and 1682, the colony passed a series of strict laws regarding slavery. Johnson feared increasing trouble for all blacks.

In 1664, Johnson decided to move. He sold most of his property to white people and moved his family to Maryland where they rented land. He did keep 50 acres in Virginia though. He gave this land to his son, Richard. But Richard never got the land. A white jury in Virginia decided that because Anthony was black, his land could be taken from him and given to a local white planter.

Strict Slave Laws

Why did the laws in Virginia about slavery get stronger? For one thing, slaves were becoming more valuable. Fewer indentured servants were coming to Virginia in the 1660s because life in England had improved.

From the diagram on page 161, you can see that planters needed a lot of workers to grow, harvest, and dry tobacco. Tobacco farmers grew tobacco as a **cash crop**—a product grown for sale rather than for the planter's own use. Eager for profits, white plantation owners supported laws that would give them full power over black tobacco workers.

Slaves and Southern Wealth

Africans were valuable workers, not only on the tobacco plantations of Virginia. They also labored on the rice plantations in the Carolina colony, founded in 1665. Some of the slaves sent to Carolina had been able rice farmers in Africa. They used their farming skills to grow rice in Carolina as well. Rice plantation owners became the richest men in the English colonies. Slaves, however, were given only small amounts of clothing and food. Because Africans were slaves, they did not share the wealth they helped create. ■

▲ *Africans were able to grow rice more effectively than the English settlers had.*

◄ *On this tobacco label, you can see slaves working and owners enjoying their wealth.*

■ *What events took place that led Virginia colonists to adopt slavery?*

R E V I E W

1. **FOCUS** How did the slave trade begin and develop in the southern colonies?

2. **CONNECT** Contrast and compare the white settlers' attitude toward the Powhatan Indians to their attitude toward African slaves.

3. **ECONOMICS** How did tobacco farmers benefit from slavery?

4. **CRITICAL THINKING** Slavery laws were passed in Virginia to prevent slaves from rebelling against their owners. How might these laws have affected the actions of slave owners?

5. **ACTIVITY** Construct a timeline that traces the history of the slave trade. If necessary, do additional research at the library.

Interpreting Flow Lines

Here's Why

Mapmakers often use arrows to show movement. When the thickness is varied to show the quantity of what is being moved, the arrows are called graduated flow lines. Graduated means the size gets larger or smaller. Flow lines show that something is flowing or moving.

Graduated flow lines on a map give you a lot of information very quickly. They show you where something comes from, where it is going, and how the quantity is divided. Graduated flow lines are not very precise ways of indicating quantity.

To find exact amounts, you might want to consult a table.

Suppose you wanted to find out about how many slaves were sent across the Atlantic Ocean from Africa and what parts of Africa they came from. You could do this easily by looking at a map that has graduated flow lines.

Here's How

The maps at the bottom of this page and the facing page show the slave trade between Africa and the Western Hemisphere. The graduated flow lines show how many African people were taken from their home-

lands in different parts of Africa and sent to colonies in North America and South America. Use a ruler or mark a piece of paper to measure the width of the arrow. Compare the ruler or paper to the legend. This tells you that the total number of slaves was a little more than 9 million.

Look at the tail of the arrow on the map on this page. It shows the places from which the slaves originally came. Look at how the tail is broken into sections. Each section shows about how many people came from a particular region in Africa.

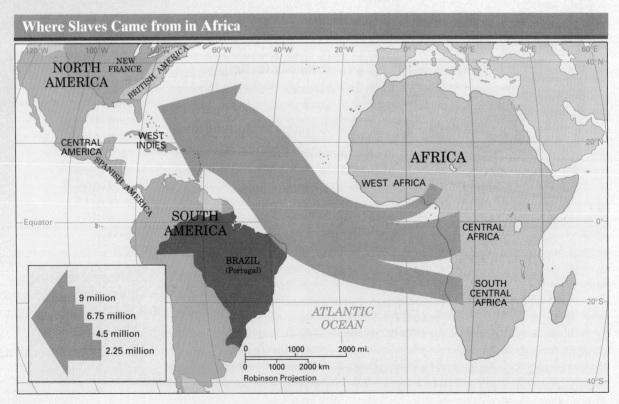

Where Slaves Came from in Africa

NORTH AMERICA

NEW FRANCE

BRITISH AMERICA

CENTRAL AMERICA

WEST INDIES

SPANISH AMERICA

SOUTH AMERICA

BRAZIL (Portugal)

AFRICA

WEST AFRICA

CENTRAL AFRICA

SOUTH CENTRAL AFRICA

ATLANTIC OCEAN

Equator

9 million
6.75 million
4.5 million
2.25 million

0   1000   2000 mi.
0   1000   2000 km
Robinson Projection

You can see that the flow line coming from Central Africa is the thickest. This means that the largest number of slaves—just over 4.5 million—came from Central Africa.

The flow line from South Central Africa is thicker than the "2.25 million" section of the legend and thinner than the "4.25 million" section. It stands for slightly more than 3 million slaves.

Now compare the line flowing from West Africa to the legend. You can see that about 1.5 million slaves came to the Western Hemisphere from West Africa.

Try It

Look at the map below. Compare the graduated flow line on this map with the one on the first map. You can see that this time the head, rather than the tail, of the arrow is broken into sections. This map focuses on where the slaves were sent rather than where they came from.

Which place in the Western Hemisphere received the most slaves from Africa? Which part received the fewest? How does the graduated flow line show you this information?

Were more African people sent as slaves to the British colonies in North America or to the Portuguese colony of Brazil in South America? About how many slaves were sent to the West Indies?

Apply It

Draw a map with a graduated flow line to show where the people in your family go during the week. The tail of the arrow will be at your home. Divide the head to show each person's destination, such as work, day care or school. If some family members stay at home, draw an arrow pointing back to your house.

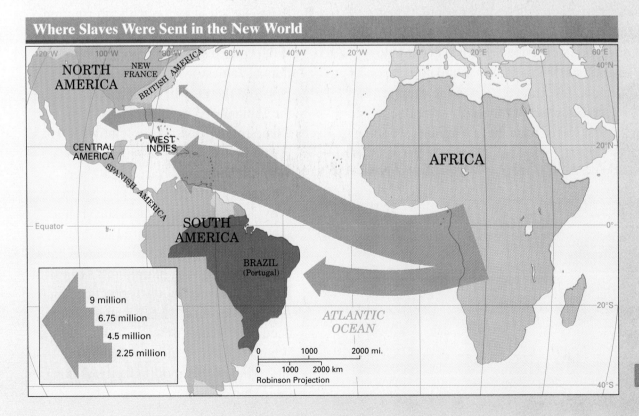

Where Slaves Were Sent in the New World

NORTH AMERICA
NEW FRANCE
BRITISH AMERICA
CENTRAL AMERICA
WEST INDIES
SPANISH AMERICA
SOUTH AMERICA
BRAZIL (Portugal)
AFRICA
Equator
ATLANTIC OCEAN

9 million
6.75 million
4.5 million
2.25 million

0   1000   2000 mi.
0   1000   2000 km
Robinson Projection

The Southern Colonies

Chapter Review

Reviewing Key Terms

cash crop (p. 173)
council (p. 163)
export (p.168)
House of Burgesses
   (p. 161)
indentured servant (p. 160)

life expectancy (p. 158)
plantation (p. 161)
rebel (p. 165)
representative (p. 161)
slavery (p. 167)

A. Each phrase below is a clue to a key term. Write a sentence giving the key term for each clue and explaining the reasons for your choice.
1. first elected government in North America
2. grown to sell for profit
3. someone elected to a lawmaking body
4. worked in return for passage to America and the promise of land.

B. Each statement below is untrue because a key term has been used incorrectly. Using information from the chapter, rewrite each sentence correctly using the key term.
1. Life expectancy describes the tobacco plant's ability to grow in wet soil.
2. Slavery was a labor system in which slaves traded work for land.
3. Governor Berkeley made people who didn't pay their taxes work in councils.
4. Rebels defended Governor Berkeley.
5. Each Indian family had a plantation on which they raised a variety of crops.
6. Exports were tools used to grow tabacco.

Exploring Concepts

A. The graph below shows population growth in Virginia during the 1600s until 1700. On your own paper, describe how each event below might have led to a jump in the population of Virginia. Use information in the chapter.
1. introduction of tobacco
2. first slaves brought to Virginia

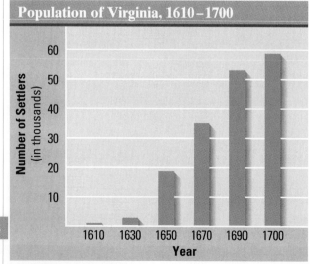

Population of Virginia, 1610–1700

Number of Settlers (in thousands) — Year: 1610, 1630, 1650, 1670, 1690, 1700

B. Answer each question with information from the chapter.
1. What caused sickness among the first settlers of Jamestown?
2. How did the growth of plantations affect the Indians of Virginia?
3. Compare the treatment of native peoples by the British and Spanish in America.
4. Why did Nathaniel Bacon challenge Governor Berkeley?
5. Why did plantation owners start using slaves instead of indentured servants?
6. What knowledge did African slaves have that made Carolina plantations successful?
7. How was slavery as it was practiced in Africa different from the way it was practiced by the colonists?
8. What were two solutions tried by the Indians to the problem of the British taking their land?

Reviewing Skills

1. Look at the map on this page of cash crops exported to Great Britain from the American colonies. The graduated flow lines show how much these crops were worth in pounds sterling, the British form of money.
   a. How much was the corn crop worth?
   b. How much was the tobacco crop worth?
   c. What was the combined worth of all three crops?
   d. What does the tail of the arrow tell you? What does the head of the arrow tell you?
2. Review the sections The Government of Virginia and The Fight for Land on pages 163 and 164. Summarize each section and combine the information in one paragraph. Who most benefited from Governor Berkeley's policies? How did his policies affect indentured servants?

3. If you wanted to show visually how quickly the number of acres of land used for raising tobacco increased in Virginia from 1612 until 1700, what would you make?

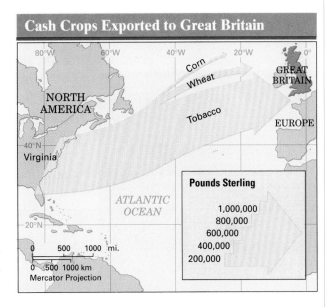

Cash Crops Exported to Great Britain

Corn
Wheat
GREAT BRITAIN
NORTH AMERICA
Tobacco
EUROPE
40°N Virginia
ATLANTIC OCEAN
20°N
0   500   1000 mi.
0   500 1000 km
Mercator Projection

Pounds Sterling
1,000,000
800,000
600,000
400,000
200,000

Using Critical Thinking

1. When indentured servants became free, they were given 100 acres of land. This land was often in Indian territory. How would you describe the events that followed from the Indians' point of view?

2. The text says, "Because Africans were slaves, they did not share in the wealth they helped to create." How is wealth created? How is it shared? Write a paragraph explaining your answers.

Preparing for Citizenship

1. **WRITING ACTIVITY** Suppose you are a geographer and that time travel is possible. Write a story in which you travel in space and time to the first Jamestown settlement. Once there, you give the settlers advice based on what you know about Virginia's geography. Imagine that they listen to your advice. Then describe what they do and what the effects are.

2. **COLLABORATIVE LEARNING** Working in groups of three to four people each, plan and stage a television news interview show. Focus on one of the following topics: (1) John Smith's first encounter with Powhatan and Pocohantas, (2) John Rolfe's marriage to Pocohantas, or (3) Nathaniel Bacon's confrontation with Governor Berkeley in the House of Burgesses.

   Divide tasks among members of the group. Report the story. Give the background on the story. That is, what led to this event? Present the point of view of each person involved in the event. As a group, describe an event that could happen today that would be like the event you have chosen for your interview.

Chapter 8
The New England Colonies

"We shall be like a city upon a hill; the eyes of all people are on us." Puritan leader John Winthrop said what many settlers in New England felt in 1630. They wanted others to see them as a strong community built on Christian beliefs. Strict Puritan values shaped almost every part of life in New England. As a result the New England colonies were different from all others in America.

1630 The town of Boston is started by 800 Puritans, including eight-year-old Anne Pollard. By the time the painting of Pollard and the map (above) were done in 1720, Boston had become the largest city in New England.

1661 The first Bible printed in North America is published in Cambridge, Massachusetts.

1625	1650	1675

1630

During this period shoes like these were worn by farmers in New England. They show how simply New Englanders lived.

During this time meetinghouses were found at the center of almost every town and village in New England.

1698 *The Bay Psalm Book,* a collection of religious songs, is the first music published in North America.

1730

L E S S O N 1

The Puritans Come to America

THINKING FOCUS

How did the religious beliefs of the New England settlers affect their way of life?

Key Terms

- covenant
- meetinghouse
- common

➤ John Winthrop became the first governor of the Massachusetts Bay Colony in 1629. He served as governor 12 times until his death in 1648.

The *Arbella* pitched and rolled on the dark waves. On board, 100 weary, seasick passengers gathered to pray. Before their ship left England in 1630, the settlers had named John Winthrop their leader. Now, as a North Atlantic storm tossed their ship from side to side, he reminded them of their Christian duty to each other:

We must love one another with a pure heart. We must bear one another's burdens, we must not look only on our own things, but also on the things of our brethren.

We must delight in each other, make others' conditions our own, rejoice together, mourn together, labor and suffer together: always having before our eyes our . . . community as members of the same body.

Puritan Beliefs

The passengers on the *Arbella* were Puritans, people who wanted to reform the Church of England. They were called Puritans because they wanted to purify, or rid, their religion of Catholic influences.

The Puritans objected to grand ceremonies and statues in church. They also believed that good Christians should follow the teachings of the Bible and strictly observe the Sabbath. In England,

The church on the left was built in Vermont in 1763. The church below, Saint Paul's in London, was completed in 1710. In which church would a Puritan be more comfortable? Why?

This letter, ink pot, and quill pen all belonged to John Winthrop. The letter is addressed "To my very Loving Husband John . . . " at a house in London. It contains news about the governor's family and the Puritan colony.

many non-Puritans preferred to dance or play cards rather than worship on the Sabbath. Such behavior shocked the Puritans.

The Puritans also believed that the Anglican church was wrong to insist that their ministers obey the rulings of the bishops. According to the Puritans, each church or congregation of worshipers should be able to choose its own minister and run its own affairs. This belief is called congregationalism.

The Puritans hoped that God would enter into a **covenant,** or agreement, with them, as He had with people in the Bible. If the Puritan colony grew and was successful, that would show that God did indeed favor them as a chosen people. Their first concern in life would be to do God's will and lead model Christian lives. Over time, the Puritans believed, their community would be copied by people throughout the New England Colonies. If they broke their covenant with God by disobeying Him, God would severely punish or even destroy the whole community. ■

■ What disagreements did Puritans have with the Church of England?

The New England Colonies

The Puritan Community

John Winthrop and 700 other people came to Massachusetts in 1630. They were the first of thousands of Puritans to settle in the Massachusetts Bay Colony. For 13 years, small ships like the *Arbella* sailed from England bringing hopeful settlers to the forested New England shores.

Settling the Land

When the ships were unloaded, the Puritans would set up camp in temporary shelters, similar to those the local Indians used. The new arrivals would camp out while their leaders arranged for a permanent settlement.

The leaders of the group would apply for a charter from colonial officials to start a new town. They would also draw up a covenant which outlined how the people would live together.

The newcomers hoped to find fertile land near pure, running water. Ten square miles would be enough to start a town. Each family head would be given several hundred acres of farmland outside the center of town. This would be enough land for each family to farm with plenty left over to pass on to grown sons.

Building Towns

Even though they farmed, the Puritans still lived together in towns so that they could help one another. In this way, the Puritans built strong communities and kept their covenant with God.

In most Puritan towns, the settlers built a **meetinghouse,** the

The homes in a typical Puritan village were built fairly close together. Fences kept the animals out of the fields.

Meetinghouse

Fields

School

Common

Ox pasture

Fields

Cow pasture

town's largest and most important building. The meetinghouse was a gathering place for religious services, celebrations, and news.

In front of the meetinghouse was a large open pasture called a **common,** which belonged to everyone. Here the townspeople could bring their livestock to graze.

Puritan families built their homes around the common on plots of land provided by the town. Most plots were large enough to include a house, a barn, and a small vegetable garden. Nearly every family also owned some land at the edge of town where they raised corn, wheat, or oats. ■

■ *Why did the Puritans live together in towns?*

Puritans and the Land

In New England the Puritan settlers were sure they had found a land that showed their special favor with God. The evergreen and hardwood forests were full of wildlife—deer, squirrels, rabbits, and other animals. Rivers, streams, and the ocean were filled with fish and other seafood.

The Puritans believed that the difficult parts of their lives were also signs from God. The cold winters and rocky soil of New England clearly meant that God wanted the Puritans to work hard together as thanks for His gift of salvation.

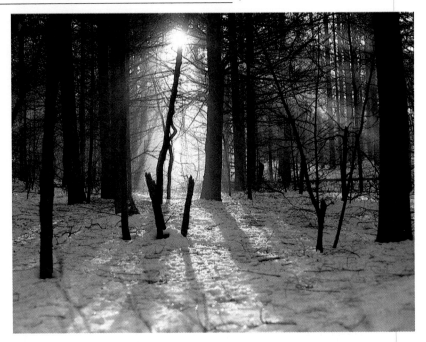

The Puritans Prosper

The Puritans were lucky to have moved to a healthy place. They had clean water from many fast-moving streams. The population in Massachusetts boomed. Soon the colony had more people than any other in English America.

Despite the healthy environment, most New Englanders did not become wealthy from farming, as the Virginia tobacco planters did. The Puritans managed to grow enough food to feed themselves, but the soil was too thin and rocky for large-scale farming.

Some settlers turned to crafts and trading to make a living. Every town had some craftspeople—men and women who made tools, home furnishings, and other equipment. Although families made their clothes, tools, soap, candles, and other everyday goods at home, it was easier to buy some goods. Blacksmiths made both horseshoes and ox-shoes. Whitesmiths made tin candleholders and tinderboxes. Joiners

▲ *Harsh but often beautiful landscapes faced the Puritans in New England winters.*

◄ *The Puritans used this cranberry rake to gather ripe berries that had fallen to the ground.*

183

Settlement in New England, 1650-1750

➤ *This map shows how Puritan settlements grew along the East Coast of what is now the United States. The Puritans established many coastal communities, including Boston, Newport, and New Haven.*

Vermont (claimed by N.Y. and N.H.)

Maine (part of Mass.)

New York

New Hampshire

•Falmouth

ATLANTIC OCEAN

•Portsmouth

Massachusetts

•Salem
•Boston

0   75 mi.
0   75 km
Lambert Conformal Conic Projection

•Plymouth

Hartford•

Providence•
R.I.

Connecticut

Newport•

New Haven

Settled before 1650

Settled 1650–1750

Settled 1700–1750

How Do We Know?

HISTORY *Ships' records reveal that the Puritans brought animals and supplies with them when they sailed to Massachusetts. They also brought military equipment, including armor and swords. They thought that they might have to defend their new homes from Indians.*

➤ *Life in the New England colonies could be harsh. Still, New Englanders enjoyed a much longer life expectancy than did the people in the southern colonies or Great Britain.*

Life Expectancy of 20-Year-Old Males, 1650

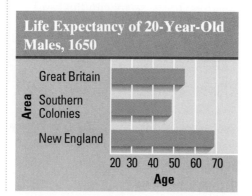

Great Britain

Southern Colonies

New England

Area

20 30 40 50 60 70
Age

fashioned furniture from wood. Cobblers repaired shoes. Cobblers who were good at their craft became cordwainers, or shoemakers.

Some settlers turned to fishing, shipbuilding, or trading to make a living. By 1664, Boston's population depended on shipping, fishing, and trading—not farming—for their livelihood.

Two Views of Nature

To the Puritans, the dense forests and rocky land of New England were wild and filled with temptation. They felt their duty was to tame nature. They cleared land, planted crops, and put up fences. They also caught, killed, and traded wild animals.

The Puritan attitude toward the land was very different from that of the Algonquin Indians. The Algonquins were comfortable with nature just as it was. They survived by fishing, farming, and hunting. They moved around the land in harmony with the seasons. In the summer they lived near the fields that the women had planted. Come winter, they set up temporary shelters in a protected location. When spring arrived, they camped near a river, so they could fish. After about 10 years in one place, the Algonquins would move on to more fertile land where wood was again plentiful.

Because they moved often and did not have horses or wagons, the Algonquins owned very little property. All they carried with them were bows, spears, planting sticks, and animal skins. The Algonquins

October–
March

March–
October

Migration

Migration

did not have a strong sense of personal property or of ownership of the land.

The Puritans misunderstood the Algonquin way of life. They thought that the Algonquins were lazy. They had not "settled" the land and, thus, did not own it. Because the two groups lived differently on the land, they did not get along well together. For example, Puritans would let their pigs and cattle roam freely to find food. They did not have to worry about these animals ruining their crops, because they fenced in their crop land. The pigs and cows did ruin Algonquin crops, however. The Algonquins did not believe in fencing their land. Small annoyances like this soon became big problems. Tensions grew, tempers flared, and eventually war broke out between the two groups. ■

▲ *As you can see in this illustration, the Algonquin Indians lived in harmony with the land.*

■ *How did the Puritans and the Algonquins view nature?*

R E V I E W

1. **FOCUS** How did the religious beliefs of the New England settlers affect their way of life?

2. **CONNECT** Why did many of Virginia's farmers become wealthier than farmers in New England?

3. **BELIEF SYSTEMS** Summarize the basic religious beliefs of the Puritans.

4. **SOCIAL SYSTEMS** Describe the Puritan communities. Why did they form their communities as they did?

5. **CRITICAL THINKING** Think about the ways the Puritans and the Algonquins lived. Why did their different ways of life lead to tensions between the two groups?

6. **ACTIVITY** Make a two-column chart comparing the attitudes of the Puritans and the attitudes of the Algonquin Indians about the land.

185

The New England Colonies

Life in New England

THINKING
F O C U S

What was everyday life like for the New England colonists?

Key Term

- apprentice

> *W*ork in that household never ceased. . . . The pewter mugs had to be scoured with reeds and fine sand. There was a great kettle of soap boiling over a fire just behind the house, and all day long Judith and her mother took turns stirring it with a long stick. Judith set Kit to tend the stirring while she readied the soap barrel. Kit tried to keep a gingerly distance from the kettle. The strong fumes of lye [from the kettle] stung her eyelids and stirring the heavy mass tired her arms and shoulders. Her stirring became more and more halfhearted till Judith snatched the stick in exasperation. "It will lump on you," she scolded, "and you can just blame yourself if we have to use lumpy soap all summer."
>
> Elizabeth George Speare,
> *The Witch of Blackbird Pond*

Like Judith and Kit in Elizabeth Speare's story, Puritan children in the Massachusetts Bay Colony worked as hard as their parents. After age six, they even dressed like adults, as you can see in the painting on page 187. In fact, Puritan society looked upon its children as serious and responsible persons. Puritan children were treated rather like miniature adults.

Children in the Puritan Family

Puritan parents were warm and loving. However, they were always concerned that their children grow up in godly ways. Parents believed that any sinful ways in their children had to be disciplined.

According to Puritan beliefs, children were born "full of sin, as full as a toad is of poison." So parents took their duties seriously and sometimes were quite strict. Puritan parents might beat their children for laziness or disrespect or for running and jumping on the Sabbath. They believed that a child is "better whipped, than damned" by the devil.

For their part, Puritan children were expected to honor their parents. In 1772, a Puritan named

The Mason children— David, Joanna, and Abigail—posed for this oil portrait in 1670. They are dressed in typical Puritan children's clothing.

Eleazer Moody wrote a book called *The School of Good Manners.* In his book, Moody set down some rules describing good behavior for Puritan children:

Approach near thy parents at no time without a bow.

Dispute not, nor delay to obey thy parents commands.

Go not out of doors without thy parents leave, and return within the time by them limited.

Quarrel not nor contend with thy brethren or sisters, but live in love, peace, and unity.

Beware thou utter not any thing hard to be believed.

Let thy words be modest about those things which only concern thee.

Even though Puritan parents were strict, they tried hard to be good parents. They felt that they had to guard against spoiling their children. For this reason, they often sent their children away at age 13 to live with relatives or friends. The children spent several years as **apprentices,** learning skills such as weaving or carpentry.

Most Puritans were educated people, more so than other groups of people who came to America. They knew how to read and write and taught their children to do so as well. See the Moment in Time on the next page to learn more about Puritan children.

This hornbook wasn't really a book at all. The alphabet is written on parchment, which is attached to a wooden paddle. A thin, transparent sheet of horn protects the parchment so the "book," which was used to teach reading, would last a long time.

Puritan Girl

10:19 A.M., September 23, 1647
Dorchester, Massachusetts

Hat
She almost forgot it when she ran out to collect bayberries this morning. Her mother scolded her by quoting a Bible passage that says a woman must be modest in her dress.

Collar
Like her hat, it's worn only when she goes outdoors.

Bayberries
The sweet–smelling fruit grows on a low bush, down the hill from her house. She'll collect several baskets for scented candles.

Apron
Made of Dutch linen, her apron is a smaller version of the ones grown women wear.

Doll
She talks softly to the corncob doll she sneaked into her basket. Her mother talks the same way to her newest brother, who is two months old.

Dress
Just like her mother's, her dress fastens down the front with hooks and eyes. She would dearly love a dress with buttons, but her father says buttons are too fancy.

Ash Smudge
Her apron hides a new smudge on the knee of her dress. Each day it's her job to clean the fireplace and collect ashes for soapmaking.

The Puritans thought of reading as a religious skill, because studying the Bible was so important. Not learning to read was "one chief project of that old deluder [deceiver], Satan, to keep men from the knowledge of the Scriptures."

Some children learned their lessons at home. Some went to school. There they studied the Lord's Prayer and learned the alphabet from hornbooks. Boys who were going to be ministers always attended school. In 1636, the Puritans founded Harvard, the first college in America, for training Puritan ministers. ■

■ *How did Puritan parents raise their children?*

Puritan Family Life

The Puritans felt that God wanted everyone to live in a family, and almost all Puritans did. Families were large. Some had as many as 15 children.

The Family Home

Most Puritan families lived in small, two-story houses made of wood. Each had a large downstairs room called the hall or keeping room. This was the only room in the house where the fireplace was kept going all the time. Families gathered in this room to eat, do chores, and study. In winter, they slept there.

If you were to visit a family in their hall, you would see a few pieces of simple furniture. The furniture would include a wicker cradle, a few ladder-back chairs, and an oak table. There would also be a stool, a spinning wheel, and a chest with a hinged lid. You might see a kettle and a bean pot near the fireplace. The fire would warm and light the room. In the summer, candles provided light.

Family Closeness

Puritan families lived and worked closely together. They passed on their way of life from

Across Time & Space

The public school system in the United States today can trace its beginnings to Massachusetts. In 1647, the Massachusetts Bay Colony set up a public school system supported by taxes.

The New England Colonies

➤ *The fireplace in the great hall of this reconstructed Puritan house both warmed the room and served as a cooking area.*

▼ *This oak footwarmer helped the Puritans to stay warm during the cold New England winters. Hot coals were placed inside and the heat came up through a grating on the top, where one's feet rested. This footwarmer has a handle on it so it could be carried to church.*

■ *Why did Puritan families live so closely together?*

one generation to the next. Boys learned from their fathers how to cultivate oats, wheat, and other crops. They also learned how to care for livestock. Girls learned from their mothers how to make candles and soap and also how to cook, sew, and care for children.

When a young man reached the age of about 23, he would ask his parents for permission to marry. When a son married, his father would give him a piece of the family's land. As the years passed, each family divided its land among several sons. After three or four generations, the land had been divided many times. The plots often were too small to farm.

With no land to work, sons began to move away from their towns in the countryside to find jobs in the cities or at sea. Sometimes they looked for land to farm farther north or west. In the late 1600s, the people of New England began to wonder whether Puritanism could survive if children continued to move away from their families and their home towns. ■

R E V I E W

1. **FOCUS** What was everyday life like for the New England colonists?
2. **CONNECT** How did life in a typical Puritan town compare to that on a southern plantation? In what ways was it similar? How was it different?
3. **HISTORY** In Puritan families, land passed from fathers to sons. How did this practice eventually cause some Puritan families to move apart?
4. **CRITICAL THINKING** Look again at Eleazer Moody's rules for Puritan children on page 187. In what ways are these rules similar to the ones children are expected to follow today?
5. **ACTIVITY** Make a chart that compares and contrasts Puritan family life with modern family life.

L E S S O N   3

Challenging Authority

A nne was delighted at this unexpected visit by her Reverend Cotton. He said he had come to ask her about the weekly meetings she was holding with many of the women in the colony. Just what did they find to talk about?

    She answered willingly. It was mainly the sermons of the preceding Sunday, the way the men did when they got together. . . . What else did Mistress Hutchinson and her women discuss?

    Why, said Anne, that each of them had the Holy Spirit within herself, and when hard-pressed, they had but to open their Bibles and God might speak to them directly through His Word.

    Cotton could hardly believe his ears. He said she must not preach such things anymore. It was the purpose of the ministers to interpret the Word.

Deborah Crawford, Four Women in a Violent Time, 1970

THINKING FOCUS

What conflicts erupted in Puritan society?

Key Terms

- democracy
- dissenter
- civil disobedience
- Great Awakening

The meeting between Anne Hutchinson and Reverend Cotton told about in this story actually took place. Anne Hutchinson was the wife of a merchant and the mother of seven children. She questioned the teachings of the ministers of the Massachusetts Bay Colony. In spite of its careful organization, the colony was soon torn by disagreement and religious conflict.

Religion and the Government

Many problems in Puritan society had to do with the relationship between the people's religion and their government. Government was to be separate from the church. Ministers, for example, could not hold political office. Even so, religion played a big role in government.

Puritan leaders did not believe in **democracy,** or rule by the will of the majority. Governor John Winthrop called democracy "the worst of all forms of Government." Winthrop believed that some men were more godly than others, and these men should have more power.

▼ *This title page is from an 1862 reprint of a book of psalms first printed in the Massachusetts Bay Colony.*

A
LITERAL REPRINT
OF THE
BAY PSALM BOOK
BEING THE
EARLIEST NEW ENGLAND VERSION
OF THE
PSALMS

In Puritan society, all the people in the colony did not vote. Only male church members could vote. Church membership was open only to those who had been admitted by other members. In this way, the colony was ruled by men who governed according to the Bible and Puritan beliefs.

Also, the Puritans did not allow any form of religious freedom. They believed that all religions other than their own were wrong and sinful in the eyes of God. For this reason, Puritans punished and banished, or sent away, people such as Quakers who did not live their lives according to Puritan beliefs. ■

➤ *This detail from an appliqué quilt shows how the church was at the center of New England life.*

■ *Why did the Puritans not believe in freedom of religion?*

UNDERSTANDING DISSENT

Roger Williams and Anne Hutchinson were not the only dissenters in America's past. Dissent has occurred throughout our country's history.

Dissent and Protest

Dissent is disagreement with established policies and speaking out about that disagreement. Anne Hutchinson disagreed with Puritan religious beliefs, and she made her views known.

When dissent is especially strong, it may take the form of protest. Protest is action meant to change established policies.

Dissent Changes History

Dr. Martin Luther King, Jr. was a Baptist minister from the South who, during the 1950s and 1960s, disagreed with many established policies toward black Americans. For example, many blacks were not allowed to vote, even though the Constitution gave them that right. In some states, blacks were not allowed to eat at the same lunch counters as whites.

Dr. King made his views on these policies known. Because his disagreement was so strong, he urged his followers to protest. They tried to register to vote. They sat down at "whites-only" lunch counters.

Because of these protests, official government policies were changed. Congress passed the Civil Rights Acts of 1964 and 1968. Because of his dissent, Dr. King, like Roger Williams and Anne Hutchinson before him, helped to change history.

Dissent in Puritan Society

Persons who could not vote or did not want to worship the same way as everyone else suffered in Puritan towns. Some **dissenters**—people who disagreed with the Puritans—spoke out.

Roger Williams

Roger Williams, a young minister, did not believe the government should support one religion over another. Williams said that requiring people to attend a particular church "stinks in God's nostrils." All people should be free to worship as they chose, he claimed. He even thought that nonchurch members should be allowed to vote and that Puritan officials should be more respectful to the Algonquin Indians.

Williams's beliefs made the colonial government nervous, so they asked him to change his views. He refused. In 1635, the government decided to ship Roger Williams back to England. Massasoit, an Algonquin chief of the Pokanoket tribe, helped Williams hide in the wilderness. The following year, Williams established a new colony in what is now Rhode Island, where religion and government were separate and people could worship freely.

Anne Hutchinson

Anne Hutchinson also challenged the authority of the male Puritan government. She believed in a personal relationship with God. Such a belief greatly reduced the power of the ministers. When the colony officials ordered her to stop preaching her beliefs, Anne Hutchinson practiced **civil disobedience**—that is, she refused to obey those colony laws she thought were unjust.

The ministers were especially upset that a woman would dare to disobey them. They believed that women should follow the advice of men and keep quiet. Massachusetts officials made Anne Hutchinson stand trial and then banished her from the

A KEY into the
LANGUAGE
OF
AMERICA:
OR,
An help to the Language of the Natives in that part of AMERICA, called NEW-ENGLAND.
Together, with briefe Observations of the Customes, Manners and Worships, &c. of the aforesaid Natives, in Peace and Warre, in Life and Death.
On all which are added Spirituall Observations, Generall and Particular by the Authour, of chiefe and speciall use (upon all occasions,) to all the English Inhabiting those parts; yet pleasant and profitable to the view of all men:
BY ROGER WILLIAMS of Providence in New-England.
LONDON,
by Dexter, 1643.

◄ Roger Williams was a friend to American Indians. In this book, published around 1643, he tried to translate Indian languages. He also wrote about their customs and the way they lived.

193

The New England Colonies

■ *Why were Roger Williams and Anne Hutchinson banished from the Bay Colony?*

Bay Colony. Like Roger Williams, she fled to Rhode Island. Later, she settled in Portsmouth with her followers and continued to preach her beliefs.

Hutchinson's friend, Mary Dyer, suffered a tragic end. Puritan officials hanged her for expressing her Quaker beliefs in the Puritan colony. As years went by, more and more dissenters challenged the iron-fisted control of Puritan ministers and officials. The Puritans found that punishing some dissenters did not stop others from speaking out. ■

Witchcraft in Salem

The tension in the Massachusetts Bay Colony reached a high point in 1692. Two young Puritan girls, Elizabeth and Abigail, began acting strangely. They both would scream and fall to the floor as if they were unable to control themselves. They said they saw rats and other creatures swarming around them. A colonial doctor decided that Elizabeth and Abigail were victims of witchcraft.

Many people in Salem got caught up in the witch craze. First children and then older people were calling their unpopular neighbors "witches." When a person was accused, a trial would be held in the town. Within a year, 19 people, mostly old women, were found guilty of witchcraft and hanged.

Historians are not sure why the people of Salem became so hysterical about witchcraft. Some historians believe that poor farmers accused rich merchants of being witches out of jealousy. Other historians think that Puritan officials used the popular belief about witches to get rid of

➤ *Cotton Mather, a Puritan minister, tried to explain witchcraft in his book* The Wonders of the Invisible World, *published in 1693.*

■ *Keeping in mind their belief in community, why do you think the Puritans killed suspected witches?*

outspoken older women who challenged their authority. There is even a possibility that moldy grain was the cause. Such grain might have brought on an illness in people that made them seem to be possessed by devils.

After about a year, the witchcraft craze in the New England colonies died down. During that time, however, many people suffered and died because of the Puritans' fear of the devil and their beliefs about witchcraft. ■

The Wonders of the Invisible World:

Being an Account of the

TRYALS

OF

Several Witches,

Lately Excuted in

NEW-ENGLAND:

And of several remarkable Curiosities therein Occurring.

Together with,

I. Observations upon the Nature, the Number, and the Operations of the Devils.
II. A short Narrative of a late outrage committed by a knot of Witches in Swede-Land, very much resembling, and so far explaining, that under which New-England has laboured.
III. Some Councels directing a due Improvement of the Terrible things lately done by the unusual and amazing Range of Evil-Spirits in New-England.
IV. A brief Discourse upon those Temptations which are the more ordinary Devices of Satan.

By COTTON MATHER.

Published by the Special Command of his EXCELLENCY the Governour of the Province of the Massachusetts-Bay in New-England.

Printed first, at Boston in New-England; and Reprinted at London, for John Dunton, at the Raven in the Poultry. 1693.

The Great Awakening

By the early 1700s, life in Puritan New England had changed. Dissenters such as Roger Williams and Anne Hutchinson had weakened the authority of ministers. Almost all of the original Puritan settlers were dead. Many younger Puritans preferred to live prosperous rather than religious lives. As one fish trader said, "My father came here for religion, but I came for fish."

Conservative Puritans, however, looked back fondly to the old days. Soon, new ministers caught their attention. The ministers spoke of sin in a very dramatic and emotional style and awakened the religious spirit in many people. For this reason, their religious revival is called the **Great Awakening.**

During the Great Awakening, new churches with new ideas popped up in Puritan towns. Everyone was encouraged to preach: women, servants, and even children. The sermons of ministers George Whitefield and Jonathan Edwards were more fiery than those of the old-time ministers.

The following is from Jonathan Edwards's famous sermon, *Sinners in the Hands of an Angry God.*

◄ *This portrait of the Reverend George Whitefield was painted around 1740. Reverend Whitefield was an important minister during the Great Awakening.*

T hus it is that natural men are held in the hand of God, over the pit of hell; they have deserved the fiery pit, and are already sentenced to it. . . . [T]he devil is waiting for them, hell is gaping for them, the flames gather and flash about them.

Edwards wasn't the only minister whose words struck fear in the hearts of his church members. One listener described the sermons of Whitefield as "sharper than a two-edged sword. The [listeners'] bitter cries and groans were enough to pierce the hardest heart." ■

■ *Why is the Puritan religious revival of the early 1700s called the Great Awakening?*

R E V I E W

1. **FOCUS** What conflicts erupted in Puritan society?
2. **CONNECT** Think about the way Puritan children were raised. Why would Puritan officials have believed that Elizabeth and Abigail were telling the truth about witchcraft in Salem?
3. **HISTORY** Were the governments of Puritan towns democracies? Why or why not?

4. **CRITICAL THINKING** Anne Hutchinson believed that people could speak directly to God. Why was her belief so threatening to Reverend Cotton?
5. **ACTIVITY** Imagine you live in Puritan New England and are being persecuted for your belief in religious freedom. Create a poster that explains why you believe all people should be able to worship freely.

195

Colonial Living

After dark, American colonists used candles to light their homes. Like soap, cloth, medicine, and butter, candles and other necessities were homemade.

Get Ready

You would need special tools to do many of the colonists' chores, tools that would be hard to find today. Some of the work they did was dangerous or very difficult. For a taste of Early American living, though, you can either make butter from cream or design a quilt.

To make butter you need heavy cream, a small deep bowl, and a wooden spoon or an egg-beater.

For a quilt design, you'll need graph paper and colored pencils.

Find Out

For butter-making, pour the cream into the bowl and beat it energetically until it thickens into butter. Write down how long this takes.

Your quilt should tell something about you. The squares can be plain patches of your favorite

▲ *Imagine this butter churn filled with cream to be turned into butter.*

Colonial women made candles using the fragrant wax of bayberries.

When the wax was heated, candlewicks were dipped into it, then lifted out to dry.

colors or your school colors. If you want to make the design more personal, use your initials, numbers such as your age or address, or a clue to your hobbies. A musical note says you sing or play an instrument. A cake or a spoon says you like to cook. A football or a bat suggests your favorite sport. Remember to keep your designs simple, so that they could easily be embroidered onto the quilt squares.

Move Ahead

How long did it take you to make butter from cream? Add everyone's time and find the average. Now look at the butter churn pictured here. Imagine it filled with cream. How much time and energy do you think it would take to turn all that into butter? Compare the taste of your homemade butter with the taste of the butter or margarine you usually eat.

Display your quilt designs. Can class members identify the person who designed each square? Discuss the pattern for a "class quilt." When you decide what you want to include, ask a group to draw the squares. Hang the finished design on the bulletin board.

Explore Some More

Make a list of things you use every day, things that colonists had to make for themselves. Find out how colonists cleaned their teeth, treated fevers, or preserved food.

This silk and velvet quilt dates from about 1704.

Colonists mixed animal fat with wood ash to make soap. It was usually done outside, because the boiling mixture smelled so bad.

The New England Colonies

Trade in New England

THINKING
FOCUS

What effect did trade have on New England life?

Key Terms

- merchant
- Parliament
- duty
- smuggle

Andrew Belcher, a wealthy New Englander, was a clever man. He knew that he could make money selling wheat in Boston. He also knew that people in the West Indies would pay twice as much money for his wheat as people in Boston. Why should he care if Bostonians didn't have enough wheat to make all the bread they needed?

Belcher bought wheat from local farmers and loaded it onto one of his ships in Boston harbor. The hungry people of Boston heard rumors of his plan to ship wheat to the West Indies. Furious, the people took action. One night, a group sawed through the rudder of Belcher's ship and tried to run it aground.

When Belcher heard of this, he tracked down the culprits and accused them in court of taking the law into their own hands. The men on the jury were as wealthy and important as Belcher. But they hadn't forgotten the Puritan belief that people should help each other, not just themselves. The jury declared his neighbors innocent and freed them.

▲ *Wheat grown by New England farmers helped to feed the northern colonists. It was also an important trade item.*

The Merchant Trade

Andrew Belcher was a **merchant,** someone who buys, transports, and sells goods. New England farmers couldn't produce cash crops like tobacco or sugar because of New England's rocky soil and cold climate. They needed a cash crop in order to buy manufactured goods from England.

The New England merchants established a trading system that allowed them to trade for these goods. They loaded their ships with fish and lumber from New England and tobacco and rice from the southern colonies. From Boston, the ships sailed to Europe or the Caribbean, where the

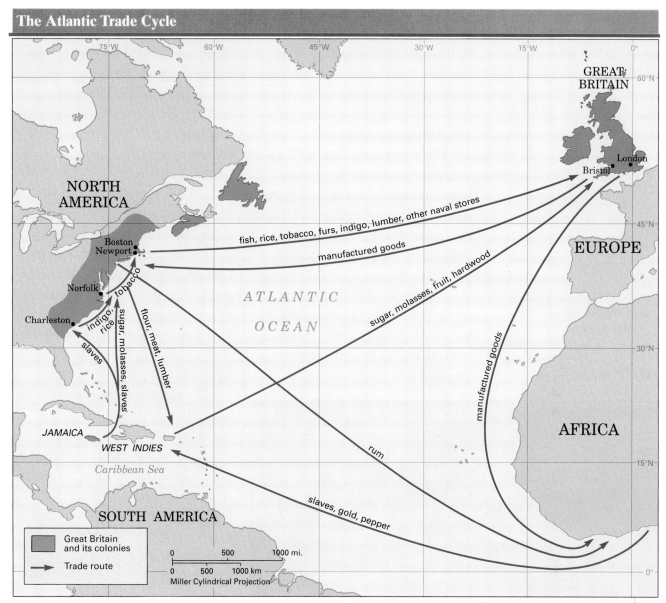

fish, rice, tobacco, furs, indigo, lumber, other naval stores

manufactured goods

sugar, molasses, fruit, hardwood

tobacco

indigo, rice

sugar, molasses, slaves

flour, meat, lumber

slaves

manufactured goods

rum

slaves, gold, pepper

NORTH AMERICA

Boston
Newport

Norfolk

Charleston

JAMAICA

WEST INDIES

Caribbean Sea

SOUTH AMERICA

ATLANTIC OCEAN

GREAT BRITAIN

London
Bristol

EUROPE

AFRICA

Great Britain and its colonies

Trade route

0   500   1000 mi.
0   500 1000 km
Miller Cylindrical Projection

merchants sold their cargoes for high profits. With these profits, the merchants bought manufactured goods like tools and glassware from England and wine, spices, coffee, and tea from other parts of the world.

Often, ships would sail between three different ports before returning to New England, as you can see on the map. A merchant might ship slaves from Africa to the Caribbean. There, he would sell the slaves and use the money he had earned to buy molasses. Next, he would ship the molasses back to New England, where distillers used it to make rum. Finally, the merchant would ship a cargo of rum to Africa and sell it. With that money, he would buy more slaves and start the cycle again. ∎

This map shows the New England merchants' trading triangle, including the usual trade routes and the goods that were bought and sold at each port.

How did the trading triangle benefit New England merchants?

Parliament and Colonial Trade

As New England merchants became successful, the English government worried that French and Dutch merchants would begin taking some of their profit. So from 1651 to 1696, the English

199

The New England Colonies

Parliament, or lawmaking body, passed a series of laws to control colonial trade.

The Navigation Acts

The Navigation Acts let England earn profits in three ways. First, the colonists had to ship their goods on English or colonial ships. No Dutch or French ship could earn money by carrying the colonies' goods.

Second, if a colonial trader wanted to buy products from any European country other than England, he had to ship the goods to England first. There he had to take everything off the ship and pay a tax to England. Then he could reload the ship and send the goods to America. He had to do the same thing when he shipped certain colonial goods, including rice and cotton, to Europe.

Finally, England demanded that the colonists pay a tax, called a **duty,** on every pound of sugar or molasses they bought in non-English colonies like the French and Dutch West Indies. These duties discouraged the colonists from buying sugar from these countries.

Smuggling Sugar

The merchants desperately needed sugar to make molasses, the main ingredient in rum. Without rum, the merchants would have a hard time trading for slaves. If the sugar became too expensive, the merchants would lose money.

The merchants preferred to buy sugar from the French or Dutch West Indies, because it was cheaper than sugar from the English West Indies. Rather than pay the high tax, many traders decided to **smuggle** the sugar, or secretly trade with the French and Dutch without paying a duty. Smugglers took risks and became richer with each success. ■

■ *How did the Navigation Acts affect the merchant trade?*

▼ *In this detail of a painting by the American artist John Greenwood, New England sea captains enjoy themselves at an inn in Surinam, on the northeast coast of South America.*

Merchants, Sailors, and Craftspeople

The richest citizens of New England were the merchants. They rode around the port cities of Massachusetts and Rhode Island in coaches pulled by fine horses. On formal occasions, they wore embroidered vests over ruffled shirts and had their hair curled and powdered. Their wives dressed in imported satins and carried silk umbrellas when they went walking.

As these merchants gained wealth they also became more powerful. By the middle 1700s,

◄ *This miniature dining room, an exact replica of the same room in the Turner-Ingersoll House, Salem, Massachusetts, 1720, shows how wealthy New Englanders lived. The elaborate porcelain bowl below was brought back from Germany as part of the merchant trade.*

merchants had replaced ministers as the most powerful people in New England society.

There would have been no rich merchants, however, without the talents of craftspeople and sailors. These people made the lifestyle of the merchants possible.

The craftspeople who supported the merchant trade included shipbuilders, sailmakers, and ropemakers. Because nearly everything was shipped in barrels, barrelmakers, or coopers, were also vital to trade. Blacksmiths forged the iron fittings for the merchants' sailing vessels.

In addition to craftspeople, sailors were needed to pilot the trading ships across the oceans. Navigators, officers, and other seafarers combined their skills to carry valuable cargoes safely to and from America's port cities. Although sailors and craftspeople never enjoyed the wealth and luxuries of the merchants, their work was vital to the success of the traders. ■

■ *How did sailors and craftspeople support the merchant trade?*

R E V I E W

1. **FOCUS** What effect did trade have on New England life?
2. **CONNECT** Compare and contrast these three ways of life: New England merchants, New England farmers, and Virginia farmers.
3. **ECONOMICS** Why was sugar an important trade item for the New England merchants?
4. **CRITICAL THINKING** Unfair taxes were one reason the colonists eventually declared their independence.

Why did the colonists think the Navigation Acts were unfair?

5. **ACTIVITY** Should Andrew Belcher have sold wheat to the West Indies when people in his native Boston were suffering from wheat shortages? Should the people of Boston have damaged Belcher's ship? Hold a debate in class, with some students defending Belcher and other students supporting the angry Bostonians.

Choosing the Right Map

Here's Why

A map uses a small space, usually on paper, to show a much larger physical area. A small-scale map gives general information about a big area. A large-scale map gives a larger picture of a small area and can show more details. Suppose you wanted to understand how a place or an event in the American Revolution related to the larger picture of the war. You could examine several maps, each drawn to a different scale. Do you know how to read different scales?

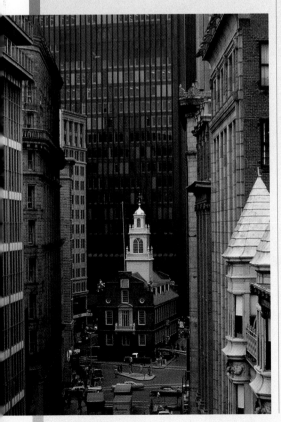

Here's How

All maps are drawn to scale. The scale can change from map to map, but it will not change within the same map. An inch on the scale might stand for 2 miles on one map, 20 miles on another map, and 200 miles on another. A large-scale map on which an inch stands for only 2 miles shows those 2 miles in much greater detail than a small-scale map on which an inch stands for 200 miles.

The picture in the bottom left corner shows the Old State House. It was built in 1713 and stands in the historic district of Boston today. You can see the modern buildings and streets around it.

Look at the maps on page 203. Each tells you something about cities settled in New England by 1750. Each map shows the city of Boston. Compare the scales on the maps.

The map of Boston has the largest scale (approximately 1 inch = $\frac{1}{2}$ mile) and gives the greatest detail. You can find the Charles River, street names, and even certain buildings in the historic district. The Old State House is one of these. You would use this kind of map to find your way in a city.

Compare the map of Boston with the map of Massachusetts (1 inch = 50 miles). The box on the map of Massachusetts outlines the area that was shown in detail in the map of Boston. The map also tells you other things. You can find other towns in Massachusetts and see how far away they are. You can also see what states border Massachusetts. You would use this kind of map to help you find cities and towns in a region.

Now look at the map of New England (1 inch = 150 miles). The box outlines the area shown in the map of Massachusetts. The scale of this map is smaller than the scale of the map of Massachusetts. For this reason, you get an even broader view of the area in which Boston is located. It shows Boston and Massachusetts in relation to all of New England and the border of Canada. It also shows important things such as the Hudson River and Lake Ontario. You would use this kind of map to find your way from one state to another.

Each map has things that are not shown in the other two. Maps of different scales can help you understand an area and the events that happened there.

Try It

Which of the three maps on this page would you use to compare the size of Massachusetts with the size of New York? Which map would help you decide if you could live in Worcester and work in Boston? Which map would you use to visit the Old State House while walking around historic Boston? Which map would you use to figure the distance for a bicycle trip from the town of Cambridge to the Paul Revere house? Explain why each map would be best for the purpose you chose it.

Apply It

Look at the maps on page 120 in your book. The larger of the two maps shows the routes of French, Dutch, and English explorers. The smaller map shows the route of the English explorer Sir Francis Drake. Which map includes more of the world? Which map contains more detailed information? Which map concentrates on only part of the world? Which map has the larger scale? Explain how you can tell.

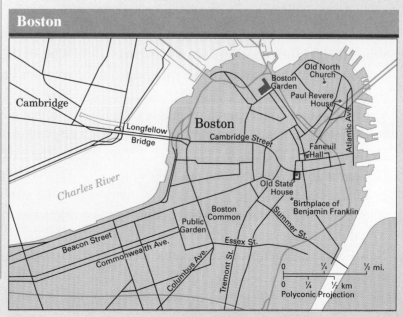

Chapter Review

Reviewing Key Terms

apprentice (p. 187)
civil disobedience (p. 193)
common (p. 183)
covenant (p. 181)
democracy (p. 191)
dissenter (p. 193)

duty (p. 200)
Great Awakening (p. 195)
meetinghouse (p. 182)
merchant (p. 198)
Parliament (p. 200)
smuggle (p. 200)

A. Write a sentence telling what role each of the following terms played in colonial New England.

1. apprentice
2. civil disobedience
3. common
4. covenant
5. democracy
6. duty
7. Great Awakening
8. meetinghouse
9. merchant
10. smuggle

B. Write a sentence to answer each question. Each sentence you write should include at least one of the key terms.

1. Who learned a craft while practicing it?
2. What did Anne Hutchinson do when Puritan officials ordered her not to preach?
3. How did Parliament discourage colonists from buying sugar in countries outside the British empire?
4. What was the religious revival in New England during the 1700s called?
5. Who passed the Navigation Acts?
6. Who bought and sold goods for profit?
7. Who disagreed with Puritan officials?

Exploring Concepts

A. On your own paper, complete the following statements using information from the chapter.

1. The passengers on the *Arbella* were called Puritans because_____.
2. Each family head was given several hundred acres of farm land in order to_____.
3. Even though they farmed, Puritans still lived together in towns since_____.
4. When their children were 13 years old, parents often sent them away to live with relatives or friends because_____.
5. The reason individual church members could not claim that God might speak directly to them was that_____.
6. Governor John Winthrop did not believe in democracy because_____.
7. The reason the Puritans punished people who did not believe in Puritanism was_____.
8. New England didn't produce valuable cash crops because_____.

B. Answer each question with information from the chapter.

1. How did the arrangement of the early Puritan towns allow the Puritans to help one another?
2. Why were there problems between the Puritan settlers and their neighbors, the Algonquin Indians?
3. Why, in the late 1600s, did Puritans wonder whether Puritanism would survive?
4. How did the Puritans make sure that their colonial government would be run according to Puritan beliefs?
5. By the early 1700s, what changes in New England society led some Puritans to turn to the ministers of the Great Awakening?
6. How did the New England trading systems work?
7. How did the power of the Puritan merchants change by the middle 1700s?

Reviewing Skills

1. Why is a city easy to show on a large-scale map, such as a road map, but hard to show in a small-scale atlas?
2. Look at the map of Boston on page 178. Suppose you were going to walk from one part of Boston to another. What scale map would you choose? What advantages does that scale have?
3. Make a timeline of these events in the history of the Massachusetts Bay Colony.
   - In 1635, the Puritan government decides to ship dissenter, Roger Williams, back to England.
   - A Quaker, Mary Dyer, is hanged in 1660 for expressing her religious beliefs.
   - Harvard, the first American college, is founded in 1636 to train Puritan ministers.
   - In 1651, Parliament passes the first of the Navigation Acts.
   - In 1638, Anne Hutchinson is banished from the Puritan colony for preaching her religious beliefs.
   - In 1630, the *Arbella* brings 700 Puritans from England.
   - Roger Williams establishes a community with religious freedom in 1636.
4. If you wanted to tell someone only the most important information in this chapter, what skill would you use?

Using Critical Thinking

1. Today many people find the help of family and friends necessary in reaching difficult goals. For example, parents may help children with their homework if the children are having difficulty in school. How is this kind of help similar to the way the early Puritans tried to help each other?
2. The Puritans punished people who did not share their religious beliefs. Today religious freedom is guaranteed by the First Amendment of the United States Constitution. Why is this protection necessary?
3. Read the entries from *The School of Good Manners* on page 187. Write down what you think each rule means. Then put a check after the rules you think are still important to parents today. Explain why you think each of the checked rules is still important.

Preparing for Citizenship

1. **COLLECTING INFORMATION** Read a library book about Puritan New England, such as *The Witch of Blackbird Pond* by Elizabeth George Speare. Make notes about the things you find most interesting. Use your notes to tell the class what you learned.
2. **GROUP ACTIVITY** Show how New England trading systems worked. Get a wall map of the world and make small, cut-out ships that look like the ones used in the 1600s and 1700s. Show where the merchants traded and tell what products they bought and sold.
3. **COLLABORATIVE LEARNING** Put on skits about different aspects of Puritan life. Form groups of three or four to decide what aspect each group will act out. Plan to have each member play a part in the skit and write his or her own lines. First meet in your group to plan how to work. For example, different members may look up information, write an outline for the skit, and make props, costumes, and scenery. Get back together as a group to share information and write your lines. Present the skit for the class.

Chapter 9
The Middle Colonies

When William Penn, a Quaker, founded Pennsylvania in 1681, he promised settlers they could worship in any way they wished. People from all over Europe—Dutch, Germans, Swedes, and others—flocked to Pennsylvania because of the offer of religious liberty. This mix of people helped Pennsylvania and other Middle Colonies grow and prosper.

During this period William Penn promised to deal fairly with American Indians living in Pennsylvania. He even put an image of an Indian on the colonial seal.

1650	1675	1700

1681

1688 Pennsylvania Quakers declare that they oppose slavery. Their statement is one of the first protests against slavery in America.

During this time immigrants brought the customs of their homelands to the Middle Colonies. German sayings and designs cover this shaving dish made in Pennsylvania in 1750.

1735 Martin Van Bergen, a Dutch settler in New York, hangs this painting of his farm. It shows the wealth many families enjoyed in the Middle Colonies.

1725

1750

1775

1728 Jewish colonists in New York City build the first synagogue in America.

1759

LESSON 1

The Land of the Middle Colonies

THINKING FOCUS

How did the geography of the Middle Colonies affect the lives of the people?

Key Terms

- navigable
- treaty

The Dutch trader walked quietly from the forest, following the smell of squirrel meat roasting over a low fire in a clearing. The Iroquois traders had to be nearby; without a doubt, this was the camp where he was to meet them.

The trader stroked his thick beard. He smiled to himself, remembering the idea most people had of fur traders: wild, dishonest. With his dark beard, dirty fingernails, and torn clothing, he thought he probably looked the part.

After a little while, three Iroquois men appeared from out of the forest on the other side of camp. They were carrying heavy loads of beaver skins. As the men spread the skins before him, the trader checked them, running the back of his hand over the thick, smooth fur. The trader knew the skins were worth a lot of money. Because of heavy fur trading, only a few beavers were left in the colony. The Iroquois probably got these from tribes much farther west. In exchange for six furs, the trader gave the men a few pieces of English wool and rum.

Before it got too dark, the trader left the Indian camp. He traveled by canoe down the Mohawk River to the Hudson River. Then he paddled down the Hudson to a fur trading company in a big cabin in Albany. There he traded the furs for cash.

The Geography of the Middle Colonies

It was the fur trade on the Hudson River that first drew many Europeans to the Middle Colonies in the 1680s. The traders noticed that plants and trees grew well in the rich soil. Soon, other Europeans came not to trade fur, but to settle down and farm. Farming was a prosperous activity in the fertile Hudson and Delaware river valleys. Peter Kalm, a Swedish naturalist and traveler to the area, described the orchards on Middle Colony farms in 1748.

Near almost every farm was a spacious orchard full of peaches and apple trees, and in some of them the fruit was fallen from the trees in such quantities as to cover nearly the whole surface. Part of it they left to rot, since they could not take it all in and consume it.

Before they picked the fruit of such orchards, though, colonists had to find and settle their land. When they first arrived in the Middle Colonies, settlers sailed up the Hudson and Delaware rivers to find good farm land. Fortunately, both the Hudson and the Delaware were **navigable**—deep and wide enough for ships to pass—for more than 100 miles upstream. Find the Delaware and Hudson rivers on the map below. Notice that these and other rivers flow through large parts of New York and Pennsylvania. Why would these rivers be important for settlement?

▲ *Rich, fertile soil helps crops grow very well in Pennsylvania.*

▼ *From this map, identify four Middle Colonies.*

The Middle Colonies

NEW FRANCE

Lake Ontario

Lake Erie

St. Lawrence R.

Lake Champlain

Mohawk R.

Vermont (Claimed by N.Y. and N.H.)

New Hampshire

New York

Albany

Massachusetts

Connecticut R.

Connecticut

Rhode Island

Hudson R.

APPALACHIAN MOUNTAINS

Allegheny R.

Susquehanna R.

Delaware R.

New York

LONG ISLAND

ATLANTIC OCEAN

Pennsylvania

New Jersey

Philadelphia

Maryland

Potomac R.

Delaware Bay

Virginia

Delaware

0   50   100 mi.
0   50   100 km
Albers Equal-Area Projection

Middle colonies

Other English colonies

Before settlers could begin to plant, they had to clear huge oaks, cedars, and other trees from the hilly land. Clearing land was slow, hard work because settlers had only axes and other simple hand tools to use. Even so, farmers of the Middle Colonies were lucky compared to farmers in New England. Their soil was much more fertile than rocky New England soil.

The fertile soil and a good climate with warm, rainy summers meant good crops. Besides the apples and peaches that Kalm mentioned, farmers also grew vegetables: squash, pumpkins, beans, onions, cabbage, turnips, and others. They made jams and pickled fruits and vegetables for their own use. They sold to traders what was left over. The geography of the river valleys favored farming so much that farmers could raise some crops just to sell. The main cash crop in Pennsylvania was wheat. In New York, it was corn.

Farmers used rivers to move their cash crops to markets in Philadelphia and New York City. Peter Kalm described the busy Hudson River.

Farmers grew many fruits and vegetables but had difficulty storing them because they had no refrigeration or ways of canning.

■ *Why did geography make the Middle Colonies a good place to settle?*

D uring eight months of the year this river is full of yachts, and other greater and lesser vessels, either going to New York or returning from thence, laden with either inland or foreign goods.

Kalm often wrote about the usefulness of the rivers and the richness of the land. Some writers, though, were more moved by its beauty.

W hoever has made a voyage up the Hudson must remember the Kaatskill Mountains. They are a dismembered branch of the great Appalachian family, and are seen away to the west of the river, swelling up to a noble height, and lording it over the surrounding country. Every change of season, every change of weather, indeed, every hour of the day produces some change in the magical hues and shapes of these mountains; and they are regarded by all the good wives, far and near, as perfect barometers [a way to predict weather].

Washington Irving,
"Rip Van Winkle"

This opening scene from the story "Rip Van Winkle" praises the Hudson River Valley. ■

Peaceful Relations with the Indians

Settlers in the Middle Colonies did well because of the fertile land and convenient rivers. However, they also prospered because they lived on good terms with native peoples.

When William Penn arrived in Pennsylvania, he encountered the Delaware, or Lenni Lenape people as they called themselves. The Delaware promised to live "in love" with the settlers: "as long as the creeks and rivers run and while the sun, moon, and stars endure." Peaceful relations with the Delaware did not last as long as "the sun, moon, and stars endure." However, they did last almost 70 years—a longer time than in the South or New England. A pleased Penn later wrote, "I have led the greatest colony into America . . . ."

Indian Relations in Pennsylvania

William Penn strongly supported the Quaker belief that war and violence are always wrong. He wanted to treat the Delaware Indians and the other tribes in Pennsylvania fairly. To make sure the Delaware felt fairly treated, Penn paid them for the land King Charles II gave to him. According to legend, Penn also made a **treaty,** or agreement, of friendship with the Delaware chiefs in 1682. The painting below shows the treaty ceremony near Philadelphia.

▼ *Edward Hicks was a wandering Quaker minister. He painted* Penn's Treaty with the Indians *in 1830.*

■ *How did settlers of the Middle Colonies avoid war with the Indians?*

In Pennsylvania, both Indians and settlers had to be treated equally and fairly in legal matters. Penn wrote about the treatment of Indians in *Concessions to the Province of Pennsylvania* in 1681:

That no man shall, by any-ways or means, in word, or deed, affront, or wrong any Indian, but he shall incur the same penalty of the law, as if he had committed it against his fellow planter, and if any Indian shall abuse, in word, or deed, any planter of this province, that he shall not be his own judge upon the Indian, but he shall make his complaint to the governor of the province. . . . That the Indians shall have liberty to do all things relating to improvement of their ground, and providing sustenance [food] for their families, that any of the planters shall enjoy.

Indian Relations in New York

During the time of peace in Pennsylvania, Indian wars did erupt in New York. However, the powerful Iroquois assured some stability in the colony of New York. Before the Europeans arrived, five different Iroquois nations had joined to form an organized government. The Iroquois had always made a living by hunting, farming, and fishing. After the Dutch arrived, the European demand for animal furs made fur trading a rich business for the Iroquois. They got guns from the Dutch and beat their enemies. Soon the Iroquois controlled the fur trade in a large area: from Maine to Michigan; from the St. Lawrence River in the north to as far south as Virginia.

Settlers and fur traders stood in awe of the Iroquois. For a time, no one dared challenge their control. The Iroquois kept control by playing the English against the French in order to avoid being taken over by either.

For a time, the English in New York were glad to have Iroquois protection from the French on the northern border of the colony. Governor Thomas Dongan praised them in 1687: "Those Five nations are very brave & the awe & Dread of all ye Indyans." Remember, too, the Dutch and English fur traders made money on the furs the Iroquois passed along to them. So they tried to stay on peaceful terms. ■

REVIEW

1. **FOCUS** How did the geography of the Middle Colonies affect the lives of the people?

2. **CONNECT** Contrast farming in the Middle Colonies to farming in New England.

3. **HISTORY** Contrast the relations between European-Americans and the native people in New York and Pennsylvania.

4. **CRITICAL THINKING** How would farming life in the Middle Colonies have been different if the colonies had not been located in a river valley?

5. **WRITING ACTIVITY** Imagine that you and your parents have just come to the colony of Pennsylvania from England in order to farm. You decide to keep a diary of your experiences in Pennsylvania. Write the first five entries of your diary. Include descriptions of the people you meet and the places you see.

L E S S O N   2

A Mixture of Many Cultures

The Reverend Andrew Burnaby of Greenwich, England, toured the Middle Colonies in 1759. He noted in his "pocket-book" every "circumstance" that impressed him. The notes in his "pocket-book" or notebook, show that he was not hopeful for peace in the colonies. He thought that the mix of many cultures meant trouble.

They [the Middle Colonies] are composed of people of different nations, different manners, different religions, and different languages. They have a mutual jealousy of each other . . . Religious zeal, too, like a smothered fire, is secretly burning in the[ir] hearts . . .

But not all visitors to the Middle Colonies felt the same way

THINKING
F O C U S

Why did the Middle Colonies have so many cultural groups?

Key Terms

- diversity
- tolerance

◄ *German fraktur is beautiful lettering used to record important events, such as weddings or baptisms.*

> *Fancy needlework was popular with the English. The sampler on the right was done with silk thread on linen.*

Burnaby did about the **diversity,** or cultural and religious variety there. Peter Kalm, for example, delighted in counting all the places of worship he saw on his journey. In 1748, he noted 12 in Philadelphia alone. Though world travelers did not agree on whether or not diversity was a good thing, all agreed that it was something new.

The mixture of cultures that we enjoy in the United States today got a good start in the Middle Colonies. You can see from the everyday objects on this page that each group brought its own special traditions and skills to the Middle Colonies.

▼ *Tulips and birds, like the ones on this coffeepot and plate, were a common decoration on Pennsylvania Dutch furniture and cookware.*

Quaker Ideals and the "Holy Experiment"

William Penn called Pennsylvania a "holy experiment" because the colony was based on a religious belief in **tolerance**—a respect for differences. As you know, experiments do not always succeed. No one knew for sure whether or not the many different peoples who settled in the Middle Colonies could live together in peace.

When William Penn set out to plan his colony, he was inspired by the ideals of his Quaker religion. He remembered that English officials had put Quakers in jail in England. William Penn wanted to make sure that people of all religions would be able to worship freely in Pennsylvania.

Quakers truly respected differences. They believed in the spiritual equality of all people. Their strong belief in equality led them to dress and act differently from most people. They wore plain black clothes without jewelry. They thought fancy dress showed special privileges. They didn't take off their hats to greet important people. Because of this, people in 17th-century England felt that Quakers had bad manners.

Quakers called everyone by the words "thee" and "thou," instead of using "thee" and "thou" for servants and children, and "you" for important adults, as was the custom. They believed that all people were equal and that no one should receive special treatment. William Penn even called King Charles II "friend Charles" instead of "Your Majesty."

214

Not everyone who came to settle in Pennsylvania agreed with Quaker beliefs. However, people of many different religions and nationalities believed that they would be treated fairly in the Quaker colony. Pennsylvania would not be a place only for English Quakers but for everyone who wanted to live in peace.

Penn's government gave citizens more power than in any of the other colonies. Most free males could vote for the Assembly, which made new laws. However, the king of England did have some say in the affairs of the colony. And laws did have to be approved by Penn or his appointed governor.

Although Penn's ideas and policies were very fair, democracy and tolerance in Pennsylvania were not perfect. Women, who often spoke forcefully at Quaker meetings, could not vote for Assembly members. Slavery existed in Pennsylvania. Even William Penn had a few slaves. So everything was not fair or just. However, Penn's holy experiment proved to be a step forward for American democracy. ■

■ *How did the beliefs of the Quakers affect life in Pennsylvania?*

▼ *Many paintings by Edward Hicks illustrate peaceful Quaker farm life.*

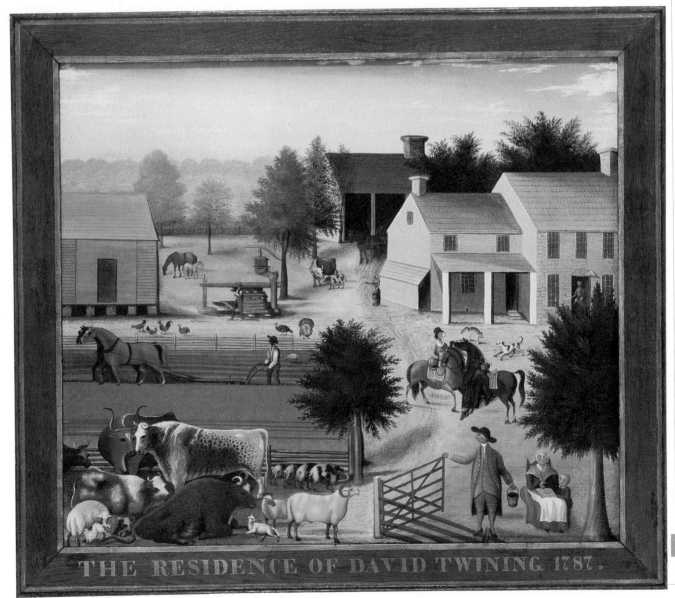

THE RESIDENCE OF DAVID TWINING 1787.

Immigration to the Middle Colonies

➤ *Travelers distributed William Penn's pamphlets all over Europe, so that many different kinds of people would know of the opportunities in Pennsylvania.*

William Penn was eager to spread the word about the benefits of his colony and attract more settlers. So he advertised Pennsylvania in several pamphlets such as the one on this page. He described Philadelphia in this way:

> The town is well-furnished with convenient mills; and what with their garden plats (the least half an acre), the fish of the river, and their labour to the countryman who begins to pay with the provisions of his own growth, they live comfortably.

Other settlers also spread the good news about Pennsylvania.

A brief Account of the **Province of Pennsylvania,** Lately Granted by the **KING,** Under the GREAT Seal of England, TO **WILLIAM PENN** AND HIS Heirs and Assigns.

UNDERSTANDING TOLERANCE

In 1750, a German traveler to Pennsylvania wrote, "That colony possesses great liberties above all other English colonies, inasmuch as all religious sects are tolerated there." Indeed, Pennsylvania's tolerance attracted settlers from many different religious and ethnic groups.

Respecting Differences

Tolerance means respecting another's beliefs and practices even though they are different from yours. It doesn't mean agreeing with someone's beliefs or even necessarily understanding them. As Voltaire *(vohl TAIR),* a famous French philosopher, said, "I disapprove of what you say but I will defend to the death your right to say it."

Benefits of Tolerance

The United States has been called a great melting pot, meaning that our country is a mixture of people from many different backgrounds. The United States is probably much more like a smorgasbord. This is a Swedish feast with many separate, wonderful kinds of food.

Practicing tolerance can keep peace and lead to prosperity. Today, for example, tolerance of different ways of life gives us lively cities filled with many types of music, food, and cultural events. In the colony of Pennsylvania, settlers enjoyed peace with the Indians because Quakers believed in tolerance and went out of their way to be fair to all groups.

Settlers often wrote letters home, urging friends and relatives to come. Here is what one Irish settler wrote to his sister Mary Valentine:

> *Land is of all prices . . . & Grows dearer every year by Reason of Vast Quantities of People that come here yearly from several Parts of the world, therefore thee & thy family or any that I wish well I wod [would] desire to make what Speed you can to come here the Sooner the better. We have traveled over a Pretty deal of this country . . . yet my father being curious & somewhat hard to Please Did not buy any Land until the Second day of 10th mo: Last and then he bought a Tract of Land consisting of five hundred Acres for which he gave 350 pounds. It is excellent good land.*
>
> Robert Parke, letter dated 1725

Letters, pamphlets, and even poems attracted Lutherans, Jews, Baptists, Amish, and other religious groups to Pennsylvania.

They came to be farmers or to work as indentured servants. By 1707, the colony numbered 20,000 settlers.

Immigrants from many nations sailed to the colony of New York, too. When it was still the Dutch colony of New Netherlands, a variety of people besides the Dutch settled the land: French Huguenots (*HYOO guh nahts*), Walloons from what is now Belgium, Swedes, Portuguese, Finns, English, and Africans. Early English and Dutch visitors to New York often wrote poems and letters home praising the colony. One poem written by Jacob Steendam, called "In Praise of New Netherlands," compared New York to the Garden of Eden. Letters encouraged friends and relatives to move to New York. One Englishman wrote, "The Country itself sends forth such a fragrant smell that it may be perceived [noticed] at Sea." ■

Across Time & Space

The state advertising slogan of Pennsylvania is "You've Got a Friend in Pennsylvania." "Friends" is another word for Quakers. The slogan also means that Pennsylvania has always thought of itself as a place that welcomes many kinds of people. Its biggest city, Philadelphia, is known as the City of Brotherly Love.

■ *What caused people to settle in the Middle Colonies?*

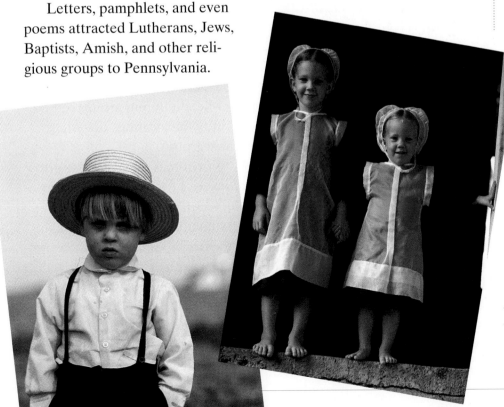

◄ *Amish people arrived in Pennsylvania in the 1720s from Switzerland and Germany. Like the children in these modern photographs, they wore plain clothes with no decorations.*

217

The Middle Colonies

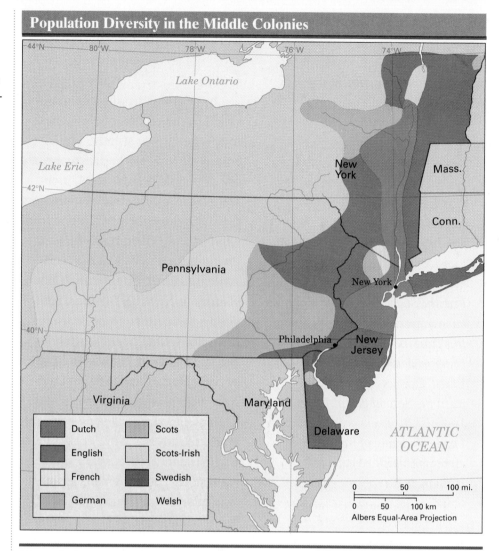

Population Diversity in the Middle Colonies

Legend:
- Dutch
- English
- French
- German
- Scots
- Scots-Irish
- Swedish
- Welsh

Albers Equal-Area Projection

Problems Among Different Groups

Although many ethnic groups lived in the Middle Colonies and tried to get along, they didn't always succeed. Also, they often didn't live near or get to know one another. They lived separately, in part, because of the way William Penn sold the land.

When William Penn advertised his land in Europe, he often promised each group a certain section of land where they could settle together and run their own community. For example, Quakers from Wales settled along the Schuylkill *(SKOOL kihl)* River. And one German group settled north of the Schuylkill. Look at the map showing where different groups settled. Identify the locations of various ethnic groups.

Sometimes ethnic groups got angry with each other. For example, German settlers, who became very numerous, tended to stick together and to speak only their own language. The Germans demanded more representatives in the Assembly. The Quakers did not like the growing power of the Germans. Such tensions among European settlers and between settlers and Indians disappointed William Penn.

After Penn died, settlers pushed the Delaware and other tribes farther and farther west. In 1748, Peter Kalm noted in his journal that "it is very possible for a person to have been to Philadelphia . . . for half a year together without so much as seeing an Indian."

New settlers, especially those on the frontier, did not share Penn's ideals and were eager to get new land. They took over Delaware and Iroquois lands in unfair ways. In 1742, the chief Canassateego (kuh nas uh TEE go) spoke against this unfair treatment:

> We know our lands are now become more valuable. The white people think we do not know their value; but we are sensible that the land is everlasting, and the few goods we receive for it are soon worn out and gone.

In addition to being driven west, many Indians died from smallpox and measles—diseases the settlers brought with them. At the time of the first English settlement, there were about 15,000 Indians in Pennsylvania. By 1790, only about 1,000 remained.

This anti-Quaker cartoon criticizes the Quakers for not considering the Bible holier than other books. The cartoon was an illustration for a poem written against Quakers in 1675.

In New York, as in Pennsylvania, ethnic problems flared up. The two largest groups, English and Dutch, often argued. When the English gained control, they let the Dutch keep speaking their own language and attending the Dutch Reformed Church. The English practiced tolerance by allowing these freedoms. However, since the two groups lived separately, they sometimes didn't understand each other.

Also, the poor people and the rich often clashed. A few rich Dutch owned most of the land. The British allowed these important landowners to keep their land. The British even lowered their taxes in order to gain their support for British rule. As a result, the poor Dutch often hated the rich Dutch as well as the British. ■

■ Why didn't settlers always get along together in the Middle Colonies?

R E V I E W

1. **FOCUS** Why did the Middle Colonies have so many cultural groups?
2. **CONNECT** Compare and contrast tolerance in the Middle and Southern Colonies and New England.
3. **HISTORY** What conditions in Pennsylvania and New York led to ethnic tensions?
4. **CRITICAL THINKING** Some people believe that ethnic tension in Pennsylvania proved that Penn's experiment had failed. Analyze this opinion and then form your own.
5. **ACTIVITY** Draw a map like the one on page 218, showing the ethnic variety in your town, county, or state.

What's the Big Idea, Ben Franklin?

Jean Fritz

Benjamin Franklin is known for his many contributions to American life and history. This story tells how Franklin developed some of his inventions and ideas. As you read, see if you can describe how Franklin was able to find work he liked. What did his father do to help him get work? Do you think Franklin's life was anything like the lives of people you know?

You have read about life in the middle colonies in this chapter. Now read about Ben Franklin, who lived and worked there.

Leather Apron a person who works with his hands
Latin School a private school, teaching Latin and Greek
pulpit a raised platform for a preacher

Benjamin was Mr. Franklin's 10th and last son. He was the youngest son of a youngest son of a youngest son of a youngest son—right back to his great-great grandfather. This made him special, Mr. Franklin thought. Besides, Benjamin was smart. Maybe he shouldn't be just another Leather Apron when he grew up.

No, Mr. Franklin decided, he shouldn't. Benjamin would be a preacher. He'd go to Latin School, then he'd go to college, then he'd climb up into a pulpit and make his father proud. So when he was 7 years old, off he went to Latin School. At the end of the year Benjamin was at the head of his class.

But he was only 8 years old. Mr. Franklin thought of all the years it would take to make Benjamin a preacher. And all the money! Besides, Mr. Franklin had been taking notice of preachers lately, especially young preachers in small churches. They had a hard time. Some went around with holes in their shoes. Now Mr. Franklin wasn't going to wait all those years and spend all that money just to have Benjamin climb up into a pulpit with holes in his shoes.

So he took Benjamin out of Latin School and put him into an ordinary writing and arithmetic school for 2 years. When Benjamin was 10, Mr. Franklin took him out of school altogether. He was old enough now to run errands, to deliver soap, to dip candles. When he was 12 years old, they'd decide what kind of a Leather Apron man he would be. Then he'd become an apprentice and learn the trade.

Benjamin didn't mind becoming a Leather Apron, but he did

dip candles to make candles
apprentice a person learning a trade from a skilled craftsman

mind becoming an apprentice. And no wonder. An apprentice had to sign a paper saying he would obey his master until he was 21 years old; he would keep his master's secrets; he would be on duty as his master demanded both day and night. In other words, an apprentice lost 9 good years of freedom to learn a trade that Benjamin thought he could learn in far less time. And if there was one thing that Benjamin liked, it was his freedom.

So when he was 12 years old, Benjamin told his father that he might go to sea.

His father didn't care for that idea. Look what happened to his brother Josiah when he went to sea, Mr. Franklin said. If Benjamin didn't want to be an apprentice, he should stay home and go into the soap and candle business.

Josiah ran away from home and drowned at sea

But Benjamin didn't care for soap and candles. Besides, look what happened to his brother Ebenezer in the soapsuds.

Ebenezer drowned in a tub of his father's soapsuds, 16 months old

Of course Benjamin knew his father had a good business. His candles sold well. Even the night watchmen in Boston carried Mr. Franklin's candles on their rounds. And his soap sold well. Barbers said it made the best lather for shaving. Housewives said it was so mild that it could be used on scarlet cloth.

scarlet bright reddish-orange color

There was, however, one thing wrong with the business. It smelled. The hot stale grease that was used to make candles had a disgusting smell. The boiling lye that was used to make soap had a sharp, nasty smell and it stung a person's nose. Benjamin was determined he was not going to spend his life smelling those smells.

lye a liquid made from wood ashes, important to making soap

So Mr. Franklin took Benjamin to different shops to show him how hatters made hats, how cutlers made knives, how coopers made barrels. All these trades seemed interesting to Benjamin, but to learn any of them he'd have to become an apprentice. And Benjamin said no.

In the end, after much arguing, Mr. Franklin talked Benjamin into becoming an apprentice to his brother James, a printer. It worked out just as Benjamin thought it would. He learned the printing business quickly. And there he was. Stuck until he was 21. Being an apprentice to his brother was no easier than being an apprentice to anyone else. James thought Benjamin was vain (which was probably true) and argumentative (which was undoubtedly true), and he treated Benjamin as strictly, if not more strictly, than the other apprentices.

vain proud
argumentative full of arguments

Benjamin could not bear to think of all those years going to waste. So he decided to use every spare moment to learn all he could about everything he could. He would read. He would write. He would observe. He would try out new ideas.

As a starter, he tried writing a poem. It was a long poem about the capture of Blackbeard the Pirate. He showed it to his father. Mr. Franklin thought it was a terrible poem. "Forget poetry," his

prose writing that is not a story or poetry

vegetarianism a diet of vegetables and grains

strokes movements

contradict disagree
opponent a person who disagrees with you

eels long, snakelike fish

father said. "Stick to prose."

To improve his prose style, Benjamin would read an essay, turn it into poetry, wait a few weeks, then turn the poetry back into his own prose. He found this increased his vocabulary. Later he would write letters to James' newspaper, signing them Silence Dogood so James wouldn't know he had written them.

Benjamin read a book on vegetarianism and decided to quit eating meat. He asked James to give him in cash half of what he had formerly paid for his meals. James agreed. Now Benjamin could not only eat by himself and read while he was eating, he could save some of his eating money and buy books. Many times a meal was only a biscuit, a handful of raisins, and a glass of water.

Once, Benjamin read a book about swimming that described unusual tricks and strokes. Benjamin was already an expert swimmer, but now he became even more expert.

He learned to swim on his belly while holding both hands still, to carry his left leg in his right hand, to show both his feet out of the water, to swim with his legs tied together, to sit in the water, to cut his toenails in the water, to show 4 parts of his body out of the water at the same time, to swim while holding up one leg, to put on his boots in the water, and to leap like a goat.

In order to swim faster he tried out an idea of his own. He made wooden paddles for his hands and feet. He went faster, but the paddles were so heavy that he didn't get far.

Then he tried lying on his back, holding a kite string, and letting the kite act as a sail and pull him across the pond. This was a great success. There was only one trouble. In those days boys went swimming naked. And if Benjamin didn't want to go home naked, he had to get a friend to carry his clothes to the other side of the pond. (It had to be a good friend because the pond was a mile wide.)

Benjamin studied arithmetic, which he had failed in his last year at school. He enjoyed it so much that in later years he made a hobby of constructing what he called magic squares. Each row of 8 numbers when added up and down or across equals 260. Each of the 4 bent rows also adds up to 260. The 4 corner numbers plus the 4 middle numbers add up to 260.

Benjamin also read a book on how to argue. The author said that person should not flatly contradict another person. Instead he should be polite and ask questions until at last he had brought his opponent around to contradicting himself. Benjamin tried this and found that it worked.

He read a book by an Englishman with all kinds of advice. It told, among other things, how to catch eels, how to cure deafness, and how to keep horses from having nightmares.

Benjamin loved books that told you how to do things. He

liked to figure out how a person could make work easier, life more comfortable, and at the same time get ahead in the world. He even read a book on how to be good and decided that being good was probably a practical idea.

Later he would make up a list of rules for good behavior: (1) Don't eat or drink too much, (2) Don't joke or talk too much, (3) Keep your things neat, (4) Do what you set out to do, (5) Don't spend too much money, (6) Don't waste time, (7) Be sincere, (8) Be fair, (9) Don't go to extremes, (10) Keep clean, (11) Keep calm, (12) Don't fool around with girls, (13) Don't show off. He kept a notebook in his pocket so he could mark down how he was doing. He didn't expect to be perfect. Each week he concentrated on one rule.

But Benjamin liked a good time and he seldom let his rules interfere. Once he spent 6 pennies to see the first lion ever brought to America. This was a lot of money, he said, but it was worth it.

interfere to stand in the way

Still, no matter what he was doing, Benjamin was always an apprentice. He couldn't forget it and he couldn't learn to like it. When he was 17, he could stand it no longer. He ran away. He boarded a boat and on one Sunday morning in October, 1723, he landed in Philadelphia, Pennsylvania.

He was free! He found a job with a printer and began earning his own money. When he had saved enough, he bought a new suit of clothes and a watch with a long gold watchchain. When he had save some more, he went to Boston to visit his family. He dropped in at the printshop to see James. He didn't come to apologize for running away; he came, in spite of his rules, to show off. He swaggered into the shop, letting James and his apprentices see what a grand thing it was to be your own master in a new suit of clothes. He twirled his watchchain. He jingled the money in his pockets and offered to treat everyone to a drink. (James was so angry that it took years for the brothers to make up.)

swaggered walk around showing off

Further Reading

Ben and Me. Robert Lawson. Amos, a mouse who lives in Franklin's old fur cap, tells the story of Franklin's life. Amos takes credit for most of Franklin's accomplishments.

Penn. Elizabeth Gray Vining. The continuing quarrel between William Penn and his father is the basis for this story, set in the time of Ben Franklin. It is about some of the younger Penn's ideas after he became a Quaker.

Poor Richard's Almanac. Benjamin Franklin. This is a collection of Franklin's wise sayings.

L E S S O N 3

Farming and Trade

THINKING FOCUS

How were farming and trade related to each other in the Middle Colonies?

Key Terms

- patroon system
- tenant farmer
- landlord

▼ *Innkeepers used wrought iron toasters and other cooking utensils to prepare breakfasts for travelers.*

> *A*ll of a sudden the inn seemed to come alive. There was the sound of heavy boots in the hall. Horses snorted and whinnied in the courtyard. Voices called back and forth. There were the deep, throaty voices of the Germans. There were the burring voices of the Scotch-Irish. But Papa's stately voice boomed above them all as he gave out duties:
>
> "Samuel, this be the day to sow the marshland with grass seed.
> "John, thee will brand the new bullocks today.
> "Thee, Thomas, will yoke the hogs so they will not stray.
> "Joseph, thee and Benjamin can pry up stones to build a fence along the upland pasture."
>
> But Benjamin was not listening. He was sniffing the air as noisily as Papa's hound dogs. The most tantalizing smells were seeping in under the door—ham and scrapple and eggs frying, pippin apples and cinnamon buns baking, and the steaming fragrance of herb tea.
>
> Marguerite Henry, from *Benjamin West and His Cat Grimalkin*

Benjamin in this story was a real person: Benjamin West. He grew up to paint pictures of Pennsylvania's history and was called the father of American painting. As a young Quaker boy, though, he worked long hours in his family's inn and on their farm.

Working on Family Farms

Every family member on Middle Colony farms in the 1700s was expected to work. Farmers not only farmed but made many different items for themselves and to sell. Women and girls, for example, churned butter and stamped it with designs from molds that the men or boys had made. Farmers often made their own furniture and tools. To earn extra income, some farm families looked for an additional trade. For example, Benjamin West's family both farmed and operated the busy Door-Latch Inn near Springfield, Pennsylvania.

Farms were usually about 200 acres, and work was heavy, as you can see in A Closer Look at Harvest Time on page 226. Farmers often had to hire or buy servants to help them. A traveler through Pennsylvania in the 1750s was a German named Gottlieb Mittelberger. He described how some terribly poor German immigrants arriving on a ship sold their children as servants to pay for their passage from Europe. "Many parents must sell and trade away their children like so many head of cattle."

Farmers needed so much help because they grew crops for people in many parts of the world. Look at the map on page 226 and notice the many places the crops went. Why might people in the West Indies and Europe need food from the Middle Colonies? ■

◄ Men made butter molds like this one. The beautiful designs they carved were stamped on blocks of butter. Stamped butter brought a higher price at market than did plain butter.

■ Why were Middle Colony farmers able to grow enough food for themselves and people far away?

Farming and the Standard of Living

The hard work of Middle Colony farmers often paid off. They lived well, compared to small farmers in Britain. Robert Parke, an Irish Quaker in Delaware County, Pennsylvania, wrote a letter to his sister in Ireland. Describing the good life in Pennsylvania of 1725, he wrote, "[N]ot one of the family, but what likes this country very well & wod [would] If we were in Ireland again come here . . ." He

The Middle Colonies

wheat, iron, naval stores, furs

meat, lumber

wheat, meat, lumber

rum, iron

GREAT BRITAIN — London — Bristol
EUROPE
FRANCE
SPAIN — Cádiz
Mediterranean Sea
AFRICA

NORTH AMERICA
MIDDLE COLONIES — New York, Philadelphia
ATLANTIC OCEAN
WEST INDIES
SOUTH AMERICA

0   750   1500 mi.
0   750 1500 km
Mercator Projection

▲ *Use this map to find out where farmers in the Middle Colonies sent their products.*

went on to explain that wages for working men were not high, but fair. Not many people became rich in Pennsylvania. The cash crops of the Middle Colonies did not bring in as much wealth as tobacco in the South, for example. But the economy of the Middle Colonies was

A CLOSER LOOK

Harvest Time

It's a hot Pennsylvania July, time to harvest the rye crop. The whole family pitches in. Whatever the family doesn't use will be sold in the nearest city or even across the ocean.

The scythe's three-foot blade and long handle let you cut grain close to the ground without having to bend over.

Harvest looks easy, doesn't it? This needlepoint scene shows a harvest in process. In real life, it took many more people to get the crop in, and harvesting was hard, sweaty work.

varied, and so many people, not just a few, enjoyed a good living. Pennsylvania became called "the best poor man's country" in the world.

Farmers in New York enjoyed this good living, even though many of them rented their farms rather than owning them. The **patroon system**—in which a few rich people owned large pieces of land—was left over from the time the Dutch colonized New York. The patroon, or owner of the land, employed **tenant farmers**—farmers who used some of the owner's land and paid him with part of their crop or with cash.

The owner they rented from—the **landlord**—gave his renters a house, tools, seeds, and supplies for free. He would also pay them if they improved the land by building a fence, adding to a house, or digging a well. For some poor farmers, renting land was a good way to start life in the Middle Colonies. ■

■ *Contrast farming in New York to farming in Pennsylvania.*

Growth of Urban Centers

As farms in the Middle Colonies were successful, farmers needed more and more help from tradesmen. For example, many farmers did not grind their own wheat. They brought the wheat to mills to be ground. The farmers, then, took the flour to market to

Grab a pitchfork and help load the cut rye onto the wagon. Even though girls and women use pitchforks to help with the harvest, they also have to do their regular dairy work. Women spend the money they earn selling milk and cheese to buy things to make their other chores easier: pins, needles, and cooking pots.

It's lunchtime! Rye bread, of course, with a hunk of homemade cheese makes a good midday meal for the harvesters. The youngest children bring lunch to the fields.

How do you get the horsepower out of the horse? The last task of the harvest is to throw the bundles of rye onto a wagon. A yoke like this enables the horse to pull the wagon.

227

▼ *This drawing,* East Prospect of Philadelphia *(1754) by George Heap, shows the largest of all colonial cities: Philadelphia. It became a center for trade and cultural activity.*

sell. Farmers traveled by boat and on land to markets in Philadelphia and New York. Since the journey was long, they might need to stop overnight in an inn, such as the Door-Latch Inn near Springfield. Keeping an inn, then, became a good business for some people, as it did for Benjamin West's mother and father.

Once the farmers got to Philadelphia or New York, they sold their goods in a town market. Then tradesmen would prepare the goods for shipping. For example, in New York, bakers took some of the farmers' flour and baked biscuits and breads to be sent overseas. Near shipyards, coopers made barrels for packing flour and

salted meat. Lumberjacks cut huge oak and cedar trees for shipbuilding—an active industry in both New York and Philadelphia.

Because farmers depended on markets and shipping, the port cities of Philadelphia and New York were busy. By the middle of the 1700s, these cities were cultural as well as trade centers. Publishers printed books and newspapers. Artists painted, sculpted, and made jewelry and decorative furniture. Educated people, such as Benjamin Franklin, made scientific experiments and discussed new political ideas. In such a creative setting, thoughts about the American Revolution began to take shape. ■

REVIEW

1. **FOCUS** How were farming and trade related to each other in the Middle Colonies?

2. **CONNECT** Analyze the reasons behind the following statement: Farmers in the Middle Colonies were neither rich nor poor. Contrast the standard of living of these farmers with those in the South.

3. **ECONOMICS** Explain how many of the jobs in the cities, such as baker, cooper, shipbuilder, and innkeeper, were related either directly or indirectly to farm life.

4. **CRITICAL THINKING** The Middle Colonies have been called the "breadbasket" of the British colonies. Why is a breadbasket a good image for the Middle Colonies?

5. **WRITING ACTIVITY** Many products were made on Middle Colony farms: candles, soap, cloth, quilts, molds, tools, furniture, and others. Choose one and research how it was made. Write a brief report to present to the class.

228

Comparing Information

Here's Why

A table can provide a quick overview of information. It can help you see similarities and differences in information easily. A table can also help you remember information. For example, a table may help you understand and remember what you have learned about the American colonies.

Here's How

Look at the table below. Pay special attention to the headings. The choice of headings in a table is very important in organizing the information.

Notice that the headings on the left have something in common. They tell you which group of colonies the information in each row describes. The colors also help you as you read across the rows.

Now look at the headings at the top of the table. Each heading tells what kind of information about the colonies is provided in the column directly below it.

Look at the heading at the top of the left column. It tells you that in this column you will find information about who came to the colonies. Now read the heading for the second column. Suppose you wanted to know where New England colonists came from. To find the answer, see where the second column meets the "New England Colonies" row.

A table helps you find information quickly. For example, suppose you wanted to find out where colonists lived who earned a living by fishing. Quickly read down the third column until you come to the word *fishing*. Since *fishing* is in the New England row, you know that New England is the answer.

Try It

Copy the table onto your own paper. Then add a row to the bottom of the table with the heading "Middle Colonies." Skim through the chapter to find the information needed for the Middle Colonies. Add the information to your table. Write short entries. Be sure that the entry in each box fits both the column heading and the row heading. What did you learn about the Middle Colonies?

Apply It

Make a table that shows how you spend your spare time. Choose a title. Use the days of the week as your column headings. Times of day—such as morning, afternoon, and evening—could be row headings.

The Early Colonies, 1600–1750				
	Who came?	**Where did they come from?**	**How did they earn a living?**	**Who did the work?**
Southern Colonies	Men and boys Indentured servants Slaves	England Africa	Tobacco farming Rice farming	Slaves Indentured servants
New England Colonies	Families	England	Trading (general) Shipbuilding Fishing	Adults and children

229

The Middle Colonies

Chapter Review

Reviewing Key Terms

diversity (p. 214)
landlord (p. 227)
navigable (p. 209)
patroon system (p. 227)
tenant farmer (p. 227)
tolerance (p. 214)
treaty (p. 211)

Some of the following statements are true. The rest are false. On your own paper, write *True* or *False* for each statement. Then rewrite the false statements to make them true.

1. A section of a river with waterfalls and rapids is quite likely to be navigable.
2. According to legend, William Penn made a treaty with the Delaware that led to 70 years of peace.
3. One thing the Middle Colonies lacked was cultural diversity, because the settlers spoke so many different languages.
4. William Penn based his colony on tolerance because he looked down upon people with different ways of life.
5. The patroon system helped new immigrants by enabling them to rent farmland they couldn't afford to buy.
6. Tenant farmers collected rent from landlords, who actually did the farming.
7. The Quaker ideal of tolerance helped bring diversity to the Middle Colonies.
8. Navigable rivers helped make Philadelphia and New York City major trade centers.

Exploring Concepts

A. Copy and complete the following outline using information from the chapter.

The Middle Colonies
I. The Land of the Middle Colonies
   A. Geography of the Middle Colonies
      1. _____
      2. _____
   B. Peaceful relations with the Indians
II. Mixture of Many Cultures
   A. Quaker ideals and the "Holy Experiment"
   B. Immigration to the Middle Colonies
   C. Problems among different groups
      1. _____
      2. _____
III. Farming and Trade
   A. _____
   B. _____
   C. _____

B. Answer each question with information from the chapter.

1. What characteristics of the geography of the Middle Colonies made it possible for many colonists to make a good living?
2. Why was tolerance an important ideal for the Middle Colonies?
3. How were the Quakers' ideals reflected in their relationships with native peoples?
4. How did Penn's "Holy Experiment" help bring prosperity to Pennsylvania?
5. Why did tensions arise among ethnic groups in the Middle Colonies?
6. How did prosperity in the Middle Colonies differ from that of the South?
7. What was the relationship between trade and farming in the Middle Colonies?
8. In what ways did farmers and city workers in the Middle Colonies depend on each other?

Reviewing Skills

1. Copy the table shown on this page onto your own sheet of paper. Complete the table using information from the chapter. Then use the table to answer the following questions.
   a. In what ways was the land of these two Middle Colonies the same?
   b. How did New York and Pennsylvania differ in their ways of farming?
   c. What major industry was important to both New York and Pennsylvania?
   d. What major exports did New York and Pennsylvania have in common?
2. Suppose you wanted to make a line graph to show the dramatic population growth in the American colonies between 1650 and 1760. Your data are as follows. The population was 52,000 in 1650. In 1700, the population had grown to 250,000. By 1760, 1,700,000 people lived in the colonies.

Make a graph using this information. How would you describe the shape of this graph?
3. Suppose you knew that the Hudson River was navigable for at least 100 miles upstream from New York City. Find a map of New York State. What part of the map will help you locate a city on the river that could ship farm products directly to New York City?

Two Middle Colonies		
	New York	**Pennsylvania**
Major city		
Major river		
Farm size and ownership		
Major crop		
Major industries		

Using Critical Thinking

1. In New York City and Philadelphia today, there are dozens of different ethnic groups speaking many different languages. Write a paragraph explaining how such ethnic diversity had its beginnings in the Middle Colonies.
2. Based on what you know and on information in the chapter, what seems to cause conflict among ethnic groups? Write a paragraph defining the problem. In a second paragraph, suggest two or three ways to reduce such conflicts.

Preparing for Citizenship

1. **COLLECTING INFORMATION** Find out in detail how one craft or trade would have been practiced in the Middle Colonies. Examples of crafts and trades in the chapter are milling (making flour), baking, keeping an inn, and managing a farm. Use an encyclopedia or contact an historical society to find the information. Write a descriptive report.
2. **COLLABORATIVE LEARNING** Make a class mural that pictures the economic life of the Middle Colonies. Divide the mural into four sections: farming, crafts, cities, and trade. Divide into four groups. Each group will be responsible for a different section of the mural. Make the mural go from west on the left to east on the right. To the left in the mural, there would be farms. To the right would be a city such as New York or Philadelphia. When the mural has been completed, list similarities and differences between the economic life of the area in colonial times and today.

The Struggle for Independence

To many people in the 1770s America was "a world turned upside down." Colonists who had once been loyal British subjects began to talk about independence. British soldiers who once had protected the colonists now threatened— even killed —some of them. While these events amazed people in America and Britain, the changes had just begun.

1720

Amos Doolittle, A View of the Town of Concord, 1775.
Engraving. Library of Congress.

1828

Chapter 10
Crisis with Britain

In 1754, Benjamin Franklin bragged that the "people in the colonies are as loyal . . . as any subjects" of the British Empire. Only 16 years later, Patrick Henry said he was ready to die for American independence. In those 16 years many things happened that changed American minds: taxes, riots, shootings. By 1775, the once-loyal colonists knew they wanted to rule themselves and would die to do so.

During this time, Americans became outraged by British laws. One colonist even made a teapot protesting the law known as the Stamp Act in 1765 (above).

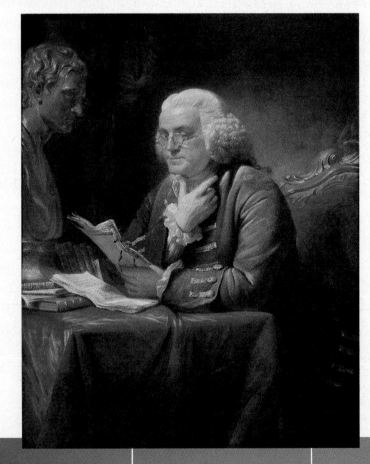

1710	1720	1730	1740

1720

1722–1775 Writer, printer, and inventor, Benjamin Franklin (above) is one of the best-known people in America. During this time, Franklin begins to call for the colonies to unite.

1754–1763 France and Britain fight over lands in North America in the Seven Years' War. Many colonists gain military experience in this war.

1775 In a fiery speech calling for American independence, Patrick Henry cries, "Give me liberty or give me death." Henry first won fame as a brilliant speaker in a 1763 court case, shown above.

1750

1760

1770

1780

1772 Phillis Wheatley, a slave, (above) writes a poem comparing America's desire for freedom to her own. Wheatley is America's first important black poet.

1775

L E S S O N   1

Ties to Great Britain

THINKING FOCUS

Why were the colonists more loyal to Great Britain than they were to each other in the 1750s?

Key Terms

- salutary neglect
- assembly
- veto

Benjamin Franklin and other Philadelphia leaders worked quickly. They were preparing to defend their city from attack in early 1764. The danger did not come from the French or any Indian tribes. Rather, the danger to the British colonists in Philadelphia came from another group of British subjects: the Paxton Boys.

The Paxton Boys were a group of 57 frontier settlers from western Pennsylvania. They were angry because the Wyalusing Indians had attacked their farms time after time. The Indians burned homes and sometimes killed settlers. The Paxton Boys were marching into Philadelphia. They wanted to force the colonial government to hire soldiers to stop the attacks.

Philadelphians had good reason to be afraid of this angry mob. In December of 1763, the Paxton Boys had attacked a group of Conestoga Indians. The Paxton Boys said that the Conestoga were helping the Wyalusing. The Conestoga Indians were Christians. When attacked, they joined hands and began to pray. But the Paxton Boys did not stop. They massacred all 20 men, women, and children as they prayed. Would the Paxton Boys attack Philadelphians next?

➤ *This 1764 engraving by Henry Dawkins shows Philadelphians lining up in battle formation and preparing their cannons to face the approaching Paxton Boys.*

On February 6, 1764, the Paxton Boys reached the edge of the city. Franklin and other government officials met with their leaders. Two long days of meetings finally produced a settlement. The colonial government agreed to pay for 1,000 troops to help defend the western settlements. The crisis ended. The Paxton Boys went home, and the people of Philadelphia felt safe again.

However, tensions remained. Why were British colonists, all of whom were loyal to the empire, so divided from each other?

Divisions Among the Colonists

In the 1750s, no "Americans" lived in the British colonies. People called themselves "Virginians," "New Yorkers," or some other name based on the colony they lived in. They did not think of themselves as "Americans" because they did not feel any special ties with other colonies.

However, colonists did feel strongly about troops and taxes. As in Pennsylvania, western settlers in several colonies feared attacks. They wanted the government to send troops to protect them. Many people in cities, though, did not agree. They felt that settlers should take care of their own problems. Conflicts between farmers and people in cities caused violent battles in Massachusetts, Virginia, North Carolina, and South Carolina.

Differences in language also separated colonists. Some English-speaking colonists were angry at the Germans, Dutch, French, and Swedish. Instead of speaking English, many of these colonists spoke their own language. For example, Benjamin Franklin's family came from England. He wondered why settlers from Germany should be allowed "to swarm into our settlements, and . . . establish their language and manners, to the exclusion of ours." According to the map below, which colonies had large German settlements?

The map key shows the largest groups of Europeans in the colonies by 1750.

Ethnic Divisions in Colonial America

NEW FRANCE

L. Huron
L. Ontario
L. Erie

Maine (part of Mass.)
N.H.
New York
Mass.
Conn.
R.I.
Pennsylvania
N.J.
Maryland
Del.
ATLANTIC OCEAN
Virginia
North Carolina
South Carolina
Georgia
FLORIDA (Spain)

80°W 75°W 70°W
45°N
40°N
35°N

English
German
Dutch
Scots
Scots–Irish

0   100   200 mi.
0 100 200 km
Lambert Conformal-Conic Projection

Colonists were also divided by religion. Many Europeans fled to the colonies to escape religious conflicts. However, they brought many of these conflicts with them to America.

Visitors noted differences among the colonists. Writing of his travels through the colonies in the 1760s, Andrew Burnaby of England said, "In short, such is the difference of character, of manners, of religion, of interest, of the different colonies, that I think . . . were they left to themselves, there would soon be a civil war, from one end of the continent to the other." ■

■ *Why were the colonists divided from each other?*

Benefits and Costs of Empire

The colonists were divided from one another. However, they were united in another way. Every colony supported Britain. In a letter to a British official in 1754, Franklin wrote:

> The people in the colonies are as loyal, and as firmly attached to the present constitution, and reigning family, as any subjects in the king's dominions [empire].

The Benefits of Empire

The need the Paxton boys felt for protection helps explain why the colonists were so loyal to Great Britain. The British army and navy were among the most powerful in the world. The army protected the colonists from the Indians and from French troops in the Ohio Valley. The navy protected colonial ships at sea.

Colonists also liked to trade with Britain. For example, British merchants bought large amounts of tobacco, fish, and grain from their American colonies. Colonists made money selling these goods to Britain.

Many colonists had another reason to be loyal. Almost half of the colonists were from England or were descended from English settlers. Most still had family living in England.

➤ *Richard Byron painted the busy Boston harbor in 1764. By then New York and Philadelphia were starting to challenge Boston's position as the leading colonial port for trade with Britain.*

For the colonists, then, being part of the empire brought great benefits but cost little. Before 1763, Great Britain followed a policy that historians now call **salutary neglect.** The British government neglected, or paid little attention to, its North American colonies. The colonies, after all, were only a small part of a large empire.

This lack of attention was salutary, or helpful, for the American colonies. The British government did not even tax the colonists to raise money to support the British government. Colonists had to pay only local taxes. They only had to pay for the government in their own colony.

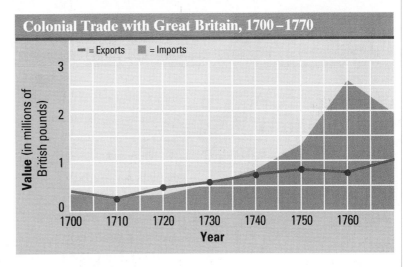

Colonial Trade with Great Britain, 1700–1770

Value (in millions of British pounds) vs. Year (1700–1760). ■ = Exports, ■ = Imports.

The Costs of Empire

Even though Britain did not govern the colonies tightly, some colonists did not like British rule. Some merchants were against laws known as the Navigation Acts.

▲ *How do the changes in colonial trade with Great Britain between 1700 and 1760 help explain why colonists were loyal to Great Britain?*

◄ *The British influenced colonial life in many ways. The painting, by John Singleton Copley, portrays colonists Mary and Elizabeth Royall wearing British-style dress. The image of George II, Britain's king from 1727 to 1760, was stamped on colonial coins.*

Crisis with Britain

These acts said that tobacco, sugar, and certain other colonial goods could be shipped only to Britain or its colonies. Colonists could not sell these items to another country.

Other acts said that colonists had to buy some goods, such as woolen goods and iron products, only from Britain. Colonists could not buy them from other countries. Colonists could not even make these goods.

Parliament also tried to rule the colonists through duties. These are taxes on goods bought from other countries. The Molasses Act of 1733 made colonists pay six pence on each gallon of molasses they bought from French or Dutch colonies in the West Indies. But the British did not make colonists obey the law. Merchants could smuggle in molasses without paying the duty.

Some colonists were also upset about British power over colonial governments. In each colony, the citizens elected an **assembly,** a group of citizens who made laws and set taxes. But, in most colonies, the king chose a governor. The governor could **veto,** or reject, colonial laws. And if the governor vetoed an act the assembly passed, it did not become a law.

Some governors did not rule their colonies wisely. In Franklin's letter to a British official, he explained how the people of the colonies viewed the governors:

> They will say . . . that governors often come to the colonies merely to make fortunes, with which they intend to return to Britain; are not always men of the best abilities or integrity [honesty]; have many of them no estates [land] here, nor any natural connections with us, that should make them heartily concerned for our welfare.

Franklin may have been right. Many governors did not rule their colonies well. But many barely ruled their colonies at all. Many colonists felt little British control over their lives. So, few disliked British rule in the 1750s. But Britain would soon have to change its policy of salutary neglect. Colonists would then think again about their ties to Britain—and to each other. ■

The family crest of the British kings in the 1700s was added to the Virginia governor's house in 1753. The crest has been rebuilt since then.

Across Time & Space

State governments today are similar to the colonial governments of the 1700s. Most states have a governor who can veto laws passed by the assembly. Today, however, governors are elected rather than appointed.

■ *How did colonists benefit from British rule?*

REVIEW

1. **FOCUS** Why were the colonists more loyal to Great Britain than they were to each other in the 1750s?
2. **CONNECT** Which colonies probably had the smallest percentage of people with relatives in England?
3. **HISTORY** How did the colonies benefit from the military strength of the British Empire?
4. **POLITICAL SYSTEMS** Explain the British policy of salutary neglect.
5. **CRITICAL THINKING** Consider how salutary neglect affected the colonists. Predict what would happen to the number of colonists who opposed British rule if Britain ended salutary neglect.
6. **WRITING ACTIVITY** Imagine you are a farmer in Pennsylvania. Write a letter to your cousin in Ireland explaining why you are glad your colony is part of the British Empire.

Chapter 10

LESSON 2

The Seven Years' War

*W*e got behind trees, logs and stumps, and covered ourselves as we could from the enemy's fire. The ground was strewed [covered] with the dead and dying. It happened that I got behind a white-oak stump, which was so small that I had to lay on my side, and stretch myself; the balls striking the ground within a hand's breadth of me every moment, and I could hear the men screaming, and see them dying all around me.

David Perry, *Life of Captain David Perry*, 1822

**THINKING
FOCUS**

What were the main results of the Seven Years' War?

David Perry was 81 years old when he remembered the deadly battle he fought in at age 17. The battle took place near Ticonderoga, New York, in 1758. It was just one conflict in a long fight

Key Terms

- import
- politics

◄ *This painting of the battle at Ticonderoga shows members of the Black Watch, a unit of British soldiers from Scotland. Over half of the members of the Black Watch were killed or wounded in the fighting.*

between Great Britain and France for the control of most of North America. As a British colonist, Perry fought alongside soldiers in the British army.

The French won the battle at Ticonderoga. Almost 500 British and colonial soldiers died in the fighting. Those who died most likely thought they were protecting the British Empire in North America. They did not know that the war would help bring an end to the empire. As they defended the empire, Perry and the other soldiers also helped destroy it.

Rivalry Between Britain and France

The Battle of Ticonderoga was one battle in a series of four wars between Britain and France. These two countries battled for power around the world. Between 1689 and 1763, the two powers fought in Europe, in India, in the Caribbean, and in North America. Study the timeline on this page. How many years were Britain and France at war from 1689 to 1763?

In North America, Britain and France fought to control the land and its wealth. Each hoped to bring into their country more of the valuable furs and fish from North America. Each of these items was an **import,** a product brought into a country. The first three wars did not settle the conflict. The fourth war began in 1754 when French soldiers attacked British colonists. These colonists had settled on land claimed by France near the Ohio River.

Fighting in America went on until 1763, a total of nine years. However, the war is called the Seven Years' War, because Britain and France fought in Europe between 1756 and 1763. The war is also called the French and Indian War. In the war, the French joined with several Indian tribes to fight the British.

The Life of Soldiers

When the Seven Years' War began, colonists rushed to join the army. Most British colonists were Protestants. They disliked the French, who were Catholics.

▼ Great Britain and France fought four separate wars between 1689 and 1763. In North America, all four wars were fought for control of land and resources.

The British–French Conflict, 1689–1763

1689–1697, King William's War. England and France fight for control of land and the fur trade in North America. Fighting stops. Neither side wins any territory.

1744–1748, King George's War. British colonists capture the French fort at Louisbourg, Canada. However, the fort is returned to France at the end of the war. Neither side gains any territory.

1700 — 1725 — 1750 — 1775

1702–1713, Queen Anne's War. Britain wins a small victory. The British gain valuable fur-trading land near Hudson Bay, fishing villages in Nova Scotia, and a sugar-producing island in the Caribbean Sea.

1756–1763, The Seven Years' War (also called the French and Indian War). Britain wins control of lands claimed by France in eastern North America.

Also, the French had forts in Canada and along the Ohio River. These forts stopped British colonists from moving westward. Study the map below. What lands did Britain and France claim in 1689?

The colonists were ready to fight. Yet few had military experience. They looked up to the British troops because many had fought before. A Connecticut man, Gideon Hawley, said, "One of the regulars is worth five of our men."

However, the colonists soon saw that even for the tough British soldiers, war was hard. Troops often had only salt pork and biscuits to eat. And sometimes the meat was spoiled by the time it reached the troops.

The poor food made soldiers more likely to get sick. And the camps they stayed in were often very crowded, so diseases like typhoid fever spread quickly from one soldier to another. In fact, during the Seven Years' War, more soldiers died from disease than from fighting.

The Role of Indian Tribes

Colonists and Europeans were not the only ones involved in fighting. Indian tribes in northeastern North America also fought in the war. To protect their trade with the French, the Huron and the Seneca

▼ *The carving on this powder horn shows the key battles fought in New York during the Seven Years' War.*

▼ *In 1707, England joined with Scotland and Wales to form the country called Great Britain. The English claims on the 1689 map, then, became the British claims after 1707.*

European Land Claims in North America, 1689 and 1763

Hudson Bay
HUDSON'S BAY COMPANY
Disputed by England and France
NEW FRANCE
Louisbourg
Quebec
Montréal
Philadelphia
LOUISIANA
Ohio R.
Missouri R.
Mississippi R.
Great Lakes
PACIFIC OCEAN
NEW SPAIN
ATLANTIC OCEAN
Gulf of Mexico
BAHAMAS
Mexico City
CUBA
JAMAICA
HISPANIOLA
Caribbean Sea
NEW GRANADA

Land claims in 1689
England
France
Spain

0   500   1000 mi.
0 500 1000 km
Azimuthal Projection

ALASKA
Disputed by Great Britain, Russia, and Spain
Hudson Bay
HUDSON'S BAY COMPANY
Missouri R.
QUEBEC
Louisbourg
Quebec
Montréal
Philadelphia
Proclamation Line of 1763
LOUISIANA
Ohio R.
PACIFIC OCEAN
NEW SPAIN
New Orleans
ATLANTIC OCEAN
Gulf of Mexico
BAHAMAS
Mexico City
CUBA
JAMAICA
HISPANIOLA
Caribbean Sea
NEW GRANADA

Land claims in 1763
Great Britain
France
Spain
Russia

0   500   1000 mi.
0 500 1000 km
Azimuthal Projection

In the picture at the bottom of the page, you can see the British preparing to attack Quebec. The engraving above it shows the death of the British general, James Wolfe, who was wounded three times in the fighting.

joined the French to fight the British.

The Seneca were part of the Iroquois Nation, a confederation of tribes. The rest of the Iroquois tried to stay out of the war when it began. The Iroquois carefully studied **politics,** the way governments act. Wars between Britain and France were good for the Iroquois. They used each country as a friend against the other country. The Iro-

quois did not want either country to win and become stronger in North America.

Early in the war, the French, the Huron, and the Seneca joined together to win several major battles. But in 1757, William Pitt became the leader of the British government. Pitt decided that Britain should send more troops to North America. He also sent better food and more guns to aid the British troops.

The Iroquois tribes who had stayed out of the war saw the change in the British army. They began to feel that the British might win the war. To protect their trade with Britain and its colonies, they joined the British to fight the French.

The Battle of Quebec

With more troops, better supplies, and the help of several Iroquois tribes, the British army began to win more battles. In 1759,

British troops, led by 32-year-old James Wolfe, got ready to attack the city of Quebec, the French capital in Canada. Quebec sat atop a 180-foot cliff and was defended by 10,000 French troops. Attacking the fort would be very dangerous for the British.

However, during the night of September 12, 1759, Wolfe's British troops secretly climbed a narrow path up the steep cliff. When the French troops got up in the morning, 5,000 British troops were waiting for them.

Fighting soon began. The inexperienced French troops fired wildly as they moved toward the British. The well-trained British troops waited until the French got within 40 yards. Then the British opened fire with deadly aim. In a short 30 minutes, the British had won the battle. And they had won the key to power over most of North America. ■

■ *What was the main goal of Britain and France in the North American wars they fought between 1689 and 1763?*

Results of the War

Britain and France ended the war with the signing of the Treaty of Paris in 1763. Britain wanted all of the French lands in North America. But the French did not want the British to become too powerful. So, the treaty gave all French land west of the Mississippi River to Spain. Britain agreed to this treaty, even though Spain had helped France during the war. According to the treaty, Britain took over the French lands east of the Mississippi River.

The Proclamation of 1763

With the French defeat, many colonists eagerly prepared to move across the Appalachian Mountains. However, the British were worried. They knew that new settlements would anger the Iroquois, Delaware, Shawnee, and other Indian tribes who already lived there. To prevent fighting, the British issued the Proclamation of 1763. This act saved all land west of the Appalachians for Indians. Colonists could not settle there.

This engraving by Henry Dawkins shows leaders of an Indian tribe negotiating with the British near the end of the Seven Years' War.

The Proclamation upset many colonists. Earlier, the French had blocked new settlements. The French had been defeated. Now, though, the British also stopped people from moving west. Many colonists wondered why they had fought the war.

The Cost of Victory

Colonial anger at Britain's Proclamation of 1763 was just one

245

➤ *This sign appeared in the* Pennsylvania Journal *two years after the Seven Years' War. It expressed the colonists' feelings about the terrible effects of the war and the general lack of money.*

The TIMES are Dreadful, Dismal Doleful Dolorous, and DOLLAR-LESS.

hardship the war caused. The British, the Indians, and the colonists each faced new troubles.

In Britain, the war had caused the government to borrow money. Between 1754 and 1763, the money Britain owed doubled. The country needed money to pay back its many loans.

Britain also had to pay the 10,000 soldiers it sent to North America. These troops were needed to protect the large new British empire. Britain now had to spend three times as much to defend its American empire as it did before the war.

For many Indian tribes, the war brought a loss of power. They could no longer use the French to help them against the British. And even 10,000 British soldiers could

■ *Name two ways the colonists benefited from the Seven Years' War.*

not stop settlers from moving onto Indian lands.

In the colonies, the war caused great suffering. Boston, a city of about 2,500 families, lost 700 men during the war. These deaths left many widows and orphans who needed help just to buy food.

The Effect on Attitudes

The war also changed the way colonists viewed Britain. Colonists no longer needed British help to fight the French. Therefore, the colonists felt less closely tied to Britain.

Also, many colonists had become skilled soldiers in the war. They had learned that they could defend themselves. One colonist who had fought for the first time was a Virginian, George Washington. After one battle, Washington wrote to his mother that the "Virginia troops showed a great deal of bravery." Yet the British troops, he said, ran from the French like "sheep pursued by dogs."

The war taught Washington something. Colonists could fight as well as British soldiers. In a few years, the whole world would know what Washington knew. ■

REVIEW

1. **FOCUS** What were the main results of the Seven Years' War?

2. **CONNECT** In 1754, why were most British colonists content to be part of the British Empire?

3. **GEOGRAPHY** How did geography make Britain's attack on Quebec difficult?

4. **HISTORY** Why did the Proclamation of 1763 fail?

5. **CRITICAL THINKING** Compare the comments about the colonial soldiers at the beginning of the Seven Years'

War with the comments about the French soldiers who attacked Wolfe's troops at Quebec. How were the two groups similar?

6. **WRITING ACTIVITY** Make two columns on your paper. In the left column, list benefits of the Seven Years' War for the colonists. In the right column, list costs of the war for the colonists. Compare the items in the two columns and explain why you think that the war helped or hurt the colonists overall.

L E S S O N 3

A New British Policy

In Boston, on January 25, 1774, a little boy stood quietly behind a sled he had been pushing. A man stood over him, "cursing, damning, threatening and shaking a very large cane . . . over his head."

George Robert Twelves Hewes, a shoemaker, hurried over. "Mr. Malcolm, I hope you are not going to strike this boy with that stick."

John Malcolm turned quickly. He stared angrily at Hewes.

Malcolm was a colonial official. He worked for the British government, managing colonial trade. Hewes was a poor working man. Malcolm shouted that poor people had no right even to speak to him.

Hewes reminded Malcolm of what happened two months earlier. An angry crowd had punished Malcolm for mistreating a poor person. The crowd had grabbed Malcolm. Then they had poured hot tar over him, and covered him with feathers.

At this comment by Hewes, Malcolm swung his cane. The blow left Hewes lying on the ground with a bloody cut in his head. A group of angry colonists rushed to punish Malcolm. For a second time, Bostonians tarred and feathered Malcolm.

Yet the colonists' anger was also directed at the British government. That anger had been building for 11 years. Before the Seven Years' War, Parliament had used duties to regulate colonial trade. Yet it had never tried to raise money from the colonists. Because of the war, though, Britain needed money. So Parliament decided to do something it had never done. It decided to tax the colonists.

THINKING
F O C U S

What caused increased conflicts between the colonies and Britain after 1763?

Key Terms

- repeal
- boycott
- propaganda

◄ *This cartoon showing the tarring and feathering of a British official in the colonies may have been based on the treatment of John Malcolm.*

247

Crisis with Britain

Britain Taxes the Colonies

➤ *Why do you think the colonists used a skull to symbolize the Stamp Act?*

In 1764, Parliament first tried to tax colonists. It changed the 1733 Molasses Act into a new law called the Sugar Act. This law increased the number of customs agents. It also increased the penalties for smuggling, though it lowered the duty on molasses. By catching more smugglers, Britain hoped to make merchants pay the duty.

Eight colonial assemblies called on Parliament to **repeal,** or do away with, the Sugar Act. They said that Parliament had no right to tax the colonists because the colonists had no representatives in Parliament. Parliament did not agree. The law remained.

The Stamp Act

In March 1765, Parliament tried again to raise money from the colonists. In Britain people had to pay a stamp tax. This was an extra charge on newspapers and other items written on paper that had to have a government stamp on them. Parliament decided that colonists should also pay a stamp tax. They expected the tax would upset a few colonists. But they were not ready for what happened.

The colonists exploded in anger. They charged that the stamp tax — or any tax—was unfair. Anger came not only from merchants, but also from large groups of citizens, such as shoemakers and tailors. Colonial men formed groups called the Sons of Liberty. Colonial women formed the Daughters of Liberty. These groups held public meetings to speak out against the Stamp Act.

In some places crowds did more than protest. In Boston, Andrew Oliver had been chosen to pass out stamps. However, a crowd

of angry citizens tore down a new building Oliver owned. Then they broke into his large home and destroyed his furniture. Oliver decided to quit. Fear of attacks caused other officials to quit as well. Soon Parliament had no one to pass out the stamped paper. Parliament had to repeal the new Stamp Act. And the act had not even taken effect yet.

The Townshend Duties

In 1767, Parliament tried a third time to tax the colonists. Parliament passed duties on paper, lead, painters' colors, and tea. The duties were named after Charles Townshend. He was the British official in charge of handling money for the government.

▲ *The British issued this stamp in 1765 for use in the colonies.*

The Effects of British Taxation, 1764–1770

Sugar Act	Stamp Act	Townshend Duties
British action 1764, Parliament tries to increase its revenue by tightening control over colonial trade.	**British action** 1765, Parliament taxes all newspapers, pamphlets, and legal documents.	**British action** 1767, Parliament taxes paper, lead, painters' colors, and tea.
Colonial reaction 1764, Colonists protest against taxation without representation.	**Colonial reaction** 1765, Patrick Henry and Sam Adams lead colonial protests. The threat of violence causes stamp distributors to resign.	**Colonial reaction** 1767, Colonists boycott British goods. The Sons of Liberty pressures all merchants to support the boycott.
British response 1766, After trying to collect the tax on molasses for almost two years, Parliament lowers it.	**British response** 1766, Parliament repeals the Stamp Act.	**British response** 1770, Parliament repeals all Townshend Duties except the tax on tea.

Again the colonists cried, "No taxation without representation!" To cause the British to repeal the duties, colonial merchants agreed to **boycott,** or not buy, anything from Britain. The boycott, they thought, would cause British businesses to lose money. British merchants would then ask Parliament to repeal the duties.

Women played an important part in the boycott of British goods. Britain had a large and profitable cloth trade in the colonies. To help the boycott of British cloth, colonial women made their own. Many held spinning contests to advertise the boycott.

The boycott worked. In 1770, Parliament decided to end all of the taxes but one. Only the tax on tea remained.

The Boston Massacre

In 1768, during the argument over the Townshend duties, Parliament got worried. They feared that the colonial protests were out of control. They sent soldiers to Boston. Some colonists welcomed the soldiers. They believed the soldiers might help keep order. Other colonists were angry. They charged that the soldiers were a danger to the rights of colonists.

Anger over the soldiers finally exploded in violence. On March 5, 1770, about 100 Bostonians moved toward some soldiers guarding the customs house. One of the Bostonians' leaders was a black man named Crispus Attucks. The crowd yelled, then threw rocks and snowballs. Fearing for their safety, the soldiers opened fire. They killed Attucks and four other colonists.

Colonial newspapers called the action the "Boston Massacre." Through **propaganda,** or telling one side of a story to win support for a cause, the newspapers stirred up anger at the British.

Not all colonists blamed the British soldiers for the five deaths.

▲ *In the chart, notice the British reaction to colonial protests against taxation. How successful were the colonists?*

Crisis with Britain

➤ *Crispus Attucks was a runaway slave who worked on the docks in Boston. He was almost 50 years old when he was killed in the Boston Massacre.*

How Do We Know?

HISTORY *The memories of George Robert Twelves Hewes were written down in the 1830s by historians Benjamin Bussey Thatcher and James Hawkes. They interviewed Hewes shortly before he died. He was nearly 100 at his death.*

■ *Why did the colonists oppose paying taxes to the British?*

▼ *The arrival of tea in colonial ports was considered, as this flyer said, an "alarming crisis."*

Lawyer John Adams of Boston defended the soldiers in court. The court punished only two of the soldiers.

John Adams' cousin, Samuel Adams, was a leader in spreading the propaganda. As a boy, Sam had learned from his father about how people had defended their rights in the past. Now he urged the Boston town meeting to set up a committee. This committee would tell other colonies of British actions. Soon the other colonies started their own groups, called Committees of Correspondence. Anger at Britain was causing people in the colonies to work more closely together.

The Tea Act

Parliament still was not getting money from the colonists. And Parliament faced another problem. The British East India Company was going broke. The company sold tea and other goods from Asia. To help the company, Parliament let it sell tea directly to colonial merchants. The merchants then sold the tea to colonists. Even with the tax, tea from the company cost less than smuggled tea.

The colonists knew that Parliament was still taxing them without their approval. In November 1773, three ships carrying East India Company tea reached Boston harbor. For almost three weeks, crowds of colonists stopped anyone from taking the hated tea off the ships. Then, in December 1773, dozens of colonists dressed up as Indians. One of these was George Robert Twelves Hewes. They silently boarded the ships. Sixty years later, Hewes described the action now known as the Boston Tea Party:

W e then were ordered by our commander to open the hatches, and take out all the chests of tea and throw them overboard, and we immediately proceeded to execute his orders; first cutting and splitting the chests with our tomahawks, so as thoroughly to expose them to the effects of the water. In about three hours from the time we went on board, we had thus broken and thrown overboard every tea chest to be found in the ship; while those in the other ships were disposing of the tea in the same way, at the same time.

The Boston Tea Party was a brave move by the colonists. You can learn more about it in A Closer Look on page 251. ■

Monday Morning, December 27, 1773.
THE TEA-SHIP being arrived, every Inhabitant, who wishes to preserve the Liberty of America, is desired to meet at the STATE-HOUSE, This Morning, precisely at TEN o'Clock, to advise what is best to be done on this alarming Crisis.

Boston Tea Party

It took three hours for American patriots to dump 90,000 pounds of tea into Boston harbor. An English woman living in Boston wrote that the event was "too shocking for me to describe." But the tea was the only thing the colonists damaged—except for one padlock, which they replaced the next day.

To mask their faces, patriots rubbed on charcoal, soot, and burnt cork.

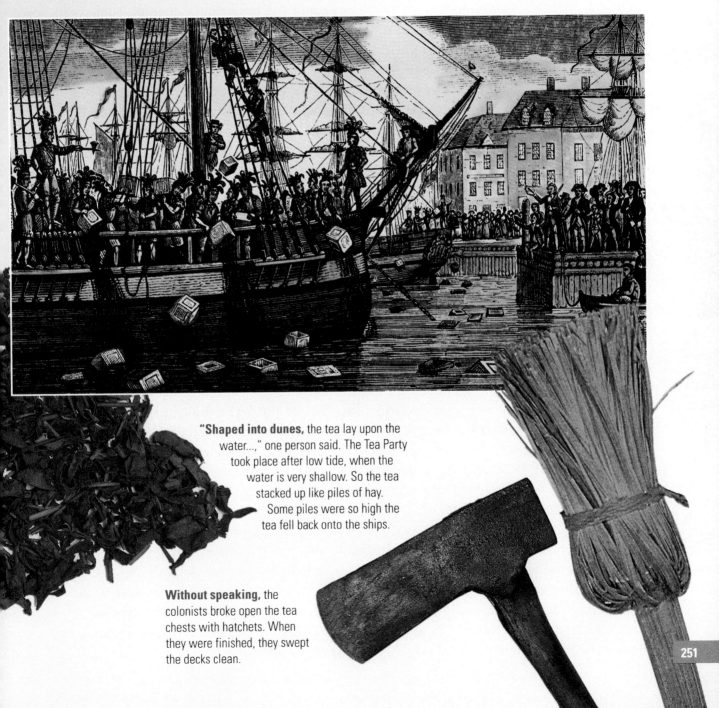

"Shaped into dunes, the tea lay upon the water...," one person said. The Tea Party took place after low tide, when the water is very shallow. So the tea stacked up like piles of hay. Some piles were so high the tea fell back onto the ships.

Without speaking, the colonists broke open the tea chests with hatchets. When they were finished, they swept the decks clean.

251

Colonists Begin to Unite

The Boston Tea Party enraged the British. To punish Boston, Parliament passed what colonists called the "Intolerable Acts." These acts ended town meetings. They took away some of the power of the Massachusetts assembly. They also closed Boston harbor to almost all shipping, except for some food and fuel. The city could not import or export most goods until it paid for the tea.

Boston was a city built on trade. Closing its harbor could be terrible for its people. What would happen to Boston's many sailors, dock workers, and merchants?

Parliament hoped that closing the Boston harbor would cause the city to pay for the tea. Instead, closing the harbor caused the other colonies to help Boston. Food and supplies poured in from the other colonies.

On September 5, 1774, delegates from every colony except Georgia met in Philadelphia to talk about the British actions. This group is now known as the First Continental Congress. They voted to stop all trade with Britain.

Most colonists expected the crisis to end peacefully. They hoped Britain would return to its policy of salutary neglect. Only a few were rebels, people who were ready to overthrow the government and set up a new one.

UNDERSTANDING TAXATION

After 1763, Britain needed money to pay for the Seven Years' War. Parliament tried to raise money as most governments do: through taxation. What is taxation? What is its goal?

Types of Taxes

Governments often pass laws that require people to pay money to them. This way of raising money is called taxation.

One type of tax is the sales tax. When you buy a notebook, you may pay a small amount for sales tax. The store sends the government the extra money.

Another tax, the income tax, is based on the money a person earns. The more money a worker earns, the more tax that person must pay.

The Use of Taxes

The government then uses money from taxation to pay for goods and services that everyone needs. For example, taxes pay for operating schools, hiring police and firefighters, and building roads. Tax money also pays the salaries of the people elected to government, such as the president and members of Congress.

In the 1700s, Britain used taxes to defend its empire. The government of Boston used tax money to support widows and orphans. Today, governments still use taxes to pay the military and to help the needy.

252

Yet how colonists viewed one another had changed in only 20 years. In 1754, before the Seven Years' War, colonists were divided from each other. By 1774, however, colonists were joining together for protection. During the First Continental Congress, Virginia delegate Patrick Henry said something that no one would have said 20 years earlier. "The distinctions between Virginians, Pennsylvanians, New Yorkers, and New Englanders are no more. I am not a Virginian, but an American."

And something else was different since 1754. Colonists' view of Britain had changed. Then, most colonists thought Britain protected them. Now, more and more colonists thought Britain was a danger to their liberties. Patrick Henry also stated this new view of Britain. In a speech in Richmond, Virginia, in March 1775, Henry boldly declared:

A British cartoon made fun of the Boston colonists. They felt caged in when Britain closed their port.

> Our chains are forged. Their clanking may be heard on the plains of Boston! The war is inevitable—and let it come! I repeat it, sir, let it come! . . . Is life so dear, or peace so sweet, as to be purchased at the price of chains and slavery? Forbid it, Almighty God! I know not what course others may take; but as for me, give me liberty, or give me death!

In less than one month, Henry's prediction came true. The war began. ■

■ *Why did the colonists begin to work with each other against the British government?*

R E V I E W

1. **FOCUS** What caused increased conflicts between the colonies and Great Britain after 1763?

2. **CONNECT** Why were colonists more confident of their ability to defend themselves in the 1770s than they had been in the 1750s?

3. **HISTORY** How was the reaction to the Stamp Act different from the protests against the Sugar Act?

4. **HISTORY** What was the British reaction to the Boston Tea Party?

5. **CRITICAL THINKING** Write one sentence summarizing the change in the relationship between the colonies and Great Britain between 1754 and 1775.

6. **WRITING ACTIVITY** With a group of three other students, prepare a skit about the Boston Tea Party.

253

Crisis with Britain

Interpreting Political Cartoons

Here's Why

Political cartoons use pictures, and often humor, to make a point about public affairs. They are fun and informative, and they can help you understand what people of the time were concerned about. For example, political cartoons from the time of the American Revolution can help you understand what was important to Americans of that time.

Here's How

Look at the cartoon on the opposite page. It was published in London, in 1776, ten months after the Battle of Lexington and Concord. The cartoon suggests that King George was greedy in trying to get more and more taxes from the American colonists. It also suggests that the king's actions caused the revolt of the colonies.

In creating cartoons, all cartoonists first depend on readers having a certain level of background knowledge. The meaning of the cartoon on the opposite page would have been clear to people who saw it in 1776.

Today, we have trouble identifying the characters in Revolutionary War cartoons, just as people 200 years from

now will have difficulty interpreting our political cartoons. In 1776, the problems between England and the colonies were known to everyone. The cartoonist could depend on the fact that people would recognize the noblemen in the picture as King George and his cabinet. Today we are not even sure who the man killing the goose is. Readers at the time would have known who that man and all the others in the picture were.

The man wearing a sash and leaning over the goose is shown on this page to give you a closer look at him. We think that he is either King George III or the British minister Lord Frederick North.

Second, cartoonists make comparisons. Here, the car-

toonist compares the American colonies to the goose that laid the golden egg in the story of "The Wise Men of Gotham and their Goose." The basket of golden eggs, shown in the upper left corner, is a symbol of the wealth England gained from the colonies.

King George III and his cabinet represent the not-so-wise men who decided to kill the goose to get more than one golden egg in a day.

Third, cartoonists sometimes use labels to identify parts of the cartoon that the reader may not understand. Find the labels "North America" and "taxes." These are parts of the cartoon that the cartoonist does not want the reader to miss.

Finally, cartoons may include written clues. Notice that the cartoonist included the story of "The Wise Men of Gotham and their Goose."

Try It

Find the cartoon on page 253. Read the caption and study the cartoon. Who are the people in the cartoon? Explain what background knowledge you need to have in order to understand the cartoon. Point out the main comparison in the cartoon.

Skill'd in the great Politic Wheel
Could pound a Magpie, drown an Eel,
With many Things of worthy Note
At present much too long to quote,
Their District was both far and wide
Which not a little swell'd their Pride
But above all that they possess'd
Was a fine Goose, by all confess'd,
A Rara Avis to behold
Who laid each Day an Egg of Gold
This made them grow immensely rich
Gave them an avaritious Itch,
The Case belongs to many more

To make the Harmless Bird lay Two,
This Glorious purpose to obtain
About her Neck they put a Chain,
And more their Folly to compleat
They Stampt upon her Wings & Feet,
But this had no Effect at all,
Yet made her struggle, flutter, squall,
And do what every Goose would do
That had her Liberty in view,
When one of more distinguish'd Note
Cry'd D—n her let us lit her Throat,
They did, but not an Egg was found
But BLOOD came pouring from y Wound.

THE WISE MEN of GOTHAM and their GOOSE

Pub.d 16th Feb.y 1776. by W. Humphrey, Gerrard Street Soho.

Review the Colonists Begin to Unite section of Lesson 3 if you need help. Explain the cartoon's message.

Apply It

Most newspapers print a political cartoon every day. Write a paragraph that explains a political cartoon from your newspaper. Share your cartoon and explanations with classmates.

Chapter Review

Reviewing Key Terms

assembly (p. 240)   propaganda (p. 249)
boycott (p. 249)   repeal (p. 248)
import (p. 242)   salutary neglect (p. 239)
politics (p. 244)   veto (p. 240)

A. Write a sentence to answer each question. Each sentence you write should include at least one key term.

1. Why were certain laws in the colonies not strictly enforced?
2. How could a governor stop a law from taking effect?
3. What group chose people to represent the colony in Parliament?
4. How did Parliament stop the Sugar Act from taking effect?
5. How could Britain and France get furs from North America?
6. How could newspapers stir up anger among the American colonists?
7. What happened when Americans refused to buy British goods?

B. Use a dictionary to find the origins of the following words. On your own paper, write one or two sentences explaining how the word can be used to describe colonial times.

1. boycott
2. propaganda
3. politics

Exploring Concepts

A. Following the Seven Years' War, important changes took place in the colonies. These changes included the colonists' attitude toward Britain and toward each other, Britain's wealth, Britain's taxation of colonists, and the Indians' power. Copy and complete the chart below using information from the chapter.

Issue	Before War	After War
1. Colonists' attitude toward Britain	Saw Britain as protector	Saw Britain as threat
2. Colonists' attitude toward each other		
3. Britain's wealth		
4. Britain's taxation of colonists		
5. Indians' power		

B. Answer each question with information from the chapter.

1. Did all the colonial governors follow the policy of salutary neglect?
2. Why were there often violent clashes among the colonists?
3. Why did very few colonists want to revolt against the British in the 1750s?
4. What effect did colonists fighting in the Seven Years' War have on their relationship with Britain later on?
5. What part did members of the Iroquois Nation play in the Seven Years' War?
6. What was the Proclamation of 1763 and what were its effects?
7. How did the British government try to raise money from the American colonists after the costly Seven Years' War?
8. What did the colonists mean by saying "No taxation without representation"?

Reviewing Skills

1. The illustration on this page is thought to be America's first political cartoon. Benjamin Franklin drew it in 1754 to support the idea of united colonies. The cartoon was based on the superstition that a cut up snake could be put back together if its pieces were joined by sunset. The cartoon reappeared in colonial newspapers in 1765 and 1774. What did the pieces of the snake mean? What written clue did Franklin add to help explain this?

2. What did people of Franklin's time need to know in order to understand his cartoon? Why do we need background information when we discuss his cartoon?

3. The graph on page 239 shows colonial trade with Britain. This graph is based on information from a table. What headings might the table have used? Why is it more helpful to show this information on a graph than on a table?

4. What special kind of map symbol could you use to show the number of immigrants that came from Europe to each colony?

Using Critical Thinking

1. Some colonists boycotted British goods for several years. What effects might the boycott have had on their everyday lives?

2. In 1770, colonists threw rocks at British soldiers. The soldiers feared for their lives and opened fire. Explain how the newspapers stirred up anger against the British.

3. In the Seven Years' War, more soldiers died from diseases than from battles. Could this happen today? Why or why not?

4. After the Seven Years' War was over in America in 1763, this country was very different. Think about what life in the colonies would have been like if the war had never happened. How might the country have been different? What changes were caused by the war? Would those changes have happened anyway?

Preparing for Citizenship

1. COLLECTING INFORMATION Think about how colonial newspapers reported the Boston Massacre. Then find three letters to the editor in your newspaper that have strong, clear opinions on one or more of these topics: the environment; state or local government; candidates running for office. After each letter, briefly tell the writer's opinion. Then paste the articles and your explanations in a booklet.

2. COLLABORATIVE LEARNING With a group of classmates, write and perform dramatic scenes that show how the colonists' relationship with Britain changed. The first scene should take place in the early 1750s in a colonial shop that sells British cloth. The second scene should take place in the same shop 20 years later. In both scenes, have the same characters talk about their attitudes toward the British.

Chapter 11

War Breaks Out

When the first shots of the Revolution were fired, America consisted of 13 very different and separate colonies. But when America faced the well-trained British army, the differences between the colonies did not seem so important. People throughout the nation—generals, farmers, politicians, and women at home—did their part to win the war.

During the war, many women took charge of farms and businesses while the men fought. Abigail Adams (above) ran her family's farm while her husband, John Adams, represented the United States in Britain.

1775 American Minutemen fight British troops at the bridge at Concord, Massachusetts (right). Three British soldiers and two Americans are killed.

1770	1775	1780

1776 The American colonies declare their independence from Britain.

1781 British troops surrender at Yorktown, Virginia.

1775

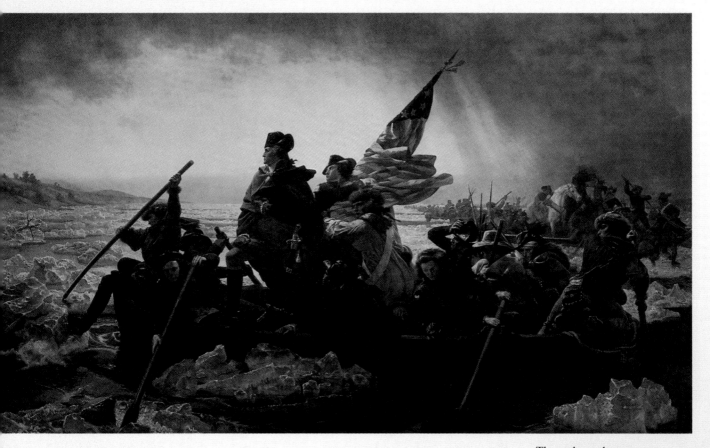

Throughout the war, George Washington led the Continental Army through dozens of battles. Above, Washington leads his troops on a surprise attack against the British on Christmas Day, 1776.

1785

1790

1795

1783 Britain and the United States sign a treaty ending the war. The picture above shows the American signers; the British refused to pose for the painting.

1792

L E S S O N   1

Forming a New Government

THINKING FOCUS

How did the colonies organize a government to lead their fight for independence?

Key Terms

- militia
- delegate
- independence
- equality

Just after midnight on April 19, 1775, the alarm bells in Lexington, Massachusetts, started to clang. Jonas Parker jumped out of bed, grabbed his musket, and ran to the common, a meadow in the center of the village. "The Redcoats are coming," he heard voices shouting.

Within minutes, Parker and 130 other farmers and shopkeepers had gathered on the common. All were clutching guns. They talked in excited whispers and stamped their feet to stay warm in the chill night air.

By 1:30 A.M., no British troops had appeared, so Captain John Parker dismissed the men. He told them to return to the green the minute they heard the beating of the drum. Men who lived nearby went home. The rest went to Monroe and Buckman taverns to keep warm and wait.

Three hours later, a scout named Thaddeus Brown galloped into town to report that the British were less than a half mile away. Immediately, 16-year-old William Diamond beat the drum, and 77 townsmen rushed to the green. There they formed two uneven lines and waited nervously. As the sun rose, a line of 300 British soldiers marched into view.

The colonists weren't sure what to do. No one had told them to stop the British. So they stood in their ranks, silently protesting the British force.

▲ In order to fire his musket, a Minuteman had to pour gunpowder from his powder horn, shown on the right, into the barrel of the gun.

The First Shot Is Fired

The farmers and shopkeepers who gathered on the green that morning were members of the **militia,** citizens who served as part-time soldiers. They were also called Minutemen because they were ready to fight any enemy at a minute's notice.

The British soldiers were a secret raiding party from Boston looking for hidden colonial weapons. They surprised no one, however. Paul Revere, Billy Dawes, and Samuel Prescott had ridden all night from Boston to warn the local militias.

The Conflict Begins

When Major John Pitcairn, the British officer in charge, spotted the Minutemen on the green, he ordered his men into battle lines. Then he urged his horse forward, shouting at the colonists "Disperse ye villains, ye rebels!"

Suddenly a shot rang out. The British troops charged forward. Eyewitnesses disagree on whether the British or the colonists fired first. In any case, the battle was over in minutes. Ten colonists were wounded and eight were killed, including Jonas Parker. One British soldier was hurt.

Pitcairn then marched his troops six miles to Concord. There they searched buildings and set fire to the town hall. At 9:30 A.M., a group of militiamen clashed with the British at North Bridge and drove them off. Two colonists and three British soldiers were killed.

Retreat to Boston

After their losses at North Bridge, the British began their retreat to Boston. However, more than 1,000 angry militiamen from other villages gathered and fired at the Redcoats from behind trees and stone walls. Before the British reached the safety of Boston at 9:30 P.M., the Americans had 95 dead and wounded, the British 273. The American Revolution had begun. ■

Farmers and towns-people took up arms to defend their homes in Lexington and Concord.

■ *Why was the militia of Lexington and Concord ready to oppose the British raiding party?*

War Breaks Out

The Continental Congress Meets

Months earlier, in September 1774, representatives of each colony had gathered at the First Continental Congress. At that time, these representatives, or **delegates,** promised to meet again in May 1775 if the problems with Britain continued. Now blood had been shed and tensions were high. The need to meet was clear. Leaders of the 13 colonies gathered in Philadelphia on May 10, 1775, for the Second Continental Congress. They had big decisions to make.

Preparing for War

Many Americans wanted the colonies and Great Britain to settle their differences. The members of Congress were prepared to try that solution. But they also knew that they had to prepare for the worst —a war for **independence,** which would free them from control by Britain.

Congress quickly began acting like an independent government.

By a small majority, they voted to organize the New England militia into an army of 20,000 "for the defense of American liberty." They named George Washington, a Virginian, to lead the forces.

Congress also agreed to issue paper money to buy gunpowder and weapons. Since they feared the British would turn the Indian tribes against them, they set up a commission to keep peace with the Indians. They also began seeking support from other European countries.

Seeking Peace

To try to avoid war, Congress sent a written request to King George III. The message stated the colonists' loyalty to the king. It blamed the king's ministers for trying to enslave the colonies. It also asked the king to help restore peace by ending the unfair laws he had imposed. This message was called the Olive Branch Petition.

▶ *Delegates from the 13 colonies gathered in Philadelphia at the Second Continental Congress. In this painting of their meeting by John Trumbull, you can see five leaders of the new nation: 1. John Adams; 2. Roger Sherman; 3. Robert R. Livingston; 4. Thomas Jefferson; and 5. Benjamin Franklin.*

The Second Continental Congress issued paper money like this to buy gunpowder and other war supplies.

It took a month for a ship to carry the colonists' message to King George. But it took only two days for the king to reject the colonists' request and to declare the colonies in rebellion. The king outlawed trade with the colonies and ordered 20,000 more troops to America. The war was under way. ■

■ Why did the colonies need a government after Lexington and Concord, and what actions did the new government take?

The Colonists Declare Independence

Fighting between the colonists and the British increased during the fall and winter of 1775. Militiamen placed cannons on Dorchester Heights near Boston and drove the British from the city. On January 1, 1776, ships of the British navy shelled Norfolk, Virginia, and caused a great fire that burned the town. But Americans were gaining confidence, and the idea of independence was gathering force.

Common Sense

In January 1776, Thomas Paine, an Englishman who had settled in Pennsylvania, published a bold call to revolution. His work, called *Common Sense,* asked the colonists to consider all the reasons to fight for independence.

Paine pointed out that it was not logical for a small island like Britain to rule a large continent like America. He argued strongly that the colonists should not feel loyal to a king who was ruling them harshly. He urged the colonists to separate from England. "A government of our own is our natural right," he wrote.

By March 1776, three months after it was printed, 120,000 copies of *Common Sense* were sold in all of the colonies. Paine's writing was simple but strong. All Americans could understand and discuss his ideas. This small pamphlet helped persuade many Americans to fight for independence.

The Declaration of Independence

As the idea of independence spread throughout the colonies, many colonies began to set up their own governments. Soon, some of the colonies began to press Congress to officially declare independence from Great Britain.

On June 7, 1776, Richard Henry Lee of Virginia made a motion to the Congress that "these unified colonies ought to be free and independent states." After much debate, Congress met on July 2, 1776, to consider a formal Declaration of Independence. It had been written by a committee of five, including Benjamin Franklin, John Adams, and Thomas Jefferson, a 33-year-old delegate from Virginia.

Jefferson began the Declaration with a short introduction. This paragraph promised that the Declaration would spell out the reasons the colonies had to separate from Britain.

Then, in three sections, Jefferson made the case for independence. In the first section, he

▼ *Thomas Jefferson penned the rough draft of the Declaration of Independence shown at the bottom of the page.*

UNDERSTANDING EQUALITY

P robably the most famous words in the Declaration of Independence are the following: "We hold these truths to be self-evident, that all men are created equal." But what did Thomas Jefferson and the other signers of the Declaration mean by equal? And what does equality mean today?

Jefferson's Equality

Equality means that all people have the same rights and privileges, such as the right to vote. Equality does not mean that everyone is the same. Obviously, some people are stronger, or more artistic, or more athletic than others. People differ also in their sex, race, religion, and country of birth. In 1776, when the Declaration of Independence was written, differences like these determined a person's rights. At that time, only white men could be citizens. When Jefferson wrote that "all men" were equal, he really meant "all citizens." Women and blacks were not included.

Equality Today

Over the years, new laws have extended the rights of citizenship to all Americans equally. After the Civil War, Congress acted to give black Americans the right to vote. In 1920, women finally received this same right.

Today, equality means that the laws of the United States apply to everyone in exactly the same way. By law, all Americans have an equal opportunity to be hired for a job. Every American also has an equal right to use public buses and subways. Though the law grants these rights to everyone, black Americans and other minorities have had to struggle to make sure that these laws are applied fairly.

◄ *Angry colonists pulled down a statue of King George. Some stories say that the colonists melted down the statue and made musket balls from the metal.*

stated a bold idea—that each citizen has natural rights that governments cannot give or take away. These included rights to "life, liberty, and the pursuit of happiness." The purpose of government was to make sure all people could enjoy these rights.

The second section was an accusation. It listed 27 ways in which King George III had misused his power. It accused him of taxing the colonists without their consent and cutting off their trade. It also said the king forced colonists to house and feed British soldiers.

The third section was a brave statement of independence. It stated that the colonies had asked the king many times to end his unfair treatment and he had refused. "We therefore declare," the Declaration then concludes, "that these united colonies are, and of right ought to be, free and independent states." You can read a copy of the Declaration of Independence on pages 528-531 of the Time/Space Databank.

Two days later, Congress voted to accept the Declaration. The date was July 4, 1776. ■

R E V I E W

1. **FOCUS** How did the colonies organize a government to lead their fight for independence?

2. **CONNECT** In what ways did King George rule the colonists harshly and unfairly before the start of the Revolutionary War?

3. **CITIZENSHIP** In the Declaration, Jefferson wrote that each citizen has natural rights. What are these natural rights, and what should government do about them?

4. **CRITICAL THINKING** Compare what Thomas Jefferson meant by equality and what this word means to Americans today. Give some examples of equality as it applies to students at your school.

5. **ACTIVITY** With other students, act out the events of the Battle of Lexington. You might start with the clanging of the alarm bell at midnight and end with the fight at dawn on the Lexington green.

Patriot or Loyalist?

> A republican form of government [elected representatives] will never suit the genius of the people or the extent of the country. The Americans are properly Britons.
>
> Elias Boudinot of New Jersey, to the Continental Congress, June, 1776

> Our Cause is the Cause of all Mankind, and we are fighting for their Liberty in defending our own.
>
> Benjamin Franklin

Background

Soldiers used tinder boxes like these to start their campfires.

The American colonists were not all alike. Some were poor, others rich, many were somewhere in the middle. Most were from England, but many had come to America from Holland or Germany or France. Some were very well educated, while others were skilled at a trade, such as carpentry, candle making, or wheel making. Still others had come to the colonies hoping to learn a trade or buy a small farm. Colonists also differed in their religious beliefs and in their politics. How did all these people ever agree to break away from England? They didn't.

Some colonists felt very "English." They missed the relatives they'd left behind. Many of them hoped to return to England some day. Others in the colonies had become "American." This was their country, not England. Some, like Thomas Paine and Benjamin Franklin, no longer accepted the idea of kings. They did not want to be forced to obey distant royalty. They believed people could and should govern themselves. Others still believed that kings were meant to rule nations.

Once it was clear that there would be war with England, families and individuals had to make a difficult choice: Would they be patriot, or would they be loyalist?

Musket balls

Musket ball mold

Conflict Over the Revolution

In this war the colonies were fighting the most powerful country in the world. If the colonies lost the war, England might demand even higher taxes and impose even stricter laws. Maybe it would be best to remain loyal to the king. When the war ended, surely this loyalty would be rewarded. Besides, the king was the rightful ruler of the British empire, and the American colonies were part of that empire.

On the other hand, there was much to be said in favor of the rebellion. The taxes were unfair, and peaceful action had brought no change. The mood of the colonies was one of great excitement. Those who were against the war would be uncomfortable at best. At worst, they could be suspected of spying or accused of treason.

England's army was strong, but the soldiers were not used to fighting as the colonists fought. Also, the English soldiers were not fighting on their own land and protecting their own homes and families. The colonial leaders also knew how harshly they could be treated if they lost the war. They intended to win.

Finally, there remained the bold idea behind the rebellion: Could people, should people, govern themselves?

Loyalist or Patriot

Loyalty to England Fear of punishment Family in England	Self-government Tax relief Create a new nation
Loyalist	Patriot

Decision Point

1. Suppose you are a colonist who wants independence, but you are opposed to war. How would you achieve your goal? What could persuade you to fight?

2. What goals and values could make a colonist decide to remain loyal to the king?

3. The colonists were fighting for certain freedoms, including the freedom to share ideas. Do you think they would allow loyalists to write and speak freely during the war? Why?

4. The colonists valued freedom of speech. They wanted to be free to criticize their government and its officials. Today we value this same freedom, but there are some limits to free speech. Can you think of at least one example? Do these limits conflict with the goals and values of free speech as the colonists saw it?

▼ *A captain in George Washington's bodyguard wore this helmet.*

L E S S O N   2

Fighting the War

▼ *Continental Army drummers beat colorful drums to signal soldiers.*

General Thomas Gage, commander of all British soldiers in North America, was angry and discouraged. On this day in June 1775, he sat at his desk in Boston writing a letter to his superiors in London. He was trying to explain what had happened.

Only days before, a ragtag army of 1,000 Massachusetts volunteers held off 2,500 British Redcoats on Bunker Hill and Breed's Hill north of Boston. Twice the Redcoats charged up the hill. Twice the volunteers threw them back with blasts of musket fire.

We captured the hills in the end, Gage reminded himself. But we lost so many—1,150 British soldiers, wounded or dead!

"You will receive an account of some success against the rebels, but attended with a long list of killed or wounded on our side," Gage wrote in his letter of explanation, "so many of the latter that the hospital has hardly hands sufficient to take care of them." In describing the American soldiers, Gage wrote, "These people are now spirited up by a rage and enthusiasm, as great as ever people were possessed of."

The Soldiers Who Fought the War

The American soldiers were so "spirited up" because they believed in their cause. They were fighting to replace the British king with a **republic,** a government in which citizens elect their leaders. To them, the war was a **revolution,** a change of government by force.

Many kinds of soldiers took part in the Revolution. On the American side were militia companies who defended Bunker Hill. Militiamen enlisted for a particular battle or at most for a year. Since many were farmers, militiamen often went home during harvest and planting times.

In contrast, young men without families joined the Continental Army, which Congress had formed. You can learn more about Continental soldiers in A Moment in Time on page 271.

In this painting by William Renney, a black soldier helps American forces win an important victory in South Carolina in January 1781.

Deborah Sampson was so eager to fight in the war that she dressed as a man and joined the Massachusetts militia.

Many men enlisted because Congress promised to give them 100 acres of land and 20 dollars in cash if they served in the army for three years. About 5,000 free blacks also joined the Continental Army. Some were slaves who were freed as a reward for enlisting.

Some American women also went into battle. Margaret Corbin accompanied the troop of her husband, John. Like many other women of the time, Corbin did chores for the troops such as cooking and washing. But John Corbin was killed at his wife's side in a battle at Fort Washington, near New York City. Margaret Corbin took over her husband's post and fought until she herself was wounded. Another woman, Deborah Sampson, disguised as a man and served in the Massachusetts militia from 1781 to 1783.

On the British side, Britain's soldiers were full-time and well trained. They were also well supplied with uniforms and weapons. In addition, Britain hired German soldiers and transported them to America. Some Americans who were still loyal to the king also fought for Britain. These **Loyalists** were also called Tories, after a group of politicians in England who supported the king. The British army also successfully recruited thousands of American slaves. ∎

Name a significant difference between the British and American soldiers who fought in the Revolutionary War.

War Rages in the North

In the first real battles of the war, the British army captured New York City. After that, they attacked Philadelphia. Washington's inexperienced soldiers fought off the British advance. However, the British took control of the city by September 1777. Thomas Paine later said, "These are the times that try men's souls."

Washington led his defeated troops to a camp at Valley Forge, 18 miles northwest of Philadelphia. The general and his weary soldiers spent the icy winter of 1777–1778 in the valley's harsh conditions. Since Valley Forge had no buildings, the soldiers fought the chilling cold to build simple huts.

War Breaks Out

Their worn-out shoes and clothing were little help against the cold. Worst of all, they had hardly any food. They survived on little but firecake, a thin bread of flour and water. Hundreds died—of starvation, frost-bite, or smallpox. As one soldier complained, "Here all [is] confusion —smoke and cold— hunger and filthiness."

Conditions were truly terrible, yet Washington's strength and determination held his army together. He was a stern leader, but Washington still had the trust and admiration of his men. See page 565 in the Time/Space Databank for more information about Washington.

Indian Strategies

Early in the Revolution, the Indians had tried not to take sides. But in 1777, General John Burgoyne and other British agents met with the leaders of the Iroquois nation. Many Iroquois were angry at American settlers who had taken their land. The Seneca, Cayuga, Mohawk, and Onondaga agreed to help the British.

Though Indian attacks hurt the colonies, Americans learned a valuable lesson from the Indians. During battle, the Indians fought differently than the British. Instead of standing in rows to shoot, they attacked by surprise from behind rocks and trees, then vanished.

Washington had seen the Indians fight during the Seven Years' War. He decided to adopt their hit-and-run strategy. It helped his soldiers stand up to the experienced British army.

British Plans

Iroquois fighters also joined an army in Canada under General Burgoyne. Burgoyne convinced King George that an attack from Canada was certain to end the Revolution. Two other British armies were supposed to meet Burgoyne at Albany, New York. The British hoped to weaken New England by cutting it off from the other colonies.

▲ *Because firecakes were cooked over a wood fire, they were often covered with ashes.*

➤ *Burgoyne told the Iroquois that the rebellious colonists were like bad children who were arguing with their father, King George.*

A Continental Soldier

5:56 P.M., September 9, 1781
At the edge of a field, half a mile
from Williamsburg, Virginia

Beard
He will shave tonight, after a week without soap and razors. He's been marching every day. The wagons holding all the equipment just caught up with him.

Hunting Shirt
Sewn by his mother, this homespun linen uniform scares the enemy. General Washington says the British think every person who wears a shirt like this is an expert with a musket.

Fish
Dinner smells delicious, after days of eating chewy dried beef. Munching on nuts and berries he found in the woods this morning only made him hungrier.

Knife
The brass-handled knife he carries on the back of his belt was a gift from his father when he joined the army four years ago. The knife was made in England, where he lived until he was seven.

Bedroll
His blanket contains his army coat and a letter from his sister telling him he is sorely missed on the farm.

Shoes
The leather dried stiff and tight after several days of slogging through the rain.

Musket
Cheap and easy to fire, his musket is fitted with a bayonet for stabbing.

Burgoyne's army marched through a wilderness. As the British cut down trees to make a road, New York militiamen shot at them from behind rocks and trees. Near Saratoga, New York, Burgoyne's army clashed with 6,000 American soldiers, led by General Horatio Gates. Burgoyne hoped for help, but the two other British armies never came. After days of fighting, Burgoyne surrendered to Gates in October 1777.

■ *What made it possible for the weaker American army to fight successfully against the British?*

The victory at Saratoga brought an important ally to the side of the Americans. The French were still angry that Britain had beaten them in the Seven Years' War. Now the French hoped to weaken Britain by helping its American colonies win their freedom. Saratoga convinced the French that America could win the war. In February 1778, French soldiers and ships joined the fight beside the Americans. ■

The War Moves South

▼ *Though the Revolutionary War began in the New England colonies, battles took place in every part of colonial America.*

After Burgoyne's defeat in the North, the British generals turned south. The British knew that the southern colonies had fewer soldiers than the North. Southern planters were not willing to leave their farms to fight because they were afraid their slaves would revolt. In fact, thousands of slaves did join the British. In Virginia, Britain formed an army unit of 600 black men. Britain also received help from the many Loyalists who lived in North Carolina and South Carolina.

As a first step in conquering the South, the British invaded Georgia with 3,500 men. They chose Georgia because it was the youngest and weakest colony. The 850 American defenders were outnumbered. In a battle near Savannah in December 1778, the British won control of Georgia.

However, the greatest prize in the South was Charleston, South Carolina. British forces under Sir Henry Clinton surrounded the city with 8,500 troops and 14 warships. They slowly closed in. On May 12, 1780, the 5,000 Americans defending the city were

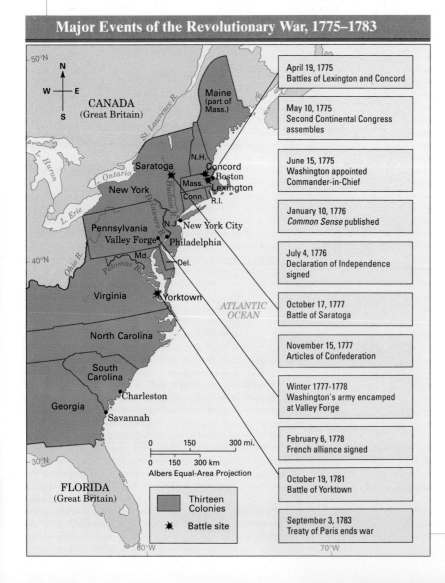

Major Events of the Revolutionary War, 1775–1783

Date	Event
April 19, 1775	Battles of Lexington and Concord
May 10, 1775	Second Continental Congress assembles
June 15, 1775	Washington appointed Commander-in-Chief
January 10, 1776	*Common Sense* published
July 4, 1776	Declaration of Independence signed
October 17, 1777	Battle of Saratoga
November 15, 1777	Articles of Confederation
Winter 1777-1778	Washington's army encamped at Valley Forge
February 6, 1778	French alliance signed
October 19, 1781	Battle of Yorktown
September 3, 1783	Treaty of Paris ends war

CANADA (Great Britain)

Maine (part of Mass.)

Saratoga
New York
N.H.
Concord
Boston
Mass.
Lexington
Conn.
R.I.

Pennsylvania
Valley Forge
New York City
Philadelphia
N.J.
Md.
Del.

Virginia
Yorktown
ATLANTIC OCEAN

North Carolina

South Carolina
Charleston

Georgia
Savannah

FLORIDA (Great Britain)

Thirteen Colonies

★ Battle site

0   150   300 mi.
0 150 300 km
Albers Equal-Area Projection

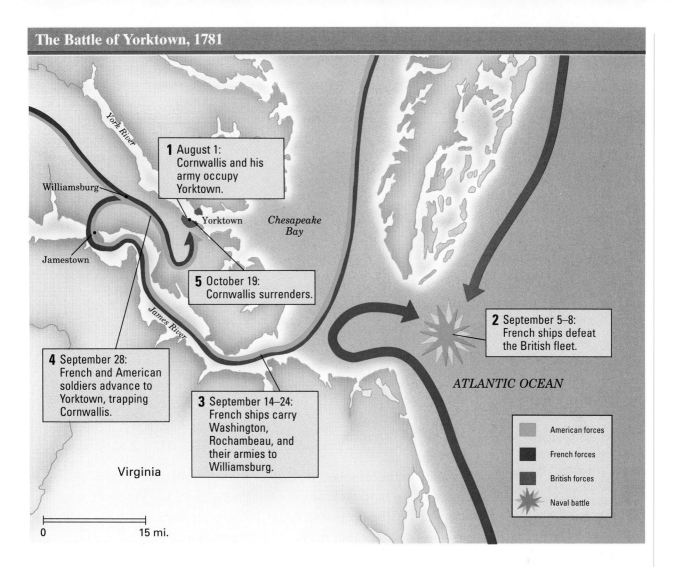

1 August 1: Cornwallis and his army occupy Yorktown.

5 October 19: Cornwallis surrenders.

4 September 28: French and American soldiers advance to Yorktown, trapping Cornwallis.

3 September 14–24: French ships carry Washington, Rochambeau, and their armies to Williamsburg.

2 September 5–8: French ships defeat the British fleet.

York River

Williamsburg

Jamestown

Yorktown

Chesapeake Bay

James River

ATLANTIC OCEAN

Virginia

American forces

French forces

British forces

Naval battle

0   15 mi.

The geography of Yorktown helped the American and French forces trap and defeat Cornwallis.

forced to surrender. It was the most serious American defeat of the war.

The Battle of Yorktown

The victory at Charleston convinced the British commander Lord Cornwallis that he could win in the South. In August 1781, Cornwallis moved his 7,200 soldiers into position at Yorktown, Virginia.

George Washington and the French generals thought that they could defeat Cornwallis at Yorktown. They made a brilliant plan. In September 1781, both Washington and French General Rochambeau (*roh sham BOH*) moved their armies swiftly south from New York. They trapped Cornwallis on the peninsula between the York and James rivers.

Cornwallis looked for help from the British navy. But he could not escape Yorktown by sea because British ships had lost control of the coast. On September 5, French Admiral DeGrasse and 28 French warships began a fierce naval battle against 18 British ships. For five days, the big cannons on the ships thundered and boomed in the heavy seas off the coast of Virginia. The French fleet outgunned and outsailed the British. In the end, the French warships were victorious.

On the morning of September 28, the French and American armies attacked Yorktown.

273

United States, 1790

CANADA
(Great Britain)

Maine
(part of
Mass.)

Vt.

N.H.

New York

Mass.

R.I.

Conn.

Pennsylvania

N.J.

ATLANTIC
OCEAN

Northwest
Territory

Md.

Del.

Virginia

LOUISIANA
(Spain)

North
Carolina

Southwest
Territories

South
Carolina

Georgia

0   200   400 km

0   200   400 km
Albers Equal-Area Projection

FLORIDA
(Spain)

Gulf of Mexico

Original 13 states

Ceded by states

▲ *The Treaty of Paris, shown above, ended the American struggle for independence from Britain. The map to the right shows the United States after the war. The new states ceded their old colonial land claims to the new government.*

■ *Why did the British concentrate their war efforts in the southern colonies after 1778?*

Cornwallis was outnumbered three-to-one on land and cut off from the sea by the French navy. Cornwallis could see that his position was hopeless. On October 19, 1781, he surrendered his army to General Washington.

The Treaty of Paris

The victory at Yorktown won the war for the Americans. In April 1782, Congress sent three Americans—Benjamin Franklin, John Adams, and John Jay—to Paris. There they met with the British and worked out a treaty, or formal agreement of peace.

Under the treaty, the colonies were given complete independence. The treaty also gave them a great deal of land. Trace the boundaries of the United States after the Revolutionary War on the map above. What natural geographic feature formed the western boundary of the new United States? ■

R E V I E W

1. **FOCUS** How did poorly equipped American soldiers defeat Britain's army and win independence for the colonies?

2. **CONNECT** How did George Washington's experiences in the Seven Years' War prepare him to lead America's fight for independence?

3. **GEOGRAPHY** How did George Washington and his French allies use the geography of Yorktown, Virginia, to help them defeat Lord Cornwallis?

4. **CRITICAL THINKING** Why did many Black Americans and American Indians choose to fight on the side of the British during the Revolutionary War? In what ways were their reasons similar?

5. **ACTIVITY** Imagine that you are a junior member of General Burgoyne's staff. Your job is to persuade a group of young Iroquois fighters to join the British army. What will you say to the Iroquois?

Organizing What You Read

Here's Why

Learning how to outlining helps you to understand and remember what you read. When you outline a lesson, you arrange the facts and ideas from the lesson under main topics and subtopics. Then by reviewing and reading over the outline, you can quickly and easily see the important points of the lesson.

Here's How

The outline on this page shows the main points of Lesson 1. Roman numerals set off the main ideas. A capital letter sets off each subtopic, which is an important point supporting the main idea. Arabic numerals set off the details that support subtopics.

■ main head
■ subtopic
■ detail

I. The first shot is fired
  A. The conflict begins
    1. The battle of Lexington
    2. The battle of Concord
  B. Retreat to Boston
    1. Militiamen fire on Redcoats
    2. Injuries and deaths are many
II. The Continental Congress meets
  A. Preparing for war
    1. Army organized
    2. George Washington named commander-in-chief
    3. Paper money printed to buy weapons and gunpowder
    4. Peace commission formed for the Indians
    5. European support sought
  B. Seeking peace
    1. The Olive Branch Petition
    2. Trade with colonies outlawed
III. The colonists declare independence
  A. Common Sense
  B. The Declaration of Independence
    1. Introduction (Preamble)
    2. Statement of human rights
    3. Accusations against the king
    4. Statement of independence

Before you begin an outline, look over the material to get an overview. Find the main ideas, important points, and supporting details. In this textbook, the headings and subheadings will help you. Sometimes, though, there aren't a lot of headings in a lesson. To make an outline in such cases, you may need to add your own subtopics based on the content .

Notice how the outline below is arranged. At least two subtopics appear under each main head. If details are listed under a subtopic, there are at least two details.

Try It

Copy the outline onto a sheet of paper. Use Lesson 2 to finish the outline.

I. The soldiers who fought the war
  A. The American side
    1. Local militia
    2. _____
  B. _____
    1. _____
    2. Hired German soldiers
    3. _____

Apply It

Outline another lesson from this textbook. Use the sample outline as a guide.

Sybil Ludington's Ride

Erick Berry

Sybil Ludington was a real person and a real hero of the Revolutionary War. Like the militiamen in Lesson 2, she was ready to fight the British.

The American Revolution was fought by famous soldiers like George Washington and ordinary people whose names we don't remember. As you have learned, many of these unknown soldiers were part-time fighters—militiamen—who had to be called together to fight a battle. How were these soldiers notified that they were needed when there was no telephone, radio, or television? Who brought the message to them? Ride with one of those ordinary people on April 17, 1777, as 14-year-old Sybil Ludington makes a 30-mile journey on horseback to deliver the message that "the British are coming."

The pitch-black night closed down like a shutter. There followed a slight struggle. For Star didn't approve of the cold wet night and wanted to return to the comfort of his stable; at least that was what Sybil hoped. But in the darkness it was quite possible she was trying to ride him through the thick trunk of the butternut tree, and to that he quite naturally objected.

No, there was a deeper dark against the black, the tree trunk. And a moment after, Star stumbled into the deep ruts of the road. Left or right? Left of course; the horse protesting only because he felt that any road was the wrong road on a night like this.

The roar of the millstream came clear above the drumming of the rain, and there on the right bulked the shape of the mill.

Jake Hunter's there on the right, she was sure of it. And here was the turn-in. There was a light too, in the kitchen. But had she really come so short a distance? For this wasn't Jake's after all, it was only the Gillettes'.

She rode Star up to the window—it was no matter that he tramped Mrs. Gillette's yarbs—and hammered noisily on the shutter with her fist. The window swung open.

"Father sent me to carry warning," she began politely, as though she were inviting the woman to supper at the Ludingtons'.

"You, gal, at this time of night!" said Mrs. Gillette. "Is aught wrong? Hitch, and come right in."

Sybil took a deep breath and tried again, this time in a firmer tone. "The British are burning Danbury. Tell Mr. Gillette that the troops are to muster immediately. Women and children to bundle

yarbs garden herbs

aught anything
hitch to tie a horse's bridle to a post
muster gather together

up their valuables and be ready to drive off livestock, if the redcoats come this way. And please spread word to your neighbors." That was her full message. She wheeled Star and headed him down the road. She hoped the woman would believe her and take warning.

Only a short ride—Star more willing now—to the Hunters'. The house was dark; could she afford time to waken them? Oh, she must, for he was a corporal in the militia and mighty dependable. But she would remember that the message she brought was military. She reined up, hammered lustily at the shutter, and shouted, "Rouse! Rouse! The British are burning Danbury!" There would be no need here to explain what that meant, what it meant to the whole countryside.

corporal military officer in charge of troops
lustily powerfully
rouse wake up

A head came out of a window, and Jake's voice said almost placidly, "That'll mean a mustering."

"And please to tell your neighbors."

She was off again, with growing sense of relief. Jake would know what to do. And she wouldn't have to stop at the next house, a half-mile farther on. Star broke into a canter, and she urged him faster, with the realization of how long it was going to take to deliver each message; even, in the darkness, to find each house. Thank goodness she had changed to trousers; by now her skirts would have been a cold, sodden mass; as it was, the shawl over her head slapped in a wet lump against her chest, carried water like a gutter along her leg; and when in passing it caught on a hanging branch she jerked away, letting it go. Hopeless to hunt for it in the dark, and anyway it was no longer protection. She could scarcely be wetter.

Two more households were wakened without difficulty, and one even remembered to thank her. Then she encountered what threatened to be a failure. Susannah Oppenshore utterly refused to waken her deaf husband.

"There's been a sight too many musterin's," she snapped at Sybil through the half-open window. "And a man's got his duty by his wife and farm. Likely enough it's a false alarm, like all the others."

sight large number

277

Disgusted, furious with the woman's selfishness, scarce able to believe anyone could be so shortsighted, Sybil tried again.

"But this time the British are at Danbury. We need every soldier—"

"Let the Danbury folk fight them, then," snapped the woman. "And you go right home and quit pesterin' folks."

Sybil, glancing anxiously along the road, desperate to be off again, noted how much clearer the bare trees showed against the sky. What was that glow? Surely not moonrise, with all this rain. She turned to the woman, about to close her window.

"If you don't believe me, ma'am," she said, "look out at the sky there. 'Tis Danbury burning. You can see the glare of it on the clouds. Like enough the redcoats are marching this way even now."

"The redcoats comin' this way?" The woman's anger changed suddenly to fear. She turned to shout back into the house, "Timothy! You there, Timothy! D'you want us all to be burned in our beds? . . ."

Sybil missed the rest of it.

At Carmel settlement she paused to summon only three; one offered to ride on with her. The thought of having a human companion on the lonely dark road was tempting, so tempting. But she told him the route she was taking, the road to the lake, and begged him to spread the alarm east along the highroad. Before she was out of the settlement she heard the raucous clamor of the village bell; it bore her reassuring company for nigh a mile.

Then came a long and cheerless stretch. The yearling's first burst of energy and her own excitement were fading into a dull, dogged purpose. She tried to sing against the pelting rain. Star pricked up his ears and seemed to move more cheerfully.

She patted his neck. "Good boy!" she told him. "I don't know what we'd have done without you. Between us we've roused at least a dozen homes, and each household is spreading the alarm to others. 'Tisn't every yearling, or even full-grown horse, can put fifty or more armed men in the field to fight the enemy." And true it was.

Was the rain really easing? Hard to tell, both she and Star were so wet. But through the dark she could hear the chime of the peepers in the swamp, and once an owl floated past her face, silent as a blown feather. Here, so far from home, she was less familiar with the countryside, and it was fortunate the sky was less dark. As it was, she couldn't spare time to halt at every clearing and search for a house. But those whom she roused promised to carry on the news.

She had by now carried the alarm over eight miles or more of countryside, but that was less than a quarter of the distance she must go. Shivering, she was, with cold and weariness. But how

raucous harsh, rough sounding
nigh almost
yearling one-year-old horse

278

about Star? He was willing enough, but could a yearling, who hadn't yet come to his full growth and strength, stay the whole course?

With almost a shock she realized that she was no longer afraid of him. Not a single trick he had tried to play on the whole ride. It was as though the urgency of her errand was understood by him, as though he knew how much and how many depended on him. On, on, he swept through the night, splashing through deep rain-filled wheel ruts, fording small streams, sure-footed in the darkness. And as she talked to him, "Good fellow. Oh, Star, that was splendid. Careful now, that branch almost swept me off. Here's a bit that's bad . . ." there had grown up between them, young rider and young mount, a sympathy, a comradeship, each understanding the other, each relying on each.

At the next clearing a light already showed in the barn. She splashed up to it, and her voice, hoarse now, delivered her urgent message.

"Danbury, is it?" said the man. "I saw the light and thought as 'twas a house in Carmel burning." He finished saddling up and set down the two buckets he had tied over his shoulder. "I won't be needing these now. Reckon a musket'll be more good against the redcoats' kind of fire."

And on again, the lake glimmering on her right through its thick fringe of trees. And after the lake, someone had told her, she must look for a sharp turn right. She found it, or hoped she had. She should be turning north here, and could judge her direction by the glow in the sky. This was the least settled, most terrifying stretch of the whole route. Here were no big clearings, no farms, no mills or well-built houses. Just a few squatters, trappers, and such living with their families in small ill-built cabins among the thick untimbered forest. And in between, for a mile at a time, the road was no more than a pitch-black tunnel, with trees close-arched above her head. Once Star shied right across the track and nearly brushed her off against a tree trunk. It might be no more than a raccoon or a wandering porcupine; but there had been wolves here, even in recent years, and in wartime when men kept their powder and ball to shoot each other such critters might easily return in force.

With murmurings and a gentling hand she steadied Star to a safer pace, though her instinct urged her to escape at full gallop. "We're important, Star. So much depends on us. If you break a leg or I get swept off and stunned by a bough, the British may catch these people helpless in their beds."

In front of her, for mile after dark mile, lay a sleeping, defenseless countryside. Behind her, kindled by her message, lights had sprung up, hearthfires had been raked to a blaze, lanterns carried at a run to barns, to neighbors lying off the route. Voices called to

squatters persons illegally living on vacant land

voices, people were dressing, women packing in haste, men shouting for their arms, for musket and powder horn and bullet bag, and saddling or hasting away on foot. Children, bundled still sleeping from their cots, or the older ones sent on errands, given tasks; this one to help grandmother, that one to catch up the hens in readiness for flight, another to bury the pewter in the garden— she could imagine a hundred such happenings.

But before her, nothing but darkness, sleep, unreadiness. No, for there was a glow ahead, more than a houselight. A glow of a firelight through the trees. Soldiers, mustering, perhaps, to march to the Ludingtons', had kindled a small blaze? But it seemed unlikely.

Whoever they were they must be told. She turned Star off the road, headed him in the direction of the bonfire, and left it to him to thread his way between the rocks and undergrowth.

She could see six men or thereabouts. And horses. And, yes, firearms were propped beside the seated men as they warmed themselves at the blaze.

But no man with farming to do would be awake and camped out in the open at this time of night, and the British could scarcely have reached here as yet. But all the same it was relief to see that the men wore no colored uniform. Which made it likely they were militia.

She was near enough now to shout. And was just about to, when a stone turned under Star's hoof and went rattling down a short slope. A man sprang up from the fireside and grabbed his musket.

Sybil jerked tight the rein. The appetizing odor of roast mutton had reached her. And there, slowly turning on a greenwood spit beside the fire, was the best part of a stolen sheep.

Not British, not militia, these men. They were thieves and robbers, cowboys or skinners.

Desperately she turned the yearling; and, eyes blinded by the firelight, headed him back into the darkness.

A chorus of shouts. The cutthroats were after her.

There was no knowing what these outlaws would do if they caught her. And if they captured her, who would spread the alarm? Her safety, Star's safety, was nothing beside the safety of the whole countryside.

She had a hundred paces' start. Add a few moments while the cutthroats were catching and saddling their horses. If only she could gallop, gallop, lose herself in the darkness.

But here under the thick trees there was no chance even of picking her direction. And at every panic attempt to make for the road, boulders, a stream bed, giant tree trunks, headed her off. Star stumbled and slipped at a scrambling walk. She was lost, but in a moment she was glad of it.

---

pewter fine metal dishes used in colonial times

cowboys or skinners guerrillas, or independent fighters

cutthroats murderers

For from eastward in the probable direction of the road came the wrathful shout of voices. "Headed south, I cal'late."

"No, north. Or I'd have seen him. You might ha' let him past."

So they had taken her for a man? That was somehow encouraging.

But how lucky that she hadn't got down to the road and been caught between the two lots of skinners. When it served their turn these outlaws murdered as freely as they robbed, and they wouldn't think twice of putting a musket ball into an unlucky witness who had caught them roasting that stolen sheep.

She pulled up Star and waited a moment, listening. The glow of the campfire was out of sight, or perhaps they had quenched it. No sound but the creak of the saddle to Star's wearied breathing; and he, the darling, was listening too, head up, ears pricked. Then she caught a sound, a man's footfall; faint though it was, she was sure of it. Not that she could hear each step. But a stone rolled, a sodden twig snapped. It came no nearer, seemed to retreat.

In the tenseness of her waiting, moments seemed hours; as long as she was silent she was safe. But someone must carry the call to arms; she couldn't wait here till daylight, when the skinners would have moved off. And which way were they going? North or south? If she only knew.

For lack of a better plan she decided to strike east, far enough east to get behind their camp, then head north, and at a safe distance circle, to cut back west to the road. But ten minutes' slow floundering as the yearling heaved himself up one slippery rock, slithered down another, convinced her that she had lost all sense of direction; and the rise of the ground to one side had blotted out any glow from Danbury. Oh, why had she been such a fool as to turn off for that campfire? Even [her sister] Ricky, reckless as she was, would have more sense than that; Ricky, safely at home, tucked in snug and warm under the covers. Sybil almost envied her.

Twice the yearling nearly fell and all but pitched her off in his efforts to recover balance. She dismounted and tried to lead him; that might be easier for Star, but it was harder, a heap harder, for Sybil. Slipping and sliding over wet leaves, wedging a foot between rocks, blundering into tree trunks, she could have cried with sheer fatigue and vexation. And every moment of delay might be bringing the enemy closer, closer; while militiamen, badly needed, slumbered in their homes.

Suddenly, from nearby, came a man's voice. "Who's that?"

One of the cattle stealers, no doubt, thinking he had come across a comrade. She could see the darker shadow in the dimness, and he must be able to see her, for the summons came again.

And more sharply this time. "Who's there?"

She stretched out an arm, as though with a pistol. "Stand, or I fire!"

wrathful angry
cal'late calculate, figure
ha' have

quenched put out

"Holy Moses!" in tones of surprise. "That ain't you, Sybil Ludington? It's me, Zeke Cowper, that you roused a while since. I'm cuttin' cross-lots to the other road, to pass on your warning. But cripes above, this is no place for you to be ridin'."

Sybil could have burst into tears with sheer relief. But fearful that his loud, cheerful voice might betray them, she begged him to be quiet and whispered her news of the skinners' camp.

"Once the war's won we'll hang 'em all, skinners and cowboys alike," he rumbled angrily. "But you let me lead your horse and you follow. It's only a step across here to the next road."

Zeke's idea of a "step" was a giant's stride, but they did reach the road at last, a road that lay east of the one she had been following. "Just head north, for Ben Hasbrouck's place," he advised her as he helped her back into the saddle. "Then turn east for Stormville; Ben'll show you." And promised, if he arrived first, to tell her father that, so far, all was well.

Frightened she was now, and she would admit as much, after that meeting with the skinners. It called for all the courage she could lay hand on to ride in off the road and rouse the next farm. At Ben Hasbrouck's, at the turn of the road, they set her on her new direction, and surprised her by telling her it was no later than midnight, when she had thought the dawn itself must be close. But more than half her ride was over; Star, who had gone lame for a while, had only caught a stone in his hoof, and once she had that out, he was striding out as gallantly as before. Never,

as long as she lived, would she forget how brave, how helpful he was. If ever there was a good patriot, it was Star this night. Heavens, how tired she was! Every muscle ached, and legs and even arms were bruised from floundering around among those rocks. But strangely enough she had never been happier in her life, though she didn't know it herself till she found herself singing.

A mile or so later and with a good hour's ride still ahead of her, her troubles were already over; someone riding from the opposite direction had already spread the alarm. First there were lighted houses; then there were armed men, in twos and threes, striding on grimly to muster for defense, to fight for freedom. They gave her a shout and some gave her a cheer as Star, spurred on by excitement, galloped past. Soon she was traveling among a little group of horsemen, men who had come from farther west. The group included a woman riding with her husband so she could lead back the much needed team after he joined his regiment.

The procession grew till there must have been a score or more, pounding the road like a troop of cavalry. Inspired by the other horses, excited perhaps by the two or three lanterns, Star threw up his head proudly and stretched his pace. South through Stormville, where a blacksmith's apprentice was still loudly pounding on a wagon tire to spread the alarm, southeast down a road that grew more and more familiar, they swung.

Into the Ludington lane, down past the mill, which had been flung open to shelter those who couldn't squeeze into either house or barn. Constant scurrying to and fro, the rumble of men's voices, the sharp bark of orders from officers: Sybil had seen and heard it all before, but this time she was a part of it. She had received her orders and carried them out like a soldier.

At the gate someone took Star and offered to stable him. Reluctantly she surrendered him. 'Twas like giving up part of herself. "Best rub him down," said Sybil. "He's done a long ride." The gathering at the house door made way for her.

"Here she is, Colonel. Here's your aide, sir." And Father himself threw down his quill and, in full regimentals, rose from the table to greet her and hear her report, just as he would for a soldier. This surely was the proudest moment of her life.

regiment large military troop
score twenty

quill feather with sharpened tip used as a pen
full regimentals military uniform

Further Reading

Johnny Tremain. Esther Forbes. Johnny, a silversmith's apprentice, is caught up in the turbulent and exciting times of Revolutionary War Boston as he mingles with Paul Revere and other heroes.

I'm Deborah Sampson: A Soldier in the War of the Revolution. Patricia Clapp. Deborah Sampson disguised herself as a man and fought for over a year as a soldier in the revolutionary army.

My Brother Sam Is Dead. James Lincoln Collier. Tragedy strikes the Meeker family when one son joins the American rebels while the rest of the family tries to remain neutral in a Tory town.

"Paul Revere's Ride." Henry Wadsworth Longfellow. "One if by land; two if by sea"—the midnight ride of Paul Revere is told in an exciting story poem.

L E S S O N   3

Building a New Society

> I long to hear that you have declared an independency. And, by the way, in the new code of laws which I suppose it will be necessary for you to make, I desire you would remember the ladies and be more generous and favorable to them than your ancestors. Do not put such un-limited power into the hands of the husbands. Remember, all men would be tyrants if they could. If particular care and attention is not paid to the ladies, we are determined to foment [stir up] a rebellion, and will not hold ourselves bound by any laws in which we have no voice or representation.
>
> Abigail Adams in a letter to her husband

Key Terms

- civilian
- constitution

When she wrote this letter on March 31, 1776, Abigail Adams was at home in Braintree, Massachusetts. She was busy managing the family farm. Her husband, John, was away at Congress in Philadelphia, arguing in favor of independence.

Abigail Adams was only half-joking when she warned that women would stir up their own revolution if the new government

➤ *Some colonial women ran shops like this one, in which tin pots, pans, and plates were made and repaired.*

did not remember their needs. Although colonial women could hire workers or sell land, they could not own the farms they managed. Women also could not vote.

The Revolution won representation for colonial men. Women's rights were not considered, even though women's efforts helped win the Revolution.

The Home Front

Like Abigail Adams, many colonial women took on new responsibilities during the war. While men were fighting on the battlefront, **civilians**—the people left at home—were struggling with new jobs and with money problems.

A New Role for Women

Many colonial women managed their households alone while their husbands were away fighting in the war. These women still did their traditional work, such as spinning cloth, making clothes, tending the garden and the dairy, and caring for the children and the house. But they also took over many jobs normally done by men. Some women rose at dawn and rode out on horseback to tell farm workers what to do. Others ran businesses, such as flour mills or tailor shops. At first, many men wrote letters home telling their wives what crops to plant and what bills to pay. But as time went on, husbands came to depend more and more on their wives' judgment.

For their part, women got used to making decisions for their families. Like Abigail Adams, they had no wish to return to the time when husbands and fathers had complete authority over their wives and children.

Money Problems

Among the decisions women had to make was how to manage the family's money. This grew more difficult as the war went on. The army bought tons of meat and flour to feed the soldiers. They

Across Time & Space

In July 1848, Elizabeth Cady Stanton and other women held a meeting at Seneca Falls, New York. Using words similar to those in the Declaration of Independence, the women declared that "woman is man's equal." Like Abigail Adams, Stanton believed that men and women should have the same political rights.

◄ *When the war began, most Americans could afford to buy brown bread at about $1.50 a loaf. After three years of war, a loaf of bread cost $9.50. At that price, few Americans could afford it.*

285

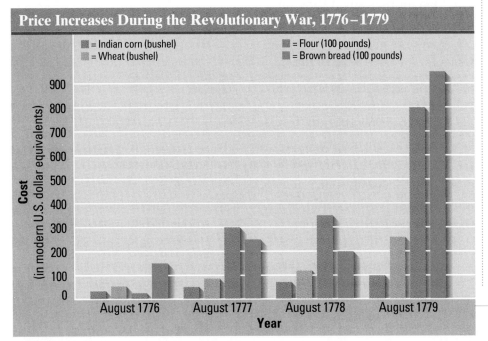

Price Increases During the Revolutionary War, 1776–1779

= Indian corn (bushel)
= Wheat (bushel)
= Flour (100 pounds)
= Brown bread (100 pounds)

Cost (in modern U.S. dollar equivalents)

900
800
700
600
500
400
300
200
100
0

August 1776   August 1777   August 1778   August 1779

Year

War Breaks Out

also purchased large quantities of shoes and clothing. The army's large purchases created shortages of many essential items at home. Women and other civilians had a hard time finding such things as coffee, tea, and grain to buy. The little that was available was very expensive, and prices rose higher every year. The chart on page 285 shows how quickly and steeply prices went up. ■

The Effects of the War

Women were not the only Americans whose lives were changed by the war. Americans loyal to the king and blacks who fought for the British often had to begin new lives after the war. Many Indians also lost everything they had as a result of the war.

➤ *Some Loyalists were beaten by hotheaded supporters of the Revolution. Others were covered with pine tar and goose feathers and paraded through the streets. The unfortunate supporter of the king, shown in the cartoon on the right, is being insulted by a crowd, which has hung him from a pole.*

Loyalists

Not all Americans supported the Revolution. About 500,000 Americans remained loyal to Britain. Some Loyalists were rich officials of the British government. Others had recently arrived in America from Britain, Scotland, or Germany. Some people who lived in towns the British controlled during the war, often found it wise to be Loyalists as well. They could buy food more easily if they supported the British.

Many Loyalists were treated badly by supporters of the Revolution. In 1777, Congress urged the states to take away the houses, land, and other property of Loyalists. Some Loyalists went to jail. In Pennsylvania, a person found guilty of persuading someone to join the British army could be fined, imprisoned, or even put to death.

After the war, nearly 80,000 Loyalists left their homes and moved to England, Canada, and the West Indies. The British government gave about $20 million to Loyalists to make up for property they left behind in the United States. But most Loyalists were paid less than half of what their property was worth.

Black and Indian Americans

About 14,000 blacks also left the United States after the war. Few got money or other help from the British government. British officials told them that freedom from slavery was payment enough for their service. Some blacks found jobs in England, Canada, and the West Indies. Others joined the British navy. A few returned to Africa. A British company offered transportation to Sierra Leone, a country on the west coast of Africa, and 20 acres of land to any black who would settle there. In 1792, about 1,200 former slaves sailed from Nova Scotia, Canada, to Africa to begin new lives.

Indians who helped the British also had to find new homes after the war. The Iroquois faced an especially hard task. To punish the Iroquois for raids against white settlements, in which they stole horses and cattle and killed settlers, American soldiers burned Iroquois houses. They also chopped down orchards and set fire to fields of ripe corn. By spring 1780, all but two of the Iroquois villages in New York state had been destroyed.

In 1784, the Americans negotiated the Treaty of Fort Stanwix with the Iroquois. The treaty gave the United States all Iroquois land west of New York and Pennsylvania and kept the Iroquois in a small area. ■

■ *In what ways were the effects of the Revolution similar for blacks, Loyalists, and Indians?*

The Pennsylvania Constitution

Now that the war was over, the task of building a new American society could begin. The Revolution won for Americans the right to form their own national government. But what form should the new government take? For guidance, Americans could look to the governments of the 13 new states. Between 1776 and 1780, each state adopted a **constitution,** or formal plan of government.

Pennsylvania's constitution, adopted in May 1776, contained many new ideas. It gave the right to vote to all white men, not just to men who owned property, as was common in other states. The Pennsylvania constitution also called for annual elections for members of the state legislature. This meant that each year voters could choose representatives who reflected their views and opinions. These ideas show the enthusiasm that the colonists felt for a new kind of government—a republic, in which voters had a great deal of power. ■

■ *Name an important new idea in the Pennsylvania constitution.*

R E V I E W

1. **FOCUS** What effect did the Revolution have on Americans who did not fight in the American army?
2. **CONNECT** Abigail Adams warned that women would not be bound by laws that they could not vote to approve. How is her argument similar to the one men made against the British government?
3. **ECONOMICS** How did the war affect the price of flour? Why was this change a problem for women?
4. **CRITICAL THINKING** The Pennsylvania constitution was adopted in 1776, the same year as the publication of Thomas Paine's *Common Sense* and the signing of the Declaration of Independence. What ideas do these three documents share?
5. **WRITING ACTIVITY** Imagine that your father is away fighting. Write a letter to a friend describing how the war has affected life in your family.

287

War Breaks Out

Chapter Review

Reviewing Key Terms

civilian (p. 285)
constitution (p. 287)
delegate (p. 262)
equality (p. 264)
independence (p. 262)

Loyalist (p. 269)
militia (p. 260)
republic (p. 268)
revolution (p. 268)

A. Use each pair of key terms in a sentence. Your sentences should show that you understand the meanings of the terms.
1. revolution, equality
2. civilian, independence
3. delegate, constitution
4. Loyalist, republic
5 militia, civilian
6. independence, Loyalist

B. Each newspaper headline contains a key term. Write the headlines on your own paper. Then write one or two sentences that could begin a newspaper article.
1. Revolution Picks Up Speed
2. Join the Militia Today
3. Our Battle for Independence Has Just Begun
4. Citizens Demand a Republic
5. Read About Pennsylvania's Constitution
6. Delegates Gather for Second Continental Congress
7. Civilians Face Problems Keeping the Home Front Going

Exploring Concepts

A. Copy and complete the following cause-and effect chart on your own paper. The first answer has been done for you.

Cause	Effect
Colonists were tired of heavy taxes and unfair treatment.	The colonists sent a petition to King George III of England.
	Thomas Paine wrote and published a pamphlet called *Common Sense*.
	The French signed an agreement to help the colonists fight the British army.
	Hundreds of Washington's soldiers died at Valley Forge.
	Prices of goods were high and there were shortages of essential items.

B. Answer each of the following questions. Use information from the chapter.
1. What were the differences in how the militia and the Continental Army joined the fight for independence?
2. In what ways did George Washington prove that he was probably the best person to lead the Continental forces?
3. How did the women of revolutionary times show they were able to handle many added responsibilities?
4. By 1775, which side seemed to be winning the war? By 1780, another side seemed to be winning. Explain what happened.
5. What losses did the Iroquois people suffer because of the war?
6. What were some important terms of the Treaty of Paris?
7. After the war, what happened to many Americans who had been loyal to Britain?

Reviewing Skills

1. Read Lesson 3 again. Then complete the following outline on your own paper.

> Building a New Society
> I. The Home Front
>   A. A new role for women
>   1. _____
>   2. _____
>   B. Money problems
> II. The Effects of the War
>   A. _____
>   1. Persecuted by patriots
>   2. Migration to England and Canada
>   B. Black and Indian Americans
>   1. _____
>   2. _____
>   3. Iroquois villages destroyed
>   4. _____

2. Using an organized approach to making an outline helps to organize your thinking. List the suggested steps for making an outline in the correct order.

3. Look at the map on page 273. Is this a large scale or a small scale map? Could you use this map as a general guide in traveling from Valley Forge, Pennsylvania to Yorktown, Virginia? Could you use it to find a particular place in Yorktown? Would you need a map with a larger scale or a smaller scale?

4. Suppose that you need to study for a test covering the battles of the American Revolution. You have to know the date of each battle, where it was fought, the names of the American and British leaders, and what the results were. Your notes include all of this information, but they are not organized. What device could you create to organize the information about the battles?

Using Critical Thinking

1. After the American victory at Saratoga in October 1777, a British leader offered to end the war. He sent a message to Benjamin Franklin saying that Britain would meet most of the American demands. His offer was refused by American leaders. If it had been accepted, what events of the Revolution would not have taken place?

2. The Second Continental Congress set up a commission to maintain peace with the Indians. Yet many Indians joined forces with the Loyalists. Why do you think this happened?

3. Review the ways that France helped the colonists on land and sea. Then tell why you agree or disagree with the statement: "If not for France, we might still be owned by England."

Preparing for Citizenship

1. **ARTS ACTIVITY** Pictures of American flags appear on pages 554 and 555 of your Minipedia. Several of the flags are from the time period you are studying in this chapter. Draw at least two of the flags. Then point out the similarities and differences.

2. **COLLABORATIVE LEARNING** Work to produce a newspaper, *The Revolutionary Times*. Form groups to include writers of news, ads, and columns representing blacks and Indians. Other groups can write Letters to the Editor or draw political cartoons. A managing editor can set deadlines. "Printers" can use typewriters or word processors and then paste up the art. Ask the school office or a copying store for help in making copies.

Chapter 12

Searching for Unity

On July 4, 1776, the American colonies declared their independence, then threw off British rule. After the Revolution, independence became America's biggest problem. The 13 British colonies had become 13 "free and independent states." But they had not become one united nation. In 1783, Americans shared little more than a name and a flag. Many people wondered: Could the states that had defeated the most powerful country in the world unite?

Throughout this time, George Washington was known as the father of the country. First as a general, then as President, Washington was an important leader in the young nation.

1760	1770	1780	1790

1775

1787 The U.S. Constitution is written. The first words of the document—"We the People"—express the idea that citizens have the power to create a government.

FIRST in WAR,
FIRST in PEACE,
&
FIRST in the HEARTS
OF HIS
COUNTRYMEN.

During this period, the eagle became the symbol of America. In 1782, Congress made the eagle the central figure on the Great Seal of the United States.

1775–1828 Americans become proud of their new nation. This painting, done in 1810, shows some symbols of the United States: the flag, the eagle, and George Washington.

| 1800 | 1810 | 1820 | 1830 |

1800 The capital of the United States moves from Philadelphia to Washington, D.C.

1828

L E S S O N   1

Forming a Government

THINKING

F O C U S

What caused Americans to want a stronger central government after the Revolutionary War?

Key Terms

- federal
- ratify
- township
- legislature

➤ *As the chart shows, several states claimed the same areas of land during the 1780s.*

Rachel Budd, her husband Benjamin, and their eight children moved from Connecticut to the Susquehanna River Valley in 1775 to start a farm. Their story is told in *Sketches of Eighteenth Century Life* by Michel Jean de Crèvecoeur *(krehv KUR)*. Between 1775 and 1778, Crèvecoeur traveled the Susquehanna talking with settlers. Later he wrote about their experiences in his book.

Today, the Susquehanna Valley is part of the state of Pennsylvania. Then, both Connecticut and Pennsylvania claimed the valley as their territory. Pennsylvania sent soldiers to force out the settlers from Connecticut. Rachel explains what happened.

My husband, though a most peaceable man, fell victim to these disputes and was carried away prisoner to Philadelphia. We lost all our horses and cows, for in these petty wars these movables are always driven off. I was ready to starve, and ashamed to become troublesome to my neighbors.

The neighbors' help saved Rachel and the children for eight months until Benjamin was let go as a part of a deal between the two states. The family then began their farm again. However, as Rachel wrote, "We had no government but what the people chose to follow from day to day." And they never knew when their lives might be disrupted again.

Disputed Land Claims in the 1780s	
States That Claimed Area	**Name of Area Today**
Connecticut, Pennsylvania	Northern Pennsylvania
New York, Connecticut, Virginia	Eastern Ohio
New York, Massachusetts, Virginia	Southern Michigan
Connecticut, Virginia	Northern Illinois
New York, North Carolina	Tennessee
Georgia, South Carolina	Mississippi
Georgia, South Carolina	Alabama

292

Chapter 12

The Articles of Confederation

States frequently fought over land or money during and after the Revolution. The Second Continental Congress had no power to settle such fights. Congress knew that it would need national laws to govern effectively. In June 1776, a congressional committee began to draw up a plan.

A National Plan

The plan was called the Articles of Confederation. It required the states to give up some powers to a **federal** government, which had power over all the states.

The states feared an overly-strong federal government. So they refused to give up two important powers: collecting taxes and making foreign trade agreements. The federal government had to get its money from the states. Often the states refused to pay.

The Articles of the Confederation gave Congress its own powers. It could declare war, deliver the mail, and sign treaties with American Indians living outside state boundaries. Congress could also settle boundary disputes between states. However, it could not force states to obey its decisions.

Before the Articles of Confederation could become law, each state had to **ratify,** or approve, them. By 1779, all but Maryland had voted approval. Maryland refused to ratify the Articles unless Congress solved a western lands dispute. Colonial charters gave seven states land west of the Appalachian Mountains. Six states,

including Maryland, had no western land. Because all the states were fighting to win the land from the British, Maryland wanted all western lands to be turned over to the federal government. The states that claimed western lands agreed, but only in order to get Maryland's approval. Maryland voted for the Articles on March l, 1781. The United States had its first official government.

The Northwest Territory

Congress could not raise money with taxes. So it had to sell some of the western land north of the Ohio River and west of Pennsylvania. This land was called the Northwest Territory.

▼ *Trace the boundaries of the Northwest Territory on this map. What natural feature forms the western boundary of the Territory?*

Northwest Territory, 1787

States

Northwest Territory

Southwest territories

Ohio States later formed in Northwest Territory

Searching for Unity

> The Ohio Company bought land under the ordinance of 1785 and laid out plans for cities. The land shown in the northern part of this map was allotted to Wyandot and Delaware Indians.

▼ This photograph of present-day midwestern farmland was taken from a plane. In it you can see roads and fields that still lie along the square lines of sections that were laid out over 200 years ago.

■ In what ways were the states more powerful than the federal government under the Articles of Confederation?

In 1785, Congress divided the Territory into square **townships** that measured six miles on a side. Each township was divided into 36 sections. Each section measured one square mile, or 640 acres. Organizing the land into townships and sections helped Congress keep track of land sales and ownership. The federal government then sold off the sections for at least $1 an acre.

Few frontier families could afford to spend $640 to buy a whole section of land. Instead land companies often bought many sections of land in a township. Then they sold small plots to individual farmers who moved their families across the Appalachian Mountains. Congress decided that the income from the sale of land in one section of each township should be used to support public schools.

Many Indian tribes lived in the Northwest Territory. So Congress passed a law that told settlers to treat Indians with "good faith," and not to try to settle on Indian lands. Another part of the law said no one could bring slaves into the Territory. Some members of Congress from Southern states agreed to this law only because they believed Congress would allow slavery in new lands south of the Ohio River.

Future States

Congress had to decide how to govern its new lands. In 1787, a committee headed by Thomas Jefferson drew up a plan.

The committee decided that the United States should never have colonies. Instead the committee divided the Northwest Territory into areas that could become new states. A governor and three judges chosen by Congress would govern each area until the number of people reached 5,000 free adult men. Then the men in the region could vote for a **legislature,** a group of people elected to make laws. When the number of people grew to 60,000 free adult men, the region could become a state. It just had to write a constitution approved by Congress. Look at the map of the Northwest Territory on page 293. How many states were formed from this land? ■

Money Problems

The sale of land in the Northwest Territory provided some money for Congress, but not enough to pay the government's large debts. Congress owed about $35 million, mostly to French and Dutch bankers. Congress had borrowed the money to buy guns, ammunition, and other supplies during the Revolutionary War. Soldiers who had fought in the war had not always been paid. They were now demanding their back pay.

To pay these debts, Congress and many state governments printed paper money during the war. However, as more money was printed, the paper money in use became less valuable. To add to the confusion, many people did not trust paper money and insisted on being paid in gold and silver coins.

A Chain of Borrowing

By the end of the Revolutionary War, the shortage of money troubled everyone. Farmers needed cash more than anyone. State taxes were high, and farmers often had large personal debts as well. Because they had little money, farmers had to buy seed and household supplies on credit. The shopkeepers in turn borrowed from rich merchants to buy more goods to sell. Then, the American merchants borrowed from English merchants. The illustration on this page shows this chain of borrowing. What happened to American farmers in 1785 when a money crisis hit Great Britain?

Shays's Rebellion

Farmers in the western part of Massachusetts had an especially hard time paying their bills. Massachusetts farmers owed about one-third of their income for state taxes, and the Massachusetts legislature refused to issue paper money as other states had done. Those farmers who could not pay their taxes had their farms taken away by state courts. Court officials then auctioned off the farms and used the money from the sale to pay the taxes. Farmers who could not pay their personal debts were often put into prison.

A chain of borrowing linked farmers in Massachusetts to bankers in London.

Chain of Debt

1 The farmer borrows money from a merchant to buy land and supplies.

2 The merchant borrows money from a London banker to lend to the farmer.

3 A financial crisis hits London.

4 The banker demands that the merchant repay the loans quickly.

5 The merchant demands that the farmer repay the loans quickly.

6 The farmer must sell land to raise money.

DEED

CRISIS

➤ Soldiers turn back a group of angry farmers led by Daniel Shays in a battle in Springfield, Massachusetts.

The farmers asked the Massachusetts legislature to lower taxes and let them pay taxes and other debts with farm produce. They begged the legislature to stop jailing people who could not pay their debts. Instead the legislature listened to merchants and bankers to whom the farmers owed money. It refused to pass laws to help the farmers.

Because they could not get help through legal means, a group of farmers decided they had no choice but to rebel. Their leader was Daniel Shays, former Revolutionary War captain. In the fall of 1786, Shays led armed farmers in marches outside county courthouses in Springfield, Northampton, and other towns in western Massachusetts. The purpose was to keep the courts from meeting. If the courts did not meet, bankers and others to whom farmers owed money could not take away their farms.

In January 1787, Shays's men attacked a Springfield building where the government stored guns. The governor of Massachusetts sent soldiers paid for by wealthy Boston merchants to fight the rebels. The soldiers shot and killed four, and soon the rest of Shays's followers fled. Several rebel leaders were caught. These men were brought to trial, found guilty, and sentenced to death. Later the court set them all free, including Shays.

Shays's Rebellion failed. But it made many Americans think a stronger central government was needed to prevent such rebellions in the future. ■

■ Why were both the federal government and farmers in Massachusetts in debt after the Revolutionary War?

R E V I E W

1. **FOCUS** What caused Americans to want a stronger central government after the Revolutionary War?

2. **CONNECT** How did the way Congress planned to govern the Northwest Territory differ from the way Spain and other European countries governed their American territories?

3. **ECONOMICS** What part of the Articles of Confederation made it especially difficult for Congress to pay its debts after the Revolutionary War?

4. **CRITICAL THINKING** Thomas Jefferson defended the farmers who took part in Shays's Rebellion by saying: "A little rebellion from time to time is a good thing." What does this statement mean? Do you agree with Jefferson? Give reasons for your answer.

5. **WRITING ACTIVITY** Imagine it is 1786. Your family may lose its farm in western Massachusetts because of unpaid bills. Write a letter to the Massachusetts legislature to explain why your family is in debt and ask for help.

LESSON 2

The Constitution

THINKING
FOCUS

How did the writers of the Constitution create a strong federal government while protecting the rights of states and individuals?

Benjamin Franklin had a startling idea. In 1751, 25 years before the Declaration of Independence was written, he suggested that the American colonies band together for defense. No one listened to his idea. Alexander Hamilton also had a similar plan. In 1780, he wrote a friend in Congress from the Revolutionary Army base at Liberty Pole, New Jersey. He begged Congress to call "immediately a convention of all the states" to plan a strong new government. Congress turned down Hamilton's plea that year and again in 1783.

In 1786, Virginia asked the states to send people to meet at Annapolis, Maryland, to talk about the trade problems of all the states. Only 12 men from 5 states came. And they agreed only to ask Congress to call another meeting. Even the 1787 Constitutional Convention in Philadelphia got off to a bad start. Most delegates arrived several days late. Nineteen never showed up at all.

"The Grand Convention"

Americans had put their trust mostly in local and state governments. But by 1787 many believed that the nation needed a stronger federal government. After saying no to the idea many times, Congress voted for a convention in Philadelphia to change the Articles of Confederation. Newspapers called the meeting "the Grand Convention," but others were not so sure. Of 74 delegates named to the convention by the states, only 55 came to Philadelphia. Rhode Island refused to send anyone.

The delegates who met on May 25, 1787, were mostly rich, well-educated young men. Like Alexander Hamilton of New York, many were lawyers. Like James Madison of Virginia, many had served in Congress. The delegates elected George Washington to lead their meetings. They also voted to keep the meetings secret. This way they could speak freely, without being criticized in public for their views. For more about the convention, see A Closer Look on the next two pages.

Key Terms

- compromise
- checks and balances
- separation of powers
- amendment

Searching for Unity

Life at the Convention

Fifty-five delegates spent the hot summer of 1787 in Philadelphia drafting a plan to govern their new nation. On September 17, the finished Constitution was read aloud for the first time.

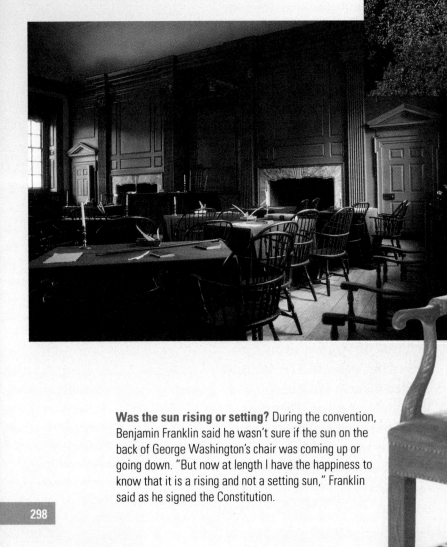

It was hot and sticky in the convention hall. The delegates had to keep the windows and doors closed so no one could hear their discussions. The windows kept in the heat but also kept out big bluebottle flies that were swarming through Philadelphia.

Was the sun rising or setting? During the convention, Benjamin Franklin said he wasn't sure if the sun on the back of George Washington's chair was coming up or going down. "But now at length I have the happiness to know that it is a rising and not a setting sun," Franklin said as he signed the Constitution.

298

Pennsylvania delegate
Gouverneur Morris wrote most of the Constitution's final wording. He was also the loudest critic of slavery at the convention.

Benjamin Franklin's voice was often too weak to be heard, so he had to write out his speeches. James Wilson, a Pennsylvania lawyer with a thick Scottish accent, read Franklin's words.

A workhorse of the convention, John Rutledge of South Carolina served on five committees. But he was so bossy the other delegates gave him the nickname Dictator John.

At 81, Benjamin Franklin was the oldest delegate at the convention and he was an important and honored figure. Franklin was one of the few delegates who was sad to see the convention end.

Searching for Unity

Although meetings of the Philadelphia convention were secret, we know a lot about what happened there thanks to a diary kept by James Madison of Virginia. In his own system of shorthand, he took notes on everything the delegates said and did each day. Each night he went back to his room and put his notes in final form.

▼ *This painting by American artist Junius B. Stearns shows George Washington addressing the Constitutional Convention.*

Divided Delegates

The delegates were divided by the different interests of their home states. On May 29, Edmund Randolph of Virginia presented a plan of government that pleased the delegates from large states. Called the Virginia Plan, it outlined a whole new government with three branches, or parts. These were an executive branch headed by a president, a judicial branch with a Supreme Court and Federal courts, and a legislative branch, or Congress. The number of representatives each state could send to Congress would depend on the population of the state. States with large populations supported the Virginia Plan.

On June 15, William Paterson from the small state of New Jersey said every state should have an equal number of representatives in Congress. His idea was known as the New Jersey Plan. States with small populations backed this plan.

The Great Compromise

In June and July of 1787, the delegates argued the Virginia and New Jersey plans. Roger Sherman of Connecticut proposed a **compromise,** an agreement in which each side gets something it wants while giving up something else. Congress should have two houses, Sherman said. To please large states, representation in the House of Representatives should be based on population. To please small states, each state should have equal votes in the Senate. On July 16, the convention agreed.

Another set of compromises ended a conflict between the North and the South. The North agreed that Southern states could include three-fifths of their slaves in population counts to give them more representatives. The South also agreed to count three-fifths of the slaves in adding up the taxes they would owe. The South agreed that the slave trade would eventually come to an end. In return, the North agreed that Congress would not outlaw the slave trade until after 1808. ■

■ *What argument divided delegates from large states and small states, and how was it resolved?*

Checks and Balances

The Great Compromise had settled how Congress would be organized. Next, the delegates worked to balance the powers of the three parts of government. They wanted to make the legislative, executive, and judicial branches equally powerful. And they wanted to protect each branch from control by the others. To accomplish this, the delegates created a system of **checks and balances.** These were ways each branch could stop, or check, the others. The delegates hoped that this system would keep any part of the government from becoming so strong it could threaten the liberty of citizens.

Look at the chart on this page. Notice how each branch can check the powers of the others. When Congress passes a law, it must be signed by the President. Only then can it can take effect. In this way, the President can check the power of Congress. How can Congress check the power of the President in return?

The delegates also balanced the government by giving each branch

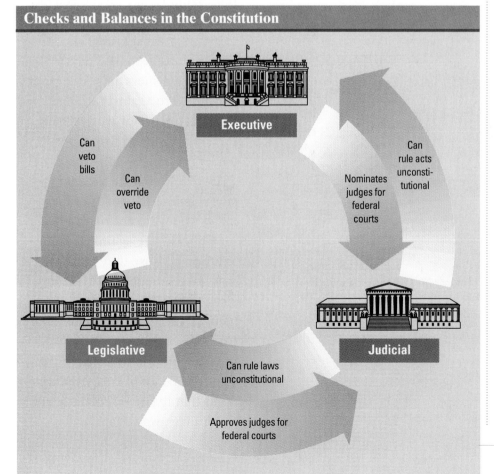

Checks and Balances in the Constitution

Executive

Can veto bills

Can override veto

Can rule acts unconstitutional

Nominates judges for federal courts

Legislative

Judicial

Can rule laws unconstitutional

Approves judges for federal courts

◄ *How does the judicial branch check the actions of the President and the Congress?*

a different job. They called this the **separation of powers.** The legislative branch would make laws that every state had to follow. The executive branch would see that the laws were obeyed. The judicial branch would rule on cases when federal laws were broken.

But who would head the executive branch? Some delegates objected to placing one person in charge. Edmund J. Randolph of Virginia said one president might be like a king. He suggested three presidents, one from each part of the country. James Wilson of Pennsylvania argued that only a single president could be an effective leader. After much debate, the delegates voted to have one president. After all, they said, George Washington would probably be chosen first. They could trust him to use his power wisely. ■

■ *What are checks and balances, and why did the delegates include them in the Constitution?*

▼ *The first states to ratify the Constitution were Delaware, Pennsylvania, New Jersey, Georgia, Connecticut, and Massachusetts.*

Ratification of the Constitution

Finally, all the debates had been settled. Then, the delegates approved a final draft of the Constitution. Now the governments and people of the states had their turn to argue about the plan. Newspapers printed the whole Constitution. And almost everyone had something to say about its good and bad points. Each state held elections to choose representatives to attend conventions. Nine state conventions had to ratify, or accept, the Constitution for it to become law.

Many farmers and other poor citizens were against ratifying the Constitution. They were afraid that only rich men would become leaders in the new government. They feared that such leaders would ignore the needs of the many who were not rich.

Others were against the Constitution because they feared the new government would be too strong. A too-powerful government might take away people's freedoms. These people wanted the Constitution to have a bill of rights—a list of liberties and freedoms that the government could never take away.

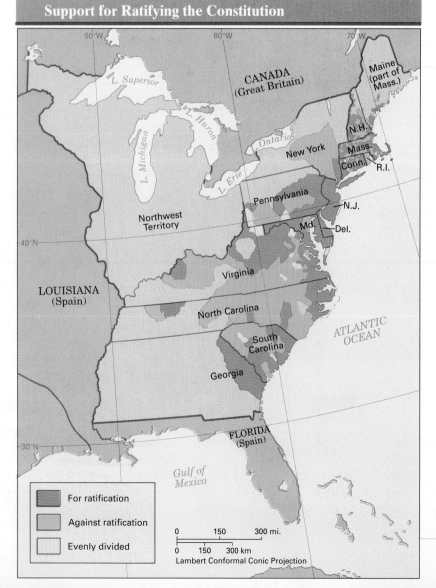

Support for Ratifying the Constitution

For ratification

Against ratification

Evenly divided

0   150   300 mi.

0   150   300 km
Lambert Conformal Conic Projection

Another group, including many merchants and wealthy farmers, favored the Constitution. They believed a strong, stable government would pass laws that would benefit their businesses. ■

■ *What arguments did citizens raise for and against the ratification of the Constitution?*

The Bill of Rights

The battle to ratify the Constitution was waged in the conventions held in each of the 13 states. Delegates to these conventions debated many of the same points raised in arguments between ordinary citizens. Six states approved the Constitution quickly. However, other states refused to go along until the Constitution included a bill of rights. James Madison of Virginia, who had worked so hard on the Constitution, was now a leader in the fight for ratification. In 1788, Madison promised that if the Constitution was ratified, he would ask Congress to add a bill of rights. Even with this promise, it took nearly two years for all 13 states to approve the Constitution.

The first Congress under the new Constitution met in April, 1789. James Madison was now a representative from Virginia in the House of Representatives. On June 8, he introduced a bill of rights as one of the first items of business. By 1791, all the states had ratified it. The Bill of Rights had become part of the Constitution.

The Bill of Rights is made up of ten **amendments,** statements added to change the Constitution or to make its intentions clearer. Here is the First Amendment:

Congress shall make no law respecting an establishment of religion, or prohibiting the free exercise thereof; or abridging the freedom of speech, or of the press; or the right of the people peaceably to assemble, and to petition the government for a redress of grievances.

Note that this amendment protects important personal liberties—freedom of religion, freedom of speech, and freedom of the press. Other parts of the Bill of Rights guarantee that people cannot be arrested without good reason and that they have the right to a trial by jury. These liberties are basic to the American way of life. ■

Across Time & Space

The Constitution has been amended only 26 times since it was written 200 years ago. The first ten amendments are the Bill of Rights. Later amendments made slavery illegal and gave black Americans, women, and people over 18 the right to vote.

■ *How did the Bill of Rights satisfy the objections of some citizens to ratifying the Constitution?*

R E V I E W

1. **FOCUS** How did the writers of the Constitution create a strong federal government while protecting the rights of states and individuals?

2. **CONNECT** In what ways was the federal government created by the Constitution stronger than the federal government created by the Articles of Confederation?

3. **HISTORY** What issues divided delegates from northern and southern states? How were these differences finally resolved by the delegates?

4. **CRITICAL THINKING** Some delegates objected to having a president because a president was too much like a king. What events in their recent history may have led delegates to make this argument?

5. **ACTIVITY** Imagine you work for a newspaper in 1788. Draw a political cartoon for your paper which illustrates why the Constitution should be approved.

Searching for Unity

Identifying Fact and Opinion

Here's Why

Every day, you must think carefully about the things you hear and read. So knowing how to evaluate, or judge, written and spoken words is an important skill. One way you can do this is by recognizing the difference between a statement of fact and a statement of opinion.

Suppose you were reading a short biographical sketch about James Madison. Being able to distinguish between fact and opinion would help you to evaluate it.

Here's How

A fact is something that has happened or that can be observed. A fact is a statement that can be proven to be true. Proof can come from many sources—direct observation, articles or books, or artifacts dug up by archaeologists.

Read the piece about James Madison and the Constitution. Identify which statements are facts and which are opinions.

The statement highlighted in blue is a fact. Records of Virginia would show that Madison was born there in 1751. Consider this statement: "In fact, he studied so hard that he finished the regular program at the College of New Jersey (now Princeton University) in only two years." This is also a fact, because it can be proven.

College records would indicate when he entered and graduated.

An opinion tells what a person feels or believes

James Madison and the Constitution

James Madison was born on March 16, 1751, at Port Conway, Virginia. He was the oldest of 12 children. As a young man, Madison was an eager student. In fact, he studied so hard that he finished the regular program at the College of New Jersey (now Princeton University) in only two years.

During his college years, Madison developed a keen interest in politics. In 1776, he served in Virginia's first legislative assembly. It was there that he met Thomas Jefferson, who became his lifelong friend. In December 1779, Madison was elected to the Continental Congress. Later, he returned to Virginia, serving in the Virginia Assembly.

James Madison was probably the most important person at the Constitutional Convention. In fact, he is often called "The Father of the Constitution." It was Madison who planned the system of checks and balances. And it was Madison who drafted the Virginia Plan presented by Edmund Randolph. Madison's role as a mediator (*MEE dee ay tur*), or person who helps to solve conflicts, was equally important. In addition, Madison's *Notes on the Federal Convention* give us a record of the debates that helped to shape the Constitution.

Later, Madison served in Congress. He was Secretary of State under Thomas Jefferson. In 1808, he was elected President of the United States. His wife, Dolley Payne Madison, was well suited for the job of first lady. The writer Washington Irving found her to be charming. He remembered her as having "a smile and pleasant word for everybody."

about something. Opinions cannot be proven. The statement highlighted in green is an opinion. It is true that Madison played a major role at the Constitutional Convention. But the idea that Madison was "probably the most important person there" is an opinion. The statement cannot be proven true or false. Instead, it tells how the author felt about the delegates to the convention. The clue words *probably* and *most important* help you to recognize the sentence as an opinion.

Although opinions can't be proven, they can still be valuable. Learning about the opinions of people from the past helps us to understand why they acted as they did. For example, the strong opinions of many colonists made them willing to fight in the Revolutionary War. It is also important to note that two people, faced with the same set of facts, may form very different opinions. Both opinions can be valuable.

A statement about the opinions of others can be a fact. Look at the last two sentences, about Washington Irving. These statements are facts. You can prove this by reading Washington Irving's

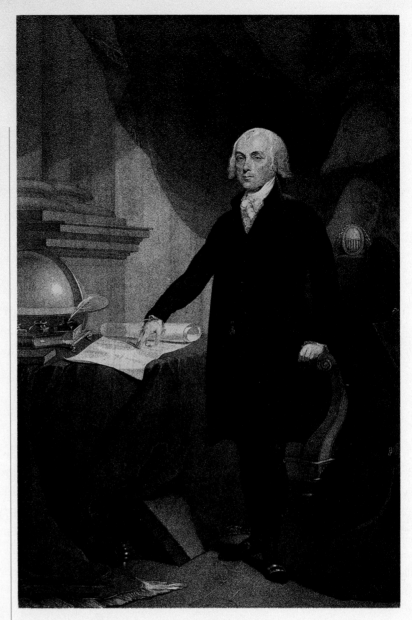

writing in which he refers to Dolley Madison as having "a smile and a pleasant word for everybody."

Try It

Reread the piece about James Madison. Write down the sentences that are facts. Next, tell which sentences express opinions. For each statement of fact, suggest where to look for proof. For each opinion, tell how you know it is an opinion. Be

sure to list any clue words that tell you a statement is an opinion.

Apply It

Find an editorial in your local newspaper. You might want to look for an editorial on a topic that you find interesting. Highlight the facts in one color and the opinions in another color. Circle any clue words that indicate opinions. Did you find more facts or opinions?

L E S S O N   3

Becoming American

THINKING
F O C U S

How did artists, writers, and government leaders help the people of the United States start thinking of themselves as Americans?

Key Terms

- hero
- patriotism

Shortly after George Washington died, Parson Mason Weems published a book about Washington's life. In his book, Weems wrote that when George was just six years old, he chopped down one of his father's cherry trees. When his father sternly asked George if he knew what had happened to the tree, the future first President of the United States replied, "I cannot tell a lie. I did it with my hatchet." Because George bravely told the truth, Weems wrote, his father was willing to forgive him.

Weems's book became quite popular. Soon everyone knew the story of George Washington and the cherry tree. Over the years, many writers and other artists repeated the story. The painting on this page, by the American artist Grant Wood, is one such example.

The cherry tree story and many other incidents in Weems's book never actually happened. Weems added made-up events to the real story of George Washington's life to make Washington seem even more of a hero to the American people than he already was.

➤ *The man drawing back the curtain in this 1939 painting by Grant Wood is Parson Weems. He is pointing to the central character in the story he made up about George Washington.*

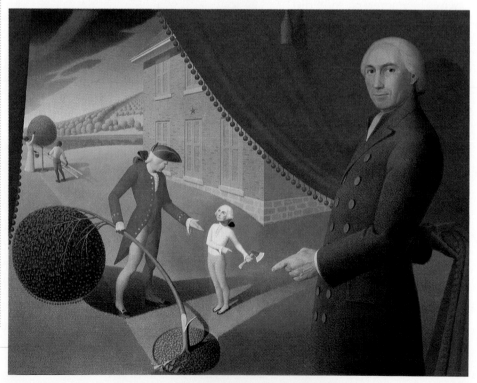

New American Heroes

A **hero** is a person who shows great strength, courage, or noble purpose. In the early days of the United States, artists and writers helped to make heroes of people who played important roles in the founding of this country. When these people were featured in stories, paintings, and sculptures, they were portrayed as brave, honest, wise, and smart.

Look at the illustration on this page. It shows a woman known today as Molly Pitcher, although her real name may have been Mary Ludwig. The painting shows Molly taking her fallen husband's place in battle during the Revolutionary War. The story of her heroism was told often and celebrated in American art and literature.

Molly Pitcher was just one of many new American heroes. Some of these celebrated Americans, like Molly, Paul Revere, and George Washington, had acted bravely during the Revolutionary

⬆ *Molly Pitcher carried water to the troops during the Battle of Monmouth in 1778. When her husband fell from heat stroke, she took his place.*

UNDERSTANDING HEROISM

George Washington and Molly Pitcher were heroes of the Revolutionary War. Americans have long admired their bravery and courage.

How a Hero Acts

Heroes are people who act bravely in dangerous or difficult situations. Sometimes, but not always, their brave actions take place in war time. During the Civil War, Clara Barton was a battlefield nurse. She continued taking care of the wounded even as cannonballs exploded around her. Clara Barton later founded the American Red Cross.

In this century, Rosa Parks, a black woman from Alabama, became a hero in the struggle for civil rights. She refused to obey the Alabama law that said black people had to sit in the back of the bus. Her refusal eventually led to a change in the law.

Why We Have Heroes

Heroes are an important part of a nation's tradition. They are people we can look up to, people whose brave actions display the best part of the human spirit. Heroes like Clara Barton and Rosa Parks serve as models for all Americans. Their acts of heroism are goals for all of us.

1776, Liberty Bell is rung to celebrate the Declaration of Independence.

1792, Great Seal is adopted.

1800, the White House is completed.

1780   1790   1800

▲ *These events and symbols helped create our American identity.*

■ *How did the creation of new heroes help people think of themselves as Americans?*

War. Others were political leaders, like John Adams, Benjamin Franklin, and Thomas Jefferson. They had acted bravely by speaking up for American independence from Great Britain.

Poems, stories, illustrations, and statues of famous people like these helped create a strong and positive image of the new Americans. These heroes had been born in America, not England. They helped Americans build new ideas of themselves. Their actions made people proud to be citizens of this new country called the United States of America. ■

An American Way of Life

Everything Americans did— from the way they talked to the holidays they celebrated—was especially their own.

An American Dictionary

Schoolmaster Noah Webster wanted Americans to have spelling books and dictionaries that listed words used by Americans. So he published *The American Spelling-Book* in 1783. It simplified spelling by leaving out the *u* in words like *colour* and spelling *wagon* with one *g*. Then in 1828 he published *An American Dictionary of the English Language*. Words in the dictionary included the names of items found only in this country. Some of these names were American Indian words, such as *wigwam, moccasin,* and *raccoon*. Other words came out of the lives of the American

▼ *Webster's dictionary included 12,000 words and 40,000 definitions that had never before been in a dictionary.*

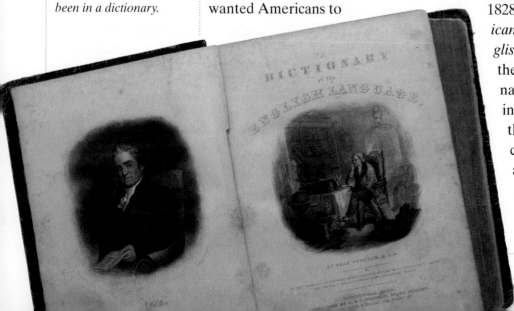

1826, John James Audubon publishes *Birds of America* and shows Americans the beauty of their land.

| 1810 | 1820 | 1830 |

1815, The term *Uncle Sam* is first used to represent the United States.

pioneers. These words included *prairie, log cabin,* and *popcorn.*

Webster's dictionary showed Americans that they shared a common and special language. Now they could discover the meanings of unfamiliar words that didn't exist in any other English-language dictionaries. In this way Webster helped Americans to write and talk to each other more easily and clearly.

Holidays and Symbols

The government of the United States helped to bring together the citizens of the new country by choosing national symbols and creating national holidays. In 1777, Congress approved a national flag.

In 1792, Congress chose another national symbol—the Great Seal of the United States. The seal is used on important government documents.

National holidays were also set aside. For example, in 1800, Congress declared July 4th to be Independence Day. This national holiday celebrates the day in 1776 when the Declaration of Independence was approved.

The creation of these symbols and holidays helped to establish a feeling of **patriotism,** or love of country. The American flag and the Great Seal reminded Americans that they were part of a proud new nation. Americans now all shared a common bond as citizens of a new nation. ■

■ *What events or ideas caused a feeling of patriotism to grow in Americans after the Revolutionary War?*

R E V I E W

1. **FOCUS** How did artists, writers, and government leaders help the people of the United States start thinking of themselves as Americans?

2. **CONNECT** What brave deeds or wise political actions were Molly Pitcher and George Washington noted for? What other men and women who took part in the Revolutionary War have become American heroes?

3. **HISTORY** In what ways did Noah Webster's Dictionary help unify Americans?

4. **CRITICAL THINKING** George Washington and other early national heroes made Americans feel proud of their country. Think of some national heroes that Americans admire today. What qualities do these heroes share?

5. **WRITING ACTIVITY** Choose a man or woman you think of as an American hero. Write a brief paragraph or two that tells in your own words what you admire about the person you have chosen.

309

Searching for Unity

Chapter Review

Reviewing Key Terms

amendment (p. 303)   legislature (p. 294)
checks and balances   patriotism (p. 309)
    (p. 301)   ratify (p. 293)
compromise (p. 300)   separation of powers
federal (p. 293)   (p. 302)
hero (p. 307)   township (p. 294)

A. Use the following terms in a paragraph about the Constitution.
1. amendment
2. federal
3. compromise
4. checks and balances
5. separation of powers

B. Write *True* or *False* for each statement. Rewrite the false statements to make them true.
1. A legislature tries criminals.
2. A township was one mile on a side.
3. Heroes' brave actions often are inspired by patriotism.
4. The Philadelphia Convention could ratify the Constitution.

Exploring Concepts

A. Fill in the missing information about the Articles of Confederation and the Constitution.

Articles of Confederation
    Powers of the States
        1. Collect taxes
        2. _____
    Powers of the Federal Government
        1. _____
        2. _____
The Constitution
    The Three Branches
        1. Executive
        2. _____
        3. _____
    The System of Checks and Balances
        1. President can veto bills
        2. _____
        3. _____
        4. _____
        5. _____
        6. _____

B. Answer each question with information from the chapter.
1. Why couldn't the Second Continental Congress govern effectively?
2. What were the states afraid would happen under the Articles of Confederation?
3. What did Shays's Rebellion accomplish?
4. What were the important points of the Virginia Plan? How was the New Jersey Plan different from the Virginia Plan?
5. What terms of the Great Compromise settled the debate between the Virginia Plan and the New Jersey Plan?
6. How does the separation of powers create a fair government?
7. What were some qualities that people admired in the first American heroes?
8. What were some words that only Americans needed in their dictionaries?
9. How did symbols and national holidays help patriotism grow among the American people?

Reviewing Skills

1. Read the following sentences. On a separate sheet of paper, tell which of the sentences express facts and which ones express opinions.
   a. The New Jersey Plan would have been better for all of the states than the Virginia Plan.
   b. Roger Sherman said that Congress should have two houses.
   c. Of the 74 delegates that were named by the states to attend the convention, only 55 actually arrived in Philadelphia for the event.
   d. By 1787, many people believed that the nation needed a stronger government.
   e. George Washington was the most important person in the colonies.
   f. The land that is now the state of Tennessee was once claimed as territory by both New York and North Carolina.
2. Every one of the delegates to the Constitutional Convention was sure that most of the people really wanted them to change the way the government was organized. Is this statement a fact or an opinion? Explain your answer.
3. Read the paragraph at the top of page 302 about the Constitutional Convention's debate about a head for the executive branch. What opinion did Edmund J. Randolph have about the subject of executive leadership? What opinion did James Wilson express? With which opinion did most of the delegates eventually agree?
4. The Constitutional Convention met in May of 1787 in Philadelphia, Pennsylvania. It was summer in Philadelphia during the convention. What season was it in the Southern Hemisphere at that time? How do you know?
5. If you were asked to explain in a few sentences the main points of a lesson from this chapter, what steps would you follow to do that?

Using Critical Thinking

1. Imagine that the Philadelphia Convention passed the Virginia Plan instead of the Sherman compromise. Which house of Congress would not exist today? How do you think your state's voice in Congress would change? Support your answer with both facts from the chapter and your own ideas.
2. Study the First Amendment to the United States Constitution on page 303. Think about all the rights that the First Amendment gives us. List the ways our lives would change if we didn't have these rights. Add any rights you think may be missing from the First Amendment.

Preparing for Citizenship

1. **COLLECTING INFORMATION** Look through newspapers for articles about the mayor of your city or town. Cut out the articles that show the mayor using the powers of his or her office. Paste them onto sheets of paper. Below each article, tell what official powers the mayor is using. Bind the sheets into your own book entitled, *Our Living Government*.
2. **COLLABORATIVE LEARNING** Plan and present a skit on the argument over whether the United States should have one or three presidents. Work in committees that do these jobs: write the script for supporting one president; write the script for supporting three presidents; perform the speaking parts; make the props.

Unit 5

Life in a Growing Nation

When George Washington became president in 1789 an exciting time in American life began. The people of the young nation were learning to use a new form of government. They were also building cities and exploring western lands. Many Americans set out to turn the rich land into farms. Farm life could be hard, but sometimes it had its rewards. Barn raising parties and fall harvest fairs, like the one shown here, helped Americans celebrate the success of their growing nation.

1763

1860

Artist unknown, Pennsylvania Dutch Harvest Festival, 1853. Courtesy of owner.

Chapter 13

Birth of a New Nation

The years following the birth of the new nation were full of new beginnings. Everything was happening for the first time: electing the first president, starting the first political parties, coining the first U.S. money. Slowly the new nation took form. Sometimes people disagreed. Sometimes they even wondered if they would succeed.

1801–1808 The nation grows during Thomas Jefferson's presidency. Earlier he had proposed a plan for 14 new states (above): 2 was called Michigania and 5 was Metropotamia.

1789 George Washington is sworn in as the first President of the United States.

1780

1790

1800

1788

1793–1795 George Washington does not want his portrait on U.S. coins. Congress uses the goddess of liberty instead.

Throughout this period one-room schoolhouses sprang up as the nation built a system of public schools.

| 1810 | 1820 | 1830 |

1807 Robert Fulton makes the first successful steamboat voyage.

1824

Launching a New Government

How did Jefferson's view of the future of the United States differ from Hamilton's view?

Key Terms

- precedent
- Cabinet
- political party
- Federalist
- Republican

➤ *People sewed special buttons on their clothes to honor Washington on the day he became president in 1788. Two of these buttons are shown above.*

George Washington became our first president on April 30, 1789 in New York City. Americans wondered what to call him. Your Excellency? His High Mightiness? His Highness, the President of the United States of America, and Protector of Their Liberties?

But Americans had just fought against Britain's king. They did not want their new leader thinking he was like a king. People knew that what they called Washington would set a **precedent,** a model to follow in years to come. Congress finally chose a plain, simple address: "Mr. President." It has been used ever since.

Setting Goals at Home

Washington's closest advisers were the men he chose to run the departments of the government. These advisers later became known as the **Cabinet.** One Cabinet leader was Alexander Hamilton, the Secretary of the Treasury. Hamilton was a lawyer from New York. He hoped that the United States would become a land of strong businesses and growing cities. He feared that a weak national government could not keep order.

The Secretary of State, Thomas Jefferson, did not agree with Hamilton. As a farmer, Jefferson thought farmers were "the chosen people of God." He dreamed of a country of farms and small towns. He feared that a strong national government could hurt liberty.

The different views of America caused conflicts between Jefferson and Hamilton. Hamilton wanted a strong national government to help businesses grow. To do this, he said he thought that the government should set up a national bank. The bank could help businesses grow by lending money to them. Jefferson did not want the bank. Small farmers had little need for it.

Washington asked each adviser to write his thoughts about the bank. Jefferson wrote that the national government should do only what the U.S. Constitution clearly allowed. The Constitution did not speak about a national bank. Thus, Jefferson said, no bank should be set up.

Hamilton stayed up all night to write an answer. Under the Constitution, he noted, Congress could make all laws that were "necessary and proper" for the United States. He said that a bank was "proper" because it would help the nation grow richer.

Washington finally agreed with Hamilton. The bank opened. Washington thus set a precedent for understanding the "necessary and proper" clause broadly. This allowed the national government to grow more powerful. ■

■ *How did Jefferson and Hamilton interpret the Constitution differently?*

Shaping Foreign Policy

Jefferson and Hamilton had another important difference. They did not agree on how the United States should act in the world.

In 1789, the citizens of France overthrew their king. The French then began a sweeping revolution. France's European neighbors feared that citizens of nations everywhere might try to get rid of their own kings. France's neighbors then went to war to defeat the revolutionaries. By 1793, France was fighting several countries. One of them was Britain.

Jefferson thought the United States should help France. The two nations had an agreement of friendship. Also, Jefferson believed that the United States should help the common people of France, who had thrown over an unfair government led by a king.

Hamilton did not want to help France. He said that the United States could lose its rich trade with

Britain if it helped France. Also, the revolution in France was the kind of fighting by common

▼ *This etching of the first Cabinet shows, from left, Henry Knox, Thomas Jefferson, Edmund Randolph, Alexander Hamilton, and George Washington.*

➤ *How do you know that the print showing the French Revolution was done by someone against the revolution?*

■ *How did Americans view France's revolution?*

▼ *Campaign posters from 1800 show that each party viewed the other as a threat to the nation. In the poster on the left, notice the snake—a sign of danger—under Jefferson.*

citizens that worried Hamilton. Revolutionaries had killed many people who were against reforms. Among those killed were the king and queen of France.

At first many Americans agreed with Jefferson. They supported the revolution in France. People remembered how France had helped them win independence. They thought it was America's turn to help France. Also, the enemy was Great Britain again. Many Americans still did not like Britain.

Washington, though, agreed with Hamilton. He felt that the young nation was too weak to fight Britain. The United States did not help France. This decision set another precedent. The United States would stay out of wars in Europe. ■

Forming Political Parties

Washington won a second term in 1792. He feared that political fighting was destroying the nation. Yet by 1796, the nation was even more sharply divided. Washington's belief in Hamilton had turned many of his old friends into bitter enemies. In a letter printed in a newspaper, Thomas Paine attacked Washington.

A*s to you sir . . . the world will be puzzled to decide . . . whether you have abandoned [given up] good principles, or whether you ever had any.*

Washington decided not to run again. The race for president became a contest between people with different goals for the United States. Like Jefferson, most small farmers and workers

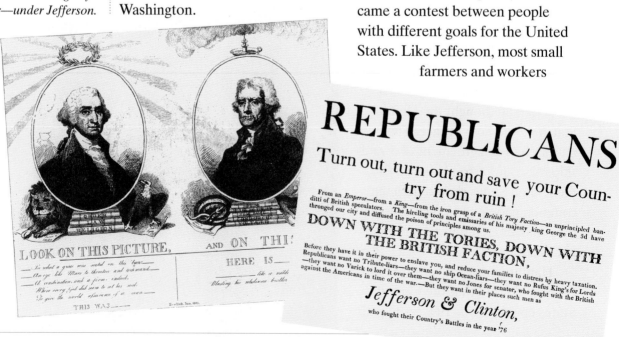

wanted a weak national government. They wanted common citizens to take part in government.

Like Hamilton, most merchants and rich landowners wanted a strong national government. They believed it would keep order and help business to grow.

Federalists and Republicans

People set up groups, now called **political parties,** to support their favorite candidates. Hamilton's friends formed the **Federalist** party and helped John Adams run for president.

Jefferson's friends formed the **Republican** party and helped Jefferson run for president. This party is not the same Republican party as today. Rather, Jefferson's party later became what is now the Democratic party.

The Sedition Act

Adams defeated Jefferson in the 1796 election. In 1798, Congress tried to stop the Republicans from attacking Federalist policies. They passed the Sedition Act, which punished people who spoke against the government. The first person thrown into prison under this law was Benjamin Franklin's grandson.

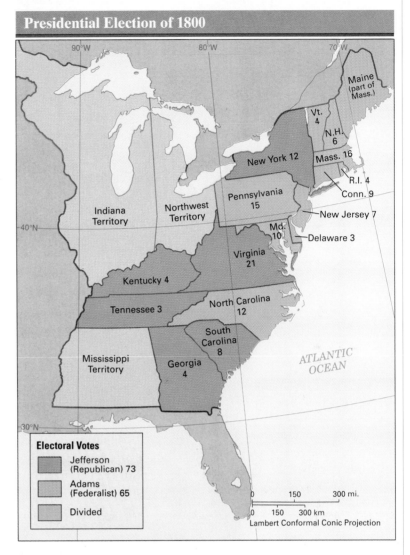

Presidential Election of 1800

Maine (part of Mass.)
Vt. 4
N.H. 6
New York 12
Mass. 16
R.I. 4
Conn. 9
Pennsylvania 15
New Jersey 7
Md. 10
Delaware 3
Indiana Territory
Northwest Territory
Virginia 21
Kentucky 4
North Carolina 12
Tennessee 3
South Carolina 8
ATLANTIC OCEAN
Mississippi Territory
Georgia 4

Electoral Votes

Jefferson (Republican) 73
Adams (Federalist) 65
Divided

0   150   300 mi.
0 150   300 km
Lambert Conformal Conic Projection

He died in prison. But the Sedition Act did not unite the country. The United States still had two parties for the next presidential election. In 1800, though, Jefferson won. Could he bring the people together? ■

▲ *Which regions voted for Jefferson in 1800?*

■ *How were the Federalists and Republicans different?*

R E V I E W

1. **FOCUS** How did Jefferson's view of the future of the United States differ from Hamilton's view?
2. **CONNECT** Compare the Sedition Act and the First Amendment.
3. **POLITICAL SYSTEMS** What did Jefferson think the phrase "necessary and proper" meant?
4. **HISTORY** Explain whether Washington acted more like a Federalist or a Republican.
5. **CRITICAL THINKING** Today, the federal government helps farmers by lending them money at a lower cost than banks do. How do you think Hamilton and Jefferson would view this program?
6. **WRITING ACTIVITY** Pretend you are either a Federalist or a Republican candidate for Congress in 1800. Write a one-minute campaign speech. Explain why people should vote for your party's candidates.

319

Birth of a New Nation

Timeline: 1780 1790 1800 1824 1830

1780   1790   **1800**   **1824**   1830

Jefferson and National Unity

THINKING FOCUS

How did the people of the United States become more strongly united in the early 1800s?

Key Terms

- nationalism
- impressment
- War Hawk
- Monroe Doctrine

► *Jefferson was the first president to begin his term in Washington, D.C. The unfinished capital city symbolized just how new and undeveloped the entire nation was in 1800.*

No guards, no coach, not even a horse waited at the door for Thomas Jefferson as he left his rented room in Washington, D.C. He wore no powdered wig and carried no sword. His clothes were simple. He looked like any other citizen out for a walk.

The tall, red-haired Virginian tried to keep his shoes clean as he strolled up muddy New Jersey Avenue. A few friends walked with him. Behind him marched some Virginia soldiers. They were the only sign that Jefferson was on important business.

When Jefferson reached the north wing of the unfinished Capitol, he entered. There he promised to serve honestly and well as the third president of the United States.

A New Party Takes Power

Jefferson's simple taking of office matched his Republican view of government. Not like Washington and Adams, he would govern as a common citizen. He would choose advisers for their skills and their belief in his ideas, not for their wealth. Federalists worried. Under Jefferson, they warned, the country would be governed by "the worthless" and "the dishonest."

The Federalists did not need to worry. Jefferson did not throw out what the Federalists had done. He tried to bring the country together. "We are all republicans," he said as he took office. "We are all federalists." During Jefferson's two terms as president, people in the United States began to feel a growing sense of **nationalism,** of belonging to a certain country.

Peace across the seas was harder to have than peace at home. In 1803, Britain and France went to war again. Each country wanted to stop the United States from trading with its enemy.

UNDERSTANDING NATIONALISM

*I*n the early 1800s, people in the United States began to feel that their country had become a nation. They came to recognize that they belonged to a common culture and shared certain interests. The feeling of being part of a nation is called nationalism.

Some people confuse nationalism with patriotism—a very positive feeling about a country. Patriots often feel that their country is the best one in the world.

Nationalism and Nations

Nationalists often feel that everyone who shares the same language, customs, and values should live under one government. In the late 1700s, the region where the Poles lived was divided into areas controlled by German, Russian, and Austrian rulers. In 1918, the Polish areas were combined to form the nation of Poland.

At other times two groups that have very different cultures may live in one country. For example, the country of Pakistan was formed in 1947. It joined the Muslims who had lived in the extreme east and west of British India. The people of East and West Pakistan shared the same religion, but they differed in many other ways. They spoke different languages and had many different customs and traditions. In 1971, the eastern part of Pakistan broke away and formed the nation of Bangladesh.

Nationalism and Heroes

Heroes help build nationalism. They remind people that they share many values. George Washington and Thomas Jefferson are two of America's most popular heroes. They helped lead the 13 colonies to declare their independence in 1776. People called the new country the United States. But only later, when nationalism developed, were the states truly united.

Britain and France each caught hundreds of American merchant ships and stole their goods. In bold acts called **impressment,** the British carried off thousands of American sailors and made them work in the British navy.

These British and French acts made Americans angry. In 1807, Jefferson stopped U.S. trade with all countries. He hoped to make Britain and France respect the rights of U.S. ships.

Yet this act hurt the United States more than it hurt Britain or France. Buildings filled up with goods that could not be sold. James Madison, elected president in 1808, opened trade again with all countries by 1810. ■

■ *What trade problems did the United States have under Jefferson?*

A Second War with Britain

Madison, like Jefferson, was a Republican from Virginia. And like Jefferson, he did not want war. But British attacks went on. Also, Britain was giving guns to the Shawnee Indians. The Shawnee were attacking U.S. settlements on Shawnee land in the territories of Indiana and Michigan. On June 18, 1812, Congress, led by a group called the **War Hawks,** declared war on Britain. Study the map on this page. Can you tell where the major battles happened?

For two years, the war was evenly fought. Then, on August 24, 1814, British soldiers stormed into Washington, D.C. They set fire to the Capitol and the White House. In just hours, the buildings were wrapped "in one sheet of fire." Fear swept the city. Madison, his wife Dolley, and the people of Washington fled into the country.

▲ *Dolley Madison took key government papers as she fled the burning White House in 1814.*

➤ *The large map shows all major battles in the War of 1812. The small map shows the Great Lakes battles.*

Across Time & Space

Two weeks after the treaty ending the War of 1812 was signed in Europe, U.S. troops defeated the British at New Orleans. Because travel across the ocean was slow, troops had not heard about the treaty. Today, our news crosses oceans in seconds.

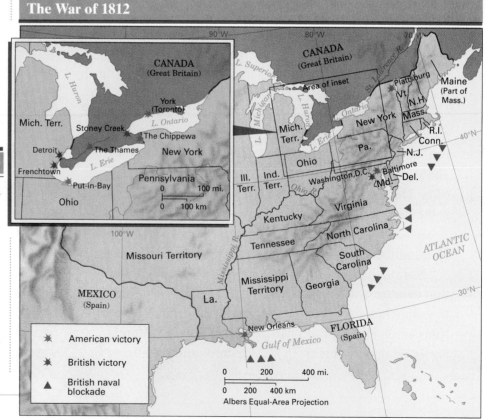

The War of 1812

★ American victory

✹ British victory

▲ British naval blockade

But in six months, the Americans drove the British off of the Atlantic coast. Again the war was even. With no victory in sight, Britain and the United States signed a treaty on December 24, 1814. This ended the fighting we now call the War of 1812. ■

■ *Why did the United States go to war against Great Britain?*

A Rise in Nationalism

At first, the War of 1812 split the United States. Many New England Federalists did not want the war. Some even said that New England should leave the country.

Yet fighting together helped to unite the country. The war reminded Americans that they shared many values. After the war political battles died down. The Federalist party almost died out. In the 1816 presidential election, Republican James Monroe won easily. One newspaper even claimed that the election began an "Era of Good Feelings."

While nationalism grew in the United States, the Spanish holdings in the Americas were falling apart. Between 1791 and 1822, most Spanish lands in the Americas became free. Monroe feared that Spain, or France, might take over these new nations. He did not want Europeans to hold land in America.

In 1823, James Monroe warned European countries to stay out of the Americas, or risk war with the United States. In return, the United States would stay out of European conflicts. This statement, now called the **Monroe Doctrine,** showed America's growing strength. ■

▲ *This flag flew over Fort McHenry, Baltimore, in the War of 1812. It inspired Francis Scott Key to write the "Star Spangled Banner."*

■ *What was the Era of Good Feelings?*

◄ *How does this carving show national pride?*

U. S. Custom House, 1805.

REVIEW

1. **FOCUS** How did the people of the United States become more strongly united in the early 1800s?
2. **CONNECT** How was Jefferson's action on trade similar to the British action on Boston trade just before the Revolutionary War?
3. **CITIZENSHIP** Define and give examples of the idea of nationalism.
4. **GEOGRAPHY** Why would merchants in New England be less likely to support a war against Britain than would people in other regions?
5. **CRITICAL THINKING** Explain whether or not you think the United States had a right to issue the Monroe Doctrine.
6. **WRITING ACTIVITY** Write a newspaper story from a Federalist viewpoint describing Jefferson's inauguration in 1801.

L E S S O N   3

Economic Life of the New Nation

THINKING

F O C U S

How was the economy of the United States changing between 1788 and 1824?

Key Terms

- surplus
- textile

The farmer's wife, and a young woman who looked like her sister, were spinning, and three little children were playing about. The woman told me that they spun and wove all the cotton and woollen garments of the family, and knit all the stockings; her husband, though not a shoe-maker by trade, made all the shoes. She manufactured all the soap and candles they used, and prepared her sugar from the sugar-trees on their farm. All she wanted with money, she said, was to buy coffee [and]tea. . . .

These words, telling of an early Ohio farm, were written by Frances Trollope, an English woman who lived in the United States in the 1820s. Trollope was interested in how farm families grew or made most of what they needed. The farmer's wife "seemed . . . proud of her independence." But she told Trollope sadly:

Tis strange to us to see company: I expect the sun may rise and set a hundred times before I shall see another human that does not belong to the family.

Agriculture and Trade

The Ohio family made most of what it needed. What they did not make, they got by trading with neighbors. Many frontier families lived on such farms.

Changes in Agriculture

Farming across the United States was changing, however. More and more farmers produced a **surplus.** That is, they raised more than they needed for themselves. Farmers usually loaded their extra flour, pork, or other goods on wagons and took them to nearby towns to sell. Soon, however, some farmers began to grow fewer crops. Instead of growing everything they needed, these farmers raised only one or two crops. They grew crops they could sell for cash. They began to depend on the money they received.

An Increase in Trade

As the farmers grew fewer crops, they needed to buy more goods that they used to make, such as shoes. And since they sold more crops, they had more money to buy things with. As they bought things, they made work for shoemakers and other skilled workers. They created a need for factory-made goods like **textiles**—cloth made from cotton or wool.

Farmers in each part of the country grew different crops. In the south more and more farmers raised cotton, especially after 1820. In the middle states such as Ohio, Indiana, and Illinois, more farmers only grew corn and raised hogs. So much pork was shipped through Cincinnati that people called it "Porkopolis." On a walk through Cincinnati one day, Frances Trollope came across a brook that she described as "red with the stream from a pig slaughter-house."

Growth of Port Cities

By 1820, farmers sold one-fourth of their goods to Britain, France, or other countries. As sales grew, port cities such as New York and New Orleans became busier. Cotton, wheat, flour, beef, and pork were the main goods sold.

New inventions made trade easier. Before 1807, shipping goods down the rivers was easy. However, boats going up the rivers, against the current, moved slowly. In 1807, Robert Fulton developed the first steam-powered boat that worked well. Steamboats went up-river much faster. Fulton's boat went about five miles per hour.

The steamboat enabled trade on the river to increase. This helped port cities grow more rapidly. A Closer Look tells you more about port cities on the next page. ■

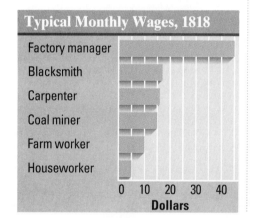

Typical Monthly Wages, 1818

Factory manager
Blacksmith
Carpenter
Coal miner
Farm worker
Houseworker

0   10   20   30   40
Dollars

Across Time & Space

America still exports farm products to the rest of the world. U.S. farmers export about 60 per cent of the wheat and about 25 per cent of the corn they grow. Japan and the Netherlands are two of the leading importers of U.S. farm products.

■ *How was farming changing in the early 1800s?*

◄ *As the chart shows, monthly wages in 1818 were low compared to today, but so were prices. Some everyday items are shown below. Bread flour was 3 cents per pound; nails, 9 cents per pound; candlesticks, 15 cents each; and coffee beans 16 cents per pound. Most cloth sold for about 16 cents a yard.*

New York Harbor, 1830

By 1830, the nation's busiest port was a forest of ship masts. Dock workers busily loaded ships with American farm products and unloaded cargo from as far away as China. Auctioneers stood on sugar barrels, shouting at the merchants who crowded the docks.

Forty cents of every dollar earned on cotton fell into the hands of New York's merchants. In 1830, they made almost $12 million! Captains stowed America's number-one export wherever they could, sometimes even using a bundle or two as a table.

Apples, cheese, and grain from the U.S. heartland made their way to Europe from northeastern ports like New York.

Belgian lace was just one of the luxury items merchants eagerly awaited on the docks. The next ship might be carrying silk and tea from China, sharp knives from Britain, or fine wine from France.

STORAGE

M⁰KIBBIN & CAYLEY GRO

South Street, New York, on the East River

Southern tobacco, America's number-two export, left New York for European markets. Ships returning from Europe carried manufactured goods like tools and clothes. Some ships carried people, too—tourists who enjoyed every shipboard luxury, and immigrants crammed into the ship's smelly hold.

Clothes for cloves: that was the swap between the United States and the East African island of Zanzibar. Trading spicy cloves for American cloth was so successful the African term *merikani* (American) came to mean cotton goods or blankets.

Birth of a New Nation

Wealth and Inequality

The changes in farming caused other changes in the economy. Though most people still lived on farms, the number of people in business was growing. And as trade grew, so did the number of very wealthy people in the nation.

One of the richest merchants in America in the 1790s was

In the early 1800s, workers used wooden plates while wealthy people could afford beautiful plates imported from China.

■ *Why did economic differences among Americans increase in the early 1800s?*

Elias Derby. He lived in the booming port city of Salem, Massachusetts. His three-story mansion had 15 rooms. It was filled with French carpets, satin-covered furniture, and marble tables. Derby was the first person in the United States to own $1 million worth of property.

The Growth of Poverty

As trade grew, people moved to cities looking for work. As cities grew, the prices of food and housing went up. Workers with little money suffered. The number of poor people in cities grew.

The South also had many very rich and very poor people. Though most people in the South were small farmers who owned no slaves, a few whites owned large plantations. These rich families lived in large homes and owned hundreds of slaves.

A New Problem for America

The growth of trade caused a problem for the United States. As merchants and plantation owners got richer, many workers, both free and slave, got poorer. Was the United States still a land of equality, as promised in the Declaration of Independence? The people had to decide what kind of country they wanted to become. ■

R E V I E W

1. **FOCUS** How was the economy in the United States changing between 1788 and 1824?

2. **CONNECT** Explain why Alexander Hamilton would support the changes occurring in the United States between 1788 and 1824.

3. **CITIZENSHIP** How did the growth of trade challenge one traditional idea about citizenship?

4. **ECONOMICS** Why would the middle states have greater equality than would port cities or the South?

5. **CRITICAL THINKING** Think about how the economic changes discussed in this lesson would influence the relationships among people. Explain whether these changes would make people in the United States more or less closely united with each other.

6. **WRITING ACTIVITY** Imagine you were an English citizen reading Frances Trollope's book just after it was written. Make a list of five questions you would like to have her answer about life in the United States.

LESSON 4

Everyday Life in the Young Nation

"Y ou will never have a correct idea of what a wilderness is till you come to visit me," wrote Elias Pym Fordham in 1817. He was describing the Illinois Territory. He went on, saying:

T o be at an unknown distance from the dwellings of man . . . and then to lie at night in a blanket, with your feet to a fire, with your rifle hugged in your arms, listening to the howling wolves, and starting at the shriek of the terrible panther: This it is to be in a wilderness alone.

The nation had thriving cities as well as rugged frontier areas. Many liked cities best. Anne Royall visited Philadelphia in the 1820s. In telling about her trip, she wrote:

T he profusion [large amount] of merchandize which lines the streets and windows is incredible. Dry goods are strewed [spread out] along the side-walks, near the store doors; flannels, cloths, muslins, silks. . . . But it is at night that the wealth and splendor of Philadelphia appears to the best advantage; the windows being lighted with numerous lamps and gaslights, which, with the lamps in the streets, and the luster [light] of the glittering wares in the windows, present a scene of astonishing beauty.

THINKING
FOCUS

How did daily life in the young republic change from 1789 to 1824?

Key Terms

- camp meeting
- common school

Changes in Religion

As the United States grew, people developed different ways of life. The differences between the frontier and the city were just one kind of difference. The nation also had people of many religious groups. Most immigrants were Christians from Europe. However, they brought several different beliefs to the United States.

Most settlers from England were Congregationalists, Quakers,

329

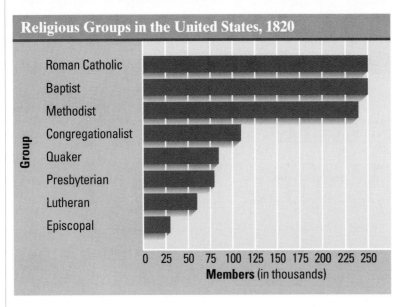

Religious Groups in the United States, 1820

Group
- Roman Catholic
- Baptist
- Methodist
- Congregationalist
- Quaker
- Presbyterian
- Lutheran
- Episcopal

Members (in thousands)
0 25 50 75 100 125 150 175 200 225 250

▲ *This chart shows some of the largest religious groups in the United States. Dozens of smaller groups also existed.*

■ *Why was religious diversity growing in the United States in the early 1800s?*

▼ *Paul Cuffee became a wealthy merchant in the early 1800s.*

or members of the Church of England. Shortly after the Revolutionary War, members of the Church of England in the United States decided to break away from the English church. They formed the Episcopal Church.

Many settlers from Scotland were Presbyterians. They followed the teachings of John Knox, a Scottish religious leader in the 1500s.

Many people from Sweden and northern Germany were Lutherans. This group got its name from

Martin Luther, a German religious leader of the 1500s. Most settlers from southern Germany and from Ireland were Roman Catholics.

In the United States, people worshiped in different ways in the early 1800s. In cities and towns, most people attended churches. In many small villages and in fields on the edges of towns, though, men and women held huge prayer meetings, or **camp meetings.** These were more like rallies than quiet church services. Preachers gave thunderous sermons. People shouted and sang hymns. Many rolled around on the ground in excitement.

Baptists or Methodists led many camp meetings. The Baptists had a long history in America. One of the first Baptists in America was Roger Williams. He founded the colony of Rhode Island in the 1630s.

Unlike the Baptists, the Methodists were new to America in the early 1800s. They followed the teachings of John Wesley, an English clergyman of the 1700s. ■

Growth of the Free Black Community

Most American settlers had come from Europe. But the new nation also had many people who traced their roots to Africa.

How Blacks Became Free

In 1820, about one-eighth of all blacks in the United States were free. Some had won freedom by serving in the army during the Revolutionary War or the War of 1812. A few owners let their slaves work for money and then buy their

freedom. Many saved enough to free their whole family.

Some slaves were freed by their owners. George Washington gave his slaves their freedom in his will. Other slaves escaped and moved north, but they lived in daily fear of being discovered.

How Blacks Lived and Worked

Many free blacks lived in northern cities. In these cities they were not as likely to be kidnapped into slavery. Also, free blacks faced fewer hardships in the north than in the south.

Even in the north, though, blacks suffered from unfair treatment by whites. Few blacks had high-paying jobs. Black women often worked as house servants. Some made a living by sewing. Black men often worked as laborers, hotel porters, waiters, and sailors. But some free blacks became skilled workers, such as shoemakers and mechanics.

Benjamin Banneker was one of the most successful free blacks. He was born in Baltimore in 1731. He attended a small private school for both black students and white students. At age 28, he built the first clock made in America. In 1791, he helped to survey the city of Washington, D.C. Banneker was also a skilled astronomer. He even printed his weather predictions in an annual book.

How Blacks Worshiped

Blacks wanted to worship in their own ways. So, beginning in the 1790s, they formed their own churches. The African heritage of blacks influenced the music that developed in their churches. The church helped blacks when they were sick or in need. ■

◀ *Elizabeth Freeman was a slave in Massachusetts. But after she was beaten, she left the family and won her freedom in a court case.*

■ *How were the lives of most free black Americans different from those of white Americans?*

◀ *Lemuel Haynes was the minister of a mostly white Congregational church in Vermont.*

Changes in the Family

Family life in the new republic also was changing. Since colonial times, women had always been responsible for raising large families. Yet that was only one of their duties. During the Revolutionary War, many women took over the family farm or other businesses while their husbands were away fighting.

Raising Children

After the war, women were also expected to raise their children as good citizens. "When our land is filled with virtuous and patriotic mothers," wrote clergyman John Abbott, "then will it be filled with virtuous and patriotic men." Women tried to teach their children the values of hard work and pride in their country.

The mother's role in the family became more important in cities and towns. The needs of trade and business often took men to jobs away from the home. As men worked outside the home, they spent less and less time with their children.

Earning Money

Even life on the farm was changing. Farmers made less of what they needed and more of what they could sell. Money became more important on the farm. To bring in money, daughters in farm families sometimes worked as servants in other people's homes. Other women made money sewing clothes or making brooms, hats, or other items for sale.

Women had time for such things as families became smaller. In one town, the common family size of the mid-1700s was nine children. By the early 1800s, the town's average family had only six children. The same change happened in many towns. Farm families, though, stayed large. ■

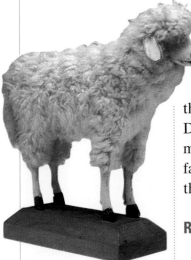

▲ *Toy animals such as this sheep were popular with children in the early 1800s.*

■ *How did the lives of farm women in the United States change as commerce developed?*

➤ *This painting was done around 1800. How does it show the different roles of men and women in the family?*

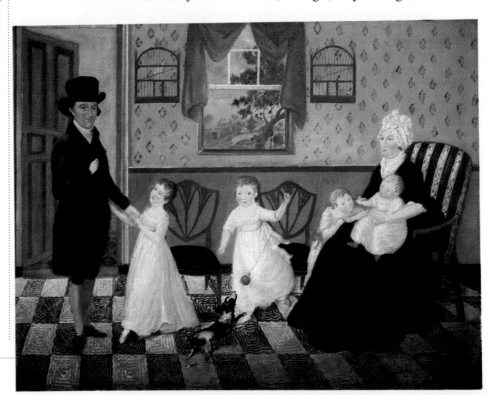

Growth of Public Schools

For children, life was also changing in other ways. Public schools were one-room buildings called **common schools.** Students of all ages and abilities studied in the same room:

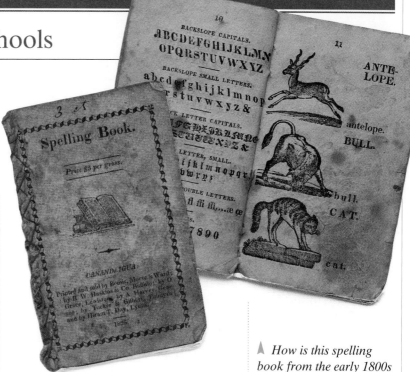

> The boys in the writing class were scratching away busily in their copy-books. In the corner by the fireplace Jonathan's own big brother, Andrew, was working over his arithmetic, setting down his figures on a large piece of birch bark. And the smallest children were standing in a straight row before the new schoolmaster, saying their spelling lesson.
>
> Enid LaMonte Meadowcroft,
> *By Wagon and Flatboat*

Not all children attended common schools. Children from rich families often went to private schools. And many children who lived on farms had to work rather than go to school. Farm families needed all hands in the fields during harvest season.

The first common schools were started by settlers in New England. They opened schools soon after arriving in America. Then, in 1787, the Northwest Ordinance set up a way to pay for schools in all the territories. As the settlers moved to the west, they set up new schools. Public schools soon gave people great pride in their nation.

People hoped that schools would do more than teach students how to read, write, and do math. They wanted schools to make young people into good citizens. ■

▲ *How is this spelling book from the early 1800s different from the books you use in school today?*

■ *What were schools like in the United States in the early 1800s?*

R E V I E W

1. **FOCUS** How did daily life in the young republic change from 1789 to 1824?

2. **CONNECT** Study the picture of Washington's cabinet shown on page 317. How were the people in the president's cabinet unlike the people of the United States as a whole in 1788?

3. **CITIZENSHIP** Think about the differences between the North and the South. Why did many free blacks live in northern cities?

4. **ECONOMICS** How did changes in the economy influence the role of men and women as parents?

5. **CRITICAL THINKING** Why do you think the followers of the Church of England became Episcopalians shortly after the Revolutionary War?

6. **WRITING ACTIVITY** Write a letter to send to an imaginary student living in the United States in 1800. Describe your own school today and explain some ways that it differs from the schools of the past.

Using Cluster Diagrams

Here's Why

Diagramming is a good way to organize and remember information. One kind of diagram is called a cluster diagram. A cluster diagram looks something like a wheel. The main idea of the diagram is in the middle. Details are placed around the main idea like the spokes of the wheel. Cluster diagrams are very helpful because they center your attention and make summarizing easier.

In Lesson 1 you read about how Alexander Hamilton and Thomas Jefferson tried to help George Washington build a new nation. You also learned that Hamilton and Jefferson strongly disagreed about many government policies. One way to arrange and summarize their political views is to build two cluster diagrams, one for Hamilton and one for Jefferson.

Here's How

In the cluster diagram below, pieces of information are connected to the figure in the middle. What can you learn at a glance from this cluster diagram?

The first step is to note the subject of the cluster diagram. The center identifies the person or main subject of the diagram. What is the subject of this diagram?

Next, note the different categories. The categories in this diagram state Alexander Hamilton's political party and his positions on the French Revolution, government, and economics. Look at page 316, paragraph 5. Find information that explains why the phrase "large, strong federal" was given as a detail under Government. Then find the material on pages 316 and 317 that explains placing the phrase "Manufacturing and trade; national bank" in the economy category.

Now copy the cluster diagram below on a separate sheet of paper. Finish the first category in the diagram by finding the name of Hamilton's political party on page 319. Finish the second category by turning to pages 317 and 318 and finding a description of Hamilton's ideas on the French Revolution.

1 — Political party

Government — Large, strong, federal

French Revolution — **2**

Economy — Manufacturing and trade; national bank

Alexander Hamilton

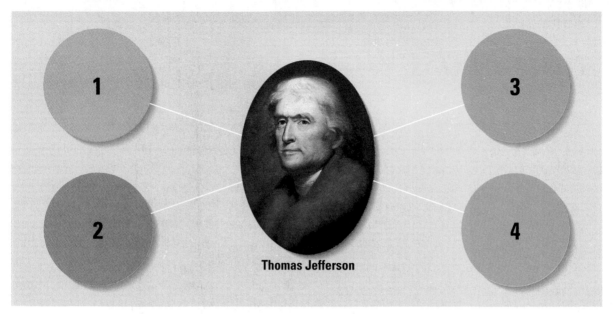

Thomas Jefferson

What other categories might be added to the cluster diagram about Hamilton?

The diagram can help you to arrange and remember information about Hamilton. Without looking at it, try to see the diagram in your mind. Then tell what you know about Hamilton.

Try It

Look at the cluster diagram above. Thomas Jefferson is the subject.

Copy the cluster diagram onto a sheet of paper. If you are comparing Jefferson's views to those of Hamilton, what should the four categories used in this cluster diagram be?

Write one category on each line. Then look through the material on pages 316, 317, and 319. Find the information to finish each of the categories. Try adding new categories to the diagram to increase the amount of information it contains.

After you have finished your cluster diagram, take a good look at it. Then turn your paper over. Try to picture your diagram. Without looking at your diagram, tell a classmate what you know about Thomas Jefferson.

Look at the cluster diagram about Hamilton and the diagram about Jefferson. How do the ideas of these two great men compare? What is one example of a subject on which they do not agree? Explain how comparing the two diagrams gives you a clearer idea of how Hamilton and Jefferson thought.

Now make your own cluster diagrams about other leaders mentioned in Chapter 13. Select George Washington, James Madison, or James Monroe.

Apply It

Cluster diagrams can help you arrange information about people who are living today. Pick a favorite political candidate or movie star. Maybe a candidate for student council would make a good subject for a cluster diagram. Think about what makes that person special and what things and ideas represent him or her. Build a cluster diagram that shows these important points.

If you choose a student council candidate, try using his or her stated beliefs about the office as the categories. Be sure to include his or her ideas about the duties involved with the office. Then find out about the other candidates running for the same office. Make a cluster diagram for each candidate. Use his or her stated beliefs in the same way as you did on the first diagram. Share your cluster diagrams with your classmates. Ask them to explain what they can tell about the candidates for student council from your cluster diagrams.

Chapter Review

Reviewing Key Terms

Cabinet (p. 316)
camp meeting (p. 330)
common school (p. 333)
Federalist (p. 319)
impressment (p. 322)
Monroe Doctrine (p. 323)
nationalism (p. 321)

political party (p. 319)
precedent (p. 316)
Republican (p. 319)
surplus (p. 324)
textile (p. 325)
War Hawk (p. 322)

A. Each of the following words is related in some way to one of the key terms. Write the correct key term next to the words on the list below.

1. unified
2. sailor
3. extra
4. religion
5. weave
6. advise
7. pattern

B. Some of the following statements are true. The rest are false. Write True or False for each statement. Then rewrite the false statements to make them true.

1. Most Federalists were workers and common citizens.
2. A War Hawk favored declaring war on Britain in 1812.
3. A common school had only one classroom for all its students.
4. Republicans wanted a weak national government.
5. The Monroe Doctrine helped schools.
6. As farmers became more efficient, they produced a surplus of crops.
7. Each political party supported a candidate in the 1796 election.

Exploring Concepts

A. Write one or two sentences to answer each of the questions below.

1. Did the growth of nationalism reduce the influence of one political party? If so, which one and why?
2. What groups of people benefited from the growth in commerce? Which groups were harmed by it?
3. Who did the Northwest Ordinance help to educate, and how?
4. What feeling brings together people who share the same culture?
5. Which two men in particular debated the course of America's future?
6. What groups of people outside the United States were affected by the Monroe Doctrine?

B. Write whether you agree or disagree with each of the following statements. If you disagree, give your reasons.

1. The early settlers in the Illinois territory felt safe in their new land.
2. Immigrants brought many different religious beliefs to the United States.
3. The only role of women in colonial America was to cook and care for children.
4. Some blacks served in the army and thus earned their freedom.
5. Benjamin Banneker was one of many well-known, successful blacks in 1790.
6. With the growth of commerce, the fathers' role in families began to change.
7. Camp meetings were a quiet time for Americans to think about religion.

336

Reviewing Skills

1. Use the cluster diagram on this page to answer this question: Why was Cincinnati called "Porkopolis" in the 1820s? Then think of an "-opolis" name for your hometown. Make a cluster diagram that illustrates why the name you created is a good one for your town.

2. Reread pages 324–333. Make one cluster diagram with "wilderness" in the center and another with "city." Make your webs compare everyday life in those two places.

3. Choose one of the groups of immigrants referred to in Lesson 4. Then find information about the history of this group in America by looking in an encyclopedia. List the name of the encyclopedia and the volume number. Write down the title of the article you found. Then write two facts from the article.

4. Imagine that you lived in the United States in the 1800s. How would you organize and present facts about the changing American economy in order to explain it to someone from another country?

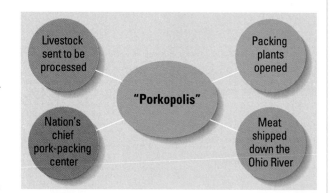

Using Critical Thinking

1. Alexander Hamilton wanted America to become a nation of merchants. Thomas Jefferson thought it should stay a nation of farms and small towns. What do you think your life would be like today if America had not become an industrial country?

2. Thomas Jefferson stated, "Difference of opinion is advantageous in religion." Many present-day immigrants bring different religions to the United States. What are the advantages of this to the communities where the immigrants live?

3. Nationalism developed in the United States after the War of 1812. Fighting in a war often strengthens people's sense of nationalism. Why do you think this happens?

Preparing for Citizenship

1. **INTERVIEWING** Interview the principal of your school. Ask him or her how the local government helps pay for the school's expenses. Present the results of the interview to the class.

2. **GROUP ACTIVITY** Meet with a small group of classmates. Discuss why a Boston newspaper claimed that the presidential election of 1816 started an "Era of Good Feeling." Do you think our country is living in an era of good feeling today? Present your main points to the class.

3. **COLLABORATIVE LEARNING** Each group of four students should choose a popular TV program about a family. The group will write and perform a scene using the characters from that show but placing them in the United States of the early 1800s. Work together to write a scene that will take four or five minutes to perform. Assign one person to play each character. Show how the family members of 200 years ago behaved differently from those on the present-day program.

Chapter 14
Moving West

Throughout this period, thousands of people poured through the Cumberland Gap in the Appalachian Mountains.

Even before America won its independence, settlers were pushing west of the Appalachian Mountains. Americans found adventure and opportunity in these new lands. Many dreamed of building a better life by starting over in places like Kentucky and Tennessee. One minister even declared: "Heaven is a Kentucky of a place!"

1803 The United States buys the Louisiana Territory from France for $15 million. The new land, shown in the map above, doubles the size of the young country.

1750   1775   1800

1763

1803–1806 Meriwether Lewis and William Clark explore the land west of the Mississippi River. Lewis is shown above with a page from a book about their trip.

1800–1832 Most settlers travel to new homes on the frontier in sturdy covered wagons.

1825

1850

1875

1832

L E S S O N 1

The Moving Frontier

THINKING
F O C U S

Why did pioneers move to settlements across the Appalachian Mountains?

Key Terms

- pioneer
- ordinance

➤ *Daniel Boone started the movement west by building the Wilderness Road through the rugged Cumberland Gap. This statue of Boone shows him as a young man wearing an animal skin hat. In fact, Boone usually wore a black felt hat.*

When the men gathered around the campfire, Daniel Boone always had an exciting story for them. He might tell about the time he was trapped by stampeding buffalo. He couldn't outrun the herd, so he aimed his rifle at the lead buffalo. He killed it with a single shot. Then he used the body as a shelter as the herd thundered past.

Or he might tell about the day a band of Shawnee closed in on him with tomahawks raised. He was on the edge of a cliff. The only way to escape was to jump, so he did. Luckily, he landed in the branches of a tree.

The Shawnee admired Daniel Boone. So did the men around the campfire. They were proud to ride with the best woodsman on the frontier.

In 1775, Daniel Boone led 30 frontiersmen into the Appalachian Mountains. They went to build the

Wilderness Road, a narrow trail winding through dense forests and steep mountain passes. The road opened the lands west of the Appalachians to settlers. It led to a region known as "Kentucky," an Iroquois word meaning great meadow. During the next 20 years, thousands of settlers would travel this road to reach the frontier and start a new life.

To the men and women who followed him west, Daniel Boone stood for boldness, courage, and the restless spirit of adventure. Americans feel the same way about him today.

> *W*hen Daniel Boone goes by, at night,
> The phantom deer arise
> And all lost, wild America
> Is burning in their eyes.
>
> Rosemary and Stephen Benét,
> *A Book of Americans*, 1933

The Appalachian Frontier

Daniel Boone reached Kentucky in April 1775. During the next few years, Boone led several groups of **pioneers,** or early settlers, to Kentucky. He later bragged that his wife Rebecca and their daughters were "the first white women that ever stood on the banks of the Kentucky River."

The region Boone explored was part of a huge territory. It stretched from the Great Lakes in the north to the Gulf of Mexico in the south, from the Appalachians in the east to the Mississippi River in the west. Trace the outline of this territory on the map on page 342. What present-day states were part of this area?

France claimed most of this land before 1763. The French were only interested in the furs they could take from the region. French hunters and trappers roamed the forests and paddled up rivers in search of beaver, deer, bear, and other animals.

Control passed to the British after the Seven Years' War. The British knew that white settlers wanted to move west. They also knew that they would need hundreds of soldiers to keep the peace on the frontier. That would be expensive.

To solve the problem, the British passed a law called the Proclamation of 1763. It said that the lands west of the Appalachians belonged to the Shawnee, Creek, Cherokee, and other Indian tribes who were already living there. Colonists were ordered to keep out. ∎

How Do We Know?

HISTORY *Daniel Boone became a legend in his own time. In 1784, a pioneer named John Filson wrote a book called* The Discovery and Settlement of Kentucky. *The book contained exciting accounts of Boone's adventures.*

■ *Who owned the lands west of the Appalachians in the 1700s?*

341

Moving West

Early Pioneers

The Proclamation of 1763 did not stop frontiersmen like Daniel Boone. It didn't stop the pioneers who followed, either. People crossed the Appalachians for many reasons. Some wanted cheap land for farming. Others were running away from bills that they couldn't pay. Some were running away from the law. All hoped the frontier would be the answer to their dreams. "Heaven is a Kentucky of a place!" one minister told his church members.

Look at the map at the bottom of the page. Trace the path of the Wilderness Road that Daniel Boone built in 1775. During the late 1700s and early 1800s, thousands of pioneers moved west along this road. The Wilderness Road was not a smooth, wide highway. It was a narrow, rocky trail barely wide enough for a horse. To learn more about the special skills of frontiersmen like Daniel Boone, see A Moment in Time on the next page.

Across Time & Space

Some of the early pioneer roads later became highways for automobiles. The route Boone took up Moccasin Gap and across the Clinch River in Virginia is now U.S. 58. In Kentucky, Boone's men cut through thickets and blazed what is now Interstate 75.

➤ *How many states were carved out of the Old Northwest? How many were carved out of the Old Southwest?*

The Appalachian Frontier, 1787–1830

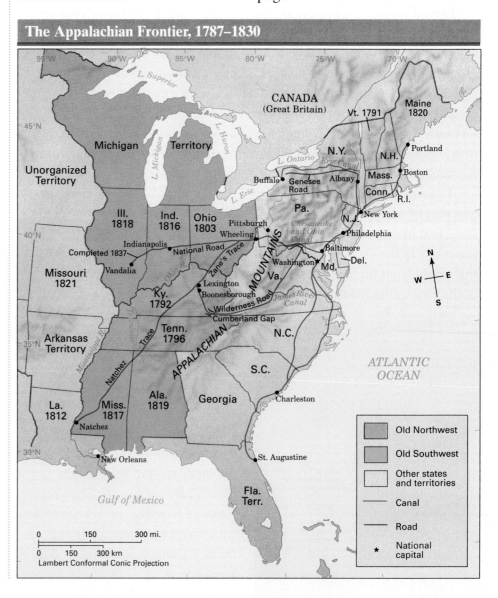

A Frontiersman

5:48 p.m., October 21, 1785
Overlooking the Auglaize River, between the
present-day cities of Dayton and Toledo, Ohio.

Shirt
The roomy chest pocket of his shirt holds
a bit of deer jerky. It tastes good with the
dried squash his wife packed when he
began his 200-mile journey 18 days ago.

Eyes
Sharp-eyed from years of
hunting, he spies a tree with
a twisted branch. This "road
sign" lets him know he's just
a three-day canoe ride from
the Shawnee village he seeks.

Buckskin Jacket
His sturdy coat protects him
from thorny branches along
the densely wooded trail.

Shot Pouch
When he's ready for supper,
he'll reach into his pouch to
get shot for his rifle. He's
learned to be careful not to
cut his finger on the needle he
uses to repair his moccasins.

Leather Bag
Inside is the compass that led him
due west into Indian territory. The
bag also holds a gift of salt the
Indians will prize and a bone wedge
he'll use to strip bark for a canoe.

Leather Rifle Case
The Indians he trades
furs with gave him this
treasured gift. He thanked
them in the Shawnee
language he learned as
a child in Pennsylvania.

Rifle
With this weapon, he'll "bark"
a squirrel for supper tonight.
When he shoots the part of the
tree right next to the squirrel,
the impact will kill the animal
without tearing up its body.

Moccasins
He stuffed his homemade
shoes with dry leaves
against the morning chill.

343

➤ *Study the graph at the right. How many people were living west of the Appalachians in 1800? In 1820?*

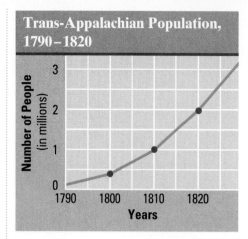

Trans-Appalachian Population, 1790–1820

■ *What was the main cause of the conflict between Indians and settlers?*

A trip over the Wilderness Road could be hard. The pioneers packed pots and pans, bedding, seed, and tools. They had to walk, but nothing could stop them. In 1775, there were only 150 pioneers living on the frontier west of the Appalachians. By 1810, the population had reached a million.

As settlers moved to the frontier, the Indians became increasingly upset. They lost more and more land each year. They tried to work out treaties with the settlers, but the treaties never lasted very long. The settlers wanted land. They were willing to buy it, but they would take it if they had to. As the years went by, the situation got worst. In the end, most Indian tribes were forced to move farther west. ■

The Northwest Ordinance

■ *How did the establishment of formal government change life on the frontier?*

As settlers moved west, the U.S. government had to decide how to organize the territory west of the Appalachians. Kentucky became the nation's 15th state in 1792. Tennessee became the 16th state in 1796.

The lands north of the Ohio River needed some kind of government. In 1787, Congress passed the Northwest Ordinance. An **ordinance** is a law. The Northwest Ordinance divided the region into separate territories. Each territory could become a state once the population reached 60,000. The ordinance guaranteed freedom of religion for the area, and it outlawed slavery. In addition, it promised to use "the utmost good faith" in protecting the rights of the Indians.

The days of the hunter and trapper in the area were drawing to a close. The frontier was moving west once again. ■

R E V I E W

1. **FOCUS** Why did pioneers move to settlements across the Appalachian Mountains?

2. **CONNECT** As settlers moved west, the U.S. government had to govern a faraway territory. In what ways was this task similar to the problem facing the British government as it tried to rule its American colonies in the 1770s? What methods did each government use?

3. **ECONOMICS** How did the needs of new settlers conflict with the needs of Indian tribes already living in the territory west of the Appalachians?

4. **CRITICAL THINKING** As more settlers crossed the Appalachians, the Indians were forced to move to hunting grounds farther west. What do you think happened as settlers also moved farther west?

5. **WRITING ACTIVITY** Suppose you were a pioneer traveling with your family along the Wilderness Road to Kentucky. Write a letter to a relative back East telling about your adventures.

LESSON 2

Life on the New Frontier

Rain was falling when the Fowlers left Pittsburgh, but Amy Fowler didn't mind. She was excited. She, her parents, and her seven brothers and sisters were bound for a new life.

The Fowlers' flatboat was one of a dozen going west that rainy April morning in 1788. The other boats belonged to Amy's aunts and uncles. They had come from central Pennsylvania to Pittsburgh, where they bought the flatboats. Now they were drifting down the Ohio River, headed for Kentucky.

Everything the Fowlers owned was on the deck of the 40-foot boat: clothes, a wagon, a horse, even a cow. The Fowlers had stretched cloth above the deck to provide shelter from storms.

Amy was only 10 years old, but she had to help her mother with the cooking and laundry. All the work was done on the boat, because Indians and other dangers might be hiding in the woods along the riverbanks. It was a risky two-week journey down the river. But the Fowlers braved the dangers to begin a new life.

THINKING FOCUS

What was life on the new frontier like for settlers in the early 1800s?

Key Terms

- tributary
- canal

◄ *In 1788, the Fowlers traveled down the Ohio River on a flatboat similar to this. Over 500 boats went down the river that year. They carried about 20,000 pioneers, 8,000 horses, 2,400 head of cattle, 1,000 sheep, and 700 wagons.*

345

River Routes and Trails West

■ *What were the two main ways of travel for pioneers heading west?*

▼ *Pioneers moved west as families. The photo shows a pioneer family in Wisconsin. They even brought the family cat.*

The Fowlers were just one family out of thousands who floated down the Ohio River to the frontier between 1780 and 1820. Rivers were major routes for moving west.

Many pioneers chose to travel on the Ohio River or one of its tributaries. A **tributary** is a small river that flows into a larger one. Pioneers who wanted to go to Tennessee, for example, could take the Cumberland, a major tributary of the Ohio River.

In the 1820s and 1830s, workers dug a number of **canals,** or waterways, to connect rivers and lakes. The Erie Canal, for example, was finished in 1825. It joined the Mohawk River to the Great Lakes. The canals encouraged even more pioneer movement.

Other pioneers traveled west by land. Many walked Daniel Boone's Wilderness Road to Kentucky and Tennessee. Others took Zane's Trace from Wheeling, West Virginia, to Lexington, Kentucky. Still others took the new National Road. It ran through Ohio and Indiana all the way to Vandalia, Illinois.

Travel over these routes was hard, and often dangerous. The roads cut through dense forests and across roaring streams. They were cold and muddy in the springtime, hot and dusty in the summer. One young woman wrote to a friend in 1810: "The reason so few are willing to return from the Western country is not that the country is so good but because the journey is so bad." ■

Pioneers on the Frontier

The pioneers of the late 1700s were the first group of settlers to move into western lands. The pioneers braved rough roads and dangerous rivers, the heat of summer and the cold of winter—all for the chance to start a new life.

A traveler on the Wilderness Road in 1796 described what he saw this way:

> Women and children in the month of December traveling a wilderness through ice and snow, passing large rivers and creeks without shoe or stocking and barely as many rags as covers their nakedness, without money or provisions except what the wilderness affords.

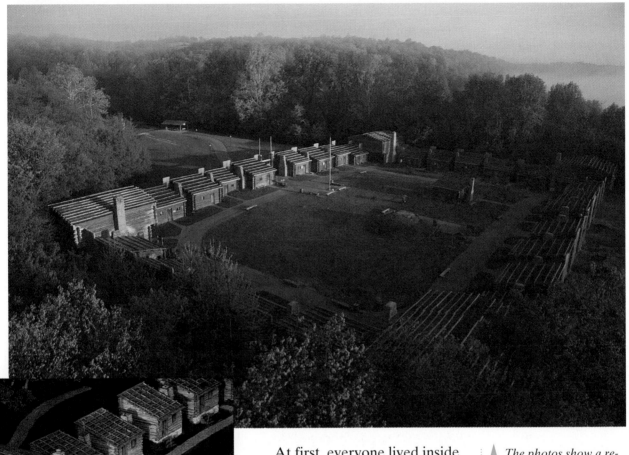

He asked some of the pioneers what they wanted in Kentucky. The answer was "land." They had never seen Kentucky, but they knew about the land. The soil was rich, and the land was cheap.

When pioneers like the Fowlers reached a spot that looked promising, they often built a small fort known as a frontier station. First they cleared the trees off a square piece of land near the river. Then they built two-story log houses at each corner of the square. They connected the buildings with high wooden walls.

At first, everyone lived inside the walls of the frontier station. Later, the settlers built log houses outside the walls. The houses were still close enough so that families could rush to the safety of the station in time of danger.

The new settlers helped each other whenever they could. They cleared land and built houses and barns. They planted crops and started fruit orchards. They grew enough food for their families, plus some extra to sell or trade.

Many of the first settlers on the Appalachian frontier were people like Daniel Boone. They got "the itching foot" when too many farmers moved to an area. When this happened, the first settlers pushed farther west.

This is the way the west was settled. Year after year, pioneers

The photos show a reconstructed frontier station at Boonesborough, Kentucky. Daniel Boone moved to Boonesborough with his wife Rebecca and their daughter in August 1775. They were the first pioneer family to settle west of the Mississippi.

pushed on from one frontier to another. After the War of 1812, they settled the rich lands of the Michigan Territory. By the 1830s, they had reached the banks of the Mississippi River. There were settlements in Illinois, Wisconsin, and Missouri. ■

Life in Early Settlements

As the frontier stations became towns, more settlers arrived to start businesses. Amy Fowler saw her Kentucky station grow into a real town as she grew up.

A year after her father started his farm, a blacksmith arrived to shoe horses. He could also make tools and other metal products. Later, a carpenter arrived to make furniture and other wooden goods.

Next, a miller constructed a gristmill for grinding grain. A gristmill was always built on a swift-running stream. The miller needed water power to turn the millstone. At harvest time Amy's family brought wagonloads of wheat and corn to the gristmill to be ground into flour.

Amy's family was happy to see a storekeeper set up shop. The store sold goods like sugar and tea, needles and thread, hammers and saws. It also sold simple machines like butter churns and spinning wheels.

UNDERSTANDING THE FRONTIER

Pioneers like the Fowlers knew that life on the frontier would be challenging. They were willing to accept the danger and hardship, however. For them, the frontier represented a chance for a better life.

The Changing Frontier

In Daniel Boone's time, the frontier was the vast western part of the country unexplored by white settlers. As pioneers moved west, the frontier moved, too. It was always a step ahead of them.

A frontier doesn't have to be land, like the western frontier. Now that America is settled, we call a frontier anything that is new and unknown.

The Frontier Spirit

The frontier experience shaped America's thinking. After settling the West, Americans developed a new spirit. They were confident they could take on any challenge.

In 1961, President John Kennedy called on America to face "the new frontier."

He meant that America should attack its problems today in the same spirit it had once settled the frontier.

The New Frontier

Today, the new frontier includes learning to care for the environment, ending poverty and hunger—any problem we want to solve. Attacking our problems with courage will lead to a better life for all.

Every few weeks, a frontier doctor arrived on horseback. The doctor was welcome. Diseases such as pneumonia, measles, and tuberculosis spread easily in small, crowded cabins. Even a simple sore throat or ear infection could turn into a serious illness.

Larger towns like Lexington, Kentucky, soon had churches and schools. Unfortunately, the Fowlers did not live near a town with a school. Amy's mother taught the children to read and write herself.

The frontier settlements brought settlers into close contact with Indian tribes living in the area. Some Indians became friendly with the settlers. They traded fur for tools and clothing, and they helped farmers with crops.

Other Indians were unhappy. They did not like to see so many settlers moving into lands that had been theirs for hundreds of years. ■

■ *What were some of the signs that a frontier station was becoming a town?*

R E V I E W

1. **FOCUS** What was life on the new frontier like for settlers in the early 1800s?

2. **CONNECT** How was life on the frontier similar to life in the early colonies?

3. **ECONOMICS** Why did people want to make the dangerous and uncomfortable trip to settle in western lands?

4. **GEOGRAPHY** How did people in the early 1800s move from place to place? Why was travel difficult?

5. **CRITICAL THINKING** Compare Amy Fowler's trip in 1788 with a trip you might take today from Pittsburgh, Pennsylvania, to Lexington, Kentucky. Study the maps on pages 572-575 to get an idea of the mountains and rivers along the way.

6. **ACTIVITY** Draw a picture of a flatboat loaded with a family's possessions. You may refer to the painting on page 345.

Davy Crockett

Anne Malcolmson

Life on the American frontier was not easy as you have learned. For entertainment the settlers told stories. Many of these were tall tales about real and imaginary people. Davy Crockett was a favorite subject.

Like Daniel Boone, Davy Crockett loved the wilderness. Here is a tall tale about this real frontiersman.

backwoodsman a person from the wilderness

comet a ball of dust and gas that circles the sun
Halley's Comet a comet seen every 76 years named for Edmund Halley
shooting star a stone or metal that travels toward Earth from outer space at a great speed

coon raccoon

When Davy Crockett went to Congress, he didn't waste his time making dull speeches. He told stories. He had a great many stories to tell, too—stories of his life as a hunter, a backwoodsman, and an Indian fighter. Sometimes he was carried away by his stories. People began to expect almost anything from him.

His fame spread far and wide. During his second term in Washington, it was feared that the world was coming to an end. Halley's Comet shone in the sky. This was a particularly bright comet with a long tail. It came fearfully close to the earth. Bits of burning metal flew off and showered fields and forests. The sky was streaked with shooting stars.

This comet had appeared before. Whenever it came close to our planet something dreadful happened. People feared it meant disaster again. But with Davy in Congress they thought they might be safe. They sent a committee to him, just as people send committees to Washington today. They asked him to help them. At last he agreed. If the comet came any closer, said he, he would climb to the top of the Appalachian Mountains. There he would stand until he could catch the old comet and wring off its tail. This made the committee feel better and they went home satisfied.

Davy Crockett was born in the Tennessee hills. As a tiny baby, he was cradled in the shell of a snapping turtle. His crib cover was a panther's skin. A crocodile curled itself up into a ball for his pillow. From the very beginning he was a remarkable person.

As a young man he fought in the Indian Wars. All over the Tennessee and Arkansas country he hunted coon and bear. He even tried his hand at farming. Everything he saw and did gave him a new story to tell.

Throughout the Shakes, as his part of Tennessee was called, Davy was famous for his grin. It spread from ear to ear. No one could look at it without smiling back. People thought that it had strange powers, and told how Davy had once grinned a coon out of a tree.

On the top branch of a pine sat the fat little coon, grinning like a Cheshire cat. Davy needed a new cap. He liked the markings on the little creature's tail. But he had left Betsey, his long rifle, at home. All he could do was to stand there and grin. He stretched his lips as far as they could go and fixed his snapping eyes on the coon. After an hour the animal gave up. The glare from Crockett's smile was too much. Down fell the raccoon. He had been out-grinned by the hunter.

On another occasion in the Shakes, Davy saw another coon. This time he decided to grin him down for the fun of it. Davy grinned and grinned, but nothing happened. He stood there all night long, grinning. Rattler, his hunting dog, who usually went wild with excitement when his master hunted a coon, acted very strangely. He paid no attention, but curled up at the foot of the tree and slept soundly.

In the morning, Hunter Crockett saw his mistake. What he thought was a coon was only a big knot on the branch. What a fool he had been, grinning at a tree all night long! His grin had not been wasted, however. It had burned all the bark off the tree.

Beside Rattler and Betsey, Crockett had two unusual hunting companions. His favorite was his old bear, Death Hug. Davy had brought him up from a tiny cub. He had a saddle and bridle made for the old creature and often rode him around the wilderness. Death Hug saved his life on one occasion. Davy was surrounded by angry Indians, who were out for his scalp. As soon as the bear saw the danger he leapt into a tree with his master on his back. From branch to branch he swung, faster than the Indians could follow. He crossed the whole forest this way and came down in friendly country.

The second was an alligator whom he called Mississippi. Davy and Death Hug were skating on the frozen Niagara River, above the falls. It was getting on toward spring. Without any warning, their piece of ice broke off from the rest and headed for the falls. They were indeed in a pickle! But Death Hug saved the day. Davy locked his arms around Death Hug's waist. He guided the chunk of ice over the great waterfall and they landed safely at the bottom, without even a ducking.

cheshire cat the grinning cat from the book *Alice in Wonderland*

cap Davy wants a hat made from fur of raccoon, including the striped tail

knot a hard lump where a branch grows out from the tree

scalp skin and hair cut from the body of an enemy

pickle a bad situation

ducking to get wet

Further Reading

By Wagon and Flatboat. Enid L. Meadowcroft. This is the story of a family who moves west to Ohio. The Burds find their travels full of adventure.

Daniel Boone. Laurie Lawlor. Many tall tales were told about Daniel Boone. This biography, however, tells about the man behind the legend.

LESSON 3

The Next Frontier

What were the main results of purchasing the Louisiana Territory?

Key Term

• Louisiana Purchase

➤ *The pocket watch contains a portrait of James Monroe, the man who made the decision to purchase the Louisiana Territory.*

In 1802, American settlers were moving west into the lands beyond the Appalachians. At the same time, events were unfolding in France that would change the future development of the United States.

Napoleon Bonaparte, the ruler of France, was worried about the French colony of Santo Domingo in the West Indies. He had already sent thousands of troops there to crush a revolt of black slaves. He would need to send thousands more. In addition, Napoleon found himself on the verge of war with Great Britain. Wars cost money, and Napoleon was going to need lots of it.

President Thomas Jefferson knew that Napoleon needed money. He sent James Monroe to Paris with orders to buy New Orleans from France. Owning this busy Mississippi River port would safeguard American trade.

When Monroe arrived in Paris, he found that Napoleon wanted to sell the entire Louisiana Territory for $15 million. Monroe thought hard. Congress had said he could spend $2 million for New Orleans. The President had given him permission to offer as much as $10 million. If Monroe spent just $5 million more, he could double the size of the United States. What should he do?

The Louisiana Purchase

Monroe decided to take the risk. On May 2, 1803, he agreed to the **Louisiana Purchase** in which he bought 830,000 square miles of land west of the Mississippi River.

Find the Louisiana Territory on the map on the next page. The United States bought this land for about four cents an acre. Compare it with the map on pages 572-573 in the Atlas. What present-day states make up this area?

President Jefferson was happy with Monroe's purchase, but some

Exploring the Western Frontier

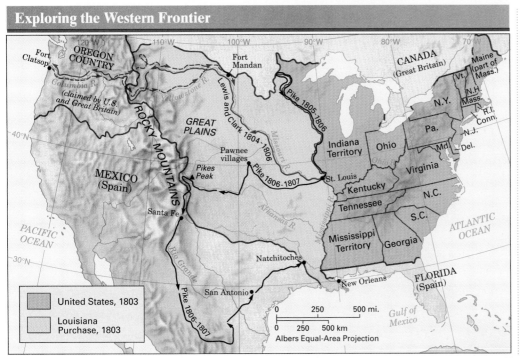

United States, 1803

Louisiana Purchase, 1803

◄ The Louisiana Purchase stretched from the Mississippi River all the way to the Rocky Mountains. Note the routes of explorers Lewis and Clark and Pike on this map.

▼ The official seal of France (below) was attached to the Louisiana Purchase document.

members of Congress were not. They said the Constitution did not allow the president to buy new territory without permission of Congress. Jefferson urged Congress to agree with his action.

This treaty must of course be laid before both Houses. . . . They, I presume, will see their duty to their country in ratifying and paying for it. . . . It is the case of the guardian [adult] investing the money of his ward [child] in purchasing an important adjacent territory, and saying to him when of age, I did this for your good!

President Jefferson knew little about the new territory. New Orleans was a trade center for the frontier west of the Appalachians. Hunters and trappers brought furs to the city by traveling down rivers that fed into the Mississippi.

President Jefferson wondered if one of the rivers flowed to the Pacific Ocean. If so, it would form a trade route across the continent. To explore this territory, Jefferson chose two men. One was Meriwether Lewis, his secretary. The other was William Clark, an army officer. ■

■ Why did people in the United States disagree about whether or not the country should buy the Louisiana Territory?

The Lewis and Clark Expedition

President Jefferson sent Lewis and Clark on an expedition, or journey of discovery. They were to travel up the Missouri River and make their way to the Pacific. They were to map the area as they traveled, and they were to find out as much as they could about the plants and animals living there. To learn more about the Lewis and Clark expedition, see A Closer Look on the following pages.

353

The Lewis and Clark Expedition

Thomas Jefferson had been eager to know about the unexplored part of America since he was a young man. As President, he was in a position to satisfy his curiosity. He insisted that Lewis and Clark take notes on climate, rivers, mountains, plants, animals, and the peoples they encountered. Without such notes, he said, "history becomes fable instead of facts."

Sacajawea, a young Shoshone woman (shown above, standing with her arms outstretched) went with the expedition. Sacajawea helped translate and buy food and horses. Most important, when other Indians saw her and her baby, they knew that the expedition was peaceful.

Map of Columbia River, from the Lewis and Clark journals

With this pocket compass, Clark recorded the exact direction the group traveled every day. Later he could draw accurate maps of the country they went through.

354

Chapter 14

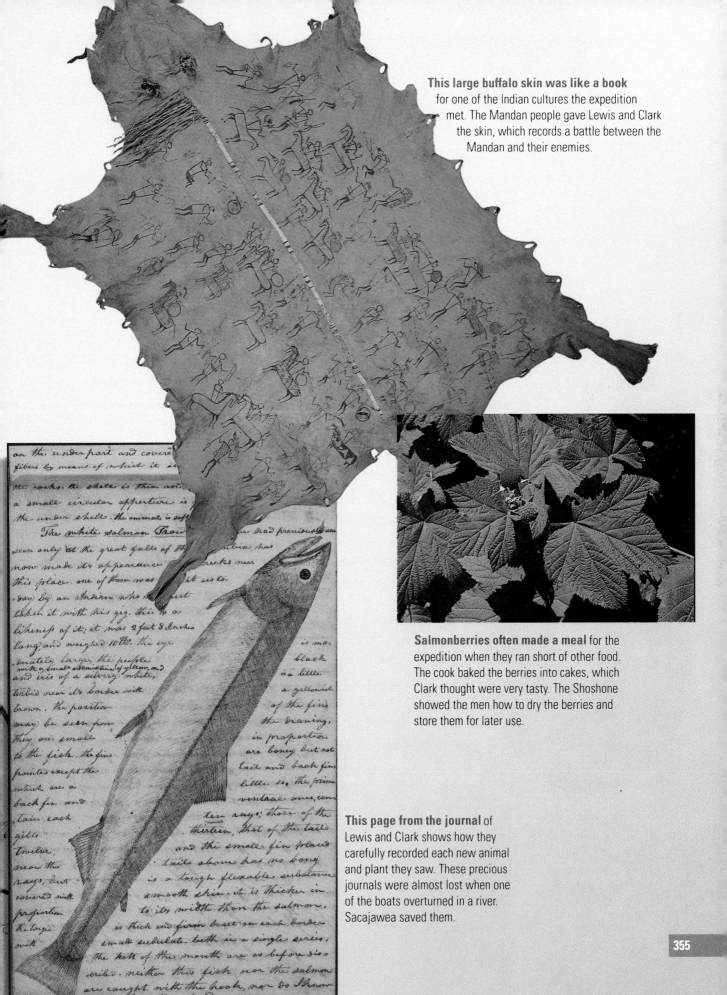

This large buffalo skin was like a book for one of the Indian cultures the expedition met. The Mandan people gave Lewis and Clark the skin, which records a battle between the Mandan and their enemies.

Salmonberries often made a meal for the expedition when they ran short of other food. The cook baked the berries into cakes, which Clark thought were very tasty. The Shoshone showed the men how to dry the berries and store them for later use.

This page from the journal of Lewis and Clark shows how they carefully recorded each new animal and plant they saw. These precious journals were almost lost when one of the boats overturned in a river. Sacajawea saved them.

Moving West

HISTORY *People today know what happened to Lewis and Clark, because the explorers kept very complete journals. Since the purpose of their expedition was to do research, they took thorough notes on much of what they saw.*

■ *What was the main goal of the Lewis and Clark expedition?*

Lewis and Clark chose 48 frontiersmen and hunters for the trip. The group included a black slave named York. In May 1804, the explorers set off from St. Louis in river boats. They spent the winter with the Mandan Indian tribe in what is now North Dakota. In the spring, they continued the journey west. By that time, Sacajawea *(sak uh juh WEE uh)*, a Shoshone, had joined the expedition with her husband.

Nez Perce *(nehz purs)* Indians showed the explorers a path through the Rocky Mountains to the Columbia River. The explorers built canoes and paddled down the river. They reached the Pacific in November 1805, after 18 exhausting months.

Lewis and Clark shipped their reports and maps back to President Jefferson. The reports gave Americans a better understanding of the huge territory that was now part of the United States. Lewis and Clark didn't find a river route to the Pacific, but they showed that overland travel was possible. They also laid a foundation for friendly relations with the Indians. ■

Zebulon Pike's Expedition

Lewis and Clark returned to St. Louis in September 1806. Even before that, President Jefferson sent other explorers to scout different parts of the Louisiana Territory. For example, he sent Zebulon Pike, a lieutenant in the army, to explore the Southwest. Pike set out in July 1806 with 23 men. These explorers made their way across present-day Kansas to Colorado. They reached the Rocky Mountains on November 15. Pike described the moment in his journal:

> *A*t two in the afternoon I could distinguish a mountain to our right. . . . When our small party arrived on the hill, they gave three cheers.

▲ *Zebulon Pike never did climb to the top of Pikes Peak. Visitors today can reach the top easily, either by road or by cog railroad.*

Pike and three of his men tried to climb the mountain, but they were unsuccessful. Today, the mountain is known as Pikes Peak.

The explorers then turned south and followed the Rio Grande down into Mexico. There, Spanish troops stopped them and made them turn back. Look back at the map on page 353. Where did Pike go next?

Explorers like Pike helped to create interest in the lands beyond the Mississippi. More and more people started thinking about moving to the next frontier. ■

■ *How did explorers like Zebulon Pike hasten the movement of settlers into the Louisiana Territory?*

The Beckoning West

In some ways, the frontier of the Louisiana Territory looked like the Northwest Territory of the late 1700s. Hunters and trappers moved in first. Later, settlers started small farms. Many of these settlers were the children of pioneers who had settled Kentucky, Ohio, and Tennessee. As in earlier times, rivers were the major routes for moving west.

One of the earliest settlers in the Louisiana Territory was the restless Daniel Boone. In 1799, even before America's purchase of the land, Boone set off for a new home west of the Mississippi. With some friends and relatives, he went west on foot, leading cattle and pack horses for more than 600 miles to what is now Missouri.

Boone and his wife Rebecca built a cabin near one of their sons. The old pioneer didn't stay long, however. Until he was nearly 80, Boone had "the itching foot." He roamed the western plains that later became Kansas and the Dakotas. Some say he even climbed the Rocky Mountains.

After Boone became too old to wander, he often sat near the banks of the Missouri River, watching the wagon trains as they headed west. Sometimes young pioneers stopped to ask Boone about his travels. Had he ever gotten lost on the frontier? The old pioneer thought for a moment. Then he answered this way: "No, can't say as ever I was lost. But I was bewildered once for three days." ■

▲ *This portrait of Daniel Boone was painted in 1820, when Boone was 85 years old.*

■ *What were the pioneers like who moved west into the Louisiana Territory?*

REVIEW

1. **FOCUS** What were the main results of the purchase of the Louisiana Territory?

2. **CONNECT** How was the pattern of settlement in the Louisiana Territory similar to the pattern in the Northwest Territory?

3. **GEOGRAPHY** Why was control of the city of New Orleans considered so important to people in the United States?

4. **CRITICAL THINKING** Why did Daniel Boone keep moving westward rather than settle down in one place?

5. **CRITICAL THINKING** Compare Jefferson's decision to send Lewis and Clark on an expedition with the decision by Ferdinand and Isabella to sponsor Columbus. What did both Jefferson and the monarchs hope the explorers would find?

6. **WRITING ACTIVITY** What do you think President Jefferson wanted to know about the Louisiana Purchase? Write a list of five questions he might have asked Lewis and Clark when they returned from their expedition.

Using Landmarks as Guides

Here's Why

The first explorers of the frontier had no maps. They had to locate places and figure out distances based on their own experience. Before long, people began to develop maps of the new territories. Those mapmaking skills are valuable today. If you can draw accurate maps, you can pass on information about places you know.

Suppose you were the first person to explore a wilderness area. If you drew a map to help others, what information would you include? How would you let travelers know what landmarks to look for?

Here's How

The painting on page 359 shows a portion of western Appalachia. The map at the bottom of these two pages shows physical features, such as mountains, rivers, and swamps that an explorer might have found in this area. Symbols for these features are included in the legend at the bottom left. The legend also includes symbols for features made by humans.

The compass rose next to the legend tells you which direction is north. The scale at the bottom left of page 359 tells you how many miles an inch on the map represents. Use the legend, compass rose, and scale to trace this route west.

From Briar Lake near the east edge, you can look north toward Trapper's Peak. Note the map's symbol for a mountain peak. About three miles downriver from the waterfall is Fort Drakes. After the river forks, cross the bridge south. You can go on south toward some cabins on the Hope River or west along Little Bird River toward a salt lick. Check the legend for the symbols for waterfall, cabin, and salt lick.

Traveling west along the Little Bird River from the salt lick brings you to another bridge. Cross the bridge north and continue west along the river. When you reach a fork in the trail, at Eagle Peak, you can go south to Sugar Lake or west to the Indian settlement. It is over two miles from Sugar Lake by river to the Indian settlement.

Around the bend in the river from the Indian settlement is Gooseneck Lake. Use the scale to measure how close the western edge

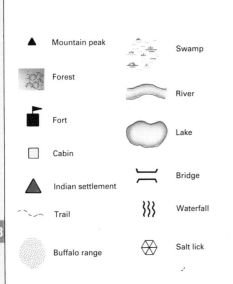

▲	Mountain peak	⌇ Swamp	
Forest		∿ River	
Fort		Lake	
□	Cabin		
▲	Indian settlement	⊐⊏ Bridge	
⌇	Trail	⟨⟨⟨ Waterfall	
Buffalo range		⬡ Salt lick	

Rabbit Island

Eagle Peak

Little Bird River

Sugar Lake

N
W — E
S

Gooseneck Lake

of Gooseneck Lake is to the nearest buffalo range. Finish your journey at Rabbit Island. The compass rose shows you that you will need to go north from Gooseneck Lake to get there. You can see that information from the legend, the compass rose, and the scale helped you on your journey, even in unfamiliar territory.

Try It

Trace the map on a separate sheet of paper. Imagine that as you travel through this area, you find some additional landmarks that you want to include on the map.

1. Draw a fort on the southern point of Rabbit Island.

2. Indicate a lake one mile north and one mile east of Fort Drakes.
3. Draw a canyon one-half mile south of Sugar Lake.
4. Beginning at the group of cabins that are along the Hope River, trace a five-mile-long trail northeast through the mountains.

If necessary, create new symbols to draw these new landmarks. Add any new symbols to the legend and to the map. Be sure to name your new features and label them on the map.

Apply It

Draw a map of a route that is familiar to you, such as the one from your house to your favorite restaurant. It could also be from your school to the public library, or from your school to your house.

Include a legend, compass rose, and scale by miles or by city block on the map you draw. Don't forget that others who use your map will need to recognize the symbols and landmarks that you include.

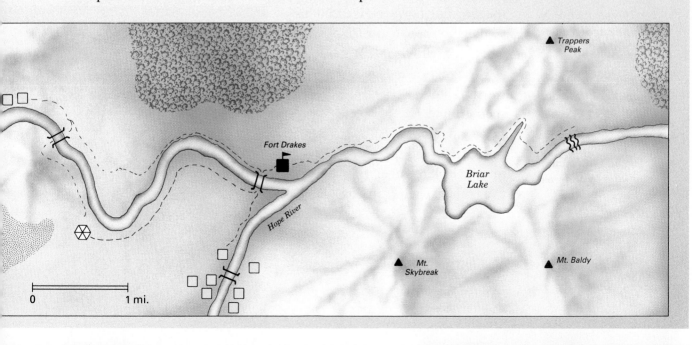

L E S S O N 4

The American Indians in Retreat

THINKING FOCUS

What caused the Indians to gradually lose control of their lands?

Key Term

- Bureau of Indian Affairs

➤ *This painting originally belonged to the family of William Clark, the man who explored the Louisiana Territory. Historians think it is a portrait of Tecumseh.*

▼ *Feathers like these were worn by Shawnee warriors.*

The meeting took place in a grove of trees near the governor's house in Vincennes, Indiana. It was August 12, 1810. William Henry Harrison, governor of the Indiana Territory, was speaking. He insisted that the United States had always been fair with the Indians. At these words, the Shawnee chief Tecumseh *(teh KUHM seh)* jumped to his feet. "Liar, liar!" he shouted.

Tecumseh was speaking in Shawnee. At first, Harrison did not know what Tecumseh was saying. An American army officer at the meeting did, however. He told his soldiers to cock their rifles and prepare to fire.

The Shawnee warriors stood their ground. For a moment, the soldiers and the Shawnee glared at each other. Then Harrison ordered the soldiers to lower their rifles. The tension eased, and the meeting ended.

Meetings like this were of little help in ending conflicts between Indians and settlers. Over the years Tecumseh had seen settlers take more and more land. They often cheated the Indians, paying far less than the land was worth. And it wasn't just the settlers who cheated the Indians. Harrison had bought three million acres of land for the government from Little Turtle, a chief of the Miami.

All Harrison paid was $7,000 in cash, with additional payments of $1,750 due each year.

Tecumseh felt that if the settlers were not stopped, they would soon push the Indians into the Great Lakes. The only hope was for Indians to join together and fight, no matter what their tribe.

Throughout 1808 and 1809, Tecumseh traveled around the frontier. He met with leaders of the Potawatomi, the Wyandot, and others. He wanted the tribes to put aside their differences and unite.

Unfair Treaties

A series of treaties signed during the late 1700s gave settlers the right to more and more Indian land. The map at the right shows the result. What were the only states with large Indian populations by 1830?

To Tecumseh a treaty was just a worthless piece of paper. Nobody could sell land, because nobody really "owned" it. If you could sell the land, Tecumseh said, "why not sell the air, the clouds, and the great sea . . .?"

Tecumseh knew that Indian leaders sometimes signed treaties giving away land that belonged to others. For instance, Iroquois living in New York signed a treaty at Fort Stanwix in 1784. The treaty gave settlers the right to live in western Pennsylvania. The Shawnee and other Indian tribes living in Pennsylvania had not signed the treaty. Yet it resulted in a rush of settlers onto their lands.

What the government could not win by treaty it was prepared to take by force. In July 1793,

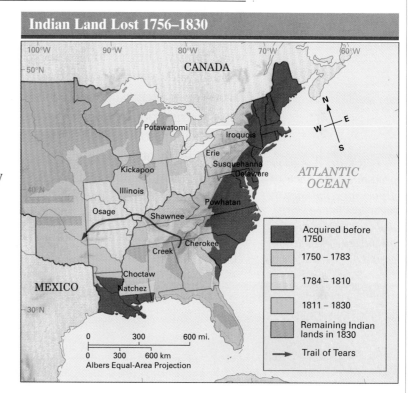

Indian Land Lost 1756–1830

CANADA

Potawatomi
Iroquois
Erie
Susquehanna
Kickapoo
Delaware
Illinois
Powhatan
Osage
Shawnee
Creek
Cherokee
Choctaw
Natchez

MEXICO

ATLANTIC OCEAN

0   300   600 mi.

0   300   600 km
Albers Equal-Area Projection

- Acquired before 1750
- 1750 – 1783
- 1784 – 1810
- 1811 – 1830
- Remaining Indian lands in 1830
- → Trail of Tears

officials met with Indians from the Shawnee, the Kickapoo, the Miami, and other tribes at Niagara, New York. The government asked the tribes to give up land east of the Muskingum River in southwestern Ohio. In return, the government would guarantee them control over other lands in Ohio. The Shawnee said no. So did the Kickapoo and the Miami.

The government would not take no for an answer. When the Indians turned down the

▲ *Each year Indian tribes were forced to surrender more and more land. Compare this map with the Minipedia map on page 560 to see the vast lands Indians once occupied.*

Moving West

proposal, the government called in the army. In 1794, General Anthony Wayne defeated the Indians at the Battle of Fallen Timbers in northwestern Ohio. As a result, the Indians were forced to sign the Treaty of Greenville. They gave up rights to most of central and southern Ohio. In return, they received $20,000 in supplies and the promise of $9,500 in yearly payments. One of the Shawnee warriors who fought in the Battle of Fallen Timbers was the young Tecumseh. ■

■ *Why was Tecumseh opposed to treaties?*

Indian Resistance

During the next ten years, Tecumseh saw the Indians lose more and more land. Many Indians were hungry. They no longer had enough land to hunt on and to farm. When Tecumseh visited villages to urge cooperation, he found people willing to listen. They also listened to Tecumseh's younger brother, called the Prophet. He preached that Indians had taken on too many of the white man's ways. He said that Indians must return "to the ways of our fathers."

Many young warriors joined Tecumseh and his brother. They built a new village in northwestern Indiana, along the Tippecanoe River. The village was called Prophetstown. By spring 1810, Tecumseh had an army of 1,000 warriors at Prophetstown.

The Battle of Tippecanoe

Governor Harrison worried when he saw more and more Indians joining Tecumseh and the Prophet. In 1811, Harrison

▼ *This Kurtz & Allison print shows the Battle of Tippecanoe. In losing the battle, the Indians lost their last chance to stop the advance of settlers east of the Mississippi.*

learned that Tecumseh had left Prophetstown to gather support from the Chickasaws in Tennessee and other southern tribes. Harrison decided to take advantage of Tecumseh's absence. He marched an army of 1,000 men up the Wabash River to the Tippecanoe. He set up camp two miles west of Prophetstown. Harrison tried to negotiate, but the Indian leaders had made up their minds to fight. On November 4, 1811, the Indians attacked.

The Battle of Tippecanoe lasted two hours. The Prophet had told the warriors that his prayers would protect them from American bullets. It didn't work that way. About 40 Indians were killed, and the rest quickly fled. Harrison's men burned Prophetstown to the ground.

The War of 1812

When Tecumseh returned to Indiana in 1812, he tried to rebuild his forces. He made an agreement with British officials in Michigan and Canada. The British offered him guns and supplies in return for his support. The British knew that war between their country and the United States was going to start again. When it did, they wanted Tecumseh's help.

During the War of 1812, Tecumseh fought on the British side. He and his followers fought against the Americans in Canada, Ohio, and Michigan. In October 1813, Tecumseh was killed in a battle near Detroit. The general leading the American army was the Shawnee chief's old enemy, William Henry Harrison. ■

■ *How did Tecumseh hope to stop the advance of the settlers?*

▲ *During this period, the U.S. government awarded the Andrew Jackson Medal to Indian chiefs who lived peacefully with the settlers.*

Peace for a Time

After the death of Tecumseh, Indian tribes like the Sauk *(sawk)*, the Fox, and the Kickapoo decided to leave their ancient tribal lands. They moved across the Mississippi River to start a new life. They wanted to get as far away from the settlers as they could.

Other tribes, including the Potawatomi, the Choctaw, and the Cherokee, wanted to stay east of the Mississippi, if possible. Between 1815 and 1830, these tribes tried to live in peace beside the Americans.

Some Indians tried to live like the settlers. Many Potawatomi in Indiana and Ohio had converted to the Catholic faith. They lived as farmers and fur traders. Some

Choctaw in Mississippi also became Christians. They sent their children to a government-run school called the Choctaw Academy.

In the Southeast the Cherokee took the lead in adopting the settlers' ways. Many Cherokee who stayed in their tribal lands in Alabama, Georgia, and Tennessee bought land and became farmers. Others opened stores and mills. Wealthy Cherokee cotton farmers even bought black slaves to work on plantations. Many Cherokee also converted to Christianity.

An educated Cherokee named Sequoyah *(sih KWOY uh)* developed a written alphabet for his

Sequoyah developed the Cherokee alphabet over a period of 12 years.

■ *In what two ways did the Indians try to keep the peace?*

people. Another Cherokee named Elias Boudinot *(BOO dnoh)* published the *Cherokee Phoenix,* a newspaper printed in both Cherokee and English. Cherokee leaders also set up a government for their people. They wrote a constitution based on the Constitution of the United States.

During this period, the U.S. government did everything it could to make sure that the Indians were treated fairly. In 1824, the government started the **Bureau of Indian Affairs.** This agency had the power to make treaties and control trade with the Indians.

At the same time, the government knew that the peace between the Indians and settlers could not last. People like President John Quincy Adams were urging Indian tribes to move to the lands west of the Mississippi. ■

Loss and Defeat

By 1830, the government was no longer asking the Indians to move away from their ancient tribal lands. It was ordering them. Making the Indians move west was now official government policy.

The Trail of Tears

Removal treaties demanded that many Indians in the Southeast move to Indian reservations in what is now Oklahoma. States were eager to take control of Indian lands. The Choctaw, Creek, and Chickasaw moved reluctantly. The Cherokee, however, decided to stay. They fought the treaties in the courts.

One case went to the Supreme Court. It ruled that the government had no right to order the Indians off their lands. President

Andrew Jackson said this decision was ridiculous. He ignored the Supreme Court and ordered the American army to move the Cherokee by force.

Soldiers with guns marched more than 18,000 Cherokee from their homes in the Southeast. Almost one-fourth of the Indians died of starvation, disease, and harsh treatment along the way. The route the Cherokee followed to Oklahoma became known as "The Trail of Tears."

Look back at the map on page 361. Trace the route of the Trail of Tears. What present-day states did the Cherokee pass through on their journey to Oklahoma?

The Black Hawk War

Many Indian tribes living in Ohio, Indiana, and Illinois were also forced to move west of the Mississippi River. The Sauk and the Fox had already moved to Iowa. Every summer some of them would cross the Mississippi to tend their old farmlands in Illinois. This upset settlers who wanted that farmland for themselves. In the summer of 1832, the settlers sent soldiers to force the Indians back to Iowa. Led by the Sauk chief Black Hawk, the Indians retreated to the west, defending themselves as they went. When they reached the Mississippi, the army attacked. Later, Black Hawk described the battle this way:

They [the Indians] tried to give themselves up—the whites paid no attention to their entreaties—but commenced slaughtering them. In a little while the whole army arrived. Our braves, but few in number, finding that the enemy paid no regard to age or sex, and seeing that they were murdering helpless women and little children, determined to fight until they were killed.

Many women drowned as they tried to swim the Mississippi with children on their backs. Some were shot from the shore. Of 2,000 Indians who had gone into Illinois to tend their fields, only about 150 made it back to Iowa. Nothing could stop the flood of settlers determined to move west and claim the Indians' land. ∎

▼ *Chief Black Hawk spent a lifetime trying to protect Indian lands from the settlers.*

■ *How did the United States government finally take over Indian lands?*

Look back at the map on page 361.

R E V I E W

1. **FOCUS** What caused the Indians to gradually lose control of their lands?
2. **CONNECT** How was what happened to Indians on the Appalachian frontier similar to what happened to Indians on the eastern seaboard?
3. **CITIZENSHIP** What did Cherokee leaders do to help their tribe? What did Sequoyah and Elias Boudinot do?
4. **CRITICAL THINKING** The Supreme Court ruled that the government had no right to remove the Indians from their land, but President Andrew Jackson ordered the army to remove them anyway. What would probably happen today if the president ignored a Supreme Court decision?
5. **WRITING ACTIVITY** Write a newspaper account of the forced march of 18,000 Cherokees from their homes in the Southwest to reservations in Oklahoma. Imagine that you are the first reporter to tell the American public what is happening to the Cherokee.

Moving West

Chapter Review

Reviewing Key Terms

Bureau of Indian Affairs (p. 364)
canal (p. 346)
Louisiana Purchase (p. 352)
ordinance (p. 344)
pioneer (p. 341)
tributary (p. 346)

A. Be sure you understand the meanings of the key terms. Then answer each question by writing one or more sentences.

1. How are pioneers and the Louisiana Purchase related?
2. How are a tributary and a canal similar? How are they different?
3. Daniel Boone seems to stand for what it meant to be a pioneer. What qualities did he have that pioneers also had?

4. What is the Bureau of Indian Affairs? When was it established and what power did it have?
5. Ordinances were passed for the frontier. How does that show that the new frontier was being settled in an orderly way?

B. The two words in each pair are related in some way. On your own paper, write a sentence explaining how the words are related.

1. pioneer, canal
2. Bureau of Indian Affairs, ordinance
3. pioneer, ordinance

Exploring Concepts

A. Copy the cluster diagram on your paper. Then write sentences that tell something about the frontier. Begin the sentences with the terms listed. The first one is done for you.

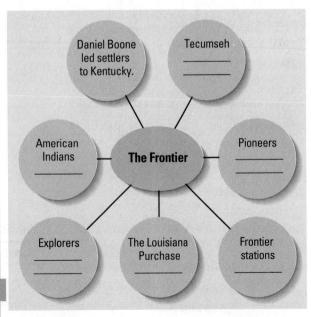

B. Answer each question with information from the chapter.

1. What were the boundaries of the Appalachian frontier?
2. How did Daniel Boone help settle the Appalachian frontier?
3. What kinds of dwellings did the settlers live in? What jobs did they do?
4. Who was sent to France to buy New Orleans? Look at the fifth entry on the chart on page 562 of the Minipedia. What happened to him in 1817?
5. What were some of the problems the American Indians faced because settlers moved into the frontier?
6. Who was Tecumseh and how did he try to help his people?
7. What did the American Indians do to live peacefully with the settlers? Did they continue to live peacefully with them? Why?

Reviewing Skills

1. Trace the map below and complete it as directed. Add new symbols to the legend.
   a. Locate a forest one-quarter mile east of Sugar Lake.
   b. Place cabins between Gooseneck Lake and the bend in the river.
   c. Mark the rapids two miles upriver from the Indian settlement.

2. Reread Lesson 3 and on your own paper, complete the outline below.
3. Suppose you wanted to see how settlers traveled from Pennsylvania to Tennessee. What might you trace or follow on a map?

I. The Louisiana Purchase
  A. _____
  B. _____
II. The Lewis and Clark Expedition
  A. _____
  B. _____
III. Zebulon Pike's Expedition
  A. _____
  B. _____
IV. The Beckoning West
  A. _____
  B. _____

Using Critical Thinking

1. You have been reading about pioneers and frontier lands. We have no more frontier lands in our country, but are there still pioneers? Explain.
2. Imagine that you were the *first* settler in an area. Soon other settlers came and a town grew up around you. List both the advantages and disadvantages of staying in the area or moving on to new frontiers.
3. The American Indians often tried to help the settlers adapt to their new location. New families, some of them from other lands, are constantly moving into our communities. What could you and your class do to help them get settled?

Preparing for Citizenship

1. **GROUP ACTIVITY** As a class, make a map showing what changes are being made or are planned for the neighborhoods in which you live. Small groups should gather information from observation, newspapers, radio and television news, organizations, and business owners. Mark the changes on the class's map.
2. **COLLABORATIVE LEARNING** With classmates, explore a part of your school. Imagine you have never seen the area before. Working in groups of four, present the results of your expedition to the class. Each person in the group should be responsible for one of the following tasks: (1) preparing maps and drawings of the area, (2) questioning the people who work there, (3) gathering samples of things found there, and (4) organizing the information in the form of a radio newscast about a newly discovered area.

Chapter 15

Settling the Far West

In the 1800s, books, magazines, and newspapers all gave Americans the same message: Go west. People seeking new farms headed for Texas and Oregon. Those hoping to get rich quickly searched for gold in California. And a group seeking religious freedom, the Mormons, settled in Utah. Whatever these people dreamed about, they believed they would find it in the American West.

Throughout this period Americans headed west in covered wagons (above) and built new lives on the frontier. The woman shown at right gathers buffalo chips for fuel on the treeless prairie.

36
Independence on the Plains.   Gathering Chips.

1790	1800	1810	1820

1792

1806 Explorer Zebulon Pike discovers Pike's Peak in present-day Colorado.

FOR PIKE'S PEAK, HO!
DAILY U.S. MAIL LINE
Through to Denver City in 6 1-2 Days!
THE CENTRAL
OVERLAND, CALIFORNIA
AND
PIKE'S PEAK EXPRESS CO.
FORMERLY JONES, RUSSELL & CO.
ARE NOW RUNNING A DAILY LINE OF COACHES
FROM ST. JOSEPH
—TO—
DENVER CITY.
ANY NUMBER OF EXTRA COACHES
FURNISHED AT SHORT NOTICE.
MEALS PROVIDED AT THE STATIONS AT REASONABLE PRICES!
THE CALIFORNIA
PONY EXPRESS
LEAVES ST. JOSEPH AT 11, P. M., EVERY SATURDAY.
TEN DAYS TO SAN FRANCISCO!
TAKING LETTERS TO
All Points in California, Salt Lake and Carson Valley!
For Further Particulars apply at Office at the PATEE HOUSE, St. Joseph, Mo.
West Job Rooms, Second Street, opposite the Post Office, St. Joseph, Mo.

1822–1860 Wagon trains and stagecoaches rolling west toward California and Oregon leave deep ruts in the trails.

| 1830 | 1840 | 1850 | 1860 |

1849 Thousands of Americans catch "gold fever" and race to California. Some find gold with tools like the mining pan shown above.

1860

L E S S O N   1

Texas and the Struggle with Mexico

THINKING FOCUS

How did the United States expand its southern border to include Texas?

Key Terms

- plain
- annex

▼ *Americans headed to Texas by the thousands after reading ads like this. They were looking for rich farmland and open grassland for cattle.*

"Free land in Texas! Climate so mild no house is needed!" Like magic, such advertisements lured thousands of Americans in the 1820s and 1830s.

The advertisements described rich Texas lands where wild horses, antelope, and buffalo roamed; where cherries, grapes, and plums grew wild. Best of all was the chance to buy land cheaply, or even get it free!

Many people were ready to believe the advertisements about Texas. It was a land where everyone could succeed. Some saw Texas as a place to get away from bill collectors or problems with the law. Others were poor farm families or struggling business owners hoping for a fresh start.

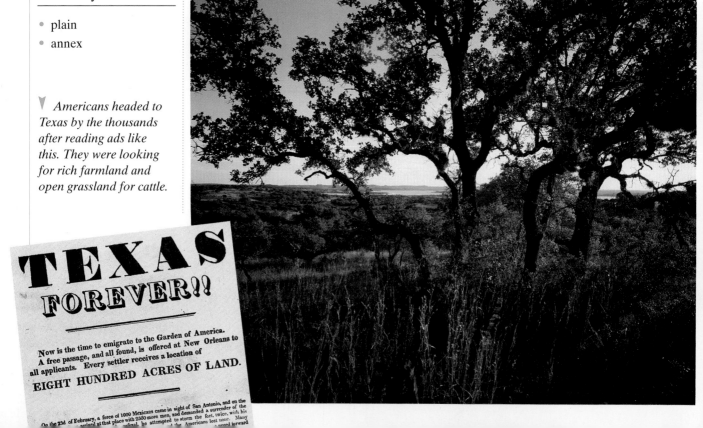

TEXAS FOREVER!!

Now is the time to emigrate to the Garden of America.
A free passage, and all found, is offered at New Orleans to
all applicants. Every settler receives a location of
EIGHT HUNDRED ACRES OF LAND.

On the 23d of February, a force of 1000 Mexicans came in sight of San Antonio, and on the
arrived at that place ... final, he attempted to storm the fort, twice, with his
... the Americans lost none. Many
... reed forward

Note the size of Mexico when American settlers first moved to Texas.

The Settlement of Texas

The settlers moved to lands that had once been part of the Spanish colony of Mexico. In 1821, Mexico won its independence from Spain. The new nation included a region called Texas, with rich farmlands and grassy **plains**—huge, flat areas without trees.

The map above shows the Mexican territory of Texas. The map on pages 572 and 573 in the Atlas shows the state of Texas. What present-day states were once part of Mexico?

In the early years of Mexican independence, Texas was hard to govern. Settlements were far apart and as much as 1,000 miles from the capital of Mexico City. Mexican leaders tried to strengthen their country by building the population of Texas. They hoped that by encouraging American settle-ment, they would also build strong ties of friendship and trade with the United States.

In 1823, Mexico offered large land grants to anyone bringing settlers to Texas. These people could sell or give away farm-sized plots to the settlers. In return, the settlers had to promise to become Mexican citizens and join the Catholic Church.

In 1823, Stephen F. Austin, an American pioneer from Missouri, arrived in Texas with 300 American families. They settled in the rich lands along the Brazos River.

One settler, Anna Maria Campbell Reynolds, recalled that the "first night's camp on the prairies was horrible to me. . . . There was no sound to greet my ears but the howling of wolves. . . . I was frightfully blue."

Across Time & Space

Early Texas settlements of the 1820s and 1830s were dangerous places. Indians might attack at any time. So Stephen Austin gathered a band of rugged Texans to protect the settlers. Out of these forces grew the Texas Rangers. Since then, the Rangers have kept the peace in Texas. Today, they are the country's oldest law enforcement agency.

371

Settling the Far West

■ *Why did the Mexican government encourage Americans to settle in Texas?*

While pioneers like Reynolds settled in, more and more Americans poured into the region. Many were Southerners from states like Georgia and Louisiana. They brought along slaves to help grow cotton in the warm Texas climate. So many settlers came to Texas that by 1830, Americans outnumbered Mexicans by about four to one. Mexican officials began to wonder if allowing Americans to settle in Texas had been such a good idea. They began to wonder if it was going to create trouble in the future. ■

Conflict with Mexico

Mexican officials decided to act. First they outlawed slavery. By doing this, they hoped to discourage Southerners from coming to Texas. When that didn't slow the flood of Americans, the Mexicans outlawed American settlement altogether.

American settlers already in Texas were upset. Many believed that they could no longer live under Mexican rule, which had become too strict. Conditions grew worse in 1834, when General Antonio López de Santa Anna became dictator of Mexico.

After Santa Anna took over, trouble between Mexicans and Americans increased. Soon, American settlers in Texas rebelled against the Mexican government. They set up their own government in 1835.

Bloodshed in Texas

In response to the settlers, Santa Anna sent several thousand soldiers to the Alamo, an old mission in San Antonio. About 200 Americans, including Davy Crockett and Jim Bowie, were holding the Alamo.

► *The illustration shows the Alamo during the final attack. Santa Anna sent one column of troops against the south wall and another against the east as a diversion. The main attack came at the north wall. The photo shows an Alamo flag that Santa Anna's troops captured.*

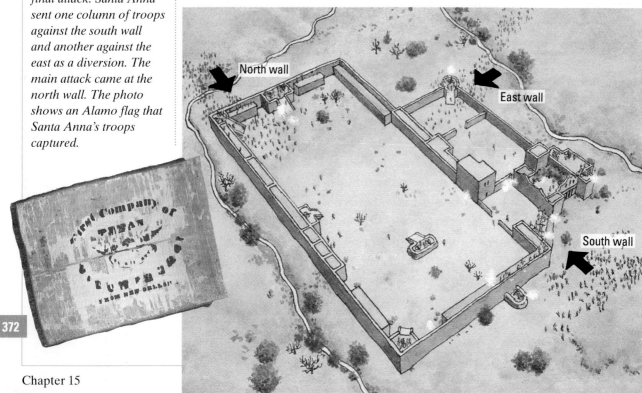

North wall

East wall

South wall

The Battle of the Alamo began on February 24, 1836. Mexican cannon pounded the Alamo walls for days. Each night the guns moved closer. By March 5, they were 200 yards away.

Early in the morning on March 6, Santa Anna directed the final attack. The Texans fought fearlessly. They threw back first one attack, then another. The Mexican troops kept coming, however, and they finally succeeded. They stormed the wall, opened the gates, and overran the defenders. They killed almost everyone, including Bowie, Crockett, and the commander William Travis. Only a few survived.

The Texans' Victory

The defeat at the Alamo aroused the feelings of the American settlers. "Remember the Alamo!" became a battle cry. The Texas army, growing stronger

every day, never stopped hoping for revenge.

Their chance came on April 21, 1836. Under the command of Sam Houston, the Texas army surprised Santa Anna near the San Jacinto *(san yuh SIHN toh)* River. After a fierce midday battle lasting only 20 minutes, they captured Santa Anna and ended the war.

In the meantime, leading American settlers met at the Texas town of Washington-on-the-Brazos to declare Texas independent. The new government moved quickly to ask the U.S. government to **annex** Texas—that is, to make it part of the United States. ■

◄ *Texas is known as the Lone Star State. This early Texas flag shows why.*

■ *Why did conflict arise between the American settlers in Texas and the Mexican government?*

The Mexican War

Most American settlers in Texas wanted to join the United States. The U.S. government, however, was in no hurry.

Statehood for Texas

One problem was that some people in Texas owned slaves. The United States contained 13 free states and 13 slave states

at this time. Making Texas a state would upset the balance. Another problem was Mexico. Some U.S. government officials believed that annexing Texas would awaken old feelings and lead to another war. In 1845, however,

▼ *Once the Mexican War started, the army asked for volunteers. Men signed up by the thousands.*

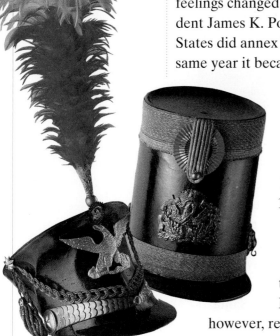

feelings changed under new president James K. Polk. The United States did annex Texas, and in the same year it became a state.

As expected, Mexico reacted angrily to the news of statehood for Texas. In November 1845, President Polk sent an ambassador to Mexico City to try to negotiate. Mexican officials, however, refused to talk.

War with Mexico

Next, President Polk ordered American forces in Texas to move down to the Rio Grande. They were now in territory that the Mexican government said was theirs. In April 1846, Mexican troops fought with an American scouting party, leaving 16 dead or wounded. The United States and Mexico were now at war.

American generals Winfield Scott and Zachary Taylor believed that an invasion of Mexico was necessary to win the war. They decided to attack from two directions. General Taylor invaded Mexico from the north. Crossing the Rio Grande, his troops won a few quick victories and took some important Mexican towns.

General Scott sailed south to Veracruz, a port on the eastern coast of Mexico. His troops won a number of battles against the badly equipped and poorly led Mexican forces. Then General Scott marched his troops over the mountains and captured Mexico City in September 1847. The Mexican government agreed to sign a peace treaty.

These hats belonged to a U.S. soldier (left) and a Mexican cavalry officer (right). The U.S. soldiers in the painting (below) are advancing on Mexico City in 1847.

Lands Gained by the United States, 1848–1853

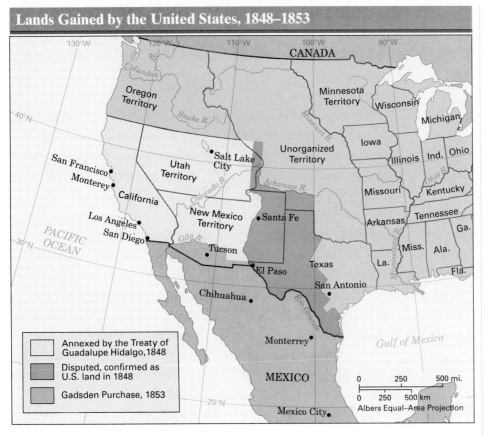

How many states were carved out of the land that the United States received from Mexico?

The Treaty of Guadalupe Hidalgo *(gwa duh LOO pay ee DAHL goh)* was signed on February 2, 1848. The map at the top of the page shows the result. Mexico gave up all claims to lands in Texas. What other lands did the United States receive?

The United States paid Mexico $15 million for all the land it received after the Mexican War. Five years later, the United States bought more land along Mexico's northern border. This time it paid Mexico $10 million. The purchase was arranged by James Gadsden, U.S. minister to Mexico. The United States wanted this land, known as the Gadsden Purchase, to build a railroad along a southern route to California. The southern border of the United States was now set. ■

What actions showed that the U.S. government was ready for a war with Mexico?

REVIEW

1. **FOCUS** How did the United States expand its southern border to include Texas?

2. **CONNECT** What qualities did the first American settlers in Texas have in common with the first settlers in Kentucky?

3. **CITIZENSHIP** Why did Mexico require new American settlers in Texas to become Mexican citizens?

4. **SOCIAL SYSTEMS** Why did the American settlers want to make Texas independent?

5. **CRITICAL THINKING** No one really wanted the Mexican War. Before the war, Polk sent an ambassador to Mexico City to negotiate. Mexican officials didn't start to fight until Polk had sent troops all the way to the Rio Grande. What else could Polk have done to prevent the war? What else could the Mexican officials have done?

6. **WRITING ACTIVITY** Write an eyewitness account of the battle of the Alamo.

Using Word Clues and Diagrams

Here's Why

Your everyday life is full of causes and effects. You forget your lunch. By late in the afternoon, you are hungry. Forgetting your lunch was the *cause*, and becoming hungry was the *effect*.

History is full of causes and effects, too. Suppose you wanted to understand what happened in the 1820s and 1830s.

Here's How

Word clues can help you to identify causes and effects. When you read, look for such phrases as: *led to, therefore, as a result of, since, brought about,* and *because.* These words suggest cause-and-effect relationships.

You can use diagrams to summarize cause-and-effect relationships. Study the diagram below. The first diagram shows how the single cause on the left resulted in the effect on the right.

Sometimes a single event sets off a "chain reaction" of other events. Look at the chain effect diagram below. It shows how the cause on the left resulted in the effect in the middle. This, in turn, became a cause for the effect on the right.

Suppose an event has more than one cause. In this case, you would use a diagram like the last one below. Note that several causes on the left resulted in the single effect on the right. Diagrams like this one are used to show complex cause-and-effect relationships that take place over long periods of time.

Try It

Use information from Lesson 1 to make a chain effect diagram. Show the defeat of the Texans at the Alamo as the first cause. End with the new government's request to annex Texas.

Apply It

Read newspaper articles to find cause-and-effect relationships. Write summaries that briefly describe each cause or effect. Make one of each of the three types of cause-and-effect diagrams based on articles you find.

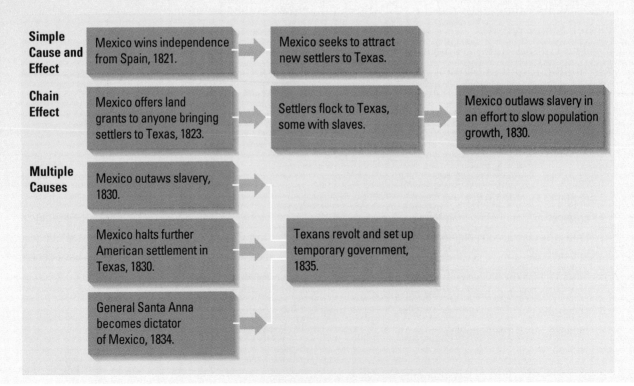

Simple Cause and Effect
- Mexico wins independence from Spain, 1821. → Mexico seeks to attract new settlers to Texas.

Chain Effect
- Mexico offers land grants to anyone bringing settlers to Texas, 1823. → Settlers flock to Texas, some with slaves. → Mexico outlaws slavery in an effort to slow population growth, 1830.

Multiple Causes
- Mexico outlaws slavery, 1830.
- Mexico halts further American settlement in Texas, 1830. → Texans revolt and set up temporary government, 1835.
- General Santa Anna becomes dictator of Mexico, 1834.

LESSON 2

The Road to Oregon

Wednesday, April 20th *Cloudy. We are creeping along slowly, one wagon after another, the same old gait [pace]; and the same thing over, out of one mud hole and into another all day. Crossed a branch where the water run into the wagons. No corn to be had within 75 miles. Came 18 miles and camp.*

Wednesday, June 1st It has been raining all day long. . . . The men and boys are all soaking wet and look sad and comfortless. (The little ones and myself are shut up in the wagons from the rain. Still it will find its way in and many things are wet; and take us all together, we are a poor looking set, and all this for Oregon. . . .)

THINKING FOCUS

Why were so many settlers willing to make the long and difficult journey to Oregon?

Key Terms

- migrate
- claim

Amelia Stewart Knight, an Iowa farm wife, wrote these notes in her diary in 1853, as her covered wagon moved across what is now western Nebraska. Knight was traveling to Oregon with her husband and their seven children. The Knights were only one family among thousands who made the long trip west during the 1840s and 1850s. These people had read newspaper stories about a

◄ *The move to Oregon was a family affair, with everyone pitching in to help with the chores. In later life, most children would look back on the journey west as a great adventure.*

377

Settling the Far West

wonderful land in the Northwest called Oregon. Many writers praised Oregon's mild weather and rich soil. One writer said that beets grew up to "three feet in diameter, while turnips were five feet around." From stories like these, many people caught "Oregon fever"—a strong desire to move west and start a new life.

■ *What was "Oregon fever" and how did people "catch" it?*

Oregon Fever

American interest in Oregon dated back to 1792, when an American explorer named Robert Gray discovered the mouth of a huge river. He named the river the Columbia after his sailing ship. The Columbia River flowed through the land that became known as the Oregon Territory. Lewis and Clark reached the area in 1805. The explorations of Gray and Lewis and Clark led to American claims of the land.

American missionaries visited Oregon in the 1830s. They hoped to bring Christianity to the Indians. The missionaries liked the region, and they sent letters back east telling of its beauty. Other travelers and explorers who visited Oregon wrote glowing descriptions that appeared in newspapers and books.

It wasn't long before people like the Knights began to think that Oregon was a place where they could get a new start in life. Thousands of families decided to **migrate**—that is, to sell their homes, pack up their belongings, and settle in the new area. ■

The Oregon Trail

Travelers to Oregon soon found that getting there was not easy. A voyage by ship was costly and took six to eight months. It was much cheaper to travel overland by covered wagon.

Most pioneers took the Oregon Trail. It stretched northwestward from Missouri for 2,000 miles over prairies, rivers, and mountains. The trip took about six months. Pioneers began the journey in the spring. That gave them just enough time to cross the western mountains before winter snows closed the mountain passes.

Preparations for the Trip

To begin the journey, families needed $600 for supplies. Many families raised the money by selling their farms. Next, they loaded their wagons and set out for Independence, Missouri, where the Oregon Trail began.

In Independence, families had to buy food for six months of travel. They stocked up on corn and beans, sugar and flour, coffee and tea, dried fruit and dried meat. When fully loaded, the wagon weighed 1,500 to 2,000 pounds.

▼ *Guidebooks like* The National Wagon Road Guide *provided pioneers with maps and practical travel tips.*

Families usually bought one or two teams of oxen. They were better than horses for pulling heavy loads. Families also bought weapons—usually shotguns and rifles—for hunting along the way and for protection.

After several days of preparation, the family loaded the wagon and set off. Rebecca West, who went to Oregon in 1853, wrote about her feelings of wonder in her diary: "The prairie, oh, the broad, the beautiful, the bounding, rolling prairie!"

Travel Along the Trail

Feelings of excitement soon gave way to the hardships of the journey. Pioneers traveled from dawn to dusk, in a wagon train of 50 or more wagons. The wagon train crawled along, averaging about 15 miles a day. At night, the pioneers pulled the wagons into a circle for safety. They often told stories, sang, or danced to help them forget the hardships of the day's travel.

The pioneers faced all kinds of problems along the trail. Bad weather, unsafe water, sickness, a broken axle—all could stop the wagon train for days. Death was always present, as one pioneer noted in her diary:

> Monday, July 28 . . . *Came past a camp of thirty-six wagons who have been camped for some time here in the mountains. They have had their cattle stampeded four or five times. There was a woman died in this train yesterday. She left six children, one of them only two days old. Poor little thing, it had better have died with its mother. They made a good picket fence around the grave.*
>
> Jane Gould Tourtillott, 1862

To learn more about the Oregon Trail, see A Closer Look on the following pages. Trace the Oregon Trail from Missouri to Oregon. Which part of the trail do you think would present the most difficulty for the pioneers?

Across Time & Space

If your family has ever taken a car trip across the United States, you may have followed part of the Oregon Trail or another famous trail. A number of today's highways follow paths taken by the great old trails that stretched west from the Missouri River. The present Interstate Highway 80 comes close to the Oregon Trail in western Nebraska and through Wyoming.

◄ *Friends and neighbors often presented departing pioneers with a memento quilt. Many were sad at the parting, feeling that they would never see each other again.*

The Oregon Trail

The Oregon Trail was a long, long road to a better life. Between 1840 and 1870, more than 350,000 people packed their belongings into covered wagons and headed west. Survivors endured 2,000 miles and six months of desert heat and mountain cold. For some, it led to tragedy. For others, it was a great adventure.

Death was a part of life on the trail. This steer may have died from exhaustion, starvation, or from drinking bad water. People died on the trail, too—usually from disease or accidents.

Going about two miles an hour, the oxen inched the wagons westward. When the oxen got tired, the men—in boots like these—got off the wagon and walked. As the oxen got weaker, the women and children often had to walk, too.

Like tracks from ghosts, these ruts carved by thousands of wagon wheels still scar the land along the Oregon Trail. Although most of them have been plowed over, hundreds of miles of trails like these remain intact.

Mile after boring mile, settlers rolled across the plains of the Platte River Valley. When they saw Chimney Rock in western Nebraska, settlers knew the mountains were near. The road was about to get tougher.

There was time to play on the trail, but little room for toys in the wagon. Children were usually allowed to bring just one. A doll like this one would have been a girl's most precious possession. What would you bring?

Point of interest

Fort

Oregon Trail

0   75   150mi

N

Northern Cheyenne

Independence Rock

Sioux

Fort Laramie

Chimney Rock

Scotts Bluff

Pawnee

Fort Kearny

St. Joseph

Westport Landing

Southern Cheyenne and Arapaho

Unorganized Territory

Lawrence

Independence

St. Louis

Missouri

CONTINENTAL DIVIDE

Iowa

Missouri R.

Platte R.

It was a good sign if settlers reached Independence Rock, Wyoming, before July 4, Independence Day. That meant they should get through the mountains before heavy snows came. Some settlers even signed their names and left messages on the rock.

W.R. WALKER
1852

Settling the Far West

The pioneers lost no time establishing stable communities once they reached Oregon. This schoolhouse dates from 1858.

While some built the cabin, others prepared the newly cleared fields for planting. After the cabin was finished, they built furniture. It took the pioneers about six months to get settled and to feel at home in Oregon.

A New State

As the number of settlers in Oregon grew, they demanded that a government be established. Most American settlers wanted Oregon to become part of the United States, but Great Britain also claimed it.

The question of who owned Oregon was settled once and for all in 1846. James K. Polk had won the 1844 presidential election. He had promised to make Oregon a state. The British protested, but they didn't want to go to war. The two countries talked over the problem. In 1846 they agreed to a border along the 49th parallel. That is the border between the United States and Canada today.

Two years later Oregon became a territory of the United States. In February 1859 Oregon joined the Union as the 33rd state. ■

The End of the Trail

The pioneers faced new challenges once they reached Oregon. They had to file a **claim,** a request to own a tract of land. Each family could get one square mile of land—640 acres. To keep the land, the family had to build a cabin within six months.

Building the cabin was backbreaking work. All family members who were old enough helped chop down trees and prepare the logs. The family lived in the covered wagon until the cabin was ready.

■ *What did a pioneer family need for a trip along the Oregon Trail?*

R E V I E W

1. **FOCUS** Why were so many settlers willing to make the long and difficult journey to Oregon?
2. **CONNECT** How did the United States and Great Britain handle the dispute over Oregon? How does this compare with the way the United States and Mexico handled the dispute over Texas?
3. **SOCIAL SYSTEMS** What did pioneer families have to do once they reached Oregon?
4. **GEOGRAPHY** Why did it take a wagon train six months to make the trip between Missouri and Oregon?
5. **CRITICAL THINKING** Suppose you are living on a farm in Iowa back in 1843. Your family is beginning to think about moving to Oregon. What are some of the questions the family should discuss before making the decision?
6. **WRITING ACTIVITY** Imagine you are about to set out on the Oregon Trail. Write a diary entry telling how you feel.

LESSON 3

Migrating to California and Utah

"GOLD MINE FOUND!" proclaimed the newspaper headline from the tiny California settlement of San Francisco on March 15, 1848. The newspaper story went on: "In the newly made raceway [wooden channel for water] of the saw mill recently erected by Captain Sutter . . . gold has been found in considerable quantities."

It took a while for news of the gold strike to spread. By May 1848, for example, only a few hundred gold seekers had come to the lands along the American River near Sutter's mill. By the end of the year, they numbered in the thousands. Before long, people had flocked to California from cities and towns throughout the United States and from countries around the world.

Gold seekers swarmed into the foothills of the Sierra Nevada Mountains. Boom towns grew up overnight. Before it was over, the gold rush would bring more than 300,000 people into California.

THINKING FOCUS

What were the goals of the people who went to California and Utah?

Key Terms

- forty-niner
- Mormon

◄ *George W. Northrup, a Minnesota schoolteacher, had his picture taken in 1849 as he prepared to "strike it rich" in California. Unfortunately, he was killed by Indians before he got out of Minnesota.*

Early California

California had been part of Spanish Mexico since the 1500s. It had been largely ignored for over 200 years. Spain finally began to encourage settlement when it learned that Russian and British fur traders had moved into the area.

Spanish priests began building a chain of missions up and down the coast in 1769. The first settlers from Mexico, called Californios, arrived shortly thereafter. By 1821, the year Mexico won its independence from Spain, there were about 3,000 Californios living in California. There were also 200,000 Indians.

During the next 20 years, most Californios lived and worked on great ranches with thousands and thousands of acres. The ranches raised cattle, not for beef but for the leather hides.

■ *Find evidence to support this statement: California was settled by diverse groups of people.*

The first settlers from the United States made their way to California at this time. Most were traders who sold hides and furs in China. They became friends with the Californios, married into Californio families, and became Mexican citizens.

More settlers from the United States began arriving in the 1840s. They came overland in covered wagons, just like the settlers who went to Oregon. These new settlers were farmers, not traders. They did not want to become Mexican citizens. In fact, they wanted to make California part of the United States.

When the Mexican War broke out in 1846, some of these American settlers rebelled against the Mexican government. They wanted to make California an independent republic—the Bear Flag Republic. The U.S. government encouraged them. It sent troops and warships to attack Mexican strongholds.

The Mexican forces in California surrendered in 1847, just months before the Mexican War ended. Under the Treaty of Guadalupe Hidalgo, the United States gained a huge territory that included California. ■

The Gold Rush

One month before the Treaty of Guadalupe Hidalgo was signed, gold was discovered at Sutter's mill. John Sutter owned a large ranch in the Sacramento Valley.

Sutter had hired a carpenter named James Marshall to build a sawmill and raceway on his property, about 40 miles northeast of present-day Sacramento.

On January 24, 1848, Marshall noticed some shiny bits of metal mixed with the sand, mud, and gravel in the raceway. He picked up the glittering fragments, wrapped them in a rag, and rushed to Sutter.

Making sure that they were alone, Marshall showed Sutter what he had found. The largest pieces were no bigger than a pea. The smallest were the size of a speck. Marshall said he thought the shiny fragments were gold. At first, Sutter didn't believe it, but Marshall was right. He had found gold.

Dreams of Striking It Rich

News of the gold strike soon brought thousands of people to California. Farmers left their plows in the field and soldiers ran away from the army, all for gold. In faraway lands like Europe and China, gold seekers boarded ships and came to California. One observer wrote that a gold miner could earn "in one day more than double a soldier's pay for a month."

The gold seekers were called **forty-niners,** for the year 1849 when the gold rush madness was at its peak. Once they reached California, the forty-niners headed straight for the gold fields. All they could think about was striking it rich. All they dreamed about was going back home with a fortune.

Not everyone who moved to California at this time wanted to work in the gold fields. Many men and women came to start a business. Some sold clothing to the miners. Others sold food or mining equipment. Some cooked and did laundry. Others ran hotels.

▼ *Teachers, farmers, mechanics—people from all walks of life were caught up in the excitement of the gold rush. In this photograph miners use pans and wooden troughs to sift gravel for gold.*

▲ *In 1840, San Francisco was a sleepy little town of 200. By 1850, it was a bustling city of 50,000. Growth was so fast that some people had to live in tents.*

➤ *The graph shows the dramatic increase in population brought on by the gold rush.*

All came to California in the hope of making a profit, as this gold rush tune suggests:

> *O*h, California,
> Thou land of glittering dreams
> Where the yellow dust and diamonds, boys
> Are found in all thy streams!

The wild rush for gold lasted just four years. It peaked in 1852, when forty-niners mined gold worth more than $80 million. Prospecting continued after 1853, but the remaining gold lay deep in the ground. Miners would need costly machines to get at it.

Violence and Injustice

California gold-mining towns usually consisted of a collection of run-down buildings—stores, restaurants, boarding houses, and the like. There were few laws in these towns, and fewer law officers. As the gold fields filled up, tempers grew short. Arguments often led to fights. Fights often led to shootings.

Prejudice also became a serious problem at this time, especially after 1852 when the gold started to give out. Mexicans, Blacks, and Indians working in the gold fields all suffered from prejudice. So did

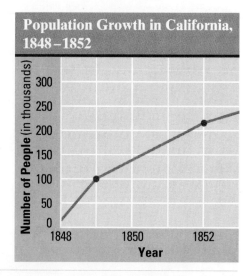

Population Growth in California, 1848–1852

forty-niners who came to California from Europe and China.

Effects of the Gold Rush

A few forty-niners struck it rich, but most were not so lucky. For example, John Sutter did not become rich from the gold discovered on his property. Forty-niners looking for gold overran his land and ruined his sawmill. Sutter lost all his money and died poor.

The most lasting result of the gold rush was the effect it had on California. The gold rush changed California from a sleepy outpost to an important western land. Many businesses came to the area, and California farmers found more and more buyers for their crops. The great increase in population made San Francisco a major city almost overnight. It helped make California ready for statehood in 1850. ■

▲ Not everyone came to California to work in the gold fields. Levi Strauss made a fortune by selling denim pants to miners.

■ How did the gold rush change California?

A "Kingdom" in Utah

Another group went west in the mid-1800s, but not to find gold. These settlers were **Mormons,** members of the Church of Jesus Christ of Latter-day Saints. They are called Mormons after their sacred scripture, the Book of Mormon. Mormons give great emphasis to the importance of the family. The Mormons went west to live and raise their families and worship God in their own way.

Early History of the Mormons

Joseph Smith founded the Mormon church in New York in 1830. The Mormons went through difficult times during their early years. They had to move from place to place in order to practice their religion freely. They lived in Ohio for a time, but they left after Smith was tarred and feathered. They moved to Missouri, but left after Smith was jailed. They settled in Illinois, but in 1844, Smith was jailed again. On June 27, a mob stormed the jail and murdered Smith and one of his brothers.

Brigham Young now became leader of the Mormons. He decided to carry out Smith's plan to move to the Great Basin in the Rocky Mountains. Once there, the Mormons could build "the kingdom of God on earth."

The Mormon Migration

Young planned the migration carefully. He would lead the first group of settlers. The rest would wait until he sent word to follow. They set out on the long trail west in April 1847.

Settling the Far West

▲ *Mormons were always ready to lend their neighbors a helping hand. The photo shows a group of Mormons raising a barn.*

■ *What does the story of the Mormons tell you about their beliefs?*

*I*n the vast, endless, rippling prairie land the column of wagons wound slowly westward, crawling over the rise and fall of the land. A thin thread of life under the hot June sun. White canvas gave off a blinding glare; the river glittered like a sheet of brown glass, this shallow, muddy Platte, all tangled in its willows and islands.

Hot, hard going. The dust made a grit in the mouth.

Annabel and Edgar Johnson, 1962
Wilderness Bride

After months of travel, Young and his followers entered the Great Salt Lake valley, a dry, treeless land where only sagebrush grew. "This is the place," Young said. Two hours later, the Mormons were hard at work building a new life. Young returned east to bring back the Mormons waiting in Iowa and Nebraska.

The Mormon settlement of Salt Lake City grew. Soon Young and his followers needed more people to help with the work. During the 1850s, thousands of Mormons from as far away as Europe made the difficult trip to Salt Lake City. Mark Twain described a wagon train of Mormons that he saw on his own travels west: "They were dusty and uncombed . . . and ragged, and they did look so tired!"

Mexico owned the Great Salt Lake valley when the Mormons settled there in 1847. It became U.S. land in the Treaty of Guadalupe Hidalgo the following year. The Mormons applied for statehood for Utah in 1849, but Congress made the area a territory instead. Utah did not become a state until 1896. ■

R E V I E W

1. **FOCUS** What were the goals of the people who went to California and Utah?
2. **CONNECT** What happened after settlers from the United States flooded into Texas in the 1820s and 1830s? How was this similar to what happened in California?
3. **HISTORY** What was the most lasting effect of the gold rush?
4. **BELIEF SYSTEMS** Why did the Mormons have to move from place to place during their early years?
5. **CRITICAL THINKING** Two groups of settlers moved to California before the gold rush. How were these groups different?
6. **WRITING ACTIVITY** Imagine that you are a Texan who went to California in 1849 hoping to strike it rich. Write a letter to your parents telling about your adventures.

L E S S O N   4

Conflicts with the American Indians

The Duwamish, an Indian tribe living in the Northwest in 1851, were forced to sell most of their ancient tribal lands to white settlers. By 1855, the U.S. government was demanding more.

Seattle, a Duwamish chief, had been friendly with the settlers. Now he was troubled. On January 9, 1855, Seattle responded to the government. His speech tells a great deal about the American Indians' special feelings for the land:

The great . . . White Chief sends us word that he wants to buy our land. . . . We will consider your offer. When we have decided, we will let you know. Should we accept, I here and now make this condition: we will never be denied the right to visit, at any time, the graves of our fathers and our friends.

Every part of this earth is sacred to my people. Every hillside, every valley, every clearing and wood, is holy in the memory and experience of my people. Even those un-speaking stones along the shore are loud with events and memories in the life of my people. The ground beneath your feet responds more lovingly to our steps than yours, because it is the ashes of our grandfathers. . . . The earth is rich with the lives of our kin.

The young men, the mothers, and girls, the little children who once lived and were happy here, still love these lonely places. And at evening the forests are dark with the presence of the dead. When the last red man has vanished from this earth, and his memory is only a story among the whites, these shores will still swarm with the invisible dead of my people.

THINKING FOCUS

How did the migration of white settlers change the lives of Indians?

Key Term

• nomad

▼ *Chief Seattle's name was given to the city of Seattle, Washington, which was founded in 1853.*

Indian Ways of Life

Across Time & Space

A number of states and cities have Indian names. The name Wyoming, for example, is an Indian word meaning "on the great plain." Its capital city of Cheyenne gets its name from the Cheyenne tribe.

▼ *Compare this map with the one on page 560 of the Minipedia. How did the western Indians live?*

As settlers on their way to Oregon and California crossed the Great Plains, they paid little attention to the American Indians. They knew little about the Indians' beliefs, their way of life, and their feelings about the land. They saw the Indians as just another obstacle on the difficult trip west.

Many different tribes were living west of the Mississippi at this time. Look at the map on this page. Find the names of various Indian tribes who lived on the Great Plains.

The Plains Indians were alike in one way. They all shared a strong belief in the importance of nature and the land. The Plains Indians had a great reverence for the land. They believed it is nature's greatest gift. The land supplied everything they needed. It had to be cared for and protected.

In other respects, the Plains Indians were quite different. Each tribe had its own territory, its own traditions, and its own language. Some Plains Indians, like the Kansas, were peaceful farmers who raised corn and other crops. Others tribes were **nomads**—people who move often in search of food.

Some Plains Indians, like the Sioux and the Cheyenne, were great warriors who fought mainly for glory. Others, like the Blackfeet, lived by stealing food and horses from their neighbors.

Indian Groups in the Western United States, 1860

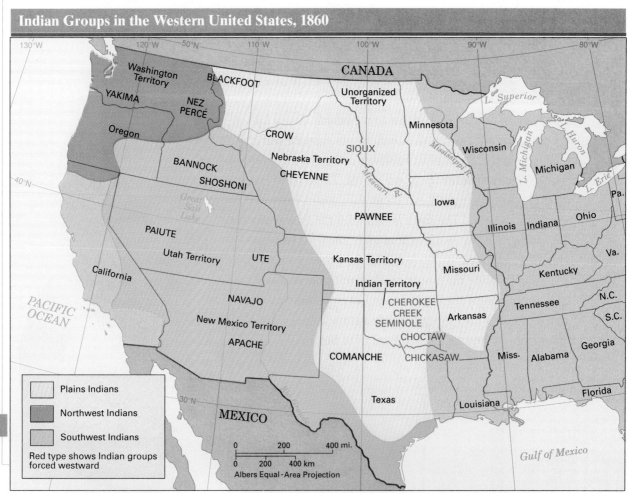

Many tribes depended on the horse for their way of life. With horses, they could hunt buffalo. They could also strike quickly at their enemies.

Life on the plains was not always peaceful. Indians had fought with one another long before the coming of the settlers. But now the situation got worse. As settlers pushed farther and farther west, they gradually pushed one tribe onto the land of another. Then the two tribes would fight over territory, water, and hunting grounds. As one chief of the Sauks stated, "Let the Sioux keep from our lands, and there will be peace."

Trade

Friend

White man

Little by little, the Plains Indians, no matter what their tribe, were beginning to understand that they all faced a common problem. More and more wagon trains were traveling across Indian land on the way to Oregon and California. How long would it be before settlers started moving onto Indian land in the Great Plains? ■

▲ *The Plains Indians often communicated by sign language. From left to right these signs mean "trade," "friend," and "white man."*

■ *How did the Indian tribes of the plains differ from each other? How were they alike?*

The Indians and the Settlers

In the early 1800s, the U.S. government made many treaties with the Indians. Time and again, however, settlers moved onto Indian land and the treaties were forgotten.

In 1824, the government tried to improve relations by starting the Bureau of Indian Affairs. Six years later, however, the government ordered several Indian tribes in the Southeast to move to Indian reservations in what is now Oklahoma. This was the time when the Cherokee were forced to make their long march west along the Trail of Tears.

Settlers who crossed the Oregon Trail in the late 1840s had mostly peaceful contacts with the Plains Indians. As the migration

◄ *These portraits show how Indian dress was affected by contact with traders. The father, at the far left, is dressed in traditional garb—a deerskin shirt with a buffalo robe. His son is wearing a colorful blanket and glass beads bought from a trader.*

> *The two horsemen on the shield represent the growing conflict between Indians and settlers.*

■ *Why did the arrival of white settlers cause conflict among Indian groups?*

increased in the 1850s, however, the settlers began to upset the Indians' way of life.

For example, the settlers' horses and oxen ate grass along the trail. The Indians depended upon the grass for their own horses. In addition, settlers began killing more and more buffalo for food. This caused further trouble. The buffalo was an important food source for the Indians.

Settlers also brought diseases like smallpox and cholera to the Plains. In 1837, a smallpox epidemic swept through one tribe of 1,600. It left only 31 survivors. Forty-niners on their way to California spread cholera. Said one Cheyenne warrior, ill with cholera: "If I could see this thing, if I knew where it was, I would go there and kill it!" ■

UNDERSTANDING DEMOGRAPHIC CHANGE

In the 1830s, the U.S. government expelled thousands of Indians from tribal lands east of the Mississippi. American settlers soon occupied the vacant land.

As a result, the population in these areas changed rapidly. Before the 1830s, American Indians lived in these lands. Afterwards, mainly European Americans lived there. Historians refer to this kind of change as a demographic change.

The study of the characteristics of human population is called demography. Historians study the size of the population, its growth, the number of people of different ages, and other features of the population.

Changes in Population

Demographic change may involve a simple increase in numbers of people. Or it may involve new people coming into an area—new people with different languages, different customs, and different values.

For example, demographic change occurred in California during the 1840s. American settlers moving into the area were very different from the Spanish-speaking Californios already living there. A similar change occurred in the 1980s, with the arrival of thousands of immigrants from the continent of Asia.

Results of the Changes

Demographic changes bring other changes. For example, people bring with them new foods, new customs, new ideas, and everyone else benefits.

This is not always the case, however. Westward expansion of the United States resulted in changes that disrupted the lives of American Indians for over a century.

Government Intervention

Settlers began to fear the Plains Indians, who now began to harass wagon trains. The settlers asked the government to step in. At the same time, the Indians complained about the settlers. They demanded that the government pay for damage done to Indian lands.

In 1851, the government called a meeting of nine western tribes at Fort Laramie, in what is now Wyoming. About 10,000 Indians attended. The government had two purposes for the meeting. It wanted to make travel safe for wagon trains, and it wanted to set boundaries for each tribe's hunting area.

The government and the tribes signed an agreement at the Fort Laramie meeting. The tribes promised to stop harassing the wagon trains. They accepted boundaries for tribal territories. They also agreed to let the government build roads and forts on Indian land. In return, the federal government promised to pay each tribe $50,000 a year in food and supplies.

Not surprisingly, the agreement soon broke down. For example,

the government reduced the amount of food and supplies promised by the treaty. The government and the Plains Indians would make other agreements in the future. They would break down, too. Neither side at the Fort Laramie meeting knew that one day settlers would flood into the Great Plains to stay. Neither side knew that one day settlers would drive the Plains Indians from their beloved land. ■

▲ *After years of treaty violations on both sides, the Sioux came to Fort Laramie in 1867 to settle differences with the settlers.*

■ *How did the government respond to the problems between Indian tribes and between Indians and settlers?*

R E V I E W

1. **FOCUS** How did the migration of white settlers change the lives of Indians?

2. **CONNECT** What trends have American settlers followed in their dealings with Indians since the first colonial settlement at Jamestown?

3. **SOCIAL SYSTEMS** What are the names of some of the Indian tribes that lived on the Great Plains? How were the names alike? How were they different?

4. **CRITICAL THINKING** How did the Plains Indians feel about land? How did settlers feel?

5. **WRITING ACTIVITY** Imagine you are a Plains Indian heading out on a buffalo hunt. One day you see a wagon train of settlers and their families passing through your hunting grounds. Write a short paragraph telling how you might feel.

6. **ACTIVITY** Get together with two or three friends. Make a mural showing a daily scene in a Sioux village. The Minipedia on page 558 shows Sioux clothing, tepees, crafts, and weapons.

Should I Go West with My Family?

A portion of the emigrants of 1846 . . . lost most of their property, barely getting here with their lives. A better way (than the old road) may be found, but it is best for men with wagons and families not to try this experiment.

George Abernethy, Governor of the Oregon Territory, 1847

W hoo ha! Go it boys! We're in a perfect Oregon fever. . . . From present evidence, we suppose that no less than two or three thousand people are congregating at this point (Independence, Missouri) previous to their start upon the broad prairie.

Independence Expositor, May 3, 1845

Background

In the mid-1800s, the American West represented both an opportunity and a challenge. It gave a second chance to many people. European immigrants were pouring into the eastern cities, competing for scarce jobs and housing. Many people moved west to get out of the cities. In the Midwest, good land had been claimed by the best farmers. If a family had not found success and security in Virginia or Ohio or Missouri, why not follow the Oregon Trail?

The U.S. government supported the desire to settle the new territories. Free land was there for anyone willing to settle on it.

What did people really know about the West? They had heard that the land was fertile. They had read letters from early settlers. They knew these lands were populated by numerous nations of native peoples. Some letters promised plenty of animals for food. Others warned that these same animals were dangerous. If they were provoked, they would attack. If they were hungry, they would steal food. The good land for grazing cattle was far off the trail. A wagon train could travel for days without finding clean water.

What Lies Ahead?

Oregon offered free land and jobs for skilled workers and farmhands. A family could earn a good living. Oregon was a way out of overcrowded cities, an escape from unpaid bills and unhappy memories. All who were willing to work hard could succeed if they got there alive.

The trail was lined with the graves of those who didn't. People froze, or starved to death, in blizzards. They fell, wagons and all, into deep mountain passes. They died of fevers caused by drinking unclean water.

Leaving bills and unemployment might also mean leaving friends and family or aging parents. Settlers also left schools and churches, doctors, and the familiar buildings of a town or neighborhood.

Travel was difficult and slow. Some who took the Oregon Trail would return eventually. Others would persuade family and friends to move west. But as they left Missouri, they left the known world behind.

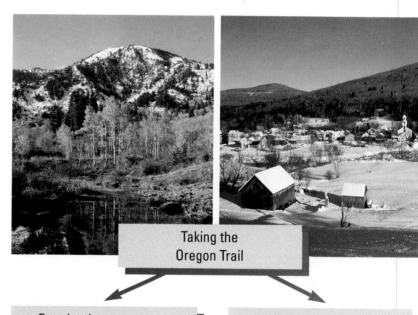

Taking the Oregon Trail

- Free land
- Jobs
- Chance of riches
- Room to grow

Go west

- Hardships of the journey
- Fear of the unknown
- Leaving friends and family
- Dangers on the trail

Stay where you are

Decision Point

1. Half your family wants to go to Oregon; half wants to stay put. What do you know that would help you decide what to do?
2. What would you want to know about Oregon? How could you get this information?
3. Find a news story about someone who risked danger to seek a new home. Why did they leave home?
4. Suppose you are grown and have a family. You are offered a job in Iceland or Peru. What do you want to know before you make up your mind? Where can you find this information?
5. What if you were asked to settle on another planet? What would be good reasons for going? For staying here?

Chapter Review

Reviewing Key Terms

annex (p. 373)
claim (p. 382)
forty-niner (p. 385)
migrate (p. 378)

Mormon (p. 387)
nomad (p. 390)
plain (p. 371)

6. nomad, traveler
7. Mormon, religion

A. The two words in each pair are related in some way. The first word is always a key term. On your own paper, write a sentence explaining how the words are related.
1. annex, add
2. claim, right
3. forty-niner, prospector
4. migrate, move
5. plain, flat

B. On your own paper, use each key term in a sentence that shows what the word means. Write each sentence as if you were a settler writing a letter to a friend back home.
1. claim
2. forty-niner
3. migrate
4. Mormons
5. plains
6. nomads

Exploring Concepts

A. Look at the timeline below. You will see dates for important historical events in the growth of the United States. Copy the timeline on a separate sheet of paper. Fill in the events for the years shown. Notice that the completed timeline will show two events each for the years 1846 and 1848.

B. Answer each question with information from the chapter.
1. Why did Americans migrate to Texas?
2. What were the events leading up to the Mexican War?

3. What effect did the Treaty of Guadalupe Hidalgo have on the southern border of the United States?
4. Why was the journey to Oregon so hard?
5. How were the goals of the people who migrated to California and Utah alike? How were they different?
6. During this time, the United States had conflicts with Mexico and with Great Britain. How were the conflicts similar? How were they different?
7. What were reasons for the friction between the settlers and the American Indians?

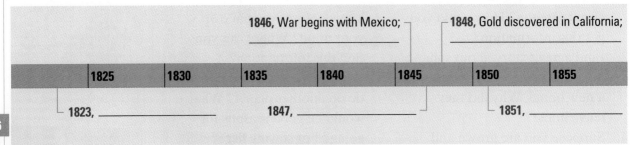

1846, War begins with Mexico;
_____

1848, Gold discovered in California;

| 1825 | 1830 | 1835 | 1840 | 1845 | 1850 | 1855 |

1823, _____

1847, _____

1851, _____

Reviewing Skills

1. Study the diagram on this page. Was the discovery of gold a cause or an effect? Which entry is both a cause and an effect?
2. Look again at Lesson 2. Make a chain-effect diagram that explains the events that led to demands for a regional government in Oregon.
3. The map on page 390 shows the location of American Indian groups in the western United States during the 1840s and 1850s. Study the map, then copy the following paragraph onto your own paper . Complete the paragraph using cardinal and intermediate directions.

   We traveled west from Texas into the land inhabited by the Apache. From there, we journeyed _____ into Navajo country. We then traveled _____ to reach the land of the Paiute.

4. Suppose you were a settler interested in bringing more people to Texas and you had decided to create an advertisement. Would you use an illustration or a photograph of Texas in your ad? Why?

The California Gold Rush 1848– 1853

Gold discovered in California, 1848.	→	250,000 people from around the world arrive in California seeking gold, 1848–1853.	→	Increased population leads to California becoming a state, 1850.

Using Critical Thinking

1. Many people moved to Texas because they believed the advertisements about Texas. Are people as influenced by advertisements today? Explain.
2. In the 1800s, people caught "Oregon fever," an intense desire to move west and start a new life. Do you think people in the 2000s will ever be infected with "planet fever"? Why?
3. The Plains Indians had a great reverence for the land. They believed it was nature's greatest gift and had to be cared for and protected. Do you think Americans today share this belief? Explain.

Preparing for Citizenship

1. GROUP ACTIVITY Advertisements persuaded thousands of Americans to settle in Texas during the 1820s and 1830s. Write an advertisement that would attract people to move to your state. Include the main advantages of living in your state.
2. ARTS ACTIVITY Look at the Alamo Flag on page 372 and other flags in American history on pages 554–555 of the Minipedia. Choose one of the groups discussed in this chapter and design a flag for that group.
3. COLLABORATIVE LEARNING As a class project, paint a mural of one family's trek west on the Oregon Trail. First, as a class, decide which scenes to show. Then, working in groups of four, choose one of the scenes to paint. Each person in a group should be in charge of researching and drawing one of the following: (1) the scenery, (2) the equipment, (3) the people, and (4) the animals. Paint your scene on a large sheet of paper. Join the scenes to form the mural.

Unit 6
A Nation in Conflict

During the 1800s, the United States enjoyed booming success. Yet the nation seemed like two different places. The North was a land of bustling cities and busy factories. Southern life was shaped by the work of slaves, such as those shown here. As the North and South began to argue about slavery, Americans wondered which direction the nation would take.

1779

Henry P. Moore, photographer, South Carolina plantation, about 1862. Courtesy of the New-York Historical Society, New York City.

1865

Chapter 16
Southern Society

Just as tobacco changed the South in the 1600s, cotton changed the South in the 1800s. Huge profits from the crop allowed a few plantation owners to live in great luxury. For poorer farmers who wanted the wealth and power of the planters, cotton was the best way to get rich. For the slaves who worked in the fields and mansions of the plantations, the cotton boom simply meant more hard work.

During this time, a few rich plantation families dominate southern society. Mary Theodosia Ford appears to be the ideal southern belle: wealthy and proper.

1793 Eli Whitney invents the cotton gin. The gin, shown in the drawing to the left, helps make cotton a profitable crop. It also leads to a huge increase in the number of slaves living in the South (above).

| 1750 | 1775 | 1800 |

1808 Congress bans the import of slaves from Africa.

1779

1820 The southern states become the world's largest producers of cotton. The South grows most of its cotton on large plantations, like the one shown above.

1860 More than three-quarters of white southerners own no slaves. Most of these people run small farms with their families, often using crude tools like this plow.

1825

1850

1875

1850 More than 3 million slaves now live in the United States.

1860

L E S S O N   1

Plantation Society

THINKING
FOCUS

How did cotton and slavery allow plantation owners to live a privileged life?

Key Terms

- cotton gin
- abolitionist

Abiel Abbot, a minister from Massachusetts, often traveled to the warm South for his health. In 1818, he visited the Elms, a South Carolina rice plantation. Abbot had seen grand southern estates before and had even attended fancy parties at several plantation houses. Still, the wealth Abiel Abbot saw at the Elms greatly impressed him.

In his journal, Abbot described a fine mansion staffed by "perfect servants" who polished his shoes and straightened his clothes. One of the daughters of the family entertained him by playing the harp, and Abbot said, "the effect was magical." He and the master of the plantation "partook of a plentiful repast of tea, hominy, John Cake, & meats." His host spoke "with much knowledge of the world and books."

Abbot's account of life at the Elms differed little from a description written 34 years later by Mrs. Henry Schoolcraft, the wife of a South Carolina planter. She wrote

➤ *Drayton Hall is the name of both this South Carolina mansion, and the plantation on which it was built. Completed in 1742, Drayton Hall is the oldest plantation house still standing in the South.*

of White Hall, another South Carolina plantation: "The entrance to White Hall from the land side was a long avenue of live oaks and a hedge of evergreen." Mrs. Schoolcraft went on to describe the splendor of the house: "The house contained 21 rooms, each thirty feet square. The imposingly large architecture, set off with wings, gave the building quite the appearance of a palace."

At a wedding in the garden, tables were "groaning" from the weight of "fish, flesh, and fowl, pies, cakes, and puddings, fruits and bouquets, nuts and wines." The wedding guests danced late into the evening, and slaves attended their every need.

The Reverend John G. Drayton grew rice, cotton, and other crops on his Drayton Hall plantation (see page 402). A southern planter and investor, he built Drayton Hall next to his family's plantation, Magnolia Gardens.

King Cotton

Tobacco, rice, wheat, and indigo were important crops on plantations like the ones Abiel Abbot and Mrs. Schoolcraft visited. But cotton was king in the South. Cotton was the crop that fueled the southern economy and made the plantation owners rich.

One drawback to growing cotton was the time it took to process the crop after harvesting. Inside the fluffy bolls, or tufts, of cotton were sticky seeds. Slaves had to remove each seed by hand.

In 1793, a Massachusetts settler named Eli Whitney solved the problem by inventing the **cotton gin.** Whitney's invention was a small, boxy machine that removed the seeds from cotton. Here's how it worked.

A worker fed a boll of cotton into the gin and turned a crank. Metal teeth grabbed the cotton and pulled it

◄ The invention of the cotton gin led to a great increase in cotton production in the South. Which states gave over half of their land to cotton?

The Cotton Kingdom, 1820 and 1860

Land cultivated in cotton by 1820

Land cultivated in cotton by 1860

0   150   300 mi.

0 150 300 km

Lambert Conformal Conic Projection

Southern Society

1 Metal teeth pull raw cotton through the grate.

2 Seeds, which cannot pass through the grate, are collected here.

3 Brushes sweep cotton out of the gin.

Growth of Cotton and Slavery, 1800–1860

🌿 = 100,000 bales of cotton

🧍 = 200,000 slaves

1800

1820

1840

1860

▲ *Eli Whitney's cotton gin made quick work of cotton seeding. The result, as the graph shows, was an increase in cotton production.*

■ *How did the invention of the cotton gin increase the need for slaves in the South?*

through narrow slits. The cotton passed through the slits easily, but the seeds could not and were left behind. Brushes swept the cleaned cotton out of the machine. One cotton gin could clean as much

cotton in a day as 50 people working by hand.

The textile mills in New England and Europe bought all the cotton the South could produce. So plantation owners planted more and more cotton, using slaves to pick it and the cotton gin to clean it. The more cotton they grew, the more slaves they demanded. Thus, Eli Whitney's time- and labor-saving invention actually increased the need for slave labor. ■

The Plantation Owners

➤ *This wealthy southern woman is shown at the time of the Civil War. The sword she holds stands for honor, an important ideal to southerners.*

The huge profits some southern planters earned from cotton, tobacco, and other crops allowed them to live a life of wealth and leisure. The diaries and letters of these rich plantation owners are filled with stories about their way of life and provide good examples of their values.

William Byrd was a planter in the South before the Revolutionary War. Byrd owned a large tobacco plantation in Virginia. In an entry in his diary dated 1726, he described what he felt was his role as a southern planter and slave owner:

> I must take care to keep all my people to their Duty, to set all the Springs in motion and to make every one draw his equal Share to carry the Machine [plantation life] forward.

William Byrd thought of himself as a wise ruler, like a father who takes care of his family. This idea of the slave owner as a father appears often in the writings of the planters. They argued that owning slaves, like being a parent, was their duty.

White southerners also felt bound to protect their honor. A gentleman might challenge another man to a duel if he felt insulted in some way.

Planters thought it was their duty to become educated and cultured—to read, listen to music, and entertain. Abbot often made mention in his journal of the well-kept plantation libraries he saw during his many travels. ■

■ *How did the wealthy southern planters live, and what were some of their beliefs?*

The Defense of Slavery

Very few southern farmers became rich enough to enjoy this special style of life. In fact, only about one-fourth of all free southerners owned slaves. Still, nearly all white southerners, rich and poor, defended slave labor.

Revolt!

One bloody August night in 1831, this "right" was challenged by an angry Virginia slave named Nat Turner. Turner, a forceful preacher who said he had visions from God, believed that God wanted him to free the slaves.

On the night of August 21, in Jerusalem, Virginia, Turner and 7 slaves began their revolt. First they murdered Turner's owner, Joseph Travis, and his family. During the next two days, about 75 slaves joined Turner's rebellion, killing over 50 white people.

A force of 3,000 white southerners put down the revolt. Six weeks later, Turner was captured.

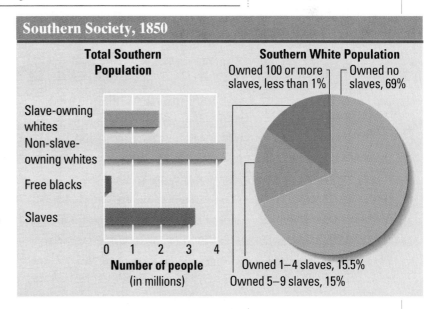

Southern Society, 1850

Total Southern Population

Slave-owning whites
Non-slave-owning whites
Free blacks
Slaves

0　1　2　3　4
Number of people
(in millions)

Southern White Population

Owned 100 or more slaves, less than 1%
Owned no slaves, 69%
Owned 1–4 slaves, 15.5%
Owned 5–9 slaves, 15%

He told authorities, "[I]t was my object to carry terror and devastation wherever we went." Although Turner was convicted and hanged for the murders, white southerners became afraid. They would never again trust that slaves would always obey and be silent.

▲ *These two graphs show the distribution of people in southern society. The graph on the right shows how few southern whites owned slaves.*

Attacks from the North

Slavery also was being attacked by some people in the northern

405

➤ *Nat Turner, an educated slave shown preaching in this 19th-century engraving, led the most infamous slave rebellion in U.S. history. The Virginia militia captured and hanged Turner and 20 of his fellow rebels.*

states. These people were called **abolitionists,** because they believed that slavery was wrong and should be abolished, or ended. One northern abolitionist, William Lloyd Garrison, wrote in his antislavery newspaper, *The Liberator:*

I will be as harsh as truth and as uncompromising as justice. On this subject [slavery], I do not wish to think, or speak, or write, with moderation. No! No!

Such attacks made whites in the South angry. Before Turner's revolt, many planters had been apologetic about keeping slaves. But now they were prepared to defend slavery. They argued that slaves were better off than northerners who worked in dark, dirty factories. They thought that blacks were an inferior race and that the Bible justified slavery. One of their strongest arguments noted that the Constitution let states make their own laws about slavery. ■

■ *In what two ways was slavery challenged during the first half of the 19th century?*

R E V I E W

1. **FOCUS** How did cotton and slavery allow cotton planters to live a privileged life?
2. **CONNECT** How were the lives of the wealthy southern planters different from the lives of prosperous farmers in the northern states? What were some reasons for these differences?
3. **ECONOMICS** Describe how the cotton gin works and how it affected the southern economy.
4. **CRITICAL THINKING** William Byrd said, "I must take care to keep all my people to their Duty." Who were

his people? What was their duty? How does this quote show that Byrd saw himself like a father?

5. **CRITICAL THINKING** How might life in the South have been different if Eli Whitney had not invented the cotton gin?
6. **ACTIVITY** Imagine you are a slave being urged to join Nat Turner's revolt. Will you join the revolt or not? Why? In a brief speech to your classmates, explain your decision and your reasons.

L E S S O N   2

A Look at Slavery

The Reverend Josiah Henson was a former slave who escaped to Canada. In his autobiography, Reverend Henson recalled the horror of being sold at a 1795 slave auction in Maryland:

My brothers and sisters were bid off first, and one by one, while my mother, paralyzed with grief, held me by the hand. Her turn came and she was bought by Isaac Riley of Montgomery County. Then I was offered. . . . My mother, half distracted with the thought of parting forever from all her children, pushed though the crowd while the bidding for me was going on, to the spot where Riley was standing. She fell at his feet, and clung to his knees, entreating [begging] him in tones that a mother only could command, to buy her baby as well as herself, and spare to her one, at least, of her little ones.

Isaac Riley was unmoved by the mother's pleas. He kicked her nearly senseless. Josiah, just five years old, was bought by another man.

THINKING FOCUS

How did slaves survive both physically and spiritually?

Key Terms

- overseer
- spiritual

VALUABLE GANG OF YOUNG **NEGROES**

By **JOS. A. BEARD.**

Will be sold at Auction,

ON WEDNESDAY, 25TH INST.

At 12 o'clock, at Banks' Arcade, 17 Valuable Young Negroes, Men and Women, Field Hands. Sold for no fault; with the best city guarantees.

Sale Positive and without reserve!

☞ TERMS CASH.

New Orleans, March 24, 1840.

◄ *Not unlike livestock, slaves were sold at public auctions like the one announced on this wall poster (far left). Slaves were forced to wear tags (left) that indicated the type of work for which they were thought to be best suited.*

407

Southern Society

Living the Life of a Slave

All slaves lived without freedom, but not all slaves lived under the same conditions. The daily lives of slaves depended on the size of the plantation they worked, the kind of work assigned to them, and the treatment they received.

Only a few plantations had more than 100 slaves; most had fewer than 10. On the smaller plantations, white owners worked side by side with black slaves. In general, this closeness meant a better quality of life for small-plantation slaves compared with those on large plantations. The owners hesitated to beat their "property" because they couldn't afford to lose workers.

Life Under the Overseer

The owners of large plantations did not work with their slaves. They hired a white or black **overseer,** or boss, to watch over the workers in the fields. When the overseer became angry or impatient, he often punished the slaves with his whip. As a slave named Solomon Northup remembered, 25 lashes was "a mere brush." Northup explained that "50 is ordinary. . . . One hundred is called severe."

▼ *Young and old field slaves, like those below and on the right, often worked 14 hours a day.*

82

The overseer organized field slaves into work crews, or gangs, of 20 to 25 men and women. During an average day on a cotton plantation, the field slaves worked 14 hours. Each slave picked about 140 pounds of cotton.

Solomon Northup described their tiring schedule after he gained his freedom. He noted that the slaves were up before dawn, and that "they are not permitted to be a moment idle until it is too dark to see, and when the moon is full, they often times labor till the middle of the night."

Women were not given time to care for their children. Often, the women strapped the babies on their backs and carried them into the fields.

Harsh Treatment

Most slaves lived in drafty, one-room cabins with dirt floors. Many times, two or more families would live together in one cabin. They slept on the ground on mattresses filled with cornhusks. Northup described his bed as "a plank 12 inches wide and 10 feet long." His

pillow was a stick. Slaves wore shabby cotton or wool clothing, which was provided by the master twice a year. They ate pork fat, molasses, and cornmeal. Sometimes they could raise vegetables. But often the food did not have important nutrients.

Most slaves worked in the fields, but a few had other jobs. House slaves cleaned, cooked, washed, sewed, and took care of children in the "big house," or plantation mansion. Their jobs were easier than working in the cotton or rice fields, but many house slaves suffered constant criticism from their watchful owners.

Some slaves were skilled craft workers. These slaves worked as blacksmiths, carpenters, weavers, and ironworkers. A few slaves worked in factories or on the docks in cities such as Charleston and Savannah. These slaves sometimes felt lucky because their work was not as hard as the work of field slaves. ■

These slave quarters on the Evergreen Plantation in Louisiana have been restored to their original condition. How do these cabins compare with Drayton Hall on page 402?

Female house slaves, like the woman at left, often became second mothers to the children of the plantation owners.

■ *How did most overseers control the slaves on large plantations?*

Southern Society

Surviving Slavery

Slaves developed a culture that helped them survive their hard lives. Congress had outlawed the slave trade from Africa after 1808, so by the 1850s, most slaves in the United States had been born here. These slaves mixed their African traditions with the culture of their slavemasters to form an African-American culture.

The Influence of Religion

Religion became an important part of their culture. The religion that most white southerners practiced promised a free and joyful life in heaven. The slaves heard the story of Moses, who led his people out of Egypt and slavery, and dreamed of the day they would be led to freedom. The slaves made their masters' religion their own. They held secret services during which they expressed their African heritage. The time and place of these meetings was communicated by code.

The Importance of Music

Christianity inspired the slaves to compose **spirituals,** religious songs expressing strong desire for a better life. One included these lines: "There's a better day a-coming, Go sound the jubilee."

The slaves also wrote songs about their daily experiences—their work, loves, and sorrows. Often these songs protested the unfairness of their lives.

A CLOSER LOOK

Slave Culture

Uprooted from their African homes, American slaves developed a culture that mixed African elements and American features. Food, fabric, music—all clearly showed the influence of cultures lost but not forgotten.

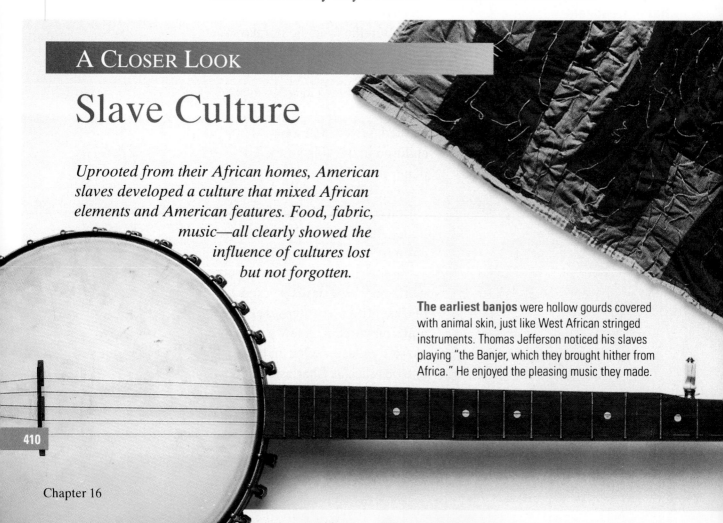

The earliest banjos were hollow gourds covered with animal skin, just like West African stringed instruments. Thomas Jefferson noticed his slaves playing "the Banjer, which they brought hither from Africa." He enjoyed the pleasing music they made.

*R*abbit in the briar patch,
Squirrel in the tree,
Wish I could go hunting
But I ain't free.

The big bee flies high,
The little bee makes the honey
The black folks make the
cotton
And the white folks get the
money.

We raise the wheat,
They give us the corn;
We bake the bread,
They give us the crust;
We sift the meal,
They give us the skin,
And that's the way
They take us in.

The pictures on these pages show how music influenced and enriched the lives of slaves. They expressed their feelings and creativity by singing, playing instruments, and dancing.

In the book *To Be a Slave*, a slave named Betty Jones told how the slaves would gather at night to dance and have fun. "Saturday nights we'd slip out the quarters and go to the woods," Jones recalled. "Was an ol' cabin 'bout five miles away from the house and us would raise all the ruckus there we wanted to." As Betty Jones remembered, music was an important part of these gatherings. "Every gal with her beau and such music! Had two fiddles, two tambourines, two banjos and two sets of bones." ■

■ *How did the spirituals help blacks survive slavery?*

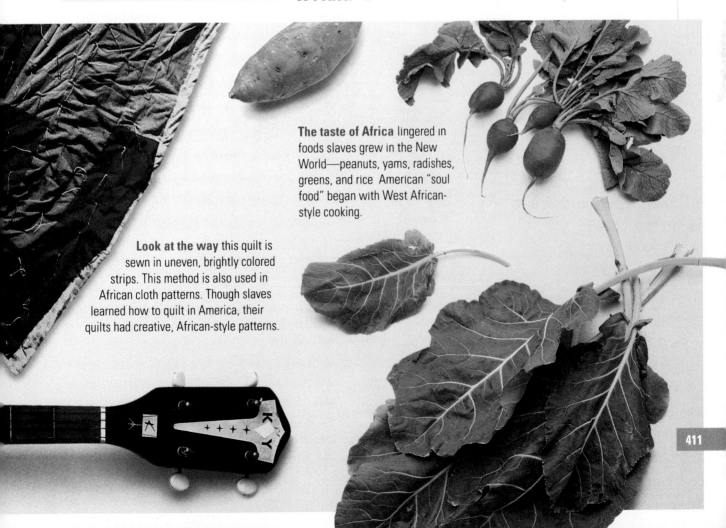

The taste of Africa lingered in foods slaves grew in the New World—peanuts, yams, radishes, greens, and rice American "soul food" began with West African-style cooking.

Look at the way this quilt is sewn in uneven, brightly colored strips. This method is also used in African cloth patterns. Though slaves learned how to quilt in America, their quilts had creative, African-style patterns.

411

Resisting Slavery

■ *How did some slaves resist slavery?*

As this poster makes clear, large amounts of money were offered to anyone who returned a runaway slave. Notice that the reward got bigger the further away the slave was caught.

Slaves learned to survive the suffering and shame of being someone else's property, but few of them were happy. They never stopped dreaming of the day when they would finally be free.

Slaves often resisted in simple ways. They pretended to be sick, or they broke farm tools needed to work the fields. House slaves often took food and liquor from their masters. One slave, Charles Ball, said he had never met a slave "who believed that he violated any rule of morality by appropriating [taking] to himself anything that belonged to his master."

Sometimes acts of resistance were quite daring. Many slaves tried to escape to freedom in the North. Trying to escape was a brave but risky act, because any slave who was caught would be severely beaten. Sometimes, a recaptured slave was even put to death as an example to other slaves.

Some slaves even attacked their masters or organized slave revolts like the one led by Nat Turner. But these revolts had little chance of succeeding. Whites usually outnumbered blacks and were always on the lookout for signs of rebellion. Slave owners would be sure to kill any slaves they caught planning a revolt.

Slave owners liked to believe that their slaves worked happily, but slave resistance proved them wrong. Solomon Northup predicted a "terrible day of vengeance," a feeling shared by all slaves who resisted their suffering at the hands of cruel slave masters. ■

$150 REWARD

RANAWAY from the subscriber, on the night of the 2d instant, a negro man, who calls himself *Henry May*, about 22 years old, 5 feet 6 or 8 inches high, ordinary color, rather chunky built, bushy head, and has it divided mostly on one side, and keeps it very nicely combed; has been raised in the house, and is a first rate dining-room servant, and was in a tavern in Louisville for 18 months. I expect he is now in Louisville trying to make his escape to a free state, (in all probability to Cincinnati, Ohio.) Perhaps he may try to get employment on a steamboat. He is a good cook, and is handy in any capacity as a house servant. Had on when he left, a dark cassinett contee, and dark striped cassinett pantaloons, new—he had other clothing. I will give $50 reward if taken in Louisvill; 100 dollars if taken one hundred miles from Louisville in this State, and 150 dollars if taken out of this State, and delivered to me, or secured in any jail so that I can get him again.   WILLIAM BURKE.
Bardstown, Ky., September 3d, 1838.

R E V I E W

1. **FOCUS** How were slaves able to survive both physically and spiritually?

2. **CONNECT** Recall how William Byrd described his duty as a slave owner. How do you think Byrd would have reacted if he had heard his slaves singing "Rabbit in the briar patch"?

3. **CULTURE** How did the slaves' family life and religious beliefs help them to live through their cruel treatment?

4. **CRITICAL THINKING** Charles Ball said that he had never met a slave who thought it was wrong to take things from a slave master. Why did slaves feel this way?

5. **WRITING ACTIVITY** Abiel Abbot and Mrs. Schoolcraft wrote descriptions of southern life. What type of description of southern life do you suppose a slave would have written? Imagine you are a slave like Josiah Henson or Charles Ball. Write a description of life in the South as you see it.

L E S S O N   3

Life in the Other South

In 1779, a twelve-year-old southern boy named Andrew Jackson and his two brothers joined the colonial army to fight for America's independence from Britain. After one of young Andrew's brothers was killed, he and his other brother were captured by British soldiers and put in prison. There, the boys caught smallpox, and Andrew's brother died. Not long after his mother won his release from prison, she also died. Andrew was an orphan at the age of 14.

He had grown up in the kind of poverty that was typical in the South. His family had shared a log cabin in the woods. Nevertheless, Andrew grew to be an adventurous and educated young man. He raced horses in Charleston, taught school in his home settlement, and started a successful law practice in Tennessee.

Before long, the young man had achieved the dream of many poor southerners. He bought a great deal of land, established a large plantation, and purchased many slaves to work it. Many years later, in 1828, this poor boy of the South was elected the seventh President of the United States.

THINKING FOCUS

Why did people who owned no slaves defend slavery?

Key Term

• sharecropper

◄ *Very few southern whites lived on plantations in big houses. For most southerners, like the family pictured here, home was a one-room log cabin in the woods.*

413

Southern Society

The People of the Other South

Across Time & Space

Before the Civil War, nearly all sharecroppers were poor white southerners. After the war, however, most sharecroppers were black. During the 1930s, black sharecroppers formed a labor union to fight for better living and working conditions.

Many white southerners shared Jackson's dream of wealth and a life of privilege. They made up the "other South"—white southerners who neither owned slaves nor lived on plantations. Three-fourths of all white southerners belonged to this other South. A few traded cotton or manufactured goods. Most lived as Andrew Jackson had, in simple cabins on small farms in the mountains or foothills.

These farmers grew a little wheat, corn, and other vegetables and owned a cow or two. If they grew any cotton at all, it was just enough for their own needs. They had no money to buy slaves, so they worked the land themselves. These southern farmers were quite poor, and their lives were hard.

Some white southerners were so poor they couldn't even afford to own their own land. Usually they rented a small area to farm and gave part of everything they grew to the land's owners. These farmers were called **sharecroppers.** Sharecroppers grew barely enough food to survive. Their lives were very different from those of the rich, independent plantation owners.

Other farmers lived on good farmland near large cotton, rice, or indigo plantations. These farmers

UNDERSTANDING LIFESTYLE

When Abiel Abbot and Mrs. Schoolcraft visited the prosperous plantations of the South, they found rich planters living lives of luxury and leisure. If they had visited other families, they would have found farmers living lives of poverty and hard work. Southern planters and poor southern farmers lived very different lifestyles.

A Way of Living

The word *lifestyle* refers to the way people live their lives. A person's lifestyle shows something about what he or she thinks and believes. It also shows something about the person's situation in life. The wealthy southern planters, for example, had time to travel, to read, to study music, and to entertain. They had the money and the freedom to choose whatever pleasures they desired. Sharecroppers, however, had few such choices. Their lifestyle was one of hard work and little leisure.

Lifestyles Today

Take a look around and you will see people living many different lifestyles. City-dwellers lead different lives than do farmers. The rich enjoy a way of life that the poor cannot afford. People living in democratic countries have freedoms that are forbidden to people living under dictators.

The way people feel about their lifestyles has sometimes affected the course of history. For example, southern planters were so committed to their lifestyle that they eventually chose to fight a bitter war against the North to protect their way of life.

earned a living by raising hogs and selling bacon and pork to local slaveowners. Most of these farmers were not poor, but the rich planters still looked down on them as just hog herders. ■

■ How did southern whites who did not own slaves make a living?

Life on Small Farms

Few free southerners were sharecroppers or hog herders. Most were small, independent farmers—frontiersmen, like Andrew Jackson, seeking a better life. Their land was not fertile enough to raise cotton, but they could grow corn and other vegetables. Other food came from the animals they hunted in the forest. In 1853, a traveler from the North named Frederick Law Olmsted described their houses: "The large majority of the dwellings were of logs, and even those of the white people were often without glass windows."

Religion gave some comfort to these poor southern farmers. Once a year they traveled to camp meetings, where thousands gathered in tents or sheds for a week of religious services. For those farmers who lived far from one another, the camp meeting became an important social occasion as well as a religious event.

Getting together at camp meetings was a special time because small farmers often moved in search of better land and more opportunity. At each new spot, their lives began again. They had to build new cabins and clear new land for their crops. They had to depend on just themselves, because they had lost touch with old friends and neighbors. Moving around made the farmers strong and independent, and they were proud of this spirit. ■

▼ *These books of Southern Methodist hymns were published in 1855.*

■ Why was an independent spirit so important to small southern farmers?

◄ *This painting shows a quilting party, a chance for southern families to get together and socialize.*

415

Southern Society

Unity in Defense of Slavery

Although most small southern farmers never owned slaves, they still defended the system of slavery. The success of Andrew Jackson helps to explain why poor whites were willing to stand up for the lifestyles of the rich southern slavemasters.

The poor knew that Jackson had once been one of them. The wealth and privilege he had achieved gave them hope, even as they worked their poor farmlands and lived in their log cabins. Perhaps one day they, too, would become rich, live on a large plantation, and own slaves.

Small farmers also defended slavery because it made them feel more important and richer than they were. In the "other South," the poorest whites lived in shacks no better than slaves' cabins, but they still thought they were better than black slaves.

In Mark Twain's novel *The Adventures of Huckleberry Finn*, Huck's father thinks that he is superior to blacks, even though he himself could not read and didn't have a job. In the speech that follows, you can sense that Huck's father feels threatened by a black man who has gained his freedom:

> *T*hey said he was a p'fessor in a college, and could talk all kinds of languages, and knowed everything. And that ain't the wust. They said he could *vote*, when he was at home. Well, that let me out. Thinks I, what is the country a'coming to?

Rich plantation owners got the support of small farmers in defending slavery because both groups hated outside interference. They especially disliked criticism from the northern states. When northerners spoke against slavery, all southern whites, rich and poor alike, felt stung by the attack. They deeply disliked what they considered the interference of the North in southern affairs. By 1860, this resentment had grown quite strong. Many southern states were now in open rebellion against the federal government. Some had even left the Union. The terrible War Between the States was just a cannon shot away. ■

■ *How did the system of slavery make poor southern whites feel important?*

R E V I E W

1. **FOCUS** Why did people who owned no slaves defend slavery?

2. **CONNECT** During the California gold rush, gold seekers dreamed of riches and power. Very few, however, realized their dreams. How was the situation of poor southern whites similar to that of the gold seekers?

3. **CULTURE** What is a camp meeting? Why were camp meetings important to southern farmers?

4. **CRITICAL THINKING** How might the South have been different if the small farmers hadn't shared the ideals of the cotton planters so closely?

5. **WRITING ACTIVITY** Imagine the year is 1840, and you are a northerner who has come to the South to visit your cousin. Your cousin's family is part of the other South described in this chapter. Write a paragraph that describes what your cousin's life is like.

Interpreting History Visually

Here's Why

Imagining what it was like to grow up during a particular historical period can give you an understanding of the people and the times. Suppose you had been the child of a plantation owner in the South before the Civil War. What if you had lived on a small farm without slaves? What would it have been like to live as a slave?

Just as you can write a report to inform others what you have learned about a topic, you also can draw a picture. In the picture you can express what you know and also what you feel.

Here's How

Paintings and works of art can help you understand how people lived in the past. They can also tell you how artists feel about the times they are portraying.

Study the details of the painting to the right. Black artist Henry Ossawa Tanner made this painting, called *The Banjo Lesson*, in 1890. The father is teaching his son to play the banjo. The bare floor and walls tell you that the family is poor. The food on the table makes you think the lesson is taking place after dinner. Note the

expressions on the faces of the father and son. How do they seem to feel about the lesson and about each other?

Try It

Plan a drawing to express some aspect of life in the South in the 1840s. Imagine being the child of a plantation owner, a slave, or a

farmer. Think carefully about what colors, figures, and actions you will use to convey your ideas. Draw a sketch.

Apply It

Work with pencil, color markers, or clay. Convey how you feel about a special moment such as when you first learned to do something.

Chapter Review

Reviewing Key Terms

abolitionist (p. 406)
cotton gin (p. 403)
overseer (p. 408)
sharecropper (p. 414)
spiritual (p. 410)

A. The following quotations express the beliefs of certain people. Write the key term that identifies each speaker.

1. "I don't own this land, I just farm it. When I sell my crops, I give some of the profits to the land owner."
2. "I'm in charge of 20 men and women. I often keep them working 14 hours a day. If they cause trouble, they better keep away from me!"
3. "No arguments will change my mind. I think slavery is absolutely wrong!"

B. Answer the questions with one or two sentences. Your answers should show that you understand the meanings of the key terms.

1. What did the sharecroppers have to share?
2. How are spirituals related to people's feelings about religion?
3. What does the cotton gin do?
4. Why did slaves probably dislike their overseers?
5. Were abolitionists upset about the treatment of plantation slaves?

Exploring Concepts

A. Copy and complete the following chart on your own paper. Compare the lifestyles of slaves, small farmers, and plantation owners. Use information from the lessons in this chapter. The first row has been done for you.

Comparing Southern Lifestyles			
	Slaves	**Small Farmers**	**Plantation Owners**
Homes	One-room cabins with dirt floors	Log cabins, often with no windows	Huge mansions with many rooms
Food			
Kinds of work			
Social life and religion			

B. The statements below are the answers to certain questions. Write the question that will make sense for each answer.

1. in palace-like houses with plenty of food
2. textile mills in New England
3. about one-fourth of free southerners
4. Nat Turner's slave revolt
5. poorly built, one-room houses; two or more families in each
6. field slaves, house slaves, craft workers, factory workers, dock workers
7. by mixing African traditions with American culture of white masters
8. in religious songs about their sorrow
9. because slaves who tried to escape were beaten severely
10. Andrew Jackson
11. comforted both slaves and poor white farmers who lived harsh lives

Reviewing Skills

1. Imagine that you are Mrs. Schoolcraft, Josiah Henson, or Andrew Jackson. Use a form of art to express something about the life of the person you have chosen.
2. Write two short journal entries. In the first entry, write about an experience in your everyday life as a young person of today. You could describe the clothes you wear for school or how you buy groceries or prepare food.

   In the second journal entry, write about a similar experience from the viewpoint of a young person who lived in the early 1800s. This person can be from either the South or the North, free or slave, wealthy or poor. Make an illustration for one of your journal entries.
3. Illustrate the differences in lifestyle on a plantation by drawing a plantation owner's house and a slave's house.
4. List five clue words or phrases that tell you when something you are reading is opinion rather than fact.
5. Suppose you want to tell about situations or events and explain what caused them to happen. You also want to tell what the result, or effect, was. For example, what changes took place in the lives of southerners because of the invention of the cotton gin? Or, what effect did Nat Turner's revolt have on slave-owners who had always trusted their slaves? Tell the device you would use to clearly show what caused a situation and what was the effect.

Using Critical Thinking

1. Some slave owners argued that slaves were better off than factory workers in the North. Imagine you are an abolitionist visiting a plantation in the South. You are talking to a wealthy planter about slavery and he gives you this argument. How would you try to convince the planter that slaves are really much worse off than northern factory workers?
2. Plantation owners grew rich selling crops. They paid little or no wages and had plenty of demand for their products. Today's business owners seldom have those advantages. Think of a business, such as a store or factory. List some problems, such as other stores selling for less or high costs for workers. Tell some ways the owner can solve the problems.

Preparing for Citizenship

1. **WRITING ACTIVITY** Write a slave narrative— a personal story by someone who lived as a slave. Imagine that your family was split up in a slave auction. Tell how you feel about being separated from your family. Describe the work you must do, either in the plantation owner's mansion or out in the cotton or rice fields. Tell about how you and other slaves live. At the end of your narrative, tell how you imagine freedom will feel someday.
2. **COLLABORATIVE LEARNING** Present an oral report with something visual as part of a project, "From Plant to Product." In groups of two or three, choose one step in cotton growing, manufacturing, or selling. Take notes and create a poster or display. Choose from one of these topics or another one: growing cotton, ginning and baling, kinds of cotton, fiber products, cottonseed products, products from cotton linters, how cotton is made into cloth, the cotton exchange.

Chapter 17

The Industrial North

As the frontier stretched to the West and plantations grew in the South, northern life also changed. In large cities new factories and businesses created new jobs. These jobs attracted people from around the nation and all over the world. This growth sometimes created problems. But the new people, businesses, and experiences also made northern cities exciting places to live.

Throughout this time, many new businesses and factories started in northern cities. The picture above shows a meat-packing plant in Cincinnati in the 1850s.

| 1750 | 1775 | 1800 |

1789

1793 Using machines like the spinning frame (above), Samuel Slater opens the first successful textile mill in the United States.

During this period, trade and travel along canals helped many businesses grow and prosper. This painting shows the Union Glass Works at Kensington, Delaware, in 1827.

1831 A steam locomotive called the DeWitt Clinton (right) travels from Albany to Schenectady in New York in under one hour.

1825

1850

1875

1842 Massachusetts passes a law stating that children under 12 years of age cannot work more than 10 hours a day.

1860

L E S S O N   1

Industrial Growth

THINKING
FOCUS

How did inventions of the late 18th and early 19th centuries change the way goods were produced and transported?

Key Terms

- Industrial Revolution
- factory

➤ *The John Bull, a locomotive built for the Camden and Amboy Railroad in New Jersey, operated between 1831 and 1866. It is now in the Smithsonian Institution.*

> T he horse was perhaps a quarter of a mile ahead when the safety valve of the engine lifted . . . The blower whistled, the steam blew off in vapory clouds, the pace increased, the passengers shouted, the engine gained on the horse, soon it lapped him . . . The race was neck and neck, nose and nose—then the engine passed the horse, and a great hurrah hailed the victory . . . But just at this time . . . the safety valve ceased to scream, and the engine for want of breath began to wheeze and pant . . . The horse gained on the machine, and passed it.
>
> John Latrobe, *The Baltimore and Ohio Railroad, Personal Recollections*

John Latrobe wrote this description of an event that occurred in 1830. During that summer, a man named Peter Cooper had invented a steam-powered locomotive. To show people that his invention worked, Cooper bragged that his locomotive could win a race against a horse. Cooper's locomotive lost. But his remarkable invention amazed America. In a few years, steam-powered locomotives would become fast enough to replace the horse-drawn cart as the quickest way to move goods over land.

Inventions for Industry

Between 1770 and 1840, many inventions, like the locomotive, changed the way people made and shipped goods. This period is called the **Industrial Revolution.**

Before 1770, most goods—such as clothing and shoes—were made by hand. At that time, most Americans lived on farms. A family member might need a shirt, for example.

So someone in the family would spin wool into thread, weave it into cloth, and sew the shirt.

Americans did not make all their own goods, however. Some things—such as glass, tools, and some cloth—were made in Britain and imported. During the mid-1700s, British inventors looked for ways to make these goods more cheaply and thus increase their sales. These inventors built many of the most important machines of the Industrial Revolution.

Some of these inventions involved new ways to make cloth. In the 1760s, James Hargreaves, an Englishman, invented the "spinning jenny," a machine that could spin 75 threads from wool at one time. Another Englishman, John Kay, invented the "flying shuttle." This device could help weave cloth hundreds of times faster than one person working by hand.

The British also developed the **factory,** a large building or group of buildings where a particular product is made. Factories had enough space to house the new machines in one location. Factories and new inventions made Great Britain one of the wealthiest and most powerful countries in the world. ■

Before the Industrial Revolution, goods like shoes were made by hand. This handmade shoe is over 250 years old.

■ How did inventions change the way people made and shipped goods?

Industry in the United States

The British tried to keep their inventions a secret. They did not allow workers, inventors, or business people to leave Britain. In 1789, however, an Englishman named Samuel Slater memorized the plans for building a textile factory. Then, disguised as a boy, he sailed to America and built the first American factory, in Pawtucket, Rhode Island.

Water from streams provided the power to run textile factories, or mills, like Slater's. The streams would turn a water wheel, which was connected to a number of belts and wheels. These belts and wheels would drive the machines. Because they needed waterpower, many of the first factories were built in New England, which has many fast rivers. In these factories workers spun thread from Southern cotton and wove it into cloth. This cloth was used to make clothing for people throughout the country.

The largest of all the New England textile mills was built in Lowell, Massachusetts, in 1813. The workers in this and many other factories were mostly unmarried young women who had been born and raised on New England farms. The chance to leave the farm and earn money excited these young women. However, working in the

▼ Slater's Mill in Pawtucket, Rhode Island, contained machinery for spinning cotton into thread. All the workers were children, ranging in age from 7 to 12.

> Women did much of the work in the early New England mills. These women used a bobbin and shuttle, like the ones pictured below, when weaving cloth on the looms.

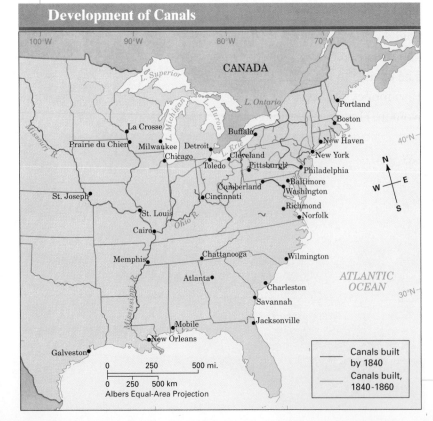

■ How did the coming of the factory system change the way young women in New England lived?

▼ The tremendous boom in canals changed the way goods were moved in the United States. By 1860, over 4,000 miles of canals crisscrossed the East.

mill wasn't easy. For a daily wage of 30 or 35 cents, New England mill girls worked 13 hours a day. They got only three half-hour breaks for meals. Lucy Larcom, who had worked at Lowell as a young girl in the 1830s, remembered: "In the sweet June weather I would lean far out of the window, and try not to hear the un-ceasing [never ending] clash of sound inside. Looking away to the hills, my whole stifled being would cry out 'Oh, that I had wings!' " ■

Changes in Transportation

By the 1820s, businessmen were building more and more factories. Farmers were growing their crops on lands that were farther and farther west. Roads were often rough and muddy. The poor roads made shipping goods by wagon slow and costly. Businessmen and farmers both needed new forms of transportation to take their products to market.

Building Canals

Americans had shipped goods on rivers throughout colonial times. However, most American rivers do not extend very far west. So people in the 19th century built canals—deep ditches filled with water and wide enough for boats. Horses walked alongside canals and pulled the boats.

The most important canal was the Erie Canal. From 1817 to 1825, workers carved the canal through 363 miles of wilderness between Al-bany and Buffalo, New York. The canal was 42 feet wide and 4 feet deep. After the Erie Canal was

Development of Canals

Canals built by 1840

Canals built, 1840-1860

completed, boats could travel from New York City through the Great Lakes and on to the West.

Canals greatly lowered the cost of shipping. Goods that once cost $100 a ton to move between Buffalo and New York now cost only $5 a ton. As a result of the Erie Canal, New York City grew rapidly and became the largest center of trade in the country.

Building Railroads

Many cities rushed to build new forms of transportation so they could compete with New York. These cities knew that they needed a link with the West if they were to grow and prosper. Some cities, such as Baltimore, tried to build canals. However, their canals were not as successful as the Erie Canal. Instead, these cities built railroads. The map at the right shows the boom in rail building in this period.

Railroads offered a number of advantages. First, trains could travel much faster than horse-drawn canal boats. Second, railroad routes were often more direct than waterways. Third, trains could travel all year, while rivers and canals often froze in the winter. By 1860, railroads had replaced canals as the largest carrier of goods.

The growth of transportation brought vast changes to the United States. Railroads and canals helped connect the different parts of the country. In 1800, for example, a trip from New York City to Pittsburgh took one week. By 1857, railroads and canals had shortened the same trip to one day. ■

Development of Railroads

| | Railroads built by 1840 |
| | Railroads built, 1840-1860 |

0 250 500 mi.
0 250 500 km
Albers Equal-Area Projection

▲ *"Rivers run only where nature pleases; railroads run wherever man pleases"* stated a St. Louis newspaper in 1867. By 1860, railroads had 30,000 miles of track, up from 73 miles in 1830.

■ *How did the development of railroads and canals change the way goods were transported across the United States?*

R E V I E W

1. **FOCUS** How did inventions of the late 18th and early 19th centuries change the way goods were produced and transported?

2. **CONNECT** Why might some New England mill owners have cooperated with southern slave owners?

3. **ECONOMICS** Why did canals save money on shipping costs?

4. **CRITICAL THINKING** How would a mill girl's life differ from life on the farm?

5. **CRITICAL THINKING** In 1830, transportation along rivers was more important than overland transportation. Today, the opposite is true. Why do you think such a change occurred?

6. **ACTIVITY** Look at the map of canals on page 424 and the map of railroads on this page. Then, list the ways goods could be transported from New York City to New Orleans.

LESSON 2

New People, New Problems

THINKING
FOCUS

What was life like for immigrants to the United States?

Key Term

- tenement

T he crossing was terrible. Three days after we had left land, we had a frightful storm, and during the night we lost the mainmast and the foremast. . . . Many of the berths on the lower deck collapsed, and water poured down through the hatchways so that coffers, trunks, sacks, and all kinds of loose objects floated around in the water and were in a great part broken against the sides of the ship because of the terribly heavy sea. That many provisions were spoilt and clothes and the like damaged by the water is easy to understand. This storm lasted two days and two nights, and during this time we had to go both hungry and thirsty, since we could not manage to prepare anything . . . [and] could not get fresh water either.

Theodore C. Blegen, *Land of Their Choice*

➤ *During the first half of the 19th century, millions of immigrants left Europe. The Irish immigrants pictured here prepare for their difficult journey from their homeland.*

EMIGRANTS ARRIVAL AT CORK.—A SCENE ON THE QUAY.

426

Chapter 17

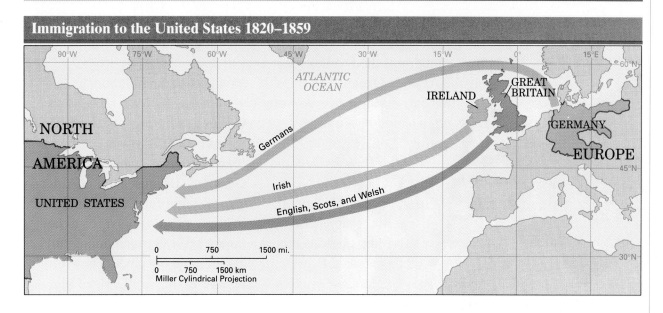

The man who wrote this letter in 1853 was an immigrant—a person who has left his or her native land and come to another country. We don't know this man's name, yet we do know that, like most other immigrants, he left his homeland and came to America to start a new life. His Atlantic crossing was probably the first of many hardships he would find as he began his life in a new country.

Immigration to the United States

From 1830 to 1850, more than 2.5 million immigrants came to America. Thousands came from England, Norway, Scotland, Sweden, and Wales. But most came from Ireland and Germany.

Irish and German immigrants came to America for different reasons. The Irish came to escape starvation. Most Germans came because they believed they could lead a better life in America than in Germany.

Immigration from Ireland

Ireland lies just west of Great Britain. Because of poor soil and harsh weather, Ireland is a hard place to farm. In the early 1800s, the Irish were particularly poor.

Most families lived almost entirely on potatoes.

In the 1840s, however, a disease attacked Ireland's potato crops. From 1847 to 1854, over one million Irish starved to death. At the time, a Roman Catholic priest called the Irish "the poorest and most wretched population that can be found in the world."

Without money or food, the Irish had little choice but to leave their homes. Between 1830 and 1860, more than one million Irish people made the difficult trip to America.

Aboard ship, the immigrants faced many horrors. Because they often could afford only the cheapest

The map above shows that from 1820 to 1859, most immigrants to the United States came from Ireland, Great Britain, and Germany. As the graph shows, few Irish emigrated in the early 1800s. Why did many more Irish leave home by 1850?

427

tickets, immigrants filled the lowest, dampest part of the ship. Many Irish immigrants died while crossing the Atlantic Ocean. The ships that carried these people were often called "swimming coffins."

After they arrived, the Irish settled first in New York, Boston, Cincinnati, and other large cities. Most had no skills other than farming. However, many Irish immigrants began to find unskilled jobs in factories. Irish women and children worked in the textile factories of New England. Some Irishmen did hard labor digging the Erie Canal and building roads and railroads.

Immigration from Germany

Unlike the Irish, most of the Germans who came to the United States before 1860 were not poor. Many had owned small farms in Germany. Because land in America was plentiful, they immigrated in hopes of starting larger, richer farms. Most German immigrants avoided the big cities. They settled instead in the farmlands of Illinois, Ohio, Pennsylvania, and Wisconsin. From 1830 to 1860, over 1.5 million Germans immigrated to America. ■

The Move to Cities

Before 1830, immigrants who came to the United States often settled in the countryside or in small towns to work on farms or in textile mills. However, after 1830, many of the newly arrived immigrants began to settle in large cities like New York, Boston, Philadelphia, and Cincinnati.

These new immigrants settled in neighborhoods with others from their homeland. Everyone shared the same customs and traditions and spoke the same language. One such neighborhood in New York City was called "Little Germany."

L ife in [Little Germany] is almost the same as in the Old Country. Butchers, bakers, druggists—are all Germans . . . The shoe-makers, tailors, barbers, physicians, grocers, and innkeepers are Germans. The residents of [Little Germany] need not even know English in order to make a living.

Albert Robbins, *Coming to America*

Many such immigrant neighborhoods were to spring up in eastern cities in the years to come. ■

Treatment of Immigrants

By the late 1700s, only five cities had more than 8,000 people. By 1860, almost a million people lived in New York City alone, partly as a result of the Erie Canal.

With such huge rises in population, cities changed dramatically. Many became overcrowded. In many ways, however, they were exciting places in which to live.

One observer wrote that New York City was the "busiest community that any man could desire to live in. In all the streets all is hurry and bustle. . . ."

Overcrowding soon became a serious problem, however. In New York, as many as four families might live in a small basement room with no heat, light, or running water.

Some landlords took advantage of people who could not afford good housing. They built **tenements,** apartment buildings with few windows and often no heat or plumbing.

In addition to poor living conditions, immigrant workers earned wages so low that they could

barely rise above their poverty. Many had been very poor in their homeland. So they were willing to work for low wages in America. This angered many native-born Americans, who feared that their own wages would be cut.

To make matters worse, native-born Americans often distrusted the new immigrants. Immigrants' ways often seemed strange and different to them. In particular, most Americans were Protestants, many of whom distrusted Catholics. Most of the Irish and many of the Germans were Catholics. Protestants were afraid that they would lose political power to these Catholic immigrants. Between 1834 and 1860, anti-Irish riots broke out in many cities. In a few places, angry rioters burned Catholic churches and schools.

Many immigrants came to the United States in search of better lives. However, once they arrived, immigrants often faced problems that neither they nor native-born Americans could solve. ∎

RESTRICT ALL **IMMIGRATION!**

PROTECT YOURSELF AND YOUR CHILDREN

AGAINST

Ruinous Labor and Business Competition

THROUGH

UNRESTRICTED IMMIGRATION.

▲ *As this pamphlet shows, many native-born Americans feared that immigrant labor might ruin American workers.*

◄ *Cities like New York, Boston, and Philadelphia all had slum districts in the mid-1800s.* Cliff Dwellers, *a painting by George Bellows, shows how crowded conditions had become by the late 1800s.*

∎ *What three conditions did immigrants face in the United States that made their lives difficult?*

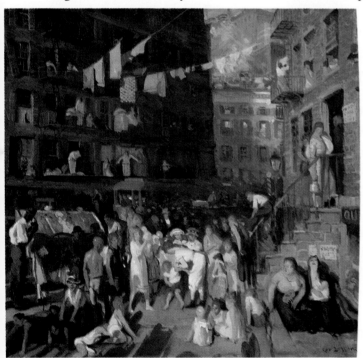

R E V I E W

1. **FOCUS** What was life like for immigrants to the United States?

2. **CONNECT** Compare and contrast the arrival of the immigrants with that of the African slaves.

3. **CRITICAL THINKING** If you could have helped Irish immigrants in 1840, what would you have done?

4. **WRITING ACTIVITY** Write a diary entry describing your first day at school as an immigrant in a big city.

L E S S O N   3

Life in Northern Cities

THINKING
F O C U S

How did cities in the North change between 1830 and 1860?

> Y*ou must button your coat tight about you, see that your shoes are secure at the heels, settle your hat firmly on your head, look up street and down street, at the self-same moment, to see what carts and carriages are upon you, and then run for your life.*

These words were written in 1837 by Dr. Asa Greene. Dr. Greene was explaining how to cross a street in New York City, which had become a crowded, noisy place. A few years before, New York and other cities had been quiet places where people could walk and talk at their leisure. But all of that had changed.

Key Terms

- walking city
- slum

A Typical American City

Let's imagine ourselves in Cincinnati, Ohio—a typical city in 1830. Cincinnati is small enough that we can walk across the whole city in one afternoon. Cincinnati in 1830 is a **walking city,** a city with no public transportation where everyone walks to work, to the store, and to visit friends.

The 25,000 people who live here are proud of their bustling downtown. On the main streets, we must step lively, for the horse-drawn carriages move quickly. The streets have no stoplights or police officers to direct traffic. As we stand on the street, we have to watch out for the mud and dust. Most streets are unpaved. No one cleans the streets, so litter lines the

roads. In addition, hogs are everywhere. A visitor to Cincinnati in the 1830s wrote:

> I *am sure I would have liked Cincinnati much better if the people had not dealt so very largely in hogs. If I determined upon a walk up Main-street, the chances were five hundred to one against my reaching the shady side without brushing by a [hog] snout fresh dripping from the kennel.*
>
> Francis Trollope,
> *Domestic Manners of the Americans*

Study A Closer Look at the Walking City to see what it was like to live in a city in 1830. ■

A Walking City

In Cincinnati during the 1830s, you'd find everything within walking distance. Strolling around town, you'd hear steam whistles from the paddle-wheel boats on the Ohio River. You'd look in the shops where they make pigskin leather or hog-bristle brushes. Every few minutes you'd be saying hello to someone you know.

More buildings go up every day, and stand proudly in their fresh paint. But look at how low they are. Elevators didn't exist yet, and nobody wanted to climb more than four flights of stairs.

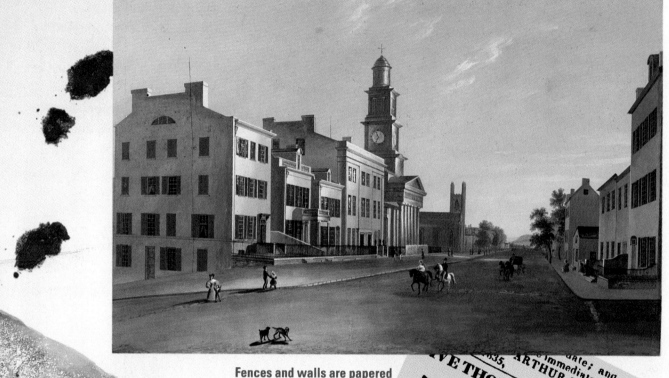

Fences and walls are papered with advertisements, and ads fill the newspaper. More jobs mean more money to spend. Cincinnati is booming!

Walk to the German neighborhood called Over the Rhine. Newcomers arrive each day, bringing their skills and customs. Can you smell the German strudel baking?

Strudel

The city is growing—and all the streets need names! Here, as everywhere, streets are being named after local pioneers and national heros. People here call one street of meat-packing houses Sausage Row.

The Changing City

If we were to have visited Cincinnati 30 years later, in 1860, we would find it greatly changed. Immigrants have flooded into the city to work in the newly built factories. The population has increased by seven times to nearly 300,000 people. Cincinnati is now the sixth largest city in the United States. It covers more than 20 square miles.

One of the changes we would notice is the public transportation. Horse-drawn omnibuses—known today as buses—and horse-drawn railroad cars carry people throughout the downtown area. For 10 cents, a person can ride across town.

Along with improvements have come problems. Cincinnati now has **slums,** places where living conditions are poor. Sewers do not work well. Slum dwellers must dump their waste from bathrooms and kitchens onto the streets. Crimes, especially riots and drunken brawls, have become common.

The problems Cincinnati faced after 1830 were typical of cities in the North. To make cities good places to live, city leaders decided to improve the services they offered their residents. ■

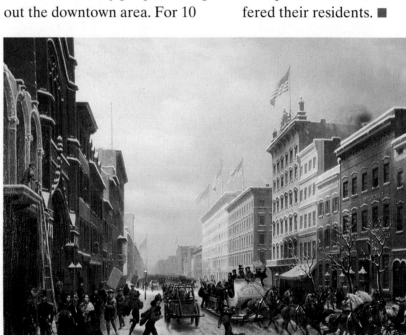

▼ Broadway and Spring Street, a painting by Hyppolite Sebron, shows a bustling New York City in 1855. New York was the largest city in the country by far. Study the graph. What was the population of New York in 1860?

Urban Population Growth, 1800–1860

■ = Boston
■ = Philadelphia
■ = New York

Population (in thousands): 900, 800, 700, 600, 500, 400, 300, 200, 100, 0

Year: 1800, 1860

■ *Name several problems resulting from sudden population growth in cities.*

New Cities, New Services

Before the 1840s, cities operated with few controls. Governments paid little attention to providing clean streets, a fresh water supply, and protection from crime and fire.

By the 1840s, however, many people understood that dirty conditions spread diseases through cities. To clean up the streets, cities built new sewer systems that carried away waste in underground tunnels. In 1849, New York City had 70 miles of underground sewers. By 1857, 158 miles of underground sewers crisscrossed the city. Even so, over three-fourths of the city still lacked good sewers.

Fresh drinking water was scarce in most big cities. Philadelphia was among the first cities to build a water system to bring in clean water. In 1845, New York City built a system that carried in water from over 40 miles away.

Many cities suffered from high crime rates. In 1844, New York City created the nation's first paid police force, with over 800 officers.

Cities also began to protect citizens against fire. Cincinnati led the way by starting a paid fire department in 1853.

Cities acted to help the poor. By 1835, New York had over 10,000 poor people. More than half were immigrants. By 1860, almost 80 percent of the very poor in the United States were immigrants. To help the poor, New Yorkers started the Association for Improving the Condition of the Poor. This group, founded in 1843, gave shelter and food. It urged governments to change housing laws. New laws and services began to improve living conditions in the changing American city. ■

Across Time & Space

In the 1980s, the government of New York City began to worry that their water supply would be inadequate for the 21st century. Since only two old tunnels carried water into the city, officials decided to build a new one.

■ *Describe three ways people in cities tried to combat problems.*

R E V I E W

1. **FOCUS** How did cities in the North change between 1830 and 1860?

2. **CONNECT** How was life in the North and Northeast generally different from life in the South?

3. **HISTORY** What steps did big cities take to fight crime in the 1840s and 1850s?

4. **CRITICAL THINKING** What problems in the cities of the 1840s are still problems in cities today?

5. **ACTIVITY** Draw two pictures contrasting an American city around 1820 and again around 1850. Think about how the city would have changed and how it would look different.

L E S S O N   4

Making a Better Society

THINKING FOCUS

How did reform movements change American society?

Key Terms

- Second Great Awakening
- utopian community
- Shaker
- reform

▼ *The Cane Ridge Meeting House was the site of an early religious revival in Kentucky.*

> I *saw two families including six or eight children burrowing in one cellar under a stable—a prey to famine [shortage of food] on the one hand and to vermin [insects] . . . on the other, with sickness adding its horrors to those of a polluted [dirty] atmosphere and a wintry [cold] temperature.*
>
> Horace Greeley, *Reflections of a Busy Life*, 1868

In the 1830s, Horace Greeley, an American newspaperman, visited the poor in New York City. He later wrote the description at left. America's cities during the 1830s were in a state of confusion, marked by crime, filth, and overcrowding. Angry and upset, people wondered where they could turn.

Some people looked to religion. Others retreated to "perfect" communities to escape the confusion. Still others tried to improve conditions throughout the country.

Awakening Religious Feelings

In the years from 1830 to 1860, America underwent massive changes. Many Americans found these changes upsetting and turned to religion for support and comfort.

In the 1830s and 1840s, thousands of Americans were influenced by a powerful religious movement known as the **Second Great Awakening.** During the Awakening, ministers urged people to think about sinfulness and salvation. Many attended "camp meetings," huge religious services often held in a tent. Thousands of people might travel for days to attend. There they would sit spellbound, day after day, to hear fiery sermons about good and evil. One man who attended a camp meeting described it in his autobiography.

*T*he noise was like the roar of Niagara. The vast sea of human beings seemed to be agitated as if by a storm. I counted seven ministers, all preaching at one time, some on stumps, others on wagons. . . . Some of the people were singing, others praying, some crying for mercy. A peculiarly strange sensation came over me. My heart beat tumultuously, my knees trembled, my lips quivered, and I felt as though I must fall to the ground.

Autobiography of James B. Finley, 1801

The traveling preachers who were part of the Awakening belonged to different Protestant churches. Yet all of them spoke of a personal struggle against sin. You could improve yourself, they argued, and you could change the world, too.

Women worked actively in the religious revival. During this time they were responsible for their family's religious life. Slowly, women brought their husbands and children into the movement.

Many religious groups formed at this time. Groups like the Bible Society urged Americans to read the Bible. All hoped to improve the country's spiritual life. ■

▲ Camp meetings such as this one from 1830 were religious revivals held outdoors. They were often attended by thousands of people.

■ What was the Second Great Awakening, and when did it occur?

Building "Perfect" Communities

During the Second Great Awakening, some people with strong religious ideas wanted to form separate communities. They believed it was possible to form a **utopian community**—a perfect village where people would live together in harmony, free from crime and poverty.

One important utopian community was formed by the United Society of Believers. This society became known as **Shakers** because many of them trembled and shook during their intense worship services. The Shakers were founded in 1784 by Ann Lee, an Englishwoman. Her followers called her Mother Ann. The Shakers are remembered today for their simple but beautiful furniture and other household goods. Shakers lived simple lives and believed that all people should work for the common

▼ This Shaker water dipper is made entirely of wood. It shows the careful attention to detail typical of all Shaker products.

435

➤ *This painting shows a utopian community at Bishop's Hill, Illinois, in 1834. The men and women are harvesting wheat.*

■ *What are utopian communities, and why did people want to form them?*

good. They lived in groups in dwellings called family houses. Men and women lived separately in different parts of the house. Shakers never married because they did not believe in having children.

More utopian communities formed in other parts of the United States. New Harmony was founded in Indiana in the 1820s. Its members tried to trade goods and services instead of paying for them with money. At Brook Farm in Massachusetts, most of the people were writers and thinkers. They believed that Americans thought too much about money and getting ahead and not enough about friendship and cooperation. ■

Changing Americans' Beliefs

For many, building a utopian community was a way of avoiding America's problems. Others wanted to **reform,** or improve, the world, not hide from it.

The Antislavery Movement

Many people believed that slavery was America's worst problem. Slavery went against America's ideal of freedom. For this reason it had to end. Abolitionists, people who wanted to end slavery, spoke and wrote of its evils. One famous abolitionist, Frederick Douglass, was born a slave. Douglass was tall and handsome, a powerful speaker and a brilliant writer. He told people

➤ *Frederick Douglass was born a slave in 1817. After escaping to the North in 1838, Douglass became a leading black abolitionist.*

436

Chapter 17

THE LIBERATOR.

VOL. I.]   WILLIAM LLOYD GARRISON AND ISAAC KNAPP, PUBLISHERS.   **[NO. 22.**

BOSTON, MASSACHUSETTS.]   OUR COUNTRY IS THE WORLD—OUR COUNTRYMEN ARE MANKIND.   [SATURDAY, MAY 28, 1831.

that a belief in slavery "brands your Christianity as a lie."

Like others who had been influenced by the Second Great Awakening, William Lloyd Garrison believed that he should work to reform the world. Garrison started *The Liberator,* a powerful antislavery newspaper, in 1831. Garrison demanded an immediate end to slavery in the United States.

Both Douglass and Garrison helped to make slavery a controversial issue in the early 19th century.

Women Fight for Their Rights

Many women took part in the abolitionist movement. Like other abolitionists, these women believed in the importance of liberty and human rights. They quickly learned, however, that most male

▲ *William Lloyd Garrison used* The Liberator *to demand that slavery be ended at once. Note how Garrison portrayed slavery in the picture over the paper's title.*

UNDERSTANDING ACTIVISM

Frederick Douglass and William Lloyd Garrison believed that slavery had to be destroyed. To reach their goal, both became activists, or people who take direct action to change society.

What Activists Do

Membership in a political party or in any group is not activism unless the member takes strong action in support of a cause. The person who works to make

lasting changes in society is an activist.

At times activists have been mistreated. For example, Garrison was once dragged through the streets of Boston by a mob.

Activists have worked hard for change throughout American history. For example, during the 1960s, civil rights activists struggled to win equal rights for blacks. Activists traveled through the South by bus on what were called

"Freedom Rides." They hoped to overturn southern laws that would not let blacks and whites sit together on buses.

Importance of Activism

Activists have always helped draw America's attention to problems. Activists in the early 1800s saw few results. Yet their actions eventually brought important changes to American society.

> *During the early 1800s, women could not attend most colleges. Later in the century, the work of women's rights activists allowed women to go to schools like the one shown here.*

abolitionists would not give political rights to women. As Elizabeth Cady Stanton, the wife of an abolitionist, said, "Many a man who advocated equality most eloquently for a Southern plantation would not tolerate it at his own fireside."

In 1830, women had few rights. They could not vote. Married women could not own property. They were not allowed to attend most colleges or hold most jobs. When one woman applied to Harvard Medical School, students of the all-male school objected. They wrote that "no woman of true delicacy" could attend lectures about the human body in the presence of men.

To fight this prejudice, Stanton and Lucretia Mott organized a meeting of women in 1848 at Seneca Falls, New York. There they wrote a declaration of independence stating that "men and women are created equal." They also demanded that women receive their rights—to go to school, to vote, to be treated equally before the law.

▲ *Sojourner Truth was born a slave in New York in 1797. She gained her freedom when New York banned slavery in 1828. For the rest of her life, she fought for rights for both blacks and women.*

■ *Name two important reform movements of the 1800s.*

Another reformer was Sojourner Truth, who worked to reform both slavery and women's inequality. In 1851, she spoke out against people who thought women were weaker than men:

> N obody ever helps me into carriages or over puddles or gives me the best place . . . and ain't I a woman? Look at my arm. I have ploughed and planted and gathered. And ain't I a woman?

Reformers worked hard to change American society. Many did not gain immediate success. But future generations, would see the results of their work. ■

REVIEW

1. **FOCUS** How did reform movements change American society?
2. **CONNECT** How were America's reform movements related to its big cities?
3. **BELIEF SYSTEMS** How did the beliefs of the Second Great Awakening contribute to the growth of reform movements and utopian communities?
4. **CRITICAL THINKING** Most utopian communities of the 1800s failed within a few years after they formed. Why do you think this happened? If a utopian community formed today, do you think it would survive?
5. **ACTIVITY** What kinds of reformers are active today? Think of people in the news. Make a chart, listing people's names and their causes.

Working Together

Here's Why

Many projects are too big for one person to do and are better completed by people working together. If a group project is to succeed, members of the group must agree on their goals and the tasks that each member should do.

Group cooperation was important to the antislavery reformers. People's lives depended on being able to trust group members. Your projects may require much less risk, but they will be easier to complete if you know how to work in a group.

Here's How

Suppose your group decides to hold a rally in favor of abolishing slavery, like the one where Sojourner Truth made her "Ain't I A Woman?" speech. Here are some things your group would need to do:

1. **Select a moderator.** The moderator's job is to make sure that everyone talks about the things that must be done.
2. **Select a scribe.** This person writes down the group's ideas and decisions.
3. **Select a timekeeper.** One person limits how long people speak, in order to keep any person or idea from taking up the whole meeting.
4. **Brainstorm.** Think of all the things that must be done to prepare for, hold, and clean up after the rally. Create a list of tasks and plan to discuss the ideas later.
5. **Agree on a plan.** Group members must agree on what needs to be done, so everyone will cooperate. When members of a group agree, that is called consensus.

By the end of the second meeting, each member should have a job. Progress reports and problems can be discussed at future meetings.

Try It

Apply steps 1–4 to another class project. What if your group were making a presentation to other classes about immigration? How would you plan it?

Apply It

Think of a project that would help your school or community. You might organize a tutoring program to help students in lower grades or a campaign to clean up litter. Then form a group and make a list of things to be done to complete the project.

Chapter Review

Reviewing Key Terms

factory (p. 423)
Industrial Revolution
   (p. 422)
reform (p. 436)
Second Great Awakening
   (p. 434)

Shaker (p. 435)
slum (p. 432)
tenement (p. 429)
utopian community (p. 435)
walking city (p. 430)

The key terms appear in the following letters between a sister and brother. The key terms are underlined. Copy the letters on your own paper and fill in the missing meanings where you see a space. The first one is done for you.

Dear Grace,

   Here I am in a <u>utopian community</u>, *a perfect village away from city problems.* I miss you but my city block became a <u>slum</u>, an area that _____. Do our parents still hope to <u>reform</u>, or _____, the world? Does Father work in the <u>factory</u>, the _____? I'm sure Mother would like to live in a <u>walking city</u> where _____.

        Your brother, Roger

Dear Roger,

   We still live in the _____ that the papers call a <u>tenement</u>. Our neighbors often discuss the <u>Industrial Revolution</u>, a time of _____. Our parents recall the <u>Second Great Awakening</u> when _____. They tell about our aunt, who was a <u>Shaker</u>. Her group _____.

        Your sister, Grace

Exploring Concepts

A. Copy this chart on your own paper. For each historical fact, list one or more reasons.

Historical Facts	Reasons
1. An Industrial Revolution took place in the United States during the 1700s and 1800s.	Increase in population and demand for goods
2. By 1860, the population of American cities had grown dramatically.	
3. In the mid-1800s, some American cities were not pleasant places.	
4. In the 1800s, Americans showed a new interest in religion, founded utopian communities, and started reform movements.	

B. Support each statement with facts and details from the chapter.

1. The American Industrial Revolution owed a great deal to people in Great Britain.
2. Girls who worked in the mills found advantages and disadvantages there.
3. After canals were built, people did not have to pay as much for goods they purchased.
4. Irish immigrants came to America just to survive; Germans came for other reasons.
5. The problems of some immigrants did not end after the difficult ocean voyage.
6. Factories and mills of the Industrial Revolution provided jobs but not always a better way of life.
7. Organizations for helping the poor were needed in American cities of the 1800s.
8. People in utopian communities had good reasons for leaving the cities.

Reviewing Skills

1. Suppose you wanted to put on a play about Frederick Douglass as a class project. Explain how you would organize classmates to complete the project.
2. Explain why it is important for a group to reach consensus. What happens when members can't agree on a goal or plan?
3. As you know, a project may require many tasks. Suggest ways the moderator and scribe can work together to assign jobs and track the progress that is made.
4. Give examples of rules a timekeeper could make to help group discussions move forward and remain orderly.
5. If your group were producing a play about a historical figure, how might it use a cluster diagram to organize the details involved? Name some main topics that your cluster would contain.
6. You've probably heard the saying, "A picture is worth a thousand words." Suppose you wanted to make a point about one of the subjects in this chapter—for example, immigration, women's rights, or the advantages and disadvantages of machines. If you wanted to get people's attention and use humor at the same time, what form of expression would you use?

Using Critical Thinking

1. Explain why you agree or disagree with this statement: Some inventions of modern times have changed American society as much as the steam engine and other inventions of the 18th and 19th centuries. Refer to at least two 20th century inventions in your explanation. Discuss the changes they caused. Then predict some inventions of the future. Tell what kinds of changes might come about as a result of those inventions.
2. Suppose a group of immigrants arrives in your community. What are some important things the new arrivals will need to learn about your way of life? How would you help them? What kinds of problems might they have as they adjust to the lifestyle of your neighborhood?

Preparing for Citizenship

1. **INTERVIEWING** Conduct an interview with someone who came from another country to live in your city. The person can be a relative, friend, or neighbor. Before you begin, have a discussion with classmates about the kinds of questions you will ask. Make a list of questions such as the following:
   What country did you come from?
   Why did you leave?
   How is this country different from your old country?
   What do you like best about this country?
   What were you most worried about when you first arrived?
2. **ARTS ACTIVITY** Create a large picture showing several means of transportation during the period studied in this chapter. You might want to attach some three-dimensional figures to part of your picture.
3. **COLLABORATIVE LEARNING** Gather articles about problems in your city, such as run-down housing, factory pollution, crowded schools, or roads in need of repair. Form groups to concentrate on one particular problem. Ask a local librarian to help you find articles about ways that problems are being solved. Share your information with classmates.

Chapter 18
A Divided Nation

As America expanded westward, people asked: Should the new territories be slave or free? That question made Americans see how different the North and South were. Many Southerners said they needed slavery. Many Northerners said they hated it. Politicians argued about slavery, and settlers fought over it. Soon people began to wonder: Can the North and the South stay together?

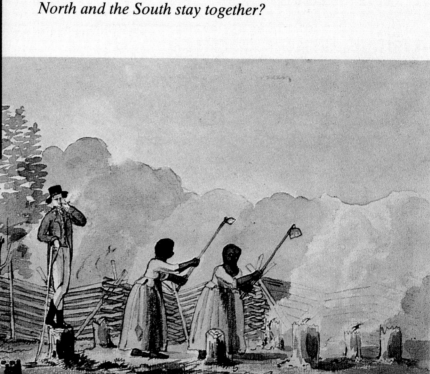

Throughout this time, more and more Americans opposed slavery. William Whipper (above), a free black, spoke out against slavery and helped runaway slaves from his home in Pennsylvania.

1750	1775	1800

1787

1790–1800 Slavery grows more important in the South with the start of a cotton boom. Most slaves work in the fields of plantations (above).

1860 Northerner Abraham Lincoln is elected President of the United States.

1861–1865 The North and the South battle in the Civil War. The photograph above shows a Northern drummer boy. The spyglass below was used by a Southern soldier.

1825

1850

1875

1818 Congress passes the Missouri Compromise. This law allows slaves in Southern territories but not in Northern territories.

1865

L E S S O N   1

Crisis and Compromise

How did Northern and Southern states resolve their differences?

Key Terms

- Union
- free state
- slave state
- secede

➤ *Slavery was an important part of the economy in Southern states. Southerners argued that slaves should be counted as part of a state's population. However, slaves did not have the rights that free men had to vote or to become citizens.*

John Quincy Adams, the Secretary of State of the United States, sat at the desk in his bedroom. He was exhausted, but he never went to bed until he had written in his diary. So, late that winter evening, Adams opened his diary in the flickering lamplight and wrote at the top of the page: *March 1, 1820.*

Earlier that day, Adams had watched President James Monroe sign a document known as the Missouri Compromise. This law allowed slavery in the new state of Missouri. Some people called it one of the most important laws ever passed by Congress, but Adams was troubled by what he had seen in the last year.

Adams had seen bitter arguments erupt in Congress. Southern congressmen wanted slavery to be allowed in Missouri. But Northern congressmen said that they would never allow it in the new state. Suddenly, the issue of slavery divided the nation.

The Missouri Compromise may have stopped the fight over slavery for a time, but Adams knew that the problem had not been solved. He wrote:

> If the Union must be dissolved, slavery is precisely the question upon which it ought to break. For the present, however, this contest is laid asleep.

The Balance of Power

The contest over slavery in the United States had begun at the Constitutional Convention in the spring of 1787. There, delegates debated and decided many issues. Slavery was one of them.

The First Compromise

The convention decided that a state's population would determine how many representatives that state could send to Congress. The Southern delegates wanted slaves counted as a part of their states' populations. Pierce Butler of South Carolina argued:

> The labor of a slave in South Carolina is as productive and valuable as that of a free man in Massachusetts. An equal representation ought to be allowed for them.

Northern delegates represented areas where few people owned slaves. They did not want them counted at all. "Why should blacks," argued a Northern delegate, "be in the rule of representation more than the cattle and horses of the North?"

The delegates put aside their differences, however, and finally agreed to a compromise. Three-fifths of the slaves in each state would be counted in deciding the number of representatives for the state. This compromise ensured that every state would accept the U.S. Constitution. It also ensured that slavery remained legal in all of the United States.

Congressional Representation of North and South, 1810–1850

= North
= South (not counting slaves)
= South (extra votes counting slaves)

At that time, most Americans thought slavery would be useful only on a few large plantations in the South. There was little conflict, then, when Congress passed the Northwest Ordinance in 1787. This law made slavery illegal in the territories north of the Ohio River.

Free States and Slave States

Over the next 30 years, these lands were settled. One by one, new states joined the **Union,** as the United States was sometimes called. The new states north of the Ohio River, where slavery was not allowed, became known as **free states.** States south of the Ohio River were called **slave states.**

In the South, agriculture—and slavery—had made some planters very wealthy. Many of these wealthy planters were elected to Congress by their states. These men, therefore, wanted to preserve the freedom of planters to buy

◄ *The U.S. Constitution gave slave-rich Southern states 20 to 30 more votes in Congress than they would have had if they counted only free, white males.*

land and slaves and to plant tobacco or cotton.

Farming was also important in free states. But the North was becoming a place of growing cities and booming industries. Merchants and manufacturers of the North produced cloth, shoes, guns, tools, and other goods. Northern Congressmen tried to pass laws that protected Northern businesses and slave-free farms.

Because the North and South were different, each side worried that the other would get more votes in Congress and pass laws harmful to its interests. It was important, therefore, to keep a balance of Northern and Southern votes in Congress. ■

■ *How were Southern and Northern states different in the 1800s?*

Conflict over the Territories

In 1819, the number of slave states and free states was equal. Southerners, however, saw signs that the balance was changing. Even with the addition of new slave states, the South was losing power in Congress. The only thing that would erase Southerners' fears of being outnumbered was the addition of a new slave state.

Southerners expected to get that state when Missouri applied for statehood in 1819. Since about one-sixth of the people living there were slaves, Southerners thought that Missouri would be admitted as a slave state.

The Fight Over Missouri

When the subject of Missouri's statehood was brought before Congress, however, Southerners were shocked. Congressman Rufus King of New York demanded that slavery not be allowed in Missouri. Any law that protected slavery, he

➤ *According to the Missouri Compromise, slavery was illegal in all territories north of 36° 30´ latitude—except Missouri. Slavery was allowed in territories south of that line.*

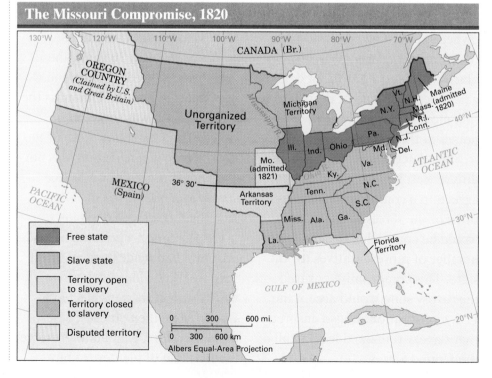

The Missouri Compromise, 1820

Free state
Slave state
Territory open to slavery
Territory closed to slavery
Disputed territory

Chapter 18

said, was "contrary to the law of nature, which is the law of God."

A huge uproar followed. Southerners complained that Congress had no right to prohibit slavery. Some Americans might not like slavery, they said, but it was protected by the Constitution.

Congress had never been so divided by an issue. Thomas Jefferson observed the discord and wrote: "This momentous question, like a fire-bell in the night, awakened and filled me with terror."

Clay's Solution

After months of arguments, no progress had been made on the Missouri issue. Finally, Speaker of the House Henry Clay decided to act. He knew that the conflict between North and South had to end if the nation was to survive.

Working behind the scenes, Clay convinced the two sides to

◄ *Representative Henry Clay of Kentucky owned slaves himself but often opposed other Southern politicians over slavery in Congress. To Clay, nothing was more important than preserving the Union.*

agree to a "Missouri Compromise." To maintain the balance of power in the Senate, Maine was admitted as a free state and Missouri joined the Union as a slave state. Free states and slave states were again equally represented in the Senate. The map on page 446 shows how Congress solved the dispute between white politicians over slavery in the territories. This compromise ended the crisis, but tensions between North and South remained. ■

■ *How did the Missouri Compromise settle the differences between free states and slave states?*

Expansion and Compromise

In the years after the Missouri Compromise, politicians kept the issue of slavery out of Congress. However, other concerns occupied the nation. In the North, industries thrived and cities grew. In the South, cotton became one of the most important and profitable crops produced in the United States. And in the west, the United States and Mexico fought a war over Texas.

Texas and California

Most Northerners opposed the Mexican War. They thought the lands gained from Mexico would

become slave states. Many Southerners supported the war for the same reason.

Texas became a slave state in 1845. Southerners reasoned that a few more slave states carved out of Mexican land would solve their problems. These new states would increase Southern power in Congress.

No new slave states came out of those lands over the next four years, however. Northern Congressmen would not upset the balance between free states and slave states—at least, not by a slave state. Southerners were furious, then,

A Divided Nation

➤ *Senator John Calhoun of South Carolina was one of the most powerful politicians of his day. His idea that a state had the right to do as it pleased gained support in the South in the 1850s.*

when California applied for statehood as a free state in 1849. The crisis had reached a new height.

Clay and Calhoun

Congress hoped to resolve the crisis in a series of debates in early 1850. Huge audiences crowded into the Capitol Building to watch some of the era's great politicians speak.

Henry Clay came out of retirement to make his speech. Once more, he asked for compromise. It was, he argued, the only way to keep the nation from splitting. "I am for staying within the Union," he said.

Senator John Calhoun claimed that a state could **secede,** or leave the Union, if it didn't agree with the rest of the

UNDERSTANDING COMPROMISE

Compromise has been useful in solving problems throughout the history of the United States. It is unlikely, for example, that the Constitution would have been able to exist without it.

Compromise in the Past

At the Constitutional Convention, delegates saw that they couldn't get everything they wanted. Each delegate gave up some of what he wanted and got some of what he wanted. The delegates recognized that the Constitution was more important than their individual needs.

Compromise is not surrender. When General Lee surrendered to General

Grant at the end of the Civil War, Lee had no choice. He gained nothing and Grant lost nothing. In a compromise, each side must give up something.

Compromise Today

In the United States, compromise is especially important. With so many people doing so many different things, no one can get everything he or she wants all the time. In order to live peacefully, everyone must compromise.

For example, a fire department needs a larger firehouse. The only place to build the firehouse is in a park. Families want to save the park for their children. A compromise

is reached when the fire department agrees to build a small firehouse on part of the park, keeping the rest open for families.

Compromise works best when both sides are equal parts of a larger group or nation. Then, each side is willing to give something up for the good of the whole group.

But if one side feels threatened by the other, compromise doesn't work. In those cases, like the United States of the 1840s, compromise doesn't solve conflicts. It delays them.

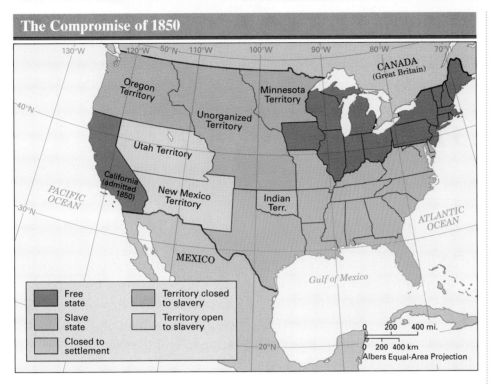

The Compromise of 1850

Free state

Slave state

Closed to settlement

Territory closed to slavery

Territory open to slavery

◀ Under the Compromise of 1850, California was admitted to the Union as a free state, and slavery was allowed in the New Mexico and Utah territories. What part of these territories lies above the 36°30′ line of the Missouri Compromise?

nation. He asked Northern Congressmen to allow slavery in the territories. If they would not, he said, they should "let the States we both represent agree to separate and part in peace."

Clay's plea for compromise eventually won. The map on this page shows how this compromise affected the issue of slavery in the territories. The compromise also strengthened the Fugitive Slave Law of 1793.

Escaping slaves had always been a problem for slave-owners, but in the 1840s, the problem grew even worse. Northerners had begun to help slaves escape. This made it almost impossible for planters to capture slaves that had run away.

The Fugitive Slave Law required Northern citizens to help catch escaped slaves. But many Northerners hated the law as much as they hated slavery. They ignored it from the time it was passed by Congress. In this way, the Fugitive Slave Law increased the tension between Northerners and Southerners. But the Compromise of 1850 did keep the two sections of the nation together. ■

Across Time & Space

In the 1800s, speeches by politicians informed, aroused, and entertained Americans. Large crowds gathered to hear the hours-long speeches of John Calhoun and Henry Clay. Today, all many Americans hear of political speeches are 5- or 10-second excerpts on TV news.

■ How did the Compromise of 1850 increase tension between free states and slave states?

REVIEW

1. **FOCUS** How did Northern and Southern states resolve their differences?

2. **CONNECT** Why was slavery important to Southerners?

3. **POLITICAL SYSTEMS** Why was it important to keep a balance between free states and slave states?

4. **CRITICAL THINKING** Compromise can be a good way to settle a dispute. However, compromise did not resolve all of the conflicts between the North and the South in the 1800s. Why didn't it work?

5. **ACTIVITY** Henry Clay and John Calhoun tried to convince people to change their minds by making speeches. Prepare a one-minute speech on the topic of slavery in the territories. Stage a debate with your classmates.

449

A Divided Nation

LESSON 2

The Growing Conflict

Key Terms

- Underground Railroad
- popular sovereignty

➤ *John Stewart Curry's portrait John Brown, shown on this page, was painted between 1938 and 1940. It hangs in the State House in Topeka, Kansas.*

John Brown was tired of the politicians' arguments. He was impatient with all the speeches about slavery. He wanted to do something about it. John Brown wanted to fight slavery like a soldier fights a war.

In 1854, that fight moved into the territory of Kansas. Congress had decided to allow the people of Kansas to choose whether theirs would be a free state or a slave state. Supporters and opponents of slavery flooded across the borders in order to influence the future of the state.

Kansas, Brown thought, was the place where the battle over slavery would be fought once and for all. In 1855, Brown and five of his sons moved to Kansas to fight slavery. Tensions between proslavery and antislavery settlers were

high. Threats of violence and murder were common. This did not discourage John Brown. As time went by, he would do almost anything to end slavery.

The Attack on Slavery

Few people felt or acted the way John Brown did. However, some Americans had always believed that slavery was wrong. In the 1680s, Pennsylvania Quakers spoke out against slavery. In the 1700s, some leaders of the

American Revolution argued that slavery did not belong in a nation where "all men are created equal." By the 1830s, more and more Americans believed that slavery should end. These people were called abolitionists.

The *Liberator*

One of these people was William Lloyd Garrison. In 1831, he started a newspaper called the *Liberator*. In its pages, Garrison demanded an immediate and total end to slavery. There could be "no Union with slaveholders," he wrote. Such statements quickly made the *Liberator* one of the most important forces in the growing antislavery movement.

In 1833, Garrison helped start the American Anti-Slavery Society. This society tried to persuade slaveowners that slavery was an evil that should be wiped out. The society did not convince many slaveowners to free their slaves. However, their speeches inspired many Northerners to join the struggle against slavery.

The Underground Railroad

Speeches were not enough for some abolitionists. Some people assisted slaves along the **Underground Railroad.** This was not a railroad or underground, but a series of secret escape routes from the South to free states and Canada. Many abolitionists acted as "conductors" and helped escaping slaves. The illustration on pages 452–453 and A Moment in Time on page 454 tell more about the Underground Railroad. The story "Carrying the Running-Aways" on pages 458–461 also tells about escaping slaves.

Frederick Douglass escaped along the Underground Railroad. Once free, he began to speak

Harriet Tubman was one of the most famous conductors on the Underground Railroad. After escaping from slavery herself, Tubman returned to the South 19 times and helped over 300 slaves escape.

out about his experiences. Over time, he became the best-known black abolitionist in the United States. Douglass fought slavery by giving lectures, publishing a newspaper, and writing his life story.

The stories of Douglass and other slaves made Northerners realize that blacks were suffering. They were people escaping from cruelty and violence.

Uncle Tom's Cabin

Harriet Beecher Stowe did more than anyone else to make the nation see the problems of

Uncle Tom's Cabin *was published in 1852. Over 3,000 copies were sold in one day when it was published. Few books have had such a strong impact on the United States.*

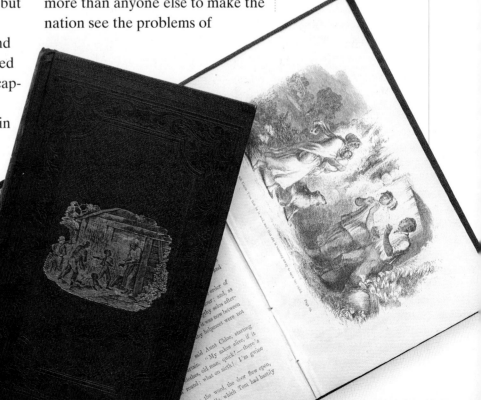

slaves. In 1851, an abolitionist magazine called the *National Era* began printing chapters of Stowe's novel called *Uncle Tom's Cabin*. The scenes of violence and brutality in Stowe's novel helped people see slavery as an evil. In this one, for example, a slave describes an encounter with his owner's son.

*T*hen he turned on me, and began striking me. I held his hand, and then he screamed and kicked and ran to his father, and told him that I was fighting him. He came in a rage, and said he'd teach me who was my master; and he tied me to a tree, and cut switches for young master, and told him he might whip me till he was tired. . . . Who made this man my master?

Each week, the story of the slaves Eliza and old Uncle Tom and the cruel boss Simon Legree

unfolded. Each week, more and more people read it. Readers wept when Uncle Tom was sold from owner to owner. They cheered as Eliza escaped across the frozen Ohio River to freedom.

Uncle Tom's Cabin was published as a book in 1852. It sold over 300,000 copies in one year. By then, nearly everyone in the country had heard about it.

The South's Response

Southerners were angered by the attacks on slavery in *Uncle Tom's Cabin* and the *Liberator.* They complained loudly that the novel's description of slavery and Southern life was wrong. It seemed to Southerners that abolitionists would attack the South, no matter what the facts were.

These attacks only created

▼ *Imagine a slave named Adam as he escapes from a plantation in Ashburn, Virginia, in May 1854. Adam rests during the day and travels at night. In the darkness he walks to the north, swims across a river, and hides in forests. He meets a conductor who feeds him and leads him to a safe house.*

➤ *Adam follows a path next to a fence, and then wades across another river. After 10 days Adam reaches the town of Oxford, Pennsylvania. There, Adam is met by an abolitionist family. They feed him, give him new clothes, and arrange to send him to safety in Canada.*

A lawn sculpture holding a lit lantern signals to Adam that it is safe to come into the house. Inside, Adam is hidden in a secret room behind a sliding panel.

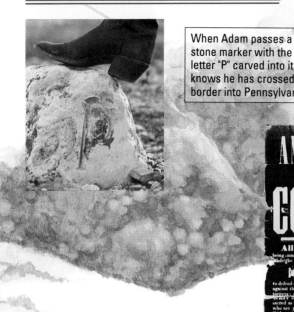

When Adam passes a stone marker with the letter "P" carved into it, he knows he has crossed the border into Pennsylvania.

ANTI-SLAVE-CATCHERS' MASS CONVENTION!

All the People of this State, who are opposed to being made SLAVES or SLAVE-CATCHERS, and to having the Free Soil of Wisconsin made the hunting-ground for *Human Kidnappers*, and all who are willing to unite in a

STATE LEAGUE,

to defend our State Sovereignty, our State Courts, and our State and National Constitutions, against the flagrant usurpations of U. S. Judges, Commissioners, and Marshals, and their Attorneys; and to maintain inviolate those great Constitutional Safeguards of Freedom—the WRIT OF HABEAS CORPUS, and the RIGHT OF TRIAL BY JURY—as old and sacred as Constitutional Liberty itself; and all who are willing to sustain the cause of those who are prosecuted, and to be prosecuted in Wisconsin, by the agents and executors of the Kidnapping Act of 1850, for the alleged crime of rescuing a human being from the hands of kidnappers, and restoring him to himself and to Freedom, are invited to meet at

YOUNGS' HALL,

IN THIS CITY.

Adam knows he has reached freedom when he sees posters for antislavery meetings.

more tensions between the two regions. Southerners stopped sending their children to Northern schools. Some Northerners stopped buying cotton from slave-holding plantations. Even the Methodist and Presbyterian churches split into Northern and Southern sections. The entire nation seemed to be splitting in two. ■

■ *Find evidence to support this statement: Abolitionism increased tensions between the North and the South.*

The Battle of Kansas

Stephen Douglas, a senator from Illinois, thought he knew how to bring the nation together again. He believed that if the people of the territories decided the issue of slavery for themselves, then the rest of the nation would not have to get involved in the problem. This idea was called **popular sovereignty** *(SAHV ur ihn tee)*.

In 1854, Douglas tested this idea. He introduced a bill organizing two new states: Kansas and Nebraska. Douglas thought his Kansas-Nebraska Act would bring the nation together, just like Henry Clay's compromises in 1820 and 1850.

Actually, the Kansas-Nebraska Act helped to pull the nation apart. Abolitionists hated the bill.

They didn't want slavery admitted into any new territory. Southerners opposed the bill because they wanted slavery to expand freely into new lands.

Most Congressmen, however, agreed that the state should decide its own fate. The Kansas-Nebraska Act became law in May 1854. The law said that elections would be held in 1855 to decide whether Kansas would be a free or a slave state. The map on page 455 shows the result this law had on the future of slavery in the territories.

Settling Kansas

Groups for and against slavery rushed into Kansas. Each side wanted to fill the state with people who would vote their way.

453

A Divided Nation

Escaping Slave

3:09 A.M., October 12, 1848
At a safe house near Baltimore

Eyes
The carpenter's eyes are accustomed to night travel. He hopes to avoid being captured by traveling at night and sleeping by day.

Back
He can still feel the scars from his master's whip after his first escape attempt.

Papers
The forged documents that he has just received say he is a free man. These papers might help if slave hunters capture him.

Feet
The journey has made his feet tired. Except for tonight's uncomfortable trip in the wagon, he has traveled on foot for the last four nights.

Stomach
The scent of coffee and fresh bread makes his hungry stomach growl. The "stationmaster" who prepared breakfast is a freed slave. He often waits up for the "passengers" that come into his "station."

Straw
Hiding for four hours in a "conductor's" hay wagon left bits of straw on his clothes. The conductor, a Maryland farmer, has transported hundreds of escaping slaves along this 20-mile stretch of the Underground Railroad.

Clothes
He is a skilled carpenter, but his clothes make him look like a field hand. Many "passengers" on the Underground Railroad wore disguises to fool slave hunters.

Tensions between the two groups of settlers grew throughout 1854. One proslavery paper invited Southerners to bring weapons and "send the scoundrels" from the North back home. A Northern minister said that rifles would be more useful than Bibles in Kansas.

Elections deciding whether Kansas would be a free state or a slave state were held in March 1855. On election day, armed men from the slave state of Missouri, called "Border Ruffians," rushed into the state and voted illegally. Every proslavery candidate in Kansas was elected with the help of "Ruffian" votes.

Bleeding Kansas

A group of antislavery settlers challenged the vote and set up a free-state capital in Lawrence, Kansas. The proslavery group set up a capital in Lecompton. Kansas was now split into two halves.

John Brown, the man who had come to Kansas to fight slavery, watched as violent bands from both sides burned crops. They destroyed buildings and threatened their opponents.

In May 1856, a proslavery group killed an antislavery settler. When John Brown heard about this, he organized a band of five men. They traveled to a proslavery settlement near a place called Pottawatomie Creek. Brown and his men dragged five of the men out of bed in the middle of the night and murdered them.

News of John Brown's massacre spread through Kansas, and the violence increased. Fighting between free-state and slave-state bands continued through the summer of 1856.

The two groups did not agree on a constitution until 1861, when Kansas was finally admitted as a free state. Douglas thought the

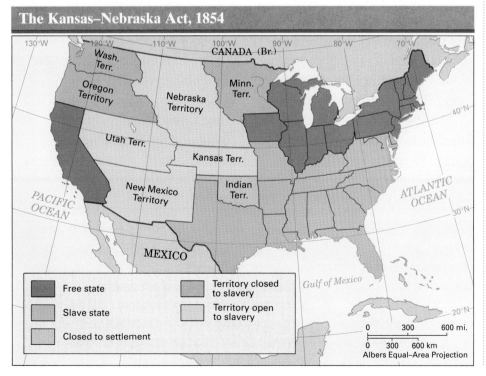

The Kansas–Nebraska Act, 1854

Free state
Slave state
Closed to settlement
Territory closed to slavery
Territory open to slavery

◄ *When Congress passed the Kansas-Nebraska Act, it meant that slavery could exist in any territory where people voted for it. This law erased the 36°30′ line of the Missouri Compromise that kept slavery out of the northern territories.*

A Divided Nation

Kansas-Nebraska Act would ease the conflicts between sections of the country. Instead, it brought civil war to the territories and created an even wider split between North and South. ■

The Geography of Politics

▼ *The Republicans' first presidential candidate was John C. Fremont. He lost the election of 1856, but won a majority of the votes in free states.*

The question of slavery had split Kansas in two. It had also begun to divide American political parties into two camps.

The Democrats were successful in all parts of the country in the late 1840s and 1850s. But now slavery divided the party.

Stephen Douglas was one of the party's leaders in the 1850s. He believed that popular sovereignty was the only way to hold the nation together.

Again, Douglas was caught between two groups. Many Southern Democrats turned to more radical candidates who would protect slavery. Many northern Democrats opposed slavery and wouldn't compromise any longer. They left the party.

In 1854, a new party—the Republican Party—was formed. It brought together abolitionists, other opponents of slavery, and former Northern Democrats. Some Republicans wanted to forbid slavery immediately. Others did not think that the United States was ready for such a sudden change. These people were willing to allow slavery where it already existed, but wanted to keep it out of the territories. This group was led by a man named Abraham Lincoln.

The tall, awkward-looking Lincoln was from Illinois. He had served a term in Congress and had spoken out against slavery throughout his career. But it was not until Lincoln joined the Republicans that he became an important political figure. His clever and forceful speeches—on slavery and other subjects—made him a leader of the new party.

Now, sectional conflicts were also political conflicts—and vice versa. The era of compromise had passed, and the split between North and South widened. ■

R E V I E W

1. **FOCUS** How did the continuing conflict between North and South affect the United States?
2. **CONNECT** In what way was the Kansas-Nebraska Act like the Missouri Compromise and the Compromise of 1850?
3. **ETHICS** How do you think the ideas of abolitionism affected the actions of people in the 1830s, 1840s, and 1850s?
4. **CRITICAL THINKING** Americans had lived with slavery for a long time before the 1850s. Why do you think reading the *Liberator* and *Uncle Tom's Cabin* made people feel so strongly about slavery?
5. **WRITING ACTIVITY** Imagine you are a slave who has escaped along the Underground Railroad to Pennsylvania. Write an account of your new life and how it differs from your life as a slave.

Asking Good Questions

Here's Why

In order to understand issues and make decisions with an informed and open mind, you need to be able to ask good questions. Listening courteously to a different viewpoint or to new information does not mean you agree with that side. It means that you are giving all points of view a fair hearing.

The ability to ask good questions is a skill used by good newspaper or television reporters. When reporters write articles about current issues, they must investigate different sides of the issue. The rule for good reporting is to always ask: Who? What? When? Where? and Why? or How?

Suppose you had to vote on the Compromise of 1850. How would you become informed about this important issue?

Here's How

The chapter presents different sides of the slavery issue. On page 446 find the question, "How were the Southern and Northern states different in the 1800s?" This is a good question because it is neutral: it helps us study both sides. The word *different* tells you to look at

both sides. Find other neutral words in the lesson that you could use in your own questions.

Here is how a reporter's five key questions could be used to compare the viewpoints of Henry Clay and John Calhoun on slavery:

Who? Henry Clay
What? He wanted states to compromise on permitting slavery in new states and territories.
When? 1850
Where? Congress
Why? He wanted the union to survive.

Who? John Calhoun
What? He wanted to allow slavery in the territories or give the states the option to leave the union.
When? 1850
Where? Congress
Why? He believed slavery was up to the people of the state or territory, not the Congress.

Try It

Imagine you are interviewing Henry Clay or John Calhoun just before the Compromise of 1850. Write two neutral questions that you could ask about the slavery issue. Tell how Clay or Calhoun might have answered.

Apply It

You are the host of a television talk show. The topic: Should parents limit the kind and amount of television children watch? To be fair to both sides of the issue, what two guests would you invite? Write two neutral questions to ask each guest.

who?
what?
when?
where?
why?
how?

Carrying the Running-Aways

Told by Virginia Hamilton

This true slave narrative about the Underground Railroad was passed down through generations in one family.

You have read about the Underground Railroad and the way it was used to help runaway slaves escape. This story is from a book of Black American folktales called The People Could Fly. *It is a true story first told by Arnold Gragston, a slave in Kentucky. This story stands for thousands of such tales of escape to the North and freedom. The man who helped the runaways was John Rankin, a Presbyterian minister who lived in Ripley, Ohio. From 1825 to 1865 more than 2,000 slaves were sheltered at Rankin's underground railroad station.*

courtin a form of dating

Never had any idea of carryin the runnin-away slaves over the river. Even though I was right there on the plantation, right by that big river, it never got in my mind to do somethin like that. But one night the woman whose house I had gone courtin to said she knew a pretty girl wanted to cross the river and would I take her. Well, I met the girl and she was awful pretty. And soon the woman was tellin me how to get across, how to go, and when to leave.

Well, I had to think about it. But each day, that girl or the woman would come around, ask me would I row the girl across the river to a place called Ripley. Well, I finally said I would. And one night I went over to the woman's house. My owner trusted me and let me come and go as I pleased, long as I didn't try to read or write anythin. For writin and readin was forbidden to slaves.

Now, I had heard about the other side of the river from the other slaves. But I thought it was just like the side where we lived on the plantation. I thought there were slaves and masters over there, too, and overseers and rawhide whips they used on us. That's why I was so scared. I thought I'd land the girl over there and some overseer didn't know us would beat us for bein out at night. They could do that, you know.

overseer a person who directed the work of the slaves
rawhide untanned cattle hide

458

Well I did it. Oh, it was a long rowin time in the cold, with me worryin. But pretty soon I see a light way up high. Then I remembered the woman told me to watch for a light. Told me to row to the light, which is what I did. And when I got to it, there were two men. They reached down and grabbed the girl. Then one of the men took me by the arm. Said, "You about hungry?" And if he hadn't been holdin me, I would of fell out of that rowboat.

Well, that was my first trip. I was scared for a long time after that. But pretty soon I got over it, as other folks asked me to take them across the river. Two and three at a time, I'd take them. I got used to making three or four trips every month.

Now it was funny. I never saw my passengers after that first girl. Because I took them on the nights when the moon was not showin, it was cloudy. And I always met them in the open or in a house with no light. So I never saw them, couldn't recognize them, and couldn't describe them. But I would say to them, "What you say?" And they would say the password. Sounded like "Menare." Seemed the word came from the Bible somewhere, but I don't know. And they would have to say that word before I took them across.

Well, there in Ripley was a man named Mr. Rankins, the rest was John, I think. He had a "station" there for escaping slaves. Ohio was a free state, I found out, so once they got across, Mr. Rankins would see to them. We went at night so we could continue back for more and to be sure no slave catchers would follow us there.

Mr. Rankins had a big light about thirty feet high up and it burned all night. It meant freedom for slaves if they could get to that bright flame.

I worked hard and almost got caught. I'd been rowing fugitives for almost four years. It was in 1863 and it was a night I carried twelve runnin-aways across the river to Mr. Rankins'. I stepped out of the boat back in Kentucky and they were after me. Don't know how they found out. But the slave catchers, didn't know them, were on my trail. I ran away from the plantation and all who I knew there. I lived in the fields and in the woods. Even in caves. Sometimes I slept up in the tree branches. Or in a hay pile. I couldn't get across the river now, it was watched so closely.

Finally, I did get across. Late one night me and my wife went. I had gone back to the plantation to get her. Mr. Rankins had him a bell by this time, along with the light. We were rowin and rowin. We could see the light and hear that bell, but it seemed we weren't gettin any closer. It took forever, it seemed.

menare a made up word

station a stop on the Underground Railroad

fugitives people who have fled

That was because we were so scared and it was so dark and we knew we could get caught and never get gone.

Well, we did get there. We pulled up there and went on to freedom. It was only a few months before all the slaves was freed.

We didn't stay on at Ripley. We went on to Detroit because I wasn't taking any chances. I have children and grandchildren now. Well, you know, the bigger ones don't care so much to hear about those times. But the little ones, well, they never get tired of hearin how their grandpa brought emancipation to loads of slaves he could touch and feel in the dark but never ever see.

emancipation to be set free

Further Reading

Brady. Jean Fritz. Brady cannot keep a secret, so his parents haven't told him they are agents for the Underground Railroad. He finds out and when his father is hurt, takes over to help with an escape.

The Drinking Gourd. Ferdinand Manjo. Tommy, sent home from church after he plays a prank, finds a runaway slave family hiding in the barn. Tommy saves the family from a search party of slave catchers.

A Gathering of Days: A New England Girl's Journal, 1830-32. Joan Blos. Catherine and her friends find a note from a fugitive slave asking for help. They leave food and a blanket where the slave will find it, thus helping someone they never meet.

To Be a Slave. Julius Lester. In the 1930s, the Federal Writers' Project interviewed ex-slaves about their experiences. Their powerful stories are presented in this stirring book.

L E S S O N   3

A House Divided

THINKING
F O C U S

Why did efforts to resolve the issue of slavery fail?

Key Terms

- secessionist
- Confederacy

➤ *Though he later won his freedom, Dred Scott spent most of his life as a slave—the property of another person.*

Throughout his long life as a slave, Dred Scott wanted freedom.

As a boy in Missouri, he knew slaves who ran away. Some of them found freedom in Northern states. Dred Scott did not run away, but he did want to be free.

When he was about 30 years old, Dred Scott was bought by John Emerson, a doctor in the U.S. Army. Scott traveled with his new owner to the free lands in Illinois and Wisconsin. They spent about four years in places that did not allow slavery. At the end of that time, Dred Scott returned to Missouri, still a slave.

When Dr. Emerson died a few years later in 1843, Dred Scott thought he might be freed. Many slaves were freed when their owners died. Dr. Emerson, however, left everything he owned—including his slaves—to his wife. For Dred Scott, there had to be a new way to find freedom.

In 1846, with the help of some abolitionists, Dred Scott sued Mrs. Emerson for his freedom. He argued that he had lived in free states for four years. That, he said, made him a free man. The case was discussed in one court after another for 11 years without a final decision. Finally, the case was brought to the U.S. Supreme Court.

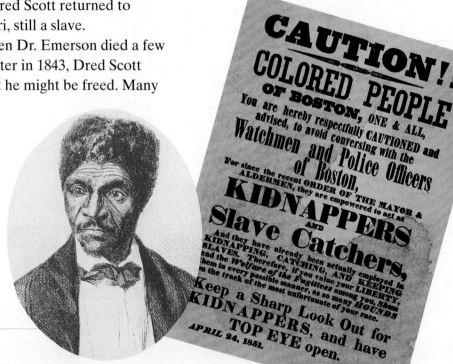

The Search for a Solution

By the time the Dred Scott case came to the Supreme Court, it was no longer just a case about one man's freedom. The entire nation looked to the court to settle the issue of slavery once and for all.

On March 6, 1857, the Supreme Court declared that Dred Scott was still a slave. Chief Justice Roger Taney, a former slaveholder, said that blacks were "beings of an inferior order" and "had no rights which white men were bound to respect." According to the court, blacks were not citizens of the United States. The court also said that Congress did not have the right to forbid slavery in U.S. territories.

In the North, reactions to the decision were violent. Frederick Douglass called the decision "a most scandalous and devilish perversion of the Constitution." Many politicians were shocked that the court no longer allowed Congress to prohibit slavery.

Stephen Douglas agreed that Congress had been wrong in forbidding slavery. He still thought popular sovereignty was the best way to resolve the question of slavery.

Abraham Lincoln, however, thought the only way to resolve the question was to keep slaves out of the territories and let slavery die

◄ *Thousands of Illinois voters came to hear the debates between Abraham Lincoln and Stephen Douglas. The rest of the nation followed these debates in newspapers.*

out in the South. People all over the nation began to learn of Lincoln's views on slavery when he challenged Stephen Douglas in the election for senator from Illinois. When he was nominated in June 1858, Lincoln told the crowd of Republicans:

> A house divided against itself cannot stand. I believe this government cannot endure, permanently half slave and half free. I do not expect the Union to be dissolved—I do not expect the house to fall—but I do expect it will cease to be divided. It will become all one thing or all the other.

In the Illinois campaign of 1858, voters learned about the candidates and their opinions though a series of seven public debates.

A Divided Nation

The two candidates traveled from town to town, discussing and arguing the greatest issue of the day: slavery.

In one debate, Douglas said that he didn't mind letting slavery go on forever. Lincoln disagreed. "I contemplate slavery as a moral, social, and political evil," he said.

Illinois voters reelected Stephen Douglas as senator in November 1858. Lincoln lost the election, but his statements on slavery in the debates made him one of the leading antislavery spokesmen in the country.

After his experiences in Kansas, John Brown still wanted to fight, not debate. Brown planned to start a slave revolt in Virginia.

He would lead an army of free blacks and escaped slaves through the South and destroy slavery once and for all. In October 1859, Brown attacked and captured a federal weapons warehouse in Harper's Ferry, Virginia. For two days he and his band fought off the U.S. Army. Finally, however, Brown was arrested. Six weeks later he was convicted of treason and hanged.

To some people, John Brown seemed to stand for the whole conflict over slavery. To some abolitionists, Brown had sacrificed his life for the cause of freedom for slaves. To Southerners, he was a dangerous man who would do anything to wipe out slavery and their way of life. ■

■ Why didn't the Dred Scott decision end the conflict over slavery?

The Election of 1860

Many Southerners believed that the presidential election of 1860 would decide the future of

The debates with Stephen Douglas in 1858 made Abraham Lincoln famous. In 1860, Lincoln was nominated as the Republican party's candidate for president.

slavery in the United States. Southern Democrats wanted a candidate who would be sure to protect slavery. They nominated John Breckinridge of Kentucky.

Northern Democrats chose Stephen Douglas. He still believed that the people of the territories should decide the issue of slavery for themselves.

Abraham Lincoln, the Republican candidate for president, knew that the two Democratic candidates might split the proslavery vote. Lincoln knew that if he could win enough votes in Northern states he had a chance to become president.

On a chilly Election Day in November, Lincoln waited for news about the election at the telegraph office in his hometown of

HANNIBAL HAMLIN. For Vice President
ABRAM LINCOLN. For President

Springfield, Illinois. Finally, the news arrived: Lincoln had won. Abraham Lincoln, the Northerner who said he hated slavery, would be the 16th President of the United States. ■

■ How did proslavery Democrats help Lincoln win the election of 1860?

The Reaction of the South

Long before Lincoln received news of his victory, Southern leaders had made plans to secede from the United States. All through the campaign, Southerners thought their worst fears were coming true. They feared that Lincoln would keep slaveholders off new land. They worried that the South would lose its political power if no new slave states were admitted. They feared that Lincoln would abolish slavery.

As much as one group of Southerners hated and feared Lincoln, they cheered when he was elected. These **secessionists,** as they were called, wanted to withdraw from the Union. They argued that a state had the right to leave the United States if the government acted against the state's interests. The secessionists believed that Lincoln's victory would convince other Southerners to join them in forming their own independent country. They

◄ A group of secessionists in South Carolina voted to take the state out of the Union in December 1860. In the next two months, six other states followed them.

were right. "People are wild," wrote one Southerner. "You might as well attempt to control a tornado as attempt to stop them."

Southern leaders didn't wait until Lincoln took office to leave

◄ By February 1861, seven Southern states had elected a president and formed a government. They had even chosen flags for their new country, shown on the left.

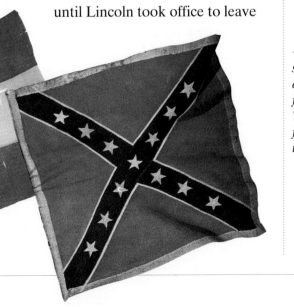

465

A Divided Nation

Secession of Southern States

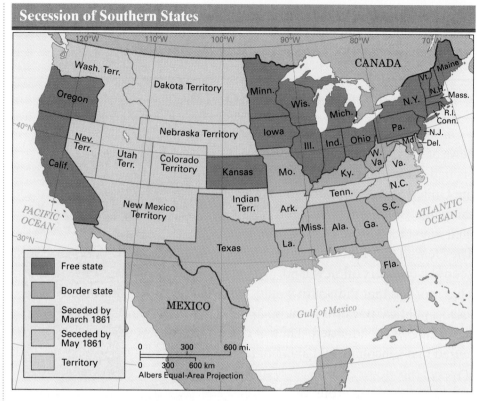

Free state

Border state

Seceded by March 1861

Seceded by May 1861

Territory

the Union. By February 1861, one month before Lincoln became president, seven Southern states had seceded. They elected a former U.S. congressman, Jefferson Davis, president of the Confederate States of America, or the **Confederacy,** as it was sometimes called. Look at the map above. Which states made up the Confederacy?

The Confederates ordered all U.S. military troops to leave the forts in their states. But Lincoln regarded those forts as U.S. property.

■ Why did Southerners leave the Union?

He refused to remove the troops. Early in April, Union ships brought supplies to Fort Sumter in Charleston, South Carolina. When the Confederate gunners saw ships flying the U.S. flag, they began firing from the shore. "Shot and shell went screaming over Sumter as if an army of devils were swooping around it," wrote one Union soldier.

On April 14 the Union troops surrendered the fort. Although no one had been killed in 33 hours of shelling, the war had begun. ■

REVIEW

1. **FOCUS** Why did efforts to resolve the question of slavery fail?

2. **CONNECT** What politician first suggested the idea of seceding from the Union? What region of the country did he represent?

3. **HISTORY** Why did the election of Abraham Lincoln frighten Southerners? Why did it also make some of them happy?

4. **CRITICAL THINKING** Speaking of slavery, Lincoln said, "It will become all one thing or all the other." Why do you think he believed that?

5. **ACTIVITY** Make a chart of the candidates for president in the election of 1860. Include the following for each: name, party, home state, beliefs or statements about slavery.

L E S S O N   4

Civil War and Freedom

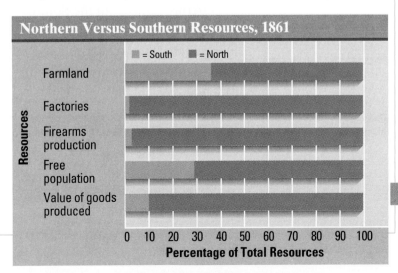

News of the war came to the Upson family of Indiana on a warm April day. "Father and I were husking out some corn," wrote 16-year-old Theodore Upson in his diary. A friend ran up to them and told them about the Confederate attack. "Rebels have fired upon and taken Fort Sumter."

They returned to the house in silence. Theodore's father "looked ten years older." Theodore's grandmother asked what the trouble was. Mr. Upson told her. "Oh, my poor children in the South!" she cried. "Oh, to think that I should have lived to see the day when brother should rise against brother."

How did the Civil War change the United States?

Key Term

- emancipation

North and South

In 1861, most Americans thought the war would not last long. Southerners thought that just one victory on the battlefield would force the Union to see that they were a separate nation now. Northerners believed one victory would convince the Confederate states to return to the Union.

Northerners thought their victory would come easily. They had many advantages over the South. Some are shown in the graph at right. In addition, the North already had a government and an army, while the South had to start

their own government and army in 1861.

The South, however, had hidden advantages. For example, many of the best officers in the

▲ *In May 1861, thousands of young men, like the one shown above, volunteered to fight. At that time, it seemed that the Union's strengths (below) ensured a quick, northern victory.*

Northern Versus Southern Resources, 1861

■ = South   ■ = North

Resources:
- Farmland
- Factories
- Firearms production
- Free population
- Value of goods produced

Percentage of Total Resources
0 10 20 30 40 50 60 70 80 90 100

467

➤ *Before the war, people said that "a lady's thimble will hold all the blood that will be shed." They were wrong. More than 600,000 men died during the war. This map shows when and where some of the important battles of the Civil War took place and how many men each side lost.*

How Do We Know?

The Civil War was the first major conflict recorded by photography, invented in the 1830s. Matthew Brady was just one of many photographers who carried heavy cameras into dangerous areas to make pictures. The thousands of images they produced help us to better understand the people who lived through, and died in, the Civil War.

■ *What advantages did the North have in fighting the Civil War?*

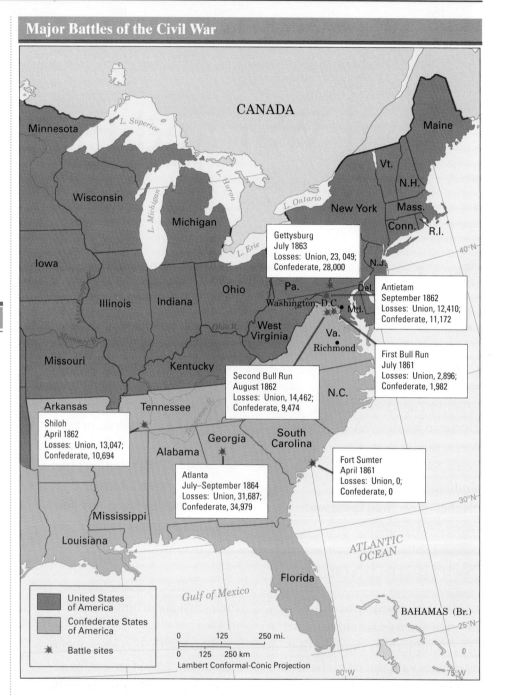

Major Battles of the Civil War

CANADA

Minnesota
L. Superior
Maine
Wisconsin
Vt.
N.H.
L. Ontario
New York
Mass.
Conn.
R.I.
Michigan
L. Erie
40°N
Iowa
Ohio
Pa.
N.J.
Indiana
Washington, D.C.
Del.
Md.
Illinois
West Virginia
Va.
Richmond
Missouri
Kentucky
N.C.
Arkansas
Tennessee
South Carolina
Alabama
Georgia
Mississippi
Louisiana
Florida
ATLANTIC OCEAN
30°N
Gulf of Mexico
BAHAMAS (Br.)
25°N
80°W
75°W

Gettysburg
July 1863
Losses: Union, 23, 049;
Confederate, 28,000

Antietam
September 1862
Losses: Union, 12,410;
Confederate, 11,172

First Bull Run
July 1861
Losses: Union, 2,896;
Confederate, 1,982

Second Bull Run
August 1862
Losses: Union, 14,462;
Confederate, 9,474

Shiloh
April 1862
Losses: Union, 13,047;
Confederate, 10,694

Atlanta
July–September 1864
Losses: Union, 31,687;
Confederate, 34,979

Fort Sumter
April 1861
Losses: Union, 0;
Confederate, 0

United States of America
Confederate States of America
✳ Battle sites

0   125   250 mi.
0   125   250 km
Lambert Conformal-Conic Projection

U.S. Army came from the South. When the war began, many of these officers joined the rebels.

These Southerners knew that the North would have to invade the South to fight the war. Soldiers tend to fight harder when they defend their own homes. Fighting on home territory thus gave the South an advantage over the North. ■

Soldiers and Citizens

The two sides only had to meet once to discover how difficult and painful the war would be. In July 1861, Union troops set out from Washington, D.C., to capture the Confederate capital at Richmond,

Virginia. They met Confederate troops at a creek called Bull Run, only 30 miles from Washington. As spectators watched the day-long battle, 5,000 men—North and South—were killed, wounded, or captured. The battle of Bull Run proved to both sides that the war would not be easily won. The battle gave the soldiers a taste of the fighting to come.

On the Battlefield

"What a medley of sounds," wrote one Civil War soldier about a battle. "The incessant roar of the rifle, the screaming of bullets, the forest on fire, men cheering, groaning, yelling, swearing, and praying!"

In most battles, soldiers stood out in the open, shooting at each other until one side pulled back. Cannonballs hit the ground and threw large chunks of sod in the air. Men fell wounded and lay for hours without medical care. After the battle, the dead lay in the field awaiting burial. The map on page 468 shows where some of these battles took place.

Confederate and Union soldiers only rarely faced the fear and

In battle soldiers loaded their rifles by hand and fired one bullet at a time. Union troops wore blue uniforms and Confederates wore grey. In the confusion of battle, it was not always possible to tell the two sides apart.

Civil War soldiers faced long hours of boredom. Here, a group of Union soldiers waits for the start of a battle.

Dinner for the Civil War soldier usually consisted of salt pork, coffee, and a biscuit called hardtack, shown below. Soldiers sometimes stole fresh food from farms near their camps.

confusion of a battle. The soldier's life was filled with endless marches, muddy camps, and bad food.

On the Home Front

As the men of the North and South survived the challenges of a soldier's life, women on the home front faced the war's trials. Many women left their homes to work in hospitals. "Nothing that I had ever heard or read had given me the faintest idea of the horrors witnessed here," wrote a young woman from Mississippi about her work with the wounded.

During the war, women in both the North and the South took on responsibilities that few women had ever had before. Women ran businesses and plantations. Some even acted as spies. However, life on the home front remained very difficult. Food and clothing were hard to find, especially in the South. Families were separated. Fathers, brothers, husbands, and sons were captured, wounded, or killed. For the women of both the North and the South, the war produced much misery and suffering. ■

■ *What challenges did the Civil War bring to soldiers on the battlefield and to women at home?*

Freedom and Victory

The war was difficult for Abraham Lincoln as well. By the end of 1862, the North seemed no closer to defeating the South. Lincoln needed a new way to attack the South. He thought maybe he could do it with laws.

Emancipation for the Slaves

Lincoln once said that a sudden end to slavery would be bad for the nation. But as the war continued, he decided to use slavery to help win the war. "What I do about slavery," he said, "I do because I believe it helps to save this Union."

On New Year's Day 1863, Lincoln called for the **emancipation,** or freeing, of the slaves in all states that did not belong to the Union. Any state that returned to the Union could keep its slaves. Lincoln's proclamation, stated that all slaves held in "any state in rebellion against the United States, shall be then, thenceforward, and forever free."

Defeat for the South

After Lincoln enacted the Emancipation Proclamation, he found a general who could lead the North to victory. Ulysses S. Grant became head of all the Union armies in March 1864.

Under Grant, the Union's advantage in men and guns led to

▼ *The Emancipation Proclamation, shown below, helped the Union win the war. About 200,000 black soldiers fought for the Union during the Civil War. Many of them were former slaves made "forever free" by the proclamation.*

470

victory. The North had more men than the South. Even the bloodiest battles could be counted as victories for the Union army.

Large parts of the South were destroyed by victorious Union armies. "There was hardly a fence left standing," wrote one woman from Georgia. "The fields were trampled down and the road was lined with carcasses [dead bodies] of horses, hogs, and cattle."

In April 1865, General Grant reached Richmond, Virginia, the Confederate capital. As Union troops marched into Richmond,

the Confederate general, Robert E. Lee, surrendered to Grant at a place called Appomattox Court-house, Virginia. The four-year civil war was finally over. The Union was preserved.

By the end of 1865, the Union was also entirely slave-free. In December, 27 states ratified the 13th Amendment to the Constitution. It stated: "Neither slavery nor involuntary servitude . . . shall exist in the United States." The question that divided the United States for 90 years was now, according to the law, resolved. ■

Defeat during the Civil War left large parts of the South in ruins. Here, rubble is all that remains of this part of Richmond.

■ *How did the Civil War resolve the conflict over slavery in the United States?*

R E V I E W

1. **FOCUS** How did the Civil War change the United States?

2. **CONNECT** President Lincoln once believed that the country wasn't ready for a sudden end to slavery. What made him change his mind?

3. **SOCIAL SYSTEMS** How would the life of a slave living in Virginia have changed in the period from 1861 to 1865?

4. **CRITICAL THINKING** If you were a ten-year-old living in 1862, how do you think your life would have changed in the last year?

5. **WRITING ACTIVITY** Read the article on Abraham Lincoln's Gettysburg Address in the Minipedia at the back of this book. Imagine you heard Lincoln give that speech. Write a short letter to a friend telling him what you heard and saw.

A Divided Nation

Early Photography

A Frenchman named Joseph Nicéphore took the first true photograph in 1826. During the Civil War, photographs became a way to store personal and national memories. Ever since, pictures have changed our lives and become part of them.

The photographer poses his client for a portrait in the 1800s.

Get Ready

Find a current magazine with many kinds of photographs. Keep the magazine open next to these pages in your textbook. All of the photographs below are from the 1800s. Use a notebook to write down what you observe about the historic prints and the current ones you found.

Find Out

Study both sets of photographs—the ones on these pages and the ones in your magazine. Notice the lighting, the backgrounds, and the people's poses. Make a list of questions to answer about each photograph. Did the

Only two of these early cameras exist in the United States. This one dates from 1839.

people in the picture know they were being photographed? Why do you think the picture was taken? Can you tell what time of day it was?

Compare your answers about the 1800s photographs to your answers about the current ones. Make a list of the differences you observed.

Move Ahead

Make a combined list of questions you and your classmates answered. Did most of you agree about the differences between historic photos and current ones?

Why are the older pictures different from the current ones? Check your school or classroom reference books to find out how you would have had your picture taken in the 1870s. How long would you have had to sit still? Ask a volunteer to sit or stand for that amount of time. What position does the person choose? What happens to his or her facial expression?

Explore Some More

To learn more about current photography, study newspaper photographs for a week. Make

a scrapbook of the pictures that you find that could not have been taken 100 years ago. Next to each picture, note the reason. You will find night scenes, action shots, candid photos of people caught unaware and beautiful color scenes.

If you also look at family or school pictures, you will see how we have come to depend on film to record our history.

Dorothy J. Rainey and her seven daughters pose rigidly for a group portrait.

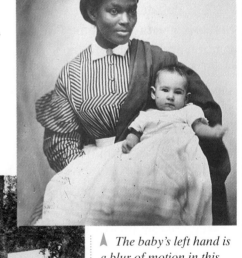

The baby's left hand is a blur of motion in this early photo of a baby girl and her nursemaid.

◄ *This picture was taken outside a traveling darkroom.*

Chapter Review

Reviewing Key Terms

Confederacy (p. 466)
emancipation (p. 470)
free state (p. 445)
popular sovereignty (p. 453)
secede (p. 448)

secessionist (p. 465)
slave state (p. 445)
Underground Railroad (p. 451)
Union (p. 445)

A. The two words in each pair are related in some way. On your own paper, write a sentence explaining how the words are related.

1. Union, Confederacy
2. free state, slave state
3. Underground Railroad, free state
4. Confederacy, secede
5. emancipation, Union
6. secessionist, secede

B. Some of the following statements are true. The rest are false. Write *True* or *False* for each statement. Then rewrite the false statements to make them true.

1. Popular sovereignty was an election in new territories to fill public offices.
2. Thousands of slaves escaped to freedom through the secret route to the North called the Underground Railroad.
3. The emancipation of the slaves refers to their journey to America on slave ships.
4. Secessionists cheered when Lincoln was elected because they believed he would keep the Union together.

Exploring Concepts

A. The debate over slavery in the United States began in 1787 at the Philadelphia Convention and lasted until 1865. The U.S. government made the following decisions regarding slavery. Copy the decisions. For each one, write an explanation of what was decided. The first one has been done for you.

1. Three-fifths Compromise
   Three-fifths of the slaves would be counted in a state's population when representation in Congress was decided. This meant that slavery remained legal in the United States.
2. Northwest Ordinance
3. Missouri Compromise
4. Compromise of 1850
5. Kansas-Nebraska Act
6. Dred Scott Decision
7. Emancipation Proclamation
8. Thirteenth Amendment

B. Answer each question with information from the chapter.

1. What three compromises did the North and the South make to keep the nation together?
2. Why did the North and the South want to avoid being outnumbered in Congress?
3. What caused John Brown to go to Kansas in 1855? How was his protest against slavery different from those before him?
4. Were Northerners pleased or angry about the Dred Scott decision? Why?
5. What stand on slavery did Lincoln take during the Lincoln-Douglas debates?
6. Why were Northerners and Southerners each convinced they would win the war?
7. What was the Emancipation Proclamation? What effect did it have on the South?
8. What was the abolitionists' goal? Was it ever achieved? If so, when?

Reviewing Skills

1. Imagine that you are a member of a state legislature considering Amendment 26 on allowing 18-year-olds to vote. What questions would you ask to decide how to vote on this question?
2. What neutral questions would you ask the following people to learn about the effects of the Dred Scott decision: Dred Scott, Abraham Lincoln, and Chief Justice Roger Taney?
3. Between 1787 and 1857, the government made several important decisions about slavery. Look back in the chapter for the dates. Make a timeline that shows the following decisions.
   a. Three-fifths Compromise
   b. Kansas-Nebraska Act
   c. Dred Scott Decision
   d. Missouri Compromise
   e. Emancipation Proclamation
4. Suppose your group is assigned to make a report on two to three events leading up to the Civil War. What steps should the group take to work together to plan the report?

Using Critical Thinking

1. Making compromises kept North and South together for years. Think of a problem, one in your town, at school, or among friends, that could be solved by each side compromising. How might the compromise work?
2. Senator John Calhoun believed that a state could secede from the Union if the state did not agree with the rest of the nation. Do you think that Senator Calhoun's policy would work in our country today? Why or why not? Describe what you think would happen.
3. Find the information about Lincoln's Gettysburg Address on page 556 of the Minipedia. Read the address on the lower right. What do you think Lincoln meant when he referred to the "new birth of freedom"? What do you think Lincoln meant when he talked of government "of the people, by the people, and for the people"?

Preparing for Citizenship

1. **WRITING ACTIVITY** Get more information about the 1858 Lincoln-Douglas debates. Then write a newspaper article in which you report the debates. Be sure to report both sides of the issues.
2. **ARTS ACTIVITY** With a partner, plan and draw two political cartoons that capture people's reactions to President Lincoln's election. In one cartoon, show the feelings of Southerners. In the other, show the reaction of Northerners.
3. **GROUP ACTIVITY** *The Liberator* and abolitionist pamphlets helped to build support for the antislavery movement. Plan and write a pamphlet about a present-day issue. Inform your readers about the issue. Then arouse support for your position. Distribute your pamphlet to other classes.
4. **COLLABORATIVE LEARNING** During the 1800s, Frederick Douglass was the best-known black abolitionist in the United States. During the 1950s and 1960s, Dr. Martin Luther King, Jr., led the civil rights movement in the United States. Form groups to study each leader. Assign some members to study the leader's life and report their findings to the group. Other members use the findings to write a brief play showing what the leader achieved. The remaining members perform the play for the class.

Finding
America's Future

In the late 1800s, the United States became bigger, richer, and more powerful than it had ever been before. People looked to the future with high hopes. But many problems remained. The Civil War had ended slavery, but few black Americans felt free or equal. Women lacked many of the rights men had. Life for immigrants could be terribly hard. Many of these people believed that solving those problems would make America even greater.

1848

Frédéric Auguste Bartholdi, Liberty Enlightening the World, 1884. New York Harbor, New York. Photo from Image Bank.

Today

Chapter 19
Life in a Changing America

A new America emerged after the Civil War. More and more people moved from farms to large cities. Other recent arrivals, the immigrants, crowded into the poorest neighborhoods of the cities. Huge new factories provided plenty of jobs—and earned millions of dollars for business leaders. Even people who felt that things were changing for the worse worked to improve their lives in the new America.

Throughout this time, the steel industry became one of the biggest businesses in America. The photograph above shows a Pittsburgh steel mill in the 1880s.

| 1860 | 1870 | 1880 | 1890 |

1860

1870–1880 Millions of immigrants arrive in America. Many brought along treasured items, like pictures of relatives (above) and traditional clothing (right).

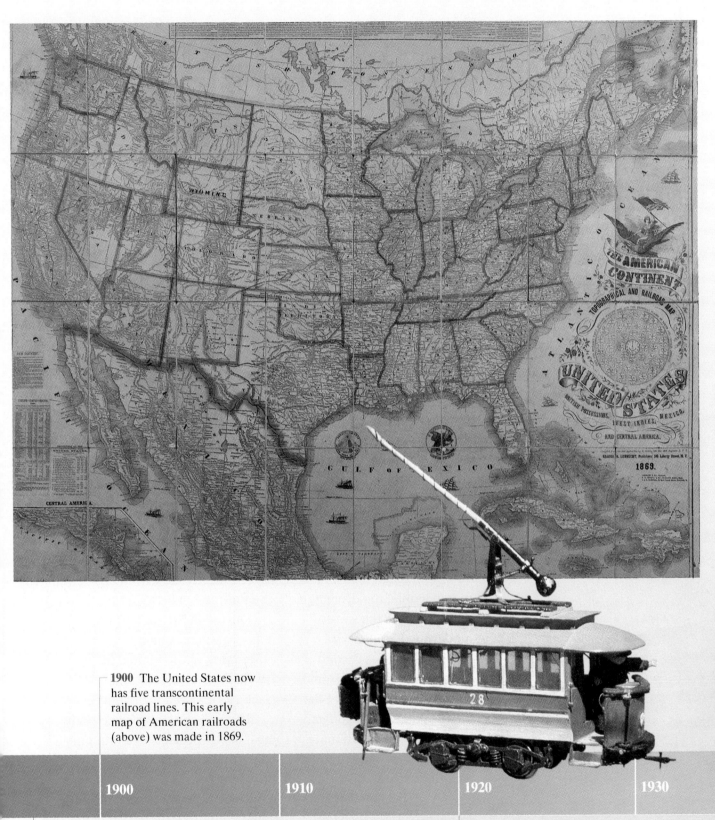

1900 The United States now has five transcontinental railroad lines. This early map of American railroads (above) was made in 1869.

1900	1910	1920	1930

1896 Charles and J. Frank Duryea build 13 gas-powered automobiles, starting the U.S. auto industry.

1890–1920 Electric trolleys replace horse-drawn streetcars in many American cities. A model of one of these new trolleys is shown above.

1914

LESSON 1

Entering the Modern Age

THINKING FOCUS

How did the rapid growth of industry affect the lives of working men and women in the United States?

Key Terms

- mechanization
- labor union
- strike

▼ *Railroads are the subject of this quilt made in 1884.*

Puffing and snorting, two black locomotives stood face to face at Promontory Point, Utah. It was a clear, cool morning in May 1869. Dozens of railroad workers stood on top of the engines. Some of them milled about on the ground. They all watched Leland Stanford get ready for the big moment.

As president of the Central Pacific Railroad, Stanford would hammer a golden spike into a special silver-banded railroad tie. That spike would complete the first railroad to stretch from the Atlantic Ocean to the Pacific Ocean.

A telegraph operator tapped out a description of the event. "Hats off! Prayer is being offered." The news traveled across telegraph wires to the rest of the nation. "We have got done praying. The spike is about to be presented."

Stanford stepped forward and drove the spike into the tie. "One, two, three—done!" tapped the telegraph operator. Across the country cannons boomed, bells rang, and parades began in celebration of the grand event.

Changes in a New Age

To many people, the driving of the golden spike was the start of a new, modern age in America. Telegraph lines carried news to and from every corner of the country. Huge factories produced materials for growing industries and cities. And, perhaps most important, railroads banded the entire nation together.

The Railroad Industry

During the 1870s and 1880s, many companies built railroads in other parts of the United States. By 1880, over 115,000 miles of track crisscrossed the country.

This rail system was one of the most costly projects ever attempted in the United States. But both private investors and the government saw how important railroads could be. People, goods, and mail would move across the nation faster than ever before on trains.

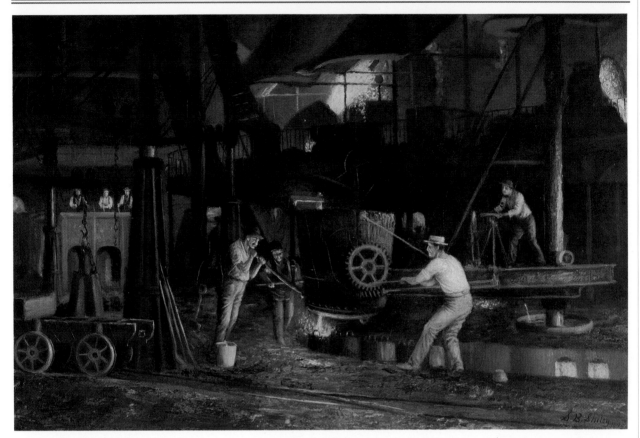

Congress gave land, and investors spent millions of dollars to build the railroads.

Once they were completed, the railroads were expensive to run. They used more machinery and employed more people than any business in America ever had. They also made more money than any American business had before. Railroads were the first big business in the United States.

The success of the railroads helped other industries to succeed as well. The steel industry, for example, was completely changed by the railroads.

The Steel Industry

The railroads needed huge amounts of steel for tracks and other equipment. This need caused the steel industry to grow as never before. Soon, steel was being made more quickly and cheaply than ever.

Steel mills were built along the railroad lines where raw materials, such as iron ore and coal, could be brought by trains. Finished steel rails were also sent by train to wherever new railroads were being built. Other steel products—wire, needles, screws, nails, pots, and pans—were shipped by train to stores throughout the country.

Carnegie's Industry

As industries grew, owners of companies looked for more profitable ways to run their businesses. Sometimes this meant having the lowest prices. Sometimes it meant paying employees the lowest wages. In the case of Andrew Carnegie, it meant controlling an entire industry.

The steel industry made men like Andrew Carnegie rich. Life for the factory workers, however, was dangerous and difficult.

Life in a Changing America

Andrew Carnegie was a Scottish immigrant. His first job was as a bobbin boy in a cotton factory. Over the next 20 years, Carnegie worked in many jobs, always climbing higher. His drive, ambition, and desire for wealth led him to become the head of a steel company. Those qualities also led him to change the steel industry.

Carnegie wanted to control every part of the steel-making process. First he bought iron and coal mines. Then he bought huge steel mills. Finally, he purchased railroads and steamships. In this way

■ *Why were railroads important to the economy of the United States in the late 1800s?*

Carnegie controlled everything—the raw materials, factories, and transportation—needed to make steel.

Carnegie was able to sell his steel at lower prices than other companies. Soon, he began to drive other mill owners out of business. By the time he retired, Carnegie controlled most of the steel production in the country.

Some of the leaders in other industries followed Carnegie's example. In time, many of them became as rich and powerful as Carnegie. ■

UNDERSTANDING MECHANIZATION

*I*n the 1870s, machines were doing many jobs that people used to do. Once workers had been paid well to do skilled jobs. Suddenly, they were paid poorly to do simple, boring tasks. They experienced firsthand one of the problems connected with **mechanization**—the use of machines to do work.

Changes on the Farm

Mechanization did help some people. In the early 1800s, wheat was harvested by hand. A farmer walked up and down the rows of wheat swinging a long, curved blade to cut the wheat. In the 1830s, Cyrus H. McCormick invented a mechanical reaper.

This mechanical reaper made the farmer's job much easier. It also meant that fewer workers were required to harvest wheat.

Changes in Factories

Mechanization allowed people to produce more goods. It kept prices for goods down and it created jobs for people to produce and service the machines.

With mechanization, however, came many problems for factory workers. For example, a woman working on an

assembly line repeated one simple job again and again. Workers once felt the satisfaction of creating a tool or a toy themselves. But in mechanized factories, workers came to feel like replaceable parts of a large machine.

Factory workers worked long hours. They earned low wages. They performed boring jobs in unsafe conditions. Workers who are bored and badly treated rarely do good work. They may begin to think about ways to get better wages and working conditions.

Mechanization helped workers produce more goods. But it also created problems of boredom and dissatisfaction for workers.

◄ *In the late 1800s and early 1900s, children often worked as long and hard as adults. These boys worked at a coal mine in Pennsylvania in 1911.*

Working in a New Age

The lives of factory workers were also changed by the growth of industry. But few people thought the change was for the better.

Men, women, and many children worked 10 hours a day, six days a week. They were usually paid less than $10 each week. The process of mechanization led factory owners to use machines for jobs that people had once done. This meant that most of the jobs that people did in factories were boring and dangerous. One worker said that he was treated "like any piece of machinery."

These poor conditions made factory workers angry. It seemed unfair that a few bosses had so much control over so many workers. As their anger increased, workers began to organize **labor unions.**

These organizations de-manded better conditions and higher pay from a company. If the company refused, workers would **strike,** or refuse to work until they got what they wanted.

A Fight for Change

Sometimes these strikes became violent. The clash between the owner and workers of the Pullman Palace Car Company of Chicago is one of the most famous.

In 1894, the Pullman Company, which made railway cars, decided to cut the wages of their workers

▼ *Labor unions organized workers into groups that could stand up against powerful factory owners. This poster invited workers to a meeting in Chicago on May 4, 1886.*

Attention Workingmen!
GREAT
MASS-MEETING
NIGHT, at 7.30 o'clock,

➤ *Unions won higher wages and better working conditions for many different people—from carpenters to garment workers (right).*

■ *What did the labor unions hope to do for workers?*

by 25 percent. Workers protested by calling a strike.

News of the strike spread through the nation. President Grover Cleveland ordered U.S. soldiers to Chicago to end the strike. In July 1894, soldiers and armed guards hired by the Pullman Company clashed with striking workers. Dozens of workers were killed and over $300,000 of railroad property was destroyed.

Workers finally ended the strike. They did not get anything they had asked for. But the strike showed the nation the problems of workers.

A Change for the Better

Between 1881 and 1905, more than 6 million workers took part in over 36,000 strikes in the United States. Slowly, unions began to win victories for workers. By 1914, for example, every state but one had a law that prevented children under 12 from working.

Labor unions remain an important force in American life today. They continue to seek better conditions for workers in every state. ■

R E V I E W

1. **FOCUS** How did the rapid growth of industry affect the lives of working men and women in the United States?

2. **CONNECT** How did railroads influence the growth of industry? How did they make transportation of products easier and faster than before 1860?

3. **ECONOMICS** Why did workers in the late 1800s form labor unions and organize strikes?

4. **CRITICAL THINKING** Why do you think that some strikes became violent?

5. **WRITING ACTIVITY** Many people in the late 1800s worked 10 hours a day, six days a week, in a factory. Write two journal entries as if you were a factory worker who lived at that time.

Making Location Decisions

Here's Why

You may have passed by a new building and wondered why it was built where it was. Maps can help you figure out why. For example, suppose you wanted to know why so many steel mills were built around Gary, Indiana. The map below can help you figure this out.

Here's How

Symbols on a map give information about places. Maps can help you figure out why activities happen in certain locations.

Look at the map of the steel industry in the Great Lakes area around 1900. The symbols stand for coal and iron ore. They show where to find these raw materials for making steel. The coal fueled the furnaces needed to melt the iron ore before making steel products.

Notice the coal deposits near Gary, Indiana. Then look at the railroad lines that meet in Gary. Coal from these deposits could easily be sent by rail to Gary's steel mills. As the mills made more steel rails and rail cars, the railroads carried more coal and iron ore to the steel mills.

Now find Duluth, Minnesota. Iron ore from the mines in Minnesota could be loaded on ships at Duluth.

Trace the route of the ore across Lakes Superior and Michigan to the ports of Gary and Chicago. Iron ore and coal could be shipped either by water or rail to the steel mills near the cities. Cities provide people to work in the mills.

Try It

Look at the map again. What cities other than Gary and Chicago would be good sites for steel mills? Where would the materials come from? How could they be transported?

Apply It

What factors would help a city sports arena be successful? Write a paragraph explaining your answer.

Steel Industry in the Great Lakes Region, 1890-1920

LESSON 2

Coming to America

*I*t was not a pleasure trip, that 14-day journey aboard ship. Crammed into a dark, stuffy cabin with four other people, we spent the nights on sheetless bunks and most of the days standing in line for food that was ladled out to us as though we were cattle. Mother, Sheyna, and Zipke were seasick most of the time, but I felt well and can remember staring at the sea for hours wondering what Milwaukee would be like.

THINKING FOCUS

What were the lives of immigrants like in the United States between 1870 and 1914?

Key Term

- racism
- nativism

➤ *This Italian mother and her children arrived in the United States with all their belongings in two clumsy bundles. Each of them was given a landing pass (shown below).*

Golda Meir, who later became the prime minister of Israel, wrote these words about her journey to America in 1906. She and her mother and two sisters traveled by ship from Russia to New York. From there they continued to Milwaukee, where they joined her father.

It took courage for Meir's family to leave everything they knew and move to a new country. "Going to America then was almost like going to the moon," Meir remembered. But thousands of others dared to do what Meir's family did. Between 1860 and 1914, about 25 million immigrants made the voyage to America.

Red Star Line
Landing Card

MAJESTIC No.

Manifest Sheet No.

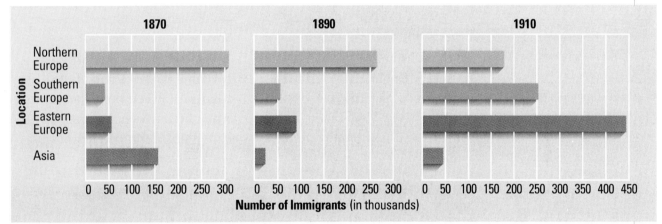

Immigrants in the United States

The immigrants who came to the United States after the Civil War were different from those who came earlier. Early immigrants had come only from Great Britain, Germany, and other countries of northern Europe. Many had moved from overcrowded European cities in search of a better living. Many of these immigrants already spoke English or learned it quickly. They settled on farms or in cities and lived much as their American neighbors did.

A New Wave of Immigrants

After 1910, however, most immigrants came from eastern and southern Europe. These people escaped from economic hardships and political problems in their home countries. The map and graphs on this page show where these immigrants came from. Many

▲ *This map shows where most immigrants to the United States came from. The graphs show how many immigrants arrived from different parts of the world between 1870 and 1910.*

487

Life in a Changing America

of these people could not speak English. Most were unskilled workers who wanted jobs in American factories. Look at the article on page 557 of the Minipedia to learn more about these new immigrants.

Some European immigrants had relatives and friends who had already settled in America. They sometimes sent money home for the boat trip. They offered to help friends from their villages find housing and jobs in America.

To unskilled European workers struggling to support their families, America promised plenty of jobs. In Eastern Europe, Jews were often persecuted for their religion. To them, America offered the promise of a place where all religions would be allowed.

With these hopes and plans, millions left their homes, families, and friends. They set off for America with their small savings and their most precious possessions—things like family portraits, an ancestor's wedding ring, and a grandmother's silver candlesticks.

A New Home for Immigrants

Immigrants faced many hardships when they arrived in America. Many were too poor to leave the crowded tenements of port cities like New York or Boston. Others traveled to cities where family members or friends lived. They settled in neighborhoods with other people from their home countries. Soon, many American cities had Jewish, Italian, Polish, and other ethnic neighborhoods.

Life in these neighborhoods gave immigrants some of the comforts of their home lands. Anna Fodorovich, a Russian immigrant, described her neighborhood in Pittsburgh.

▲ *Immigrants often brought items from their homeland with them to America. These painted Easter eggs, for example, came from Russia.*

Across Time & Space

A hundred years ago, most immigrants to the United States came from Europe. Today, about one-third of all immigrants come from Mexico. Like European immigrants, many Mexicans cross the border looking for better jobs and a better life. Another large group of immigrants comes from Asian countries such as China, the Philippines, Korea, and Vietnam.

➤ *This photograph of a New York neighborhood is from the early 1900s. A Jewish shopkeeper advertises with signs printed in Hebrew.*

488

The Russian Church was in the Hill District then. So every Sunday morning my brother would take me and we would walk over the bridge to church. . . . And there were all kinds of Russian stores. So, we bought herring and black bread and we got together. That's how we met people.

Nicolette DiLucente told how her neighborhood celebrated an Italian saint's day. "All the people were from the same town," she said. "We decorated the whole street, made special foods, and we celebrated."

Immigrant neighborhoods were often run down and over-crowded. But they were also filled with familiar languages, customs,

and foods of the old country. These ethnic neighborhoods helped make the immigrants' new land seem a little less strange. To learn more about the lives of immigrants look at A Closer Look at Immigrant Children on page 490. ■

◄ This shop in San Francisco's Chinatown sold such ethnic foods as Chinese cabbage, mushrooms, tea, and ginger.

■ *Why did immigrants often settle in ethnic neighborhoods?*

Immigrants and Politics

As immigrant neighborhoods became more crowded, they needed more city services. People needed protection from fire and crime. They needed garbage collection, street repairs and schools.

Bosses Help Immigrants

Many immigrants turned to local politicians, called bosses, to get these services. These politicians often made important improvements in the immigrant neighborhoods. In return, immigrants would vote for the boss that helped them in the next election.

Many immigrants had never before had the right to vote in Europe. Voting meant little to them

at first. But as time went on, they were happy to give their votes to whomever would help them.

Bosses Help Themselves

Bosses became very powerful as a result of these immigrant votes. Some bosses took advantage of the immigrants and made themselves very rich.

The most famous of these bosses was William Tweed of New York. Tweed promised to make city improvements, just as all bosses did. But Tweed kept the money he raised. After he swindled New York out of millions of dollars, Tweed was arrested and sent to jail.

Life in a Changing America

Immigrant Children

Farms, small towns, and big cities provided new homes for children who came to the United States. Whether or not they went to school, all had to learn how to get along in America.

City streets were classrooms for a lot of immigrant children. They learned American business methods by selling newspapers, matches, or candy on street corners. When "class" was over, the children gathered in courtyards for fast and furious games of stickball.

McGuffey's Reader, an English textbook, was the first American book many immigrants read. Its success stories about poor-but-honest children gave immigrants the hope that they, too, could succeed in America.

What did you have for lunch? A pickle and a piece of bread was all some children got in their lunch bags. Bad food and long working hours were blamed for the poor health of many immigrant children.

McGUFFEY'S
FIFTH READER

I. THE GOOD READER.

1. IT is told of Frederick the Great, King of Prussia, that, as he was seated one day in his private room, a ___ition was brought to him with the request that ___ediately read. The King had just re- (29)

Bosses were often the first experience immigrants had of politics and democracy in America. Some bosses took advantage of immigrants, but others helped them in their new homes. ■

■ *How did political bosses get immigrants to vote for them?*

Immigrants and Other Americans

Many immigrants faced problems because of the attitudes of other Americans. Some people disliked immigrants because of **racism**—the belief that one's own race or ethnic group is better than others. Other people simply feared that immigrants would steal their jobs by working for lower wages.

Because of racism and fear, some Americans treated people born in the United States better than they treated immigrants. This policy is called **nativism.** For example, some western states would not allow Japanese immigrants to own property. Some clubs and colleges did not accept Jewish immigrants as members or students.

Racist and nativist beliefs led Americans to pass laws keeping many immigrants from coming to the United States. In 1882, Congress passed a law that stopped Chinese immigration. In 1917, Congress voted to require

immigrants to pass a reading test in English. Other laws passed in the 1920s limited the number of immigrants from southern and eastern Europe. As a result of these laws, immigration to the United States slowed down.

Millions of immigrants came to the United States between 1860 and 1914. Their experiences, joys, and problems have been shared by the millions of immigrants who have come to America since that time. ■

This cartoon shows that many of the people who were most prejudiced against immigrants were the children of immigrants themselves .

■ *Why did some labor union members fear immigrants?*

R E V I E W

1. **FOCUS** What were the lives of immigrants like in the United States between 1870 and 1914?

2. **CONNECT** How was immigration before 1880 different from immigration after 1880?

3. **CULTURE** Why did immigrants from the same country tend to live in the same neighborhood?

4. **CRITICAL THINKING** What are some of the reasons for nativism? Can you think of any groups of immigrants who meet with hostility when they arrive in the United States today? What do you think are the reasons for this?

5. **WRITING ACTIVITY** Interview someone who can tell you how they or their ancestors traveled to this country. This can be someone in your own family or in the family of a friend. Ask these questions: Why did they leave their old country? Where did they settle? What work did they do? What did they like best and least about their new home?

491

Life in a Changing America

Immigration: Open or Restricted?

> *L*et them come, then, as the
> waves come . . . It is easy for
> every man of them to have a farm
> which they can soon call their
> own.
>
> Boston Evening Transcript

> *W*e need to keep our voting
> power and our reserves of
> public land out of the reach . . . of
> the hordes of half-educated and
> wholly unreliable foreigners now
> bribed to migrate here.
>
> John Murray Forbes,
> railroad builder

Background

Anna Maria Gavin came to America in 1866. As a child, she had heard that in America you could become rich, practice the religion you chose, and eat meat and bread every day! In Ireland Anna Maria often ate only dry bread with watercress, a plant like lettuce.

The 40 million immigrants who poured in from 1820 to 1920 had high hopes. Most, like Anna Gavin, became citizens.

But for citizens born in America, the waves of immigration were disturbing, even frightening. The newcomers would compete for jobs, housing, and land. They might dress and speak differently. No one knew what political beliefs they might have. Would they really be loyal to this country rather than to the place where they were born? Would they understand how democracy worked?

Many immigrants had been extremely poor. Would they work for less money and bring down wages of native-born American workers? Would they take over whole towns and neighborhoods with their different ways of life?

Conflict Over Immigration

The argument over immigration was heating up by the time Anna Gavin arrived. From one point of view, it seemed that the nation's doors must remain open. The country's founders were, after all, immigrants or the children of immigrants. They had come to escape poverty and unjust laws.

More than that, they had come to find freedom and opportunity. How could they or their children turn away other people who shared the same goals? Railroads were opening the West. Industry was growing rapidly. Surely, there were jobs and space enough for anyone willing to work. Why not let the immigrants come in?

On the other hand, numbers are important in a democratic country. What if the newcomers took control of the country with their votes? They might want to change the laws and customs. They might settle in the crowded cities and take the jobs the native-born Americans wanted. Pressure was building for new laws, laws that would limit immigration. Americans were pleased with the new nation they were building, and they wanted to keep it as it was.

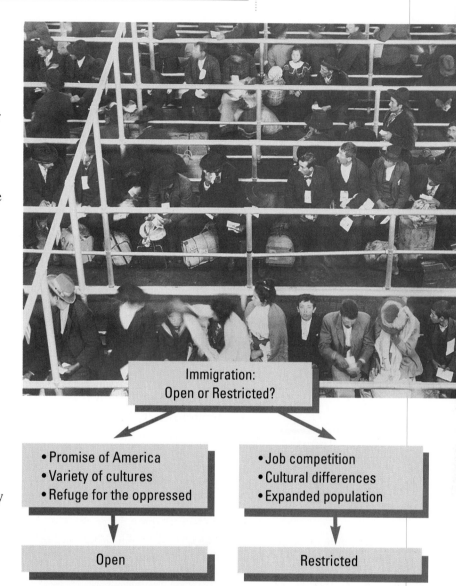

Immigration:
Open or Restricted?

- Promise of America
- Variety of cultures
- Refuge for the oppressed

Open

- Job competition
- Cultural differences
- Expanded population

Restricted

In 1882, Congress passed the first law to limit immigration. Was the land of the free now less free? Or was freedom being protected?

Decision Point

1. What made immigration disturbing to "born" Americans?
2. What goals and values of the American-born citizens helped them accept the newcomers?
3. Find a newspaper or magazine article about immigration today.

What goals and values make present-day immigrants want to come to America?

4. What information could help you decide about open immigration? Where might you find this information?

Life in a Changing America

L E S S O N   3

Into Growing Cities

THINKING FOCUS

How did cities grow and change in the years between 1870 and 1914?

Key Terms

- ghetto
- middle class

➤ *Good jobs and new opportunities drew people into Chicago and other growing American cities. Some things, like this beaded purse, were available only in big cities.*

> hen Caroline Meeber boarded the afternoon train for Chicago, her total outfit consisted of a small trunk, a cheap imitation alligator-skin satchel, a small lunch in a paper box, and a yellow leather snap purse, containing her ticket, a scrap of paper with her sister's address in Van Buren Street, and four dollars in money. It was in August, 1889. She was eighteen years of age. . . .
>
> Theodore Dreiser, *Sister Carrie*, 1900

The main character in Theodore Dreiser's novel felt restless in her hometown. Carrie Meeber longed for the fashionable clothes and glamorous life that she hoped to find in the big city.

Carrie spoke English, but in many ways she was as much a

foreigner in Chicago as immigrants from Russia and Italy. The city was not at all like the world she had known. She had no working skills. Still, Carrie set out to find a job in Chicago's business district. She wandered all day, looking for jobs and finding none. Finally, she found work in a factory for $4.50 a week.

Growth of Cities

To many Americans, cities promised good jobs and new opportunities. The excitement of busy city life drew many native-born Americans away from their farms and small towns. As a result, cities grew at an amazing rate. In 1860, only about 6 million people lived in U.S. cities. By 1920, more than 54 million people were city dwellers. The map to the right shows how much cities changed in the years between 1880 and 1900.

For example, by 1889 over 500,000 people already lived in Chicago. Its streets, houses, and businesses covered 75 square miles. Factories were built all around the city. Many railroads ran through Chicago. Railroad companies bought huge pieces of land in this booming city.

Leaving the Farm

In America's rural areas, well-paying jobs for farm workers were hard to find. The main reason was mechanization. Mechanical reapers and harvesters allowed farmers to produce more with fewer workers. Farms no longer needed armies of seasonal workers to prepare the land and to harvest the crops. As a result, many farm workers lost their jobs.

The farmers who could not afford new machines looked for other opportunities. They saw the city as a place to start over.

Moving North

In addition to white farmers and their families, many black Americans moved from the rural

▼ *More and more Americans made their homes in big cities in the late 1800s, as these maps show.*

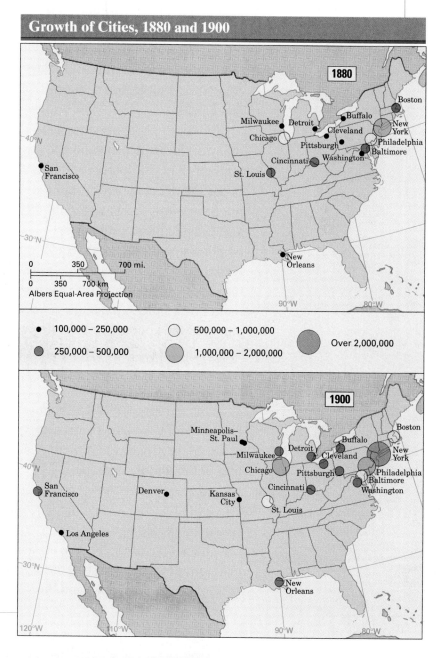

Growth of Cities, 1880 and 1900

Population Changes, 1870–1910

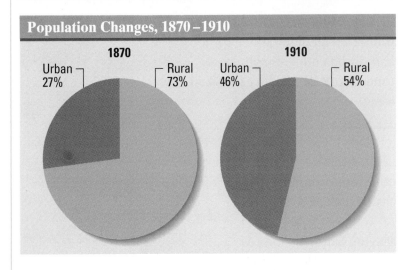

1870

Urban 27%
Rural 73%

1910

Urban 46%
Rural 54%

These graphs show how the population shifted from rural to urban areas between 1870 and 1910.

Many black families moved from southern farms to northern cities in the early 1900s.

How did mechanization affect farm workers?

South to northern cities. Blacks moved to the cities to find better jobs, just as so many other Americans had.

By 1920, a majority of blacks had moved to industrial cities like New York, Philadelphia, Detroit, and Chicago.

Black people experienced many of the same problems the immigrants had. But blacks had one big problem that other groups did not have. Most European immigrants could move into better neighborhoods when they could afford to. But blacks could not easily move to better parts of the city, no matter how much money they earned. Many people refused to sell or rent houses to blacks. Blacks who did move met with racial prejudice from white neighbors.

Most black people stayed in decaying neighborhoods. The parts of a city where minority groups are forced to live because of prejudice are called **ghettos.**

Black ghettos were overcrowded and run-down. Streets were often dirty and dangerous. Still, black culture blossomed in the ghetto. Jazz clubs, storefront churches, and sports helped people cope with the difficulties of ghetto living. ■

Growth of the Middle Class

Not everyone in the city was an immigrant or came from rural areas. Many city dwellers were part of the **middle class,** people who were neither rich nor poor.

Living in the City

The people of the middle class held jobs as file clerks, secretaries, or bookkeepers in banks and business offices. Others owned their own small businesses, such as grocery or clothing stores. As cities grew and more businesses were located there, the middle class grew as well.

Gradually, more and more middle-class people saw the problems of the city. Some felt that greedy politicians hurt honest

496

Chapter 19

businesses. Many people feared that crime and sickness in poorer neighborhoods would spread to their homes.

Improving the City

To protect their neighborhoods and their families, some middle-class people formed civic organizations. These groups worked to improve city government. They worked to clean up city water and milk supplies, build parks and playgrounds, and improve schools.

As hard as they tried, there were some things that reformers could not change. America's cities were centers for manufacturing. Railroads cut through cities and factories grew up next to them. No one wanted to live close to a rail line or a large factory. But for a long time, it was not possible for most people to move away.

Escaping the City

In the 1860s, most workers had to walk to and from their jobs. By the 1870s and 1880s, however, public transportation systems were operating in most large cities. Cable cars and trolley cars made it possible for people to live miles away from their jobs.

In the 1880s and 1890s, trolley lines were built into the country around large cities. Developers bought land along the trolley lines and built the first suburbs. Suburbs had houses for single families, yards, and quiet tree-lined streets.

Changing the City

As middle-class families moved away, cities changed. Stores, offices, factories, and warehouses lined the inner-city streets.

But not only the cities changed in the late 1800s. Railroads connected the nation. By 1914, telephones and electric light bulbs appeared in homes. The lives of many workers and immigrants proved that not all these changes were good. But in both the good and bad changes, Americans saw that they had entered a new, modern age. ■

▲ *Some people escaped the problems of growing cities by moving to suburbs like Maywood, Illinois, outside of Chicago.*

■ *What made it possible for middle-class families to move to the suburbs?*

R E V I E W

1. **FOCUS** How did cities grow and change between the years 1870 and 1914?

2. **CONNECT** What were some reasons rural people had for moving to the city?

3. **ECONOMICS** Why did people of the middle class feel they had a stake in solving a city's problems?

4. **CRITICAL THINKING** Europeans came to America as immigrants, blacks moved north, rural people moved to cities, and middle-class people moved to the suburbs. Why were so many people doing so much moving?

5. **WRITING ACTIVITY** In the late 1800s and early 1900s, many people moved into cities. At the same time, many people were moving out of the city into suburbs. Make a chart listing reasons for moving into cities in one column and reasons for moving out of cities in another.

Life in a Changing America

An Orphan for Nebraska

Charlene Joy Talbot

You have learned that the cities grew in the late 1800s because of immigration and movement of people from farms. The problem of homeless children grew as well, and a Children's Aid Society was formed to take orphans from the cities and settle them in the towns and farms of the western United States. The Society found homes or work for them. In this story, Kevin, an Irish orphan who worked as a newspaper boy and lived on the streets of New York City, finds a new life in Nebraska in the 1860s.

Millions of immigrants came to America with their dreams of a better life. Here is a story about one 11-year-old immigrant boy.

buffalo robe a blanket made of buffalo skins

The next thing Kevin knew, Elizabeth was screeching, "Be we there, Mister? Is this Nebraska?"

He threw back the buffalo robe to see sun streaming through the depot window. Elizabeth, George and Maggie were crowding out the door. He heard them running on the platform.

Kevin tied his shoes, fumbling in his haste. Then he, too, was flying out the door.

The countryside was so flat that the station platform felt like a hilltop. Shining steel rails cut across the prairie in both directions. Away over some fields Kevin saw a scattering of one- and two-story buildings. Everywhere else snowy wastelands spread to the horizon, except for one line of bare trees.

George was looking bewildered. "Where's Cottonwood City?"

Kevin, used to the villages of Ireland, said, "That's it."

Hiram came running at them.

"That's not a city! There's more of us than there is houses!" Which wasn't really true.

"Come on!" Kevin set off at top speed toward some clumps of tall weedstalks surrounding snow-covered piles of lumber. The three boys ran past Maggie and Elizabeth, who were galloping round and round a shock of corn in the nearest field. Maggie stopped suddenly. She picked up an ear that had fallen to the ground. Yellow corn peeked from beneath the pale, dried husk.

"Look at this!" She ran shrieking to Mr. Carter.

Elizabeth found the winter remains of a patch of prairie roses.

shock a bundle of cornstalks standing upright

"Berries!" she screeched. The red-orange rose hips did indeed look like fruit. She bit one. Her face scrunched, and she spat.

"Breakfast!" Mr. Carter called from the platform. "Whoever wants breakfast, come along!" Hannah, Mr. Carter and Peter set out along the road to town. The others straggled after, running from side to side, making tracks in the unmarked snow.

The hotel, which was the largest building in town, was beginning to stir when the group trailed across the porch. A man opened the door, exclaiming, "Land alive, these must be the orphans! Molly!" he called over his shoulder. "Breakfast customers!" He directed them to a hallway where they hung their coats. A bench held two big washpans and a bucket of water. A big girl came from the kitchen with a steaming kettle and poured hot water into the basins. Beside the bench hung a long strip of toweling. A mirror was nailed beside it. Hands and faces were washed; Hannah combed the girls' hair and Peter's, and the comb was passed among the rest of the boys. From the neck up, they looked respectable, Kevin thought. The boys had barber's haircuts before leaving New York. Their clothes, however, were a different story—wrinkled, dirty and even torn, having been lived in for so many days and nights.

They sat on either side of a long, bare table. Pitchers of milk and coffee came from the kitchen, followed by platters of buckwheat cakes and sausage, with sorghum syrup to pour over. There was a pitcher of cream for the coffee and molded hills of butter to spread on the pancakes. After all that, Molly brought out dried apple pies.

Some of the town's bachelors boarded at the hotel. One by one men drifted in, sat at the long table and stared at the children while they cut through stacks of pancakes. They were bearded and booted. Kevin wished his new shoes had been boots.

When the youngsters had eaten all they could hold, Mr. Carter inquired the way to the church, and they filed into the main street, which was wide and rutted and ran east to west like the railroad track. Whichever way Kevin looked, he could see open prairie beyond the houses.

"How can they call this a city?" he whispered to Mr. Carter.

"They're hoping lots of people will move here and make it one."

Despite the cold and the early hour, saddle horses were tied to the hitching rails along the street. Men stood gossiping in twos and threes on the board sidewalks, and families drove past in wagons.

Everyone stared. Mr. Carter led the children into the church. Everywhere they heard whispering: "There's the orphans!" "—little, ain't he? They must not have any food in New York City."

rose hips part of a rose bush

sorghum syrup a sweet, sticky syrup

bachelor unmarried man

hitching rails a long pole for tying animals

The preacher, wearing a black suit, welcomed them. He shook hands with Mr. Carter and sent them all to the empty second row. The first row was full of small, pale-haired children who eyed them over the back of the pew. One pointed at Kevin's hair and they all giggled.

Kevin's breakfast was now a lump in his stomach as big as a washtub. Maggie had thrown hers up. Peter's bruises still showed, and Dolly looked ready to cry.

Could anybody possibly want any of us, Kevin wondered. James and Hiram were acting too smart for their britches, as if they didn't care whether anyone wanted them or not.

The children had to sit through Sunday school and then church. It passed in a blur. Everyone but Peter knew they were being inspected. The actual choosing would be that afternoon at the courthouse, which was to be opened even though it was Sunday.

After church Mr. Carter took his group back to the hotel. The owner had offered them a free meal, but no one did justice to it, partly due to the *mammoth* breakfast, but mostly to the *ordeal* ahead. The dining room seemed full of silent, staring faces. Used to loud city voices, the children found these quiet people frightening. No one had any desire to explore. They waited *docilely* for what would happen.

The courthouse was one big room. It stood in the corner of an empty square. "The building's only temporary," the preacher apologized as they trailed toward it. "We plan to build a fine stone one. Everything's booming; taxpayers, churchgoers moving in so fast a person can't keep count."

"How are the schools?" Mr. Carter asked.

The preacher beamed. "We have a fine one here in town— fifteen pupils. In the country . . . well, each *township* does the best it can. Have to educate the young, you know. They're the most important crop the prairie produces, after all." He smiled.

The youngsters stared back amazed. George's mouth actually dropped open, and Hiram nudged James. Never had any of them, except Kevin, been considered anything but a nuisance, an extra mouth to feed.

A crowd was standing about the door, so Kevin was not surprised to see that inside the room was full and men were lining the wall. If *this* many people wanted children . . . perhaps they did have a chance.

The orphans were led to two railed-off benches at the front of the room. The preacher stepped to the platform.

"Ladies and gentlemen," he began. "We are happy to see so many faces this crisp and sunny afternoon." And he began to tell them how wonderful their community was. Kevin heard *guffaws* from the back row at some of the more *extravagant* praise. When

---

mammoth huge
ordeal difficult situation

docilely quietly

township an area 36 miles square

guffaws hearty laughs
extravagant grand

500

he said that southern Nebraska was on the same world parallel as Italy, some wag said, "You sure you don't mean Switzerland, mister?" People chuckled, because everyone knew that Italy was warm and sunny and Switzerland was full of ice and snow. But in general his listeners seemed to enjoy being told about their wonderful choice of a home. He was loudly clapped, after which he introduced Mr. Carter.

Mr. Carter told his audience that thousands of homeless children roamed the streets of New York City. He explained that the Children's Aid Society worked to move them into the country where they could grow into useful men and women instead of beggars and criminals. "These are not young criminals or paupers," he said. "They are simply homeless, unfortunate boys and girls. They are the best material, folks, that a farmer or a master could desire to make into good workers on the farm or in the house."

"How about the little 'uns, mister?" the same voice called. "What's they good for?"

There was some good-natured laughter, but Dolly threw her head into Hannah's lap and began to cry.

Mr. Carter glanced toward her and then said with dignity, "They are good for loving. As our Saviour said, 'Even as you do it unto the least of these, you do it unto me.' I know there are warmhearted people here who will want to do just that."

He sat down beside the children on the bench, and the preacher stood up.

"Let us pray. . . ."

After the prayer he announced: "Mr. Carter and I will be here for the rest of the afternoon. Those who wish to interview a child or apply for one will please come forward."

Immediately a big, black-bearded man made his way down the aisle. He was followed by a nicely dressed woman with happy black eyes.

"This is Mr. Thayer, our blacksmith, and this is his wife." The preacher introduced them to Mr. Carter. "He also runs the livery stable."

The boys caught their breath at that. To be taking care of horses was what they all wanted.

"So you folks want a boy?" the preacher said.

Mr. Thayer's laugh rang through the room like a hammer on an anvil. He looked down at his wife and then back toward the bench where he'd been sitting. Following his glance Kevin saw a row of young men, as like to their father as a family of blackbirds.

"Ain't five boys enough? What we want is that black-haired gal." And Mrs. Thayer stepped to the railing and looked straight at Hannah. "Would you like to come to us, my dear? It's all menfolk but me, but you could have your own room."

parallel latitude
wag a smart aleck

'uns ones

blacksmith maker of iron tools and horse-shoes
livery stable boarding stable for horses

anvil an iron block on which metal is shaped

And so Hannah was the first one chosen. Hiram, George and James were speechless with envy. Except for Dolly's tears, the farewells were cheerful. Her new family bundled her away.

After that some farmers came forward. The preacher vouched for the standing of each one in the community, and the men described their farms, their horses and other livestock. Each boy was to get his schooling, his board and room, and one hundred dollars if he stayed until he was twenty-one. In that way the futures of James, Hiram, and even George were settled. The boys thanked Mr. Carter, promised to write to the society, and went away to their new lives without a backward glance.

"I have one more boy here old enough to do farm work," Mr. Carter told the gathering. But the remaining farmers shook their heads. "That lad!" one said. "There ain't enough of him to hold down a plow." "Look at that white skin," another scoffed. "One day in the sun would sizzle him like a fried tomato."

Elizabeth was picked next.

"My wife wants a girl old enough to help with the children," announced the next man. Mr. Carter suggested Elizabeth. "Kind of small for eight, ain't she?" the man said. "But if that's the oldest one left, she'll have to do. My young'uns is two and three."

"Mr. Phelps is our general storekeeper," the preacher explained. "He and his family live over the store."

Kevin was watching a young couple. The man kept looking toward Dolly or Peter. Then he would confer with his wife again. He seemed to be urging her. She was quietly crying.

The courtroom was clearing out. A bank of snowclouds had come up in the west, people reported. Kevin heard teams brought up outside, and men came stomping in to collect their families. The people who remained, sitting or standing about, were apparently townsfolk, making the most of the entertainment. Who took the children and why would be something to talk about for months.

The sad couple, as Kevin thought of them, came up and asked for Peter. "Their only child died last fall of diphtheria," the preacher said after they left.

Kevin was beginning to wonder if he and Dolly and Maggie would have to sleep at the railroad station again when there was a stir at the door. A snow-powdered figure burst through the crowd and came striding towards the platform. Kevin's heart leaped. Here was a purposeful man, just the kind he, Kevin, would like to work for. The man was small, dark and energetic, his coat was belted closely, his cap had ear flaps, and his legs were encased in leggings.

"I've got orders for two girls," he shouted when he was halfway down the aisle. "I'm a rancher up on Deer Creek. My wife wants one, and Mrs. Higgins wants the other. I'm not too

---

vouched guaranteed

scoffed made fun of

team horses harnessed together

diphtheria serious disease of the throat

leggings leather pants

502

late, am I?" He looked towards the youngsters. "Those two will do fine. Snow's been following me all the way in. If I'm gonna get back, I've got to take 'em and skedaddle."

Mr. Carter looked at the preacher.

"Mr. Jacques," the preacher said quickly.

Mr. Jacques bounded to the railing. "Here's a pair of pretties!" he exclaimed. "My wife and Mrs. Higgins are just a-setting up there on Deer Creek waiting for you."

The little girls looked at him round-eyed.

Everything was quickly arranged. Mr. Carter helped bundle the girls into Mr. Jacques's sleigh, and they dashed away with a jingle of sleighbells.

Kevin shrank back on the bench and wished he could disappear. What would Mr. Carter do with him?

Mr. Carter came back into the room and made his way around the railing. He sat beside Kevin and patted his hand. Kevin caught his lower lip between his teeth. He *would* not cry. He was *not* a criminal, set off from these strangers by a railing.

"I always save my best till last," Mr. Carter said with a smile.

Another stir at the door made them both look up. The man who came in was slim and black-bearded and walked with a limp. Like the other young men, he was bundled into a worn blue army overcoat. An alertness in his manner reminded Kevin of the men who worked on Newspaper Row. He was not surprised when the preacher introduced the newcomer as "the editor of the *Cottonwood Clarion*, our lively newspaper."

The man shook hands with Mr. Carter. "Euclid Smith's my name. I expected to get back to town last night, but my horse threw a shoe. I was over at Grand Island," he explained, "picking up a load of newsprint. The editor there bought more than he could pay for." He glanced at Kevin. "Are they all gone but this one?"

The preacher nodded. "We found fine homes for all the rest," he bragged. "Not one of these children will ever regret coming to our community."

"I'm sure they won't," Mr. Carter agreed.

"I'd like the names of the families who took them," Euclid Smith said, "for next week's paper." The preacher showed him the list.

"Mr. Smith," the preacher said while the editor was copying the list, "weren't you looking for a printer's devil a while back?"

The editor glanced at Kevin. "I need an older lad, one who's had more schooling."

"This boy's eleven and reads very well," Mr. Carter said quickly. "Come here, Kevin. He's small for his age, that's all. The farmers say he'd burn to a crisp in the fields." Mr. Carter put his arm across Kevin's shoulders.

skedaddle to hurry

sleigh horse-drawn carriage with runners instead of wheels for use on snow

printer's devil errand boy in a print shop

503

Euclid Smith straightened from his task of copying and looked Kevin up and down. Kevin stared back, liking what he saw. He hoped suddenly, desperately, that the newspaperman would like *him*.

"I don't have time to look after a child," the editor protested. "Don't even have time to look after myself."

"He won't need looking after," Mr. Carter said. "This boy's bright and quick. It's my guess you can teach him just about anything."

Euclid Smith fingered his beard. Then he asked a surprising question. "Can you cook?"

"Some, sir." Kevin's mother had taught him to peel potatoes and make tea.

"Mr. Smith's a bachelor," the preacher explained.

"What can you read?" Euclid Smith asked.

"Newspapers, sir. . . . books."

"How about handwriting? Here—read this." He put the half-copied list into Kevin's hands.

Kevin read aloud: "Hannah Moore, ten, to Mr. and Mrs. Lije Thayer; James Albert, thirteen to Mr. Harold Connor; Hiram Hostetter, twelve, to Mr. John Swenson—"

"All right, that's enough." He fingered his beard again. "I don't know. Think you'd like printshop work?"

Kevin was nearly speechless with yearning. His 'yes' came out in a whisper from his dry throat.

Euclid Smith looked at the other two men as though he'd been backed into a corner. "I only came to get the story. I'm not sure—I hardly make ends meet as it is."

One of the onlookers lounged up. "Go on, take him, Yuke—What are you waiting for?"

"By George, Jake, I'm waiting for you to pay for your subscription!"

The man called Jake dug in his pocket, produced two quarters, and handed them over. "There you are—four bits." He winked at Kevin.

"All right, by gum, I'll take him," Euclid Smith told Mr. Carter. "I hope you like beans and cornmeal, boy."

Kevin nodded. His throat was too full to speak. He had never thought of such a thing as working in a newspaper office. Mr. Carter was right: the best offer *had* come last.

While Euclid Smith finished copying the list, Kevin said goodbye to Mr. Carter and promised to write.

"Ready to go?" Euclid Smith asked. "We'll stop at the store and get you a tick to sleep on. You're lucky I've got some spare bedding. I suppose you haven't had supper?"

"No, Mr. Smith."

"You don't have to call me Mister," the editor said. "You

subscription an agreement to receive issues of a publication
bit 12½ cents
by gum mild swearing, no specific meaning

tick cloth mattress cover

504

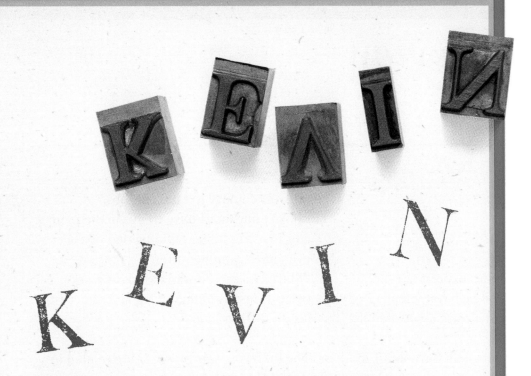

KEVIN

might as well call me Yuke. Everyone else does, except the preacher. Well, I usually have popcorn and apples for Sunday supper. That's bachelor fare for you."

Not even the promise of bread and water could have marred Kevin's happiness.

Further Reading

Call Me Ruth. Marilyn Sachs. In the early 1900s, Rifka and her mother come to the U.S. from Russia. Rifka adapts easily and even takes an American name. Her mother has a difficult time adjusting and only when she becomes involved with the unionization movement does she accept her new life.

The Great Wheel. Robert Lawson. An Irish boy seeking adventure in America comes to Chicago. He finds work on the construction of the great wheel invented by George Ferris which is a highlight of the Columbian Exposition in 1893.

The Long Winter. Laura Ingalls Wilder. Part of the "Little House on the Prairie" series, this story tells of the winter of 1880–81 in the Dakota Territory. The Ingalls have moved to town because of the harsh weather. A series of blizzards bury the town stopping all travel in and out. Shortages of food and fuel threaten the Ingalls and the townspeople.

My Prairie Year. Brett Harvey. Nine-year-old Eleanor Plaisted moves with her family from Maine to the Dakotas in 1889. This true story describes the perils and pleasures of homesteading.

Chapter Review

Reviewing Key Terms

ghetto (p. 496)   nativism (p. 491)
labor union (p. 483)   racism (p. 491)
mechanization (p. 482)   strike (p. 483)
middle class (p. 496)

A. The following quotations express the feelings of various people. For each statement, identify the key term most closely associated with it.

1. "I'm not the richest person in town, but I'm not the poorest, either—and I have a pretty good job in a business office."
2. "I believe those people are smarter than any other group of people."
3. "We do all the work, and the factory owners want to keep all the money. But if we stick together, we'll get what we deserve."
4. "We should stop letting so many immigrants into our country to take our jobs."
5. "It isn't fair that I have to live in the inner city, in a crumbling building that doesn't even have running water."
6. "Machines can do some kinds of work twice as fast as humans can, and they cost less in the long run."

B. The following sets of words are related in some way. For each set, write a short paragraph explaining how the words are related.

1. mechanization
   labor union
   strike
2. racism
   ghetto
   nativism

Exploring Concepts

A. Copy the following cause-and-effect chart on your paper. Then write one effect for each cause. Some causes may have more than one effect.

Cause	Effect
The number of factories increased.	The demand for unskilled workers grew.
Workers wanted improved working conditions.	
Europeans sought jobs and freedom.	
Farming became mechanized.	
Middle-class people wanted better neighborhoods. Transportation improved.	

B. Support each of the following statements with facts and details from the chapter.

1. Railroads grew quickly all over the nation.
2. Labor unions helped to improve the lives of workers.
3. Mechanization affected both factory workers and farm workers.
4. Immigrants moving to city neighborhoods led to the rise of political bosses.
5. Some Americans were prejudiced against the new immigrants.
6. Black culture developed even in the ghetto.
7. Cities grew quickly from 1860 to 1920.
8. By the 1870s, workers no longer had to live very close to their jobs.
9. As the suburbs grew, the nature of cities changed.

Reviewing Skills

1. What three factors should you consider when you choose a location for any purpose?
2. What would you look for on a map if you were trying to decide where to locate:
   a. a shopping center?
   b. a paper factory?
   c. a wild animal park?
3. The railroads had a major effect on American society. What had an effect on the growth of railroads? Use the information from pages 480–482 in your book to draw a multiple-causes diagram that illustrates the causes for the following effect: The railroads grew quickly.
4. Suppose you wanted to understand more about the lives of people in three different economic classes—factory workers, middle-class workers, and farm workers—in the years after the Civil War. What kind of diagram might you draw to record details about the lives, work, and problems of the three groups?

Using Critical Thinking

1. Golda Meir wrote of her family's immigration to America in 1906 that the journey "was almost like going to the moon." What do you think she meant? Do you think immigrants to the United States today experience similar feelings?
2. Today, many people still move to the edges of the city because they want to escape the problems of the city. What do you think are some of the advantages of living in present-day suburbs? What do you see as some disadvantages?
3. Most immigrants today no longer come from southern and eastern Europe. Look in the Minipedia (p. 557) to find out where they do come from and why they leave their native lands. Why do you think the areas from which immigrants come change over time?
4. Political bosses were sometimes greedy and dishonest, but they also did some good. In what ways were the bosses helpful? Do you think politicians today do a better job of serving the public than the bosses did?

Preparing for Citizenship

1. **WRITING ACTIVITY** Imagine you are a factory worker in the 1870s. How do you spend your time? Where do you live? How is life different from your real life in the 1990s? Look for descriptions and facts in an encyclopedia. Then write a short story about what might happen if you were transported to the past as a factory worker.
2. **GROUP ACTIVITY** Choose a partner and debate the roles of a machine you or your family use today. Your subject might be, for example, a vacuum cleaner or a computer. One person should present the advantages of the machine and the other person should present the disadvantages. Base your views on personal experiences. Use examples to support your opinions.
3. **COLLABORATIVE LEARNING** In groups of three, survey the immigrant influences in the neighborhood where you live. Assign one person to listen for different languages and music styles, one to list the names of residents, and one to notice how homes and restaurants are decorated and what the buildings look like. What countries are represented? Clip photos that show ethnic influences from local newspapers. Then meet in large groups to combine them into a poster.

Chapter 20

Keeping America's Promise

The United States is a land of promise—the promise of freedom and equality for all. Since the founding of the country, citizens have struggled to make sure that all Americans have the rights they need to fulfill this promise. Understanding these rights means understanding how Americans make the dream of freedom and equality come true.

During this time, many Americans used the political system to help solve the nation's problems. Electing candidates—whose faces and names appear on everything from lanterns to buttons—is the first step in this process.

1870 Passage of the Fifteenth Amendment to the U.S. Constitution gives black men the right to vote.

1825	1850	1875	1900

1848

1888 Women cast their votes in a Cheyenne, Wyoming, election (above). At this time, Wyoming and Utah are the only states where women have full voting rights.

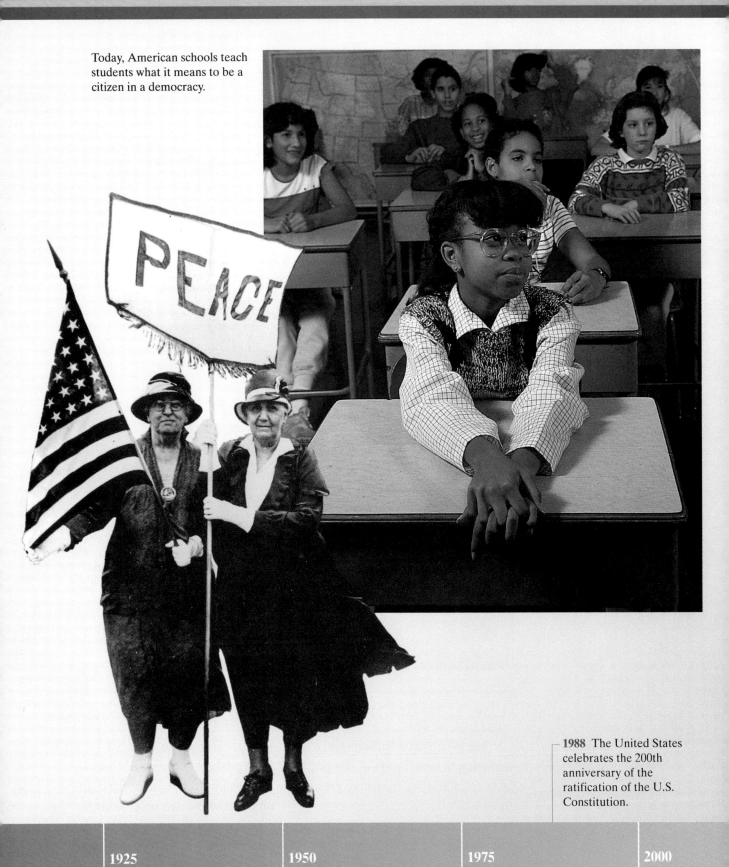

Today, American schools teach students what it means to be a citizen in a democracy.

1988 The United States celebrates the 200th anniversary of the ratification of the U.S. Constitution.

1925	1950	1975	2000

1889–1930 Jane Addams (above right) devotes her career to helping others win their rights. During this time, Addams fights to improve life for children, women, immigrants, and blacks.

Today

509

L E S S O N   1

Struggle for Freedom

THINKING
F O C U S

*How are the legal rights
of citizens different from
their rights in reality?*

Key Terms

- minority
- civil rights
- discrimination
- registration
- segregation

▲ *The painting of Chief
Joseph shown above was
done by Cyrenius Hall in
1878. The chief was about
38 years old.*

In 1879, the leader of the Nez
Perce Indians, Chief Joseph,
traveled to Washington,
D.C. With these words, he
challenged the United States to
live up to its promises.

> Treat all men alike. Give them
> all the same law. Give them
> an even chance to live and grow.
> . . . Let me be a free man—free to
> travel, free to stop, free to work,
> free to trade, where I choose, free
> to choose my own teachers, free to
> follow the religion of my fathers,
> free to think and talk and act for
> myself—and I will obey every law,
> or submit to the penalty.
>
> Chief Joseph, speech to
> government leaders, 1879

The Nez Perce chief knew
something that many others had
learned earlier in U.S. history. He
believed that people often must
struggle if they hope to have their
rights respected.

The Importance of Rights

The Nez Perce Indians were a
minority, or small part of the population. Like other minority groups,
the Nez Perce were supposed to
have certain rights. Yet they did
not really have these rights. For
example, the Declaration of Independence promised that "all men
are created equal." Yet Indians
never truly had equal rights with
whites. Time after time, white settlers pushed Indians off their land.
Whites could live anywhere. Indians had to live on reservations.

The U.S. Constitution also
promises basic liberties, or **civil
rights,** for all. The Constitution
protects each person's freedom to
speak, to worship, and to vote. It
also guarantees that newspapers

can print what they want. By protecting how people state their ideas, civil rights make democracy possible.

However, basic rights have not always been honored. In 1917, the United States went to war against Germany. This conflict is now called World War I. In 1918, Congress passed a law to stop all protests against the war. The government arrested over 6,000 people for antiwar protests.

The Struggle by Helen Keller

Laws are only one limit on the rights of people. In addition, without information, people cannot vote wisely. Blind and deaf people have extra challenges in getting information and in using their rights fully.

Helen Keller showed how people with disabilities can face these challenges. Keller was born in 1880. At age two, illness caused her to lose both her sight and her hearing. Keller learned to use her fingers to read Braille. Braille is a writing system using raised dots on a piece of paper. By age 16, Keller even learned to speak. As an adult, Keller raised money for the education of blind and deaf people. Through her travels around the country, she showed how the disabled could be active citizens.

The Struggle by Blacks

Like many other minorities, blacks have often faced **discrimination,** actions based on an unreasonable dislike of a group of people. In his poem, "Let America Be America Again," black writer Langston Hughes attacked discrimination:

> *O,* let my land be a land where Liberty
> Is crowned with no false patriotic wreath,
> But opportunity is real, and life is free,
> Equality is in the air we breathe.
> (There's never been equality for me,
> Nor freedom in this "homeland of the free.")

With these words, Hughes showed that he wanted what Chief Joseph wanted. Both hoped that the United States would keep its promise of equality. ■

▲ *This stamp showing Helen Keller as a young girl was issued in 1980 to honor her on the 100th anniversary of her birth. She is holding the hand of Anne Sullivan, the teacher who taught her to speak.*

■ *What problems have Indians, antiwar protesters, and the disabled had getting their civil rights?*

◄ *This material in Braille explains how to register to vote.*

Keeping America's Promise

Du Bois Challenges Racism

One leader of the black movement for equality was William Edward Burghardt (W.E.B.) Du Bois. He was born in a small town in Massachusetts in 1868. Most people in the town were white. There, he learned that not everyone believed in equality. As an adult, he remembered learning about the "shadow" of discrimination:

▼ *How much did the percentage of blacks registered to vote in Louisiana go down between 1896 and 1904?*

> I remember well when the shadow swept across me. I was a little thing, away up in the hills of New England. . . . In a wee wooden schoolhouse, something put it into the boys' and girls' heads to buy gorgeous visiting cards—ten cents a package—and exchange. The exchange was merry, till one girl, a tall newcomer, refused my card,— refused it peremptorily [without discussion], with a glance. Then it dawned upon me with a certain suddenness that I was different from the others.
>
> W.E.B. Du Bois, *The Souls of Black Folks*, 1904

After finishing his education, Du Bois taught history at Atlanta University. While there, Du Bois studied the nation's black communities. He asked questions, made observations, and wrote articles. Du Bois hoped that such knowledge would help improve race relations.

Yet Du Bois eventually decided that it would take more than knowledge and understanding to end racism. Black Americans had to stand up for their rights. Du Bois became a leader of the black protest movement. Blacks, he said, should "claim for ourselves every single right that belongs to a freeborn American."

The Importance of Voting

The key to winning these rights, he claimed, was voting. If blacks voted, they would have power in government. Leaders would then pass laws to protect blacks' other rights as well.

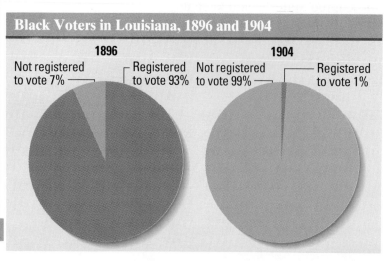

Black Voters in Louisiana, 1896 and 1904

1896 Not registered to vote 7% — Registered to vote 93%

1904 Not registered to vote 99% — Registered to vote 1%

In 1868, the Fifteenth Amendment to the Constitution had given blacks the right to vote. Many blacks did vote during the 1870s and 1880s.

However, in the 1890s, many states wrote new laws to stop blacks from voting. **Registration,** the process of signing up to vote, dropped quickly among blacks. The Constitution still gave blacks the right to vote. But by the early 1900s, few really could.

The Role of the NAACP

Du Bois and other leaders fought for the rights of blacks. In 1909, they started the National Association for the Advancement of Colored People (NAACP). The NAACP fought all kinds of **segregation,** the separation of people by race.

From 1910 to 1934, Du Bois edited the journal of the NAACP, *The Crisis.* This journal printed stories about the fight for freedom. It also had stories about black people who were successful in fields such as business and art.

Du Bois and the NAACP believed that the Constitution gave blacks the same rights as whites. Thus, lawyers for the organization challenged laws that went against the Constitution.

In 1915, the NAACP won its first major victory. The Supreme Court ruled that several laws that

Du Bois believed that blacks needed to develop strong leaders. So The Crisis often had stories on important black men and women. How does the button show one way for blacks to become leaders?

stopped black Americans from voting were unconstitutional. According to the Court, these laws went against the Fifteenth Amendment. This victory was one step in helping blacks vote again.

The work of the NAACP and Du Bois showed the gap between what the Constitution promised and what really happened. Today, the struggle goes on to keep the American promise. ■

■ *How did black Americans fight for their rights?*

R E V I E W

1. **FOCUS** How are the legal rights of citizens different from their rights in reality?

2. **CONNECT** What basic rights are protected by the First Amendment to the U.S. Constitution?

3. **HISTORY** Why was Langston Hughes disappointed with the United States?

4. **CITIZENSHIP** Describe one group's efforts to gain their Constitutional rights today.

5. **CRITICAL THINKING** Explain whether this statement is a fact or an opinion: Black Americans should have been treated more fairly in the early 1900s.

6. **WRITNG ACTIVITY** Make a two-column chart. In one column, list three basic rights you think all people should have. In the second column, list individuals or groups of people in United States history that have not always had these rights.

L E S S O N   2

Patterns of Change

THINKING
FOCUS

Why does change in a democracy often take a long time?

Key Terms

- self-interest
- suffrage

▼ *The four examples on this timeline show how long changes take in a democracy.*

Germantown, Pennsylvania, 1688: A small group of German Quakers meet. They write a protest against "traffic of mens-body," or slavery. Opposition to slavery spreads slowly. Finally, 177 years after the first antislavery protest, the United States ends slavery.

Philadelphia, 1697: William Penn suggests that the English colonies in North America should unite. Unity would improve trade and defense for each colony. Not until the Seven Years' War ends in 1763, however, do people take this idea seriously. Finally, 79 years after the first call for unity, 13 colonies join together to form the United States of America.

Boston, 1836: State legislators talk of the harm done to children in factory jobs. Children work 14 hours a day, six days a week. They pass a law limiting the use of child labor. By the end of the century, citizens call for a law ending child labor throughout the country. Finally, 102 years after the first Massachusetts law, Congress passes a national child labor law.

What do the three examples of change have in common? Each change began with the idea of one person or group. Then many people—often many generations of people—worked for the change before it finally came. These examples show that societies often change slowly. And they show that change often needs the work of many people.

The Process of Change

| 1650 | 1700 | 1750 | 1800 |

1697, William Penn proposes that the English colonies in North America unite.

1776, Thirteen British colonies join together to form the United States of America.

1688, Quakers in Pennsylvania issue the first written protest against slavery in America.

1778, Hannah Lee Corbin suggests to her brother that women be given the right to vote.

Why Change Takes Time

One reason that societies change slowly is that each person has a **self-interest,** or personal concern, about an issue. Ending slavery was in the self-interest of slaves. They wanted freedom. However, ending slavery was not in the self-interest of slave-owners. They did not want to end a system from which they made money.

Slave-owners, like other citizens in a democracy, could defend their self-interests. People have many different interests. Thus, almost every change goes against someone's self-interest. The slave-owners who were wealthy had power in the national government. They delayed the end of slavery until 1865. ■

■ *How can the self-interests of citizens slow down or stop change?*

How Women Fought for the Vote

The fight to end slavery took generations. So did the struggle of women to win **suffrage,** or the right to vote. As early as 1778, Hannah Lee Corbin wrote a letter asking her brother, political leader Richard Henry Lee, to help women win their voting rights. Her letter got no action.

The Movement Begins

For the next 70 years, few politicians even thought of allowing women to vote. But in 1848, Elizabeth Cady Stanton, Lucretia Mott, and 300 other women held a meeting in Seneca Falls, New York, to discuss women's rights. Stanton read a changed version of the

Declaration of Independence: "We hold these truths to be self-evident: that all men and women are created equal."

The Seneca Falls meeting was a success. It started a drive to win the vote for women. Politicians began to think about the issue. However, not until 21 years later did the movement win its first big victory. In 1869, the Wyoming Territory became the first part of the United States to give women full voting rights.

The Struggle Continues

In 1872, Susan B. Anthony and 16 other women in Rochester, New York, claimed that, as citizens, they

KEEP COOL AND RAISE **A Breeze for Suffrage!**

Vote for Woman Suffrage Nov. 6th   Vote for Woman Suffrage Nov. 6th

▲ *In New York, supporters of suffrage carried fans advertising their cause.*

1836, Massachusetts passes the first law limiting the use of child labor in the state.

1938, Congress passes a federal law limiting the use of child labor throughout the United States.

| 1800 | 1850 | 1900 | 1950 |

1865, The Thirteenth Amendment abolishes slavery in the United States.

1920, The Nineteenth Amendment gives women the right to vote throughout the United States.

Stanton worked for the rights of her daughter and granddaughter as well as for her own rights.

How Do We Know?

HISTORY *No opinion polls were taken in the early 1900s. So historians study election results, newspaper editorials, and other sources. From these sources they get an idea of people's opinions about issues like suffrage for women.*

➤ *Notice the people in this photograph. What can you learn about support for the suffrage movement?*

had a right to vote. So they voted. Three weeks later, police arrested Anthony. She was not even allowed to speak at the trial. The judge found her guilty. He fined her $100. But she never paid the fine.

With meetings, speeches, and articles, Stanton, Anthony, and others slowly built their movement. In 1878, they convinced a senator to bring up a suffrage

amendment in Congress. The Senate voted it down. Yet from then on, supporters raised the "Anthony Amendment" often. Politicians could no longer avoid the issue. They had to take a position.

By 1897, only four states had given women full voting rights. Still, Anthony was confident:

> *I t may be delayed longer than we think, it may be here sooner than we expect; but the day will come when man will recognize woman as his peer, not only at the fireside but in the councils of the nation.*
>
> Susan B. Anthony,
> *The Arena, 1897*

Not everyone was hopeful. Some worried about the opposition to suffrage. Many factory owners were against it. They feared that women would support laws to stop children from working in factories. Children worked for much lower wages than did adults. Ending child labor would cost factory owners money.

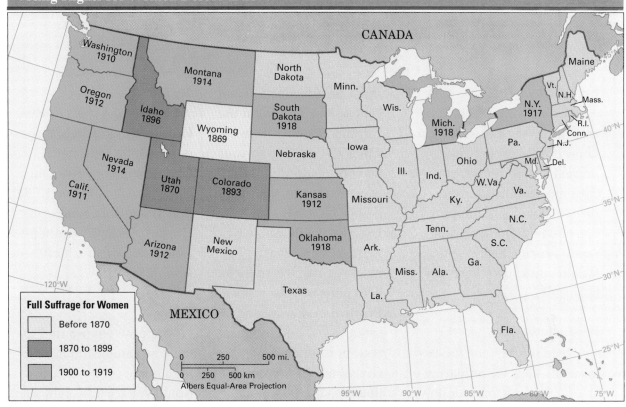

Voting Rights for Women Before 1920

Full Suffrage for Women
- Before 1870
- 1870 to 1899
- 1900 to 1919

0   250   500 mi.
0   250   500 km
Albers Equal-Area Projection

The Final Drive

In the early 1900s, Stanton and Anthony died. However, they left a strong base for new leaders to build on. After 1910, support for the suffrage movement grew more rapidly. On the map on this page, locate the ten states that had given women the vote by 1916. What part of the country were these states in?

The successes in the states showed that the years of effort were paying off. In 1919, Congress once again considered the Anthony Amendment. This discussion was different than all the earlier ones, though. For the first time, each house of Congress approved the proposed amendment.

By 1920, enough states ratified the proposal that it became the Nineteenth Amendment. Finally, 142 years after Corbin had written her brother about suffrage, women won the right to vote. ■

▲ *Most states did not give women full voting rights until the ratification of the Nineteenth Amendment in 1920. These states are shown on the map in light brown.*

■ *How does the campaign for women's suffrage show how changes occur in a democracy?*

REVIEW

1. **FOCUS** Why does change in a democracy often take a long time?

2. **CONNECT** How was Stanton's version of the Declaration of Independence unlike the original?

3. **HISTORY** Explain how self-interest both sped up and slowed down the suffrage movement.

4. **CITIZENSHIP** Explain whether or not you think Anthony should have been punished for breaking the law when she voted in 1872.

5. **CRITICAL THINKING** How is the struggle by black Americans for equal rights similar to the struggle by women for the right to vote?

6. **ACTIVITY** Draw a timeline of the main events in the struggle by women for the right to vote.

517

Giving an Oral Report

Here's Why

You will often make oral reports in your classes. If you know how to prepare and present a good report, you can enjoy and learn from these assignments. Suppose you had to prepare an oral report about Chief Joseph. Would you know where to begin?

Here's How

Read through the following eight steps for preparing an oral report. Consider how you might use each step to prepare your report.

1. **Narrow the topic.** You might choose to talk about Chief Joseph's speech when he called for fair treatment of Indians.
2. **Collect information.** Start with your textbook. Then look at encyclopedias, books and magazine articles about the Nez Perce Indians.
3. **Take notes.** Make a detailed outline of all the ideas you want to include in your report.
4. **Prepare a set of note cards.** Write down the ideas from your outline that you want to present in your talk. You can refer to these note cards while presenting your report.
5. **Write an introduction and conclusion.** You might use a dramatic quote from Chief Joseph to grab your audience's attention. End by summarizing your main points.
6. **Use visual aids.** Show pictures, posters, charts, maps, or artifacts to highlight parts of your report.
7. **Practice.** Ask someone to listen to you and to time your presentation.
8. **Give the final presentation.** Be sure to look directly at your audience and speak clearly.

Try It

Follow the steps in Here's How to prepare an oral report about a reformer. Choose someone from this chapter such as Helen Keller, W.E.B. DuBois, Langston Hughes, Susan B. Anthony, Jane Addams, or Chief Joseph.

Apply It

Suppose you wanted to tell your family about uses for a home computer. How would you use the eight steps to convince your family to buy a computer?

L E S S O N   3

Role of Citizenship

> *I dreamed night after night that every one in the world was dead excepting myself, and that upon me rested the responsibility of making a wagon wheel. . . . I always stood in the same spot in the blacksmith shop, darkly pondering as to how to begin, and never once did I know how, although I fully realized that the affairs of the world could not be resumed until at least one wheel should be made and something started.*
>
> Jane Addams, *Twenty Years at Hull House,* 1935

THINKING
F O C U S

What is the meaning of good citizenship?

Even at age six in 1866, Jane Addams felt she had to get something started. She grew up wanting to change her world, and she did.

According to Theodore Roosevelt, president from 1901 to 1909, Addams became "the most useful citizen."

Key Terms

- citizenship
- petition

What Is Citizenship?

When Jane Addams finished college, she hoped to become a doctor. She wanted to give health care to the poor. However, a bad back stopped her from going to medical school.

Getting Involved

But at age 29, Addams bought a large, old house—Hull House—in a poor immigrant area of Chicago. Neighbors wondered about her. Why would she want to live in such a run-down house?

They soon found out. Addams wanted to help poor people solve the problems they faced. Sometimes Addams helped people directly. For example, one time a man tried to rob her. He needed money to feed his children. Addams did not call the police. Instead, she helped the man find a job.

More often, though, she helped people through programs at Hull House. At Hull House, immigrants could learn English. Working parents could leave their babies

▲ *The detail of a photograph of Jane Addams shown above was taken in 1892, about three years after Hull House opened.*

519

the alleys near Hull House. The piles of trash caused disease and death among the children who played in the alleys. So, Addams took a city job as a garbage inspector. Each morning, she followed the garbage wagons to be sure they got to the dump.

Defining Citizenship

Addams showed the full meaning of **citizenship.** In part, citizenship belongs to a person who lives in a certain country and has certain rights. U.S. citizens have freedom of speech, freedom of religion, and other rights. In addition, though, citizenship includes the duty to help solve problems, just as Addams did. In A Moment in Time on page 521, you will see another citizen in action. ■

Today, the Hull House Association in Chicago continues the work started by Jane Addams.

➤ *Many Hull House programs served neighborhood children such as these shown on the right.*

■ *How was Jane Addams a good citizen?*

there during the day. Children could take art classes. Families could gather for weddings and other events. Addams raised money from people across the country to pay for these programs.

Many problems that people faced needed government action. So Addams tried to change the government. She often worked in campaigns for people running for office. She wrote letters to members of Congress. She went to meetings to support giving women the right to vote. She lead marches to support laws ending the use of child labor in factories.

Addams even served in government herself. She worried about the garbage that filled

A School Reformer

*2:11 P.M., Saturday, May 13, 1905
On a temporary stage in a field in
Chesterfield County, Virginia*

Spectacles
She needs the glasses to read her
speech. It's the first time she has
ever spoken in public. She wants
to make a strong argument to the
audience of 359 people, including
a state legislator.

Pin
She is proud to wear the badge of
her women's literary club. The club
used to meet just to talk about
books. But she has been urging
members to become active in
state politics.

Dress
No decent southern lady would
dream of exposing her ankles
in public. The bottom of her
long dress got mud stained
during stops on her bumpy
coach trip from Richmond.

Flyer
The first two lines
boldly announce: "Our
children are the future
of our state. It pays to
educate the children of
every class."

Flower
Today she received this gift from
a barefoot nine-year-old girl who
has never been to school.

Speech
She tries to remember to say her
opening lines slowly and loudly:
"We must build clean, safe schools
for all the children in Virginia."

How Can Citizens Bring Change?

Many of the problems that Addams fought still exist. For example, hunger is still a serious problem. In 1985, the Physician Task Force on Hunger in America estimated that as many as 20 million Americans go hungry at least part of each month.

Around the world, the problem of hunger is even worse. From 13 to 18 million people die from lack of food each year. Studying the ways Addams fought problems in the past can show citizens how to fight hunger today.

Addams helped people directly. Today, religious groups and organizations like the Boy Scouts often help others through food drives. They provide food for hungry people in their communities.

Jane Addams also worked to raise money for the programs at Hull House. Today, many students and other citizens collect money for groups that feed hungry people in the United States and around the world.

Finally, Addams tried to influence the government. People

UNDERSTANDING CITIZENSHIP

Jane Addams was an excellent citizen because she helped improve her neighborhood, her city, and her country. Citizenship is a combination of rights and responsibilities that go along with living in a particular country.

Meaning of Citizenship

Not everyone who lives in a country is a citizen. For example, tourists from foreign countries who visit the United States are not citizens. They cannot vote or run for public office.

Who a country defines as its citizens may differ in different times and different places. For example, democracy began 2,000 years ago in Athens, Greece. In Athens, each citizen voted on the city's laws. But only free men could be citizens. Most people who lived in Athens—slaves, foreigners, women, and children—were not citizens. And non-citizens had no role in government.

Changes in Citizenship

In the United States, the idea of citizenship has changed over time. In 1776, most blacks, Indians, and white women could not vote. These groups, and others, have struggled to become full citizens. And through their struggle, they have won a right and responsibility—the vote.

Citizenship thus requires activism, from wearing buttons to running for office. As Jane Addams said, "Progress is not automatic; the world grows better because people wish that it should and take the right steps to make it better."

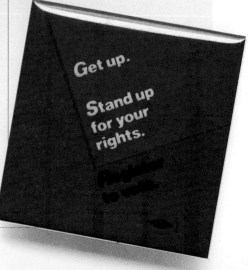

Get up.

Stand up for your rights.

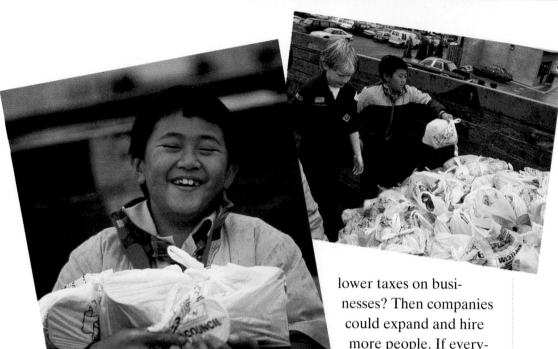

How are these Scouts showing good citizenship?

today can still **petition,** or try to influence the policies of government. Petitioning is one of the basic rights of all citizens protected by the United States Constitution.

Before citizens petition the government, though, they must first choose the best way to fight problems like hunger. Should the government spend less money on weapons? The money it saved could be used to help feed the poor. Or should the government lower taxes on businesses? Then companies could expand and hire more people. If everyone had a job, few people would go hungry.

To decide which approach works best, citizens can study how each solution worked in the past. Studying history, then, is a key part of effective citizenship.

Addams understood something quite important about good citizenship. She realized that helping people meant giving them the skills and knowledge to become active citizens themselves. Close to the end of her life Addams said, "Democracy is perhaps not an attainment, but a process—the process according to which we do not force law upon others, but make it for ourselves." ■

■ *How can a young person be a good citizen?*

R E V I E W

1. **FOCUS** What is the meaning of good citizenship?
2. **CONNECT** In what ways were W.E.B. Du Bois and Elizabeth Cady Stanton good citizens?
3. **HISTORY** List three ways Addams helped the poor.
4. **CITIZENSHIP** Name someone alive today that you consider a good citizen. Explain your choice.
5. **CRITICAL THINKING** Name a problem your school or community faces. Explain how you and your classmates could help solve that problem.
6. **ACTIVITY** Draw a picture showing the activities occurring in Hull House on a busy night. Label activities that show good citizenship.

Recognizing Others' Feelings

Here's Why

Have you ever been in a situation in which you were the newest person in the group and everyone but you knew what to do? Perhaps you were learning a new hobby, or had joined a new club. Did others in the group help you? Or did you struggle to catch on, feeling all alone?

If you have been in that kind of a situation, then you know a little bit about how to help newcomers. But even if you haven't, you can still learn to consider other people's feelings.

Jane Addams's background was very different from those of the people she helped at Hull House. But she learned how to recognize the needs of others.

Here's How

One way to experience the feelings of other people is to mentally put yourself in their place and consider their problems. This is what Jane Addams did at Hull House. She understood that to get along in the United States people needed to be able to read, write, and speak English. By mentally putting herself in their place, Addams was able to see what she needed to do to help immigrants.

Think what it would be like to be a new person in your school, someone who

Tips for Newcomers
1. Dress code
2. Hall passes
3. Absence procedure
4. Library procedure
5. Tardiness policy
6. Lunchroom procedure

needs to learn the rules and customs. One thing you could do to help is to put yourself in the new person's place. Think about what you might need to know and make a checklist. Above is an example of such a checklist. Would such a list help you if you were the new student? Can you think of other items to put on it?

Try It

Copy the checklist from this page and add items you think would be useful. Then fill in the information that you think a newcomer would need to know about each item.

Apply It

School is not the only place to which people are new. Make a checklist to help a newcomer participate in an activity you are involved in outside of school.

Chapter Review

Reviewing Key Terms

A. The key terms in each pair below are related in some way. On your own paper, write a sentence explaining how the words are related.
1. registration, suffrage
2. self-interest, segregation
3. minority, civil rights
4. citizenship, petition
5. discrimination, civil rights

B. Some of the following statements are true. The rest are false. Write *True* or *False* for each statement. Then rewrite the false statements to make them true.
1. The policy of discrimination allowed blacks to enjoy their civil rights fully.
2. When citizens petition, they threaten the safety of a democratic government.
3. In a democracy, citizenship carries with it responsibilities as well as rights.
4. The Constitution promises civil rights to everyone in the United States.
5. The campaign for women's suffrage was not successful after 70 years.

Exploring Concepts

A. Copy the diagram on your own paper. Notice the title and the names and activities given. Using information from the chapter, add a name and activities to complete the diagram.

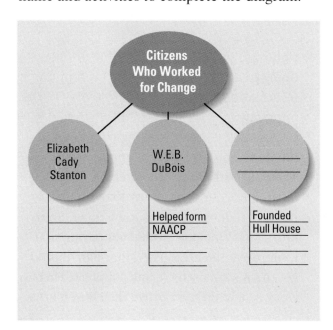

B. Answer each question with information from the chapter.
1. What are two of the civil rights promised in the United States Constitution?
2. What are some of the groups in this country whose civil rights have not always been respected?
3. Why did it take so long for women to receive the right to vote?
4. Struggle involving change often takes time. For example, the fight to end slavery and the effort to pass child-labor laws each took a long time. Why is this so?
5. In what ways did Jane Addams act as a "most useful citizen"?
6. How can citizens influence the government in a democracy?
7. How were the people discussed in this chapter good citizens? Why is it important to learn about them?

Reviewing Skills

1. Write an introductory paragraph for an oral report about women's suffrage.
2. Suppose you were preparing a report about the struggle for civil rights. Give two different possible subjects that narrow the topic.
3. Draw a picture of a group of people during the 1800s who are demonstrating for a cause they believe in. Include details that will help people guess what the cause is.
4. Suppose a new person has joined your soccer team. Make a list of things you could tell that person to make her or him feel welcome on the team.
5. What resources would you use to learn what foods are appropriate to serve when you invite someone from India to your home for dinner?
6. You and your best friend are having a discussion about civil rights. You make a statement that your friend says is just your opinion. You say it's a fact. How can you determine who is right?

Using Critical Thinking

1. The Constitution expresses the basic principles of our government. Look at the First Amendment to the Constitution on page 543. What rights are guaranteed? Why do you think these rights were chosen?
2. Imagine that freedom of the press has been taken away. What changes might there be in the materials you read?
3. In a democracy, change is often slow because freedom of speech gives everyone the right to comment on suggested changes. One way to speed up change would be to limit the number of people who can comment on a proposed change. Would this be a good idea? Explain.
4. In the past, people fought for the right to vote. However, many people in the United States who have that right do not vote. Why do you think people do not exercise their right to vote?
5. Name three problems that stores in your neighborhood face. What could you do to help solve them?

Preparing for Citizenship

1. **COLLECTING INFORMATION** Interview people in your community to determine what is being done to provide places for people your age to go after school, on weekends, and during vacations. Take pictures of existing places or make drawings to show places you would like to see made available to you. Present your findings in a scrapbook.
2. **GROUP ACTIVITY** Identify a group of people who are still fighting for their civil rights. Such a group might include immigrants from another country, blacks, and women. Interview someone who is a member of that group. Ask these questions: What rights are you fighting for? What are you doing to achieve those rights? Present the information to the class as a role-play of the interview.
3. **COLLABORATIVE LEARNING** Making your community look good is a part of good citizenship. Team up with three other people. Think of an area in your community that needs attention. Plan what needs to be done. Split into pairs. One pair should get permission to improve the area. The other pair should get the necessary tools and supplies. Then work as a team to improve the chosen area.

Time/Space Databank

U. S. Custom House. 1805.

★ ★ ★ ★ ★ ★ ★ ★ ★ ★

The Declaration of Independence

In Congress, July 4, 1776
The unaimous declaration of the thirteen united States of America

INTRODUCTION*

In the Declaration of Independence, the colonists explained why they were breaking away from Britain. They believed they had the right to form their own country.

W hen, in the course of human events, it becomes necessary for one people to dissolve the political bonds which have connected them with another, and to assume, among the powers of the earth, the separate and equal station to which the laws of nature and of nature's God entitle them, a decent respect to the opinions of mankind requires that they should declare the causes which impel them to the separation.

BASIC RIGHTS

The opening part of the Declaration is very famous. It says that all people are equal. Everyone has certain basic rights that are unalienable. That means that these rights cannot be taken away. Governments are formed to protect these basic rights. If a government does not do this, then the people have a right to begin a new one.

We hold these truths to be self-evident: That all men are created equal, that they are endowed by their Creator with certain unalienable rights; that among these are life, liberty, and the pursuit of happiness; that, to secure these rights, governments are instituted among men, deriving their just powers from the consent of the governed; that whenever any form of government becomes destructive of these ends, it is the right of the people to alter or to abolish it, and to institute new government, laying its foundation on such principles, and organizing its powers in such form, as to them shall seem most likely to effect their safety and happiness. Prudence, indeed, will dictate that governments long established should not be changed for light and transient causes; and accordingly all experience hath shown that mankind are more disposed to suffer, while evils are sufferable, than to right themselves by abolishing the forms to which they are accustomed. But when a long train of abuses and usurpations, pursuing invariably the same object, evinces a design to reduce them under absolute despotism, it is their right, it is their duty, to throw off such government, and to provide new guards for their future security. Such has been the patient sufferance of these colonies; and such is now the necessity which constrains them to alter their former systems of government. The history of the present King of Great Britain is a history of repeated injuries and usurpations, all having in direct object the establishment of an absolute tyranny over these states. To prove this, let facts be submitted to a candid world.

Forming a new government meant ending the colonial ties to the king. The writers listed the wrongs of King George III to prove the need for their actions.

*Titles have been added to the Declaration to make it easier to read. These titles are not in the original document.

★ ★ ★ ★ ★ ★ ★ ★ ★

CHARGES AGAINST THE KING

He has refused his assent to laws, the most wholesome and necessary for the public good.

He has forbidden his governors to pass laws of immediate and pressing importance, unless suspended in their operation till his assent should be obtained; and, when so suspended, he has utterly neglected to attend to them.

He has refused to pass other laws for the accommodation of large districts of people, unless those people would relinquish the right of representation in the legislature, a right inestimable to them, and formidable to tyrants only.

He has called together legislative bodies at places unusual, uncomfortable, and distant from the depository of their public records, for the sole purpose of fatiguing them into compliance with his measures.

He has dissolved representative houses repeatedly, for opposing, with manly firmness, his invasions on the rights of the people.

He has refused for a long time, after such dissolutions, to cause others to be elected; whereby the legislative powers, incapable of annihilation, have returned to the people at large for their exercise; the state remaining, in the mean time, exposed to all the dangers of invasions from without and convulsions within.

He has endeavored to prevent the population of these states; for that purpose obstructing the laws for the naturalization of foreigners; refusing to pass others to encourage their migration hither, and raising the conditions of new appropriations of lands.

He has obstructed the administration of justice, by refusing his assent to laws for establishing judiciary powers.

He has made judges dependent on his will alone, for the tenure of their offices, and the amount of payment of their salaries.

He has erected a multitude of new offices, and sent hither swarms of officers to harass our people and eat out their substance.

He has kept among us, in times of peace, standing armies, without the consent of our legislatures.

He has affected to render the military independent of, and superior to, the civil power.

He has combined with others to subject us to a jurisdiction foreign to our constitution and unacknowledged by our laws, giving his assent to their acts of pretended legislation:

For quartering large bodies of armed troops among us;

For protecting them, by a mock trial, from punishment for any murders which they should commit on the inhabitants of these states;

For cutting off our trade with all parts of the world;

For imposing taxes on us without our consent;

For depriving us, in many cases, of the benefits of trial by jury;

Colonists said the king had not let the colonies make their own laws. He had limited the people's representation in their assemblies.

The king had made colonial assemblies meet at unusual times and places. This made going to assembly meetings hard for colonial representatives.

In some cases the king stopped the assembly from meeting at all.

The king stopped people from moving to the colonies and into new western lands.

The king prevented the colonies from choosing their own judges. Instead, he sent over judges who depended on him for their jobs and pay.

The king kept British soldiers in the colonies, even though the colonists had not asked for them.

The king and Parliament had taxed the colonists without their consent. This was one of the most important reasons the colonists were angry at Britain.

★ ★ ★ ★ ★ ★ ★ ★ ★ ★ ★ ★ ★

For transporting us beyond seas, to be tried for pretended offenses;

For abolishing the free system of English laws in a neighboring province, establishing therein an arbitrary government, and enlarging its boundaries, so as to render it at once an example and fit instrument for introducing the same absolute rule into these colonies;

For taking away our charters, abolishing our most valuable laws, and altering fundamentally the forms of our governments.

For suspending our own legislatures, and declaring themselves invested with power to legislate for us in all cases whatsoever.

The colonists felt that the king had waged war on them.

He has abdicated government here, by declaring us out of his protection and waging war against us.

He has plundered our seas, ravaged our coasts, burned our towns, and destroyed the lives of our people.

The king had hired German soldiers and sent them to the colonies to keep order.

He is at this time transporting large armies of foreign mercenaries to complete the works of death, desolation, and tyranny already begun with circumstances of cruelty and perfidy scarcely paralleled in the most barbarous ages, and totally unworthy the head of a civilized nation.

He has constrained our fellow-citizens, taken captive on the high seas, to bear arms against their country, to become the executioners of their friends and brethren, or to fall themselves by their hands.

He has excited domestic insurrection among us, and has endeavored to bring on the inhabitants of our frontiers, the merciless Indian savages, whose known rule of warfare is an undistinguished destruction of all ages, sexes, and conditions.

RESPONSE TO THE KING

In every stage of these oppressions we have petitioned for redress in the most humble terms; our repeated petitions have been answered only by repeated injury. A prince, whose character is thus marked by every act which may define a tyrant, is unfit to be the ruler of a free people.

The colonists said that they had asked the king to change his policies, but he had not listened to them.

Nor have we been wanting in our attentions to our British brethren. We have warned them, from time to time, of attempts by their legislature to extend an unwarrantable jurisdiction over us. We have reminded them of the circumstances of our emigration and settlement here. We have appealed to their native justice and magnanimity; and we have conjured them, by the ties of our common kindred, to disavow these usurpations, which would inevitably interrupt our connections and correspondence. They, too, have been deaf to the voice of justice and of consanguinity. We must, therefore, acquiesce in the necessity which denounces our separation, and hold them, as we hold the rest of mankind, enemies in war, in peace friends.

★ ★ ★ ★ ★ ★ ★ ★ ★ ★ ★ ★

INDEPENDENCE

We, therefore, the representatives of the United States of America, in General Congress assembled, appealing to the Supreme Judge of the world for the rectitude of our intentions, do, in the name and by the authority of the good people of these colonies, solemnly publish and declare, that these United Colonies are, and of right ought to be, FREE AND INDEPENDENT STATES; that they are absolved from all allegiance to the British crown, and that all political connection between them and the state of Great Britain is, and ought to be, totally dissolved; and that, as free and independent states, they have full power to levy war, conclude peace, contract alliances, establish commerce, and do all other acts and things which independent states may of right do. And for the support of this declaration, with a firm reliance on the protection of Divine Providence, we mutually pledge to each other our lives, our fortunes, and our sacred honor.

John Hancock

The writers declared that the colonies were free and independent states, equal to the world's other states. They had the powers to make war and peace and to trade with other countries.

The signers pledged their lives to the support of this Declaration. The Continental Congress ordered the Declaration of Independence to be read in all the states and to the army.

NEW HAMPSHIRE
Josiah Bartlett
William Whipple
Matthew Thornton

MASSACHUSETTS
John Adams
Samuel Adams
Robert Treat Paine
Elbridge Gerry

NEW YORK
William Floyd
Philip Livingston
Francis Lewis
Lewis Morris

RHODE ISLAND
Stephen Hopkins
William Ellery

NEW JERSEY
Richard Stockton
John Witherspoon
Francis Hopkinson
John Hart
Abraham Clark

PENNSYLVANIA
Robert Morris
Benjamin Rush
Benjamin Franklin
John Morton
George Clymer
James Smith
George Taylor
James Wilson
George Ross

DELAWARE
Caesar Rodney
George Read
Thomas McKean

MARYLAND
Samuel Chase
William Paca
Thomas Stone
Charles Carroll of Carrollton

NORTH CAROLINA
William Hooper
Joseph Hewes
John Penn

VIRGINIA
George Wythe
Richard Henry Lee
Thomas Jefferson
Benjamin Harrison
Thomas Nelson, Jr.
Francis Lightfoot Lee
Carter Braxton

SOUTH CAROLINA
Edward Rutledge
Thomas Heyward, Jr.
Thomas Lynch, Jr.
Arthur Middleton

CONNECTICUT
Roger Sherman
Samuel Huntington
William Williams
Oliver Wolcott

GEORGIA
Button Gwinnett
Lyman Hall
George Walton

★ ★ ★ ★ ★ ★ ★ ★ ★ ★

The Constitution of the United States

PREAMBLE
INTRODUCTION*

We the people of the United States, in order to form a more perfect union, establish justice, insure domestic tranquility, provide for the common defense, promote the general welfare, and secure the blessings of liberty to ourselves and our posterity, do ordain and establish this Constitution for the United States of America.

ARTICLE 1
LEGISLATIVE BRANCH

SECTION 1. CONGRESS

All legislative powers herein granted shall be vested in a Congress of the United States, which shall consist of a Senate and House of Representatives.

SECTION 2. HOUSE OF REPRESENTATIVES

Election and Term of Members *The House of Representatives shall be composed of members chosen every second year by the people of the several States, and the electors in each State shall have the qualifications requisite for electors of the most numerous branch of the State legislature.*

Qualifications *No person shall be a representative who shall not have attained to the age of twenty-five years, and been seven years a citizen of the United States, and who shall not, when elected, be an inhabitant of that State in which he shall be chosen.*

Number of Representatives per State *Representatives and direct taxes shall be apportioned among the several States which may be included within this Union, according to their respective numbers,* which shall be determined by adding to the whole number of free persons, including those bound to service for a term of years, and excluding Indians not taxed, three-fifths of all other persons.** *The actual enumeration shall be made within*

---

* The titles of the Preamble, and of each article, section, clause, and amendment have been added to make the Constitution easier to read. These titles are not in the original document.

** Parts of the Constitution are printed in regular type rather than italics to show that they are not in force anymore. They have been changed by amendments or they no longer apply.

Introduction The Preamble states the purposes of the Constitution. The writers wanted to strengthen the national government and to secure peace for the United States.

Congress Section 1 gives Congress the power to make laws. Congress has two parts, the House of Representatives and the Senate.

Election and Term of Members Citizens elect the members of the House of Representatives every two years.

Qualifications Representatives must be at least 25 years old. They must have been United States citizens for at least seven years. They also must live in the state they represent.

Number of Representatives per State The number of representatives each state has is based on its population. The biggest states have the most representatives. Each state must have at least one representative.

three years after the first meeting of the Congress of the United States, and within every subsequent term of ten years, in such manner as they shall by law direct. The number of representatives shall not exceed one for every thirty thousand, but each State shall have at least one representative; and until such enumeration shall be made, the State of New Hampshire shall be entitled to choose three, Massachusetts eight, Rhode Island and Providence Plantations one, Connecticut five, New York six, New Jersey Four, Pennsylvania eight, Delaware one, Maryland six, Virginia ten, North Carolina five, South Carolina five, and Georgia three.

Vacancies *When vacancies happen in the representation from any State, the executive authority thereof shall issue writs of election to fill such vacancies.*

Special Powers *The House of Representatives shall choose their speaker and other officers, and shall have the sole power of impeachment.*

SECTION 3. SENATE

Number, Term, and Selection of Members *The Senate of the United States shall be composed of two senators from each State, chosen by the legislature thereof, for six years; and each senator shall have one vote.*

Overlapping Terms and Filling Vacancies Immediately after they shall be assembled in consequence of the first election, they shall be divided as equally as may be into three classes. The seats of the senators of the first class shall be vacated at the expiration of the second year, of the second class at the expiration of the fourth year, and of the third class at the expiration of the sixth year, *so that one-third may be chosen every second year;* and if vacancies happen by resignation, or otherwise, during the recess of the legislature of any State, the executive thereof may make temporary appointments until the next meeting of the legislature, which shall then fill such vacancies.

Qualifications *No person shall be a senator who shall not have attained to the age of thirty years, and been nine years a citizen of the United States, and who shall not, when elected, be an inhabitant of that State for which he shall be chosen.*

President of the Senate *The Vice President of the United States shall be President of the Senate, but shall have no vote, unless they be equally divided.*

Other Officers *The Senate shall choose their other officers, and also a President pro tempore, in the absence of the Vice President, or when he shall exercise the office of President of the United States.*

Impeachment Trials *The Senate shall have the sole power to try all impeachments. When sitting for that purpose, they shall be on oath or affirmation. When the President of the United States is tried, the Chief Justice shall preside: and no person shall be*

Number, Term, and Selection of Members In each state, citizens elect two members of the Senate. This gives all states, whether big or small, equal power in the Senate. Senators serve six-year terms. According to the original Constitution, state legislatures choose the senators for their states. Today, however, people elect their senators directly. The Seventeenth Amendment made this change in 1913.

Qualifications Senators must be at least 30 years old and United States citizens for at least nine years. Like representatives, they must live in the state they represent.

President of the Senate The Vice President of the United States acts as the President, or chief officer, of the Senate. The Vice President votes only in cases of a tie.

Impeachment Trials If the House of Representatives impeaches an official with a crime, the Senate holds a trial. If two-thirds of the senators find the official guilty, then the person is removed from office. The only President ever impeached was Andrew Johnson in 1868. He was found not guilty.

convicted without the concurrence of two-thirds of the members present.

Penalties *Judgment in cases of impeachment shall not extend further than to removal from office, and disqualification to hold and enjoy any office of honor, trust or profit under the United States: but the party convicted shall nevertheless be liable and subject to indictment, trial, judgment and punishment, according to law.*

SECTION 4. ELECTIONS AND MEETINGS

Election of Congress *The times, places and manner of holding elections for senators and representatives shall be prescribed in each State by the legislature thereof; but the Congress may at any time by law make or alter such regulations, except as to the places of choosing senators.*

Annual Sessions *The Congress shall assemble at least once in every year, and such meeting* shall be on the first Monday in December, unless they shall by law appoint a different day.

SECTION 5. RULES OF PROCEDURE

Organization *Each house shall be the judge of the elections, returns and qualifications of its own members, and a majority of each shall constitute a quorum to do business; but a smaller number may adjourn from day to day, and may be authorized to compel the attendance of absent members, in such manner, and under such penalties as each house may provide.*

Rules *Each house may determine the rules of its proceedings, punish its members for disorderly behavior, and, with the concurrence of two-thirds, expel a member.*

Journal *Each house shall keep a journal of its proceedings, and from time to time publish the same, excepting such parts as may in their judgment require secrecy; and the yeas and nays of the members of either house on any question shall, at the desire of one-fifth of those present, be entered on the journal.*

Adjournment *Neither house, during the session of Congress, shall, without the consent of the other, adjourn for more than three days, nor to any other place than that in which the two houses shall be sitting.*

SECTION 6. PRIVILEGES AND RESTRICTIONS

Pay and Protection *The senators and representatives shall receive a compensation for their services, to be ascertained by law, and paid out of the treasury of the United States. They shall in all cases, except treason, felony and breach of the peace, be privileged from arrest during their attendance at the session of their respective houses, and in going to and returning from the same; and for any speech or debate in either house, they shall not be questioned in any other place.*

Restrictions *No senator or representative shall, during the time for which he was elected, be appointed to any civil office under the authority of the United States, which shall have been created, or the emoluments thereof shall have been increased during such time; and*

Election of Congress Each state decides where and when to hold elections. Today congressional elections are held in even-numbered years, on the Tuesday after the first Monday in November.

Annual Sessions The Constitution requires Congress to meet at least once a year. In 1933, the Twentieth Amendment moved the required meeting date of Congress to January 3.

Organization A quorum is the smallest number of members that must be present for an organization to hold a meeting. For each house of Congress, this number is the majority, or more than one-half, of its members.

Journal The Constitution requires each house to keep a record of its proceedings. *The Congressional Record* is published every day. It allows any person to look up the votes of his or her representative.

Pay and Protection Congress sets the salaries of its members, and they are paid by the federal government. No member can be arrested for anything he or she says while in office. This protection allows members to speak freely in Congress.

Restrictions Members of Congress cannot hold other federal offices during their terms. This rule protects the checks and balances system set up by the Constitution.

★ ★ ★ ★ ★ ★ ★ ★ ★

no person holding any office under the United States shall be a member of either house during his continuance in office.

SECTION 7. MAKING LAWS

Tax Bills *All bills for raising revenue shall originate in the House of Representatives; but the Senate may propose or concur with amendments as on other bills.*

Passing a Law *Every bill which shall have passed the House of Representatives and the Senate, shall, before it becomes a law, be presented to the President of the United States; if he approve he shall sign it, but if not he shall return it, with his objections to that house in which it shall have originated, who shall enter the objections at large on their journal, and proceed to reconsider it. If after such reconsideration two-thirds of that house shall agree to pass the bill, it shall be sent, together with the objections, to the other house, by which it shall likewise be reconsidered, and if approved by two-thirds of that house, it shall become a law. But in all such cases the votes of both houses shall be determined by yeas and nays, and the names of the persons voting for and against the bill shall be entered on the journal of each house respectively. If any bill shall not be returned by the President within ten days (Sundays excepted) after it shall have been presented to him, the same shall be a law, in like manner as if he had signed it, unless the Congress by their adjournment prevent its return, in which case it shall not be a law.*

Orders and Resolutions *Every order, resolution, or vote to which the concurrence of the Senate and House of Representatives may be necessary (except on a question of adjournment) shall be presented to the President of the United States; and before the same shall take effect, shall be approved by him, or being disapproved by him, shall be repassed by two-thirds of the Senate and House of Representatives, according to the rules and limitations prescribed in the case of a bill.*

SECTION 8. POWERS DELEGATED TO CONGRESS

Taxation *The Congress shall have power to lay and collect taxes, duties, imposts, and excises, to pay the debts and provide for the common defense and general welfare of the United States; but all duties, imposts and excises shall be uniform throughout the United States;*

Borrowing *To borrow money on the credit of the United States;*

Commerce *To regulate commerce with foreign nations, and among the several States, and with the Indian tribes;*

Naturalization and Bankruptcy *To establish a uniform rule of naturalization, and uniform laws on the subject of bankruptcies through the United States;*

Coins and Measures *To coin money, regulate the value thereof, and of foreign coin, and fix the standard of weights and measures;*

Counterfeiting *To provide for the punishment of counterfeiting the securities and current coin of the United States;*

Post Offices *To establish post offices and post roads;*

Tax Bills A bill is a proposed law. Only the House of Representatives can introduce bills that tax the people.

Passing a Law A bill must be passed by the majority of members in each house of Congress. Then it is sent to the President. If the President signs it, the bill becomes a law.

The President can also veto, or reject, a bill by not signing it. However, if each house of Congress repasses the bill by a two-thirds vote, it becomes a law. Passing a law after the President has vetoed it is called overriding a veto. This process is an important part of the checks and balances system set up by the Constitution.

Orders and Resolutions Congress can also pass orders and resolutions that have the same power as laws. Such acts are also subject to the President's veto.

Taxation Only Congress has the power to collect taxes.

Commerce Congress controls trade with foreign countries.

Naturalization and Bankruptcy Naturalization is the process by which a person from another country becomes a United States citizen. Congress decides the requirements for this procedure.

Copyrights and Patents Patents allow inventors to profit from their work by keeping control over it for a certain number of years. Congress grants patents to encourage scientific research.

Declaring War Only Congress can declare war on another country.

Militia Today the militia is called the National Guard. The National Guard often helps people after floods, tornadoes, and other disasters.

National Capital Congress makes the laws for Washington, D.C., the nation's capital.

Necessary Laws This clause allows Congress to make laws on issues, such as television or radio, that are not mentioned in the Constitution.

Slave Trade This clause was another compromise between the North and the South. It prevented Congress from regulating the slave trade for 20 years. Congress outlawed the slave trade in 1808.

Habeas Corpus A writ of habeas corpus requires the government to either charge a person in jail with a particular crime, or else let the person go free. Except in emergencies, Congress cannot deny the right of a person to a writ.

★ ★ ★ ★ ★ ★ ★ ★ ★

Copyrights and Patents To promote the progress of science and useful arts by securing for limited times to authors and inventors the exclusive right to their respective writings and discoveries;

Courts To constitute tribunals inferior to the Supreme Court;

Piracy To define and punish piracies and felonies committed on the high seas, and offenses against the law of nations;

Declaring War To declare war, grant letters of marque and reprisal, and make rules concerning captures on land and water;

Army To raise and support armies, but no appropriation of money to that use shall be for a longer term than two years;

Navy To provide and maintain a navy;

Military Regulations To make rules for the government and regulation of the land and naval forces;

Militia To provide for calling forth the militia to execute the laws of the Union, suppress insurrections and repel invasions;

Militia Regulations To provide for organizing, arming, and disciplining the militia, and for governing such part of them as may be employed in the service of the United States, reserving to the States respectively the appointment of the officers, and the authority of training the militia according to the discipline prescribed by Congress;

National Capital To exercise exclusive legislation in all cases whatsoever, over such district (not exceeding ten miles square) as may, by cession of particular States and the acceptance of Congress, become the seat of the government of the United States, and to exercise like authority over all places purchased by the consent of the legislature of the State in which the same shall be, for the erection of forts, magazines, arsenals, dockyards, and other needful buildings; and

Necessary Laws To make all laws which shall be necessary and proper for carrying into execution the foregoing powers, and all other powers vested by this Constitution in the government of the United States, or in any department or officer thereof.

SECTION 9. POWERS DENIED TO CONGRESS

Slave Trade The migration or importation of such persons as any of the States now existing shall think proper to admit, shall not be prohibited by the Congress prior to the year one thousand eight hundred and eight, but a tax or duty may be imposed on such importation, not exceeding ten dollars for each person.

Habeas Corpus The privilege of the writ of habeas corpus shall not be suspended, unless when in cases of rebellion or invasion the public safety may require it.

Special Laws No bill of attainder or ex post facto law shall be passed.

Direct Taxes No capitation, or other direct, tax shall be laid, unless in proportion to the census or enumeration herein before directed to be taken.

★ ★ ★ ★ ★ ★ ★ ★ ★

Export Taxes *No tax or duty shall be laid on articles exported from any State.*

Ports *No preference shall be given by any regulation of commerce or revenue to the ports of one State over those of another; nor shall vessels bound to, or from, one State be obliged to enter, clear, or pay duties in another.*

Ports When regulating trade, Congress must treat all states equally. Also, states cannot tax goods traveling between the states.

Regulations on Spending *No money shall be drawn from the treasury, but in consequence of appropriations made by law; and a regular statement and account of the receipts and expenditures of all public money shall be published from time to time.*

Regulations on Spending Congress controls the spending of public money. This clause checks the President's power.

Titles of Nobility and Gifts *No title of nobility shall be granted by the United States: and no person holding any office of profit or trust under them, shall, without the consent of the Congress, accept of any present, emolument, office, or title, of any kind whatever, from any king, prince, or foreign State.*

SECTION 10. POWERS DENIED TO THE STATES

Complete Restrictions *No State shall enter into any treaty, alliance, or confederation; grant letters of marque and reprisal; coin money; emit bills of credit; make anything but gold and silver coin a tender in payment of debts; pass any bill of attainder, ex post facto law, or law impairing the obligation of contracts, or grant any title of nobility.*

Complete Restrictions The Constitution prevents the states from acting like individual countries. States cannot make treaties with foreign nations. They cannot issue their own money.

Partial Restrictions *No State shall, without the consent of the Congress, lay any imposts or duties on imports or exports, except what may be absolutely necessary for executing its inspection laws: and the net produce of all duties and imposts laid by any State on imports or exports, shall be for the use of the treasury of the United States; and all such laws shall be subject to the revision and control of the Congress.*

Partial Restrictions States cannot tax imports and exports without approval from Congress.

Other Restrictions *No State shall, without the consent of Congress, lay any duty of tonnage, keep troops, or ships of war in time of peace, enter into any agreement or compact with another State, or with a foreign power, or engage in war, unless actually invaded, or in such imminent danger as will not admit of delay.*

Other Restrictions States cannot declare war. They cannot keep their own armies.

ARTICLE II
EXECUTIVE BRANCH

SECTION 1. PRESIDENT AND VICE PRESIDENT

Term of Office *The executive power shall be vested in a President of the United States of America. He shall hold his office during the term of four years, and, together with the Vice President, chosen for the same term, be elected as follows:*

Term of Office The President has the power to carry out the laws passed by Congress. The President and the Vice President serve four-year terms.

Electoral College *Each State shall appoint, in such manner as the legislature thereof may direct, a number of electors, equal to the whole number of senators and representatives to which the State may be entitled in the Congress; but no senator or representative, or person holding an office of trust or profit under the United States, shall be appointed an elector.*

The Electoral College A group of people called the Electoral College actually elect the President. The number of electors each state receives equals the total number of its representatives and senators.

Election Process Today electors almost always vote for the candidate who won the popular vote in their states. In other words, the candidate who wins the popular vote in a state also wins its electoral votes.

Time of Elections Today we elect our President on the Tuesday after the first Monday in November.

Qualifications A President must be at least 35 years old, a United States citizen by birth, and a resident of the United States for at least 14 years.

Vacancies If the President resigns, dies, or is impeached and found guilty, the Vice President becomes President.

Salary The President receives a yearly salary that cannot be increased or decreased during his or her term. The President cannot hold any other government positions while in office.

Oath of Office Every President must promise to uphold the Constitution. The Chief Justice of the Supreme Court usually administers this oath.

★ ★ ★ ★ ★ ★ ★ ★ ★

Election Process The electors shall meet in their respective States, and vote by ballot for two persons, of whom one at least shall not be an inhabitant of the same State with themselves. And they shall make a list of all the persons voted for, and of the number of votes for each; which list they shall sign and certify, and transmit sealed to the seat of the government of the United States, directed to the President of the Senate. The President of the Senate shall, in the presence of the Senate and House of Representatives, open all the certificates, and the votes shall then be counted. The person having the greatest number of votes shall be the President, if such number be a majority of the whole number of electors appointed, and if there be more than one who have such majority, and have an equal number of votes, then the House of Representatives shall immediately choose by ballot one of them for President; and if no person have a majority, then from the five highest on the list the said house shall in like manner choose the President. But in choosing the President, the votes shall be taken by States, the representation from each State having one vote; a quorum for this purpose shall consist of a member or members from two-thirds of the States, and a majority of all the States shall be necessary to a choice. In every case, after the choice of the President, the person having the greatest number of votes of the electors shall be the Vice President. But if there should remain two or more who have equal votes, the Senate shall choose from them by ballot the Vice President.

Time of Elections. The Congress may determine the time of choosing the electors, and the day on which they shall give their votes; which day shall be the same throughout the United States.

Qualifications No person except a natural-born citizen, or a citizen of the United States at the time of the adoption of this Constitution, *shall be eligible to the office of President; neither shall any person be eligible to that office who shall not have attained to the age of thirty-five years, and been fourteen years a resident within the United States.*

Vacancies In case of the removal of the President from office, or of his death, resignation, or inability to discharge the powers and duties of the said office, the same shall devolve on the Vice President, and the Congress may by law provide for the case of removal, death, resignation, or inability, both of the President and Vice President, declaring what officer shall then act as President, and such officer shall act accordingly, until the disability be removed, or a President shall be elected.

Salary The President shall, at stated times, receive for his services a compensation, which shall neither be increased nor diminished during the period for which he shall have been elected, and he shall not receive within that period any other emolument from the United States, or any of them.

Oath of Office Before he enter on the execution of his office, he shall take the following oath or affirmation:—"I do solemnly swear

★ ★ ★ ★ ★ ★ ★ ★ ★

(or affirm) that I will faithfully execute the office of President of the United States, and will to the best of my ability, preserve, protect and defend the Constitution of the United States."

SECTION 2. POWERS OF THE PRESIDENT

Military Powers The President shall be commander in chief of the army and navy of the United States, and of the militia of the several States, when called into the actual service of the United States; he may require the opinion, in writing, of the principal officer in each of the executive departments, upon any subject relating to the duties of their respective offices, and he shall have power to grant reprieves and pardons for offenses against the United States, except in cases of impeachment.

Treaties and Appointments He shall have power, by and with the advice and consent of the Senate, to make treaties, provided two-thirds of the senators present concur; and he shall nominate, and by and with the advice and consent of the Senate, shall appoint ambassadors, other public ministers and consuls, judges of the Supreme Court, and all other officers of the United States, whose appointments are not herein otherwise provided for, and which shall be established by law: but the Congress may by law vest the appointment of such inferior officers, as they think proper, in the President alone, in the courts of law, or in the heads of departments.

Temporary Appointments The President shall have power to fill up all vacancies that may happen during the recess of the Senate, by granting commissions which shall expire at the end of their next session.

SECTION 3. DUTIES

He shall from time to time give to the Congress information of the State of the Union, and recommend to their consideration such measures as he shall judge necessary and expedient; he may on extraordinary occasions, convene both houses, or either of them, and in case of disagreement between them with respect to the time of adjournment, he may adjourn them to such time as he shall think proper; he shall receive ambassadors and other public ministers; he shall take care that the laws be faithfully executed, and shall commission all the officers of the United States.

SECTION 4. IMPEACHMENT

The President, Vice President and all civil officers of the United States, shall be removed from office on impeachment for, and conviction of, treason, bribery, or other high crimes and misdemeanors.

ARTICLE III
JUDICIAL BRANCH

SECTION 1. FEDERAL COURTS

The judicial power of the United States shall be vested in one Supreme Court, and in such inferior courts as the Congress may from time to time ordain and establish. The judges, both of the Supreme and inferior courts, shall hold their offices during good behavior, and

Military Powers The President is the leader of the country's military forces.

Treaties and Appointments The President can make treaties with other nations. However, treaties must be approved by a two-thirds vote of the Senate. The President also appoints Supreme Court Justices and ambassadors to foreign countries. The Senate must approve these appointments.

Duties The President must report to Congress at least once a year and make recommendations for laws. This report is known as the State of the Union Address. The President delivers it each January.

Impeachment The President can be forced out of office only if found guilty of particular crimes. This clause protects government officials from being impeached for unimportant reasons.

Federal Courts The Supreme Court is the highest court in the nation. It makes the final decisions in all of the cases it hears. Today nine judges sit on the Supreme Court. Congress also has the power to set up a system of lower federal courts. All federal judges hold their offices for as long as they live.

539

shall, at stated times, receive for their services, a compensation which shall not be diminished during their continuance in office.

SECTION 2. AUTHORITY OF THE FEDERAL COURTS

General Jurisdiction *The judicial power shall extend to all cases, in law and equity, arising under this Constitution, the laws of the United States, and treaties made, or which shall be made, under their authority;—to all cases affecting ambassadors, other public ministers and consuls;—to all cases of admiralty and maritime jurisdiction;—to controversies to which the United States shall be a party;—to controversies between two or more States;—between a State and citizens of another State; between citizens of different States;—between citizens of the same State claiming lands under grants of different States, and between a State, or the citizens thereof, and foreign states, citizens or subjects.*

The Supreme Court *In all cases affecting ambassadors, other public ministers and consuls, and those in which a State shall be party, the Supreme Court shall have original jurisdiction. In all the other cases before mentioned, the Supreme Court shall have appellate jurisdiction, both as to law and fact, with such exceptions, and under such regulations as the Congress shall make.*

Trial by Jury *The trial of all crimes, except in cases of impeachment, shall be by jury; and such trial shall be held in the State where the said crimes shall have been committed; but when not committed within any State, the trial shall be at such place or places as the Congress may by law have directed.*

SECTION 3. TREASON

Definition *Treason against the United States shall consist only in levying war against them, or in adhering to their enemies, giving them aid and comfort. No person shall be convicted of treason unless on the testimony of two witnesses to the same overt act, or on confession in open court.*

Punishment *The Congress shall have power to declare the punishment of treason, but no attainder of treason shall work corruption of blood, or forfeiture except during the life of the person attainted.*

ARTICLE IV
RELATIONS AMONG THE STATES

SECTION 1. OFFICIAL RECORDS

Full faith and credit shall be given in each State to the public acts, records, and judicial proceedings of every other State. And the Congress may by general laws prescribe the manner in which such acts, records, and proceedings shall be proved, and the effect thereof.

SECTION 2. PRIVILEGES OF THE CITIZENS

Privileges *The citizens of each State shall be entitled to all privileges and immunities of citizens in the several States.*

The Supreme Court One of the Supreme Court's most important jobs is to decide whether a law passed is constitutional. This power is another example of the checks and balances system in the federal government.

Trial by Jury The Constitution guarantees everyone the right to a trial by jury. The only exception is in impeachment cases, which are tried in the Senate.

Definition People cannot be convicted of treason in the United States for what they think or say. To be guilty of treason, a person must rebel against the government by using violence or helping enemies of the country.

Official Records Each state must accept the laws, acts, and legal decisions made by other states.

Privileges Citizens have all the rights of the citizens of whichever state they are in.

★ ★ ★ ★ ★ ★ ★ ★ ★

Return of a Person Accused of a Crime *A person charged in any State with treason, felony, or other crime, who shall flee from justice, and be found in another State, shall on demand of the executive authority of the State from which he fled, be delivered up, to be removed to the State having jurisdiction of the crime.*

Return of Fugitive Slaves No person held to service or labor in one State, under the laws thereof, escaping into another, shall, in consequence of any law or regulation therein, be discharged from such service or labor, but shall be delivered up on claim of the party to whom such service or labor may be due.

SECTION 3. NEW STATES AND TERRITORIES

New States *New States may be admitted by the Congress into this Union; but no new State shall be formed or erected within the jurisdiction of any other State; nor any State be formed by the junction of two or more States or parts of States, without the consent of the legislatures of the States concerned as well as of the Congress.*

Federal Lands *The Congress shall have power to dispose of and make all needful rules and regulations respecting the territory or other property belonging to the United States; and nothing in this Constitution shall be so construed as to prejudice any claims of the United States, or of any particular State.*

SECTION 4. GUARANTEES TO THE STATES

The United States shall guarantee to every State in this Union a republican form of government, and shall protect each of them against invasion; and on application of the legislature, or of the executive (when the legislature cannot be convened) against domestic violence.

ARTICLE V
AMENDING THE CONSTITUTION

The Congress, whenever two-thirds of both houses shall deem it necessary, shall propose amendments to this Constitution, or, on the application of the legislatures of two-thirds of the several States, shall call a convention for proposing amendments, which, in either case, shall be valid to all intents and purposes, as part of this Constitution, when ratified by the legislatures of three-fourths of the several States, or by conventions in three-fourths thereof, as the one or the other mode of ratification may be proposed by the Congress; provided *that no amendments which may be made prior to the year one thousand eight hundred and eight shall in any manner affect the first and fourth clauses in the ninth section of the first article, and* that no State, without its consent, shall be deprived of its equal suffrage in the Senate.

ARTICLE VI
GENERAL PROVISIONS

Public Debt *All debts contracted and engagements entered into, before the adoption of this Constitution, shall be as valid against the United States under this Constitution, as under the Confederation.*

Return of a Person Accused of a Crime If a person charged with a crime escapes to another state, he or she must be returned to the original state to go on trial. This act of returning someone from one state to another is called extradition.

New States Congress has the power to create new states out of the nation's territories. All new states have the same rights as the old states. This clause made it clear that the United States would not make colonies out of its new lands.

Guarantees to the States The federal government must defend the states from attacks by other countries and from rebellions.

Amending the Constitution An amendment to the Constitution may be proposed either by a two-thirds vote of each house of Congress or at the request of two-thirds of the states. To be ratified, or approved, an amendment must be supported either by three-fourths of the state legislatures or by three-fourths of special conventions held in each state.

Once an amendment is ratified, it becomes a part of the Constitution. Only a new amendment can change it. Amendments have allowed people to change the Constitution to meet the changing needs of the nation.

CONSTITUTION

541

Federal Supremacy The Constitution is the highest law in the nation. Whenever a state law and a federal law are different, the federal law must be obeyed.

Oaths of Office All state and federal officials must promise to obey the Constitution.

Ratification The Constitution went into effect as soon as nine of the thirteen states approved it.

Each state held a special convention to debate the Constitution. The ninth state to approve the Constitution, New Hampshire, voted for ratification on June 21, 1788.

★ ★ ★ ★ ★ ★ ★ ★ ★

Federal Supremacy This Constitution, and the laws of the United States which shall be made in pursuance thereof; and all treaties made, or which shall be made, under the authority of the United States, shall be the supreme law of the land; and the judges in every State shall be bound thereby, anything in the constitution or laws of any State to the contrary notwithstanding.

Oaths of Office The senators and representatives before mentioned, and the members of the several State legislatures, and all executive and judicial officers, both of the United States, and of the several States, shall be bound by oath or affirmation to support this Constitution; but no religious test shall ever be required as a qualification to any office or public trust under the United States.

ARTICLE VII
RATIFICATION

The ratification of the conventions of nine States shall be sufficient for the establishment of this Constitution between the States so ratifying the same.

Done in Convention by the unanimous consent of the States present the seventeenth day of September in the year of our Lord one thousand seven hundred and eighty-seven and of the independence of the United States of America the twelfth. In witness whereof we have hereunto subscribed our names.

George Washington, President and deputy from Virginia

DELAWARE
George Read
Gunning Bedford, Junior
John Dickinson
Richard Bassett
Jacob Broom

MARYLAND
James McHenry
Daniel of St. Thomas Jenifer
Daniel Carroll

VIRGINIA
John Blair
James Madison, Junior

NORTH CAROLINA
William Blount
Richard Dobbs Spaight
Hugh Williamson

SOUTH CAROLINA
John Rutledge
Charles Cotesworth Pinckney
Charles Pinckney
Pierce Butler

GEORGIA
William Few
Abraham Baldwin

NEW HAMPSHIRE
John Langdon
Nicholas Gilman

MASSACHUSETTS
Nathaniel Gorham
Rufus King

CONNECTICUT
William Samuel Johnson
Roger Sherman

NEW YORK
Alexander Hamilton

NEW JERSEY
William Livingston
David Brearley
William Paterson
Jonathan Dayton

PENNSYLVANIA
Benjamin Franklin
Thomas Mifflin
Robert Morris
George Clymer
Thomas FitzSimmons
Jared Ingersoll
James Wilson
Gouverneur Morris

★ ★ ★ ★ ★ ★ ★ ★ ★

FIRST AMENDMENT (1791)*
BASIC FREEDOMS

Congress shall make no law respecting an establishment of religion, or prohibiting the free exercise thereof; or abridging the freedom of speech, or of the press; or the right of the people peaceably to assemble, and to petition the government for a redress of grievances.

SECOND AMENDMENT (1791)
WEAPONS AND THE MILITIA

A well-regulated militia being necessary to the security of a free State, the right of the people to keep and bear arms shall not be infringed.

THIRD AMENDMENT (1791)
HOUSING SOLDIERS

No soldier shall, in time of peace, be quartered in any house, without the consent of the owner, nor in time of war, but in a manner to be prescribed by law.

FOURTH AMENDMENT (1791)
SEARCH AND SEIZURE

The right of the people to be secure in their persons, houses, papers, and effects, against unreasonable searches and seizures, shall not be violated, and no warrants shall issue, but upon probable cause, supported by oath or affirmation, and particularly describing the place to be searched, and the persons or things to be seized.

FIFTH AMENDMENT (1791)
RIGHTS OF THE ACCUSED

No person shall be held to answer for a capital or otherwise infamous crime, unless on a presentment or indictment of a grand jury, except in cases arising in the land or naval forces, or in the militia, when in actual service in time of war or public danger; nor shall any person be subject for the same offense to be twice put in jeopardy of life or limb; nor shall be compelled in any criminal case to be a witness against himself, nor be deprived of life, liberty, or property, without due process of law; nor shall private property be taken for public use without just compensation.

SIXTH AMENDMENT (1791)
RIGHT TO A FAIR TRIAL

In all criminal prosecutions, the accused shall enjoy the right to a speedy and public trial, by an impartial jury of the State and district wherein the crime shall have been committed, which district shall have been previously ascertained by law, and to be informed of the nature and cause of the accusation; to be confronted with the witnesses against him; to have compulsory process for obtaining witnesses in his favor, and to have the assistance of counsel for his defense.

* The date beside each amendment is the year that the amendment was ratified.

Basic Freedoms The government cannot pass laws that favor one religion over another. Nor can it stop people from saying or writing whatever they want. The people have the right to openly gather and discuss problems they have with the government.

Weapons and the Militia This amendment was included to prevent the federal government from taking away guns used by members of state militias.

Housing Soldiers The army cannot use people's homes to house soldiers unless it is approved by law.

Search and Seizure This amendment protects people's privacy in their homes. The government cannot search or seize anyone's property without a warrant, or a written order, from a court. A warrant must list the people and property to be searched and give reasons for the search.

Rights of the Accused A person accused of a crime has the right to a fair trial. A person cannot be tried twice for one crime. This amendment also protects a person from self-incrimination, or having to testify against himself or herself.

Right to a Fair Trial Anyone accused of a crime is entitled to a quick and fair trial by jury. This right protects people from being kept in jail without being convicted of a crime. Also, the government must provide a lawyer for anyone accused of a crime who cannot afford to hire a lawyer.

Jury Trial in Civil Cases Civil cases usually involve two or more people suing each other over money, property, or personal injury. A jury trial is guaranteed in large lawsuits.

Bail and Punishment Courts cannot treat people accused of crimes in ways that are unusually harsh.

Powers Reserved to the People The citizens keep all rights not listed in the Constitution.

Powers Reserved to the States Any rights not clearly given to the federal government by the Constitution belong to the states or the people.

Suits Against States A citizen from one state cannot sue the government of another state in a federal court. Such cases are decided in state courts.

Election of the President and Vice President Under the original Constitution, each member of the Electoral College voted for two candidates for President. The candidate with the most votes became President. The one with the second highest total became Vice President.

The Twelfth Amendment changed this system. Members of the electoral college distinguish between their votes for President and Vice President. This change was an important step in the development of the two-party system. It allows each party to nominate its own team of candidates.

★ ★ ★ ★ ★ ★ ★ ★ ★

SEVENTH AMENDMENT (1791)
JURY TRIAL IN CIVIL CASES

In suits at common law, where the value in controversy shall exceed twenty dollars, the right of trial by jury shall be preserved, and no fact tried by a jury shall be otherwise reexamined in any court of the United States, than according to the rules of the common law.

EIGHTH AMENDMENT (1791)
BAIL AND PUNISHMENT

Excessive bail shall not be required, nor excessive fines imposed, nor cruel and unusual punishments inflicted.

NINTH AMENDMENT (1791)
POWERS RESERVED TO THE PEOPLE

The enumeration in the Constitution of certain rights shall not be construed to deny or disparage others retained by the people.

TENTH AMENDMENT (1791)
POWERS RESERVED TO THE STATES

The powers not delegated to the United States by the Constitution, nor prohibited by it to the States are reserved to the States respectively, or to the people.

ELEVENTH AMENDMENT (1795)
SUITS AGAINST STATES

The judicial power of the United States shall not be construed to extend to any suit in law or equity, commenced or prosecuted against one of the United States by citizens of another State, or by citizens or subjects of any foreign State.

TWELFTH AMENDMENT (1804)
ELECTION OF THE PRESIDENT AND VICE PRESIDENT

The electors shall meet in their respective States, and vote by ballot for President and Vice President, one of whom, at least, shall not be an inhabitant of the same State with themselves; they shall name in their ballots the person voted for as President, and in distinct ballots the person voted for as Vice President, and they shall make distinct lists of all persons voted for as President, and of all persons voted for as Vice President, and of the number of votes for each, which lists they shall sign and certify, and transmit sealed to the seat of government of the United States, directed to the President of the Senate;—The President of the Senate shall, in the presence of the Senate and House of Representatives, open all the certificates and the votes shall then be counted;—The person having the greatest number of votes for President shall be the President, if such number be a majority of the whole number of electors appointed; and if no person have such majority, then from the persons having the highest numbers not exceeding three on the list of those voted for as President, the House of Representatives shall choose

★ ★ ★ ★ ★ ★ ★ ★ ★

immediately, by ballot, the President. But in choosing the President, the votes shall be taken by States, the representation from each State having one vote; a quorum for this purpose shall consist of a member or members from two-thirds of the States, and a majority of all the States shall be necessary to a choice. And if the House of Representatives shall not choose a President whenever the right of choice shall devolve upon them, before the fourth day of March next following, *then the Vice President shall act as President, as in the case of the death or other constitutional disability of the President. The person having the greatest number of votes as Vice President shall be the Vice President, if such number be a majority of the whole number of electors appointed, and if no person have a majority, then from the two highest numbers on the list, the Senate shall choose the Vice President; a quorum for the purpose shall consist of two-thirds of the whole number of senators, and a majority of the whole number shall be necessary to a choice. But no person constitutionally ineligible to the office of President shall be eligible to that of Vice President of the United States.*

THIRTEENTH AMENDMENT (1865)
END OF SLAVERY

SECTION 1. ABOLITION

Neither slavery nor involuntary servitude, except as a punishment for crime whereof the party shall have been duly convicted, shall exist within the United States, or any place subject to their jurisdiction.

SECTION 2. ENFORCEMENT

Congress shall have power to enforce this article by appropriate legislation.

FOURTEENTH AMENDMENT (1868)
RIGHTS OF CITIZENS

SECTION 1. CITIZENSHIP

All persons born or naturalized in the United States, and subject to the jurisdiction thereof, are citizens of the United States and of the State wherein they reside. No State shall make or enforce any law which shall abridge the privileges or immunities of citizens of the United States; nor shall any State deprive any person of life, liberty, or property, without due process of law; nor deny to any person within its jurisdiction the equal protection of the laws.

SECTION 2. NUMBER OF REPRESENTATIVES

Representatives shall be apportioned among the several States according to their respective numbers, counting the whole number of persons in each State, excluding Indians not taxed. But when the right to vote at any election for the choice of electors for President and Vice President of the United States, representatives in Congress, the executive and judicial officers of a State, or the

Abolition This amendment ended slavery in the United States. It was ratified right after the Civil War.

Citizenship This amendment defined citizenship in the United States. "Due process under law" means that no state can deny its citizens the rights and privileges they enjoy as United States citizens. The goal of this amendment was to protect the rights of the recently freed blacks.

Number of Representatives: This clause replaced the Three-Fifths Compromise in Article 1. Each state's representation is based on its total population. Any state denying its male citizens over the age of 21 the right to vote will have its representation in Congress decreased.

★ ★ ★ ★ ★ ★ ★ ★ ★

members of the legislature thereof, is denied to any of the male inhabitants of such State, being twenty-one years of age, and citizens of the United States, or in any way abridged, except for participation in rebellion, or other crime, the basis of representation therein shall be reduced in the proportion which the number of such male citizens shall bear to the whole number of male citizens twenty-one years of age in such State.

SECTION 3. PENALTY FOR REBELLION

No person shall be a senator or representative in Congress, or elector of President and Vice President, or hold any office, civil or military, under the United States, or under any State, who, having previously taken an oath, as a member of Congress, or as an officer of the United States, or as a member of any State legislature, or as an executive or judicial officer of any State, to support the Constitution of the United States, shall have engaged in insurrection or rebellion against the same, or given aid or comfort to the enemies thereof. But Congress may by a vote of two-thirds of each house, remove such disability.

SECTION 4. GOVERNMENT DEBT

The validity of the public debt of the United States, authorized by law, including debts incurred for payment of pensions and bounties for services in suppressing insurrection or rebellion, shall not be questioned. But neither the United States nor any State shall assume or pay any debt or obligation incurred in aid of insurrection or rebellion against the United States, or any claim for the loss or emancipation of any slave; but all such debts, obligations, and claims shall be held illegal and void.

SECTION 5. ENFORCEMENT

The Congress shall have power to enforce, by appropriate legislation, the provisions of this article.

FIFTEENTH AMENDMENT (1870)
VOTING RIGHTS

SECTION 1. RIGHT TO VOTE

The right of citizens of the United States to vote shall not be denied or abridged by the United States or by any State on account of race, color, or previous condition of servitude.

SECTION 2. ENFORCEMENT

The Congress shall have power to enforce this article by appropriate legislation.

SIXTEENTH AMENDMENT (1913)
INCOME TAX

The Congress shall have power to lay and collect taxes on incomes, from whatever source derived, without apportionment among the several States, and without regard to any census or enumeration.

Penalty for Rebellion Officials who fought against the Union in the Civil War could not hold public office in the United States. This clause tried to keep Confederate leaders out of power. In 1872, Congress removed this limit.

Government Debt The United States paid all of the Union's debts from the Civil War. However, it did not pay any of the Confederacy's debts. This clause prevented the southern states from using public money to pay for the rebellion or to pay citizens who lost their slaves.

Right to Vote No state can deny its citizens the right to vote because of their race. This amendment was designed to protect the voting rights of blacks.

Income Tax Congress has the power to tax personal incomes.

★ ★ ★ ★ ★ ★ ★ ★ ★

SEVENTEENTH AMENDMENT (1913)
DIRECT ELECTION OF SENATORS

SECTION 1. METHOD OF ELECTION

The Senate of the United States shall be composed of two sena-tors from each State, elected by the people thereof, for six years; and each senator shall have one vote. The electors in each State shall have the qualifications requisite for electors of the most numerous branch of the State legislatures.

Direct Election of Senators In the origi-nal Constitution, the state legislatures elected the senators. This amendment gave citizens the power to elect their sen-ators directly. It made senators more responsible to the people they represented.

SECTION 2. VACANCIES

When vacancies happen in the representation of any State in the Senate, the executive authority of such State shall issue writs of election to fill such vacancies: Provided, that the legislature of any State may empower the executive thereof to make temporary appointments until the people fill the vacancies by election as the legislature may direct.

SECTION 3. EXCEPTION

This amendment shall not be so construed as to affect the elec-tion or term of any Senator chosen before it becomes valid as part of the Constitution.

EIGHTEENTH AMENDMENT (1919)
BAN ON ALCOHOLIC DRINKS

SECTION 1. PROHIBITION

After one year from the ratification of this article the man-ufacture, sale, or transportation of intoxicating liquors within, the importation thereof into, or the exportation thereof from the United States and all territory subject to the jurisdiction thereof for beverage purposes is hereby prohibited.

Prohibition This amendment made it against the law to make or sell alcoholic beverages in the United States. This law was called Prohibition. Fourteen years later, the Twenty-First Amendment ended Prohibition.

SECTION 2. ENFORCEMENT

The Congress and the several States shall have concurrent power to enforce this article by appropriate legislation.

SECTION 3. RATIFICATION

This article shall be inoperative unless it shall have been ratified as an amendment to the Constitution by the legisla-tures of the several States, as provided in the Constitution, within seven years from the date of the submission hereof to the States by the Congress.

Ratification This amendment was the first one to include a time limit for ratifi-cation. To go into effect, the amendment had to be approved by three-fourths of the states within seven years.

NINETEENTH AMENDMENT (1920)
WOMEN'S SUFFRAGE

SECTION 1. RIGHT TO VOTE

The right of citizens of the United States to vote shall not be denied or abridged by the United States or by any State on account of sex.

Women's Suffrage This amendment gave the right to vote to all women 21 years of age and older.

547

★ ★ ★ ★ ★ ★ ★ ★ ★

SECTION 2. ENFORCEMENT

The Congress shall have power to enforce this article by appropriate legislation.

TWENTIETH AMENDMENT (1933)
TERMS OF OFFICE

SECTION 1. BEGINNING OF TERMS

The terms of the President and Vice President shall end at noon on the twentieth day of January, and the terms of senators and representatives at noon on the third day of January, of the years in which such terms would have ended if this article had not been ratified; and the terms of their successors shall then begin.

SECTION 2. SESSIONS OF CONGRESS

The Congress shall assemble at least once in every year, and such meeting shall begin at noon on the third day of January, unless they shall by law appoint a different day.

SECTION 3. PRESIDENTIAL SUCCESSION

If, at the time fixed for the beginning of the term of the President, the President-elect shall have died, the Vice President-elect shall become President. If a President shall not have been chosen before the time fixed for the beginning of his term, or if the President-elect shall have failed to qualify, then the Vice President-elect shall act as President until a President shall have qualified; and the Congress may by law provide for the case wherein neither a President-elect nor a Vice President-elect shall have qualified, declaring who shall then act as President, or the manner in which one who is to act shall be selected, and such persons shall act accordingly until a President or Vice President shall have qualified.

SECTION 4. ELECTIONS DECIDED BY CONGRESS

The Congress may by law provide for the case of the death of any of the persons from whom the House of Representatives may choose a President whenever the right of choice shall have devolved upon them, and for the case of the death of any of the persons from whom the Senate may choose a Vice President whenever the right of choice shall have devolved upon them.

SECTION 5. EFFECTIVE DATE

Sections 1 and 2 shall take effect on the fifteenth day of October following the ratification of this article.

SECTION 6. RATIFICATION

This article shall be inoperative unless it shall have been ratified as an amendment to the Constitution by the legislatures of three-fourths of the several States within seven years from the date of its submission.

Beginning of Terms The President and Vice President's terms begin on January 20 after being elected. The terms for senators and representatives begin on January 3. Before this amendment, an official defeated in a November election stayed in office until March.

Presidential Succession A President who has been elected but has not yet taken office is called the President-elect. If the President-elect dies, the Vice President-elect becomes President. If neither the President-elect nor the Vice President-elect can take office, then Congress decides who will act as President.

★ ★ ★ ★ ★ ★ ★ ★ ★

TWENTY-FIRST AMENDMENT (1933)
END OF PROHIBITION

SECTION 1. REPEAL OF EIGHTEENTH AMENDMENT

The eighteenth article of amendment to the Constitution of the United States is hereby repealed.

SECTION 2. STATE LAWS

The transportation or importation into any State, territory, or possession of the United States for delivery or use therein of intoxicating liquors, in violation of the laws thereof, is hereby prohibited.

SECTION 3. RATIFICATION

This article shall be inoperative unless it shall have been ratified as an amendment to the Constitution by conventions in the several States, as provided in the Constitution, within seven years from the date of submission hereof to the States by the Congress.

TWENTY-SECOND AMENDMENT (1951)
LIMIT ON PRESIDENTIAL TERMS

SECTION 1. TWO-TERM LIMIT

No person shall be elected to the office of the President more than twice, and no person who has held the office of President, or acted as President, for more than two years of a term to which some other person was elected President shall be elected to the office of the President more than once. But this article shall not apply to any person holding the office of President when this article was proposed by the Congress, and shall not prevent any person who may be holding the office of President, or acting as President, during the term within which this article becomes operative from holding the office of President or acting as President during the remainder of such term.

SECTION 2. RATIFICATION

This article shall be inoperative unless it shall have been ratified as an amendment to the Constitution by the legislatures of three-fourths of the several States within seven years from the date of its submission to the States by Congress.

TWENTY-THIRD AMENDMENT (1961)
PRESIDENTIAL VOTES FOR WASHINGTON, D.C.

SECTION 1. NUMBER OF ELECTORS

The District constituting the seat of government of the United States shall appoint in such manner as the Congress may direct:

A number of electors of President and Vice President equal to the whole number of senators and representatives in Congress to which the District would be entitled if it were a State, but in no event more than the least populous State; they shall be in addition to those appointed by the States, but they shall be considered, for the

End of Prohibition This amendment repealed, or ended, the Eighteenth Amendment. It made alcoholic beverages legal once again in the United States. However, states can still control or stop the sale of alcohol within their borders.

Two-Term Limit George Washington set a precedent that Presidents should not serve more than two terms in office. However, Franklin Roosevelt broke the precedent. He was elected President four times between 1932 and 1944. Some people feared that a President holding office for this long could become too powerful. This amendment limits Presidents to two terms in office.

Presidential Votes for Washington, D.C. This amendment gives people who live in the nation's capital a vote for President. Washington, D.C.'s electoral votes are based on its population. However, it cannot have more votes than the state with the smallest population. Today Washington, D.C. has three electoral votes.

purposes of the election of President and Vice President, to be electors appointed by a State; and they shall meet in the District and perform such duties as provided by the twelfth article of amendment.

SECTION 2. ENFORCEMENT

The Congress shall have power to enforce this article by appropriate legislation.

TWENTY-FOURTH AMENDMENT (1964)
BAN ON POLL TAXES

SECTION 1. POLL TAXES ILLEGAL

Ban on Poll Taxes A poll tax requires a person to pay a certain amount of money to register to vote. These taxes were used to stop poor blacks from voting. This amendment made any such taxes against the law in federal elections.

The right of citizens of the United States to vote in any primary or other election for President or Vice President, for electors for President or Vice President, or for senator or representative in Congress, shall not be denied or abridged by the United States or any State by reason of failure to pay any poll tax or other tax.

SECTION 2. ENFORCEMENT

The Congress shall have power to enforce this article by appropriate legislation.

TWENTY-FIFTH AMENDMENT (1967)
PRESIDENTIAL SUCCESSION

SECTION 1. VACANCY IN THE PRESIDENCY

In case of the removal of the President from office or of his death or resignation, the Vice President shall become President.

SECTION 2. VACANCY IN THE VICE PRESIDENCY

Vacancy in the Vice Presidency If the Vice President becomes President, he or she may nominate a new Vice President. This nomination must be approved by both houses of Congress.

Whenever there is a vacancy in the office of the Vice President, the President shall nominate a Vice President who shall take office upon confirmation by a majority vote of both houses of Congress.

SECTION 3. DISABILITY OF THE PRESIDENT

Disability of the President This section tells what happens if the President suddenly becomes ill or is seriously injured. The Vice President takes over as Acting President. When the President is ready to take office again, he or she must tell Congress.

Whenever the President transmits to the President pro tempore of the Senate and the speaker of the House of Representatives his written declaration that he is unable to discharge the powers and duties of his office, and until he transmits to them a written declaration to the contrary, such powers and duties shall be discharged by the Vice President as Acting President.

SECTION 4. DETERMINING PRESIDENTIAL DISABILITY

Whenever the Vice President and a majority of either the principal officers of the executive departments or of such other body as Congress may by law provide, transmit to the President pro tempore of the Senate and the speaker of the House of Representatives their written declaration that the President is unable to discharge the powers and duties of his office, the Vice President shall immediately assume the powers and duties of the office as Acting President.

Thereafter, when the President transmits to the President pro tempore of the Senate and the speaker of the House of Representatives his written declaration that no inability exists, he shall resume the powers and duties of his office unless the Vice President and a majority of either the principal officers of the executive departments or of such other body as Congress may by law provide, transmit within four days to the President pro tempore of the Senate and the speaker of the House of Representatives their written declaration that the President is unable to discharge the powers and duties of his office. Thereupon Congress shall decide the issue, assembling within 48 hours for that purpose if not in session. If the Congress, within 21 days after receipt of the latter written declaration, or, if Congress is not in session, within 21 days after Congress is required to assemble, determines by two-thirds vote of both houses that the President is unable to discharge the powers and duties of his office, the Vice President shall continue to discharge the same as Acting President; otherwise, the President shall resume the powers and duties of his office.

TWENTY-SIXTH AMENDMENT (1971) VOTING AGE

SECTION 1. RIGHT TO VOTE

The right of citizens of the United States, who are eighteen years of age or older, to vote shall not be denied or abridged by the United States or by any State on account of age.

SECTION 2. ENFORCEMENT

The Congress shall have power to enforce this article by appropriate legislation.

Right to Vote This amendment gave the vote to everyone 18 years of age and older.

Canada

The flag of Canada   **The Canadian coat of arms**

Facts in brief

Capital: Ottawa.
Official languages: English and French.
Area: 3,849,674 sq. mi. (9,970,610 km²), including 291,577 sq. mi. (755,180 km²) of inland water. *Greatest distances*—east-west, 3,223 mi. (5,187 km), from Cape Spear, Nfld., to Mount St. Elias, Y.T.; north-south, 2,875 mi. (4,627 km), from Cape Columbia on Ellesmere Island to Middle Island in Lake Erie. *Coastline*—151,485 mi. (243,791 km), including mainland and islands; Atlantic Ocean, 28,019 mi. (45,092 km); Arctic Ocean, 82,698 mi. (133,089 km); Hudson Bay, Hudson Strait, and James Bay, 24,786 mi. (39,890 km); Pacific Ocean, 15,985 mi. (25,726 km). *Shoreline*—Great Lakes, 5,251 mi. (8,452 km).
Elevation: *Highest*—Mount Logan, 19,524 ft. (5,951 m) above sea level. *Lowest*—sea level.
Population: *Estimated 1990 population*—26,279,000; density, 7 persons per sq. mi. (3 per km²); distribution, 76 per cent urban, 24 per cent rural. *1986 census*—25,354,064. *Estimated 1995 population*—27,483,000.
Chief products: *Agriculture*—apples, barley, beef cattle, chickens, corn, eggs, hogs, milk, oats, potatoes, rapeseed, wheat. *Fishing*—cod, lobster, salmon, scallops. *Forestry*—cedar, fir, hemlock, pine, spruce. *Fur industry*—beaver, fox, mink, muskrat. *Manufacturing*—aluminum, dairy products, industrial chemicals, livestock feed, lumber and plywood, meat products, motor vehicles and parts, newsprint and other paper products, petroleum products, printed materials, steel. *Mining*—coal, copper, gold, iron ore, natural gas, natural gas liquids, nickel, petroleum, potash, sand and gravel, sulfur, uranium, zinc.
National anthem: "O Canada."
National symbols: Maple leaf and beaver.
National holiday: Canada Day, July 1.
Money: *Basic unit*—dollar. For its price in U.S. dollars, see Money (table: Exchange rates). See also **Dollar**.

Important dates

A.D. 1000's Vikings sailed along the northeast coast, possibly establishing a temporary settlement.
1497 John Cabot of England landed on Canada's east coast. Britain laid claim to all of Canada.
1534 French explorer Jacques Cartier reached the Gulf of St. Lawrence and claimed the surrounding territory for France.
1610 Henry Hudson of England sailed into Hudson Bay.
1642 French missionaries founded Montreal.
1689-1763 A series of wars between British and French colonists ended with Britain's conquest of New France, the French empire in America.
1774 The Quebec Act gave French Canadians political and religious rights.
1867 The British North America Act established the Dominion of Canada.
1869 Louis Riel led the métis in the Red River Rebellion in Manitoba.
1870 The North West Territories (now Northwest Territories) was established.
1885 Riel led a métis revolt in Saskatchewan. The Canadian Pacific Railway (now CP Rail) spanned Canada.
1898 The Yukon area became a territory of Canada.
1914-1918 More than 600,000 Canadians served in World War I.
1920 Canada became a member of the League of Nations.
1931 The Statute of Westminster made Canada an independent nation.
1939-1945 More than a million Canadians served during World War II.
1945 Canada joined the United Nations (UN).
1949 Canada signed a treaty that set up the North Atlantic Treaty Organization (NATO).
1959 The St. Lawrence Seaway, a joint U.S.-Canadian project, opened.
1962 The Trans-Canada Highway, the country's first ocean-to-ocean road, was completed.
1964 A national pension plan was introduced.
1965 A new official Canadian flag flew for the first time on February 15.
1967 Canadians celebrated the 100th anniversary of Confederation with Expo 67, a world's fair in Montreal.
1969 The Official Languages Act required federal facilities in Canada to provide service in both French and English if 10 per cent of the people in a particular area speak either language.
1982 The Constitution Act ended British control over amendments to Canada's Constitution. The act included a new bill of rights.

The provinces and territories of Canada

Provinces

Province	Capital	Area In sq. mi.	Area In km²	Rank in area	Population (1986 census)	Rank in pop.	Floral emblem	Date became province	Province abbr.
Alberta	Edmonton	255,287	661,190	4	2,375,278	4	Wild rose	1905	Alta.
British Columbia	Victoria	365,900	947,800	3	2,889,207	3	Flowering dogwood	1871	B.C.
Manitoba	Winnipeg	250,947	649,950	6	1,071,232	5	Pasqueflower	1870	Man.
New Brunswick	Fredericton	28,355	73,440	8	710,422	8	Violet	1867	N.B.
Newfoundland	St. John's	156,649	405,720	7	568,349	9	Pitcher plant	1949	Nfld.
Nova Scotia	Halifax	21,423	55,490	9	873,199	7	Trailing arbutus	1867	N.S.
Ontario	Toronto	412,581	1,068,580	2	9,113,515	1	White trillium	1867	Ont.
Prince Edward Island	Charlottetown	2,185	5,660	10	126,646	10	Lady's-slipper	1873	P.E.I.
Quebec	Quebec	594,860	1,540,680	1	6,540,276	2	White garden lily	1867	Que.
Saskatchewan	Regina	251,866	652,330	5	1,010,198	6	Prairie lily	1905	Sask.

Territories

Territory	Capital	Area In sq. mi.	Area In km²	Population (1986 census)	Floral emblem	Territory abbreviation
Northwest Territories	Yellowknife	1,322,910	3,426,320	52,238	Mountain avens	N.W. Ter. or N.W.T.
Yukon Territory	Whitehorse	186,661	483,450	23,504	Fireweed	Y.T.

Explorers of the great age of European discovery

Explorer	Nationality	Main achievements	Date
* Balboa, Vasco Núñez de	Spanish	Led expedition across Isthmus of Panama; sighted Pacific Ocean.	1513
* Cabeza de Vaca, Álvar Núñez	Spanish	Explored Gulf Plains from Texas to Mexico.	1528-1536
* Cabot, John	Italian	Sailed across the North Atlantic to what is now Canada.	1497-1498
* Cabot, Sebastian	Italian	Explored South American coast to the Río de la Plata.	1526-1530
* Cabral, Pedro Álvares	Portuguese	Reached Brazilian coast; sailed around Africa to India.	1500-1501
* Cartier, Jacques	French	Sailed up the St. Lawrence River.	1535
* Columbus, Christopher	Italian	Made four voyages to the West Indies and Caribbean lands.	1492-1504
* Coronado, Francisco de	Spanish	Explored the American Southwest.	1540-1542
* Cortés, Hernando	Spanish	Conquered Mexico.	1519-1521
* Da Gama, Vasco	Portuguese	First European to reach India by sea.	1498
* De Soto, Hernando	Spanish	Explored American Southeast; reached Mississippi River.	1539-1542
* Dias, Bartolomeu	Portuguese	First European to round the Cape of Good Hope.	1487-1488
* Drake, Sir Francis	English	First English explorer to sail around the world.	1577-1580
* Frobisher, Sir Martin	English	Searched North American coast for a Northwest Passage.	1576-1578
* Magellan, Ferdinand	Portuguese	Commanded first globe-circling voyage, completed in 1522 after his death.	1519-1521
* Oñate, Juan de	Spanish	Explored American Southwest.	1598-1605
* Orellana, Francisco de	Spanish	Explored Amazon River.	1541
* Pizarro, Francisco	Spanish	Conquered Peru; founded Lima.	1531-1535
* Ponce de León, Juan	Spanish	Explored Florida.	1513
* Verrazano, Giovanni da	Italian	Searched for a Northwest Passage.	1524
* Vespucci, Amerigo	Italian	Sailed to the West Indies and South America.	1499-1504

*Has a separate biography in WORLD BOOK.

Famous explorers of North America

Explorer	Nationality	Main achievements	Date
* Bridger, James	American	Probably the first white person to reach Great Salt Lake.	1824-1825
* Champlain, Samuel de	French	Explored eastern coast of North America, and St. Lawrence River west to Lake Huron; reached Lake Champlain.	1603-1616
* Clark, William	American	Led an expedition across the Rocky Mountains to the Pacific Ocean with Meriwether Lewis.	1804-1806
Duluth, Sieur	French	Explored Lake Superior region.	1678-1687
* Frémont, John Charles	American	Explored the American West.	1842-1846
* Hennepin, Louis	Belgian	Explored upper Mississippi River region.	1680
* Hudson, Henry	English	Explored Hudson Bay, Hudson River, and Hudson Strait.	1609-1611
* Jolliet, Louis	French Canadian	Explored northern Mississippi River region with Jacques Marquette.	1673
* La Salle, Sieur de	French	Explored the Great Lakes region and tracked the Mississippi River to the Gulf of Mexico.	1679-1682
* La Vérendrye, Sieur de	French Canadian	Explored western Canada.	1731-1743
* Lewis, Meriwether	American	Led an expedition across the Rocky Mountains to the Pacific Ocean with William Clark.	1804-1806
* Mackenzie, Sir Alexander	Canadian	Explored western Canada; followed the Mackenzie River to the Arctic Ocean.	1789-1793
* Marquette, Jacques	French	Explored northern Mississippi River region with Louis Jolliet.	1673
* Pike, Zebulon	American	Explored Middle West and Rocky Mountain region.	1805-1807
* Radisson, Pierre Esprit	French	Explored Lake Superior and northern Mississippi River regions.	1659-1661
* Smith, Jedediah Strong	American	Explored Great Basin region; blazed trails across the Rocky Mountains to California and the Pacific Northwest.	1824-1829
* Thompson, David	Canadian	Explored western Canada.	1789-1812
* Tonti, Henri de	French	Explored the Great Lakes region and the Mississippi River with de La Salle.	1679-1682

*Has a separate biography in WORLD BOOK.

Famous space explorers

Explorer	Nationality	Main achievements	Date
* Aldrin, Edwin E., Jr.	American	Landed on the moon with Neil A. Armstrong.	1969
Anders, William A.	American	Orbited the moon with James A. Lovell, Jr., and Frank Borman.	1968
* Armstrong, Neil A.	American	First person to set foot on the moon.	1969
* Borman, Frank	American	Commanded the first space flight to orbit the moon.	1968
Crippen, Robert L.	American	Piloted the first space shuttle flight with John W. Young.	1981
* Gagarin, Yuri A.	Soviet	First person to travel in space.	1961
Leonov, Alexei A.	Soviet	First person to leave a spacecraft and float freely in space.	1965
* Lovell, James A., Jr.	American	Orbited the moon.	1968
* Tereshkova, Valentina V.	Soviet	First woman to travel in space.	1963
* Young, John W.	American	Commanded the first space shuttle flight.	1981

*Has a separate biography in WORLD BOOK.

Excerpted from the Exploration article in *World Book.* Copyright © 1990 by World Book, Inc.

Flags in American history

The Viking flag of Leif Ericson was the first flag in North America, in the 1000's.

The Spanish flag carried by Columbus in 1492, *left,* combined the arms of Castile and Leon. Columbus' own flag, *right,* bore the initials F and Y for Ferdinand and Isabella (Ysabel).

This French flag was one of many flown in North America between 1604 and 1763.

The English flag of John Cabot, *left,* flew in Canada in 1497. The British flag, *right,* adopted in 1606, flew over the British colonies in North America, beginning with Jamestown, 1607.

Dutch-East India Company flag of Henry Hudson flew in the New York area in 1609.

Russian-American Company flag flew at Russian settlements in Alaska in 1806.

The Continental Colors served as America's first national flag from 1775 to 1777.

The flag of 1777 had no official arrangement for the stars. The most popular design had alternating rows of 3, 2, 3, 2, and 3 stars. Another flag with 13 stars in a circle was rarely used.

The flag of 1795 had 15 stripes, as well as 15 stars, to stand for the 15 states.

New England flags. The Taunton Flag, *left,* was raised at Taunton, Mass., in 1774. The Bedford Flag, *above,* flown in 1775, bears the words *vince aut morire,* meaning *conquer or die.* The

Rhode Island Flag, *above,* was carried in battle until 1781. The Bennington Flag, *right,* a variation of the original Stars and Stripes, may have flown during the Battle of Bennington in 1777.

Navy flags. American ships in New England waters flew a liberty tree flag, *left,* in 1775. Later that year, the Continental Navy began using a striped flag with a rattlesnake design.

Southern flags often had rattlesnake designs, as in the flag of Virginia's Culpeper Minutemen, 1775. William Moultrie's flag was flown by defenders of Charleston, S.C., in 1776.

Flags of the United States

The *Stars and Stripes* is the most popular name for the red, white, and blue national flag of the United States. No one knows where this name came from, but we do know the origin of several other names. Francis Scott Key first called the United States flag the *Star-Spangled Banner* in 1814 when he wrote the poem that became the national anthem. William Driver, a sea captain from Salem, Mass., gave the name *Old Glory* to the U.S. flag in 1824.

The Stars and Stripes stands for the land, the people, the government, and the ideals of the United States, no matter when or where it is displayed. Some other flags also stand for the United States, or its government, in certain situations. The *Navy Jack,* a blue flag with white stars, stands for the United States whenever it flies from a U.S. Navy ship. The stars, stripes, and colors of the U.S. flag appear in many federal and state flags.

The colors. The Continental Congress left no record to show why it chose red, white, and blue as the colors for the flag. But, in 1782, the Congress of the Confederation chose these same colors for the newly designed Great Seal of the United States. The resolution on the seal listed meanings for the colors. *Red* is for hardiness and courage, *white* for purity and innocence, and *blue* for vigilance, perseverance, and justice.

The stripes in the flag stand for the thirteen original colonies. The stripes were probably adopted from the flag of the Sons of Liberty, which had five red and four white stripes. The British Union Jack was added to show

Today's 50-star United States flag has the following dimensions: hoist (width) of flag, 1.0 unit; fly (length) of flag, 1.9; hoist of union, .5385 (7/13); fly of union, .76; width of each stripe, .0769 (1/13); and diameter of each star, .0616.

that the colonists did not at first seek full independence.

The stars. The resolution passed by Congress in 1777 stated that the flag should have 13 stars. But Congress did not indicate how the stars should be arranged. The most popular arrangement showed the stars in alternating rows of three, two, three, two, and three stars. Another version had 12 stars in a circle with the 13th star in the center. A flag with 13 stars in a circle is often associated with the period. But there is little evidence that such a design was used. There is also no historical basis for assigning each star to a particular state.

The flag of 1818 went back to 13 stripes, and had 20 stars for the 20 states. One design had four rows of five stars each. The Great Star Flag, *right,* formed the 20 stars in a large star.

The flag of 1861, used in the Civil War, had stars for 34 states, including the South.

The 48-star flag served as the national flag the longest of any flag, from 1912 to 1959.

Perry's flag in 1813 bore the last words of James Lawrence, a hero of the War of 1812.

Texas flags. A Texas flag that flew when Texas was part of Mexico, *left,* bore the date of Mexico's constitution. The Texas Navy Flag, *right,* had a lone star.

The Bear Flag flew over an independent California republic for a few months in 1846.

Confederate flags. The Stars and Bars, *left,* adopted in 1861, had stars for 7 seceding states. It looked too much like the U.S. flag, so troops carried a battle flag, *above.* It had stars for 11 states and for secession governments in Kentucky and Missouri, as did the flag of 1863, *above.* This looked too much like a flag of truce, so a red bar was added in 1865, *right.*

Excerpted from the Flag article in *World Book.* Copyright © 1990 by World Book, Inc.

Gettysburg Address

Detail of a lithograph (1905); Granger Collection.

Abraham Lincoln delivered the Gettysburg Address four months after the historic Civil War battle was fought.

Gettysburg Address is a short speech that Abraham Lincoln delivered on Nov. 19, 1863, at the site of the Battle of Gettysburg in Pennsylvania. He delivered the address at ceremonies to dedicate a part of the battlefield as a cemetery for those who had lost their lives in this Civil War battle. Lincoln chose his simple, noble words with such care that, ever since that day, they have stirred the deepest feelings of Americans.

Lincoln made five handwritten copies of the speech. He wrote most of the first version in Washington, before traveling to Gettysburg. At Gettysburg, he probably revised the first version, and then made a second. Lincoln planned to read the second version, and he held it in his hand while speaking. But he made several changes as he spoke. The most important change was to add the phrase "under God" after the word "nation" in the last sentence.

Historians are reasonably sure they know which version of the speech Lincoln actually gave at Gettysburg. Several reporters were present at the ceremonies and took down his words while he spoke. Although the reports vary somewhat, they all include the phrase "under God." Lincoln added that phrase to the copies of the address that he later made after the ceremonies at the Gettysburg battlefield.

Lincoln made the last copy of the address in 1864. This was the only copy he signed. This fifth version is the one carved on a stone plaque in the Lincoln Memorial.

Many false stories have grown up about this famous speech. One story says that the President wrote it in pencil on the back of an old brown envelope while on the train going to Gettysburg. According to another story, the people of Lincoln's time did not appreciate his speech. But Edward Everett, the principal speaker at the dedication, wrote to Lincoln: "I should be glad if I could flatter myself that I came as near to the central idea of the occasion in two hours as you did in two minutes." Many newspapers also immediately recognized the inspired nobility of the President's brief remarks.

Paul M. Angle

★   ★   ★   ★   ★

Two versions of the Gettysburg Address

Lincoln wrote five different versions of his famous Gettysburg Address. He held the second version, *left below,* in his hand while he spoke at Gettysburg. The fifth version, *right below,* perhaps represents as exactly as can be known the speech he gave.

Four score and seven years ago our fathers brought forth, upon this continent, a new nation, conceived in Liberty, and dedicated to the proposition that all men are created equal.

Now we are engaged in a great civil war, testing whether that nation, or any nation, so conceived, and so dedicated, can long endure. We are met here on a great battle-field of that war. We have come to dedicate a portion of it as a final resting place for those who here gave their lives that that nation might live. It is altogether fitting and proper that we should do this.

But in a larger sense we can not dedicate—we can not consecrate—we can not hallow this ground. The brave men, living and dead, who struggled here, have consecrated it far above our poor power to add or detract. The world will little note, nor long remember, what we say here, but can never forget what they did here. It is for us, the living, rather to be dedicated here to the unfinished work which they have, thus far, so nobly carried on. It is rather for us to be here dedicated to the great task remaining before us—that from these honored dead we take increased devotion to that cause for which they here gave the last full measure of devotion—that we here highly resolve that these dead shall not have died in vain; that this nation shall have a new birth of freedom; and that this government of the people, by the people, for the people, shall not perish from the earth.

Four score and seven years ago our fathers brought forth on this continent, a new nation, conceived in Liberty, and dedicated to the proposition that all men are created equal.

Now we are engaged in a great civil war, testing whether that nation, or any nation so conceived and so dedicated, can long endure. We are met on a great battlefield of that war. We have come to dedicate a portion of that field, as a final resting place for those who here gave their lives that that nation might live. It is altogether fitting and proper that we should do this.

But, in a larger sense, we can not dedicate—we can not consecrate—we can not hallow—this ground. The brave men, living and dead, who struggled here, have consecrated it, far above our poor power to add or detract. The world will little note, nor long remember what we say here, but it can never forget what they did here. It is for us the living, rather, to be dedicated here to the unfinished work which they who fought here have thus far so nobly advanced. It is rather for us to be here dedicated to the great task remaining before us—that from these honored dead we take increased devotion to that cause for which they gave the last full measure of devotion—that we here highly resolve that these dead shall not have died in vain—that this nation, under God, shall have a new birth of freedom—and that government of the people, by the people, for the people, shall not perish from the earth.

Immigration is the act of coming to a foreign country to live. The act of leaving one's country to settle in another is called *emigration*. Immigrants who flee their country because of persecution, war, or such disasters as famines or epidemics are known as *refugees* or *displaced persons* (DP's).

Most people find it extremely difficult to pull up roots in their native land and move to a strange country. But throughout history, countless millions of people have done so. The heaviest immigration worldwide took place from the early 1800's to the Great Depression—the economic hard times of the 1930's. During that period, about 60 million people moved to a new land. Most of them came from Europe. More than half emigrated to the United States. Other destinations included Canada, Argentina, Brazil, Australia, New Zealand, and South Africa.

Today, the availability of fast, safe, and cheap transportation helps make migration easier in many parts of the world. Asia is replacing Europe as the major immigrant-sending area. The United States remains the chief receiving nation.

Number of legal immigrants admitted to the United States annually

Legal immigration to the United States has varied in a wavelike pattern. These ups and downs have occurred in response both to economic and political conditions in the United States and in the major immigrant-sending nations. Statistics on legal immigration have been kept since 1820.

Source: U.S. Immigration and Naturalization Service.

Major immigration movements to the United States

Who	When	Number	Why
Irish	1840's and 1850's	About 1½ million	Famine resulting from potato crop failure
Germans	1840's to 1880's	About 4 million	Severe economic depression and unemployment; political unrest and failure of liberal revolutionary movement
Danes, Norwegians, and Swedes	1870's to 1900's	About 1½ million	Poverty; shortage of farmland
Poles	1880's to 1920's	About 1 million	Poverty; political repression; cholera epidemics
Jews from eastern Europe	1880's to 1920's	About 2½ million	Religious persecution
Austrians, Czechs, Hungarians, and Slovaks	1880's to 1920's	About 4 million	Poverty; overpopulation
Italians	1880's to 1920's	About 4½ million	Poverty; overpopulation
Mexicans	1910 to 1920's 1950's to 1980's	About 700,000 About 2 million	Mexican Revolution of 1910; low wages and unemployment Poverty; unemployment
Cubans	1960's to 1980's	About 700,000	Communist take-over in 1959
Dominicans, Haitians, and Jamaicans	1970's and 1980's	About 900,000	Poverty; unemployment
Vietnamese	1970's and 1980's	About 500,000	Vietnam War (1957-1975); Communist take-over

Source: U.S. Immigration and Naturalization Service.

Indian ways of life

The Indians had many ways of life. This chart shows some details of tribal life in the 11 major Indian culture areas. It pictures Indian clothing, buildings and shelters, and crafts and weapons.

	Far North	Eastern Woodlands	Plains	Northwest Coast	California-Intermountain	
Clothing	Naskapi	Iroquois	Sioux	Tlingit	Hupa	
Buildings and shelters	Cree bark tepee Cree bark lodge Chippewa domed bark lodge	Kickapoo wigwam Iroquois long house Seminole house Creek house	Omaha earth lodge Wichita grass house Sioux buffalo-hide tepee	Haida plank house Kwakiutl plank house	Diegueño summer hut Interior Salish earth house Paiute brush wickiup	
Crafts and weapons	Snow-shoe Bow Toboggan	War club Bow Corn mortar Wam-pum Blowgun Birchbark container	Hide shield Honor feather Hide boat Sinew-backed bow Medicine pipe	Wooden armor Wooden adz Copper knife Salmon spear Fish-hook	Water basket Yew bow Digging stick Woven basket	

Indian, American

WORLD BOOK illustrations by Anthony Saris

Southwest	Middle America	Caribbean	Andes	Tropical Forest	Marginal areas
Hopi	Aztec	Carib	Inca	Yagua	Ona
Pueblo adobe village / Navajo hogan / Apache brush lodge	Maya ceremonial building / Maya thatch hut	Guaymí hip-roofed house / Arawak thatch hut	Inca masonry temple / Inca masonry and thatch house	Panoan house / Yamamadi communal house	Ashluslay hut / Tehuelche hut / Yahgan hide and driftwood shelter
Grinding stones / Pottery / Throwing stick / Gourd rattle / Stick for planting corn	Grinding stone / Pottery vessel / Sword (obsidian blades) / Gold jewelry	Hammock / Gold nose clip / Shell ring / Manioc strainer / War club / Bow	Pottery vessel / Foot plow / Metal smelter / Quipu / Reed boat	Bow / Spear point / Blow-gun / Paddle / Wooden drums	Bow / Bird snare / Coiled basket / Pipe / Guanaco bola

Indian, American

Where the Indians lived

The Indians of North and South America formed hundreds of tribes with many different ways of life. The location of many major tribes is shown below. Scholars divide the various tribes into groups of similar tribes that they call *culture areas*. Each culture area is shown as a different color.

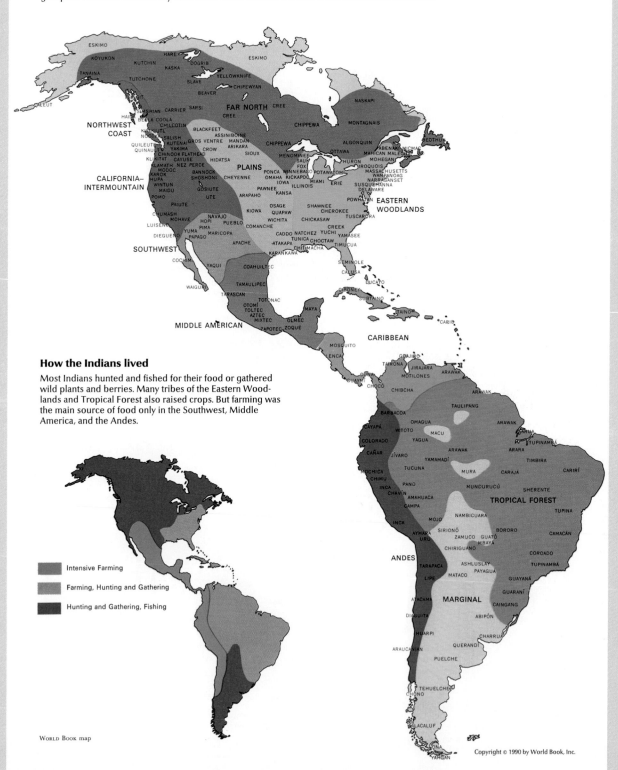

How the Indians lived

Most Indians hunted and fished for their food or gathered wild plants and berries. Many tribes of the Eastern Woodlands and Tropical Forest also raised crops. But farming was the main source of food only in the Southwest, Middle America, and the Andes.

- Intensive Farming
- Farming, Hunting and Gathering
- Hunting and Gathering, Fishing

WORLD BOOK map

Flag Research Center

Mexico's flag, adopted in 1821, features a version of the country's coat of arms. The green stands for independence, white for religion, and red for union.

Coat of arms. A legend says the Aztec Indians built their capital Tenochtitlán (now Mexico City) where they saw an eagle perched on a cactus and devouring a snake.

Facts in brief

Capital: Mexico City.
Official language: Spanish.
Official name: *Estados Unidos Mexicanos* (United Mexican States).
Area: 756,067 sq. mi. (1,958,201 km²), including 2,210 sq. mi. (5,073 km²) of outlying islands. *Greatest distances*—north-south, 1,250 mi. (2,012 km); east-west, 1,900 mi. (3,060 km). *Coastline*—6,320 mi. (10,170 km).
Elevation: *Highest*—Orizaba (Citlaltépetl), 18,701 ft. (5,700 m) above sea level. *Lowest*—near Mexicali, 33 ft. (10 m) below sea level.
Population: *Estimated 1990 population*—88,560,000; density, 117 persons per sq. mi. (45 per km²), distribution, 73 per cent urban, 27 per cent rural. *1980 census*—66,846,833. *Estimated 1995 population*—98,740,000.
Chief products: *Agriculture*—bananas, beans, beef cattle, chickens and eggs, coffee, corn, cotton, mangoes, milk, oranges, potatoes, rice, sorghum, sugar cane, tomatoes, wheat. *Fishing*—anchovies, oysters, sardines, shrimp, tuna. *Forestry*—chicle, ebony, mahogany, pine, rosewood. *Manufacturing*—automobiles, beer, cement, chemicals, clothing, fertilizers, iron and steel, household appliances, processed foods, wood pulp and paper. *Mining*—copper, fluorite, gold, iron ore, lead, manganese, natural gas, petroleum, salt, silver, sulfur, zinc.
National anthem: "Himno Nacional de México" ("National Anthem of Mexico").
National holidays: Independence Days, September 15 and 16.
Money: *Basic unit*—peso. For the price of the peso in U.S. dollars, see **Money** (table: Exchange rates). See also **Peso.**

Important dates in Mexico

c. 2000 B.C. Village life developed in the Valley of Mexico.
c. A.D. 250-900 Great Indian civilizations thrived during the Classic Period.
c. 900-1200 The Toltec empire controlled the Valley of Mexico.
Mid-1300's The Aztec founded Tenochtitlán (now Mexico City).
1519-1521 Hernando Cortés conquered the Aztec empire for Spain.
1810 Miguel Hidalgo y Costilla began the Mexican struggle for independence.
1821 Mexico won independence.
1824 Mexico became a republic.
1836 Texas won independence from Mexico.
1846-1848 The United States defeated Mexico in the Mexican War, and won much Mexican territory.
1855 A liberal government under Benito Juárez began a period of reform.
1863 French troops occupied Mexico City.
1864 Maximilian of Austria became emperor of Mexico.
1867 Liberal forces led by Benito Juárez regained power.
1876-1880 and **1884-1911** Porfirio Díaz ruled Mexico as dictator.
1910-1911 Francisco I. Madero led a revolution that overthrew Díaz.
1914 United States forces occupied Veracruz.
1917 A revolutionary constitution was adopted.
1920 The government began making revolutionary social and economic reforms.
1929 The National Revolutionary Party was formed.
1934 The government began a major program of land distribution to farmers.
1938 Mexico took over foreign oil-company properties.
1942-1945 Mexico's industries expanded rapidly during World War II to supply the Allies with war goods.
1953 Women received the right to vote in all elections.
1968 The Summer Olympic Games were held in Mexico City.
1970's Major new petroleum deposits were discovered on the Gulf of Mexico coast.
1985 Two earthquakes struck south-central Mexico, killing about 7,200 people.

States and Federal District of Mexico

States

Name	Area In sq. mi.	In km²	Population	Capital	Name	Area In sq. mi.	In km²	Population	Capital
Aguascalientes	2,112	5,471	503,410	Aguascalientes	Oaxaca	36,275	93,952	2,518,157	Oaxaca
Baja California					Puebla	13,090	33,902	3,279,960	Puebla
Norte	26,997	69,921	1,225,436	Mexicali	Querétaro	4,420	11,449	726,054	Querétaro
Baja California					Quintana Roo	19,387	50,212	209,858	Chetumal
Sur	28,369	73,475	221,389	La Paz	San Luis Potosí	24,351	63,068	1,670,637	San Luis
Campeche	19,619	50,812	372,277	Campeche					Potosí
Chiapas	28,653	74,211	2,096,812	Tuxtla	Sinaloa	22,520	58,328	1,880,098	Culiacán
Chihuahua	94,571	244,938	1,933,856	Chihuahua	Sonora	70,291	182,052	1,498,931	Hermosillo
Coahuila	57,908	149,982	1,558,401	Saltillo	Tabasco	9,756	25,267	1,149,756	Villahermosa
Colima	2,004	5,191	339,202	Colima	Tamaulipas	30,651	79,384	1,924,934	Ciudad Victoria
Durango	47,560	123,181	1,160,196	Durango					
Guanajuato	11,773	30,491	3,044,402	Guanajuato	Tlaxcala	1,550	4,016	547,261	Tlaxcala
Guerrero	24,819	64,281	2,174,162	Chilpancingo	Veracruz	27,683	71,699	5,264,611	Jalapa
Hidalgo	8,036	20,813	1,516,511	Pachuca	Yucatán	14,827	38,402	1,034,648	Mérida
Jalisco	31,211	80,836	4,293,549	Guadalajara	Zacatecas	28,283	73,252	1,145,327	Zacatecas
México	8,245	21,355	7,545,692	Toluca					
Michoacán	23,138	59,928	3,048,704	Morelia					
Morelos	1,911	4,950	931,675	Cuernavaca					
Nayarit	10,417	26,979	730,024	Tepic	**Federal District**				
Nuevo León	25,067	64,924	2,463,298	Monterrey	Federal District	571	1,479	10,061,000	Mexico City

Source for population figures: 1982 estimate for federal district; 1980 census for states.

Compiled from the Mexico article in *World Book.* Copyright © 1990 by World Book, Inc.

The Presidents of the United States

President	Born	Birthplace	Political party	Age at inaugur- ation	Served	Died	Age at death
1. George Washington ...	Feb. 22, 1732	Westmoreland County, Va.	None	57	1789-1797	Dec. 14, 1799	67
2. John Adams	Oct. 30, 1735	Braintree, Mass.	Federalist	61	1797-1801	July 4, 1826	90
3. Thomas Jefferson	Apr. 13, 1743	Albemarle County, Va.	Democratic-Republican	57	1801-1809	July 4, 1826	83
4. James Madison	Mar. 16, 1751	Port Conway, Va.	Democratic-Republican	57	1809-1817	June 28, 1836	85
5. James Monroe	Apr. 28, 1758	Westmoreland County, Va.	Democratic-Republican	58	1817-1825	July 4, 1831	73
6. John Quincy Adams	July 11, 1767	Braintree, Mass.	Democratic-Republican	57	1825-1829	Feb. 23, 1848	80
7. Andrew Jackson	Mar. 15, 1767	Waxhaw settlement, S.C. (?)	Democratic	61	1829-1837	June 8, 1845	78
8. Martin Van Buren	Dec. 5, 1782	Kinderhook, N.Y.	Democratic	54	1837-1841	July 24, 1862	79
9. William H. Harrison	Feb. 9, 1773	Berkeley, Va.	Whig	68	1841	Apr. 4, 1841	68
10. John Tyler	Mar. 29, 1790	Greenway, Va.	Whig	51	1841-1845	Jan. 18, 1862	71
11. James K. Polk	Nov. 2, 1795	near Pineville, N.C.	Democratic	49	1845-1849	June 15, 1849	53
12. Zachary Taylor	Nov. 24, 1784	Orange County, Va.	Whig	64	1849-1850	July 9, 1850	65
13. Millard Fillmore	Jan. 7, 1800	Locke, N.Y.	Whig	50	1850-1853	Mar. 8, 1874	74
14. Franklin Pierce	Nov. 23, 1804	Hillsboro, N.H.	Democratic	48	1853-1857	Oct. 8, 1869	64
15. James Buchanan	Apr. 23, 1791	near Mercersburg, Pa.	Democratic	65	1857-1861	June 1, 1868	77
16. Abraham Lincoln	Feb. 12, 1809	near Hodgenville, Ky.	Republican	52	1861-1865	Apr. 15, 1865	56
17. Andrew Johnson	Dec. 29, 1808	Raleigh, N.C.	Natl. Union†	56	1865-1869	July 31, 1875	66
18. Ulysses S. Grant	Apr. 27, 1822	Point Pleasant, Ohio	Republican	46	1869-1877	July 23, 1885	63
19. Rutherford B. Hayes ...	Oct. 4, 1822	Delaware, Ohio	Republican	54	1877-1881	Jan. 17, 1893	70
20. James A. Garfield	Nov. 19, 1831	Orange, Ohio	Republican	49	1881	Sept. 19, 1881	49
21. Chester A. Arthur	Oct. 5, 1829	Fairfield, Vt.	Republican	51	1881-1885	Nov. 18, 1886	57
22. Grover Cleveland	Mar. 18, 1837	Caldwell, N.J.	Democratic	47	1885-1889	June 24, 1908	71
23. Benjamin Harrison	Aug. 20, 1833	North Bend, Ohio	Republican	55	1889-1893	Mar. 13, 1901	67
24. Grover Cleveland	Mar. 18, 1837	Caldwell, N.J.	Democratic	55	1893-1897	June 24, 1908	71
25. William McKinley	Jan. 29, 1843	Niles, Ohio	Republican	54	1897-1901	Sept. 14, 1901	58
26. Theodore Roosevelt ...	Oct. 27, 1858	New York, N.Y.	Republican	42	1901-1909	Jan. 6, 1919	60
27. William H. Taft	Sept. 15, 1857	Cincinnati, Ohio	Republican	51	1909-1913	Mar. 8, 1930	72
28. Woodrow Wilson	Dec. 29, 1856	Staunton, Va.	Democratic	56	1913-1921	Feb. 3, 1924	67
29. Warren G. Harding	Nov. 2, 1865	near Blooming Grove, Ohio	Republican	55	1921-1923	Aug. 2, 1923	57
30. Calvin Coolidge	July 4, 1872	Plymouth Notch, Vt.	Republican	51	1923-1929	Jan. 5, 1933	60
31. Herbert C. Hoover	Aug. 10, 1874	West Branch, Iowa	Republican	54	1929-1933	Oct. 20, 1964	90
32. Franklin D. Roosevelt .	Jan. 30, 1882	Hyde Park, N.Y.	Democratic	51	1933-1945	Apr. 12, 1945	63
33. Harry S. Truman	May 8, 1884	Lamar, Mo.	Democratic	60	1945-1953	Dec. 26, 1972	88
34. Dwight D. Eisenhower	Oct. 14, 1890	Denison, Tex.	Republican	62	1953-1961	Mar. 28, 1969	78
35. John F. Kennedy	May 29, 1917	Brookline, Mass.	Democratic	43	1961-1963	Nov. 22, 1963	46
36. Lyndon B. Johnson	Aug. 27, 1908	near Stonewall, Tex.	Democratic	55	1963-1969	Jan. 22, 1973	64
37. Richard M. Nixon	Jan. 9, 1913	Yorba Linda, Calif.	Republican	56	1969-1974		
38. Gerald R. Ford‡	July 14, 1913	Omaha, Nebr.	Republican	61	1974-1977		
39. Jimmy Carter	Oct. 1, 1924	Plains, Ga.	Democratic	52	1977-1981		
40. Ronald W. Reagan	Feb. 6, 1911	Tampico, Ill.	Republican	69	1981-1989		
41. George H. W. Bush	June 12, 1924	Milton, Mass.	Republican	64	1989-		

†The National Union Party consisted of Republicans and War Democrats; Johnson was a Democrat.
‡Inaugurated Aug. 9, 1974, to replace Nixon, who resigned that same day.

Each President has a separate biography and picture in *World Book*.

Symbols of the United States include the American flag and the Great Seal. The eagle holds an olive branch and arrows, symbolizing a desire for peace but the ability to wage war. The reverse side bears the Eye of Providence, representing God, and a pyramid dated 1776.

Facts in brief

Capital: Washington, D.C.
Form of government: Republic. For details, see **United States, Government of the.**
Area: 3,618,770 sq. mi. (9,372,571 km²), including 79,481 sq. mi. (205,856 km²) of inland water but excluding 60,788 sq. mi. (157,440 km²) of Great Lakes and Lake Saint Clair and 13,942 sq. mi. (36,110 km²) of coastal water. *Greatest distances excluding Alaska and Hawaii*—east-west, 2,807 mi. (4,517 km); north-south, 1,598 mi. (2,572 km). *Greatest distances in Alaska*—north-south, about 1,200 mi. (1,930 km); east-west, about 2,200 mi. (3,540 km). *Greatest distance in Hawaii*—northwest-southeast, about 1,610 mi. (2,591 km). *Extreme points including Alaska and Hawaii*—northernmost, Point Barrow, Alaska; southernmost, Ka Lae, Hawaii; easternmost, West Quoddy Head, Me.; westernmost, Cape Wrangell, Attu Island, Alaska. *Coastline*—4,993 mi. (8,035 km), excluding Alaska and Hawaii; 12,383 mi. (19,929 km), including Alaska and Hawaii.
Elevation: *Highest*—Mount McKinley in Alaska, 20,320 ft. (6,194 m) above sea level. *Lowest*—In Death Valley in California, 282 ft. (86 m) below sea level.
Physical features: *Longest river*—Mississippi, 2,348 mi. (3,779 km). *Largest lake within the United States*—Michigan, 22,300 sq. mi. (57,757 km²). *Largest island*—island of Hawaii, 4,038 sq. mi. (10,458 km²).
Population: *Estimated 1990 population*—250,372,000; density, 69 persons per sq. mi. (27 per km²); distribution, 74 per cent urban, 26 per cent rural. *1980 census*—226,545,805. *Estimated 1995 population*—259,259,000.
Chief products: *Agriculture*—beef cattle, chickens, corn, cotton, eggs, hogs, milk, soybeans, wheat. *Fishing industry*—crabs, salmon, shrimp. *Manufacturing*—airplanes, broadcasting equipment, cameras, computers and computer parts, fabricated metal products, gasoline, guided missiles, industrial chemicals, industrial machinery, motor vehicles, paper, pharmaceuticals, plastics, printed materials, processed foods, steel. *Mining*—coal, natural gas, petroleum.
Flag: Adopted June 14, 1777.
Motto: *In God We Trust,* adopted July 30, 1956.
National anthem: "The Star-Spangled Banner," adopted March 3, 1931.
Bird: Bald eagle, adopted June 20, 1782.
Flower: Rose, adopted Oct. 7, 1986.
Money: *Basic unit*—dollar.

Important dates

1492 Christopher Columbus sailed from Spain to the Western Hemisphere. Europeans honored him as the discoverer of America.
1497 John Cabot made the first voyage to North America for England.
1513 Ponce de León of Spain began exploring Florida, seeking the Fountain of Youth.
1540-1542 Francisco Coronado of Spain explored the American Southwest.
1565 Spaniards founded St. Augustine, Fla., the oldest city in what is now the United States.
1607 About 100 colonists founded Jamestown, the first permanent British settlement in North America.
1619 Virginia established the House of Burgesses, the first representative legislature in America.
1620 The Pilgrims founded Plymouth Colony, the second permanent British settlement in North America.
1624 The Dutch established the settlement of New Netherland.
1636 Harvard—the first college in the colonies—was founded.
1638 People from Sweden established the settlement of New Sweden.
1647 Massachusetts established the first colonial public school system.
1649 Maryland passed the first religious toleration act in North America.
1664 England took control of New Netherland and New Sweden.
1704 *The Boston News-Letter,* the first successful colonial newspaper, began publication.
1763 Britain defeated France in the French and Indian War and gained control of eastern North America.
1763 Britain stationed a standing army in North America and prohibited colonists from settling west of the Appalachian Mountains.
1765 The British Parliament passed the Stamp Act, taxing newspapers, legal documents, and other printed matter in the colonies.
1770 British troops killed American civilians in the Boston Massacre.
1773 Colonists staged the Boston Tea Party, dumping British tea into Boston Harbor.
1774 The Intolerable Acts closed Boston Harbor and included other steps to punish the colonists.
1774 The First Continental Congress met to consider action against the British.
1775 The Revolutionary War between the colonists and the British began.
1776 The colonists adopted the Declaration of Independence and formed the United States of America.
1781 The Americans defeated the British at Yorktown, Va., in the last major battle of the Revolutionary War.
1783 The Treaty of Paris officially ended the Revolutionary War.
1787 The Founding Fathers wrote the Constitution.
1790's The first U.S. political parties developed.
1800 Washington, D.C., became the national capital.
1803 The Louisiana Purchase almost doubled the size of the United States.
1811 Work began on the National Road, which—when completed—linked the East and the Midwest.
1812-1814 The United States and Great Britain fought the War of 1812.
1820 The Missouri Compromise ended a slavery dispute.
1823 The Monroe Doctrine warned Europeans against interference in Western Hemisphere affairs.
1825 The Erie Canal opened, providing a water route from the Atlantic Ocean to the Great Lakes.
1832 South Carolina threatened secession over a tariff.
1846 Britain ceded the southern part of the Oregon Country to the United States.
1848 Victory in the Mexican War gave the United States vast new territory in the West.
1848 The discovery of gold in California triggered the Gold Rush.

Compiled from articles on the United States in *World Book.* © Copyright 1990 by World Book, Inc.

United States

1850 The Compromise of 1850 temporarily ended a national crisis over the slavery question.

1854 Passage of the Kansas-Nebraska Act led to nationwide turmoil over the slavery issue.

1860 Pony express riders began carrying mail from St. Joseph, Mo., to the Far West.

1861-1865 The North and the South fought each other in the Civil War.

1863 The Emancipation Proclamation declared freedom for all slaves in Confederate-held territory.

1865 The 13th Amendment outlawed slavery throughout the United States.

1867 The United States bought Alaska from Russia.

1868 The House of Representatives impeached President Andrew Johnson, but the Senate did not remove him from office.

1898 The United States defeated Spain in the Spanish-American War.

1913 The 16th Amendment gave the federal government the power to levy an income tax.

1914 World War I began in Europe.

1917-1918 The United States fought in World War I.

1920 The U.S. Senate rejected American participation in the League of Nations.

1920 The U.S. Census showed that, for the first time, the majority of Americans lived in urban areas.

1920 The 18th Amendment, prohibiting the sale of alcoholic beverages nationwide, became effective; the 19th Amendment gave women complete suffrage.

1929 The stock market crash brought financial ruin to thousands of investors.

1930's The United States suffered through the Great Depression.

1933 President Franklin D. Roosevelt began the New Deal program to try to end the depression.

1941-1945 The United States fought in World War II.

1945 An American airplane dropped the first atomic bomb used in warfare on Hiroshima, Japan.

1945 The United States became a charter member of the United Nations (UN).

1947 President Truman announced the Truman Doctrine, which pledged American aid to nations threatened by Communism.

1950 Senator Joseph R. McCarthy gained national fame by charging that Communists had infiltrated the federal government.

1950-1953 The United States fought in the Korean War.

1954 The Supreme Court ruled compulsory segregation in public schools unconstitutional.

1955 Martin Luther King, Jr., began organizing a movement to protest discrimination against blacks.

1957 The Soviet Union launched *Sputnik I*—the first space satellite—causing the United States to place more emphasis on space research.

1962 The Soviet Union removed missiles from Cuba, ending a threat of war with the United States.

1964 Congress passed a flood of important civil rights laws.

1965 American combat troops entered the Vietnam War.

1969 Astronaut Neil A. Armstrong became the first person to set foot on the moon.

1973 The United States removed its last ground troops from Vietnam. The war ended in 1975.

1974 Richard M. Nixon became the first American President to resign from office.

1976 The United States celebrated its bicentennial.

1986 The U.S. spacecraft *Challenger* exploded, and all seven crew members were killed.

1987 The United States celebrated the bicentennial of the signing of the U.S. Constitution.

The United States after the Revolutionary War

WORLD BOOK map

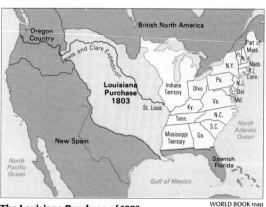

The Louisiana Purchase of 1803

WORLD BOOK map

Expansion in the mid-1800's

WORLD BOOK map

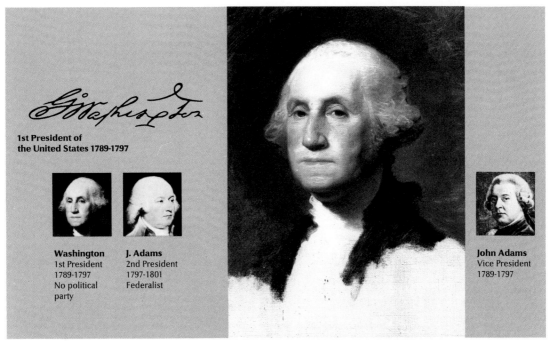

1st President of
the United States 1789-1797

Washington
1st President
1789-1797
No political
party

J. Adams
2nd President
1797-1801
Federalist

John Adams
Vice President
1789-1797

Oil painting on canvas (1796) by Gilbert Stuart; Jointly owned by the National Portrait Gallery, Smithsonian Institution, and the Museum of Fine Arts, Boston

Washington, George (1732-1799), won a lasting place in American history as the "Father of our Country." For nearly 20 years, he guided his country much as a father cares for a growing child.

In three important ways, Washington helped shape the beginning of the United States. First, he commanded the Continental Army that won American independence from Great Britain in the Revolutionary War. Second, Washington served as president of the convention that wrote the United States Constitution. Third, he was elected the first President of the United States.

The people of his day loved Washington. His army officers would have made him king if he had let them. From the Revolutionary War on, his birthday was celebrated each year throughout the country.

Washington lived an exciting life in exciting times. As a boy, he explored the wilderness. When he grew older, he helped the British fight the French and Indians. Many times he was nearly killed. As a general, he suffered hardships with his troops in the cold winters at Valley Forge, Pa., and Morristown, N.J. He lost many battles, but led the American army to final victory at Yorktown, Va. After he became President, he successfully solved many problems in turning the plans of the Constitution into a working government.

Washington went to school only until he was about 14 or 15. But he learned to make the most of all his abilities and opportunities. Washington's remarkable patience and his understanding of others helped him win people to his side in times of hardship and discouragement.

There are great differences between the United States of Washington's day and that of today. The new nation was small and weak. It stretched west only to the Mississippi River and had fewer than 4,000,000 people. Most people made their living by farming. Few children went to school. Few men or women could read or write. Transportation and communication were slow. It took Washington 3 days to travel about 90 miles (140 kilometers) from New York City to Philadelphia, longer than it now takes to fly around the world. There were only 11 states in the Union when Washington became President and 16 when he left office.

Important dates in Washington's life

1732	(Feb. 22) Born in Westmoreland County, Virginia.
1749	Became official surveyor for Culpeper County, Virginia.
1751	Went to Barbados Island, British West Indies.
1753	Carried British ultimatum to French in Ohio River Valley, as a major.
1754	Surrendered Fort Necessity in the French and Indian War, as a colonel.
1755	(July 9) With General Edward Braddock when ambushed by French and Indians.
1755-1758	Commanded Virginia's frontier troops, as a colonel.
1759	(Jan. 6) Married Mrs. Martha Dandridge Custis.
1774	Elected delegate to First Continental Congress.
1775	Elected delegate to Second Continental Congress.
1775	(June 15) Elected commander in chief of Continental Army.
1781	(Oct. 19) Victory at Yorktown.
1787	(May 25) Elected president of the Constitutional Convention.
1789	Elected first President of the United States.
1792	Reelected President of the United States.
1796	(Sept. 19) Published *Farewell Address,* refusing a third term.
1798	(July 4) Commissioned lieutenant general and commander in chief of new United States Army.
1799	(Dec. 14) Died at Mount Vernon at age 67.

WORLD: *Political*

ABBREVIATIONS

CEN. AFR. REP.
Central African Republic
DEN. Denmark
FR. France
GR. Greece
IT. Italy
N. North, Northern
NETH. Netherlands
P.D.R. YEMEN
People's Democratic
Republic of Yemen
PORT. Portugal
S. South
SP. Spain
TERR. Territory
U.A.E. United Arab
Emirates
U.K. United Kingdom
U.S. United States
W. Western

— National boundary

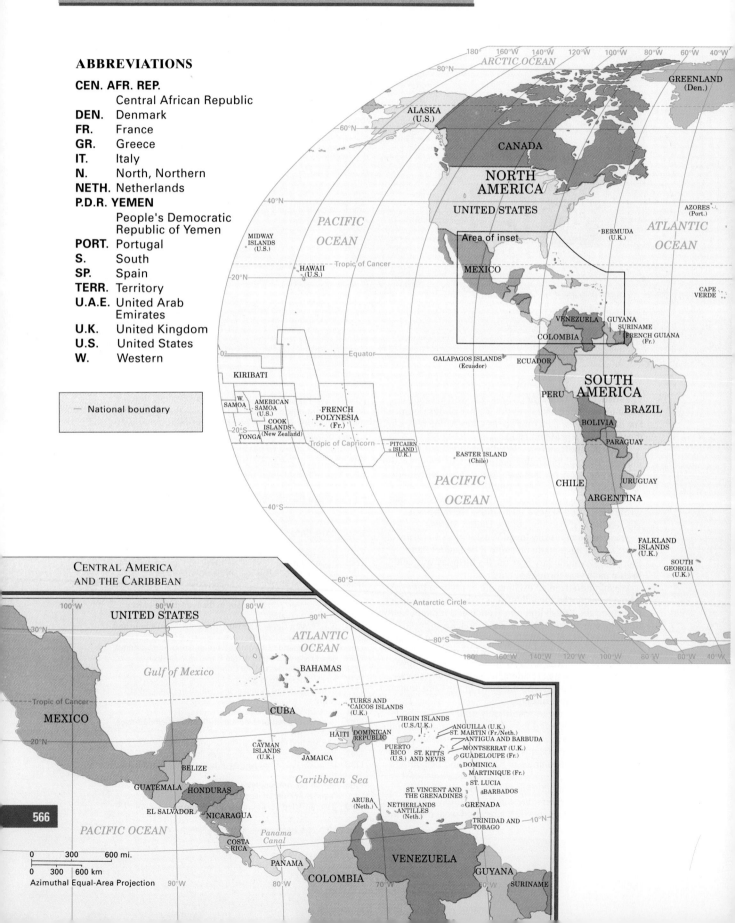

566

CENTRAL AMERICA
AND THE CARIBBEAN

0   300   600 mi.

0   300   600 km

Azimuthal Equal-Area Projection

20°W 0° 20°E 40°E 60°E 80°E 100°E 120°E 140°E 160°E 180°

ARCTIC OCEAN

80°N

Arctic Circle

ICELAND

Area of inset

60°N

UNION OF SOVIET SOCIALIST REPUBLICS
(SOVIET UNION)

EUROPE

ASIA

MONGOLIA

40°N

TURKEY

N. KOREA

PEOPLE'S REPUBLIC OF
CHINA

S. KOREA

JAPAN

CYPRUS SYRIA

MOROCCO

TUNISIA

LEBANON
ISRAEL

IRAQ

IRAN

AFGHANISTAN

PACIFIC

CANARY IS.
(Sp.)

ALGERIA

LIBYA

JORDAN

KUWAIT
QATAR

PAKISTAN

NEPAL

BHUTAN

TAIWAN

OCEAN

20°N

EGYPT

BAHRAIN
SAUDI
ARABIA

U.A.E

BANGLADESH

HONG
KONG
(U.K.)

WESTERN
SAHARA
(Morocco)

OMAN

INDIA

MYANMAR
(BURMA)

N. MARIANA
ISLANDS
(U.S.)

MAURITANIA

NIGER

AFRICA

P.D.R.
YEMEN YEMEN

LAOS

THAILAND

VIETNAM

SENEGAL

MALI

CHAD

SUDAN

DJIBOUTI

CAMBODIA

PHILIPPINES

GUAM (U.S.)

MARSHALL
ISLANDS

GAMBIA
GUINEA
BISSAU

BURKINA
FASO

NIGERIA

CEN. AFR. REP.

ETHIOPIA

SRI
LANKA

BRUNEI

FEDERATED
STATES OF
MICRONESIA

GUINEA

IVORY
COAST

TOGO
BENIN

SIERRA
LEONE

GHANA

MALAYSIA

TRUST TERR.
OF THE PACIFIC
ISLANDS (U.S.)

LIBERIA

CAMEROON

UGANDA

SOMALIA

MALDIVES

SINGAPORE

0°

EQUATORIAL GUINEA

SÃO TOMÉ AND
PRINCIPE

GABON

KENYA

RWANDA

PAPUA
NEW GUINEA

NAURU

CONGO

ZAIRE

BURUNDI

INDONESIA

CABINDA
(Angola)

TANZANIA

SEYCHELLES

INDIAN OCEAN

TUVALU

ATLANTIC

ANGOLA

MALAWI

COMOROS

SOLOMON
ISLANDS

20°S

OCEAN

ZAMBIA

VANUATU

FIJI

ZIMBABWE

MOZAMBIQUE

MADAGASCAR

MAURITIUS

NEW
CALEDONIA
(Fr.)

WALVIS BAY
(S. Africa)

NAMIBIA

BOTSWANA

SWAZILAND

AUSTRALIA

Prime Meridian

SOUTH
AFRICA

LESOTHO

N

W   E

S

0   1000   2000 mi.

0   1000   2000 km.

Robinson Projection

NEW
ZEALAND

60°S

ANTARCTICA

80°S

20°W 0° 20°E 40°E 60°E 80°E 100°E 120°E 140°E 160°E 180°

EUROPE

20°E 30°E 40°E

10°E

NORWAY

SWEDEN

FINLAND

North
Sea

60°N

IRELAND

UNITED
KINGDOM

DENMARK

Baltic Sea

SOVIET UNION

0   300   600 mi.

0   300   600 km.

Azimuthal Equal-Area Projection

NETHERLANDS

BELGIUM

EAST
GERMANY

POLAND

WEST
GERMANY

CZECHOSLOVAKIA

50°N

LUXEMBOURG

FRANCE

LIECHTENSTEIN

AUSTRIA

HUNGARY

SWITZERLAND

ROMANIA

ATLANTIC

MONACO

SAN
MARINO

YUGOSLAVIA

Black
Sea

OCEAN

40°N

ANDORRA

Adriatic Sea

BULGARIA

567

PORTUGAL

SPAIN

CORSICA
(Fr.)

ITALY

ALBANIA

BALEARIC IS.
(Sp.)

VATICAN
CITY

SARDINIA
(It.)

Mediterranean Sea

GREECE

TURKEY

GIBRALTAR
(U.K.)

SICILY
(It.)

CRETE
(Gr.)

10°W

MOROCCO

ALGERIA

MALTA

20°E

30°E

Land Elevation

Feet	Meters
9,840	3,000
6,580	2,000
3,280	1,000
656	200
0	0
Below sea level	Below sea level

Ice–covered land

▲ Mountain Peak

ARCTIC OCEAN

80°N

SVALBARD
Barents Sea

NOVAYA ZEMLYA

ICELAND
Arctic Circle

SIBERIA

60°N

KAMCHATKA

North Sea

Baltic Sea

BRITISH ISLES

EUROPE

URAL MOUNTAINS

CARPATHIANS

ASIA

Sea of Okhotsk

Mt. Blanc ▲ALPS

PYRENEES

CAUCASUS MTS.

GOBI (DESERT)

40°N

Sea of Japan

HOKKAIDO

BALKAN PEN.

Black Sea

Mt. Ararat ▲

Caspian Sea

HONSHU

Strait of Gibraltar

Mediterranean Sea

Mt. ▲Damavand

KUNLUN SHAN PLATEAU OF TIBET

SHIKOKU

KYUSHU

MADEIRA IS.

ATLAS MTS.

HIMALAYAS

Mt. Everest▲

East China Sea

CANARY IS.

SAHARA

ARABIAN DESERT

THAR DESERT

TAIWAN

20°N

NUBIAN DESERT

DECCAN PLATEAU

Arabian Sea

Bay of Bengal

HAINAN

SAHEL

SUDAN

AFRICA

SRI LANKA

South China Sea

PHILIPPINE ISLANDS

MICRONESIA

PACIFIC OCEAN

MALAY PEN.

GREAT RIFT VALLEY

Mt. Kirinyaga ▲

CONGO BASIN

▲Mt. Kilimanjaro

SEYCHELLES

INDONESIA

NEW GUINEA

ATLANTIC OCEAN

INDIAN OCEAN

MELANESIA

MADAGASCAR

20°S

KALAHARI DESERT

GREAT SANDY DESERT

Prime Meridian

AUSTRALIA

NULLARBOR PLAIN

NORTH ISLAND

Cape of Good Hope

N
W   E
S

0   1000   2000 mi.
0   1000   2000 km.
Robinson Projection

TASMANIA

SOUTH ISLAND

60°S

ANTARCTICA

ARCTIC OCEAN

160°W

160°E

180

SOVIET UNION

Alaska

Arctic Circle

Bering Sea

PACIFIC OCEAN

Washington

Oregon

Nevada

California

⊛ National capital

— National boundary

— State boundary

N

W E

S

Hawaii

Tropic of Cancer

160°W

140°W

120°W

140°W 120°W 100°W 80°W 60°W 40°W 20°W

GREENLAND

Hudson Bay

CANADA

Superior

Montana

North Dakota

Minnesota

Michigan

L. Huron

Maine

Idaho

South Dakota

Wisconsin

Vermont

New Hampshire

Wyoming

L. Michigan

New York

Massachusetts

Rhode Island

Connecticut

Nebraska

Iowa

Illinois

Indiana

Ohio

Pennsylvania

New Jersey

Utah

Colorado

Kansas

Missouri

West Virginia

Washington

Delaware

Maryland

Virginia

Kentucky

ATLANTIC OCEAN

Arizona

New Mexico

Oklahoma

Arkansas

Tennessee

North Carolina

South Carolina

Texas

Mississippi

Alabama

Georgia

Louisiana

Florida

40°N

60°W

0   250   500 mi.

0   250   500 km

Azimuthal Equal-Area Projection

BAHAMAS

Gulf of Mexico

MEXICO

CUBA

20°N

PUERTO RICO (U.S.)

100°W 80°W

UNITED STATES: *Political*

ALASKA

U.S.S.R.

ARCTIC OCEAN

0 300 600 mi.
0 300 600 km

Alaska

• Fairbanks

CANADA

• Anchorage

★ Juneau

ALEUTIAN ISLANDS

PACIFIC

OCEAN

HAWAII

KAUAI

NIIHAU

OAHU

Honolulu ★

MOLOKAI

LANAI

MAUI

PACIFIC

OCEAN

KAHOOLAWE

Hawaii

HAWAII

• Hilo

0 100 200 mi.
0 100 200 km

• Seattle

Washington

★ Olympia

Portland •

★ Salem

Oregon

Columbia River

Helena ★ Montana

• Billings

Idaho

Boise ★

Snake River

• Pocatello

Wyoming

Casper •

Cheyenne ★

Nevada

★ Carson City

San
Francisco •

• Sacramento

★ Salt Lake City

• Provo

Utah

Denver ★

Colorado

Pueblo •

California

Las Vegas •

Colorado River

• Los Angeles

Arizona

Santa Fe ★
Albuquerque •

New Mexico

• San Diego

★ Phoenix

• Tucson

MEXICO

⊛ National capital

★ State capital

• Major city

— National boundary

— State boundary

105°W 100°W 95°W 90°W 85°W 80°W 75°W 70°W 55°N 65°W 60°W

50°N

CANADA

North Dakota
Bismarck Fargo
Minnesota
Pierre
South Dakota
Sioux Falls
Minneapolis St. Paul
Wisconsin
Milwaukee
Madison
Lake Superior
Michigan
Lake Huron
Lansing
Detroit
Lake Michigan
Lake Erie
Lake Ontario

Maine
Augusta
Vermont
Burlington Montpelier New Hampshire Portland
Concord
Boston
Albany Massachusetts Providence
Hartford Rhode Island
New Haven Connecticut
New York
New York

Nebraska
Sioux City
Omaha
Lincoln
Platte River
Missouri River

Iowa
Des Moines
Chicago
Illinois
Springfield
Indiana
Indianapolis

Ohio
Cleveland
Columbus
Pennsylvania
Harrisburg
Pittsburgh
New Jersey
Trenton
Philadelphia
Wilmington Dover
Baltimore Delaware
Washington Annapolis
Maryland

40°N

Kansas
Topeka
Wichita
Arkansas River

Kansas City
Jefferson City
Missouri
St. Louis
Louisville
Evansville
Kentucky
Frankfort
Ohio River

West Virginia
Charleston
Virginia
Richmond
Norfolk

35°N

Oklahoma
Oklahoma City
Tulsa
Red River

Arkansas
Fort Smith
Little Rock
Nashville
Tennessee
Memphis
Mississippi River

North Carolina
Raleigh
Charlotte
South Carolina
Columbia
Charleston

ATLANTIC
OCEAN

70°W

Texas
Dallas
Austin
Houston
Rio Grande

Louisiana
Jackson
Mississippi
Baton Rouge
New Orleans
Greenville
Birmingham
Alabama
Montgomery
Atlanta
Georgia
Savannah
Tallahassee

30°N

N
W E
S

Gulf of Mexico

Florida
Tampa
Miami

BAHAMAS

25°N

0 200 400 mi.
0 200 400 km
Albers Equal-Area Projection

CUBA

20°N

100°W 95°W 90°W 85°W 80°W 75°W

573

UNITED STATES: *Physical*

ALASKA

U.S.S.R.

ARCTIC OCEAN

BROOKS RANGE

SEWARD PEN.

Arctic Circle

CANADA

Bering Strait

Mt. McKinley
20,320 ft.
6,194 m

ALASKA RANGE

ALEUTIAN ISLANDS

KODIAK

300   600 mi.

300   600 km

PACIFIC OCEAN

San Francisco Bay

COASTAL RANGES

CENTRAL VALLEY

SIERRA NEVADA

Mt. Shasta
14,162 ft.
4,317 m

Mt. Whitney
14,494 ft.
4,418 m

DEATH VALLEY

MOJAVE DESERT

CHANNEL ISLANDS

CASCADE RANGE

Mt. Rainier
14,410 ft.
4,392 m

Mt. St. Helens
8,364 ft.
2,549 m

Mt. Hood
11,239 ft.
3,426 m

COLUMBIA PLATEAU

Snake River

GREAT BASIN

Great Salt Lake

WASATCH RANGE

UINTA MTS.

BITTERROOT RANGE

ROCKY MOUNTAINS

Missouri River

Yellowstone River

BIG HORN MTS.

CONTINENTAL DIVIDE

Pikes Peak
14,110 ft.
4,310 m

SANGRE DE CRISTO MTS.

GRAND CANYON

PAINTED DESERT

Colorado River

Rio Grande

SACRAMENTO MTS.

Pecos River

MEXICO

HAWAIIAN ISLANDS

KAUAI

NIIHAU

OAHU

MOLOKAI

LANAI   MAUI

KAHOOLAWE

PACIFIC OCEAN

HAWAII

100   200 mi.

100   200 km

Land Elevation

Feet	Meters
13,120	4,000
6,560	2,000
1,640	500
656	200
0	0
Below sea level	Below sea level

Ice-covered land

▲ Mountain Peak

105°W 100°W 95°W 90°W 85°W 80°W 75°W 70°W 55°N 65°W 60°W

50°N

CANADA

Lake of
the Woods

MESABI
RANGE

Lake Superior

Lake
Huron

Lake
Michigan

St. Lawrence River

WHITE
MTS.
▲ Mt. Washington
6,288 ft.
1,917 m

ADIRONDACK
MTS.

NANTUCKET

CATSKILL
MTS.

MARTHA'S
VINEYARD

Lake Ontario

Lake Erie

Susquehanna River

LONG ISLAND

40°N

G
R
E
A
T

BLACK
HILLS

BADLANDS

SAND HILLS

Red River

Mississippi

Des Moines River

Missouri River

Platte River

Arkansas River

P
L
A
I
N
S

CENTRAL PLAINS

OZARK
PLATEAU

ALLEGHENY PLATEAU

APPALACHIAN MOUNTAINS

BLUE RIDGE MTS.

CUMBERLAND PLATEAU

Ohio River

▲ Mt. Mitchell
6,684 ft.
2,037 m

Delaware
Bay

Chesapeake Bay

35°N

FALL LINE

ATLANTIC COASTAL PLAIN

ATLANTIC

OCEAN

70°W

OUACHITA
MOUNTAINS

Red River

LLANO
ESTACADO

Brazos River

Sabine River

Colorado River

EDWARDS
PLATEAU

River

GULF COASTAL PLAIN

Galveston
Bay

Mobile
Bay

Pensacola
Bay

N

Tampa
Bay

Lake
Okeechobee

BAHAMAS

25°N

30°N

W   E

S

Gulf of Mexico

EVERGLADES

FLORIDA KEYS

CUBA

20°N

0   200   400 mi.

0   200   400 km
Albers Equal-Area Projection

100°W 95°W 90°W 85°W 80°W 75°W

NORTH AMERICA: *Political/Physical*

ASIA

EUROPE

ARCTIC OCEAN

Bering Sea

Bering Strait

BROOKS RANGE

Beaufort Sea

QUEEN ELIZABETH ISLANDS

ELLESMERE ISLAND

GREENLAND (Denmark)

Yukon River

ALASKA RANGE
• Fairbanks

BANKS ISLAND

Baffin Bay

• Anchorage

Gulf of Alaska

KODIAK ISLAND

VICTORIA ISLAND

BAFFIN ISLAND

ALEXANDER ARCHIPELAGO

Mackenzie River

Great Bear Lake

Labrador Sea

QUEEN CHARLOTTE ISLANDS

Great Slave Lake

UNGAVA PENINSULA

VANCOUVER ISLAND

COAST MOUNTAINS

LAURENTIAN SHIELD

LABRADOR

Vancouver
Seattle
Puget Sound

• Edmonton

CANADA

NEWFOUNDLAND

Portland •

• Calgary

Hudson Bay

PRINCE EDWARD ISLAND

CAPE BRETON ISLAND

Lake Winnipeg

• Winnipeg

Quebec •

ROCKY MOUNTAINS

BLACK HILLS

• Minneapolis

L. Superior

Montreal •
Ottawa ⊛

Bay of Fundy

San Francisco •

SIERRA NEVADA

Great Salt Lake

Salt Lake City •

Missouri River

Milwaukee •
Chicago •

Toronto •
L. Huron
L. Michigan

Boston •
Cape Cod

COAST RANGES

Omaha •

Detroit •
Cleveland •

L. Ontario
L. Erie

New York •
Philadelphia •

• Denver

Indianapolis •

APPALACHIAN MTS.

Baltimore •
Washington ⊛

ATLANTIC OCEAN

Los Angeles •
San Diego •

MOJAVE DESERT

GRAND CANYON

Kansas City •

Ohio River

St. Louis •

Louisville •

• Wichita

UNITED STATES

Nashville •

Charlotte •

Cape Hatteras

Colorado River

• Phoenix

Fort Worth •

Atlanta •
Birmingham •

BERMUDA (U.K.)

PACIFIC OCEAN

Ciudad Juárez •
Chihuahua •

Rio Grande

Austin •

Red River

Houston •

Jacksonville •

Cape Canaveral

San Antonio •

New Orleans •

Tropic of Cancer

BAJA CALIFORNIA

SIERRA MADRE OCCIDENTAL

Monterrey •

Miami •

⊛ Nassau
BAHAMAS

Cabo San Lucas

Gulf of California

MEXICO
PLATEAU OF MEXICO

SIERRA MADRE ORIENTAL

Gulf of Mexico

Havana ⊛
CUBA

San Juan

VIRGIN ISLANDS (U.S., U.K.)

ANGUILLA (U.K.)
ANTIGUA AND BARBUDA

Guadalajara •

Santiago de Cuba •

PUERTO RICO (U.S.)

ST. KITTS-NEVIS

GUADELOUPE (Fr.)

Mexico City ⊛

Veracruz •

YUCATÁN PENINSULA

CAYMAN ISLANDS (U.K.)

Port-au-Prince ⊛
HAITI

DOMINICAN REPUBLIC

Kingston •
Santo Domingo •

DOMINICA Roseau ⊛

MARTINIQUE (Fr.)

Castries ST. LUCIA

Puebla •

JAMAICA

ST. VINCENT AND THE GRENADINES

Kingstown ⊛

Bridgetown
BARBADOS

Acapulco •

ISTHMUS OF TEHUANTEPEC

Belmopan ⊛
BELIZE

Caribbean Sea

NETHERLANDS ANTILLES (Neth.)

St. George's ⊛
GRENADA

Port of Spain ⊛
TRINIDAD AND TOBAGO

GUATEMALA

HONDURAS

ARUBA (Neth.)

Guatemala City ⊛
San Salvador ⊛
EL SALVADOR

Tegucigalpa •
NICARAGUA

MOSQUITO COAST

Managua ⊛

Lago de Nicaragua

San José ⊛

ISTHMUS OF PANAMA

Panama City ⊛

SOUTH AMERICA

COSTA RICA

PANAMA

N
W   E
S

Equator

⊛ National capital

• Major city

— National boundary

0   400   800 mi.

0   400   800 km

Azimuthal Equal-Area Projection

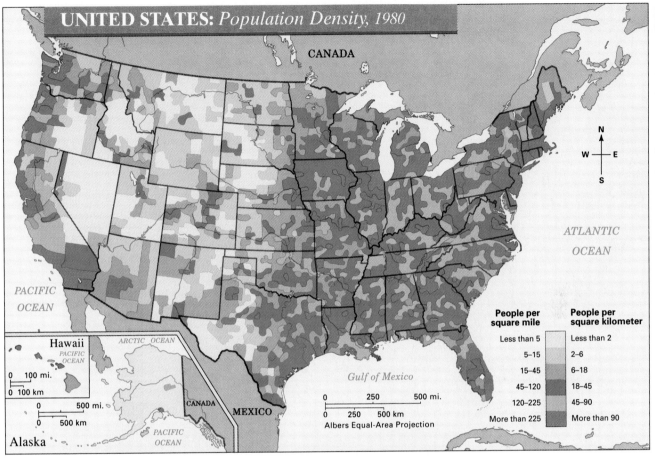

UNITED STATES: *Population Density, 1980*

CANADA

ATLANTIC OCEAN

PACIFIC OCEAN

Gulf of Mexico

CANADA

MEXICO

People per square mile

Less than 5
5–15
15–45
45–120
120–225
More than 225

People per square kilometer

Less than 2
2–6
6–18
18–45
45–90
More than 90

Hawaii
PACIFIC OCEAN
0   100 mi.
0   100 km

ARCTIC OCEAN

Alaska
CANADA
PACIFIC OCEAN
0   500 mi.
0   500 km

0   250   500 mi.
0   250   500 km
Albers Equal-Area Projection

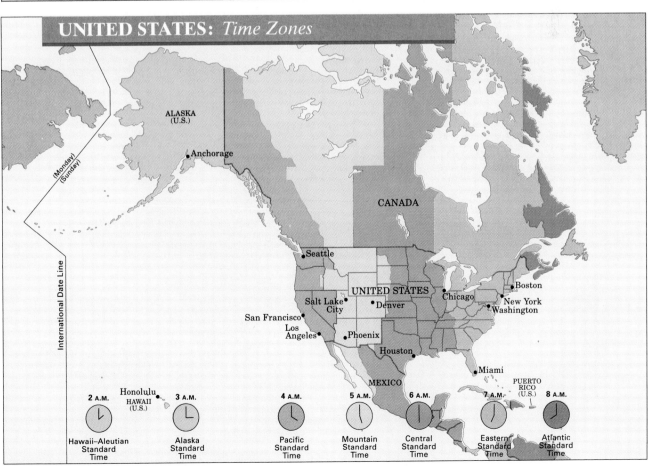

UNITED STATES: *Time Zones*

ALASKA (U.S.)

Anchorage

(Monday)
(Sunday)

International Date Line

CANADA

Seattle

Salt Lake City

UNITED STATES

Denver

Chicago

Boston

New York
Washington

San Francisco

Los Angeles

Phoenix

Houston

Miami

PUERTO RICO (U.S.)

MEXICO

2 A.M.
Honolulu
HAWAII (U.S.)
Hawaii–Aleutian Standard Time

3 A.M.
Alaska Standard Time

4 A.M.
Pacific Standard Time

5 A.M.
Mountain Standard Time

6 A.M.
Central Standard Time

7 A.M.
Eastern Standard Time

8 A.M.
Atlantic Standard Time

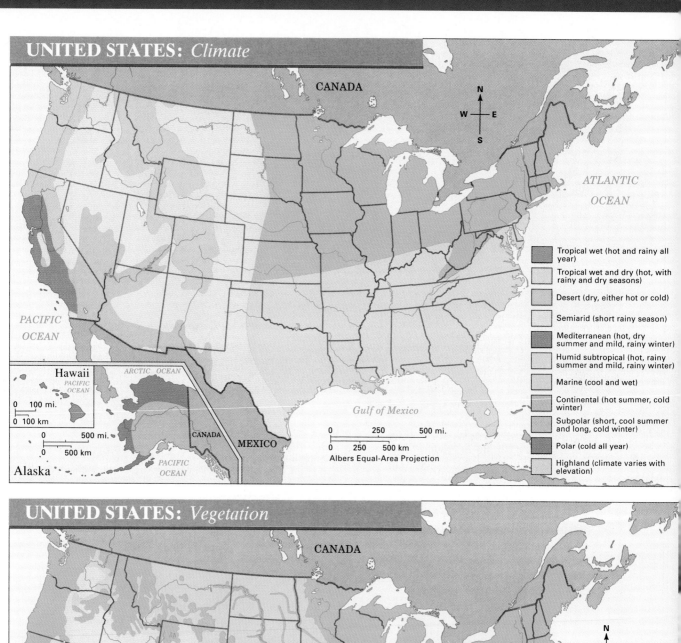

UNITED STATES: *Climate*

CANADA

N
W · E
S

ATLANTIC OCEAN

PACIFIC OCEAN

Gulf of Mexico

Tropical wet (hot and rainy all year)

Tropical wet and dry (hot, with rainy and dry seasons)

Desert (dry, either hot or cold)

Semiarid (short rainy season)

Mediterranean (hot, dry summer and mild, rainy winter)

Humid subtropical (hot, rainy summer and mild, rainy winter)

Marine (cool and wet)

Continental (hot summer, cold winter)

Subpolar (short, cool summer and long, cold winter)

Polar (cold all year)

Highland (climate varies with elevation)

Hawaii
PACIFIC OCEAN
0   100 mi.
0   100 km

ARCTIC OCEAN

CANADA

MEXICO

PACIFIC OCEAN

Alaska

0   500 mi.
0   500 km

0   250   500 mi.
0   250   500 km
Albers Equal-Area Projection

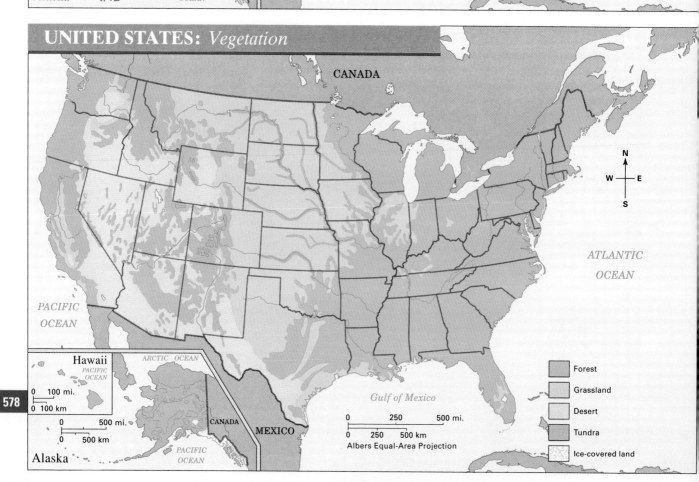

UNITED STATES: *Vegetation*

CANADA

N
W · E
S

ATLANTIC OCEAN

PACIFIC OCEAN

Gulf of Mexico

Hawaii
PACIFIC OCEAN
0   100 mi.
0   100 km

ARCTIC OCEAN

CANADA

MEXICO

PACIFIC OCEAN

Alaska

0   500 mi.
0   500 km

0   250   500 mi.
0   250   500 km
Albers Equal-Area Projection

Forest

Grassland

Desert

Tundra

Ice-covered land

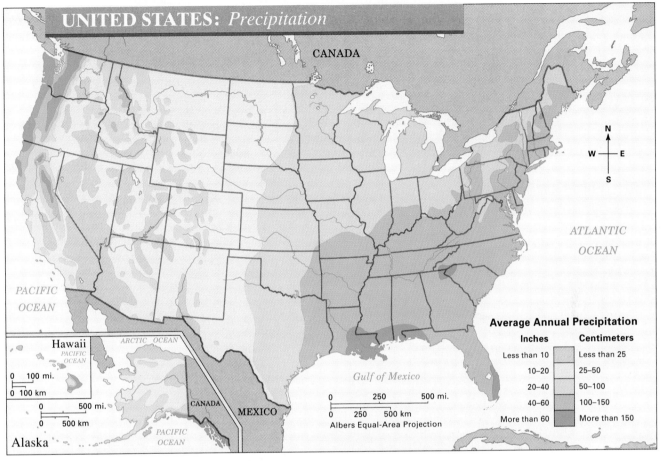

UNITED STATES: *Precipitation*

CANADA

PACIFIC
OCEAN

ATLANTIC
OCEAN

Hawaii
PACIFIC
OCEAN

ARCTIC OCEAN

0   100 mi.
0   100 km

CANADA

MEXICO

Gulf of Mexico

0   250   500 mi.
0   250   500 km
Albers Equal-Area Projection

Alaska
0   500 mi.
0   500 km
CANADA
PACIFIC
OCEAN

Average Annual Precipitation

Inches	Centimeters
Less than 10	Less than 25
10–20	25–50
20–40	50–100
40–60	100–150
More than 60	More than 150

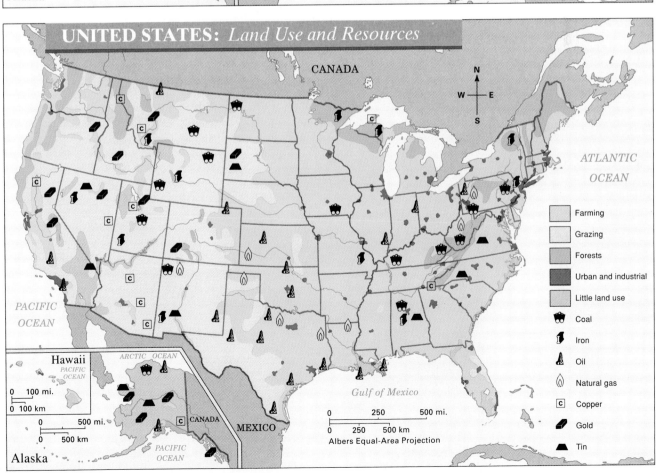

UNITED STATES: *Land Use and Resources*

CANADA

ATLANTIC
OCEAN

PACIFIC
OCEAN

Hawaii
PACIFIC
OCEAN

ARCTIC OCEAN

0   100 mi.
0   100 km

0   500 mi.
0   500 km

CANADA

MEXICO

Gulf of Mexico

0   250   500 mi.
0   250   500 km
Albers Equal-Area Projection

Alaska
PACIFIC
OCEAN

Farming

Grazing

Forests

Urban and industrial

Little land use

Coal

Iron

Oil

Natural gas

Copper

Gold

Tin

mountain
a steeply raised land mass, much higher than the surrounding country

glacier
a large ice mass that moves slowly down a mountain or over land

ocean or **sea**
a salty body of water covering a large area of the earth

mountain range
a row of mountains

tree line
on a mountain, the area above which no trees grow

valley
low land between hills or mountains

mountain pass
a gap between mountains

basin
a bowl-shaped area of land surrounded by higher land

hill
a raised mass of land, smaller than a mountain

prairie
a large, level area of grassland with few or no trees

mesa
a wide, flat-topped mountain with steep sides, found mostly in dry areas

desert
a dry area of land where few plants grow

plain
a broad, flat area of land

volcano
an opening in the earth, often raised, through which lava and gasses from the earth's interior escape

sea level
the level of the surface of the ocean

strait
a narrow channel of water connecting two large bodies of water

harbor
a sheltered body of water where ships can safely dock

coast
the land next to the ocean

bay
part of a lake or ocean extending into the land

island
a body of land completely surrounded by water

delta
a triangular area of land formed by deposits at the mouth of a river

isthmus
a narrow strip of land connecting two large bodies of land

river
a large stream that runs into a lake, ocean, or another river

tributary
a stream or river that empties into a larger river

plateau
a large area of flat land higher than the surrounding land

lake
a body of water completely surrounded by land

This Gazetteer will help you locate many of the places discussed in this book. Latitude and longitude given for large areas of land and water refers to the centermost point of the area; latitude and longitude of rivers refers to the river mouth. The page number tells you where to find each place on a map.

PLACE	LAT.	LONG.	PAGE
A			
Albany (capital of New York, on Hudson R.)	43°N	74°W	**209**
Appalachian Mts. (range stretching from Maine to Alabama)	37°N	82°W	**5**
Atlanta (capital of Georgia)	34°N	84°W	**424**
Augusta (city in Georgia on Savannah R.)	33°N	82°W	**51**
B			
Bahamas (group of islands in the Atlantic Ocean)	26°N	76°W	**468**
Bering Strait (waterway connecting Arctic Ocean and Bering Sea)	65°N	170°W	**576**
Boonesborough (fort in Kentucky; founded by Daniel Boone in 1775; south of present-day Lexington)	37°N	85°W	**342**
Boston (capital and largest city in Massachusetts)	42°N	71°W	**139**
Bristol (city in England)	51°N	3°W	**199**
Buffalo (city in western New York; on Lake Erie and Niagara R.)	43°N	79°W	**424**
C			
Canada (country bordering U.S. on north)	50°N	100°W	**36**
Cape Cod (peninsula in southeastern Massachusetts between Cape Cod Bay and the Atlantic Ocean; landing place of Pilgrims on the *Mayflower*)	41°N	70°W	**139**
Catskill Mts. (part of the Appalachian Mts. in New York)	42°N	75°W	**97**
Charleston (port city in South Carolina on Atlantic Ocean)	33°N	80°W	**272**
Chesapeake Bay (between Virginia and Maryland; about 190 miles long)	39°N	77°W	**133**
Chicago (city in Illinois on Lake Michigan; third largest U.S. city)	42°N	88°W	**5**
Cincinnati (city in Ohio; on Ohio R.)	39°N	85°W	**424**

PLACE	LAT.	LONG.	PAGE
Cleveland (largest city in Ohio; on Lake Erie)	42°N	82°W	**424**
Colorado Plateau (in New Mexico and Arizona)	36°N	109°W	**36**
Columbia R. (forms Washington-Oregon border)	46°N	124°W	**375**
Concord (city in Massachusetts near Boston, site of early Revolutionary War battle)	42°N	71°W	**272**
Connecticut R. (longest in New England)	41°N	72°W	**139**
Cumberland Gap (pass through the Appalachian Mts. in Tennessee)	36°N	83°W	**342**
D			
Delaware R. (in New York and Delaware)	39°N	75°W	**209**
Detroit (largest city in Michigan)	42°N	83°W	**425**
District of Columbia (site of U.S. capital)	39°N	77°W	**572**
E			
El Paso (city on the Rio Grande in Texas)	32°N	106°W	**375**
England (island country in Europe; largest unit of the United Kingdom of Great Britain)	52°N	2°W	**120**
Erie Canal (artificial waterway in New York; 525 miles long)	43°N	79°W	**342**
F			
Fort Sumter (site of first Civil War battle)	33°N	80°W	**468**
France (country in southeastern Europe)	47°N	1°E	**487**
G			
Germany (country in Europe)	52°N	9°E	**427**
Grand Banks (fishing area off Newfoundland)	47°N	56°W	**130**
Grand Canyon (deep canyon in Arizona formed by the Colorado R.)	36°N	112°W	**574**
Great Britain (England, Scotland, and Wales)	57°N	0°W	**199**

PLACE	LAT.	LONG.	PAGE
Great Lakes (five freshwater lakes between U.S. and Canada)	45°N	83°W	**88**
Great Plains (large, flat, dry area in western U.S.)	45°N	104°W	**36**
Gulf of Mexico (body of seawater along southern U.S. and Mexico)	25°N	94°W	**5**

H

PLACE	LAT.	LONG.	PAGE
Hudson R. (in New York; named for explorer Henry Hudson)	41°N	74°W	**209**

I

PLACE	LAT.	LONG.	PAGE
Ireland (country in Europe)	54°N	13°W	**487**
Italy (country in southern Europe; bordered by the Adriatic and Mediterranean Seas)	44°N	11°E	**487**

J

PLACE	LAT.	LONG.	PAGE
James R. (in central Virginia; flows into Chesapeake Bay)	43°N	97°W	**165**
Jamestown (first permanent English settlement in America; founded in 1607 on the shore of the James R. in Virginia)	37°N	78°W	**165**
Japan (island country off east coast of Asia)	37°N	134°E	**487**

L

PLACE	LAT.	LONG.	PAGE
Lake Erie (one of the five Great Lakes)	42°N	81°W	**342**
Lake Huron (one of the five Great Lakes)	45°N	83°W	**342**
Lake Michigan (one of the five Great Lakes)	43°N	87°W	**342**
Lake Ontario (one of the five Great Lakes)	44°N	79°W	**342**
Lake Superior (one of the five Great Lakes)	48°N	89°W	**342**
Lexington (city near Boston; site of first Revolutionary War battle)	42°N	71°W	**272**
London (capital and most populated city in England)	52°N	0°W	**199**
Los Angeles (largest city in California)	34°N	118°W	**5**

PLACE	LAT.	LONG.	PAGE
Louisiana Territory (western half of Mississippi R. basin; purchased by U.S. in 1803 from France)	37°N	92°W	**302**

M

PLACE	LAT.	LONG.	PAGE
Mexico (country bordering U.S. to the south)	24°N	104°W	**371**
Mexico City (capital of Mexico)	19°N	99°W	**371**
Mississippi R. (one of the longest rivers in U.S.)	29°N	89°W	**5**
Missouri R. (flows from Montana to Missouri; tributary of the Mississippi R.)	39°N	90°W	**5**

N

PLACE	LAT.	LONG.	PAGE
Netherlands (provinces united under leadership of largest province, also called Holland; in western Europe)	52°N	6°E	**120**
New Amsterdam (founded by Dutch settlers in 1624; now New York City)	41°N	74°W	**144**
Newfoundland (island in Atlantic Ocean off coast of Canada)	48°N	57°W	**120**
New Netherland (Dutch North American colony in present New York, New Jersey, and Connecticut)	41°N	74°W	**144**
New Orleans (largest city in Louisiana; on Mississippi R.)	30°N	90°W	**5**
New York City (largest city in U.S.)	41°N	74°W	**209**
Nogales (city in southern Arizona)	31°N	111°W	**15**
Norfolk (city in southeastern Virginia)	37°N	76°W	**424**
Northwest Territory (land north of Ohio R., west of Pennsylvania, east of Mississippi R.)	41°N	85°W	**302**

O

PLACE	LAT.	LONG.	PAGE
Oakland (city in California)	38°N	122°W	**51**
Ohio R. (in Pennsylvania and Ohio)	37°N	89°W	**342**
Oregon Territory (also Oregon Country; area from Rocky Mts. to Pacific Ocean)	45°N	120°W	**375**

This dictionary lists many of the important people introduced in this book. The page number refers to the main discussion of that person in the book. For more complete references see the Index.

Pronunciation Key

This chart presents the system of phonetic respellings used to indicate pronunciation in the Biographical Dictionary and in the chapters of this book.

Spellings	Symbol	Spellings	Symbol	Spellings	Symbol
pat	a	kick, cat, pique	k	thin, this	th
pay	ay	lid, needle	l	cut	uh
care	air	mum	m	urge, term, firm, word, heard	ur
father	ah	no, sudden	n		
bib	b	thing	ng	valve	v
church	ch	pot, horrid	ah	with	w
deed, milled	d	toe	oh	yes	y
pet	eh	caught, paw, for	aw	zebra, xylem	z
bee	ee	noise	oy	vision, pleasure, garage	zh
life, phase, rough	f	took	u		
gag	g	boot	oo	about, item, edible, gallop, circus	uh
hat	h	out	ow		
which	hw	pop	p	butter	ur
pit	ih	roar	r		
pie, by	eye, y	sauce	s	Capital letters indicate stressed syllables.	
pier	ihr	ship, dish	sh		
judge	j	tight, stopped	t		

A

Adams, Abigail 1744–1818, American First Lady, wife of John (p. 284).

Adams, John 1735–1826, 2nd U.S. President, 1797–1801 (p. 319).

Adams, John Quincy 1767–1848, 6th U.S. President, 1825–1829 (p. 444).

Adams, Samuel 1722–1803, American Revolutionary leader (p. 250).

Addams, Jane 1860–1935, American social reformer (p. 519).

Anthony, Susan B. 1820–1906, American reformer (p. 516).

Argell, Samuel 1572?–1626, English colonial governor of Virginia (p. 63).

Attucks, *(AT uhks)* **Crispus** 1723–1770, former slave killed in Boston Massacre (p. 249).

Austin, Stephen F. 1793–1836, political leader in Texas (p. 371).

B

Bacon, Nathaniel 1647–1676, English-born colonist; led Bacon's Rebellion (p. 165).

Balboa, Vasco Nuñez de 1475–1517, Spanish discoverer of Pacific Ocean (p. 114).

Baltimore, George Calvert. *See* Calvert, George.

Banneker, Benjamin 1731–1806; Black-American scientist (p. 331).

Belcher, Andrew American merchant and colonial governor (p. 198).

Berkeley, William 1606–1677, English colonial governor of Virginia (p. 163).

Black Hawk 1767–1838, American Indian leader (p. 365).

Bodmer, Karl Swiss artist; traveled with Prince Maximilian in 1833 (p. 70).

Boone, Daniel 1734–1820, American frontiersman; helped settle Kentucky (p. 357).

Boudinot *(BOO dnoh)*, **Elias** early 19th-century Cherokee Indian newspaper publisher (p. 364).

Bowie, Jim 1799–1836, American-born Mexican colonist; died at the Alamo (p. 372).

Bradford, William 1590–1657, English Puritan colonist in America (p. 139).

Breckinridge, John 1821–1875, U.S. Vice President, 1857–1861 (p. 464).

Brown, John 1800–1859, American abolitionist (p. 450).

Burgoyne *(bur GOYN)*, **John** 1722–1792, English general; surrendered at Saratoga in October 1777 (p. 270).

Burnaby, Andrew 18th-century English preacher; wrote about the Middle Colonies (p. 213).

C

Cabot, John 1450–1498, Italian-born explorer and cartographer (p. 121).

Henry VII 1457–1509, King of England, 1485–1509 (p. 139).

Henry VIII 1491–1547, King of England, 1509–1547 (p. 121).

Henson, Josiah 1789–1883, slave who escaped to Canada; published his autobiography (p. 407).

Hicks, Edward 1780–1849, American primitive painter (p. *211*).

Houston, Sam 1793–1863, President of Republic of Texas (p. 373).

Hudson, Henry d.1611, English explorer (p. 120).

Hutchinson, Anne 1591–1643, English-born American colonist and religious leader (p. *193*).

I

Isabella 1451–1504, Queen of Castile and Aragon; sponsored Christopher Columbus (p. 110).

J

Jackson, Andrew 1767–1845, 7th U.S. President, 1829–1837, called "Old Hickory" (p. 413).

James I 1566–1625, ruled England, 1603–1625, ruled Scotland as James VI, 1567–1625 (p. 162).

James II 1633–1701, ruled England, 1685–1688 (p. 144).

Jay, John 1745–1829, American diplomat; signed treaty with England (p. 274).

Jefferson, Thomas 1743–1826, 3rd U.S. President, 1801–1809; author of Declaration of Independence; scientist, architect, and educator (p. *262*).

Joseph, Chief 1840–1904, Nez Perce leader (p. *510*).

K

Kay, John 1733–1764, English inventor of flying shuttle used in weaving (p. 423).

King, Rufus 1755–1827, American politician and diplomat (p. 446).

Knox, Henry 1750–1806, American revolutionary soldier and public official p. *317*).

L

Lee, Ann 1736–1784, "Mother Ann," English founder of American Shaker sect (p. 435).

Lee, Richard Henry 1732–1794, American revolutionary leader (p. 264).

Lee, Robert E. 1807–1870, American Confederate general; surrendered to Grant (p. 471).

Lewis, Meriwether 1774–1809, American northwest explorer (p. 353).

Lincoln, Abraham 1809–1865, 16th U.S. President, 1861–1865; passed 13th Amendment; assassinated (p. *463*).

M

Madison, Dolley 1768–1849, American First Lady, wife of James (p. *322*).

Madison, James 1751–1836, 4th U.S. President, 1809–1817 (p. 297).

Magellan, Ferdinand 1480?–1521, Portuguese navigator, killed while circumnavigating the globe (p. 114).

Malcolm, John colonial official twice tarred and feathered by Bostonians (p. 247).

Marshall, James 1810–1885, American pioneer; first to find gold in California (p. 384).

Massasoit 1580?–1661, Chief of Wampanoag Indians who negotiated peace with the Pilgrims (p. 142).

Mather, Cotton 1663–1728, American clergyman and author (p. 194).

Meir, Golda 1898–1978, Russian-born American; Israeli Prime Minister (p. 486).

Mercator, Gerardus 1512–1594, Flemish geographer (p. 45).

Mittelberger, Gottlieb German traveler in America (p. 225).

Moctezuma 1480?–1520, last Aztec emperor in Mexico (p. 115).

Monroe, James 1758–1831, 5th U.S. President, 1817–1825 (p. 352).

Morris, Gouverneur 1752–1816, American diplomat and political leader (p. *299*).

Mott, Lucretia 1793–1880, American social reformer (p. 515).

N

Napoleon Bonaparte 1769–1821, French general and emperor (p. 352).

North, Frederick 1732–1792, English prime minister, 1770–1782 (p. 254).

O

Oliver, Andrew 1706–1774, American colonial political leader (p. 248).

Oñate, Juan de *(aw NYAH teh)* 1549–1624?, Spanish explorer, conquistador (p. 128).

P

Paine, Thomas 1737–1809, English-born American author of *Common Sense* (p. 263).

Paterson, William 1745–1806, Irish-born American revolutionary leader (p. 300).

Penn, William 1644–1718, Quaker leader; founded Commonwealth of Pennsylvania (p. *146*).

Philip II 1527–1598, King of Spain, 1556–1598 (p. 128).

Pike, Zebulon 1779–1813, American army officer and explorer (p. *356*).

Pitt, William 1759–1806, British Prime Minister, 1783–1801, 1804–1806 (p. 244).

Pocahontas 1595?–1617, American Indian princess (p. *162*).

Polk, James K. 1795–1849, 11th U.S. President, 1845–1849 (p. 374).

Powell, John Wesley 1834–1902, American geologist and explorer (p. 30).

Powhatan 1550?–1618, American Indian chief (p. 162).

Ptolemy 2nd century A.D. Greek astronomer and geographer (p. 110).

R

Raleigh, Sir Walter 1552?–1618, English navigator, colonizer (p. 133).

Randolph, Edmund 1753–1813, American Revolutionary leader (p. 300).

Revere, Paul 1735–1818, American revolutionary patriot (p. 261).

Rolfe, John 1585–1622, English colonist in America (p. 161).

S

Sacajawea (*sak uh juh WEE uh*) 1788?–1812, Shoshone Indian guide, aided Lewis and Clark expedition (p. 356)

Samoset d.1653?, American Indian chief and friend of Pilgrim colonists at Plymouth (p. *142*).

Scott, Dred 1795?–1858, American slave involved in Supreme Court case (p. 462).

Scott, Winfield 1786–1866, American general (p. 374).

Seattle 1786?–1866, American Indian leader (p. 389).

Sequoya (*sih KWOY uh*) 1766?–1843, leader of Cherokee Indians (p. 363).

Shays, Daniel 1747?–1825, American soldier at Bunker Hill; leader of Shays's Rebellion (p. 296).

Slater, Samuel 1768–1835, English-born textile pioneer in America (p. 423)

Smith, John 1580?–1631, English adventurer, mapmaker, colonist, explorer, and author (p. 158).

Smith, Joseph 1805–1844, American Mormon religious leader (p. 387).

Squanto (*SKWAHN toh*) ?–1622, American Indian of Pawtuxet tribe, gave vital aid to Plymouth colony, Massachusetts (p. 142).

Stanford, Leland 1824–1893, American politician, financier, railroad promoter (p. 480).

Stanton, Elizabeth Cady 1815–1902, American feminist and social reformer (p. 285).

Stowe, Harriet Beecher 1811–1896, American novelist; author of *Uncle Tom's Cabin* (p. 451).

Strauss, Levi 1829?–1902, American clothing manufacturer who gave the world blue jeans (p. 387).

Stuyvesant (*STY vih suhnt*), **Peter** 1592?–1672, Dutch administrator in America (p. 144).

Sullivan, Anne Mansfield 1866–1936, American teacher of deaf and blind, especially Helen Keller (p. 511).

Sutter, John Augustus 1803–1880, immigrant pioneer, found gold on his California land in 1848 (p. 383).

T

Taney, Roger B. 1777–1864, American jurist involved in Dred Scott decision (p. 463).

Taylor, Zachary 1784–1850, 12th U.S. President, 1849–1850 (p. 374).

Tecumseh (*teh KUHM suh*) 1768–1813, Shawnee Indian chief (p. 360).

Travis, William Barret 1809–1836, commander of the Texans in battle of the Alamo (p. 373).

Trollope, Frances (*TRAHL uhp*) 1780–1863, English author on American manners (p. 324).

Truth, Sojourner 1797–1883, American abolitionist and feminist (p. 438).

Tubman, Harriet 1820–1913, American abolitionist (p. 451).

Turner, Nat 1800–1831, American leader of slave revolt (p. 405).

Twain, Mark 1835–1910, pen name of American author born Samuel Clemens (p. 34).

Tweed, William Marcy 1823–1878, American politician; "Boss Tweed" of New York (p. 489).

V

Verrazano (*vehr uh ZAH noh*), **Giovanni da** 1485?–1528? Italian explorer of U.S. Atlantic coast (p. 119).

Vespucci (*vehs POO chee*), **Amerigo** 1454–1512, Italian navigator, explorer of New World, mapmaker (p. 114).

Voltaire (*vohl TAIR*), **Francois Marie Arouet de** 1694–1778, French author, dramatist, and philosopher (p. 216).

W

Washington, George, 1732–1799, 1st U.S. President, 1789–1797, American Revolutionary commander (p. 270).

Wayne, Anthony 1745–1796, American Revolutionary general (p. 362).

Webster, Noah 1758–1843, lexicographer; compiled first American dictionary (p. 308).

Weems, Mason 1759–1825, American clergyman; biographer of G. Washington (p. 306).

Wesley, John 1703–1791, British founder of Methodism (p. 330).

West, Benjamin 1738–1820, American painter (p. 224).

Wetherill, Richard discoverer of Mesa Verde (p. 86).

White, John ?–1593?, English painter and cartographer in America (p. 132).

Whitefield *(HWIHT feeld),* **George** 1714–1770, British religious leader (p. 195).

Whitney, Eli 1765–1825, American inventor of cotton gin (403).

Williams, Roger 1603?–1683, English preacher in America; founded Rhode Island (p. 193).

Wilson, James, 1742–1798, American Revolutionary leader; member first U.S. Supreme Court, 1789–1798 (p. 302).

Winslow, Edward 1595–1655, founder and later governor Plymouth colony, Massachusetts (p. 138).

Winthrop, John 1588–1649, leader of Puritan settlers in New England; founded Salem, Massachusetts (p. 180).

Wolfe, James 1727–1759, British army officer, defeated French in Quebec (p. 245).

Y

York, Duke of 1633–1701, became King James II, 1685–1688 (p. 144).

Young, Brigham 1801–1877, American Mormon leader; led trek to Utah (p. 387).

GLOSSARY

A

abolitionist (ăb´ə-lĭsh´ə-nist) a person who wanted to abolish, or do away with, slavery (p. 406).

agriculture (ăg´rĭ-kŭl´chər) the science and business of raising plants and animals for food; farming (p. 83).

amendment (ə-mĕnd´mənt) a statement added to change the Constitution or make its meaning clearer (p. 303).

annex (ə-nĕks´) to attach something to something larger (p. 373).

apprentice (ə-prĕn´tĭs) a person working for a skilled worker in order to learn the skill (p. 187).

archives (är´kīvz´) a collection of important records about a place or organization (p. 64).

artifact (är´tə-făkt´) an object made by humans, especially one of historical interest (p. 68).

assembly (ə-sĕm´blē) citizens gathered for a purpose, such as making laws and setting taxes (p. 240).

B

boycott (boi´kŏt´) to refuse to buy, sell, or use an item in order to force a change (p. 249).

Bureau of Indian Affairs (byōōr´ō ŭv ĭn´dē-ən ə-fâr´z) a U.S. government agency established in 1824 with authority to make treaties and regulate trade with the Indians (p. 364).

C

Cabinet (kăb´ə-nĭt) the council that advises the President, made up of the heads of government departments (p. 316).

camp meeting (kămp mē´tĭng) a large religious gathering held outdoors or in a tent, often lasting several days (p. 330).

canal (kə-năl´) a waterway made by humans and used for shipping, travel, or irrigation (p. 346).

cartographer (kär-tŏg´rə-fər) a person who makes maps (p. 35).

cash crop (kăsh krŏp) a product grown for sale and not for the farmer's own use (p. 173).

checks and balances (chĕks ənd băl´əns-əz) a system in which each branch of government—legislative, executive, or judicial—keeps the others from misusing their power (p. 301).

chronology (krə-nŏl´ə-jē) the order in which things happen; the arrangement of events in time order (p. 61).

citizenship (sĭt´ĭ-zən-shĭp´) the status of a citizen, one who is born in a country or has become a citizen by law; a U.S. citizen has certain rights, such as the protection of the government (p. 520).

civil disobedience (sĭv´əl dĭs´ə-bē´dē-əns) refusal to obey certain laws that one regards as unjust (p. 193).

civil rights (sĭv´əl rītz) the individual freedoms of each citizen; for U.S. citizens these include the right to vote and to have equal protection under the law (p. 510).

civilian (sǐ-vǐl´yən) a person who does not belong to the armed forces (p. 285).

claim (klām) a formal request to own a tract of public land; a tract of land staked out by a miner or settler (p. 382).

colonization (kŏl´ə-nǐ-zā´shən) the process of starting a colony or colonies by sending settlers to a new place, usually a distant one (p. 129).

colony (kŏl´ə-nē) a territory under the rule of another country, usually a distant one (p. 111).

common (kŏm´ən) a large public pasture in the center of a Puritan town (p. 183).

common school (kŏm´ən skōōl) a public elementary school in which students of all ages and abilities sat together and studied in the same room (p. 333).

compromise (kŏm´prə-mīz´) to settle an argument by each side giving up some demands (p. 300).

Confederacy (kən-fĕd´ər-ə-sē) the eleven states that seceded from the United States in 1860–1861; also called the Confederate States of America (p. 466).

confederation (kən-fĕd´ə-rā´shən) a group of states or nations united for a common goal (p. 95).

constitution (kŏn´stǐ-tōō´shən) the basic law and plan for governing a country or state (p. 287).

contagious disease (kən-tā´jəs dǐ-zēz´) an illness that tends to spread from one person to another (p. 122).

cotton gin (kŏt´n jǐn) a machine that cleans cotton by separating the seeds from the fibers (p. 403).

council (koun´səl) a group of people called together to give advice (p. 163).

covenant (kŭv´ə-nənt) an agreement with God; an agreement between two persons (p. 181).

culture (kŭl´chər) the attitudes, beliefs, and customs of a group of people that are passed from one generation to another (p. 6).

D

delegate (dĕl´ǐ-gāt´) a person who acts for a group or individual; a representative or agent (p. 262).

democracy (dǐ-mŏk´rə-sē) rule by the majority; a system of government in which the people rule, either directly or through elected representatives (p. 191).

descendant (dǐ-sĕn´dənt) a person who is born to particular parents, grandparents, and more distant ancestors (p. 13).

discrimination (dǐ-skrǐm´ə-nā´shən) the act of making a clear distinction; often, mistreatment of people based on prejudice (p. 511).

dissenter (dǐ-sĕn´tər) a person who disagrees with the accepted ideas of a society or government; a person who refuses to follow certain beliefs (p. 193).

diversity (dǐ-vûr´sǐ-tē) variety; the condition of being different or varied (p. 214).

duty (dōō´tē) a tax paid on goods brought into a country (p. 200).

E

emancipation (ǐ-măn´sə-pā´shən) the act of freeing people from oppression or slavery (p. 470).

empathy (ĕm´pə-thē) an understanding of other people's feelings, actions, and situations (p. 71).

encomienda (ĕn-kō´mē-ĕn´də) large tracts of land owned by wealthy Spanish settlers in North America; some included Indian villages and their inhabitants (p. 129).

epoch (ē´pŏk´) a period of time, especially one that is remarkable in some way (p. 82).

equality (ǐ-kwŏl´ǐ-tē) the state of having the same rights, privileges, and responsibilities (p. 264).

ethnic custom (ĕth´nǐk kŭs´təm) a practice of a certain cultural group that is passed from one generation to another (p. 19).

evidence (ĕv´ǐ-dəns) something that proves a belief; something that indicates what happened (p. 58).

expedition (ĕk´spǐ-dǐsh´ən) an organized journey with a specific purpose, such as exploration (p. 110).

export (ĕk´spôrt´) a product grown or manufactured in one country and sold to another (p. 168).

F

factory (făk´tə-rē) a building or group of buildings in which products are manufactured (p. 423).

fault (fôlt) a break or crack in the earth's crust (p. 52).

federal (fĕd´ər-əl) relating to a central government (p. 293).

Federalist (fĕd´ər-ə-lǐst) a member of a political party led by Alexander Hamilton that supported a strong federal government (p. 319).

fort (fôrt) a place of defense; a permanent army post (p. 131).

forty-niner (fôr´tē-nī´nər) a California gold seeker; the name comes from the year 1849, when gold-rush fever was at its peak (p. 385).

free state (frē stāt) one of the states north of the Ohio River where slavery was not allowed (p. 445).

G

geography (jē-ŏg´rə-fē) the study of the earth and its features and of life on the earth, including the relationship between people and their environment (p. 31).

ghetto (gĕt´ō) a part of a city where members of a minority group are forced to live because of poverty or social prejudice (p. 496).

glacier (glā´shər) a huge mass of ice moving slowly over land (p. 81).

Great Awakening (grāt ə-wā´kən-ĭng) the Puritan religious movement of the early 1700s, characterized by an awakening of interest in spiritual matters (p. 195).

H

hemisphere (hĕm´ĭ-sfîr´) half the earth: the Northern or Southern hemisphere; the Eastern or Western hemisphere (p. 42).

hero (hîr´ō) a person admired for strength, noble purpose, or brave actions (p. 307).

historian (hĭ-stôr´ē-ən) a person who studies the events of the past (p. 59).

historical map (hĭ-stôr´ĭ-kəl măp) a map that gives information about a historical period (p. 52).

history (hĭs´tə-rē) the study of what happened in the past; a record of past events (p. 59).

House of Burgesses (hous ŭv bûr´jĭs-z) a lawmaking body in colonial Virginia (p. 161).

I

immigrant (ĭm´ĭ-grənt) a person who leaves his or her own country to live permanently in another (p. 13).

import (ĭm´-pôrt) a product brought into a country for sale or use (p. 242).

impressment (ĭm-prĕs´mənt) the act of seizing people and forcing them into service (p. 322).

indentured servant (ĭn-dĕn´chərd sûr´vənt) a person who agreed to provide five to seven years of unpaid labor in return for free passage across the ocean, food, clothing, and shelter (p. 160).

independence (ĭn´dĭ-pĕn´dəns) the state of being free of the influence, guidance, or control of others; state of being free of political control or rule (p. 262).

Industrial Revolution (ĭn-dŭs´trē-əl rĕv´ə-loo´shən) a period of great social and economic change that began in the late 1700s, when steam, oil, and electricity began to replace human and animal power and when products began to be made in factories by machines (p. 422).

interpret (ĭn-tûr´prĭt) to explain the meaning or importance of something (p. 59).

investor (ĭn-vĕs´tôr) a person who provides money for a business, usually to gain income or make a profit (p. 134).

J

journal (jûr´nəl) a personal record of experiences kept on a regular basis (p. 70).

L

labor union (lā´bər yoon´yən) an organization formed by workers to obtain better wages and working conditions (p. 483).

landlord (lănd´lôrd´) the owner of land, houses, or apartments that are rented to tenants (p. 227).

latitude (lăt´ĭ-tood´) the distance north or south of the equator, expressed in degrees (p. 44).

legislature (lĕj´ĭ-slā´chər) a governmental body made up of persons elected to make laws (p. 294).

life expectancy (līf ĭk-spĕk´tən-sē) The number of years a person is expected to live, as predicted by statistics (p. 158).

long house (lông hous) a long wooden house in which several Iroquois families lived together (p. 95).

longitude (lŏn´jĭ-tood´) the distance east or west of the Prime Meridian expressed in degrees (p. 44).

Louisiana Purchase (loo-ē´zē-ăn´ə pûr´chĭs) land between the Mississippi River and the Rocky Mountains that the United States purchased from France in 1803 (p. 352).

Loyalist (loi´ə-lĭst) an American who remained faithful to the British government during the Revolution (p. 269).

M

mechanization (mĕk´ə-nĭz-ā´-shən) using machines to do work; equipping factories with machines (p. 482).

meetinghouse (mē´tĭng-hous´) a large building used by the Puritans as a gathering place for religious services, celebrations, and town meetings (p. 182).

merchant (mûr´chənt) a person whose business is buying and selling goods for profit (p. 198).

meridian (mə-rĭd´ē-ən) one of a series of imaginary lines that run north and south from the North Pole to the South Pole and measure distance east and west of the Prime Meridian (p. 44).

mesa (mā´sə) a flat-topped hill or mountain with steep sides, common in the southwestern United States (p. 86).

middle class (mĭd´l klăs) a social and economic class made up of people who are neither rich nor poor (p. 496).

migrate (mī´grāt´) to move from one country or region to another (p. 378).

militia (mə-lĭsh´ə) a nonprofessional army made up of citizens who serve during emergencies (p. 260).

minority (mə-nôr´ĭ-tē) a group of people, particularly a racial, ethnic, or religious group, who are less than half the total population; a smaller group regarded as different from the larger group of which it is a part (p. 510).

mission (mĭsh´ən) a place, usually including a church and a school, that is established for religious and humanitarian purposes (p. 130).

Monroe Doctrine (mən-rō´ dŏk´trĭn) a statement by President Monroe opposing European interference in the Americas and U.S. interference in Europe (p. 323).

Mormon (môr´mən) a member of the Church of Jesus Christ of Latter-day Saints, founded in 1830 by Joseph Smith (p. 387).

mound (mound) a large, steep platform built for protection, burial, or religious purposes (p. 90).

N

nationalism (năsh´ə-nə-lĭz´əm) devotion to the interests or culture of a particular nation; emphasis on national rather than international goals (p. 321).

nativism (nā´tĭ-vĭz´əm) the policy of favoring native-born inhabitants over immigrants, especially in America in the 1800s (p. 491).

navigable (năv´ĭ-gə-bəl) broad and deep enough for a ship to pass through (p. 209).

navigate (năv´ĭ-gāt´) to plan and control the course of a ship or aircraft (p. 107).

nomad (nō´măd´) one of a group of people who move with their flocks and herds as the seasons change to find water and pasture (p. 390).

Northwest Passage (nôrth-wĕst´ păs´ĭj) a legendary water route through North America; Europeans in the 1500s believed it would lead to China (p. 119).

O

oral history (ôr´əl hĭs´tə-rē) information about the past gathered from interviews with people (p. 65).

ordinance (ôr´dn-əns) a law or regulation, especially one made by a city or town (p. 344).

overseer (ō´vər-sē´ər) a person who directed the work of the slaves (p. 408).

P

pacifism (păs´ə-fĭz´əm) opposition to war and violence; the belief that war is the wrong way to solve differences between nations (p. 145).

parallel (păr´ə-lĕl´) one of a series of imaginary east-west lines that circle the globe and measure distance north and south of the equator (p. 43).

Parliament (pär´lə-mənt) the lawmaking body of England, consisting of the House of Lords and the House of Commons (p. 200).

patriotism (pā´trē-ə-tĭz´əm) love and loyal support for one's country (p. 309).

patroon system (pə-trōōn´ sĭs´təm) a plan of the Dutch West India Company for colonizing New Netherland, which included New York; any member of the company who brought 50 families over could have a large tract of land; he would rule over the settlers, who would farm the land (p. 227).

petition (pə-tĭsh´ən) to make a formal request to an authority, often a government, for a change in a policy; the request is called a petition (p. 523).

physical map (fĭz´ĭ-kəl măp´) a map that shows land and water features, such as mountains and lakes (p. 50).

Pilgrim (pĭl´grəm) one of the English Puritans who founded the colony of Plymouth in New England in 1620 (p. 139).

pioneer (pī´ə-nîr´) one of the first persons to explore or settle a region (p. 341).

plain (plān) a broad area of flat, open land (p. 371).

plantation (plăn-tā´shən) a large farm where one crop is grown. A plantation includes the home of the owner and residences for workers (p. 161).

pluralism (plŏŏr´ə-lĭz´əm) the existence within a society of a number of different ethnic, racial, religious, and social groups (p. 6).

political party (pə-lĭt´ĭ-kəl pär´tē) a group organized to promote candidates for political office (p. 319).

politics (pŏl´ĭ-tĭks) the study of governments; the activities of governments (p. 244).

popular sovereignty (pŏp´yə-lər sŏv´ər-ĭn-tē) the belief that the power or authority in a nation rests with its people (p. 453).

potlatch (pŏt´lăch´) a ceremony among the Native Americans of the northwest Pacific coast in which the host distributes gifts (p. 89).

precedent (prĕs´ĭ-dənt) an action or decision used later as an example for similar cases (p. 316).

prejudice (prĕj´ə-dĭs) an unfavorable opinion formed without knowledge of the facts (p. 21).

primary source (prī´mĕr´ē sôrs) information about events recorded at the time of those events (p. 64).

profit (prŏf´ĭt) the amount of money made by a business after all the expenses have been met (p. 134).

projection (prə-jĕk´shən) a way of drawing the curved surface of the earth on a flat map (p. 45).

propaganda (prŏp´ə-găn´də) the spread of ideas, often in a biased or one-sided form, to win support for a particular cause (p. 249).

Puritan (pyŏŏr´ĭ-tn) a member of a Protestant group in England and the American colonies. Puritans believed in simple creeds and ceremonies, strict discipline, and high moral standards (p. 139).

Q

Quaker (kwā´kər) a religious group, also called the Religious Society of Friends, founded in 1647. Quakers believe in equality and pacifism (p. 145).

R

racism (rā´sĭz´əm) the idea that one's own race or ethnic group is superior to another (p. 491).

ratify (răt´ə-fī´) consent to officially; to make valid (p. 293).

rebel (rĕb´əl) a person who uses force to oppose a government or another authority; a rebel is someone who rebels (rĭ-bĕlz´) (p. 165).

reform (rĭ-fôrm´) to change for the better (p. 436).

region (rē´jən) an area with certain characteristics —such as physical features, language, or climate— that set it apart from surrounding areas (p. 35).

registration (rĕj´ĭ-strā´shən) the act of signing up officially; for example, to enroll in a class or to vote in an election (p. 513).

repeal (rĭ-pēl´) to officially cancel or to do away with a law or tax (p. 248).

representative (rĕp´rĭ-zĕn´tə-tĭv) an elected member of a lawmaking body in a government, acting for the people in a certain geographical area (p. 161).

republic (rĭ-pŭb´lĭk) a nation in which political power lies with the citizens, who elect leaders and representatives (p. 268).

Republican (rĭ-pŭb´lĭ-kən) a member of a political party led by Thomas Jefferson that became what is now the Democratic party (p. 319).

revolution (rĕv´ə-lōō´shən) the overthrow of a government by force and the establishment of a new one (p. 268).

S

salutary neglect (săl´yə-tĕr´ē nĭ-glĕkt´) Britain's policy, which proved salutary, or helpful, of neglecting its North American colonies and not collecting taxes from them (p. 239).

secede (sĭ-sēd´) to withdraw formally, especially as a group, from an organization or country (p. 448).

secessionist (sĭ-sĕsh´-ə-nist) a person who believes in the right of a state to secede, especially those Southerners who wanted to withdraw from the Union (p. 465).

Second Great Awakening (sĕk´ənd grāt ə-wā´kən-ing) a religious movement of the 1830s and 1840s characterized by a rebirth of interest in spiritual matters (p. 434).

segregation (sĕg´rĭ-gā´shən) the policy of keeping people of different races apart (p. 513).

self-interest (sĕlf´ĭn´trĭst) concern about how an issue affects one personally; a selfish regard for one's own interests over those of others (p. 515).

separation of powers (sĕp´ə-rā´shən ŭv pou´ərz) the division of responsibilities among the branches of the government, giving each branch a different job (p. 302).

Separatist (sĕp´ər-ə-tĭst) a person belonging to a Protestant church that had left the Church of England (p. 139).

Shaker (shā´kər) the common name for a religious sect called the United Society of Believers (p. 435).

sharecropper (shâr´krŏp´ər) one of the poor southern farmers who rented land and gave part of the crops to the owner (p. 414).

slave state (slāv stāt) one of the states south of the Ohio River where slavery was allowed (p. 445).

slavery (slā´və-rē) a system in which people are owned by other people. Slaves work without pay and have no rights (p. 167).

slum (slŭm) a crowded section of a city, with run-down housing and generally poor living conditions (p. 432).

smuggle (smŭg´əl) to take goods into or out of a country secretly and unlawfully in order to avoid paying a duty (p. 200).

spiritual (spĭr´ĭ-chōō-əl) a religious song of slaves, often expresses hope for a better life (p. 410).

strike (strīk) to refuse to work until certain demands, such as higher wages, are met (p. 483).

suffrage (sŭf´rĭj) the right to vote (p. 515).

surplus (sûr´pləs) an extra amount; more than is needed (p. 324).

T

tax (tăks) money, or occasionally property, that people pay to their government (p. 130).

technology (tĕk-nŏl´ə-jē) the tools, machines, and methods used to manufacture things or in other ways to improve people's lives (p. 105).

tenant farmer (tĕn´ənt fär´mər) a farmer who works land that is owned by someone else and pays rent either in cash or in a share of the crops (p. 227).

tenement (tĕn´ə-mənt) a low-rental apartment building, overcrowded and run down (p. 429).

textile (tĕks´tīl´) fabric; woven cotton or wool (p. 325).

tolerance (tŏl´ər-əns) willingness to accept beliefs or practices different from one's own (p. 214).

township (toun´shĭp´) an area of land measuring 36 square miles (p. 294).

treaty (trē´tē) a formal written or spoken agreement, especially between nations (p. 211).

tributary (trĭb´yə-tĕr´ē) a stream or small river that flows into a larger river (p. 346).

U

Underground Railroad (ŭn´dər-ground´rāl´rōd´) a series of secret escape routes used by slaves fleeing from the South to free states and Canada (p. 451).

Union (yōōn´yən) the United States of America, especially during the Civil War (p. 445).

utopian community (yōō-tō´pē-ən kə-myōō´nĭ-tē) a perfect community; a planned community where people were meant to live together in peace and harmony (p. 435).

V

veto (vē´tō) to reject a law passed by a lawmaking body, preventing it from going into effect (p. 240).

W

walking city (wôkĭng sĭt´ē) a community with no public transportation (p. 430).

War Hawk (wôr hôk) a senator or congressman who favored war with Britain in 1812 (p. 322).

Italic numbers refer to pages on which illustrations appear.

601

Credits *(continued from page iv)*

i "Let America Be America Again" by Langston Hughes. Reprinted by permission of Harold Ober Associates Incorporated. Copyright 1938 by Langston Hughes. Copyright renewed 1965 by Langston Hughes.

8 From *Nine-Twenty O'Farrell Street* by Harriette Lane Levy, 1947. Reprint. New Hampshire: Ayer Co., 1975.

12, 14, 16, 21 From *Barrio Boy* by Ernesto Galarza. Copyright © 1989 by The University of Notre Dame Press. Reprinted by permission of University of Notre Dame Press.

17, 20 From *In the Year of the Boar and Jackie Robinson* by Bette Bao Lord. Copyright © 1984 by Harper & Row.

22 *Gooseberries to Oranges* by Barbara Cohen, illus. by Beverly Brodsky. Text Copyright © 1982 by Barbara Cohen. Ill. Copyright © 1982 by Beverly Brodsky. By permission of Lothrop Lee & Shepard Books (A Division of William Morrow & Co.).

27 Excerpt from the speech, "I Have a Dream" by Martin Luther King, Jr. Reprinted by permission of Joan Daves. Copyright © 1963 by Martin Luther King, Jr.

64 From *American Slavery, American Freedom* by Edmund Morgan, New York: Knopf, 1976.

72 "Fighting for Yellowstone" by George Hackett, *Newsweek* 112, no. 12 (Sept. 19): 18–20.

84 "How the Turtle Beat the Rabbit." Reproduced by permission of the Smithsonian Institution Press. From *Bureau of American Ethnology, Bulletin 19*, "Myths of the Cherokee," by James Mooney. Smithsonian Institution, Washington, D.C. 1893. Illustration from the book *Why the Possum's Tail Is Bare and Other North American Indian Nature Tales* by James E. Connolly. Illustrations Copyright © 1985 by Andrea Adams. Reprinted by permission of Stemmer House Publishers, Inc.

98 From *The Death and Rebirth of the Seneca* by Anthony Wallace, New York: Knopf, 1970.

143 From *Old Silver Leg Takes Over* by Robert Quakenbush, New Jersey: 1986.

160 From *The Serpent Never Sleeps* by Scott O'Dell, Boston: Houghton Mifflin, 1987.

186 From *The Witch of Blackbird Pond* by Elizabeth George Speare. Copyright © 1958 by Elizabeth George Speare. Reprinted by permission of Houghton Mifflin Company.

191 Except from *Four Women in a Violent Time* by Deborah Crawford. Copyright © 1970 by Deborah Crawford.

220 From *What's the Big Idea, Ben Franklin?* by Jean Fritz, text copyright © 1976 by Jean Fritz. Reprinted by permission of Coward-McCann, Inc.

224 Reprinted by permission of Macmillan Publishing Company, a Division of Macmillan, Inc. From *Benjamin West and His Cat Grimalkin* by Marguerite Henry. Copyright © 1947 by The Bobbs-Merrill Company; Copyright renewed 1975 Marguerite Henry.

276 From *Sybil Ludington's Ride* by Erick Berry. Copyright © 1952 by Erick Berry. Reprinted by permission of William K.H. Coxe.

341 "Daniel Boone" from *A Book of Americans* by Rosemary and Stephen Vincent Benét. Copyright 1933 by Rosemary and Stephen Vincent Benét. Copyright renewed © 1961 by Rosemary Carr Benét. Reprinted by permission of Brandt & Brandt Literary Agents.

350 Excerpts from *Yankee Doodle's Cousins* by Anne Malcolmson. Copyright 1941 by Anne Burnett Malcolmson. Copyright renewed ©

1969 by Anne Malcolmson von Storch. Reprinted by permission of Houghton Mifflin Company.

377, 379 From *Women's Diaries of the Westward Journey* ed. by Lillian Schlissel, New York: Schocken, 1982.

388 From *Wilderness Bride* by Annabel and Edgar John, New York: Harper and Row, 1962.

426 From *Land of Their Choice* by Theodore C. Blegen, Minneapolis: Minnesota, 1955.

428 From *Coming to America: Immigrants from Northern Europe* by Albert Robbins, New York: Delacorte Press, 1981.

458 "Carrying the Running-Aways" from *The People Could Fly: American Black Folktales* by Virginia Hamilton. Illustrated by Leo and Diane Dillon. Text Copyright © 1985 by Virginia Hamilton. Illustrations Copyright © 1985 by Leo and Diane Dillon. Reprinted by permission of Alfred A. Knopf, Inc.

498 "The Choosing" reprinted with permission of Atheneum Publishers, an imprint of Macmillan Publishing Company from *An Orphan for Nebraska* by Charlene Joy Talbot. Copyright © 1979 Charlene Joy Talbot.

511 "Let America Be America Again" by Langston Hughes. Reprinted by permission of Harold Ober Associates Incorporated. Copyright 1938 by Langston Hughes. Copyright renewed 1965 by Langston Hughes.

519 From *Twenty Years at Hull House* by Jane Addams, New York: Macmillan, 1935.

590 Copyright © 1985 by Houghton Mifflin Company. Adapted and reprinted by permission from *The American Heritage Dictionary*, Second College Edition.

Illustrations

Literature border design by Peggy Skycraft

Ligature 149 ©, 334, 335, 337, 482, 505, 525. **Precision Graphics** 6, 8, 13, 26, 54, 99, 106, 107, 121, 124, 138, 139, 148, 149 (b), 151, 158, 176, 184 (b), 229, 231, 239, 242, 249, 256, 285, 288, 292, 301, 308, 325, 330, 344, 366, 376, 397, 404 (tr), 405, 418, 427, 432, 440, 445, 467, 487, 496, 506, 512, 514, 525. **Alex Bloch** 185. **Jeani Brunnick** 521. **John T. Burgoyne** 112, 113, 271. **Susan David** 83, 452. **Randall Fleck** 118, 157, 262. **Simon Galkin** 95, 160, 182. **Dale Glasgow** 93, 161, 295. **Phil Jones** 482. **Guy Kingsbery** 81, 404 (l). **Joe Le Monnier** 38, 80, 358–359. **Yoshi Miyake** 96. **Edward Parker** 267, 273. **Frederick Porter** 343. **Mike Rodericks** 454. **Joseph Scrofani** 108, 196–197. **Scott Snow** 90. **Lee Steadman** 112. **Gary Torrisi** 41. **Kyuzo Tsugami** 372. **Brent Watkinson** 188.

Maps

R. R. Donnelley & Sons Company Cartographic Services 566–79. **Mapping Specialists** 5, 15, 39, 48, 51, 53, 55, 82, 88, 97, 111, 120, 123, 125, 130, 133, 139, 144, 165, 174, 175, 177, 184 (t), 199, 203, 209, 218, 226, 237, 243, 272, 274, 293, 302, 319, 322, 342, 353, 361, 371, 375, 390, 403, 424, 425, 427, 446, 449, 452, 455, 466, 468, 485, 487, 495, 517. **Precision Graphics** 42, 43, 44, 45, 46. **Susan Johnston Carlson** 170–171, 380–381. **Other**: 35 From *WE THE PEOPLE: An Atlas of America's Ethnic Diversity* by James P. Allen and Eugene J. Turner, Copyright © 1988, Macmillan Publishing Company, a division of Macmillan, Inc. Reprinted with permission of Macmillan Publishing Company. Additional source: National Geographic Society.

Photographs

GC—The Granger Collection; **LC**—Library of Congress; **RJB**—Ralph J. Brunke; **TIB**—The Image Bank, Chicago

Front cover Peter Bosy, Missouri School for the Blind. **Back cover** The Newberry Library, Chicago. **v** Laurie Platt Winfrey, Inc. **1** The Gerald Peters Gallery. **2** © Grafton M. Smith, TIB (l); RJB (r); GC (b). **3** © Paul E. Loven, TIB (t); RJB (b). **4** © Louis Sahuc, Stock Options (l); © Jackson Hill (r). **5** © Lowell Georgia, Photo Researchers, Inc. **7** RJB (tr,c,bl,cl). **10** RJB (t,b). **11** RJB (t,br); © Francis M. Cox, Stock Boston (bl). **12** University of Notre Dame Press. **14** LC, Newsweek Books (t); The New-York Historical Society, Newsweek Books (b). **15** Museum of the City of New York. **16** California State Library. **17** Bette Bao Lord. **18** RJB (tl,bl,tr,br). **19** RJB (tl,tr,bl,br). **20** © Lincoln Park Zoological Society (cl,bl); Susan Reich, © Lincoln Park Zoological Society (br). **21** © Joanna McCarthy, TIB. **28–29** The Henry Francis du Pont Winterthur Museum. **29** Earth Satellite Corporation/Science Photo Library, Photo Researchers, Inc. (t); Solomon D. Butcher Collections, Nebraska State Historic Society (cr); RJB (bc). **30–31** © David Hiser, TIB. **31** © Jerry Jacka Photography. **32** © Jerry Jacka Photography. **33** Bettmann Archive. **37** © Karl Hentz, TIB (l); © Don King, TIB (r). **38** RJB (tr,bl,br). **39** RJB (l); © John Schekler (r). **40** SuperStock. **41** NASA/Science Source, Photo Researchers, Inc. **45** RJB. **47** Private Collection. **49** Northwestern University Library, RJB. **50** © New York City Transit Authority (l); RJB (r). **52** © Ernest Braun, Comstock. **56** GC (l); The Shelburne Museum (b). **56–57** University of Oregon. **57** Museum of the American Indian, Heye Foundation (r); American Numismatic Society (b). **58** RJB. **59** © The Bostonian Society (l); Boston Parks and Recreation Department (r). **60** LC, Laurie Platt Winfrey (tr); The Newberry Library, Chicago (b). **61** Boston Public Library. **62** California State Library (t); © Peter Newark's Western Americana (b). **63** New York Public Library, Newsweek Books (l,c); American Numismatic Society (r). **65** Jamestown-Yorktown Foundation. **66** LC (l); Smithsonian Institution, Art Resource (br). **66–67** RJB. **67** RJB (tl,tc,c,br); Old Sturbridge Village (tr). **68** AR (l); LC (r). **69** RJB (t, b). **70** New York Public Library. **71** Joslyn Art Museum (tl); LC (c); Smithsonian Institution (r). **72** Jim Peaco, © Yellowstone National Park (l, r); © Yellowstone National Park (c). **73** Bozeman Daily Chronicle, RJB (l); RJB (r). **75** Glenbow Archives. **76–77** © Jerry Jacka Photography. **78** © Jerry Jacka Photography (tl); Southwest Museum, Los Angeles, (c,b). **78–9** Comstock. **79** Art Resource. **81** © NASA, Grant Heilman Photography, Inc. **83** © Smithsonian Institution. **86** © Comstock. **87** © P. Hollembeak, American Museum of Natural History (r); RJB (b). **88** © Art Wolfe, Allstock. **89** © Sharon Gerig, Tom Stack & Associates (l); RJB (r). **90** Ohio Historical Society (t); © Gary Irving, TSW-Click/Chicago Ltd. (b). **91** RJB (t); © Richard & Mary Magruder, TIB (b). **92** © Kathleen O'Donnell, Stockphotos, Inc. **94** © Benn Mitchell, TIB. **95** © W.A. Banaszewski, Finger Lake Images. **97** RJB (t,b). **98** The New York State Museum. **102** Robert Harding Picture Library (l); AR (r); **102–3** GC **105** British Museum (t); New York Public Library, Map Division (b). **106** Galdiano Museum, AR (l); GC (r). **107** Science Museum, Florence, AR (c); RJB (b). **109** Bibliotheque Nacionale. **110** Biblioteca Nacional, Madrid (t); Naval Museum, Pegli, AR (b). **111** GC. **112** Randolph Goodlett, Pittsburgh Aqua Zoo. **112–13** RJB. **113** RJB. **115** Laurie Platt Winfrey, Inc. (t); Biblioteca Escorial, Newsweek Books (c). **116** British Museum, Michael Holford (c); © David Manso Martin, Prado (bl,bc); American Numismatic Society (b). **117** NASA. **119** New York Hispanic Society (t); New York Public Library, Rare Book Division (b). **120** GC. **121** Ovieda, Historia Natural. **122** Biblioteca Medicea Laurenziana, Italy. **126** National Portrait Gallery, London (t); American Numismatic Society (r); © Doug Keats (b). **127** Laurie Platt Winfrey, Inc. **128** Archivo de Indias, Seville, Laurie Platt Winfrey, Inc. **129** British Museum, The Bridgeman Art Library. **131** The Plimoth Plantation (t,b). **132** New York Public Library, Newsweek Books. **134** GC (tl); New York Public Library, Rare Book Room (tr); The Jamestown-Yorktown Foundation (bc,bl). **135** Ashmolean Museum, Oxford. **137** Northwestern University Library, RJB. **140** © Farrell Grehan, Photo Researchers, Inc. **141** The Pilgrim Society, Plymouth, Massachusetts (tl,tr,cl,br); RJB (bl). **142** American Antiquarian Society (l); The New England (r). **143** LC. **145** Atwater-Kent Museum (c); British Museum (b); **146** Historical Society of Pennsylvania. **147** Historical Society of Pennsylvania. **149** © Dan D. Briere, SuperStock. **152–53** Private Collection. **154** Laurie Platt Winfrey, Inc. (t); Colonial Williamsburg (c); RJB (br). **154–55** © David King Gleason. **156** New York Public Library, Rare Book Division. **157** Colonial National Historical Park (t); Colonial Willliamsburg (b). **158**

Virginia State Library and Archives. **158–59** Jamestown-Yorktown Foundation. **159** Library of Congress. **160** Colonial Williamsburg Foundation. **161** © John Colwell, Grant Heilman Photography, Inc. (t); Smithsonian Institution (c). **162** National Portrait Gallery, Art Resource. **163** Bettmann Archive. **164** RJB (t); LC (b). **166** GC. **167** GC. **168** RJB (t,b). **169** New York Public Library. **170** Museum of African Art, Newsweek Books (t); © Aldo Tutino, Smithsonian Institution, Art Resource (b). **171** Nelson Gallery-Atkins Museum (Nelson Fund) (tr); The Metropolitan Museum of Art (c); Colorphoto Hinz Allschwil-Basil (b). **172** GC. **173** GC (l); Rice Council for Market Development (r). **178** Massachusetts Historical Society (tl); The Newberry Library, Chicago (r); Plimouth Plantation (b). **179** Henry Ford Museum and Greenfield Village. **180** American Antiquarian Society. **181** © F.B. Grunzweig, F Stop Pictures (tl); © Homer Sykes, Woodfin Camp & Associates (tr); © Massachusetts Historical Society (b). **183** SuperStock (c); LC (b). **187** The Fine Arts Museum of San Francisco (t); The Henry Francis du Pont Winterthur Museum (b). **189** GC (l,lc,rc,r). **190** Mystic Seaport, Mystic, Connecticut (t); Smithsonian Institution (c). **191** The Newberry Library, Chicago. **192** Henry Ford Museum and Greenfield Village. **193** © John Jenkins III (c); RJB (r). **194** GC. **195** Ipswich Historical Society, Ipswich, Massachusetts. **196** RJB. **197** Mark Sexton, Essex Institute (c); RJB (b). **198** RJB. **200** St. Louis Art Museum. **201** Miniature Dining Room, 1720, Turner-Ingersoll House, Salem, Mass., Workshop of Mrs. James Ward Thorne. Gift of Mrs. James Ward Thorne, 1942.483. © 1988 The Art Institute of Chicago (t); The Metropolitan Museum of Art (c). **202** TIB. **206** LC (tl,cl). **206–7** New York State Historical Association, Cooperstown, New York. **207** Philadelphia Museum of Art. **209** © TIB. **210** RJB. **211** Yale University Art Gallery. **213** The Henry Francis du Pont Winterthur Museum. **214** The Metropolitan Museum of Art, Rogers Fund, 1914. (14.26) (t); National Gallery of Art (c); Philadelphia Museum of Art (b). **215** Colonial Williamsburg. **216** Library Company of Philadelphia. **217** © Jerry Irwin, Photo Researchers, Inc. (l,r). **219** Haverford College Library. **224** Smithsonian Institution (l); Philidelphia Museum of Art (r). **225** Princeton University Library (t); The Shelburne Museum (c). **226** Colonial Williamsburg (tr); © Vic Kumma, Quiet Valley Living Historical Farm (tl). **227** © Vic Kumma, Quiet Valley Living Historical Farm (tl); John Deere Museum (r); RJB (l). **228** Historical Society of Pennsylvania. **232–233** LC. **234** Colonial Williamsburg (l); The White House Collection (r). **235** Virginia Historical Society (t); GC (b). **236** New York Public Library, Prints Division. **238** The Bostonian Society. **239** The Museum of Fine Arts, Boston (l); American Numismatic Society (c); Smithsonian Institution, Straub Collection (r). **240** Colonial Williamsburg. **241** © Continental Insurance. **243** Breton Littlehales, © National Geographic Society. **244** North Wind Picture Archives (c); Private Collection (b). **245** LC, Laurie Platt Winfrey, Inc. **246** New York Public Library. **247** Laurie Platt Winfrey, Inc. **248** GC (l); LC, Newsweek Books (r). **250** Historical Pictures Service, Inc., Chicago (t); GC (b). **251** RJB (t,bl); GC (c), © Vic Kumma, Quiet Valley Living Historical Farm (bc,br). **252** Historical Pictures Service, Inc., Chicago (l,r). **253** Brown University Library, Laurie Platt Winfrey, Inc. **255** The John Carter Brown Library, Brown University. **257** LC. **258** Mrs. John Adams; Gilbert Stuart; National Gallery of Art, Washington; Gift of Mrs Robert Homans (l); Photri (r). **259** Photri (t); The National Archives (c); The Henry Francis du Pont Winterthur Museum (r). **260** The Concord Museum (l,r). **261** GC. **262** Architect of the Capitol. **263** American Numismatic Society (tl); GC (tr). **264** LC. **265** Private Collection (l); RJB (r). **266** © Vic Kumma, Quiet Valley Living Historical Farm (l); The Concord Museum (r). **267** Essex Institute, Salem, Massachusetts. **268** Guilford Courthouse National Military Park. **269** Capitol, State of South Carolina (t); Rhode Island Historical Society (c). **270** RJB (t); LC (b). **274** The National Archives (l,c). **282** The Concord Museum. **284** GC. **286** LC. **290** Joseph Szaszfai, Yale University Art Gallery (l); Photri (r). **291** Laurie Platt Winfrey, Inc. (l); © Jonathan Wallen Photography, The National Archives (r). **294** © Harald Sund, TIB (l); The National Archives (r). **296** GC. **298** © Daniel S. Brody, Stock Boston (t); © Erich Hartmann, Magnum Photos (c); Independence National Historic Park Collection (b). **299** Independence National Historic Park Collection (t); GC (c); The National Archives (b). **300** Virginia Museum of Art. **305** Historical Pictures Service, Inc. **306** Amon Carter Museum, Fort Worth, Texas. **307** Bettmann Archive (t); NASA (b). **308** © G. Glander, F.P.G. International (tl); GC (tr); RJB (b). **309** Bettmann Archive (l);